Marketing

Real People, Real Decisions

Updated First Canadian Edition

Michael R. Solomon, Auburn University

Elnora W. Stuart, Winthrop University

Auleen Carson, Wilfrid Laurier University

J. Brock Smith, University of Victoria

Prentice
Hall

Toronto

To Gail, Amanda, Zachary, and Alexandra—my favorite market segment. —M.S.

To Sonny, Patrick, and Marge. —E.S.

To Paul, Emma, and Thomas. —A.C.

To Claudia, Ford, and Reed. —J.B.S.

National Library of Canada Cataloguing in Publication Data

Marketing: real people, real decisions

Updated 1st Canadian ed.
Includes bibliographical references and indexes.
ISBN 0-13-046086-9

1. Marketing. I. Solomon, Michael R.

HF5415.M3696 2003   658.8   C2002-901104-3

Vice President, Editorial Director: Michael J. Young
Senior Acquisitions Editor: Kelly Torrance
Marketing Manager: Deborah Meredith
Developmental Editor: Paul Donnelly
Production Editor: Mary Ann McCutcheon
Copy Editor: Elaine Freedman
Production Coordinator: Andrea Falkenberg
Page Layout: B.J. Weckerle
Permissions Research: Alene McNeill
Art Director: Mary Opper
Interior Design: Lisa LaPointe
Cover Design: Julia Hall
Cover Image: Robert Holmgren/Stone

4 5   07 06 05 04

Printed and bound in USA.

Brief Contents

Contents

Part VI Communicating about the Product 442

Preface

The complexity of the decisions faced by Canadian marketers in today's technology intensive, hyper-competitive, global business environment is both exciting and challenging. The main goal of this textbook is to help students develop the skills necessary to meet that challenge, and to capture the excitement of the challenge by immersing students in authentic decision-making experiences.

Unlike other introductory marketing textbooks, *Marketing: Real People, Real Decisions* focuses on the decision *maker*, not just on decision making. Students are encouraged to assume the role of a marketing manager and practise making *real* marketing decisions supported by key theories, concepts, and principles. Students also learn from decisions made by others—experienced, successful Canadian marketers in a variety of industries, companies, and contexts. We believe that this combination of learning by doing and learning from others will engage students in active learning and excite them about careers in marketing, both in Canada and internationally.

We have undertaken a significant revision of the US text to reflect the Canadian decision environment and its international perspective. We believe that marketing in the Canadian context is not simply a scaled down version of US practices, so we have attempted in this book to capture the uniqueness of the Canadian decision environment in which students will be working. The discussion of multicultural marketing in Chapters 6 and 8, for instance, presents a uniquely Canadian perspective. Similarly, the text has been updated to reflect the rapidly changing technological context of marketing decisions—particularly as it relates to the way Canadian companies are using the Internet. Additionally, the role of marketing in small and medium-sized businesses is well integrated throughout the book in recognition of the importance of these businesses to the Canadian economy. The examples, vignettes, and cases in the book provide a broad array of Canadian and international decision environments and represent a variety of industries: for-profit and not-for-profit; large established firms and entrepreneurial start-ups; and services, durable goods, packaged goods, retail and e-tail businesses.

Much has happened since the initial printing of the first Canadian edition. The events of September 11, 2001, for example, have had a profound effect on how we think about marketing and on the marketing decisions we make. In this updated edition we revisit key people and issues and introduce new ones, to ensure the book's currency and, where possible, to deepen its Canadian perspective. Here are the highlights:

- We have updated our *Real People, Real Decisions* profiles of key decision makers at Army & Navy (Chapter 1), Meal Exchange (Chapter 2), SurveySite (Chapter 5), Ford Motor Company of Canada (Chapter 8), Canada Cutlery (Chapter 10), IKEA (Chapter 15), and Raincoast Books (Chapter 18)

- We have introduced two new decision makers in our series of *Real People, Real Decisions* profiles, Michel Bendayan of Ritvik Holdings Inc. (Chapter 7), and Ryan Hobenshield of HARTMANN Group (Chapter 14)

- We have updated our *Spotlight on Real People* features on JobDirect, Daydream Software, NRG Group, and Shenetworks.com

- New to *Spotlight on Real People* are features on Worldbid.com's efforts to become the leading global B2B web portal (Chapter 7), pricing strategies adopted by General Motors in the wake of "9/11" (Chapter 12), and Canadian Tire's latest integrated marketing communications campaign (Chapter 1)

- Six new *Marketing in Action* cases discuss such subjects as the strategic issues facing companies entering Ontario's deregulated energy market (Chapter 2), how to conduct market research effectively using surveys (Chapter 5), Airborne Entertainment's target marketing of wireless content (Chapter 6), Microsoft's development and positioning of Xbox (Chapter 9), the competitive pricing of Ekati Diamonds (Chapter 12), and the challenges of marketing "Brand Canada" (Chapter 17)

- We have significantly updated the e-tailing discussion to reflect the recent "dot.bomb" fallout and more recent e-tailing statistics (Chapter 15)

- We have rewritten existing *Marketing in Action* cases that deal with such topical issues as genetically modified foods (Chapter 3), Krispy Kreme's entry into the Canadian market (Chapter 4), Krave's Candy's re-branding strategy (Chapter 10), the fortunes of WestJet Airlines since the terrorist attacks of September 11 (Chapter 13), the current positioning crisis faced by the Gap (Chapter 15), and Molson's post-"Rant" ad campaigns (Chapter 18)

To complement the updates to the text, we are also pleased to offer the following:

- *Real Marketing* CD-ROM, containing 16 video segments and written cases, together with a guide that matches the cases by topic with the chapters in the book

- A more robust package of supplements, completely revised to reflect the changes to the updated edition, and now available together in a box

Approach and Organization

The text is organized into 18 chapters grouped into six Parts. Part I (Making Marketing Decisions) provides an overview of the world of marketing (Chapter 1), marketing decisions (Chapter 2), and the environment in which these decisions are made (Chapters 3 and 4). Part II (Understanding and Identifying Markets) explores the heart of marketing decision making: market research (Chapter 5), consumer behaviour (Chapter 6), organizational buying behaviour (Chapter 7), and market segmentation (Chapter 8). These chapters help students identify creative segmentation schemes, develop rich segment profiles, and evaluate the appropriateness of alternative targeting strategies. Once armed with tools for detailed market segmentation, students are introduced to marketing mix decisions. Part III (Creating and Managing a Product: Goods and Services) includes separate chapters on product creation (Chapter 9) and management (Chapter 10) and on services marketing (Chapter 11). Part IV (Assigning Value to the Product) offers two pricing chapters that help students to recognize the strategic role of pricing (Chapter 12) and to make strategic pricing decisions (Chapter 13). Part V (Delivering the Product) consists of two chapters: one on channel management and physical distribution (Chapter 14), and one on retailing that includes in-depth coverage of e-tailing as a distribution alternative (Chapter 15). Part VI (Communicating about the Product) focuses on marketing communications, taking an integrated marketing communications perspective. Chapter 16 provides the foundation in terms of theory and concepts of the integrated marketing communications approach. Chapter 17 focuses on advertising strategy, a key element of an integrated marketing communications strategy. Chapter 18 discusses other key tools including sales promotion, public relations, and personal selling. Significant attention is paid throughout Part VI to electronic media and their communication implications.

Each chapter starts with a profile of a marketing decision maker who occupies a position students might expect to have within a few years after graduation. Midway through the chapter a decision is described that this marketer has recently faced and alternative courses of action are proposed. At this point students are asked to step into the shoes of the profiled marketer, evaluate the alternatives, and recommend and defend a course of action. At the end of the chapter we discuss what decision the marketer made and why, and provide a summary of the known consequences of that decision. We have attempted to make it clear that the decision made by the marketer is not necessarily the most appropriate one. Our aim is to show the rationale underpinning the decision and to help students understand how that rationale is informed by the decision maker's perspective. This format allows students to take an active role in applying the marketing concepts they are reading about, such as deciding what target market(s) to choose (Army & Navy Department Stores, Chapter 1; Ford of Canada, Chapter 8; Charity.ca, Chapter 11), whether to use a company brand or co-branding strategy (Canada Cutlery, Chapter 10) or whether or not a company should open a new retail concept (Roots, Chapter 9) or a new distribution channel (HARTMANN Group, Chapter 14).

We have chosen to include decision makers from a variety of organizations, ranging from large, well-known companies like Roots and Ford of Canada, to small not-for-profit organizations like Meal Exchange, and from family businesses like Army & Navy Department

Stores to Internet-based businesses like Chapters Online Inc. and Charity.ca. This allows students to see how marketing issues and decisions change across organizations, and also how they are similar.

One of our objectives for this book was to be as up to date as possible so that the content is relevant for the marketplace that students will face when they graduate. To that end, we have integrated Internet marketing throughout the book in addition to devoting a major part of Chapter 15 (Retail and E-tail) to business to consumer electronic commerce.

Key Features

This book contains many special features that will facilitate learning and enhance understanding of core concepts and their applications.

- **Chapter Objectives** at the beginning of each chapter clearly summarize the core concepts explored in that chapter.

- **Key Terms** are boldfaced where they are defined in the text, and are listed at the end of each chapter for easy reference.

- **Figures, Tables, and Exhibits** throughout the book each carry explanatory captions.

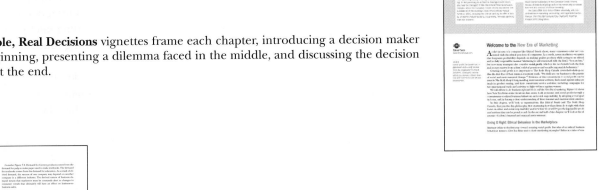

- **Real People, Real Decisions** vignettes frame each chapter, introducing a decision maker at the beginning, presenting a dilemma faced in the middle, and discussing the decision reached at the end.

- **Spotlight on Real People** boxes profile entrepreneurs in small and medium-sized businesses. Wherever possible we have highlighted the activities of young Canadian entrepreneurs to whom students can relate as peers.

- Recognizing that ethics play an increasing role in marketing, we have included **Good or Bad Decision?** boxes in each chapter that prompt students to consider ethical dilemmas faced by decision makers.

- A **Running Case** at the end of each of Part charts the development of **Computer Friendly Stuff (CFS)**, a small toy and software company now in its fifth year of operation. This case, written by the CFS management team, allows students to follow the progress of a small start-up company as it grapples with marketing issues such as choice of target market, business to business marketing, pricing, packaging, selling on the Internet, promotion, and sales force decisions. The CFS Marketing Plan is included in Appendix A and in the CFS cases throughout the book students use this Plan to determine what changes are necessary in the future in order to cope with environmental and internal changes.

- **"Marketing in Action"** cases at the end of each chapter provide an opportunity for students to make marketing decisions related to key chapter concepts in up-to-date, relevant decision situations.

- **Video cases**, two at the end of each Part, are based on segments from the CBC shows *Venture* and *Undercurrents* that deal topically with the practice of marketing, often in a small business context. A supplementary video case is included in the Instructor's Manual.

• **Weblinks** in the margins direct users to useful and relevant Internet sites.

- Extensive **Chapter Review** material helps students understand chapter concepts and issues. **Testing Your Knowledge** and **Choices and Issues** stimulate recall and critical thinking. **Applying What You've Learned** exercises ask students to assume the role of the marketing professional and apply concepts and theory to marketing decisions. **Learning by Doing** invites the student to learn outside the classroom by talking with marketing professionals, observing phenomena in the marketplace, or conducting primary and secondary research.

- **Real People, Real Surfers** exercises help students learn about resources available on the Internet and encourage them to explore first-hand the many permutations of Web-based marketing.

- **Appendix A** offers a sample marketing plan integrated with the CFS case that runs throughout the text.

- **Appendix B**, Marketing Math, supplements the pricing chapters by summarizing the basic financial analyses and calculations that marketers use in determining price decisions.

Supplements

The following outstanding supplements have been prepared to accompany this book:

- The *Instructor's Manual* provides an overview of each chapter's suggested activities, projects, and topics for class discussions. It also includes teaching notes for the end-of-chapter and CBC video cases.

- **NEW!** *Faculty Activities and Classroom Teaching Strategies (F.A.C.T.S.) Guide*, a complete set of supplemental learning and teaching aids to support the instructor's preparation and enhance the lecture experience. It provides helpful hints on overcoming barriers to effective learning, assigning in-class projects, working with the PowerPoint presentations, and developing class plans.

- *Study Guide*, organized by chapter, provides students with outlines, overviews, review questions and application exercises to aid in understanding of the textbook and encourage class discussion.

- *Electronic Transparencies in PowerPoint* incorporate exhibits from the text, weblinks, and video clips.

- The *Test Item File*, containing over 2700 questions, has been thoroughly revised to provide the optimum number of questions of each format (true/false, multple choice, and short answer), degree of difficulty (easy, moderate, difficult), and type of cognitive skill tested (recall/application).

- *Pearson Education Canada TestGen*, a special computerized version of the Test Item File, enables instructors to edit existing questions, add new questions, and generate tests.

- *CBC/Pearson Education Canada Video Library* is a compilation of 13 video segments drawn from the CBC's *Venture* and *Undercurrents* programs upon which the video cases in the book and Instructor's Manual are based.

- **NEW!** *Bessies Video*. The 2000–2001 Bessies, featuring all the award-winning entries in the 2000–2001 Canadian Television Commercial Festival.

- *Companion Website* contains numerous resources for students, including review exercises and quizzes, online access to the transparencies, hyperlinks to the text's weblinks, and search tools that facilitate further research into key organizations and topics discussed in the text. For instructors, it additionally provides access to the Instructor's Resource Manual and TestGen, and contains a syllabus builder as well as other materials.

- A *Course Management System (CMS)* is available in WebCT, BlackBoard, and CourseCompass. Instructors can use our CMS to enhance traditional course content with an online component, or to deliver the entire course onlline. The CMS created for this text features a number of study resources for students (review questions and exercises, weblinks), and valuable teaching and course administration tools for instructors (all instructor's supplements that accompany this text, including the Test Item File for online testing, Communication Tools including threaded discussion areas and e-mail accounts for each student instructor.

Acknowledgements

We would first of all like to express our thanks to the US authors of this text, Michael R. Solomon and Elnora W. Stuart, for their vision of a marketing text that would reflect the activities and priorities of real marketers. Their student-centred approach to the text was refreshing and inspiring, and we hope we have maintained their vision in the Canadian edition.

We also would like to thank the many other people who have made significant contributions to this book. We greatly appreciate the time that each of the "Real People" generously spent to help us write the *Real People, Real Decisions* cases. Without their willingness to be involved, we could not have provided students with the decision maker focus that is so central to this book. In particular, we extend our thanks to Jacqui Cohen of Army & Navy Department Stores, Rahul Raj of Meal Exchange, Margaret Yee of Ethical Funds, Marshall Rice and Jeff Hohner of SurveySite, Robert Barnard and Shelley of d~Code, Michel Bendayan of Ritvik Holdings Inc., Candace Fochuk-Barey of Ford of Canada, Marshall Myles, Sarah Cutcliffe, and Jennifer Cornwell of Roots, Mary Louise Huebner of Canada Cutlery, Susan Brekelmans and Vaughn McIntyre of Charity.ca, Astrid de Bruyn of Palliser Furniture, Stephen Webb of the Clarion Hotel Grand Pacific, Ryan Hobenshield of HARTMANN Group, David Edward of Cormark Communications, and Desiree Walsh and Tessa Vanderkop of Raincoast Books.

We would also like to thank the people at Pearson Education Canada who worked so hard on the preparation of the book, especially Paul Donnelly, Mary Ann McCutcheon, Kelly Torrance, and Andrea Falkenberg.

Additional thanks go to our student assistants: Tim Underwood, Steve Dryburgh, Rachel Khanna, Hillary Samson, Rhys Leonard, and Ian Munro, who provided valuable research for the book. Thanks also to Jeff Fila who wrote the case on genetically modified food for the end of Chapter 3, and to Marianne Sipione, who provided research support on the Microsoft Xbox case at the end of Chapter 9.

We are grateful to the following reviewers who provided valuable feedback on all or part of the manuscript:

Ann Bonnell (New Brunswick Community College); Kathleen Byrne (Grant MacEwan College); Gary Dover (Georgian College); C. Shannon Goodspeed (Mount Royal College); Linda Hoffman (Northern Alberta Institute of Technology); Mary Louise Huebner (Seneca College); Henry Klaise (Durham College); Steve Janisse (St. Clair College); Stephen R. Lee (Algonquin College); Elaine MacNeil (University College of Cape Breton); Peter Mitchell (British Columbia Institute of Technology); Lesley J. Moffitt (Assiniboine Community College); Deborah Reyner (Conestoga College); Ted Seath (Durham College); Diana Serafini (Dawson College); Peter Yannopoulos (Brock University); Mark Valvasori (Mohawk College); Padma Vipat (Douglas College)

Our families also deserve a great deal of thanks for enduring with us through the writing process and for being understanding in spite of too many evenings and weekends spent working. To Paul, Emma, and Tommy Lupinacci and Claudia, Ford, and Reed Smith, we thank you for your patience and support.

Finally, we have had the privilege, through 30 years of combined teaching, to interact with outstanding students of marketing. It is those students who have provided much of the inspiration for this book. We wish to thank all of our previous and current students for providing us with the motivation to do this book, and for helping us better understand what students need and want in a marketing textbook.

Auleen Carson
Wilfrid Laurier University

J. Brock Smith
University of Victoria

A Great Way to Learn and Instruct Online

The Pearson Education Canada Companion Website is easy to navigate and is organized to correspond to the chapters in this textbook. Whether you are a student in the classroom or a distance learner you will discover helpful resources for in-depth study and research that empower you in your quest for greater knowledge and maximize your potential for success in the course.

Companion Website

[www.pearsoned.ca/solomon]

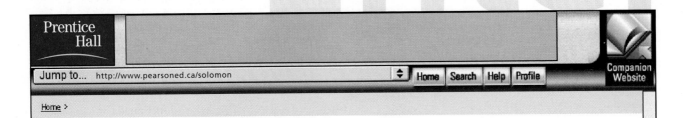

Prentice Hall

Jump to... http://www.pearsoned.ca/solomon ▲▼ | Home | Search | Help | Profile |

Companion Website

Home >

PH Companion Website

Marketing: Real People, Real Decisions, Updated First Canadian Edition, by Solomon, Stuart, Carson, and Smith

Student Resources

The modules in this section provide students with tools for learning course material. These modules include:

- Chapter Objectives
- Destinations
- Quizzes
- Internet Exercises
- Net Search

In the quiz modules students can send answers to the grader and receive instant feedback on their progress through the Results Reporter. Coaching comments and references to the textbook may be available to ensure that students take advantage of all available resources to enhance their learning experience.

Instructor Resources

The modules in this section provide instructors with additional teaching tools. Downloadable PowerPoint Presentations, Electronic Transparencies, and an Instructor's Manual are just some of the materials that may be available in this section. Where appropriate, this section will be password protected. To get a password, simply contact your Pearson Education Canada Representative or call Faculty Sales and Services at 1-800-850-5813.

SINCE 1919

ARMY & NAVY

ISSUE 1 11/01

A STORE IS BORN

**LANGLEY, B.C. OPENS
SATURDAY, NOVEMBER 3**

GOOD JEANS
**WE HAVE THE BLUES
FROM $12**

CAREER GEAR
**CORPORATE CLASSICS
FROM KAREN ELISE**

BARGAINS WITH BITE
FABULOUS FOOD SAVINGS

SALE STARTS:
SATURDAY
NOVEMBER 3RD

Low rise jeans $29

You won't believe what's in store.

1

Welcome to the World of Marketing

When you have completed your study of this chapter, you should be able to

CHAPTER OBJECTIVES

1. Define the marketing concept.

2. Define the objective of marketing.

3. Describe the marketing mix.

4. Understand the basics of marketing planning.

5. Describe the evolution of the marketing concept.

6. Explain how marketing is important to both individual and business customers in the marketplace, in our daily lives, and in society.

7. Explain marketing's role within an organization.

Real People, Real Decisions ✔ ✗

Meet Jacqui Cohen
A Decision Maker at Army & Navy

Jacqui Cohen has good instincts. A self-described "trust fund brat," who spent years living the high life with the international and Hollywood jet set, Cohen is now president of Army & Navy Department Stores, a chain her grandfather Sam Cohen built into a Western Canadian retail empire. The only surviving grandchild, Jacqui Cohen felt a strong pull to continue the family legacy and, in 1998, assumed the presidency of the $50 million operation after it had been managed by non-family members for three decades. She is the charismatic visionary who sets the direction for the organization and generally makes things happen. She makes all the major corporate decisions after seeking input from her management team. This flat structure allows Cohen to stay close to suppliers, store managers, and customers and keep her finger on the pulse of the 800-employee operation.

She grew up in the business, attended board meetings, and worked as a buyer for a year. With no formal business education, Cohen has relied on her instincts, knowledge of trends and fashion picked up during her years of travel, and marketing street smarts picked up growing up in the retail business and from her celebrity friends and their advisors. She is actively involved in the marketing strategy of the chain and works closely with her marketing team to make key marketing mix decisions. She is well respected for listening to ideas and suggestions from others, but is the creative spark behind Army & Navy's marketing strategy.

The Who of Marketing: Marketers and Customers

Army & Navy is a great example of a company that has succeeded for many years because its products provide value to customers. This book is about marketing. After you have read it, you will understand why companies like Army & Navy succeed in today's competitive business environment. You will have taken the first steps on the road to developing and executing marketing strategies that will benefit you, your organization, and society. First, you need to know more about marketing as a business function.

Marketers are drawn from many different backgrounds: Although many have earned business diplomas or degrees, others have backgrounds in other areas, such as engineering or computer science. Retailers and fashion marketers may have training in merchandising or design. Advertising copywriters often have degrees in English.

Although many students assume that the "typical" marketing job is in a large, consumer-oriented packaged goods company like Procter & Gamble, in fact, marketers work in other types of organizations, too—service organizations, such as Rogers Cable, e-commerce organizations, such as Chapters Online, technology companies, such as Nortel Networks, industrial equipment companies, such as Komatsu, agricultural companies, such as B.C. Hot House, not-for-profit organizations, such as the Canadian Cancer Society, or marketing services companies, such as Palmer Jarvis DDB advertising. In smaller organizations, one person (perhaps the owner) may handle all of the marketing responsibilities. In larger organizations, several marketers may work on different aspects of marketing strategy. Marketing was recently identified by *Canadian Business* magazine as one of the "cool careers" on the Canadian business scene. Marketers are currently in great demand, in both small and large Canadian organizations, providing future marketers with some great opportunities.[1] An extended discussion of career paths in marketing can be found on the Internet at www.pearsoned.ca.

At the beginning of each chapter, we will introduce you to professionals like Jacqui Cohen in a box called "Real People, Real Decisions." In the middle of the chapter, we'll tell you about a specific decision the marketer had to make and give you the possible options that person considered. That way, you'll be able to form your own opinion about which choice is the best. To conclude each chapter, we'll tell you what the decision maker decided and what happened. It is important to recognize that the decision maker may not have made the most appropriate decision. In fact, there are no "right answers" and, ultimately, consumers are the only judges of whether we as marketers have made good decisions. What you want to practise is making and defending your decisions based on appropriate analysis, application of marketing theory, concepts, and principles, and your judgment. Do not worry if you think that you might not have good judgment yet. That comes with experience and practice in making decisions.

What Is Marketing?

Marketing. Lots of people talk about it, but what is it? When you ask people to define marketing, you get many answers. Some say, "That's what happens when a pushy salesperson tries to sell me something I don't want." Others say, "Oh, that's simple—advertising." Others might say "merchandising," "pricing," "packaging," or "telephone soliciting." While each of these responses has some truth in it, none is complete. The term *marketing* means different things to different people (in England, it is even used as a synonym for shopping) and is used to refer to a business function, a business philosophy, and a decision-making process. As a business function, marketing involves activities within organizations relating to product or brand management, sales, advertising, and public relations. Larger firms may have separate departments for each of these marketing activities.

As a business philosophy, the **marketing concept** is concerned with the mindset, or orientation, business people have with respect to operating their business. The marketing concept suggests that organizational objectives such as long-term profitability are best met by understanding what consumers need and want, and the associated costs of satisfying them—thus making informed decisions of whether to provide products that satisfy those needs and wants.

As the marketing concept suggests, marketing is primarily a decision-making process that allows organizations to achieve objectives by satisfying consumer needs and wants. The American Marketing Association, the world's largest professional marketing association, uses this definition of marketing: "**Marketing** is the process of planning and executing the conception, pricing, promotion, and distribution of ideas, goods, and services to create exchanges that satisfy individual and organizational objectives."[2] To better understand the process of marketing, it is helpful to examine this definition in some detail. Let's start at the end of the definition and work backwards.

Marketing Satisfies Needs

The most important part of the definition is "...satisfy individual and organizational objectives." It tells us about the central aspect of marketing: satisfying the needs of both buyers and sellers. A **consumer** is the ultimate user of a good or service. Consumers can be individuals or organizations (although we usually use the term customer when referring to an organization), whether a company, government, or charity, all with different needs. But the seller, or marketer, also has needs—to make a profit, achieve organizational goals, and to remain in business. So products are *sold* to satisfy marketers' objectives. Thus, marketing is all about satisfying needs. A **need** is the difference between a consumer's actual state and some ideal or desired state. When the difference is big enough, the consumer is motivated to take action to satisfy the need. When you're hungry, you buy a snack. If you're not happy how your hair looks, you get a new haircut.

Needs can be related to physical functions, such as eating, or to psychological ones, such as wanting to look good. Research has shown, for example, that people wear such clothes as Roots hats to say important things about themselves and their desired image; the clothes satisfy the wearer's need for self-expression. Consumers can become very attached to their clothes; Levi Strauss, for example, occasionally receives in the mail a pair of beat-up pants with a letter from the owner requesting that they be given a proper burial.[3]

The specific way a need is satisfied depends on an individual's history, learning experiences, and cultural environment. A **want** is a desire for a particular product to satisfy a need

❖ ❖ ❖
marketing concept A management orientation that focuses on achieving organizational objectives by understanding consumer needs and wants and the associated costs of satisfying them.

❖ ❖ ❖
marketing The process of planning and executing the conception, pricing, promotion, and distribution of ideas, goods, and services to create exchanges that satisfy individual and organizational objectives.

❖ ❖ ❖
consumer The ultimate user of a good or service.

❖ ❖ ❖
need Recognition of any difference between a consumer's actual state and some ideal or desired state.

❖ ❖ ❖
want The desire to satisfy needs in specific ways that are culturally and socially influenced.

in specific ways; it is influenced culturally and socially. For example, two classmates' stomachs rumble during a lunchtime lecture and both need food. However, how each person satisfies this need might be quite different. The first student may be concerned about their health and so they think about munching on a big handful of trail mix, whereas the second person may be equally enticed by a greasy cheeseburger and fries. So, the first student's want is trail mix, while the second student's want is fast food.

benefit The outcome sought by a customer that motivates buying behaviour.

A product delivers a **benefit** when it satisfies a need or want. For marketers to be successful, they must develop products that provide one or more benefits. The challenge is to identify what benefits people look for, develop a product that delivers those benefits, and then convince buyers that it does so better than a competitor's. As the management expert Peter Drucker wrote, "The aim of marketing is to make selling superfluous."[4]

If we succeed in creating a product that meets the needs of the customer, he or she will happily buy it without any "persuasion" from a salesperson. For example, the Swiss firm Ste. Suisse Microélectronique et d'Horlogerie S.A. (S.M.H.) changed the face of the low-priced watch market when it introduced the Swatch watch. These inexpensive pieces of "time-keeping jewellery" satisfy consumers' need for a reliable time piece at a reasonable price, at the same time giving them the benefit of wearing a colourful and trendy fashion accessory. Another benefit is that these watches can be bought at drugstores, department stores, and fashion boutiques rather than at intimidating high-end jewellery stores.[5]

demand Customers' desire for products coupled with the resources to obtain them.

market All of the customers and potential customers who share a common need that can be satisfied by a specific product, who have the resources to exchange for it, who are willing to make the exchange, and who have the authority to make the exchange.

Everyone can want your product, but that doesn't ensure sales unless they have the means to obtain it. When desire is coupled with the buying power or resources to satisfy a want, the result is **demand**. So, the potential customers for a snappy red BMW convertible are the people who want the car *minus* those who can't afford to buy or lease one. A **market** consists of all the consumers who share a common need that can be satisfied by a specific product or service, who have the resources, willingness, and authority to make the exchange.

marketplace Any location or medium used to conduct an exchange.

A **marketplace** used to be a location where buying and selling occurred face-to-face. In today's wired world, however, buyers and sellers might not even see each other. Today's marketplace has assumed a variety of forms in which merchants, distributors, brokers, agents, and other third parties conduct the exchanges. The modern marketplace may be a shopping mall, a mail-order catalogue, a television shopping network, a home page on the Internet, or even a neighbourhood garage sale like the one shown in Exhibit 1.1.

social marketing concept An orientation that focuses on satisfying consumer needs while also addressing the needs of the larger society.

SATISFYING SOCIETY'S NEEDS, TOO

The marketing definition talks about satisfying both individual and organizational objectives. A recent movement in marketing is the **social marketing concept**, which emphasizes that customer needs must be satisfied in ways that also benefit society. Large and small firms

Exhibit 1.1

Even a garage sale is a marketplace.

alike practise this philosophy (see Exhibit 1.2). These efforts include: satisfying society's environmental and social needs for a cleaner, safer environment by developing recyclable packaging; adding extra safety features like car air bags; voluntarily modifying a manufacturing process to reduce pollution; and sponsoring campaigns to address social problems. For example, McCain Foods Ltd., one of the world's largest makers of frozen french fries, refuses to process genetically altered potatoes.[6]

Marketing Is an Exchange of Value

Central to the philosophy reflected in the marketing concept is an understanding that organizations exist to create value for consumers where it is neither efficient nor effective for consumers to attempt to satisfy their needs themselves.[7] The phrase "to create exchanges..." in our definition of marketing identifies the heart of every marketing act. An **exchange** occurs when something of value is obtained by one party for something of value offered in return to another. Typically, a buyer receives an object, service, or idea that satisfies a need, and a seller receives money in exchange.

For an exchange to occur, at least two people or organizations must be willing to make a trade, and each must have something the other wants. Both parties must perceive the exchange as being a good deal—that is, each must believe that what they are receiving in an exchange is worth the same or more than what they are offering in return. Both parties can feel this way because value is perceived—different parties have different ideas about how to best satisfy their needs. **Customer value**, the value perceived by a customer, is an assessment of what the customer gets from a product (benefits or utility) relative to what they have to give up to purchase and use it (price and such other costs as operating costs, and such sacrifices as the time and effort required to buy and use the product). Parties must also agree on the value of the exchange and how it will be carried out and be free to accept or reject the other's terms for the exchange.

Today, most exchanges occur in the form of a *monetary transaction*, where currency (in the form of cash, cheque, debit or credit card) is surrendered in return for a good or service. Even the nature of this basic act is evolving, as electronic commerce systems (*e-money*) permit sales exchanges without coins and paper money ever changing hands. Some of the most rapid and exciting changes in marketing are occurring on the Internet, where consumers search for and buy products directly. E-commerce allows merchants selling virtually anything to reach customers around the world.

(Almost) Anything Can Be Marketed

The "...ideas, goods, and services..." part of the marketing definition shows that just about anything can be marketed. Indeed, some of the best marketers come from the ranks of services companies such as American Express or not-for-profit organizations such as Greenpeace. Even politicians, athletes, and performers use marketing to their advantage. Ideas, such as democracy, religion, and art, also compete for acceptance in a "marketplace." In this book, we'll refer to any good (physical product), service (intangible product), or idea that can be marketed as a **product**, even though what is being sold may not take a physical form. These products may be directed at consumers for personal or family use, or at other organizations for use in their operations (such as office equipment) or for incorporation in their consumer products (such as component parts). Although consumer goods are more visible, in reality more goods are sold to businesses and other organizations than to consumers.

NOT-FOR-PROFIT MARKETING

You don't have to be a businessperson to use marketing principles. Many not-for-profit organizations, including museums, churches, and even zoos (see Exhibit 1.3), practise the marketing concept. Even local governments are getting into the act, as they adopt marketing techniques to create more effective taxpayer services and to attract new businesses and industries to their regions and cities. The intense competition for support of civic and

Exhibit 1.2

Social marketing, such as Durex Condoms' sponsorship of Saskatoon band Wide Mouth Mason, applies marketing principles to the promotion of social ideas and issues.

✳ ✳ ✳
exchange The process by which some transfer of value occurs between a buyer and a seller.

✳ ✳ ✳
customer value What the customer gets in the purchase, use, and ownership of a product relative to the costs and sacrifices incurred.

✳ ✳ ✳
product A tangible good, a service, an idea, or some combination of these that, through the exchange process, satisfies consumer or business customer needs; a bundle of attributes including features, functions, benefits, and uses.

Exhibit 1.3

Calgary Zoo: Not-for-profit organizations also practise the marketing concept.

charitable activities means that only those not-for-profits that meet the needs of their constituents and donors will survive.

IDEA, PLACE, AND PEOPLE MARKETING

Marketing principles are also used to get people to endorse ideas or to change their behaviours in positive ways. Many organizations work hard to convince consumers to use seat belts, engage in safe sex, not litter, not smoke, and not drink and drive.

In addition to ideas, places and people also are marketed. We are all familiar with tourism marketing, whether for resorts like Club Med, or for provinces such as "explore, relax, indulge, enjoy" Prince Edward Island and "Super-Natural" British Columbia. Indeed, tourism is an important industry for Canada. Tourists spend over $47 million a year in Canada on goods and services, and tourism industries employ over 500 000 people in Canada.[8]

Tourist events, sports, and other entertainment activities do not just happen; people must plan them. Whether for a sports team or a ballet company, the application of sound marketing principles helps ensure that fans will continue to support the activity and buy tickets. Today, sports and the arts are hotbeds of activity for marketing. A big part of these efforts involves promoting the athletes and artists who create these experiences. You may have heard the expression, "Stars are made, not born." It means that many of the famous people you pay to see got famous with the help of some shrewd marketing: They (and their handlers) developed a "product" that they hoped would appeal to some segment of the population. For example, basketball player Shaquille O'Neal's marketing strategy is to be the biggest fish in any pond (see Exhibit 1.4).

Exhibit 1.4

Shaquille O'Neal is part of a marketing machine intended to promote "Team Shaq"— people marketing at its best.

SPOTLIGHT ON REAL PEOPLE *JobDirect*

People are "products" that need to be marketed, and that's especially true in the job market. After watching the hassles their friends experienced while searching for entry-level jobs after graduating, 21-year-old undergraduates Rachel Bell and Sara Sutton had an idea. They believed that the Internet was the answer to matching up student job seekers with employers. For many, blanketing companies with letters and making hours of unproductive phone calls to surly company receptionists was a real dead end. So, Bell and Sutton put their last year of school on hold, swallowed hard, and started JobDirect, an Internet-based service that is now the largest database of entry-level student jobs on the Web.

The service is free to students, but companies—including IBM, Xerox, and Lotus—pay a fee to access the resumé data-base. These clients can search for resumés fitting specific criteria, such as students who speak French and have at least a B average.

Although all of the jobs in the JobDirect database are currently located in the US, students from Canada and other countries around the world are able to use the database free of charge, providing they are willing and able to accept a job in the US.

The largest Canadian sites for job postings and career information is Workopolis.com, a joint venture between The Globe and Mail and Torstar Corporation (www.workopolis.com). However, Monster.ca is challenging Workopolis.com for Canadian market supremacy. Other sites include CACEE WorkWeb (www.cacee.com) and the Canadian government site for Human Resources Development Canada (www.hrdc-drhc.gc.ca).

1. What is JobDirect's market?
2. What benefits does a service such as JobDirect provide to these customers?
3. How does this chapter's concept of "people marketing" fit in with what JobDirect does?
4. Compare the Workopolis.com and Monster.ca websites. What is the positioning of each site? How could each be improved to meet the needs of its target market?

He and his agent developed a marketing concept they called "Team Shaq," in which they designed a Shaq logo and copyrighted the name "Shaq" and the phrase "Shaq Attaq."[9] Wayne Gretzky, probably Canada's most famous athlete, works with the marketing arm of The International Management Group to devise an overall marketing strategy, which includes personal endorsements, lending his name and image to products, promoting his own clothing line, and establishing equity positions with companies. He has now joined forces and linked his image with those of Michael Jordon and John Elway in an online retail venture MVP.com.

Although it may seem strange to think about the marketing of people, in reality we often talk about ourselves and others in marketing terms. It is common for people to speak of "positioning" themselves for job interviews, or telling others not to "sell themselves short." In addition, many consumers hire personal image consultants to devise a "marketing strategy" for them, while others undergo plastic surgery, physical conditioning, or cosmetic makeovers, to improve their "product images." This desire by consumers to package and promote themselves is the reason for goods and services markets ranging from cosmetics and exercise equipment to resumé specialists and dating agencies.[10]

JobDirect
www.jobdirect.com

The Premier Online Sports and Outdoor Store
www.mvp.com

How Are Marketing Decisions Made?

"Marketing is a process of planning and executing..." This part of the definition of marketing suggests that marketing is a series of steps and decisions that entail both careful thought (planning) and action (executing). When it's done right, marketing is a strategic decision process in which marketing managers determine the market strategies that will help the organization meet its long-term objectives. To do this, marketers develop and implement a *marketing plan*.

The Objective of Marketing

The overall objective of this plan (and marketing in general) is to achieve objectives—individual, organizational, and societal—by creating superior customer value, for exchange with customers in one or more target market segments, with a sustainable strategy. Consistent with the marketing concept, this suggests that organizational objectives are best met by creating superior value for customers—that is, creating products that satisfy the needs and wants of consumers better than alternatives available to them. Because consumers have different needs and wants and different ideas on how best to satisfy them, marketers need to decide which consumers they are going to try to satisfy and which they are not. This concept of target market segments will be discussed in more detail in Chapter 8. This definition also suggests that marketing is primarily about facilitating exchange relationships. Finally, it suggests that the decisions marketers make about objectives, target markets, and value creation, need to be made with sustainability in mind—in a way that allows an organization to maintain ongoing superiority in the minds of their target consumers until all of the objectives of the organization have been met. This overall objective is met through marketing planning.

Marketing Planning

The objective of marketing suggests that marketing is primarily a creative task, focused on identifying and producing valued products, but doing this in a sustainable way that allows the organization to achieve long-term objectives. To accomplish this, marketers engage in strategic planning, a process of identifying and analyzing alternative ways of achieving objectives. The first phase of strategic marketing planning involves analyzing the organization's current strengths (S) and weaknesses (W) by assessing factors that might help or hinder the development and marketing of products. The analysis must also take into account the opportunities (O) and threats (T) the organization will encounter in the marketplace, such as the actions of competitors, cultural and technological changes, the economy, and so on. These issues and SWOT analysis will be the focus of Chapters 2 and 3, but to see how far-reaching these concerns can be, consider some of the many factors a firm like Levi Strauss has to think about when planning and developing its marketing strategy:

Levi Strauss & Co.
www.levistrauss.com

- What jeans styles will our core customers of young people be looking for in three to five years?

- Which customer groups that don't currently buy a lot of blue jeans might we target for Levi's products?

- How will new developments in computerized production technologies affect the denim manufacturing process?

- Will the current trend for many companies to institute "Casual Fridays," when employees can wear jeans to work, affect long-term demand for Levi's products?

- How will consumers' growing awareness about the use of child labour in Third World countries affect their attitudes toward manufacturers that locate plants overseas?

Answers to these and other questions provide the foundation for developing an organization's marketing plan. It supports management's decisions for setting specific marketing objectives and determining how the organization will meet these objectives.

Finding and Reaching a Target Market

✳ ✳ ✳

market segment A distinct group of customers within a larger market, who are similar to one another in some way and whose needs differ from other customers in the larger market.

The most critical decision marketers make is in the selection of the specific target market segment(s) on which they will focus their customer value creation efforts. All other decisions depend on the particular needs, wants, preferences, and behaviour of the target market(s). A **market segment** is a distinct group of customers within a larger market who have similar needs, wants, preferences, and behaviours, who seek similar product solutions, and whose needs differ from other customers in the larger market. Parents with young children, for example, typically seek different entertainment products than teenagers and young

Real People, Real Decisions
Decision Time at Army & Navy

Army & Navy was once a $100-million business that provided value to customers by buying merchandise from bankrupt or overstocked merchants and passing on the savings. Sales are now about half that. Large retailers such as Wal-Mart and Zellers are rapidly increasing their market share with the cost-conscious customer, and discount clubs such as Costco have adopted a similar strategy to that which made Army & Navy successful.

The location of the flagship Army & Navy store on Hastings Street in downtown Vancouver has also changed, not physically, but demographically. Once the upscale business centre of Vancouver, Hastings Street, next to trendy Gastown, is now run down and dirty, the centre of Vancouver's drug trade, and is perceived by many to be seedy and unsafe. Woolworth's, Woodwards, and Sears, once retail neighbours of Army & Navy, have moved or have gone out of business, replaced by pawn shops, tattoo parlours, and offices for social programs. Loyal Army & Navy customers, once young parents, are now seniors, and new generations of customers are unaware of what Army & Navy is all about. Declining sales were not just observed in the downtown Vancouver store; sales had been declining throughout the Army & Navy chain. They had lost touch with their traditional customer base and had lost their unique positioning in the marketplace.

Army & Navy was in trouble, and Jacqui Cohen and her team realized that something had to be done—walk away or try to fix it. Although a new marketing strategy was clearly needed, it was uncertain if the store should risk a large investment when cash flow was short. They also had to decide whom to target—current older shoppers or, going back to their roots, young adults and parents with young families.

The first thing Cohen decided to do was gather information from potential customer groups to find out what they thought about the stores. Mostly, the researchers were given the task of finding out why particular shoppers did not think to visit Army & Navy. They asked four focus groups of six people each to spend $20 at the Army & Navy store in Vancouver or New Westminster. Two groups were shoppers aged 25 to 35, and two were shoppers aged 35 to 49. All of the guest shoppers made regular purchases at Zellers or Wal-Mart and none of them had ever been to an Army & Navy store. The study concluded that the problem for Army

& Navy was in brand perception—no one knew what to expect going into Army & Navy; the name had no meaning to them. Also, the stores were perceived to be untidy and disorganized. Armed with this information, Cohen needed to decide what to do with the chain.

Option 1. The first option Cohen considered was selling the stores. She could live very comfortably on the proceeds of selling the business and could spend more time with her daughter and in running her "Face the World" charity. "Sell" was the advice from her peers, some of whom were heirs of other prominent department store families. This, however, would end 80 years of Cohen ownership and the family legacy.

Option 2. Re-establish the traditional positioning of Army & Navy as a place for young adults and young families to buy unique merchandise, find "deals," and have an original retro-style destination shopping experience. This would require a million-dollar advertising campaign aimed at enticing younger, "hipper" clientele to come into the store for the first time. It would also require a revitalized merchandizing strategy, presenting the current mix of unique and interesting retro merchandise in a way that made for a fun shopping adventure, with neat stuff around every corner. With cash flow being tight, this option was financially risky. Attracting younger consumers could also alienate their current older shoppers if they perceived that the store was no longer for them. Certainly there were no guarantees that younger shoppers would come back to Army & Navy.

Option 3. A third option was to try to re-establish the traditional positioning of Army & Navy, with a scaled down advertising campaign focusing on just the Vancouver market. Cohen was not sure whether customers in Calgary, Edmonton, Regina, and Saskatoon had the same shopping preferences and values as those in Vancouver and was concerned that young adults in those cities may not be attracted to an "original-retro" concept store. The strategy for the other cities would be to focus on current and previous customers, reminding them of the value of shopping at Army & Navy.

Now, join the Army & Navy decision team: Which option would you choose, and why?

***

adults. Depending on its goals and resources, a company may choose to focus on one or more market segments. The chosen market segment(s) become the organization's **target market(s)** toward which it directs its product development efforts. Because different target markets have different and sometimes conflicting needs, wants, and preferences, marketers

target markets
The market segment(s) on which an organization focuses its marketing plan and toward which it directs its marketing efforts.

typically have to choose among alternative segments on which to focus. This is one of Jacqui Cohen's dilemmas at Army & Navy department stores—how to attract new consumers without turning off other consumers at the same time. Similarly, Canadian fashion designer Linda Lundstrom and her company, Linda Lundstrom Ltd., doesn't make clothes for everyone. First, she designs clothing only for women. Lundstrom further narrows her market by focusing on the needs of women with less-than-perfect figures. She also gears her line toward working women who need clothes that can wear and travel well. Her most successful item is an extremely warm winter coat that combines comfort and function with a style based on First Nation's artist Norval Morriseau's traditional patterns.

***
mass market All possible customers in a market, regardless of the differences in their specific needs and wants.

Some firms choose to reach as many customers as possible by offering their products to a **mass market**, which consists of all possible customers in a market, regardless of the differences in their specific needs and wants. This strategy, however, is only effective with products such as Coca-Cola that have very broad appeal—and usually competitors of mass marketers, or even the mass marketers themselves, bring alternative products to market that have greater appeal to a subset of the people in the mass market (such as Barq's root beer), eroding the market share of the mass market product.

SEGMENTING THE MARKET

As will be discussed in more detail in Chapter 8, market segmentation is a process of dividing the overall market into groups of consumers who have similar needs and wants (seek similar benefits) or have similar purchase or consumption behaviours (buy or use products similarly) that are different from consumers in other groups. Consumers can be grouped by characteristics such as sex, age, income, place of residence, or even hobbies and leisure activities, if these characteristics reflect differences in underlying needs, wants, or behaviours. One way that Levi Strauss slices up the market is in terms of age segments—this makes sense, since different age groups have different clothing wants and may wear jeans for different purposes. Business-to-business markets are sometimes divided into segments using characteristics such as type of business, size, or sales volume, if these characteristics reflect differences in the needs, wants, or behaviours of organizations.

SELECTING A TARGET MARKET

Marketers weigh each of the segments in terms of profitability potential against the organization's resources and ability to satisfy the needs of the segments. On the basis of this analysis, the organization decides whether it will focus on a single segment or several segments. For example, the athletic shoe company Kaepa, Inc. was on the verge of going under, outrun by such shoe giants as Nike and Reebok, when it began receiving calls from cheerleaders requesting special orders of sneakers that could be customized with snap-on logos. Market research revealed that there are about 40 000 aspiring cheerleaders attending training camps every summer. This was an attractive but untapped segment of the athletic shoe market. As seen in Exhibit 1.5, Kaepa executives successfully redid the company's marketing strategy to target this market, including the development of a special Radical Grip shoe that features finger grooves on soles to help enthusiastic cheerleaders build people pyramids during the game.

Exhibit 1.5

Kaepa evaluated potential market segments and targeted cheerleaders.

Many companies know that they must look for potential target markets beyond their own geographical borders to compete in today's world economy. Modern marketers are busy meeting the needs of people all around the world, especially when the demand for products at home flattens. Throughout the text we will emphasize marketing's need to think globally.

Expanding internationally is desirable, for example, to the Mattel Corporation, as you can see in Exhibit 1.6. The average North American girl owns eight Barbies, making it the best-selling toy ever. The domestic market is starting to become saturated, so Mattel is diversifying to offset the company's reliance on North American Barbie sales. It recently acquired Fisher-Price for $1.1 billion and has plans to expand around the world. Europe has nearly twice as many children as North America; and numbers in Mexico, South America, Japan, and Southeast Asia are even greater. Mattel now manufactures 75% of its toys in plants around the world, including Indonesia, Malaysia, China, Mexico, and Italy.[11]

Exhibit 1.6

Mattel is exporting the Barbie craze to consumers around the world.

DEVELOPING AND POSITIONING THE PRODUCT

After choosing the target market(s), marketers need to develop a product that appeals to the needs, wants, and preferences of that target market better than alternatives provided by competitors. They do this by first setting a **market position**—how the product will be different and superior to competitors' products in the mind of the customer. This is the key issue faced by Jacqui Cohen at Army & Navy department stores. Many products have well-established positions in the minds of consumers as the result of long-running, carefully crafted promotional campaigns. A BMW is viewed by many as a high-status, serious driving machine, while a Civic del Sol is carefree and a little funky. The Mark Anthony Group wanted to position its new vodka-based lemon-flavoured cooler as an approachable, fun, and cheerful brand that men, particularly those aged 18 to 24, wouldn't feel "too dorky" drinking at a party.[12] With assistance from the M5 Design Group, they evaluated eight different concepts and chose "Mike's Hard Lemonade", "Mike" being a fun, party, happy-go-lucky guy who is infatuated with lemons.

Following the overall positioning decision, marketers make a set of decisions about the product itself, its price, the place it is available for purchase, and the activities that introduce it to consumers. These decisions, collectively called the **marketing mix**, establish the positioning of the product offering, create superior customer value, and create a desired response among members of the target market. Just as a radio DJ puts together a collection of separate songs (a musical mix) to create a certain mood, the idea of a mix in this context reminds us that no *single* marketing activity is sufficient to accomplish the organization's objectives, and that consistency among the decisions is critical to the overall marketing (or music) program.

Marketing's Tools: The Marketing Mix

The "...conception, pricing, promotion, and distribution..." in the definition of marketing means that whether it's a box of detergent, a sports medicine clinic, an alternative rock song, or a Roots sweatshirt, a product must be invented or developed, assigned value and meaning, and made available to interested consumers. The elements of the marketing mix are commonly known as *the four Ps*: product, price, promotion, and place. Together, the bundle of marketing mix elements represents an offer value to the consumer, what the customer will receive in an exchange. As shown in Figure 1.1, each is a piece of the puzzle that must be combined with other pieces. We will examine these components of the marketing mix in detail later in this book. For now, let's briefly look at each element of the four Ps to gain some insight into its meaning and role in the marketing mix.

✳ ✳ ✳

market position The way in which the target market perceives the product in comparison to competitors' brands.

✳ ✳ ✳

marketing mix A combination of the product itself, the price of the product, the place where it is made available, and the activities that introduce it to consumers, which creates a desired response among a set of predefined consumers.

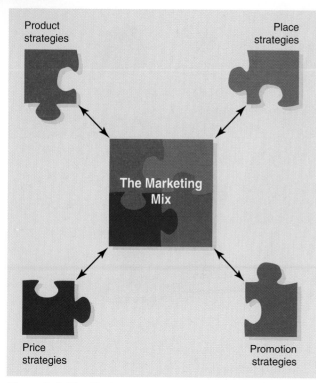

Figure 1–1 The Marketing Mix

PRODUCT

The product is a good, service, idea, place, person—whatever is offered for exchange. This aspect of the marketing mix includes the design and packaging of a good, as well as its physical features and any associated services, such as free delivery. The Mark Anthony Group, for example, had to design a product and its packaging that would be consistent with their "hip party drink beer alternative" positioning. They decide on a seven percent alcohol content (not a sissy drink), a closed four-pack package (more like beer, less like traditional coolers), hip graphics on the bottle and packaging that conveyed "hard attitude," and a "tag line" (positioning summary) on the bottle that reads: "Mike's Hard Lemonade—An excellent source of vodka." These decisions are all consistent with the intended positioning and target market.

PRICE

Price is the seller's assessment of the value of a product, what they would like to receive from the buyer in exchange for the product. The decision about how much to charge for something is not simple. For example, jeans costing $30 have a different image than those that cost $80. Procter & Gamble, which used to determine its prices based on what a product actually cost to develop plus a profit, now does research on what consumers in different countries can afford and develops products that it can offer at lower prices when the market is unwilling to buy the regular-priced ones. For example, in Brazil, P&G launched Pampers Uni, a less expensive version of its Pampers brand of diapers to expand the number of tiny customers in that country who sported its brand on their bottoms.[13] Mike's Hard Lemonade is priced competitively with imported beers. This helps maintain an image that it's a premium product and that consumers of the product are sophisticated and are not cheap.

* * *
price The seller's assignment of value to a product.

PLACE

Place is the availability of the product to the customer at the desired time and location. As we'll see in Chapter 14, this *P* is also known as the *channels of distribution*, which are the firms that work together to get a product from a producer to a consumer. For consumer goods like Roots clothing products, this channel includes retailers such as The Bay, as well as their own Roots retail outlets and the Roots Web site (www.roots.com). Part of Mike's success is its wide distribution—available at liquor stores, beer stores, bars, and restaurants, it's easy to find.

* * *
place The availability of the product to the customer at the desired time and location.

PROMOTION

Promotion refers to the communication activities undertaken to inform consumers or organizations about goods, services, or ideas, and to encourage potential customers to buy these goods, services, or ideas. Communication activities can take many forms, including personal selling, advertising, in-store displays, coupons, billboards, and public relations. Mike's communication strategy supports the brand image by developing and supporting the "personalities" of Mike and the lemonade. Cute stories about Mike and lemons were included on the packaging, and the product was brought to consumers' attention with print advertising, in-store displays, and on-shelf signage. After Mike's initial success, television advertising was created that showed "lemons being hurt real bad in the making of this product" and investigators trying to determine "who has been hurting the lemons." These quirky light-hearted ads helped make Mike's the leading brand in the Canadian cooler market. They also have a hip Internet site (www.mikeshardlemonade.com), which further supports the brand personality.

* * *
promotion The coordination of communication efforts by a marketer to inform or persuade consumers or organizations about goods, services, or ideas.

Marketing as a Process: Final Thoughts

The idea of marketing being a process has taken on new importance today. It tells us that successful marketing exchanges occur continuously over time. For many marketers, the view that doing business is a one-time transaction in which a company tries to "put one over" on its customers by delivering a minimal product at a maximum price is no longer acceptable. As will be discussed further in Chapter 16, the concept of **relationship marketing** sees marketing as a process of building long-term relationships, not only with key customers but also with suppliers, distributors, employees, and other **stakeholders**, who are integral to the value creation process. Managing customer, supplier, distributor, and other relationships is so critical to the success of most organizations that a fifth *P*—people—is often considered part of the "marketing mix." Part of the success of Mike's Hard Lemonade, for example, can be attributed to the working relationships The Mark Anthony Group have with the M5 Design Group, their advertising agency, and key retailers. It would have taken a lot trust in these relationships to launch a cooler named "Mike."

✳ ✳ ✳
relationship marketing A marketing philosophy that focuses on building long-term relationships with customers, suppliers, distributors, and other key stakeholders to satisfy mutual needs.

✳ ✳ ✳
stakeholders Individuals or organizations who affect, or are affected by, the activities of a firm.

When Did Marketing Begin?
The Evolution of a Concept

Now that we have an idea of how the marketing process works, let's take a step back and see how this process has developed over time. Although it may sound like common sense, the notion that businesses and other organizations succeed when they satisfy customers' needs is a recent one. Let's look at how the marketing discipline has developed from a product orientation to a New Era orientation. This evolution has certainly not been universal—you can still find many examples of companies today that have the marketing mindset associated with each of these orientations.

The Product Orientation

Organizations that focus on the most efficient production and distribution of products, and not whether these products best satisfy consumers' needs, have a **product orientation**. This focus works best in a **seller's market**, when demand is greater than supply. Essentially, consumers have to take whatever is available. Under these conditions, marketing plays a relatively insignificant role; the goods literally sell themselves because people have no other choices. This was the case in the formerly communist countries, where the centralized government set production quotas, and shoppers lined up (often for hours) to take whatever happened to be on a store's shelves at the time. Many of today's technology-oriented companies have a product orientation—they make technologically "neat" products without much thought to consumer needs and wants.

✳ ✳ ✳
product orientation Management philosophy that emphasizes the most efficient ways to produce and distribute products.

✳ ✳ ✳
seller's market A market in which demand is greater than supply.

Firms that focus on a product orientation tend to view the market as a homogeneous group that will be satisfied with the basic function of a product. Sometimes this view is too narrow. For example, Procter & Gamble's Ivory Soap has been in decline for some time, because P&G viewed the brand as plain old soap, not as a cleansing product that could provide other benefits as well. Ivory Soap lost business to newer deodorant and "beauty" soaps containing cold cream that appealed to different customer needs in this market.[14]

The Selling Orientation

When product availability exceeds demand in a **buyer's market**, businesses may engage in the "hard sell," in which salespeople aggressively push their products. During the Depression in the 1930s, firms shifted their focus from a production orientation to selling their goods any way they could. This **selling orientation** means that management views marketing as a sales function, or a way to move products out of warehouses so that inventories don't pile up.

✳ ✳ ✳
buyer's market A market in which product availability exceeds demand.

✳ ✳ ✳
selling orientation A managerial view of marketing as a sales function, or a way to move products out of warehouses to reduce inventory.

This orientation began after World War II. During the war, Canada dramatically increased its industrial capacity to manufacture tanks, combat boots, parachutes, and countless other wartime goods. After the war, the peacetime economy boomed—Canadians had more disposable income, and manufacturers used the increased factory capacity to turn out an abundance of civilian favourites. Suddenly, people had lots of choices and a bounty of products, such as the car pictured in Exhibit 1.7, to choose from.

Consumers eagerly bought all the things they hadn't been able to get during the war years; but once these initial needs and wants were satisfied, people became more selective. The race for consumers' hearts and pocketbooks was on. The selling orientation prevailed well into the 1950s. But consumers, as a rule, don't like to be pushed, and the hard sell approach gave marketing a bad image.

Companies that still follow a selling orientation tend to be more successful at making one-time sales rather than building repeat business. This focus is most likely to be found among companies that sell **unsought goods**, such as cemetery plots that people don't tend to buy without some prodding.

The Consumer Orientation

Grocery retailer Thrifty Foods enjoys a 25% market share on Vancouver Island by focusing on quality meats and produce, selection, value, and service. Over the past 23 years, president Alex Campbell has introduced unique services and programs for his customers, including home delivery, composting and recycling, and "kiddie-friendly" tills that offer Sesame Snaps and colouring books instead of candy.[15] Thrifty Foods has found that it pays to have a **consumer orientation**—being proactive and responsive in identifying and satisfying customers' needs and wants.

The effect of this consumer orientation, which began in the early 1950s, gave management a way to outdo the competition, and it elevated marketing's importance. Marketers researched segment markets, assisted in tailoring products to the needs of different consumer

✷ ✷ ✷

unsought good A good or service for which a consumer has little awareness or interest until the product or a need for the product is brought to his or her attention.

✷ ✷ ✷

consumer orientation A management philosophy that focuses on being proactive and responsive in identifying and satisfying consumer needs and wants.

groups, and did an even better job of designing marketing messages than in the days of the selling orientation. The marketing concept was born.

The marketing world was humming along nicely, but then inflation in the 1970s and recession in the 1980s took their toll on company profits. The marketing concept by itself was becoming insufficient. Firms had to do more than meet consumers' needs; they had to do it better than the competition. They increasingly concentrated on improving the quality of their products, and by the early 1990s, total quality management (see Chapter 3), a management effort to involve all employees from the assembly line onward in continuous product quality improvement, was well entrenched in the marketing community.

The New Era Orientation

Yet another fundamental change in marketing is occurring right now, as the goal of long-term growth continues. While the customer is still "number one," many of today's forward-thinking organizations are seeing their commitment to quality as more than simply satisfying consumers' needs. This **New Era orientation** to marketing means a devotion to excellence in designing and producing products that benefit the customer, *plus* the firm's employees, shareholders, and communities. For example, Tim Collings, while a professor at Simon Fraser University, invented the "V-chip," a device that allows parents to regulate TV programs viewed by children, in response to the December 6, 1989, student massacre at Montreal's École Polytechnique.

One outgrowth of this new way of thinking is the focus on relationship marketing; another is the emphasis on social marketing, which includes efforts to promote consumers' health, safety, and well-being. New Era managers support such efforts as encouraging cultural diversity and ethical business practices, and helping the environment even as they pursue financial profitability. IKEA, for example, insists that their worldwide suppliers, including Canadian forest companies, provide solid wood materials in environmentally friendly ways.[16]

New Era firms embrace the principles of the social marketing concept, seeking both economic and social profit. Consider, for example, Levi Strauss's decision to develop its Naturals line of jeans, which don't use any chemical dyes to colour the pants. Consumers found that the natural colour actually looked nicer with repeated washing, and demand for the jeans during the line's first year was overwhelming. Clearly, the marketing strategies underlying Naturals resulted in benefits for the environment, the consumer, and the company.[17]

> ✳ ✳ ✳
> **New Era orientation** A management philosophy in which marketing decision making means a devotion to excellence in designing and producing products and creating products that benefit the customer plus the firm's employees, shareholders, and fellow citizens.

Why Is Marketing Important?

Levi Strauss has come a long way from the days when its basic pants were piled on pushcarts and sold to miners, and the company owes much of its success to astute marketing. But the lessons learned by companies like this can be applied in many areas of our lives, so let's turn our attention to explaining why these principles benefit us in many ways. The basic principles of marketing apply to the sale of canned peas, to the delivery of food and clothing to needy people, to the fortunes of a symphony orchestra. Because meeting the needs of consumers and society in an efficient way touches on so many aspects of our daily experience, it's important to think about the role marketing plays in our lives.

Marketing Creates Value

Marketing activities play a major role in the creation of value for customers. Part of the value created is **functional value**, which is concerned with the extent to which a product has desired features and characteristics (such as aesthetics or quality), is useful (available, understandable, and helpful), performs appropriately (such as reliably or economically), and results in desired outcomes (satisfied wants and other outcomes such as consumer safety or product recyclability). Benefits relating to the usefulness of a product are also called **utility**. Form utility is the benefit provided by transforming raw materials into finished products. Place utility is the ben-

> ✳ ✳ ✳
> **functional value** Consumer benefits relating to product features, characteristics, utility, performance, and outcomes.
>
> ✳ ✳ ✳
> **utility** The usefulness or benefit received by consumers from a product.

✳ ✳ ✳
experiential value Consumer
benefits relating to sensory,
emotional, relational, and epistemic experiences.

✳ ✳ ✳
symbolic or expressive value
Consumer benefits relating to
self-concept or self-identity, self-
expression, social meaning,
personal meaning, or conditional
meaning.

✳ ✳ ✳
cost or sacrifice value
Consumer benefits relating to
economic costs, psychological
costs, personal investment, and
risk.

efit provided by making products available where customers want them. Time utility is the benefit provided by storing products until they are needed. Possession utility is the benefit provided by allowing the consumer to own, use, and enjoy the product.

Marketers also create **experiential value** for customers: appropriate experiences, feelings, and emotions. Restaurants and night clubs, for example, often create sensory experiences to appeal to customers. Vacation products such as Club Med provide emotional experiences, such as fun, pleasure, excitement, or adventure. Entertainment products such as Trivial Pursuit facilitate social-relational experiences, such as "togetherness." Tourism products such as the Ontario Science Centre provide experiences that satisfy needs for curiosity, novelty, knowledge, or fantasy, collectively known, albeit esoterically, as epistemic experiences.

Marketers also create **symbolic or expressive value** for customers, psychological meaning that is associated with or attributed to a product. Luxury goods, such as a new car, often make us feel good about ourselves and enhance our self-concepts and self-worth. Other products have more personal meaning—associations with people or events—such as a consumer's preference for Tide detergent because his or her mother uses that brand. Other branded products such as Roots clothing, Calvin Klein fragrances, or Body Shop lotions allow consumers to reflect or express their personalities, tastes, and beliefs. Brands such as a BMW car or Birks jewellery have social meaning—prestige or status, or reflect a particular image. Finally, some products, such as roses on Valentine's Day, have conditional meaning, symbolism relating to socio-cultural-ethnic events and traditions.

Finally, **cost or sacrifice value** is created by marketers by focusing on the economic costs, psychological costs, personal investment, and risk incurred by consumers in buying and using a product. Warehouse concept retailers like Costco or Home Depot try to minimize the economic costs to the consumer by buying in large quantities and passing on the savings. Many traditional retailers, such as The Bay, try to minimize the psychological costs (stress and hassle) involved in buying and using a product, by means of convenient locations, ample parking, and "no hassle" return policies. Internet companies, such as Chapters Online, try to minimize the personal investment of time, effort, and energy required to navigate the marketplace. Finally, electronics retailers, such as Future Shop, among many other companies in other industries, attempt to reduce the risk in buying and using products through the use of guarantees, warranties, and price protection policies.

Marketing's Role in the Firm

The importance assigned to marketing depends on whether the organization has adopted the marketing concept. Top management in some firms is very marketing oriented (especially when the chief executive officer came from the marketing ranks), while in others, marketing is an afterthought. Sometimes the company uses the term "marketing" when what it really means is sales or advertising. In the case of organizations, particularly not-for-profit ones, that are just waking up to the idea of marketing, there may not be anyone in the company specifically designated as "the marketing person." In contrast, some firms that focus on total quality are realizing that the basic marketing concept applies to all aspects of the firm's activities. As a result, there has been a trend toward integrating marketing with other business functions instead of setting it apart as a separate function.

A firm's marketing-related decisions must affect—and be affected by—its other operations. Marketing managers must work with financial and accounting officers to figure out whether products are profitable, to set marketing budgets, and to determine prices. They must work with people in manufacturing to be sure that products are produced on time, in the right quantities, and to quality specifications. Anticipating demand is very important, especially when marketers do too good a job at creating desire for a product, and production is unable to keep up. For example, in 1997, McDonald's almost had a disaster on its hands when the company drastically underestimated how many millions of fanatic collectors would line up for the Teenie Beanie Babies it was giving away—many UnHappy Meals resulted before corrections could be made.

Marketers also must work with research and development (R&D) specialists to create products that meet consumers' needs. The experience of Stratos Product Development, a

Seattle industrial design firm, illustrates how teamwork creates products that offer more value. When it set about developing a passenger video player for British Airways, Stratos brought together mechanical specialists, customers, and British Airways personnel in brainstorming sessions, where everyone could propose new ideas. The system came together in four months, one-third of the time estimated for the project.[18]

Marketing's Role in Our Daily Lives: Opera to Oprah

We are surrounded by marketers' creations in the form of advertisements, stores, and products competing for our attention and our dollars. Much of what we learn about the world is filtered by marketers—we see images of rich or beautiful people in TV commercials or magazines. Ads show us how we should act and what we should own. This influence extends from such "serious" goods and services as health care to such "fun" things as sports and music (though many people take these products as seriously as their health).

POPULAR CULTURE

Popular culture consists of the music, movies, sports, books, celebrities, and other forms of entertainment consumed by the mass market. Marketers play an important role in providing the materials that become part of this culture. For example, professional wrestling, as seen in Exhibit 1.8, has upgraded its image from a cheesy, lowbrow sport to an entertainment spectacular. It attracts about 40 million viewers a week in North America.[19] About 18% of Canadians watch wrestling at least once a month, but teens aged 12 to 17 watch 86% more than the average Canadian.[20] Advertisers such as Molson, Nintendo, Hasbro, McCain Foods, and Sony are climbing in the ring to reach young, predominately male, viewers.

The relationship between marketing and popular culture is a two-way street. The goods and services that are popular at any time often mirror changes in the larger society. Consider, for example, some North American products that reflected underlying cultural changes at the time they were introduced.

- The TV dinner, which hinted at changes in family structure, such as a movement away from the traditional family dinner hour filled with conversation about the day's events.
- Cosmetics made of natural materials and not animal tested, which reflected social concerns about pollution and animal rights.
- Condoms marketed in pastel carrying cases for female buyers, which signalled changing attitudes toward sexual responsibility.

MARKETING AND MYTHS

Marketing messages often communicate **myths**, stories containing symbolic elements that express the shared emotions and ideals of a culture.[21] Consider, for example, how McDonald's takes on mythical qualities. To some, the golden arches are virtually synonymous with North American culture: They offer sanctuary in foreign lands to Canadians and Americans, who are grateful to know exactly what to expect once they enter. Basic struggles involving good versus evil are played out in the fantasy world created by McDonald's advertising, as Ronald McDonald confounds the Hamburglar. McDonald's even has a "seminary" (Hamburger University) where inductees go to learn how to make the perfect burger.[22]

As Exhibit 1.9 shows, singer-songwriter Jimmy Buffett is turning the Margaritaville myth into a marketing empire. Just where is Margaritaville? It's not a place, it's a state of mind. The song "Margaritaville" immortalized a mythical tropical paradise ("...wasting away in Margaritaville...") that is still beloved by "parrotheads," Buffett fans sporting gaudy Hawaiian shirts and flip-flops, who are Florida's answer to Dead Heads, Grateful Dead fans.[23]

Marketing's Role in Society

It might be fun to be a parrothead, but what about marketing's impact on more serious issues? In many ways, we are at the mercy of marketers because we trust them to sell us products that are safe and perform as promised and to price and distribute these products fairly.

Exhibit 1.8

Professional wrestling is a part of popular culture.

✳ ✳ ✳

popular culture The music, movies, sports, books, celebrities, and other forms of entertainment consumed by the mass market.

✳ ✳ ✳

myths Stories containing symbolic elements that express the shared emotions and ideals of a culture.

McDonald's
www.mcdonalds.com

Exhibit 1.9

The Margaritaville myth is the basis of a marketing empire devoted to "parrotheads."

Conflicts often arise in business when the goal to succeed in the marketplace provokes dishonest business practices. This is why many colleges and universities and corporations are teaching and reinforcing ethical behaviour.

ETHICAL BEHAVIOUR IS GOOD BUSINESS

Companies usually find that stressing ethics and social responsibility is good business, at least in the long run. Some find out the hard way. For example, the Chrysler Corporation was accused of resetting the odometers of supposedly new cars because they had actually been driven by managers prior to sale. The company admitted the practice only after some managers tried to get out of paying speeding tickets by claiming that their speedometers didn't work because the cable was disconnected.[24] These actions caused the company great embarrassment, and it took years of hard work to restore the public's trust.

In contrast, Procter & Gamble voluntarily withdrew its Rely tampons from the market following reports of women who had suffered toxic shock syndrome (TSS). Although scientists did not claim a causal link between the usage of Rely and the onset of TSS, the company decided to undertake extensive advertising notifying women of the symptoms of TSS and asking them to return their boxes of Rely for a refund. The company took a $75 million loss and sacrificed an unusually successful new product that had already captured about one-quarter of the billion-dollar sanitary product market.[25]

SOCIAL AND ETHICAL CRITICISMS OF MARKETING

Whether intentionally or not, some marketers do violate their bond of trust with consumers, and unfortunately the "dark side" of marketing is often the subject of criticism. In some cases, these actions are illegal, such as when a retailer adopts a "bait-and-switch" selling strategy, whereby consumers are lured into the store with promises of inexpensive products with the sole intent of getting them to switch to higher-priced goods.

In other cases, marketing practices have detrimental effects on society even though they are not illegal. Some companies erect billboards for alcohol and tobacco products in low-income neighbourhoods where abuse of these products is a big problem; others sponsor commercials depicting groups of people in an unfavourable light to get the attention of a target market. Palmer Jarvis and KOKO Productions, for example, were the target of considerable outrage by children's advocates, sports associations, and the advertising industry in general when they placed an advertisement in *Marketing Magazine,* intended

good OR bad DECISION?

To promote an online game, Segasoft created a fictional cult called the Cyber Diversion movement, which encourages the primal urge to kill. The firm developed a set of Web sites that were designed to look like they were put up by members of the cult. A company executive commented, "...there is some validity to the concept [that] you need an outlet for aggressive urges. If it becomes a movement, all the better. Starting a movement is a good way to market a product."[26] What do you think? Is encouraging violence, online or otherwise, an appropriate way to market a product?

to be satirical and absurdist, that depicted a bloodied baseball bat with matted hair on it, and a caption of "disappointed coach." Let's consider some of the criticisms of marketing you may have heard.

1. *Marketers create artificial needs.* The marketing system has come under fire from both ends of the political spectrum. On the one hand, some members of the religious right believe that advertising contributes to the moral breakdown of society by presenting images of sinful pleasure. On the other hand, some leftists argue that the same deceitful promises of material pleasure function to buy off people who would otherwise be revolutionaries working to change the system.[27] They argue that the system creates demand that only its products can satisfy.

    A Response: A need is a basic motive, while a want represents one way that society has taught us the need can be satisfied. For example, while thirst is biologically based, we are taught to want Coca-Cola to satisfy that thirst rather than, say, goat milk. Thus, the need is already there; marketers simply recommend ways to satisfy it. The ad shown in Exhibit 1.10 was created by the American Association of Advertising Agencies, an industry group, to combat this perception. The Canadian equivalent, the Institute of Canadian Advertisers, does not perceive a need for such advocacy. In some circumstances, however, the marketer can engineer an environment to make it more *probable* that a need will arise. This occurs, for example, when bars supply free peanuts to patrons to stimulate thirst.

2. *Marketing teaches us to value people for what they own rather than who they are.* Goods are arbitrarily linked to desirable qualities, so we learn that we can be popular, happy, and fulfilled only if we buy these products.

    A Response: Products meet existing needs, and advertising only helps to communicate their availability. Advertising is an important source of consumer information.[28] It is a service for which consumers are willing to pay because the information it provides reduces the time and effort needed to learn about the product.

3. *Marketers promise miracles.* Marketing leads consumers to believe that products have magical properties, that they will transform their lives. Marketers provide simplistic answers to complex problems.

    A Response: Marketers do not know enough about people to manipulate them. In testimony before the US Federal Trade Commission, one executive observed that while people think that advertisers have an endless source of magical tricks and scientific techniques to manipulate people, in reality, the industry is successful when it tries to sell good products and unsuccessful when selling poor ones.[29]

Exhibit 1.10

The American Association of Advertising Agencies tries to fight the perception that marketers make people buy things they don't want or need.

Real People, Real Decisions
How it worked out at Army & Navy

Jacqui Cohen, president of Army & Navy, decided to re-establish the traditional positioning of Army & Navy as a place for young adults and young families to buy unique merchandise, find deals, and have an original retro-style destination shopping experience (Option 2). They invested a million dollars to entice 18- to 25-year-olds and young parents into the store. Lanyon-Phillips Advertising created a humorous ad campaign, "You won't believe what's in store," that was irreverent, cheeky, campy, and fun, and emphasized the unique, bizarre, and cheap products at Army & Navy and the retro shopping experience. Print advertising, billboards, and transit shelter ads depicted items like: a $1 Virgin Mary night light ("she lights the way for millions"), Heinz beans ("cheap gas"), children's pacifiers ("for back-seat drivers"), and at Christmas, leopard underwear ("now we don our gay apparel"). The chain's original 1920s logo and orange and black colour scheme were revived to add to the retro feel of the brand. Flyers were redone, focusing on sharp images and clear sell lines, with promo-

tions taking effect on Saturday to entice young families to come to the store. Although the merchandising mix was not changed dramatically (learning from retailers such as Eaton's that failed when they tried to shift their inventory drastically), they did ensure that 30% of merchandise was directed at younger shoppers. Finally, they changed the address and front entrance of the downtown Vancouver store to 36 West Cordova and refer to it as their Gastown location.

The strategy worked well in three flagship stores—Vancouver, New Westminster, and Calgary—attracting new, younger customers, but it did not work well in the Prairies. Overall sales rose by five to ten percent with sales per customer increasing significantly. The company received several letters a week with positive comments about their innovative campaign. Based on this success, Cohen recently opened the first new Army & Navy store in 22 years in Langley, B.C. She must now decide what to do with the Prairie stores.

Chapter Summary

1. Define the marketing concept.

   Marketing is the process of planning and executing the conception, pricing, promotion, and distribution of ideas, goods, and services to create exchanges that satisfy individual and organizational objectives. Organizations that seek to assure their long-term profitability by identifying and satisfying customers' needs and wants have adopted the marketing concept. Today, the societal marketing concept is being adopted by many firms that try to satisfy customers in a way that is also beneficial to society. Marketing activities are important to firms that provide goods and services to individual and business consumers, as well as not-for-profit organizations and those that focus on sports, entertainment places, people, and ideas.

2. Define the objective of marketing.

   The overall objective of marketing is to achieve success (individual, organizational, and societal) by creating superior customer value, for exchange with customers in one or more target market segments, with a sustainable strategy. This objective is consistent with the marketing concept. It suggests that marketing is primarily focused on achieving objectives through value creation. Because consumers have different ideas about what they need and want, marketers focus their value creation strategy on the needs and wants of a specific group of consumers. Value is created through marketing mix decisions and, for a company to sell anything at all, some consumers must perceive that the value offered in the marketing mix is superior to all other ways of satisfying their needs or wants.

3. Describe the marketing mix.

The marketing mix is the four *P*s of marketing: product, price, place, and promotion. Elements of the marketing mix constitute an offer of value to the consumer to satisfy their needs and wants. Products can be goods, services, or ideas. The price is the assigned value or amount to be exchanged for the product. The place or channel of distribution gets the product to the customer. Promotion is the organization's communication efforts to persuade customers to buy the product. "People" could be considered a fifth *P*, as managing relationships with customers, suppliers, distributors, and other key stakeholders is critical for meeting long-term objectives.

4. Understand the basics of marketing planning.

The strategic process of marketing planning begins with an assessment of factors within the organization and in the external environment that could help or hinder the development and marketing of products. Based on this analysis, marketers set objectives and develop strategies. Many firms use a target marketing strategy in which they divide the overall market into segments and then target the most attractive one. They then design the marketing mix to gain a competitive position in the target market.

5. Describe the evolution of the marketing concept.

Early in the twentieth century, companies followed a production orientation in which they focused on the most efficient ways to produce and distribute products. Beginning in the 1930s, some firms adopted a sales orientation that encouraged salespeople to aggressively sell products to customers. In the 1950s, organizations adopted a customer orientation that focused on customer satisfaction. This led to the development of the marketing concept. Today, many firms are moving toward a New Era orientation that includes not only a commitment to quality but also concern for both economic and social profit. Outgrowths of this orientation are relationship marketing, which focuses on building long-term relationships with customers, and social marketing, which advocates social changes and promotes worthy causes.

6. Explain how marketing is important to both individual and business customers in the marketplace, in our daily lives, and in society.

Marketing creates several kinds of utility, which is the usefulness or benefit provided by a product or service. By transforming raw materials into desirable products, marketing provides form utility. Place and time utility mean that products are available when and where customers desire. Possession utility means that customers can own and use products obtained in the exchange process. Marketing systems facilitate the exchange by making it easier for buyers and sellers to come together.

Marketing influences popular culture, and popular culture influences marketing. Marketing messages are often based on cultural myths, or stories about things or behaviours valued by a society. Although many companies are stressing ethics and social responsibility, some firms have brought criticisms to marketing by creating artificial needs, teaching people to value things too much, and promising miracles.

7. Explain marketing's role within an organization.

The importance of marketing within an organization depends on whether the firm has adopted the marketing concept. Firms that haven't may see marketing as a sales or advertising function, while firms that focus on total quality integrate the marketing concept into all business functions. Marketing decisions cannot be made in isolation from an organization's other operations. Marketing, finance, manufacturing, research and development, and other functional areas must work together to achieve the organization's goals.

KEY TERMS

benefit (6)

buyer's market (15)

consumer (5)

consumer orientation (16)

cost or sacrifice value (18)

customer value (7)

demand (6)

exchange (7)

experiential value (18)

functional value (17)

market (6)

marketing (5)

marketing concept (5)

marketing mix (13)

marketplace (6)

market position (13)

market segment (10)

mass market (12)

myths (19)

need (5)

New Era orientation (17)

place (14)

popular culture (19)

price (14)

product (7)

product orientation (15)

promotion (14)

relationship marketing (15)

seller's market (15)

selling orientation (15)

social marketing concept (6)

stakeholders (15)

symbolic or expressive value (18)

target markets (11)

unsought good (16)

utility (17)

want (5)

Chapter Review

Marketing Concepts: **Testing Your Knowledge**

1. Briefly explain what marketing is.

2. What is the marketing concept? How is it different from the social marketing concept?

3. How does marketing facilitate exchange?

4. Define these terms: consumer goods, services, and industrial products.

5. What are the elements of the marketing mix?

6. What are target markets? How do marketers select and reach target markets?

7. Trace the evolution of the marketing concept.

8. What is customer value? How does marketing create different types of value?

9. How is marketing related to popular culture?

10. What are some criticisms of marketing?

Marketing Concepts: **Discussing Choices and Issues**

1. The marketing concept focuses on the ability of marketing to satisfy customer needs. As a student, how does marketing satisfy your needs? What areas of your life are affected by marketing? What areas of your life (if any) are not affected by marketing?

2. Do you think students should study marketing even if they are not planning a career in marketing or business? Explain your reasoning.

3. In this chapter, a number of criticisms of marketing were discussed. Have you heard these criticisms? What other criticisms of marketing have you heard? Do you agree or disagree with these criticisms, and why?

4. In this chapter, we talked about how marketing communicates myths. What exactly is a myth? What are some popular myths depicted in marketing? Does marketing create some myths?

Marketing Practice: **Applying What You've Learned**

1. An old friend of yours has been making and selling leather handbags and bookbags to acquaintances and friends of friends for some time and is now thinking about opening a shop in your town. But he is worried about whether he'll have enough customers who want handcrafted bags to keep a business going. Knowing that you are a marketing student, he's asked you for some advice. What can you tell him about product, price, promotion, and distribution strategies that will help him get his business off the ground?

2. Assume that you are employed by your city's chamber of commerce. A major focus of the chamber is to get industries to move to your city. As a former marketing student, you know that there are issues involving product, price, promotion, and even distribution that can attract business. Next week, you have an opportunity to speak to the members of the chamber, and your topic will be "Marketing a City." Develop an outline for that presentation.

3. As a marketing professional, you have been asked to write a short piece for a local business newsletter about the state of marketing today. You think the best way to address this topic is to review how the marketing concept has evolved and to discuss the New Era orientation of marketing. Write the short article you will submit to the editor of the newsletter.

4. You and your friends sometimes discuss the various courses you are taking. One of your friends says to you, "Marketing's nothing but selling stuff. Anybody can do that without taking a course." Another friend says, "Yeah, all marketers do is write ads." As a role-playing exercise, present your arguments against these statements to your class.

Marketing Mini-Project: **Learning by Doing**

The purpose of this mini-project is to develop an understanding of the importance of marketing to different organizations.

1. Working as a team with two or three other students in your class, select an organization in your community that practises marketing. It may be a manufacturer, service provider, re-

tailer, not-for-profit organization—almost any organization will do. Schedule a visit with someone in the organization who is involved in the marketing activities. Ask that person to give your group a tour of the facilities and explain the organization's marketing activities.

2. Divide the following topics among your team, and ask each person to be responsible for developing a set of questions to ask during the interview to learn about the company's program:

   · What customer segments the company targets

   · How it determines needs and wants

   · What products it offers, including features, benefits, and goals for customer satisfaction

   · What its pricing strategies are, including any discounting policies

   · What promotional strategies it uses, and what these emphasize to position the product(s)

   · How it distributes products, and whether it has encountered any problems

   · How marketing planning is done and who does it

   · Whether social responsibility is part of the marketing program and, if so, in what ways

3. Develop a team report of your findings. In each section of the report, share what you learned that is new or surprising to you compared to what you expected.

4. Develop a team presentation for your class that summarizes your findings. Conclude your presentation with comments on what your team believes the company was doing well and where they could make improvements.

Real People, Real Surfers: Exploring the Web

The New Era orientation means that a firm like Levi Strauss is devoted to excellence in designing and producing products that benefit customers as well as the firm's employees, shareholders, and fellow citizens. Many firms share this on their Internet Web pages. Visit the Web site for Levi Strauss (www.levistrauss.com). Then visit the Web site for one of their competitors such as Lee Jeans (www.leejeans.com) or Wrangler jeans (www.wrangler.com). Follow the links in the sites to learn as much as you can about the company. You might first check the site map to see what links are provided on the site. Look for answers to the following questions:

1. What evidence do you find on the firms' Web sites that each is a New Era firm?

2. Which company has the better Web site? What makes it better? Based on your visit to the Web sites, what do you think is the major purpose of each company's site? To promote their products? To sell on the Web? To develop a brand image? Something else?

3. How do the companies use their Web sites for promoting their products? Is the Web site a unique form of promotion or just an extension of their normal advertising?

4. What market segments do you think each firm is targeting with its Web site? What features of the Web sites gave you this idea?

5. Do the Web sites provide an opportunity for the firm to gather information about customers so that they can customize contact with them?

6. Are there any features of the Web site that will cause consumers to come back again and again?

7. What are your major criticisms of each of the Web sites? What would you do to improve each site?

Sooke Region Museum

When Terry Malone became director of the Sooke Region Museum, he took on responsibility for the operation and management of an organization facing some tough decisions. An integral part of the Sooke, British Columbia, community since 1977, not only were the small museum and its exhibits becoming rundown, but there were also concerns about the safety of the main museum building and the lack of quality artifact storage space. The volunteer board of directors were considering plans to refurbish and expand the museum, but it was not clear how the museum should be modified to better meet its mandate.

The original mandate of the museum was to serve the Sooke Community by portraying the history and culture of the region, providing an archive of community information, offering visual and cultural arts programs for the local public, and providing full public access. The museum, a collection of rustic and heritage buildings enhanced by well-landscaped grounds featuring indigenous plants, is now a hub for the tourism industry in the area. The museum manages the Sooke Visitor Information Centre and hosts one of the largest juried fine arts shows in BC. More than 40 000 people-visits are recorded by the museum each year.

Funded at a level of about $265 000 by municipal and provincial grants, a region tax levy, donations, profits from a gift shop, and entrance fees for the annual fine arts show, the museum relies heavily on volunteers from the community to augment staff in the exhibit areas, and gift shop and in fundraising activities. Gift shop profits had traditionally contributed about 20% of the budget, but Malone thought it could contribute a third of the budget if it made merchandising changes and more than that if more people visited the museum. The museum relies a lot on word-of-mouth recommendations, but also tries to attract people to the museum by advertisements in the local newspaper and brochures placed at tourist accommodations and attractions.

Recognizing that a big part of the challenge in getting more people to visit the museum lies in determining what "product" is sought by community residents and visitors, the museum board hired three business students to find out basic needs and wants. The market research found that the museum was well received in the Sooke community, and the public had good awareness of museum programs and functions. However, in Victoria, the closest major city, awareness of the museum dropped sharply. Signage for the museum was also identified as a problem: Trees surrounding the museum made it difficult to see from the road, and small signs were difficult to read by passing car traffic. Although there were some children's programs at the museum, there were few activities for adolescents or young adults. While Sooke was becoming known for its eco-tourism (for example, kayaking, mountain biking, hiking), museum programs or exhibits did not reflect these interests. Most respondents felt that the rustic exterior was a good reflection of the museum's focus on logging, fishing, and Native heritage. Respondents liked the hands-on aspect of the current displays but felt that displays needed updating, the space was cluttered, and information was difficult to read. Some of the respondents were concerned with the number of functions the museum performed and were confused about the museum's mandate.

The museum board was committed to increasing the profile and viability of the museum but needed to decide just how to do that. The product needed redefining, and additional space was needed for exhibit storage. The price was set at "free" for regular exhibits, but there might be an opportunity to charge for special programs. The place was set in terms of physical location, but consideration might be given to increasing the size of the museum and improving its layout, the location and size of the gift shop, and hours of operation. Finally, a lot more could be done to better promote the museum. The museum board had about $71 000, including grants from government, to spend on expansion and improvements. Any additional required funds would need to be raised—but these would be matched by government funding.

MARKETING IN ACTION

THINGS TO THINK ABOUT

1. What are the problems facing the Sooke Region Museum?
2. What factors are important in understanding this problem?
3. What are the alternatives?
4. What are both short- and long-term recommendations for the museum?
5. What are some ways to implement your recommendations?

Feed the hungry. Donate your meal plan points.

www.mealexchange.com

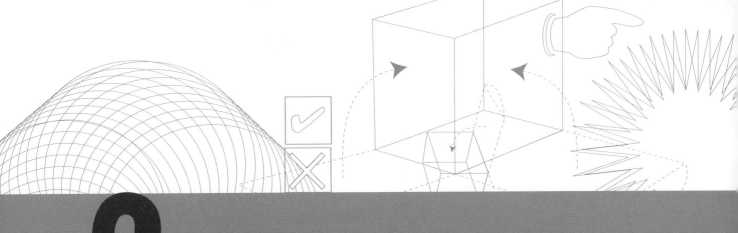

2 Strategic Planning: Making Choices in a Dynamic Environment

When you have completed your study of this chapter, you should be able to

CHAPTER OBJECTIVES

1. Explain the strategic planning process.

2. Tell how firms gain a competitive advantage and describe the factors that influence marketing objectives.

3. Describe the steps in the marketing planning process.

4. Explain the factors involved in the implementation and control of the marketing plan.

Real People, Real Decisions ✔ ✘

Meet Rahul Raj
A Decision Maker at Meal Exchange

Developing a strategic plan for marketing an idea is a priority for Rahul Raj, founder and chair of the board of Meal Exchange. Meal Exchange is a not-for-profit organization, dedicated to motivating post-secondary students to increase their involvement in fighting social problems, such as hunger. In the 1990s, as a first-year honours business administration student at Wilfrid Laurier University, Raj had the idea of Meal Exchange, when he realized that he, like many university students, had money left on his university debit-style meal card at the end of the school year. Raj organized students at his own university to donate the unused money on their meal cards to local food banks, who could then purchase food for those in need. During that

first year, $2100 was donated to community organizations from students at Wilfrid Laurier, and the Meal Exchange organization was born.

By 1997, when Raj was ready to graduate and accept a job as assistant brand manager at Procter & Gamble, donations to Meal Exchange were up to $9000. Convinced that the idea was a good one, he continued to develop the Meal Exchange concept after graduation, with the goal of expanding it to other Canadian universities and colleges. The marketing work that Raj continues to do at Meal Exchange is strictly on a volunteer basis. His current full-time job is as brand manager for the Nutella and Tic Tac brands at Ferrero Canada.

Meal Exchange
www.mealexchange.com

"Plan Well and Prosper"

Whether a firm is a small not-for-profit social organization like Meal Exchange, a family-based retailer like Army & Navy, or a major manufacturer like Nortel Networks, planning for the future is a key to prosperity. It's true that a firm can be successful even if it makes some mistakes in planning. It is also true that some "seat-of-the-pants" businesses are successful. But without good planning for the future, firms, at a minimum, will be less successful than they could be. In the worst-case scenario, a lack of planning can be fatal for both large and small businesses.

All firms operate in a dynamic environment. In today's world of business, consumer interests, technologies, the competition, and the economy are changing faster than ever. This makes good planning that enables a firm to meet the challenges of this dynamic environment and to control its own destiny more important than ever.

In this chapter, we'll look at the different steps in creating a business plan. First we'll see how managers make the decisions that guide the entire organization. Then, we'll examine the marketing planning process and the stages in that process that lead to the development and implementation of a marketing plan.

In successful firms, large and small, business planning is an ongoing process of making decisions that guide the firm both in the short term and for the long haul. Planning identifies and builds on a firm's strengths and helps managers at all levels make informed decisions in a changing business environment. Planning means that an organization develops objectives before it takes action. In large firms, such as IBM, Sony, and Nortel, that operate in many markets, planning is a complex process involving many people from different areas of the company's operations. In a small business like Mac's Diner, however, planning is quite different; Mac himself is chief cook, occasional dishwasher, and the sole company planner. With mid-size firms, the planning process falls somewhere in between, depending on the size of the firm and the complexity of its operations.

We all know, in general, what planning is—we plan a vacation or a great Saturday night party or how we are going to get work completed. When businesses plan, the process is more complex. Business planning usually occurs at three levels—strategic, tactical, and operational. **Strategic planning** is the managerial decision process that matches the organiza-

✳ ✳ ✳
strategic planning A managerial decision process that matches an organization's resources and capabilities to its market opportunities for long-term growth and survival.

tion's resources (such as its manufacturing facilities, financial assets, and skilled workforce) and capabilities (the things it is able to do well because of its expertise and experience) to its market opportunities for long-term growth. These decisions focus on the firm's ability to respond to changes and opportunities in its environment. In a strategic plan, the top management team (the chief executive officer, or CEO, president, and other top executives) defines the firm's purpose and specifies what the firm hopes to achieve over the next five or so years, increasingly in consultation with a cross-section of employees who bring varied perspectives and knowledge to the process. For example, a firm's strategic plan may set a goal of increasing the firm's total revenues by 10 or even 20% in the next five years.

In large firms, strategic planning can actually occur at two different levels. First, there is overall corporate strategic planning, which determines the organization's different business and product pursuits and may even provide guidelines for its major marketing strategies. Second, the individual business units do strategic planning for their products. Strategic planning at Disney, for example, involves an assessment of resources and capabilities for starting new businesses. In addition to making movies and running theme parks, Disney is now in the cruise ship business and operates a number of Disney vacation resorts. Disney's corporate planning expanded its theme park business to Europe and Japan—separate business units. So at Disney there are separate strategic plans for each of the different Disney businesses.

Figure 2.1 Planning at Different Management Levels

The next level of planning, shown in Figure 2.1, is tactical planning. **Tactical planning**, sometimes called functional planning, is done by middle-level managers, the vice-presidents or department directors. Tactical planning typically includes both a broad five-year plan to support the firm's strategic plan and a detailed annual plan for the coming year.

Still further down the planning ladder are the first-line managers. For example, there may be a benefits manager, safety director, and wage and salary manager in the human resource department. A quality control manager might be a first-line manager in operations, while marketing communications managers and sales managers might be first-line managers in the marketing department. These lower-level managers are responsible for a third level of planning, **operational planning**, which focuses on the day-to-day execution of the tactical plans. Planning at this level outlines the activities necessary to implement the tactical plan and includes detailed annual, semiannual, or quarterly plans. For example, operational plans might show exactly how many units of a product the firm will produce a day or how many television commercials the firm will place on certain networks during a season.

Marketing managers and other planners don't just sit in their offices and dream up their plans without any concern for the rest of the organization. Although we've described each layer separately, all business planning is an integrated activity—the organization's strategic, tactical, and operational plans must work together. For example, to develop a strategic plan for Harley Davidson Motorcycles, Franc Cimermancic, the director of business planning, has to understand operations (exactly how Harleys are built), distribution (what it takes to make a Harley dealership successful), and how Harley marketers put Harley on top. Because marketing is such an important part of a firm's overall strategies, it is practically impossible to separate marketing (tactical) planning from strategic planning. It is marketing's responsibility to monitor changes in the marketing environment and assess the firm's capability to seize opportunities. Top business planners must also consider good principles of accounting, the value of the company to its stockholders, and the requirements for staffing and human resource management—and all of the other functional departments of the organization.

Similarly, tactical planners have to make sure that their plans both support the overall organization's mission and objectives and work well together, that they are integrated. For example, if marketing planners want to boost sales during the first quarter of the year, they must make sure that operations can meet the increased production demands required by their sales goals. In fact, many firms practise **cross-functional planning**, which means that

tactical planning A decision process that concentrates on developing detailed plans for strategies and tactics for the short term that support an organization's long-term strategic plan.

operational planning A decision process that focuses on developing detailed plans for day-to-day activities that carry out an organization's tactical plans.

cross-functional planning An approach to tactical planning in which managers work together in developing tactical plans for each functional area in the firm, so that each plan considers the objectives of the other areas.

instead of working alone, middle managers actually work together as a team to develop tactical plans that consider the objectives of all the functional areas.

As an example of the three levels of planning, consider how planning might occur in a company that manufactures bicycles. In the strategic plan, the firm has a corporate goal of increasing revenues by 15% over the next five years by developing new bicycles for new markets. The marketing director, a middle manager, is responsible for tactical marketing planning. One of her objectives is to gain 20% of the racing bike market by successfully introducing three new models during the coming year. Cross-functional planning is necessary for the new bike models—she must work with the finance and manufacturing departments. At the operational planning level, the director of marketing communications, who works under the marketing director, will develop plans to promote the new bikes to potential customers, while the sales manager will develop a plan for the company's sales force.

So far, we have a general understanding of the three levels of planning. Now we'll discuss in more detail strategic planning and the important role that marketing plays in it.

Strategic Planning: Guiding the Business

Marketers don't work and plan in isolation. Before we talk about the marketing planning process, therefore, we need to understand how firms develop strategic plans.

The strategic plan focuses on the long-term horizon—five or more years into the future—but the process also includes annual planning and sets the firm's total budget and profitability goals for the year. In this section, we'll take a closer look at the four key stages in top-level strategic planning: defining the organization's business mission, evaluating the environment, setting organizational objectives, and planning the business portfolio.

Defining the Organization's Business Mission

In the first stage of strategic planning, a firm's top executives define the mission of the organization, top management's vision of why the firm exists, how it is different from other firms, and the place in the market it wants to take. Decision making in the strategic planning stage revolves around such "soul-searching" questions as: What business are we in? What customers should we serve? What kinds of value and products can we create for them? How should we develop the firm's capabilities and focus its efforts? In many firms, the answers to questions like these become the lead items in the organization's strategic plan. They become part of a **mission statement**, a formal statement that describes the organization's overall purpose and what it hopes to achieve in terms of its customers, products, and resources. Figure 2.2 shows examples of mission statements.

Robert Goizueta headed the Coca-Cola Company for 17 years; during that time, sales more than quadrupled, going from $4 billion to $18 billion. It seems like he knew what he was doing. When Goizueta took on that job, one of his first actions was to create a mission statement for the company. It began, "Our challenge will be to enhance and protect the Coca-Cola trademark, giving shareholders an above-average return and entering new businesses only if they can perform at a rate substantially above inflation."[1] By focusing all company efforts on building brand value, satisfying customers, and profitability, that mission statement led Coke into two decades of phenomenal worldwide growth. The ideal mission statement is neither too broad, too narrow, nor too shortsighted. A mission that is too broad will not provide adequate focus for the organization. It doesn't do much good to claim: "We are in the business of making high-quality products"; yet it's hard to find a firm that doesn't make this claim. But a mission statement that is too narrow may inhibit managers' ability to visualize possible growth opportunities. If, for example, a firm sees itself in terms of its product only, consumer trends or technology can make that product obsolete—and the firm is left with no future.

The term *marketing myopia* is often used to describe firms that develop shortsighted visions of who they are.[2] For example, in the 1980s, Kodak faced intense competition from Japanese film and camera companies, which had developed electronic cameras capable of

✳ ✳ ✳
mission statement A formal statement in an organization's strategic plan that describes the overall purpose of the organization and what it intends to achieve in terms of its customers, products, and resources.

Coca-Cola
www.coca-cola.com

- *AT&T:* We aspire to be the most admired and valuable company in the world. Our goal is to enrich our customers' personal lives and to make their businesses more successful by bringing to market exciting and useful communications services, building shareowner value in the process. (www.att.com/factbook/co_mission.html)

- *Sierra Club:* To explore, enjoy, and protect the wild places of the Earth; to practise and promote the responsible use of the Earth's ecosystems and resources; to educate and enlist humanity to protect and restore the quality of the natural and human environment; and to use all lawful means to carry out these objectives. (www.sierraclub.org/planet/199512/steward.html)

- *MADD:* The mission of Mothers Against Drunk Driving is to stop drunk driving and to support the victims of this violent crime. (www.charweb.org/organizations/madd/mission.htm)

- *First National Bank of Bowie:* Our mission is to be a profitable, sound, responsive, locally owned community bank that provides ultimate protection for depositors' funds. Our goals are to grow and create shareholder value. (www.fnbbowie.com/keepmiss.htm)

- *Blackhawk Controls Corporation:* The aim of Blackhawk Controls is to provide motion solutions to industry. This includes AC and DC drives, servos, steppers, controllers, and complete systems. We specialize in single and multiple axes. We have designed applications for web converting, plastics, profile and sheet lines, wire, boxboard, print presses, bindery lines, and woodworking machinery. (www.blackhawkcontrols.com/mission/htm)

- *Huff Realty, Inc.:* Jim Huff Realty is a company dedicated to excellence; using innovative real estate marketing skills and state-of-the-art technology to provide the highest-quality services to our clients and customers; above all, preserving a belief in people. (www.huff.com/info/mission/html)

- *The Quaker Oats Company:* To meet the needs of consumers through innovative marketing and manufacturing of healthful, good-tasting products that contribute to a healthy lifestyle and consumer well-being around the world, yielding above-average returns over time for our shareholders. (www.quakeroats.com/vis_mis.htm)

- *Pfizer Inc.:* Over the next five years, we will achieve and sustain our place as the world's premier research-based health care company. Our continuing success as a business will benefit patients and our customers, our shareholders, our families, and the communities in which we operate around the world. (www.pfizer.com/pfizerinc/about/vision/mission.html)

- *First Union Corporation:* Our strategic priorities are to provide our customers unparalleled service, convenience and responsiveness, balance earnings power through geographic and product diversity; provide the most innovative financing solutions and a broad array of products; increase the production of our specialty businesses; maximize operating efficiency; and emphasize capital strength and loan quality with growth in fee income, deposits, and loans. (www.firstunion.com/profile/strprior/html)

- *Spina Bifida Association of Saskatchewan:* Our mission is to improve the quality of life of all individual with spina bifida and/or hydrocephalus, and their families, through awareness, education and research. (firebar.sasknet.sk.ca/~sbass/mission.html)

Figure 2.2 Examples of Organizational Mission Statements

storing images digitally on compact disks. The future of filmless photography came a giant step closer—an exciting advancement but not the greatest news for Kodak, which viewed itself as being in the film business. Abandoning its product-oriented, myopic mission, Kodak now says it is in the "imaging" business—a consumer-oriented mission—with a focus on products that process and convert images both on film and in the form of electronic data.[3] This broader view led to the development of successful new products for its core business

Kodak
www.kodak.com

and has caused Kodak to venture into electronic publishing, medical and graphics arts imaging, printing, and digital scanning.

Evaluating the Environment: SWOT Analysis

✽ ✽ ✽
SWOT analysis An analysis of an organization's strengths and weaknesses and the opportunities and threats in its external environment.

✽ ✽ ✽
internal environment The controllable elements inside an organization, including its people, its facilities, and how it does things that influence the operations of the organization.

✽ ✽ ✽
external environment The uncontrollable elements outside of an organization that may affect its performance either positively or negatively.

The second step in strategic planning is an assessment of an organization's internal and external environments. Chapter 1 mentioned the **SWOT analysis**, a tool often used by managers and other strategic planners in this task. SWOT analysis seeks to identify meaningful strengths (S) and weaknesses (W) in the organization's internal environment, and opportunities (O) and threats (T) coming from outside the organization, the external environment. A SWOT analysis enables a firm to capitalize on opportunities and minimize threats, because it can develop strategies that successfully match what the firm does best with profitable new market opportunities.

The **internal environment** is all of the controllable elements inside an organization that influence how well the organization operates. Internal strengths and weaknesses often reside in the firm's current strategy and performance. How superior is the current value created by the firm's products? What is the relative market share of these products? What has been their financial performance? Internal strengths and weaknesses also reside in the resources, technology, intellectual capital, and other assets of the firm. For example, firms need to have appropriate technical skills to compete in their industry. Their employees need to have appropriate skills, abilities, and training to produce the firm's products. A firm's physical facilities can be an important strength or weakness, as can its level of financial stability, its relationships with suppliers and channel members, its corporate reputation, and its ownership of strong brands in the marketplace. Internal strengths may also lie in the organization of the firm—its structure, culture, and systems (how they get work done). Some firms, for example, have a positive work climate that encourages creativity, innovation, and teamwork. Other firms find they have a "chilly" climate, characterized by negativity, work-to-rule, and in-fighting among employees—which can seriously affect product quality and relationships with customers, suppliers, distributors, and other stakeholders. Finally the beliefs, values, and preferences of senior management in an organization can be a strength or weakness, as these senior people provide leadership, vision, and direction for the activities of the organization.

The **external environment** consists of those uncontrollable elements outside of the organization that may affect it either positively or negatively. The external environment includes everything from consumers to government regulations to competitors to the economy. Opportunities and threats can come from any part of the external environment. Sometimes trends or currently unserved customer needs provide opportunities for growth, while others signal possible danger or threats down the road. For entrepreneur Shabazz Fuller, a changing fashion trend provided a "phat" opportunity. In 1991, Fuller was an unlicensed street vendor, hawking T-shirts in Harlem, New York, and designing flashy outfits for local rap performers. When black urban culture took root among mainstream youth across America, Fuller and his partner saw an opportunity and turned their T-shirt business into a $5 million success called Shabazz Brothers Urbanwear. The spread of hip hop presented an opportunity for major clothing manufacturers like Fila USA and Tommy Hilfiger who have also cashed in with their own urbanwear designs.[4] We'll talk more about environments in Chapter 3.

Marketers use SWOT analysis to help them make strategic and tactical decisions. Internal strengths and external opportunities provide rationale to support a particular course of action. Internal weaknesses and external threats provide reasons why a particular course of action might not be appropriate. Differences in college and university policies regarding the redemption of meal cards, for example, might be a threat in the external environment of Meal Exchange that could limit expansion plans for the organization. Although weaknesses and threats could have negative impact on a proposed strategy, it should be recognized that some weaknesses and threats can be mitigated or overcome with a good strategic plan. Lobbying by supporters of the Meal Exchange concept, for example, might get colleges and universities to change their policies so that they could participate in the Meal Exchange program. The key to SWOT analysis is to not get bogged down in analysis paralysis. Firms face hundreds, if not thousands, of internal and external environmental considerations that shape and have an impact on their business. You will want to try to identify the top six to ten issues that might have the greatest implications for the marketing decisions you have to make. Ask yourself: Does this fact or piece of information have a major implication for a decision I have to make? If not, it's probably not worth documenting in a SWOT analysis.

Setting Organizational Objectives

In the next stage in the strategic planning process, top management translates the firm's business mission into specific goals called **objectives**. These are specific accomplishments or outcomes that an organization hopes to achieve by a specific time.

Organizational objectives are a direct outgrowth of the mission statement and broadly identify what the firm hopes to accomplish within the general time frame of the firm's long-range strategic business plan. For example, to turn around the hard times in the 1980s and assure its future for the 1990s and beyond, Harley-Davidson's managers set objectives calling for a new emphasis on quality, the redesign of its touring bikes, and investing in marketing to soften Harley's "Hell's Angels" image and attract new customers.

Organizational objectives can be as varied as the organizations that develop them. Thus, they may relate to revenue/sales, profitability, the firm's standing in the market, return on investment (ROI), productivity, innovation, use of the firm's resources, product development/introduction, customer relations/satisfaction, or even social responsibility. Often objectives are quantitative—they state the specific levels of measurable business accomplishments that are to be achieved by the organization as a whole. For example, a firm might have as an objective a 10% increase in profitability by increasing productivity, by reducing costs, or by divesting itself of an unprofitable division. Or it might meet this objective by developing new products, investing in new technologies, or entering new markets.

In 1990, Campbell Soup was hovering near the bottom of the food industry, when David W. Johnson became president and CEO of the company. Johnson saw Campbell as a firm that had lost its direction and focus, and his first act was to develop a set of measurable business objectives focusing on growth. Johnson jettisoned business divisions that didn't fit in with Campbell's core products and undertook a large-scale restructuring of the company into divisions that unified and coordinated business activities. As a result, Campbell exceeded its growth goals in both 1991 and 1992 while launching 122 new products.[5] That's a lot of chicken soup.

A firm's mission statement, the resources it has available, and top management's view of the business environment all influence the firm's objectives. The strategic plan, however, does not specify how to *reach* the objectives. This task falls to lower-level managers, who develop the tactical and operational plans—the "nuts and bolts"—for achieving organizational objectives.

Planning for Growth: The Business Portfolio

In small companies that offer a single good or service, the firm's business strategy is simple. But many large firms realize that relying on only one product can be risky, so they have become multiproduct firms with self-contained divisions organized around products or brands. These businesses or **strategic business units (SBUs)** are individual units within the firm, each having its own mission, business objectives, resources, managers, and competitors. For companies with a number of different SBUs, strategic planning means making decisions about how to best allocate resources among these different businesses to ensure growth for the total organization.

As illustrated in Figure 2.3, each SBU has its own strategic focus within the firm's overall strategic plan, and each has its own target market and strategies for reaching its goals. Just like an independent business, each SBU is a separate profit centre within the larger corporation—each SBU is responsible for its own costs, revenues, and profits.

Successful marketing strategies depend on understanding a firm's environment, and that means learning as much as you can about the competition. For example, former Staples Inc. chairman, Thomas G. Stemberrg, had his wife Dola apply for a job with rival Office Depot Inc's delivery-order centre to confirm rumours that Office Depot was starting its own delivery service. The Boehringer Mannheim Corp. filed suit when Johnson & Johnson's Life Scan Inc. employees were caught eavesdropping on a sales meeting to learn about a new Boehringer product. How far should a company be allowed to go to learn about its competitors?

✳ ✳ ✳
objectives Specific accomplishments or outcomes that an organization hopes to achieve by a specific time.

✳ ✳ ✳
strategic business units (SBUs) Individual units within the firm that operate like separate businesses, with each having its own mission, business objectives, resources, managers, and competitors.

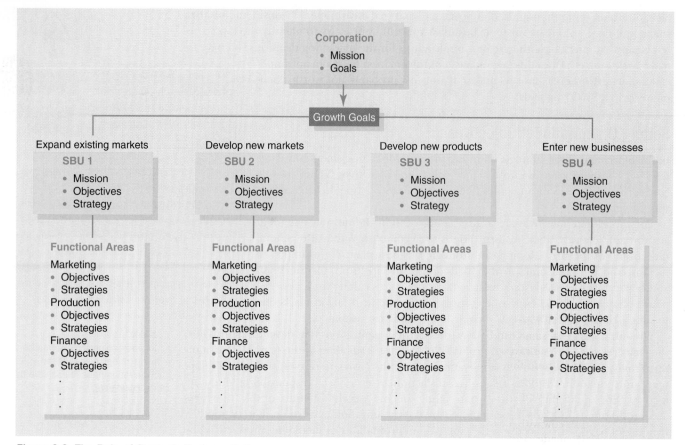

Figure 2.3 The Role of Strategic Business Units

Large corporations often have many divisions or SBUs. For example, Harley-Davidson is a firm with several SBUs. While mostly known for its "hogs," the company also owns the Holiday Rambler Corporation, which makes motor homes, and the Utilimaster Corporation, a subsidiary of Holiday Rambler, which manufactures parcel delivery vans, truck bodies, and specialty vehicles. As is often the case, Harley's SBUs produce very different products—it's hard to confuse a "hog" with a squat delivery van. Just as the collection of different stocks an investor owns is called a portfolio, the different products owned by a larger firm is called its **business portfolio**. Having a diversified portfolio of products with different revenue-generating and revenue-using characteristics reduces the firm's dependence on one product or one group of customers.

Portfolio analysis is a management tool for assessing the potential of a firm's products or businesses. It helps management decide which of its current products should receive more—or less—of the firm's resources, and which of its lines of business are consistent with the firm's mission. Several models are available to assist management in this process. Each in its own way suggests a strategy for portfolio development based on a product's position relative to competitors.

One of the most popular models is the *growth–market share matrix* developed by the Boston Consulting Group (BCG). The BCG method focuses on the potential of a firm's existing successful products to generate cash that the firm can then use to invest in new products. New products are chosen for their potential to become future cash generators. In the BCG matrix, shown in Figure 2.4, the vertical axis represents the *market growth rate*, a measure of the attractiveness of a market. The horizontal axis shows the firm's *relative market share*—its sales relative to its largest competitor's—an indicator of the company's current strength in the market. Combining the two axes creates four quadrants, which represent four different types of products or businesses. Each quadrant of the BCG grid has a special meaning, indicated by a symbol.

✳ ✳ ✳

business portfolio The group of different products or brands owned by an organization and characterized by different income-generating and growth capabilities.

✳ ✳ ✳

portfolio analysis A management tool for evaluating a firm's business mix and assessing the potential of an organization's strategic business units.

- *Stars*: Like Hollywood celebrities, stars get all the firm's attention and huge investments. Stars are business units with a dominant market share in *high-growth* markets. Because they have a dominant share of the market, stars generate large revenues, but they also require large amounts of funding to keep up with production demands and to promote them. Because the market has a large growth potential, managers design strategies to maximize market share in the face of increasing competition. The firm aims at getting the largest share of loyal customers, so the product will become a "cash cow" and generate money to be plowed into other parts of the company. For example, the BCG matrix might suggest that Viacom should continue to invest in its MTV Networks business that operates MTV: Music Television, M2: Music Television, VH1, Nickelodeon, Nick at Nite, TV Land, MTV Europe, MTV Latin America, Nickelodeon Latin America, Nickelodeon Nordic, and VH-1 UK.[6]

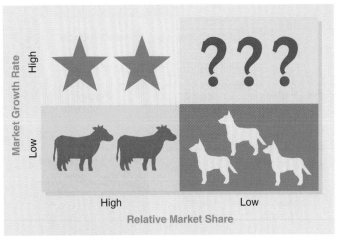

Figure 2.4 BCG Growth–Market Share Matrix

- *Cash cows:* Cash cows have a dominant market share in a *low-growth* potential market. Because there's not much opportunity for new products, competitors don't often enter the market. At the same time, the product is well established and enjoys a high market share, which the firm can sustain with minimal funding. Firms usually "milk" cash cows of their profits to fund the growth of other products in a portfolio. If the goal of a firm is to increase revenues, cash cows can become a liability. For example, Colgate-Palmolive, a multinational producer of toothpaste, deodorant, pet food, and soap, earns 70% of its $9 billion in sales outside the US and Canada. Colgate's North American business was a cash cow with little growth potential. New management, installed in the division in 1994, made sweeping changes. It closed five plants, eliminated redundant activities, and linked marketing, purchasing, distribution and customer service to each other. It also began to invest in neglected brands such as Colgate toothpaste, Palmolive detergent, Ajax cleanser, and Science Diet pet food. The result: Colgate made a comeback in its home market and turned its cash cows into stars.[7]

MTV Networks
www.mtv.com

- *Question Marks*: Question marks (or *problem children* as they are sometimes called) are products with low market shares in fast-growth markets. When a business unit is a question mark, it suggests that the firm has failed to compete successfully. Perhaps the product offers fewer benefits than competing products. Maybe its price is too high, the distributors are ineffective, or the advertising is too weak. The firm could pump more money into marketing the product and hope that market share will improve. But the firm may find itself throwing good money after bad, gaining nothing but a negative cash flow and disappointment. Adolph Coors Co., for example, invested heavily in the launch of its Zima beer targeting Generation Xers. But Zima sales never materialized— Zima became a question mark. Coors's decision was to not continue high levels of investment in the brand but to provide only minimal support to Zima as a niche product.[8]

- *Dogs*: By dog, BCG really means a mongrel, a product nobody wants. Dogs have a small share of a *slow-growth* market. They are products in limited markets that are not likely to grow quickly. When possible, large firms may sell off their dogs to smaller firms that may be able to nurture them, or a firm may take the product off the market. For example, after Quaker Oats Co. bought Snapple in 1994, the company determined that the brand was a dog and sold Snapple to Triarc Cos. losing over $1 billion.[9] Old dogs can learn new tricks—by finding new, higher-growth markets, by stimulating market growth with innovative communications strategies, and by revitalizing the product to capture the attention of consumers.

Developing Growth Strategies

While the BCG matrix helps managers decide which SBUs they should grow, it doesn't tell them much about how to go about making that growth happen. Should the growth of an

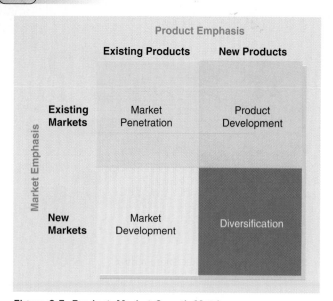

Figure 2.5 **Product–Market Growth Matrix**

✳ ✳ ✳
market penetration Growth strategies designed to increase sales of existing products to current customers, non-users, and users of competitive brands in served markets.
✳ ✳ ✳
market development Growth strategies that introduce existing products to new markets.
✳ ✳ ✳
product development Growth strategies that focus on selling new products in served markets.
✳ ✳ ✳
diversification Growth strategies that emphasize both new products and new markets.

SBU come from finding new customers, from developing new variations of the product, or from some other growth strategy?

The product–market growth matrix shown in Figure 2.5 is a useful way to look at different growth strategies. The vertical axis represents opportunities for growth in markets that are currently being served or in new markets. The horizontal axis considers whether the firm would be better off putting its resources into existing products or if it should develop or acquire new products. Thus the matrix provides four different fundamental marketing strategies: market penetration, market development, product development, and diversification.

- **Market penetration** strategies seek to increase sales of existing products to current customers, non-users, and users of competing brands in served markets. For example, a soup company can advertise new uses for soup in lunches and dinners, encouraging current customers to eat more soup and prodding non-users to find reasons to buy it. Other ways a firm might try to capture a larger share of purchases in a served market include cutting prices, improving distribution convenience, and conducting promotions aimed at increasing consumption at the expense of competitors.

- **Market development** strategies introduce existing products to new markets. This can mean reaching new customer segments within an existing geographic market, or it may mean expanding into new geographic areas. For example, after 40 years in business, IKEA, Sweden's $5.8 billion home furnishings giant, has used ads such as the one shown in Exhibit 2.1 to launch a big expansion into children's furniture and toys while expanding geographically to sites ranging from Warsaw to Montreal.[10]

- **Product development** strategies create growth by selling new products in existing markets. Product development may mean that the firm improves a product's performance, or it may mean extending the firm's product line by developing new variations of the item. One company that has been successful with a market penetration strategy is Loblaw Companies Ltd., with their President's Choice line of products. Their strategy for the past 20 years has been to provide a steady stream of new grocery products with ideas on how to use them. The President's Choice line of products now has more than 2000 items including cookies, snacks, desserts, pastas, prepared meals, sauces, soft drinks, beer, breakfast cereals, ice cream, cheese, pet food, potting soil, and financial services.

- **Diversification** strategies emphasize both new products and new markets to achieve growth. Loblaws has expanded the distribution of President's Choice products (see Exhibit 2.2) beyond Canada, and these are now sold in the United States, Hong Kong, Israel, Bermuda, Barbados, and Columbia. Loblaws recently diversified into banking by joining forces with the Canadian Imperial Bank of Commerce (CIBC) to create President's Choice Financial, a virtual bank that offers a wide range of financial services, in-store for Loblaws customers via the Internet and telephone.

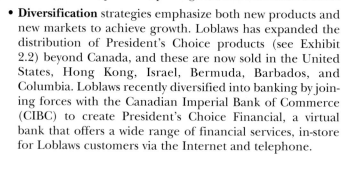

Exhibit 2.1

To grow, IKEA has identified a new market for children's furniture.

SPOTLIGHT ON REAL PEOPLE *Aliah, Inc.*

Big companies and consulting firms work hard and spend hard to transform knowledge into strategy. An entrepreneur named Aly Abulleil goes a step farther—he develops strategic planning software that captures emotions as well.[11]

As a young planner with an Egyptian oil company, Abulleil worked on the mathematical concepts of game theory, which explores how conflicts in decision making can be resolved. After entering a PhD engineering program at the University of Pittsburgh, he began to build a business, called Aliah, Inc., to help middle management make decisions. His first client was Timken, a large manufacturer of ball bearings. To combat a production problem the company was having, Abulleil analyzed the choices engineers were making. He broke every issue down into a series of questions, each with only two alternatives. The engi-

neers not only had to choose an option, they had to indicate how strongly they felt about their choice, which incorporated the intensity of managers' emotions. This approach was quite different from other planning programs.

The business was running on a shoestring, but his staff stuck with him—partly because they could see how the planning method worked in their own lives. For example, his technical chief used it to solve problems in his church, and his general manager relied on the software to help junior high students set personal priorities. In 1996, everything changed: IBM adopted the software as a planning tool, and soon other major firms like Boeing and Lubrizol were using it to develop strategy. Abulleil and his supporters plan to take Aliah public by 2002, with a share of the proceeds going toward charities.

1. How does Aliah help managers in the strategic planning process?
2. What role should emotions or intuition versus rational, objective analysis play in this process?
3. How can Aliah best convey its different approach so that the company can increase its own market share among products and services used to facilitate strategic planning? Are there other potential customers besides corporate planners who might be convinced to use the software?

Many firms ultimately rely on more than one of these strategies to achieve growth. Harley-Davidson, for example, was able to grow with a market development strategy that successfully targeted rich urban bikers *and* with a market penetration strategy that called for redesigning and improving the quality of its bikes to generate sales among existing hogs. When the firm realized that its customers not only wanted to ride Harleys, they wanted to let others know this as well, it embarked on a product development strategy. By expanding its line of Motorclothes and souvenirs, Harley dealers sell more of its products to the same customers.[12]

To review, strategic planning includes developing an organizational mission statement, assessing of the internal and external environments with a SWOT analysis, setting objectives, developing strategic business units, and planning for growth. In the next section, we'll look at the tactical planning done by marketing departments.

Harley Davidson
www.harley-davidson.com

100,000 POUNDS WON'T LAST LONG!

New **President's Choice Colossal Butterflied Garlic Shrimp** are so big and so flavourful that we're concerned there won't be enough to go around! What a fabulous convenience—shell-on, butterflied shrimp marinated in a simple yet flavourful mixture of garlic and herbs, and individually quick frozen. They're ridiculously easy to cook. Simply crack open a box straight from the freezer, throw them on the grill or in a grill basket, and enjoy them 4 to 6 minutes later! (Like we said, ridiculous.) These shrimp are

"colossal" in flavour, convenience and in size, since "colossal" is a description bestowed on the really big ones—and these average 13 to 15 to the pound! How big is that? Let's just say you'd have to stuff TWO ordinary size shrimp into your mouth to get as much meat as you get on ONE of these babies! Colossal shrimp are in such limited supply that one inevitably pays a premium for them. You'll be amazed that we are able to deliver these to you already cleaned, deveined, butterflied and marinated for the grill—for about

what you'd pay for raw shrimp you'd have to fuss with yourself! With PC **Colossal Butterflied Garlic Shrimp**, you don't have to know anything about preparing shrimp—except that you love them!—to wow your guests. Our **Chef's Challenge recipe below** pairs them with eggplant *Imam Bayildi* (Turkish for "the priest fainted," with delight!). Don't miss out on the shrimp experience of a lifetime! They're in the frozen seafood section, and when they're gone, they are *gone*!

NEW

COLOSSAL BUTTERFLIED GARLIC SHRIMP SHELL-ON MARINATED *Ideal for the grill* 13-15 sh/g UNCOOKED 454 g 1 lb

STOCK UP EARLY

12.99 454 g frozen

Exhibit 2.2

Loblaws follows an aggressive product development strategy with its President's Choice line of products.

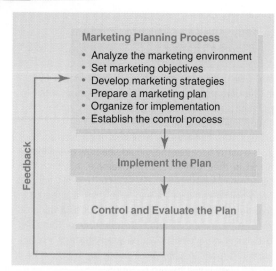

Marketing Planning Process

- Analyze the marketing environment
- Set marketing objectives
- Develop marketing strategies
- Prepare a marketing plan
- Organize for implementation
- Establish the control process

Feedback

Implement the Plan

Control and Evaluate the Plan

Figure 2.6 The Marketing Planning Process

✳ ✳ ✳

competitive advantage The ability of a firm to outperform the competition, providing customers with a benefit the competition cannot.

✳ ✳ ✳

distinctive competency A capability of a firm that is superior to that of its direct competitors.

The Marketing Planning Process

Solid planning means that a firm has a viable product at a price consumers are willing to pay, the means to get that product to the place consumers want it, and a way to promote the product to the right consumers. Figure 2.6 outlines the steps in the marketing planning process: analyzing the marketing environment, setting marketing objectives, and developing marketing strategies.

Creating a Competitive Advantage: Marketing's Strategic Focus

Before we discuss the steps in marketing planning, it's important to understand that the underlying goal of *all* marketing strategies and plans is to create a **competitive advantage** for the firm—to take what the company does really well and outperform the competition, thus providing customers with a benefit the competition cannot. A competitive advantage gives consumers a reason to choose one product over another again and again.

Andersen Windows developed a competitive advantage in its industry. Over the years, Andersen developed many choices of window designs to meet customers' ever-changing tastes, as illustrated in Exhibit 2.3. Because of this complexity, Andersen got so many orders wrong that its reputation was at stake. To solve this problem, Andersen created an interactive computerized version of its catalogue that allows customers to add, change, or strip away window features, check the window for structural soundness, and then generate a price. Each order is then electronically transmitted to the factory, where it receives a unique control number ensuring that the order gets built and shipped accurately. Andersen has cut errors to only one wrong order per 200 truckloads shipped. Customers can select from 188 000 different windows with confidence that Andersen will get their order right—an "open-and-shut case" for competitive advantage.[13]

How does a firm go about creating competitive advantage? The first step is to identify **distinctive competency**, a firm's capability that is superior to that of its competition. For example, Coca-Cola's success in global markets—Coke has 50% of the world's soft drink

If your patio doors have always stuck, squeaked or leaked, these could take some getting used to.

Exhibit 2.3

Andersen Window— offering customers more designs makes the firm distinctive in the market.

business—is related to its distinctive competencies in distribution and marketing communications. Coke's distribution system got a jump on the competition during World War II, when the firm decreed that every soldier would have access to a five-cent Coke. The US government liked this morale-building effort, and assisted Coke in building 64 overseas bottling plants. Coke's skillful marketing communications program is another distinctive competency that has contributed to its global success. In addition to its glitzy television commercials, Coke has created a commanding presence worldwide by blanketing countries like Tanzania (see Exhibit 2.4) with signs to ensure that even people without access to TV will think of Coke when they get thirsty.

The second step in developing a competitive advantage is to turn a distinctive competency into a differential benefit, one that is important to customers. **Differential benefits** set a firm's products apart from their competitors' products by providing something unique that customers want. Differential benefits provide reasons for customers to pay a premium for a firm's products or exhibit a strong brand preference.

A differential benefit does not necessarily mean simply offering something *different*. For example, Mennen marketed a deodorant with a distinctive feature: It contained vitamin D. Unfortunately, consumers did not see any reason to pay for the privilege of spraying vitamin D under their arms. Despite advertising claims, they saw no benefit and the product failed. The moral: Effective product benefits must be both *different* from the competition and *wanted* by customers.

✳ ✳ ✳
differential benefits Properties of products that set them apart from competitors' products by providing unique customer benefits.

Evaluating the Marketing Environment

Good marketing planning, just like strategic planning, has as its foundation, an understanding of the marketing environment. Thus, the first step in marketing planning is to conduct a comprehensive analysis of the marketing environment. An organization conducts a SWOT analysis to better understand its internal and external environments; marketing managers build on the company's SWOT analysis by searching out information about the environment that specifically affects the marketing plan.

For example, to develop effective marketing communications programs, marketing managers must know about competitors' advertising, sales promotion, and public relations activities. And it's not enough to have a general understanding of the target market: Marketing managers need to know what TV shows they watch; whether a coupon, rebate, or sweepstakes is most likely to make them buy; and whether they prefer buying their jeans at Zellers or on the Internet.

Setting Marketing Objectives

Once marketing managers have a thorough understanding of the marketing environment, the next step in the planning process is to develop marketing objectives. These objectives state what the marketing function must accomplish if the firm is to achieve its overall objectives.

Many marketing objectives are quantitative—they are stated in terms of dollar or unit sales or percent market share. With

Exhibit 2.4

Coca-Cola— creating a presence around the globe.

quantitative objectives, marketers can easily determine whether the marketing plan has met its goals. In some situations, however, marketing has important objectives that are more difficult to quantify, such as: "To improve the image of our brand" or "To improve customer loyalty."

Still, even these "fuzzy" objectives are measurable. Marketing researchers can assess improvement in brand image, for example, by polling customers to determine whether their feelings about a brand have changed or stayed the same. When General Motors (GM) developed a new model of its mid-size sport-utility vehicle, the Blazer, it set a quantitative objective of a sales increase from 226 000 to 300 000 units annually.[14] To achieve this growth, GM set a qualitative marketing objective during the early stages of product development—to identify ways to make the Blazer more attractive to customers by finding out what its existing customers wanted in a mid-size utility vehicle.

SALES OBJECTIVES

Regardless of the overall organizational strategies, marketing objectives normally include one or more sales objectives. After all, without sales, there are no profits; and without profits, there is no business. Some examples of sales objectives are: "To increase sales of our deluxe model toy by 15% during the next 12 months"; "To increase our toy market share by five percent each year for the next three years"; "To sell one million toys during the holiday season."

Sales objectives need to be challenging and yet achievable. First, manufacturing capacity and inventory levels are based on sales objectives; therefore, if firms set sales objectives too low, they may not be able to meet demand. Advertising, sales force, and other budgets are also set according to sales objectives, so if sales objectives are so high that they are unattainable, profits will suffer. Sometimes errors can lead to disaster, as when Coleco underestimated sales of its Cabbage Patch dolls, causing desperate parents to line up for long hours at retail stores trying to score a precious doll for their kids.

PRODUCT-ORIENTED OBJECTIVES

If a firm has decided that its growth strategy is to focus on product development—new or improved products for existing customers—it will develop product objectives. Because it is more profitable to retain customers than it is to replace them, firms often set objectives for improvements in quality or service to develop customer loyalty. In the breakfast cereal market, where consumers are more fickle than loyal, firms like Kellogg and General Mills may set objectives for developing new brands to suit the tastes of everyone—children, teens, and adults—or they may set goals for a new product to retain customers who are being lured away by a competitor's new honey-coated, fruit-and-fibre cereal. In other cases, a firm may decide to modify a product by taking advantage of trends, as when Frito-Lay developed its line of "lite" snacks.

MARKET OBJECTIVES

In some instances, firms find that their best opportunities for growth are stated in the form of market objectives. These goals can involve entering new markets or increasing product usage in

Exhibit 2.5

The RV industry believes that baby boomers can be their next big market.

Real People, Real Decisions
Decision Time at **Meal Exchange**

Rahul Raj knew that strategic planning was important to ensure that Meal Exchange understood its market and set realistic marketing objectives and plans. Although Meal Exchange was small—essentially a one-person operation—with no formal planning process in place, Raj believed that without planning, success would be limited. But he was also realistic about the capacity of such a small organization to engage in planning. So his first steps were to get the organization to a point where strategic planning could take place in a more formalized way. He wanted Meal Exchange to move from an ad hoc, volunteer organization, to a more formalized one. That move required money and people.

Raj's priority was to build Meal Exchange into a credible charitable organization. Credibility would facilitate expansion to other schools and help get cash donations from businesses and government to finance the expansion of Meal Exchange across Canada. Raj registered Meal Exchange as an official Canadian charitable organization, which meant that the organization would have to undergo an annual audit by Revenue Canada to ensure that money was being spent as it should be. Charitable status also provided for all donations to Meal Exchange to be tax deductible, a practical consideration for trying to raise money. Raj also applied for money from a large granting agency, and received a $25 000 grant to be used to help expand Meal Exchange.

Once Raj had money for personnel, he started recruiting for a full-time executive director. Having an executive director would allow the organization to move forward more quickly than if Raj did everything himself. He also set up a board of directors of 18 people, each representing a key stakeholder group for Meal Exchange: there were six business people, six students, and six people from not-for-profit and government organizations. Raj carefully chose members of the board so that each one could provide valuable information for the planning and operations of Meal Exchange.

With a team in place to assist in planning, Raj began to consider how to achieve growth for Meal Exchange. He defined two options for its future growth:

Option 1. Follow a market development strategy in the short run and expand Meal Exchange to universities and colleges across Canada. In the long term, the organization would expand throughout North America and internationally. This option would keep the strategic focus of Meal Exchange on its core "product" and would grow the organization through geographic expansion. By concentrating on the original Meal Exchange concept and refining it, the organization would become more effective and efficient. Raj realized that such concentration of resources was a good way for small organizations to be effective.

Option 2. The second option that Raj considered was a combination of product development and market development strategies. This option would see Meal Exchange develop four separate "products" at the same time that geographic expansion was taking place. Raj believed that having a broader portfolio of products would help Meal Exchange achieve the overall objective of getting post-secondary students involved in social issues. The original Meal Exchange concept represented only one way for students to be involved with social issues; by broadening the opportunities for involvement, the organization might reach more students. The four products he considered were: the original Meal Exchange concept where students would donate money from their meal plans; a volunteerism program which would provide specific opportunities for students to volunteer in not-for-profit organizations, perhaps through an Internet registry process; an annual essay contest on the topic of how to fight hunger in Canada, whose winners would be given money to help put their ideas into practice; a recognition product, whereby Meal Exchange would sponsor awards to recognize college and university students across the country who exhibited a commitment to community development and volunteerism. This broadened vision of Meal Exchange provided for several future opportunities, but Raj was concerned about the ability of a small organization to effectively operate four related products.

Now, join the Meal Exchange decision team: Which option would you recommend, and why?

served markets, through using either market development strategies (existing products sold to new customers) or diversification strategies (new products for new customers). Manufacturers of recreational vehicles (motor homes and travel trailers), for example, used a market development strategy in targeting baby boomers (see Exhibit 2.5). Joining together in a "Go RVing Coalition," they spent US $15 million on advertising aimed at this under-50 market in a three-year period.[15]

Developing Marketing Strategies

In the next stage of the marketing planning process, marketing managers develop the marketing strategies—they make decisions about what activities they must accomplish to achieve the marketing objectives. Usually, this means deciding which markets to target and how to develop the marketing mix—product, price, promotion, and distribution—to reach that market.

SELECTING A TARGET MARKET

A critical component of the planning process is selecting the group(s) of customers the organization will go after—its target market. The target market is a market segment the firm selects because it believes that its offerings are most suited to winning those customers. That is, the firm assesses the potential demand—the number of consumers it believes are willing and able to pay for its products—and decides if it has the distinctive competencies that will create a competitive advantage in the minds of these consumers. Target markets can change over time. The maker of Crayola crayons, recognizing that 90% of its products are purchased by mothers rather than by their kids, uses a nostalgia approach with an ad that targets parents, asking them to remember their first box of Crayolas.[16]

Developing Marketing Mix Programs

Marketing mix decisions identify how marketing will accomplish its objectives in the firm's target markets. Typically, marketers tailor the marketing mix—product, price, promotion, and place—to meet the needs of each target market.

Product Strategies: Because the product is the most fundamental part of the marketing mix—firms simply can't make a profit without a good, service, idea, or something else of value to exchange—carefully developed product strategies are essential to achieving marketing objectives. For goods, product strategies include decisions about the best product design, its packaging, branding, and what its warranty will be. Product strategy decisions also determine what services (such as maintenance) will accompany the product, how the product will be positioned relative to the competition, if there will be variations of the product, and what product features will provide the unique benefits targeted customers want. For example, product planners for a number of airlines, including Air Canada, sought to increase

Exhibit 2.6

The new Corvette—developed to be better but not more expensive.

their attractiveness through improved in-flight cuisine with larger portions of tastier, even exotic, dishes. Passengers may dine on such fare as Harvey's burgers, egg rolls, maple carrots, Second Cup coffee, and Montreal-style bagels.

These and other product decisions are closely tied to the other parts of the marketing mix. For example, Chevrolet sought to attract new buyers when it introduced its 1997 Corvette, the first one in 14 years. The new Corvette shown in Exhibit 2.6 has an improved ride, is far easier to get into and out of, and has twice as much trunk space for luggage and groceries as Corvettes of old. At the same time, GM marketers realized that to be successful, they needed to keep the price down. To make this pricing strategy possible, GM engineers designed the new Corvette to use 34% fewer parts, and developed a manufacturing process for the Corvette that reduced labour costs.[17]

Pricing Strategies: In a nutshell, the pricing strategy determines what specific price a firm charges for a product. That price has to be one that customers are willing to pay. If not, all of the other marketing efforts are worthless. In addition to setting prices for the final consumer, pricing strategies must establish prices that will be charged to wholesalers and retailers. A firm's pricing strategies may be based on costs or demand or pegged to the price of competing products.

In the US, Southwest Airlines, "the little airline that could," used demand-based pricing and successfully targeted customers who could not previously afford air travel. Southwest does more than compete on low price—it also provides dependable service while keeping costs down. The airline flies point-to-point instead of to a central hub; its planes are never idle at the gate waiting for connections; and few routes are longer than 800 kilometres. Southwest gets high ratings from its passengers for its on-time service and baggage handling. What's more, even passengers of other airlines win because many carriers have been forced to match this upstart's low fares.[18]

Communication Strategies: A communication (promotion) strategy is how marketers inform their target market of the nature of the "offer" represented by other elements of the marketing mix. Communication strategies address such issues as what message about the product should be developed, how to deliver the message, and the mix of advertising, sales promotion, and personal selling that will be used. Communication strategies need to be consistent with the other marketing mix strategies. For example, if consumer focus is expected to be on the multiple features of a product, then informative advertising—and print advertising in particular—might be appropriate to deliver a complex message. A communication strategy connoting high quality, luxury, or prestige would be consistent with a premium pricing strategy, where a product will sell at a higher price than its competitors.

A critical part of communication strategy is creating a brand image that will set the brand apart from the competition. Office Depot licensed the comic-strip character Dilbert to create a brand image and to buy "star power" with their $100 million–plus marketing budget. And its sales rose by 12% during the first quarter that the Dilbert ads, such as the one in Exhibit 2.7, ran. This explains why competitor Office-Max has banned Dilbert products from its stores.[19]

Exhibit 2.7

Office Depot is using a licence agreement with Dilbert creators to create a strong brand image.

Exhibit 2.8

Chapters and Barnes &
Noble offer Starbucks
many new locations with
the right image.

Distribution Strategies: The distribution (place) strategy outlines how, when, and where the firm will make the product available to targeted customers. In developing a distribution strategy, marketers must decide whether to sell the product directly to the final customer through their own retail stores or non-store alternatives, such as the Internet, or to sell through distributors, such as wholesalers or independent retailers. Which retailers will be selected depends on the product, pricing, and promotion strategies. If the firm is producing a high-quality, top-of-the-line product, it would be distributed through specialty stores rather than through discount merchandisers.

Starbucks
www.starbucks.com

Cappuccino grande to go? Starbucks Coffee has stolen market share from companies like Kraft, Procter & Gamble, and Nestlé through a distribution strategy that makes its gourmet coffees available to customers in stores, on planes, and in their homes. The retail chain went from 50 stores in 1989 to over 2000 in 1999, but avid Starbucks fans can also have regular shipments of their favourite coffee blends delivered to their doors. In addition, Starbucks coffee is now poured on many airlines and, as seen in Exhibit 2.8, in bookstores such as Chapters and Barnes & Noble. At the same time, Starbucks protects its gourmet image by refusing to be sold in convenience stores such as 7-Eleven.[20]

Distribution plans must also include how the firm will transport the product to the members of the distribution channel, where to locate distribution centres, and even how to display the product once it gets to the point-of-sale. For example, with help from Harley-Davidson, many motorcycle dealerships changed from dark and menacing caverns to bright and friendly retail environments complete with neon lights, mirrored dressing rooms, and stylish clothing.

Preparing a Marketing Plan

✳ ✳ ✳

marketing plan A document
that describes the marketing environment, outlines the marketing objectives and strategy, and
identifies who will be responsible for carrying out each part of
the marketing strategy.

The final stage of the marketing planning process is preparing the formal **marketing plan**, a written document that describes the marketing environment, outlines the marketing objectives and strategy, and identifies who will be responsible for carrying out each part of the marketing strategy. In large firms, top management often requires a written plan for marketing, because it encourages marketing managers to formulate concrete objectives and strategies. In small entrepreneurial firms, such as Computer Friendly Stuff (CFS), a well-thought-out marketing plan is often a key factor in attracting investors who will help turn the firm's dreams into reality. Check out CFS's marketing plan in Appendix A.

✳ ✳ ✳

situation analysis The first part
of a marketing plan, which provides a thorough description of
the firm's current situation including its internal and external
environments; also called a
business review.

The parts of the written marketing plan correspond to the earlier steps in the planning process. The first part of the plan, called a **situation analysis** or a business review, is a thorough description of the firm's current situation, including the results of the analysis of the internal and external environments. Based on the situation analysis, the plan describes the marketing problems and opportunities and outlines the marketing objectives.

The next part of the plan details specific strategies and action plans, or *tactics* for the elements of the marketing mix—product, price, place, and promotion. Finally, information about how and by whom the plan is to be implemented and controlled, including budgets and timing, is included. Sometimes organizations require that marketing plans include contingency plans, a predetermined change in direction should monitoring of marketing activities show that the objectives are not being met.

Implementation and Control of the Marketing Plan

In our discussion of marketing planning, we've talked about how a competitive advantage is the underlying goal. We've looked at how marketing planners examine the marketing environment, set objectives, and develop product, price, place, and promotion strategies before writing the formal marketing plan. But, the best plan ever written is useless if it's not properly carried out. Now we'll look at some of the critical issues in implementing and controlling that plan.

One reason for a firm's failure to carry out its plan may be that planning has been limited to top managers, who don't have a clear understanding of the day-to-day operations of the firm. They may be out of touch with what *really* happens on the factory floor or in the store, so the objectives they set up are easier said than done. Another problem occurs when marketers devise short-term objectives for their personal gain. Because management rewards and incentives are often tied to short-term profit objectives, implementation of the marketing plan may focus too heavily on short-term results to the detriment of the firm's long-term goals.

In this section, we'll look at two key factors in the successful implementation of marketing plans: the marketing budget and the organization of the marketing function. We'll also look at the ways in which marketing managers control and evaluate the marketing plan. These activities assess the performance of the marketing function, and they also provide valuable feedback for the development of future plans.

Implementing the Marketing Plan

Implementation means putting plans into action—bringing the strategies to life on a day-to-day basis. The implementation sections of a marketing plan contain a marketing budget, the development of specific action plans, and the assignment of major areas of responsibility to individuals or teams.

THE MARKETING BUDGET

The **marketing budget** is a statement of the total amount a firm spends on marketing and allocation of money for each activity under the marketer's control. The best, most carefully thought-out marketing strategies are not much good if there isn't money to support them. Usually decisions about the allocation of funds within the organization are made by the top-level executives and finance managers. And all of the different functional area managers need financial resources and all tend to feel that their needs are the most important. It is critical for marketing managers to understand the other functional areas of the company and to communicate to other functional managers the importance of marketing activities to the success of the overall organizational objectives.

Generally, the budgeting process in medium and large organizations goes through a series of steps. First, the marketing managers need to have a basic understanding of how much money they'll have to spend. It makes no sense to develop strategies above budget. In reality, the starting point for planning the marketing budget is often the amount allocated to marketing during the previous budget planning period. From this starting point, marketing managers determine their needs for such marketing activities as new product development, for developing and maintaining channels of distribution, and for the various promotional activities included in the marketing plan. If the overall organizational goals are to grow revenues through introduction of new products, larger budgets will be required. For example, in 1993, when Robert Louis-Dreyfus became president of Adidas, the amount earmarked for marketing was only six percent of sales.[21] Louis-Dreyfus believed in marketing enough to double the budget and develop new ads. But if the firm's overall objectives are to control costs, it will be difficult to justify increasing marketing budgets in the short term.

✳ ✳ ✳
implementation The stage of the strategic management process in which strategies are put into action on a day-to-day basis.

✳ ✳ ✳
marketing budget A statement of the total amount to be spent on marketing and the allocation of money for each activity under the marketer's control.

Marketing budgets don't always go up from one year to the next. For example, in 1998, Nike cut its global marketing budget by $100 million, as CEO Phil Knight blamed ineffective marketing for sales declines.[22] Although it's hard to understand how spending less on marketing makes a firm's marketing efforts more effective, performance-based cuts like that are often the reality marketing managers must face.

ORGANIZING THE MARKETING FUNCTION

Another important element of successful marketing plan implementation is the organization of the marketing function. Marketing organization is how a firm divides marketing tasks into different jobs and assigns people to departments or geographic territories. There are several philosophies about the best way to do this.

A *functional structure* separates marketing into distinct components, such as advertising, sales promotion, sales force management, and marketing research. Some firms feel that customer needs differ by geographic region and prefer a *geographic structure*, perhaps setting up one marketing department for, say, Eastern Europe and another for Western Europe. Firms that choose a *product structure* may have a number of different brand managers and product group or product line managers, each of whom is responsible for an entire brand. Procter & Gamble, a firm that markets products around the globe, divides its marketing operations into different product category divisions in different geographic markets. For example, each of the separate dish care divisions, laundry detergent divisions, and hard surface cleaning divisions in North America, Latin America, and in Asia are managed by individual product category managers who do the marketing planning for their product category in that region of the world.[23]

Controlling the Marketing Plan

Control means measuring actual performance, comparing it to planned performance, and making necessary changes in plans and implementation. This process requires that marketing managers obtain feedback on whether activities are being performed well and in a timely manner. Gathering such feedback allows managers to determine whether they should continue with the marketing plan, activate the contingency plan, or go back to the drawing board. It also provides feedback for the next year's planning activities. Let's briefly review some of the tools and techniques that help managers control the marketing plan.

TREND ANALYSIS

Sometimes, firms develop trend analyses to better understand patterns of change in their company, the industry, or the market. A trend is a general direction or pattern or change in events or conditions. In a **trend analysis**, marketers use data such as industry or company sales over a period of years to understand past directions that may continue into the future. For example, a trend analysis may show that industry sales have been rising, been falling, or remained about the same. An understanding of industry trends can be very important for setting sales goals, developing strategies, and measuring company performance, while a company's own sales trends show whether the overall marketing program is on track.

To understand a trend analysis at work, consider changes made by the Lotus Development Corp. Lotus saw its spreadsheet software market share plummet from 80 to 55% in the late 1980s. Though the firm had shown an ability to quickly update its software, as with its spreadsheet application Lotus 1-2-3, Lotus was losing customers. By analyzing industry sales data, however, Lotus identified a trend for *groupware* (software tools to support groups of people working together, often at different locations) and unified software packages (software suites or groups of applications designed to work together). As a result, Lotus marketers scrapped their old plans and developed new marketing plans that included successful products for these markets.

MARKETING RESEARCH

Sometimes firms conduct primary marketing research to obtain feedback on marketing plans. These efforts range from simple interviews with customers to complicated statistical analyses of thousands of responses to questionnaires. Honda, maker of the highly success-

✳ ✳ ✳
control Measuring actual performance, comparing it to planned performance, and making necessary changes in plans and implementation.

✳ ✳ ✳
trend analysis An analysis of past industry or company sales data to determine patterns of change that may continue into the future.

ful Accord, even went so far as to have its factory workers call more than 47 000 Accord owners to see if they were happy with their cars and to get ideas for improvements.[24] We'll explore marketing research techniques in more detail in Chapter 5.

THE MARKETING AUDIT

The **marketing audit** is a comprehensive review of a firm's marketing function. It can also give feedback on specific marketing plans The purpose of the audit is to determine if a firm can improve its marketing programs. Because a marketing audit should be objective and unbiased, it is best conducted by an independent consulting organization rather than by the firm itself. Alternatively, employee teams drawn from non-marketing positions can conduct the audit. In either case, those who conduct the audit systematically examine the marketing environment, as well as the objectives, strategies, and activities of the marketing plan. Auditors interview managers, customers, salespeople, and others. Table 2.1 shows the areas of the firm's marketing function that a marketing audit can evaluate.

✳ ✳ ✳
marketing audit A comprehensive review of a firm's marketing function.

Table 2.1 Information Gathered in a Marketing Audit

1. Marketing philosophy
    - Support organizational objectives
    - Focus on customer needs
    - Social responsibility included in decision making
    - Different offerings for different segments
    - A total system perspective

2. Marketing organization
    - Integration of different marketing functions
    - Integration of marketing with other functional areas of the organization
    - Organization for new product development
    - Qualifications and effectiveness of marketing management personnel

3. Marketing information systems
    - Effective use of marketing research
    - Current study data available
    - Timely communication of relevant information to marketing planners
    - Knowledge of sales potential and profitability for various market segments, territories, products, channels, and order sizes
    - Monitor effectiveness of marketing strategies and tactics
    - Cost-effectiveness studies

4. Strategic orientation
    - Formal marketing planning
        - Objectives
        - Environmental scanning
        - Sales forecasting
        - Contingency planning
    - Quality of current marketing strategy
        - Product strategies
        - Distribution strategies
        - Promotion strategies
        - Pricing strategies
    - Contingency planning

5. Operations
    - Communications and implementation of planning
    - Effective use of resources
    - Ability to adapt to changes

Source: Adapted from Philip Kotler, "From sales obsession to marketing effectiveness," *Harvard Business Review*, November–December 1977: 70–1.

Real People, Real Decisions
How it worked out at Meal Exchange

Rahul Raj and the team at Meal Exchange chose Option 1, pursuing geographic expansion of the original Meal Exchange concept as a market development strategy. The organization adopted a new mission statement, "To identify and implement student solutions to hunger in Canada", and Raj applied for more grants to finance the plans that would support the fulfillment of this mission.

By the beginning of 2002, 22 universities and colleges were running a Meal Exchange chapter, and more than $250 000 had been raised through the program to help fight hunger. The organization had also hired an executive director, had over 250 active volunteers across the country,

and had raised an additional $121 000 in grants to cover operational expenses. Meal Exchange won recognition as "one of Canada's most innovative non-profit organizations" in a 2001 article in *Maclean's*, and was one of six organizations featured in *Time* in 2001 as part of an article called "Canada, The Next Generation: People Who Do Good Things the Canadian Way." Given the success thus far of geographic expansion within Canada, Rahul Raj is now considering how to continue to achieve growth for Meal Exchange in the long run by entering the much larger college and university market in the United States.

Chapter Summary

1. Explain the strategic planning process.

   Business planning includes strategic planning by top-level managers, tactical planning by middle managers, and operations planning by lower-level managers. Strategic planning begins with defining the firm's business mission. From the firm's mission statement and an evaluation of the firm's internal strengths and weaknesses as well as its external opportunities and threats called a SWOT analysis, planners develop broad corporate objectives that identify what the firm hopes to achieve.

   Decisions about the firm's portfolio of strategic business units are often made with the help of such planning tools as the Boston Consulting Group matrix, which assesses SBUs on market growth potential and the firm's relative market share. Managers may determine the business growth strategy with the product–market growth matrix, which identifies four strategies for market penetration, market development, product development, and diversification.

2. Tell how firms gain a competitive advantage and describe the factors that influence marketing objectives.

   Creating a competitive advantage is the strategic focus of an organization's marketing planning process. A competitive advantage means that a firm has developed reasons for customers to select its product over all others in the market. A firm gains a competitive advantage when it has distinctive competencies or capabilities that are stronger than those of the competition, which it uses to create differential benefits or product benefits, which are uniquely different from the competition.

3. Describe the steps in the marketing planning process.

   Marketing planning begins with an evaluation of the internal and external environments. Marketing managers then set quantitative and qualitative market objectives, such as desired levels of sales, development of new or improved products, or growth in new or existing markets. Next, marketing mangers select the target market(s) the organization will go after and decide what marketing mix strategies they will use. Product strategies include decisions about products and product characteristics that will appeal to the target market. Pricing strategies state the specific prices to be charged to channel members and final consumers. Communication strategies include plans for advertising, consumer and trade sales promotion, the sales function, publicity, point-of-purchase materials, and other marketing communications activities to reach the target market. Distribution strategies outline how the product will be made available to targeted customers, when and where they want it. The final step in the marketing planning process is the development of a written marketing plan.

4. Explain the factors involved in the implementation and control of the marketing plan.
Implementation, or putting the plan into action, includes development of the marketing budget. Also essential to successful implementation is effective organization of the marketing function—how the work is broken up into different jobs and assigned to different people. Control is the measurement of actual performance and comparison with planned performance. Planners may use trend analyses or other forms of marketing research to obtain performance feedback. A comprehensive review of the marketing system is sometimes conducted using a marketing audit.

Chapter Review

Marketing Concepts: Testing Your Knowledge

1. What are strategic, tactical, and operational planning? What is cross-functional planning?

2. What is a mission statement? Why is a mission statement important to an organization?

3. What is a SWOT analysis? What role does it play in the planning process?

4. What is a business portfolio? Why do firms develop SBUs? Describe the planning tools firms use to plan and assess its portfolio of SBUs and to develop growth strategies?

5. Why is marketing planning important to a firm?

6. What does it mean for a firm to have a competitive advantage? What gives a firm a competitive advantage?

7. What are marketing objectives? What types of marketing objectives do firms normally include in marketing planning?

8. What are some of the factors that firms consider when developing product strategies? What are some influences on pricing strategies? What are some issues involved in developing promotion strategies? What do firms consider when developing distribution strategies?

9. What are the elements in a formal marketing plan?

10. What are the important elements in the implementation and control of marketing plans?

Marketing Concepts: Discussing Choices and Issues

1. The Boston Consulting Group matrix identifies products as stars, cash cows, question marks, and dogs. Do you think this is a useful way for organizations to examine their businesses? What are some examples of products that fit in each category?

2. Do you agree with the idea that marketing is a firm's most essential functional area, or do you think a firm's success depends equally on all of its functional areas? Explain your reasoning.

3. Do you think firms should concentrate on developing products that are better in some way than competitors' products, or should each firm focus on making the best product it can without regard to competing products? As a consumer, which approach is more likely to produce products that satisfy you the most?

4. Most planning, whether by businesses or by not-for-profit organizations, involves strategies for growth. But is growth always the right direction? Can you think of some organizations that should have contraction rather than expansion as their goal? Do you know of any organizations that have planned to get smaller rather than larger to be successful?

Marketing Practice: Applying What You've Learned

1. Assume that you are the marketing director for a local micro-brewery and that your boss, the company president, has decided to develop a mission statement to add to this year's annual report. He's admitted that he doesn't know much about developing a mission statement and has asked you to help guide him in this process. Write a memo outlining what exactly a mission statement is, why firms develop such statements, how firms use missions statements, and your thoughts on what the firm's mission statement might be.

KEY TERMS

business portfolio (36)

competitive advantage (40)

control (48)

cross-functional planning (31)

differential benefits (40)

distinctive competency (40)

diversification (38)

external environment (34)

implementation (47)

internal environment (34)

market development (38)

market penetration (38)

marketing audit (49)

marketing budget (47)

marketing plan (46)

mission statement (32)

objectives (35)

operational planning (31)

portfolio analysis (36)

product development (38)

situation analysis (46)

strategic business units (SBUs) (35)

strategic planning (30)

SWOT analysis (34)

tactical planning (31)

trend analysis (48)

2. As a marketing student, you know that large firms often organize their operations into a number of strategic business units (SBUs). A college or university might develop a similar structure where different academic units are seen as separate businesses. Working with four to six classmates, consider how your college or university might divide its total academic units into separate SBUs. What would be the problems with implementing such a plan? What would be the advantages and disadvantages for students and for faculty? Present your analysis of university SBUs to your class.

3. Working with four to six classmates, select a product that you all use, such as toothpaste or shampoo. Identify the different brands of the product used by each person in the group, and find out what product features and benefits caused each person to choose the particular brand. Then combine your responses to create a list of all possible product attributes a manufacturer might consider in developing a new brand for that product.

4. Assume you are the new marketing assistant in a small metropolitan hospital whose market consists of the residents in the city district and the students and faculty of a large nearby college or university. You have been asked for ideas that the organization might use in promotional activities to draw clients who might otherwise choose a larger facility across town. Develop a list of the consumer segments in the hospital's market (for example, elderly, children, college or university athletes, international students), and for each segment, identify possible features and benefits the hospital might emphasize in its promotions to attract that segment.

5. Successful firms have a competitive advantage because they are able to identify distinctive competencies and use these to create differential benefits for their customers. Consider your college or university. What distinctive competencies does it have? What differential benefits does it provide for students? What is its competitive advantage? What are your ideas as to how your college or university could create or improve its competitive position? Write an outline of your ideas.

Marketing Mini-Project: **Learning by Doing**

The purpose of this mini-project is to gain an understanding of marketing planning through actual experience.

1. Select one of the following for your marketing planning project:
   - yourself (in your search for a career)
   - your college or university
   - a specific department in your college or university

2. Next, develop the following elements of the marketing planning process:
   - a mission statement
   - a SWOT analysis
   - objectives
   - a description of the target market(s)
   - a brief outline of the marketing mix strategies—product, pricing, distribution, and promotion strategies—that satisfy the objectives and address the target market

3. Prepare a formal, but brief, marketing plan using Appendix A as a guide.

Real People, Real Surfers: **Exploring the Web**

Visit the home pages of one or more of the firms whose mission statements are given in Figure 2.2. Follow the links to find out about the company's products, pricing, distribution, and marketing communications strategies. Do a search of the World Wide Web for other information about the company. Based on your findings, answer the following questions:

1. What is the organization's "business"? What is the overall purpose of the organization? What does the organization hope to achieve?

2. What customers does the organization want to serve?

3. What elements of the Web page specifically reflect the business of the organization? How is the Web page designed to attract the organization's customers?

4. Do you think the marketing strategies and other activities of the organization are consistent with its mission? Why do you feel this way?

Develop a report based on your findings and conclusions about the organization. Present your report to your class.

MARKETING IN ACTION

Ontario Energy Deregulation

How do you market something that can't be seen, touched, smelled, tasted, or heard and costs $1000 to $2000 for the average consumer and tens of thousands of dollars for business customers? That's the challenge facing up to 40 energy services in Ontario's newly deregulated $10 billion energy market. The recent implementation of Bill 35 by the Ontario government ended the near monopoly status enjoyed by crown corporation Ontario Hydro and 257 municipally owned partner utilities. The push is on to differentiate new brands and build customer loyalty.

The incumbent is Hydro One, a company created from the broken up pieces of Ontario Hydro. It has several spinoffs, such as Hydro One Networks (electricity delivery), Hydro One Remote Communities, and Hydro One Telecom. Ontario Hydro Energy Services is the retail subsidiary of Hydro One that retains the historic Ontario Hydro name. Hydro One is trying to position itself as a "progressive" energy company. In its communication strategy it has adopted The Who's rock anthem "I Can See for Miles" and is using the tag line "Connecting at the speed of life." Ontario Hydro Energy Services is offering the convenience of bundled services: electricity, natural gas, long distance telephone, Internet services, cellular phone, home security, and satellite TV—all on one bill. It is focusing on the most profitable Ontario Hydro customers with direct marketing: direct mail and door-to-door soliciting (to meet requirements that signatures be obtained from customers changing suppliers).

Toronto Hydro Corp. is planning to compete on customer service and responsiveness. Michael O'Connor, vice president of marketing, is drawing on six years of experience in the cellular phone industry with Rogers-Cantel. Unlike competitors who have started with positioning and brand preference communication objectives, Toronto Hydro spent $1 million on a campaign to raise awareness of why consumers might want to choose a new energy provider. Getting consumers to perceive a need to switch is a challenge as differences in electricity prices are only in the range of $10 a month for most households.

Direct Energy Marketing Ltd. of Oakville, Ontario is planning to compete on its reputation of reliability and value in delivering natural gas to 800 000 customers. Greengrid Electric Ltd. of Toronto is claiming the environmental ground—with solutions for wind power, solar energy, biomass, and small-scale water generation of hydro. All of the players recognize the need to build trust and be more responsive than utilities have been in the past. Drawing on lessons from the natural gas industry, which was deregulated in Ontario in the mid 1990s, many competitors are following the lead of Ontario Hydro Energy Services and are focusing on direct marketing rather than paid advertising to reach consumers.

Communication strategy is not the only issue. The players need to formulate a product strategy that appeals to particular target markets. Some companies will choose to produce and sell electricity. Others will just sell it. Competitors will also need to decide in what markets they are going to compete. While there are much fewer industrial customers than household consumers, industrial customers use more electricity—and some of these, like aluminum smelters, greenhouses, and frozen meat packers, use a lot of electricity and other forms of energy. Similarly, some consumer segments might be more appropriate for some companies than others. Pricing is likely to be regulated within Ontario but opportunities may exist for differential pricing in different regions of the province and there are opportunities to produce and sell electricity in other markets. Consumers in California, for example, have recently paid up to 10 times more for electricity than consumers in Canada.

Source: Adapted from Astrid Van Den Broek, "Marketing Power Surge," *Marketing Magazine Online*, June 19, 2000.

THINGS TO THINK ABOUT

1. What are the strategic issues facing companies entering the deregulated energy market?
2. What are some alternative target markets on which these companies might focus?
3. What objectives would you have if you were running Ontario Hydro Energy Services?
4. What objectives would you have if you were running Toronto Hydro Corp.?

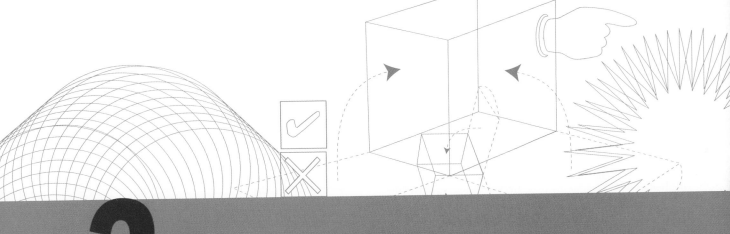

3 Decision Making in the New Era of Marketing: **Enriching the Marketing Environment**

When you have completed your study of this chapter, you should be able to

1. Explain why organizations have adopted a New Era marketing focus on ethics and social responsibility.

2. Describe the New Era emphasis on quality.

3. Discuss some of the important aspects of an organization's internal environment.

4. Explain why marketers scan an organization's external business environment.

Real People, Real Decisions ✔ ✘
Meet Margaret Yee
A Decision Maker at Ethical Funds

Margaret Yee is vice-president of Ethical Funds, the largest group of socially responsible mutual funds in Canada. In this role, she is responsible for all of the marketing decisions for the company's products, including the product development, channel management, and advertising decisions for Registered Retirement Savings Plans (RRSPs) and Registered Educational Savings Plans (RESPs). Yee has a long history of being involved with ethical investing. In her previous job at VanCity Savings Credit Union, she was the manager of the first ethical fund launched in Canada. When the Canadian Credit Unions decided to consolidate all of the existing Credit Union ethical mutual funds, including the one at VanCity, to offer a family of ethical mutual funds to consumers, Yee was asked to lead the initiative.

Ethical Funds, based in Vancouver, BC, uses six main Ethical Principles to determine which companies and economies it will invest in. These principles include not investing in companies involved in weapons development or tobacco manufacturing, or that have damaging environmental policies. Ethical Funds also invests only in companies that have progressive employee relations policies, including non-discriminatory employment practices. Ethical Funds is a wholly owned subsidiary of the Canadian Credit Unions, whose philosophy of giving back to the community is consistent with the concept of ethical investing.

Yee has a BBA from Simon Fraser University, with concentrations in marketing, accounting, and organizational behaviour. She has also achieved the Chartered Financial Analyst (CFA) designation.

Ethical Funds
www.ethicalfunds.com

❋ ❋ ❋

social profit The benefit an organization and society receive from the organization's ethical practices, community service, efforts to promote cultural diversity, and concern for the natural environment.

Welcome to the New Era of Marketing

As the success of a company like Ethical Funds shows, many consumers today are concerned with the ethical practices of companies. As a result, astute marketers recognize that long-term profitability depends on making quality products while acting in an ethical and socially responsible manner. Marketing is *still* concerned with the firm's "bottom line," but now many managers also consider **social profit**, which is the net benefit both the firm and society receive from a firm's ethical practices and socially responsible behaviour.[1]

Creating social profit is so important to The Body Shop Canada (www.thebodyshop.ca) that the first line of their mission statement reads, "We dedicate our business to the pursuit of social and environmental change."[2] Evidence of this commitment to social profit can be seen in The Body Shop's long-standing environmental activism, their stand against using animals in product testing, and their community service activities, including campaigns for fair international trade and activities to fight violence against women.

We call efforts to do business *right* and do it *well* the *New Era of marketing*. Figure 3.1 shows how New Era firms make decisions that create both economic and social profit through a commitment to ethical business behaviour and social responsibility, by adopting a total quality focus, and by having a clear understanding of their internal and external environments.

In this chapter, we'll look at organizations, like Ethical Funds and The Body Shop Canada, that practise this philosophy, first examining how these firms do it right with their focus on ethics and social responsibility and how they do it well by producing quality goods and services they can be proud to sell. In the second half of the chapter, we'll look at the elements of a firm's internal and external environments.

Doing It Right: Ethical Behaviour in the Marketplace

Business ethics is the first step toward creating social profit. But what does ethical business behaviour mean to New Era firms and to their marketing strategies? Ethics are rules of con-

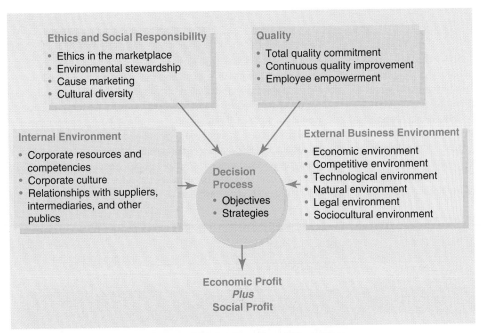

Figure 3.1 Decision Model for Firms in the New Era of Marketing

duct—how most people in a culture judge what is right and what is wrong. **Business ethics** are basic values that guide a firm's behaviour, and these beliefs govern the decisions managers make about what goes into their products, how they are advertised and sold, and how they are disposed of.

In the New Era of marketing, we are witnessing greater concern about business decisions based solely on short-term profits. It has been suggested that business now operates in an "ethics era"—a period in which both executives and consumers are becoming concerned about the downside of "business as usual."[3] For example, a 1998 study of business executives in Canada showed that 85% of the companies represented in the sample had formal statements of values and principles to guide their business decision making.[4] Similarly, a 2002 report from the Canadian Democracy and Corporate Accountability Commission revealed that 74% of Canadian shareholders believe that business executives should "embrace a broader social ethic" in their corporate responsibilities.[5]

The emphasis on ethical business practices means that sometimes firms must make decisions that hurt them in the short term. Despite robust sales of a video game called Night Trap made by Sega, executives at Toys 'R' Us pulled the product from store shelves. This costly action was taken after the store chain received complaints from parents, who objected to their children playing a game in which scantily dressed sorority sisters fight off zombies who try to suck out their blood with a giant syringe.[6]

Notions of right and wrong differ between organizations and cultures. Some businesses, for example, believe it is acceptable for salespeople to use any means to persuade customers to buy, even giving them partly true or even false information, while other firms feel that anything less than total honesty with customers is wrong. Because each culture has its own set of values, beliefs, and customs, ethical business behaviour varies in different parts of the world. Transparency International, an organization dedicated to fighting corruption in business around the world, created an International Corruption Perceptions Index, which highlights the differences in the perceptions of corrupt business practices around the world. Out of the 91 countries ranked in their recent Index, Finland was identified as number one, the country perceived to have the least corrupt business practices, and Canada ranked as number seven, ahead of both the UK (number 13) and the US (number 16).[7]

To reduce the confusion about what is right and wrong in international and domestic business operations, many firms develop their own **code of ethics**, or written standards of

✳ ✳ ✳
business ethics Rules of conduct for an organization.

Transparency International
www.transparency.org

✳ ✳ ✳
code of ethics Written standards of behaviour to which everyone in the organization must subscribe.

SPOTLIGHT ON REAL PEOPLE *Daydream Software*

Computer games are big business, but many of the best sellers like Sega's Night Trap are filled with gore and violence that may not be the best things for children to see. Is there an alternative? One company, formed by five young people in Sweden, thinks so. They are succeeding by offering product alternatives that prove you don't need to be bloody to be the best. The company, called Daydream Software, got its start when one of the programmers gave a computer to his little sister for Christmas, but then had a hard time finding appropriate games for her to play. This frustrating discovery led to discussions with friends about finding methods to push players' thrill buttons other than with endless blood and splatter. All of Daydream's founders have children, and they design games they would want their own kids to play. They want the player to come away with more than just the echo of machine guns and a sore trigger finger.

The group started by designing Safecracker, a puzzle game with superior graphics. Adapted for both Macintosh and PC, Safecracker has been translated into seven different languages and has received enthusiastic reviews. After Safecracker, Daydream developed Traitors Gate, in which the player has to break into the Tower of London, outsmart the guards, and remove some of

the jewels. The game is designed to reward a player who thinks more strategically and punish the player who is trigger happy. No huge machine guns here: The player is given only pacifying weapons, such as tranquilizing darts. Daydream's newest game, Ski-Doo X-Team Racing, was developed in collaboration with Canadian Ski-Doo maker Bombardier and offers an "exciting competitive experience." To learn more about how a start-up company can succeed by offering non-violent products in a violent world, visit www.daydream.se.[8]

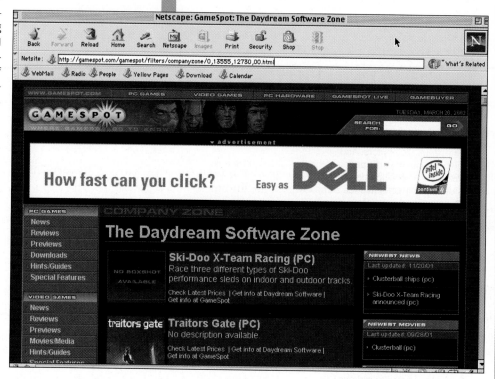

1. What are some ethical problems facing a game software company?
2. Why is Daydream a New Era company?
3. Who would be the most likely market for software games like Traitors Gate and Ski-Doo X-Team Racing?

behaviour, to which everyone in the organization must subscribe. The Canadian high-tech company Nortel Networks (www.nortelnetworks.com) has developed an extensive code of ethics to guide employee actions worldwide. The code, called Living the Commitments, includes guidelines on relationships with customers and suppliers, gathering competitive information, and general conflicts of interest.[9]

Professional associations also often establish codes of ethics to guide the behaviour of members. For instance, to help members of the marketing profession in North America and elsewhere adhere to ethical behaviour in their marketing efforts, the American Marketing Association (AMA), the largest professional marketing association in the world, has developed its own Code of Ethics, which is shown in Figure 3-2.[10]

Members of the American Marketing Association are committed to ethical, professional conduct. They have joined together in subscribing to this Code of Ethics embracing the following topics:

Responsibilities of the Marketer
Marketers must accept responsibility for the consequences of their activities and make every effort to ensure that their decisions, recommendations, and actions function to identify, serve, and satisfy all relevant publics: customers, organizations and society.

Marketers' professional conduct must be guided by:
1. The basic rule of professional ethics: not knowingly to do harm;
2. The adherence to all applicable laws and regulations;
3. The accurate representation of their education, training and experience; and
4. The active support, practice, and promotion of this Code of Ethics.

Honesty and Fairness
Marketers shall uphold and advance the integrity, honor, and dignity of the marketing profession by:
1. Being honest in serving consumers, clients, employees, suppliers, distributors, and the public;
2. Not knowingly participating in conflict of interest without prior notice to all parties involved; and
3. Establishing equitable fee schedules including the payment or receipt of usual, customary, and/or legal compensation for marketing exchanges.

Rights and Duties of Parties in the Marketing Exchange Process
Participants in the marketing exchange process should be able to expect that:
1. Products and services offered are safe and fit for their intended uses;
2. Communications about offered products and services are not deceptive;
3. All parties intend to discharge their obligations, financial and otherwise, in good faith; and
4. Appropriate internal methods exist for equitable adjustment and/or redress of grievances concerning purchases.

It is understood that the above would include, but is not limited to, the following responsibilities of the marketer:
In the area of product development and management,
- disclosure of all substantial risks associated with product or service usage;
- identification of any product component substitution that might materially change the product of impact on the buyer's purchase decision;

- identification of extra cost-added features.

In the area of promotions,
- avoidance of false and misleading advertising;
- rejection of high pressure manipulations, or misleading sales tactics;
- avoidance of sales promotions that use deception or manipulation.

In the area of distribution,
- not manipulating the availability of a product for purpose of exploitation;
- not using coercion in the marketing channel;
- not exerting undue influence over the reseller's choice to handle a product.

In the area of pricing,
- not engaging in price fixing;
- not practicing predatory pricing;
- disclosing the full price associated with any purchase.

In the area of marketing research,
- prohibiting selling or fundraising under the guise of conducting research;
- maintaining research integrity by avoiding misrepresentation and omission of pertinent research data;
- treating outside clients and suppliers fairly.

Organizational Relationships
Marketers should be aware of how their behavior may influence or impact on the behavior of others in organizational relationships. They should not demand, encourage, or apply coercion to obtain unethical behavior in their relationships with others, such as employees, suppliers, or customers.
1. Apply confidentiality and anonymity in professional relationships with regard to privileged information;
2. Meet their obligations and responsibilities in contracts and mutual agreements in a timely manner;
3. Avoid taking the work of others, in whole, or in part, and represent this work as their own or directly benefit from it without compensation or consent of the originator or owner;
4. Avoid manipulation to take advantage of situations to maximize personal welfare in a way that unfairly deprives or damages the organization of others.

Any AMA member found to be in violation of any provision of this Code of Ethics may have his or her Association membership suspended or revoked.

Figure 3.2 AMA Code of Ethics

THE HIGH COSTS OF UNETHICAL MARKETPLACE BEHAVIOUR

Ethical business is good business. New Era marketers understand that unethical practices can wind up costing dearly in the long run both to the firm's finances and to its reputation. Honda found this out the hard way, when a recent lawsuit spotlighted how former executives of the car company allegedly accepted bribes from dealers in exchange for preferential treatment. Sixteen former employees pleaded guilty to receiving "gifts," including a helicopter tour of Hawaii and a $25 000 shopping spree in Hong Kong. To ensure that this type of activity would not occur again, Honda set up a financial disclosure policy for its senior executives and established a corporate ethics committee. In addition, employees must sign Honda's revised Business Ethics and Conflict of Interest Policy every year to certify that their conduct is appropriate.[11] Such policies go a long way toward keeping a firm's behaviour ethical and maintaining customers' trust and loyalty.

Consumers appreciate companies that practise ethical behaviour, but sometimes we forget that ethics in the marketplace is a two-way street. About $2 billion worth of goods is taken from Canadian stores every year, making shoplifting a considerable problem for Canadian retailers.[12] This problem is so widespread that an entire industry has developed devoted to reducing shoplifting. Security consultants, training programs for employees, spy cameras, and clothing tags that spray ink unless removed with a special tool, are some techniques that retailers are using to combat this problem. Many retailers also lose money through *retail borrowing*, in which the consumer purchases an item such as a party dress or an expensive business suit, wears it for a special occasion, and returns it the next day as if it had not been worn. Consumers ultimately pay the price for such practices, when retailers and manufacturers raise prices to cover their losses.

CONSUMERISM: FIGHTING BACK

Organized activities that bring about social and political change are not new to the Canadian scene. Women's right to vote, child labour laws, universal medicare, minimum wage, and equal employment opportunities have all resulted from social movements in which citizens, public and private organizations, and business work to change society. **Consumerism** is the social movement directed at protecting consumers from harmful business practices.

The modern consumerism movement in Canada began in the late 1940s, when the Consumers' Association of Canada (CAC) (www.consumer.ca) was established. The mission of the CAC is to inform and educate consumers, and also to advocate on their behalf.[13] Since its inception, the CAC has been active in helping to establish protective legislation for consumers, related to labelling and packaging, bans on the use of certain pesticides, and improved quality standards for agricultural and manufactured goods. Recent activities of the CAC have focused on fighting the practice of negative-option marketing by the cable industry, in which consumers were automatically charged for services that they did not sign up for unless they contacted the cable company to cancel, and conducting a national consumer survey regarding Canadians' perceptions of the quality of goods and services.

The CAC outlines seven Consumer Rights, which it argues that both government legislation and ethical businesses should recognize and provide:

- *The Right to Safety*: Consumers should be confident that products are not dangerous when used as intended.

- *The Right to Be Informed*: Businesses should provide consumers with adequate information to make intelligent product choices. This right means that product information provided by advertising, packaging, and salespeople should be honest and complete.

- *The Right to Be Heard*: Consumers should have the means to complain or express their displeasure to obtain redress or retribution from companies. Government agencies and industry self-regulatory groups should respond to every customer complaint.

- *The Right to Redress*: Consumers should be provided with the opportunity to take action if their needs are not met in the marketplace.

- *The Right to Choose*: Consumers should be able to choose from a variety of products. No one business should be allowed to control the price, quality, or availability of goods and services.

- *The Right to a Healthy Environment*: Consumers have the right to expect that government and businesses will make choices that ensure a healthy environment.

- *The Right to a Consumer Education*: Consumers have a right to expect that they will be provided with the skills necessary to make educated choices in the marketplace.

The Consumers Council of Canada, another consumer organization that strives to improve the marketplace for Canadian consumers, has suggested an eighth consumer right to

---

✳ ✳ ✳

consumerism A social movement that attempts to protect consumers from harmful business practices.

be protected: The right to privacy, an increasingly important right in the age of information technology.[14]

Consumers continue to have a vigorous interest in consumer-related issues, and New Era marketers are responding by voluntarily making changes to prevent both consumer anger and government intervention. New Era marketers avoid both the financial losses and loss of reputation that consumerism activities may cause by having their customers' best interests in mind from the start.

Ethics in the Marketing Mix

As we've seen in previous chapters, marketing mix strategies are crucial to a firm's success in achieving its objectives. Marketing managers are responsible for determining the most ethical way to price, package, promote, and distribute their offerings to reach profit and market share objectives. Let's examine how ethical considerations can influence marketing mix decisions.

MAKING A PRODUCT SAFE

In product strategies, a key ethical decision concerns product safety. It may be tempting to cut costs on design, safety testing, and production to be able to rush a new product to market or to beat competitors on price. However, responsible companies realize that product safety needs to be a priority. They do everything to ensure that their product meets safety standards when it goes to market, and they react swiftly if a product is found to be unsafe after it is on the market. In any month in Canada, there are several product recalls: Manufacturers recognize safety problems with their products and ask consumers to return them. For example, in January 2002 alone, there were 18 product recalls in Canada, including baby clothing that could pose a safety hazard, contaminated food that could cause illness, and drug products that are considered a health risk.[15]

PRICING THE PRODUCT FAIRLY

The potential for unethical pricing strategies is so great that many shady pricing practices are illegal. For example, firms that compete in a market in which there are only a few other firms are not allowed to decide in advance on a common price for their product. This practice, called **price fixing**, eliminates price competition, which otherwise would keep prices down. Another pricing strategy is *price discrimination*, charging lower prices to larger customers. This is acceptable only if it reflects real cost savings for the manufacturer or is necessary to meet competitors' pricing.

> ✻ ✻ ✻
> **price fixing** An illegal business practice in which firms decide in advance on a common price for their product.

A pricing strategy that is unethical but not illegal is *price gouging*—raising the price of a product to take advantage of its popularity. We saw this with some Beanie Babies, toys designed to be collectors' items. In the late 1990s, for example, each authorized Beanie Baby retailer received a shipment of only 12 of the Princess Diana Beanie Babies. Beanie Babies are supposed to sell at retail for about $10 each; however, many retailers apparently took advantage of the short supply to secretly sell the Princess Di model at much higher prices, since Beanie fanatics were willing to pay up to $500 each for the fuzzy purple bears.[16]

New Era firms price their products fairly—and they have been known to cut their prices in times of need. When a hurricane hit the southern US in 1992, many local firms selling building materials raised their prices, knowing that residents would pay anything to protect what was left of their possessions. Home Depot, however, did just the opposite. The stores sold materials for restoring walls and roofs at cost. In the process, Home Depot gained the loyalty of many consumers throughout North America who had heard the story.[17] During an eastern Canadian ice storm in 1998, some Ontario and Quebec businesses didn't just lower prices; they gave away products for free. St. Viateur Bagel Shop in Montreal, for example, gave away their famous bagels to people without power, and IGA stores gave away baked goods to those in need.[18]

PROMOTING THE PRODUCT ETHICALLY

Marketing management's decisions on how to promote the firm's products are likely to draw the most criticism from consumers. To promote ethical behaviour on the part of advertisers

good OR bad DECISION?

One life insurance company encourages its agents to scan local newspapers for stories of violent crimes. The agents then call on households in the affected neighbourhoods, showing clippings of the crimes as part of their sales pitch.[20] Another company has its agents scan local newspapers for birth announcements, knowing that people who have just had children are more likely to sign up for life insurance policies. When the agents phone these new parents, they use a fear technique to sell their policies by talking about what might happen to the child if their parents were to die without leaving them any money. Are these practices ethical? Why or why not?

and to provide consumers with a forum for expressing complaints about advertising, the Canadian advertising industry follows a process of self-regulation through Advertising Standards Canada (ASC) (www.canad.com). The Canadian Code of Advertising Standards, which ASC administers, has specific guidelines regarding unfair or deceptive advertising to ensure the accuracy and appropriateness of claims. For example, ASC recently heard a complaint against Gone Hollywood Video, of Burnaby, BC, regarding a newspaper ad that the organization had run to recruit franchisees. The ads promised "100% success rate" and claimed that franchisees could "Earn Jurassic Profits." Gone Hollywood Video was unable to substantiate the claims made in the ad, so the complaint against them was upheld.[19]

ASC also enforces guidelines with respect to appropriate gender portrayal in ads.[21] These Gender Portrayal Guidelines state that advertising should not include sexual exploitation and should always portray women and men as equals. Although these guidelines were originally intended to fight negative portrayals of women in advertising, increasingly complaints by consumers have related to the portrayal of men. In 1999, just prior to its demise, a complaint was lodged against Eaton's, and the company agreed to stop showing an ad that ASC found to sexually objectify men. The ad depicted a glamorous woman going off to work, while her husband remained behind, shackled to the kitchen. Although Eaton's claimed that the ad was meant to fight gender myths by using humour, ASC reinforced the Gender Portrayal Guidelines, which state that the use of humour "should not serve as an excuse to stereotype women or men or portray behaviour that is not acceptable today."[22]

GETTING THE PRODUCT WHERE IT BELONGS

Channels of distribution decisions can also create ethical dilemmas. For example, because their size gives them bargaining power in the channel of distribution, many large retail chains are forcing manufacturers to pay a **slotting allowance**, a fee paid in exchange for agreeing to place the manufacturer's products on the retailer's valuable shelf space. While the retailers claim that such fees pay the cost of adding products to their inventory, many manufacturers feel slotting fees are unethical. Certainly the practice prevents smaller manufacturers who cannot afford the slotting allowances from reaching consumers.

❊ ❊ ❊
slotting allowance A fee paid by a manufacturer to a retailer in exchange for agreeing to place products on the retailer's shelves.

Doing It Right: A Focus on Social Responsibility

We've learned how New Era firms gain social profit by practising business ethics when making marketing mix decisions. The second part of social profit is **social responsibility**, a management process in which organizations engage in activities that have a positive effect on society and promote the public good. These activities include environmental stewardship, cause marketing, and encouraging cultural diversity. Firms like Ethical Funds that believe in social responsibility represent a business value system that goes beyond the short-term bottom line. Instead, they consider the short- and long-term effects of decisions on the company, its employees, consumers, the community, and the world at large.

❊ ❊ ❊
social responsibility A management practice in which organizations seek to engage in activities that have a positive effect on society and promote the public good.

Serving the Environment

When New Era firms make socially responsible business decisions that also protect the environment, they assume a position of **environmental stewardship**. The Body Shop Canada practises this through "sustainability" strategies, the development of products that use resources sparingly to sustain those resources for future generations.[23] Toy maker Mattel has started investigating environmentally friendly materials as an alternative to plastics for use in both its products, like Buzz Lightyear shown in Exhibit 3.1, and packaging.[24]

The term **green marketing** describes efforts by firms to choose packages, product designs, and other aspects of the marketing mix that are earth friendly but still profitable. The

❊ ❊ ❊
environmental stewardship A position taken by an organization to protect or enhance the natural environment as it conducts its business activities.

❊ ❊ ❊
green marketing A marketing strategy that supports environmental stewardship by creating an environmentally founded differential benefit in the minds of consumers.

Real People, Real Decisions

Decision Time at Ethical Funds

Hundreds of mutual funds operate in Canada, and all of them try to take advantage of an increase in consumer demand for this product. Recently there has been a shift in the Canadian "household balance sheet" from short-term to long-term investments. In particular, aging baby boomers are interested in investing for their future through RRSPs, and for the future of their children through RESPs. But the growth in this market has also been fuelled by other external environmental factors: A low interest rate environment in Canada has made GICs and term deposits less attractive investment vehicles than mutual funds, and government tax incentives have encouraged consumers to invest in RRSPs and RESPs.

In response to the growing demand for mutual funds, competitive activity has increased. In addition to traditional mutual fund companies, all of the financial services companies—banks, trust companies, and credit unions—have introduced mutual funds. Getting noticed by consumers in this competitive market, therefore, is a key marketing challenge. And although most companies offering products in this market strive to stand out from the competition, there is surprisingly little differentiation in their advertising. Most mutual funds ads communicate the same messages to consumers: Healthy rates of return and a guarantee that the investments are safe.

Despite the competitive pressure, Margaret Yee felt that Ethical Funds had a real competitive advantage in the mutual fund market. One study of Canadian consumers that she commissioned found that 98% of those surveyed would prefer to invest in companies that are socially responsible over those that are not. These results showed her the potential for her products, but Yee knew that building a strong brand presence would be key to realizing that potential.

The internal environment at Ethical Funds also supported efforts to start building a strong brand presence with consumers. From the time of its inception in 1992 until the late 1990s, Ethical Funds did not advertise directly to consumers. Instead, it focused on establishing and strengthening its channels of distribution. Ethical Funds are sold through credit unions across Canada, so marketing activities had concentrated on educating credit union employees (the

Ethical Funds "salesforce") about the advantages of Ethical Funds, so that they could communicate these advantages to consumers. Now that the channels of distribution were well entrenched and running smoothly, the time was right to begin to advertise directly to consumers.

Yee set as her goal the creation of awareness of the company and the advantages of its products among English-speaking Canadian consumers of mutual funds. In considering how she could achieve her goal within a very limited budget, Yee outlined two options for the theme and tone of her communications plan.

Option 1. Ethical Funds has traditionally provided a very strong rate of return for its investors. In fact, Ethical Funds has been recognized by several industry analysts as one of the best-managed mutual funds in Canada because of its high returns. Yee felt that she had a good "statistics" story to tell consumers about rates of return, a story that would fit well with consumers' existing perceptions of what is important in the mutual fund category. A communications message under this option would focus on the fact that consumers could do well financially by investing in the products offered by Ethical Funds. Yee felt this conservative message would be well accepted by both consumers and the credit unions that were selling her products.

Option 2. The other option Yee was considering was more risky—a hard-hitting emotional advertising campaign to appeal to consumers' sense of ethics and social responsibility. The campaign would show strong images of the negative effects of unethical business (such as environmental damage), a strategy she knew might make consumers uncomfortable. However, she also thought that such a campaign would ensure that Ethical Funds was perceived as different from competitors. Given the conservative nature of this market, though, she wasn't sure if consumers would perceive this difference in a positive or negative way.

Now join Margaret Yee and the Ethical Funds decision team. Which option would you choose, and why?

Canadian government, through Environment Canada, encourages Canadian companies to practise green marketing through such programs as the EcoLogo (www.environmental-choice.com). This program promotes stringent, environmentally friendly guidelines for industries, ranging from automotive products to office supplies. If a business meets the guidelines, it may use the EcoLogo on its product to signal its environmental soundness to consumers. Companies that have been granted the right to use the EcoLogo include

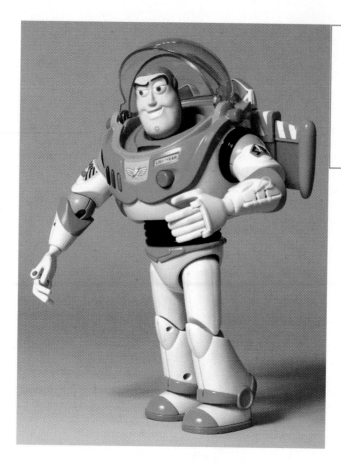

Exhibit 3.1

Mattel is investigating
the use of environmen-
tally friendly materials
for its products.

Frigidaire Canada, which manufactures energy-efficient dishwashers and washing machines, and Fuji Graphics Systems, which has developed photoprocessing systems that are gentle to the environment.[25]

Green marketing practices can indeed be successful for a firm's bottom line. For example, Electrolux found that profits from its solar-powered lawn mowers, chain saws lubricated with vegetable oil, and water-conserving washing machines actually were 3.8% higher than profits from the company's conventional products.[26] Here's how some other firms are "turning green":

- Sonoco Products Co.(www.sonoco.com), one of the world's largest packaging companies with operations in five Canadian provinces, began its "We make it, we take it back" program in 1990. The company takes its used boxes back from customers, who don't have to worry about disposing of them. Sonoco benefits because it uses recycled packaging for more than two-thirds of its raw materials.[27]

- Nortel Networks (www.nortelnetworks.com) recently received two prestigious environmental awards, including one from the United Nations, for being the first multinational corporation in the telecommunications industry to eliminate the use of ozone-depleting CFCs in its manufacturing and research operations.[28]

- Toyota (www.toyota.com) unveiled its new super energy-efficient car, the Prius, in the late 1990s. The Prius has both an internal combustion engine and an electric motor, which turn on and off independently to provide peak efficiency. Because the Prius gets excellent gas mileage, owners can save money while they're doing their part to save the planet.[29]

Do New Era firms practise environmental stewardship because they're "good" or because they will benefit financially? The answer is: a little of both. There are many business leaders who simply believe in doing the right thing, but most also see financial benefits. Customers who are concerned about the future of the planet will buy "green" products, even if the price is higher.

Serving Society: Cause Marketing

Cause marketing is a strategy of joining forces with a not-for-profit organization to tackle a social problem. In the past, this practice usually meant running a short-term promotion and then donating profits to a charity. But consumers often saw these programs as gimmicky and insincere, especially when there was no apparent connection between the company and the cause. As a result, sales increased during the promotion, but there were no long-term benefits to either the sponsoring firm or the cause it was trying to help.

Today, New Era firms have abandoned this one-shot approach and instead make a long-term commitment to tackle a social problem, such as illiteracy or child abuse.[30] Avon Canada's Flame Crusade against Breast Cancer is one example of cause marketing. Since its inception in 1993, the program has raised over $5.2 million for breast cancer research through the sales of such products as the Flame pin (see Exhibit 3.2).[31] Avon hopes that its long-term involvement with breast cancer awareness will result in both health benefits for women and increased good will for the company—a "win–win" situation.

New Era firms believe that sales of their products increase as a result of cause marketing activities. According to one survey of 2000 consumers, they are right: 84% believed that cause marketing creates a positive image of a company, and 78% said they would be more likely to buy a product associated with an important cause.[32]

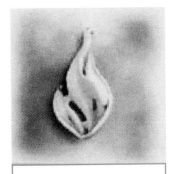

Exhibit 3.2

Avon Flame: a successful cause marketing program that women customers appreciate.

Serving the Community: Promoting Cultural Diversity

In a country as culturally diverse as Canada, promotion of **cultural diversity** is not only the right thing to do, it's also important to the long-term financial health of the organization. When firms adopt cultural diversity programs, they make sure that marketing policies and hiring practices give people an equal chance to work for the company and buy its products.

As six Toronto-area hotels found out, having a multicultural workforce can help firms reach their marketing goals. The diversity of their workforce enabled them to meet the needs of many different groups of customers, and they found that new market segments were attracted to culturally diverse hotels.[33] Warner-Lambert Canada, manufacturer of such brands as Listerine, Trident, and Dentyne, also embraces cultural diversity; as one company document states, "The more our organization reflects the consumer population, the more it will be in sync with what customers want, need and are looking for."[34] The photo of the staff at a Delta Hotel in Toronto (see Exhibit 3.3) reflects the company's goal of diversity.

The diversity philosophy also extends to the disabled. Smart marketers view the disabled as both customers and valued employees. Hertz, for example, offers cars that disabled people

✳ ✳ ✳
cause marketing A marketing strategy in which an organization serves its community by promoting and supporting a worthy cause or by allying itself with a not-for-profit organization to tackle a social problem.

✳ ✳ ✳
cultural diversity A management practice that actively seeks to include people of different sexes, races, ethnic groups, and religions in an organization's employees, customers, suppliers, and distribution channel partners.

Exhibit 3.3

Delta's goal of cultural diversity is reflected in this photo of the staff at the reception desk.

can drive at nearly 800 Hertz rental locations and has worked to equip shuttle buses and vans with lifts to transport these customers.[35]

We've seen that New Era firms create social profit by adhering to ethical business practices. Social profit is also created when firms practise social responsibility by being concerned about the environment, promoting diversity, and serving their communities through cause marketing. In the next section, we'll see how New Era firms enhance their ability to create economic profit by focusing on quality.

Doing It Well: A Focus on Quality

quality The level of performance, reliability, features, safety, cost, or other product characteristics that consumers expect to satisfy their needs and wants.

Quality is the level of performance, reliability, features, safety, cost, or other product characteristics that consumers expect to satisfy their wants and needs.

While the concept of quality is not new, its importance has increased in the past few decades. Because companies today must compete in a global marketplace in which they face a vast number of competitors, it is imperative that they understand what quality means to their customers—and that they supply it. If they don't, someone else will. For marketers, this means continuously monitoring the changing wants and needs of customers and prospective customers and making sure that they are giving those customers the quality they expect.

Although many Canadian companies take quality seriously, a recent national survey of over 10 000 Canadians conducted by the National Quality Institute found that a majority (62%) of respondents felt that companies are not responsive to consumer feedback about the quality of goods and services.[36] When asked to rate service industries, consumers rated pharmacies, hotels, credit unions, and small retailers as the most responsive to customer quality demands. At the bottom of the list were the government, postal services, cable companies, and large retailers. Personal computers and audio-visual equipment were rated as the highest-quality product categories, whereas clothing was rated as the lowest. This survey highlights the fact that Canadian organizations need to take quality seriously to better satisfy consumer demands.

National Quality Institute
www.nqi.ca

Total Quality Management

total quality management (TQM) A management philosophy that focuses on satisfying customers through empowering employees to be an active part of continuous quality improvement.

One way for organizations to embrace a quality focus is to adopt the principles and practices of **total quality management (TQM)**, a philosophy that calls for company-wide dedication to the development, maintenance, and continuous improvement of all aspects of the company's operations. TQM seeks to assure customer satisfaction by involving *all* employees, regardless of their function, in efforts to continually improve quality. For example, TQM firms encourage employees—even the lowest-paid factory workers—to suggest ways to improve products, and reward them for good ideas. Many top-level managers see TQM as the key to winning in today's global marketplace. But some marketing managers suggest that a focus on constantly finding better ways to meet customers' needs is really just the marketing concept put into practice. Whatever you call it, though, the search for quality leads a firm to long-term economic profits and makes sound business sense.

But how do you know when you've attained your goal of quality? A few key benchmarks have been established to recognize firms that are committed to quality. Around the world, many companies look to the uniform standards of the International Standards Organization (ISO) for quality guidelines. This Geneva-based organization developed a set of quality guidelines, known as **ISO 9000**, which pertain to the manufacture and installation of products, as well as post-sale servicing.[37] ISO certification, which is administered in Canada by the Standards Council of Canada (www.scc.ca), has become an important way for manufacturing organizations to work toward quality and communicate that quality to their customers in Canada (see Exhibit 3.4) and around the world. Companies become registered as ISO 9000 by undergoing an audit by an independent third party, known as a *quality system registrar*, who ensures that the company meets the ISO guidelines for quality.

Another recognition of the achievement of quality in a firm can come from quality awards, such as those presented annually by the National Quality Institute. A recent winner

ISO 9000 Criteria developed by the International Standards Organization to regulate product quality internationally.

Exhibit 3.4

The ISO 9000 banner communicates product quality to this manufacturer's customers.

of this quality award is Delta Hotels, an organization that is committed to providing employees with a productive and positive working environment so that they can in turn create a positive experience for every hotel guest.[38]

ADDING A DOSE OF QUALITY TO THE MARKETING MIX

A firm's marketers play a big part in maintaining its quality. Marketing is typically responsible for consumer research that identifies what quality characteristics consumers want and need, and what price they are willing to pay. Marketing is also responsible for informing consumers about product quality through the firm's marketing communications.

But keeping on top of what customers want is just the beginning. The more important task in quality marketing programs is to deliver a customer-perceived quality product at the right place and at the right price. Instead of being satisfied with doing things the same way year after year, New Era marketers continuously seek ways to improve product, place, price, and promotion. Here is how quality concerns have an impact on the marketing mix:

- *Product*: New Era firms can offer quality for their customers by improving their customer service support. Telus Mobility Service of Alberta has recently won a quality award for its commitment to listen to customers and respond quickly to their needs.[39]

- *Place*: Clark-Reliance Corporation produces industrial products, such as high-tech electronic sensors used by utility companies and refineries. Clark-Reliance used teamwork to improve its distribution. Sales and production departments met and reviewed how customers obtained the company's products, and employees came up with ways to boost the firm's on-time delivery rate from 30 to 90%.[40]

- *Price*: Taco Bell Corp., a subsidiary of PepsiCo Inc., is the largest Mexican fast-food restaurant in the world. In Taco Bell restaurants, making a burrito is "a high-tech happening," that uses the TACO (Total Automation of Company Operations) system. When a customer places an order, the cashier enters it into a register. The order is immediately displayed on several screens in the food preparation area so that workers can prepare the food. This system means that Taco Bell restaurants can accurately fill a larger number of food orders with fewer workers, reducing labour and food waste costs. As a fringe benefit of the system, Taco Bell can monitor exactly what is sold in each of its 4000 restaurants, so that the company can reduce costs by supplying each store with the right mixture of food products for its clientele.[41]

- *Promotion*: New Era firms realize that customers want information when it is convenient for them, not just for the company.[42] Web sites are becoming an increasingly popular way to provide information to customers, so that they can access it when they need it. For example, when DaimlerChrysler introduced the Chrysler PT Cruiser in Canada (see Exhibit 3.5), it encouraged consumers to visit the company Web site (www.daimlerchrysler.ca) to learn more about the car. Kraft Canada uses its Web site to inform consumers about new products; but the site is also used to establish a stronger relationship with consumers. Kraft's "virtual kitchen" provides product information, a recipe book, and tips on making fast meals using ingredients that consumers indicate

DaimlerChrysler Canada
www.daimlerchrysler.ca

Kraft Canada
www.kraftcanada.com

they have on hand. The site also provides opportunities for customers to give feedback on Kraft products, an important source of information on how the company can improve the quality of its products.

The Internal Business Environment

We've discussed ethics and social responsibility and how firms practise total quality management. Now we'll look at the other inputs into New Era decision making, understanding the environments in which the firm operates. First, we examine the elements of a firm's internal environment.

For New Era marketers, examining the internal environment is especially important, because it identifies the strengths and weaknesses of the organization that determine the firm's ability to create both economic and social profit. Figure 3.1 shows that the important elements in the firm's internal environment include the resources and competencies of the firm, its corporate culture, and the relationships the firm has with the outside world—other businesses, customers, and the public in general.

Corporate Resources and Competencies

As we discussed in Chapter 2, a firm's resources include its money, people, reputation, brand image, and physical facilities. Competencies refer to what the organization does well. Accurate appraisals of these two parts of a firm's internal environment are essential for making good decisions. When firms underestimate their resources and competencies, they miss opportunities. But overestimating resources and competencies can lead a firm to develop objectives that are doomed to fail. For example, after General Electric began manufacturing mainframe computers in the 1960s, the firm found it simply didn't have the financial resources to sustain that business along with its other investments. GE was forced to leave the computer business.

Corporate Culture

A firm's **corporate culture** is the ethical values, norms, and beliefs that influence the behaviour of everyone in the organization. For instance, a firm's corporate culture may dictate whether new ideas are welcomed or discouraged, the importance of individual ethical behaviour, and even the appropriate dress for work. For many years, IBM was known as "the white shirt company" due to its unwritten rule that all employees must wear only white shirts. Fortunately, corporate cultures do evolve over time, and even "radical" changes like casual workdays are now are common.

RISK-TAKING CULTURES

Some corporate cultures, like those that exist in many Canadian high-tech companies, are more inclined to take risks than others. These firms value individuality and creativity, recognizing that nurturing these characteristics often leads to the creation of important competitive advantages. A risk-taking culture is especially important to the marketing function, because firms must continually improve their product, their distribution channel, and their pricing and promotion programs to remain successful in a competitive environment. In firms with more traditional corporate cultures, getting managers to accept a new way of doing things can be difficult, thereby creating a potential barrier to effective marketing decision making.

PROFIT-CENTRED VERSUS PEOPLE-CENTRED CULTURES

If the firm's business mission is only economic profit and its chief objectives are increasing revenues and decreasing costs, management attitudes are profit centred, often at the expense of employee morale. In New Era firms, whose business mission includes a concern for employees, customers, and society, as well as shareholder profits, the internal atmosphere is quite different. Managers build employee satisfaction through training and incentive programs, and often include amenities like day-care centres and benefits like parental leave.

Relationships with Publics

The relationships a firm develops with others outside the organization—suppliers, intermediaries, and the public—are an important measure of its internal strengths. These **publics** are groups that have either a current or a potential interest in an organization and its objectives. In addition to customers and employees, a firm's publics include shareholders, business partners, public agencies, the media, the general public, and even competitors.

RELATIONSHIPS WITH SUPPLIERS AND INTERMEDIARIES

New Era firms know that they can't make quality products if they can't get quality parts and materials from their suppliers. Motorola found that some suppliers pretended they knew how to use quality methods and agreed to parts specifications that they couldn't meet. As a manager at one of Motorola's plants observed, "We used to usually end up hating each other." The remedy was to develop a class to teach suppliers about process control-measurement techniques, so that they could ensure that their products met Motorola's quality specifications.[43] Suppliers relevant to the marketing function include advertising agencies, marketing research firms, and outside firms hired to conduct special promotions and distribute coupons.

RELATIONSHIPS WITH COMPETITORS

Spirited competition is part of business, but no company benefits from an ugly marketing war. When a firm sets out to destroy a competitor, everyone gets hurt. In the worst case, the reputations of both companies are damaged, and consumers lose confidence in the competitive market system, believing that no one plays fairly. Even when competition is less brutal, the resources of both firms may be wasted in the battle. Long-distance telephone service

***
corporate culture The set of values, norms, and beliefs that are held by an organization's managers and that influence the behaviour of everyone in the organization.

***
publics Groups of people—including suppliers, channel intermediaries, customers, employees, shareholders, financial institutions, government, the media, and public interest groups—that have an interest in an organization.

Exhibit 3.6

Primus fights the "telephone war" for millions in long-distance dollars.

providers have come close to blows with their pricing strategies, as Exhibit 3.6 shows. Competitive ads on television have tried to convince consumers that the "other company" is misleading them about pricing, while telemarketing and direct mail programs offer customers lucrative incentives for switching long-distance carriers. As a result, many customers have come to distrust all long-distance provider messages, while others have figured out how to take advantage of the special offers by regularly switching from carrier to carrier.

While they compete for sales, many rivals often co-operate with one another in other spheres, often banding together to lobby for legislation that affects an entire industry. For example, companies in the direct marketing industry came together in the late 1990s through the Canadian Marketing Association to lobby the government to keep the Internet free of regulation.[44] When firms maintain good relationships with their competitors through such organizations as industry associations, the needs of all can be better served.

RELATIONSHIPS WITH THE PUBLIC

Companies need to be sensitive to the concerns of consumer groups. Building good relationships with these groups benefits an organization in two ways. First, by understanding their concerns, the firm is able to develop its own socially responsible programs and practices that will gain the favour of the groups and others in the community. Second, when problems arise, such as a potentially dangerous product design flaw, activist groups are more likely to work with the firm to make changes and less likely to organize some form of public protest against it.

Adolph Coors, the beer manufacturer, developed good relationships with several consumer groups when it promoted a romance novel as part of a $40 million, five-year cause-marketing program against illiteracy. The book, titled *Perfect*, was highly successful and became a best-seller. Coors's literacy program campaign elicited thousands of inquiries, improved their reputation in the community, and favourably influenced their other important relationships with customers, employees, and shareholders.

To review, evaluating a New Era firm's internal environment includes assessing corporate resources and competencies, understanding the corporate culture, and looking at the relationships a firm has with its various publics. In this way, New Era marketers identify the strengths and weaknesses of the firm that can create (or not create) both economic and social profit. In the next section, we'll build on that by looking at how firms scan the external environment.

Scanning the External Business Environment

New Era firms know that they must keep up to the minute on what is happening in their external environment and respond to trends in a way that results in both economic and social profit. Figure 3.1 shows the major elements of the external business environment. One of these elements is the natural environment, which we discussed earlier in this chapter. Others are the economic, competitive, technological, legal, and sociocultural environments.

The Economic Environment

Assessing the economic environment means evaluating factors that influence consumer and business buying patterns, such as the amount of confidence people have in the health of the economy. This "crystal ball" must be a global one, because events in one country can influence the economic health of other countries. For example, the downturn of Asian economies in 1997 and 1998 affected the fortunes of Canadian businesses, especially those in BC and Saskatchewan, two provinces with strong direct trade links with Asia-Pacific countries.[45]

THE BUSINESS CYCLE: WHAT GOES AROUND, COMES AROUND

The state of the economy in which a firm does business is vital to the success of its marketing plans. The overall pattern of changes or fluctuations of an economy is called the **business cycle**. All economies go through cycles of *prosperity* (high levels of demand, employment, and incomes), *recession* (falling demand, employment, and incomes), and *recovery* (gradual improvement in production, lowering unemployment and increasing income).

A severe recession is a *depression*, in which prices fall, but there is little demand because few people have money to spend and many are put out of work. *Inflation* occurs when prices and the cost of living rise, while money loses its purchasing power because the cost of goods escalates. During inflationary periods, dollar incomes may increase, but real income—what the dollar will buy—decreases because goods and services cost more.

Understanding the business cycle is especially important to marketers because of its direct effect on customer purchase behaviour. During times of prosperity, both consumers and business customers buy more goods and services. Marketers are busy during this part of the business cycle, trying to grow the business and to maintain inventory levels to meet customer demand. Marketers may also develop new versions of existing products or entirely new products to take advantage of customers' willingness to spend. Prosperity is especially kind to businesses that provide vacations, entertainment, and other luxury products, because many customers want to enjoy the good life and have the money to do so.

During periods of recession, consumers and business customers buy less. The challenge to most marketers is to effectively maintain their firm's level of sales by convincing the few customers who are buying to select the firm's product over the competition. Even recessions aren't bad for all businesses. While it may be harder to sell luxury items, firms that make basic necessities are not likely to suffer losses, and sales of used products and do-it-yourself items, such as many of the products sold at Canadian Tire, may actually increase.

THE POWER OF EXPECTATIONS

Many economists suggest that changes in the economy are primarily a "self-fulfilling prophecy." When consumers feel that the economy is getting better, they spend money to buy goods and services, industry flourishes, and the economy improves. Similarly, if consumers fear a recession will occur in the next year or so, they may begin saving their money and stop making purchases. In that case, inventories of goods grow, industries slow production, and the recession begins—simply because people expect it to. Consumer beliefs about what the future holds determine **consumer confidence**, or the extent to which people are optimistic or pessimistic about the future health of the economy and how they personally will fare down the road.

Statistics Canada and private research firms periodically conduct surveys of consumer confidence and make forecasts, which wise marketers heed. One on-going study is conducted by a business organization called The Conference Board of Canada. This survey attempts to "take the pulse" of Canadian consumers to let companies know what people will be in the mood to buy—if, in fact, they're in a buying mood at all. Many business-to-business managers also rely on The National Association of Purchasing Management's survey of the buying intentions of more than 300 corporate purchasing managers, which signals growth or decline in the manufacturing sector of the economy and allows marketers to plan for changes in demand.[46]

✱ ✱ ✱
business cycle The overall patterns of change in the economy—including periods of prosperity, recession, depression, and recovery—that affect consumer and business purchasing power.

✱ ✱ ✱
consumer confidence An indicator of future spending patterns, measured by the extent to which people are optimistic or pessimistic about the state of the economy.

Statistics Canada
www.statcan.ca

Conference Board of Canada
www2.conferenceboard.ca

The Competitive Environment

A second important part of a New Era firm's external environment is the competitive environment—staying ahead of the competition is necessary for success. For example, an airline that is losing business to a competitor that offers lower fares will quickly develop competitive strategies, perhaps offering an even lower fare, half-price fares for family members, or discounts on hotels.

ANALYZING THE COMPETITION

Before a firm can begin to develop strategies that will create a competitive advantage in the marketplace, it has to know who its competitors are and what they're doing. Marketing managers size up the competitors according to their strengths and weaknesses, monitor their marketing strategies, and try to predict their future strategic activities.

About 10% of all firms engage in **competitive intelligence (CI)** activities, the process of gathering and analyzing public information about rivals. CI activities can include talking with competitors' customers and suppliers, reading competitors' newsletters and career advertisements, talking to people at trade shows, researching on the Internet, and reading articles on competitors in newspapers and magazines.[47] Successful CI means that a firm learns about a competitor's new products, its manufacturing, or the management styles of its executives and then uses this information to develop superior marketing strategies. But good CI is defensive as well as offensive. Part of the role of a CI professional is to ensure that there are few information leaks from their own company, by reviewing speeches, publications, and any other company information that will be public to ensure that no competitive secrets are being revealed.

Many of the Canadian industries where CI is widely practised are those that have been recently deregulated, such as energy utilities and telephone companies. Teleglobe Canada, for instance, established its Centre de Renseignement Stratégique (CRS) in the early 1990s to ready itself for what it knew would be the deregulation of wholesale long-distance telephone services in Canada. Since Teleglobe Canada had enjoyed a monopoly in this market, they knew that they had a lot to learn about competition in their business. With a staff of eight researchers and a budget of about $1 million, CRS helped Teleglobe Canada compete successfully in this increasingly competitive market.[48]

COMPETITION IN THE MICROENVIRONMENT

To be successful in a competitive marketplace, marketers must have a clear understanding of exactly who their competition is. Competition in the microenvironment refers to the product alternatives from which members of a target market can choose. These choices occur at three different levels. At a broad level, many marketers compete for consumers' **discretionary income**, the amount of money people have left over after paying for necessities, including housing, utilities, food, and clothing. Few consumers are wealthy enough to buy anything and everything, so each is constantly faced with choices: whether to use any "leftover" money to buy a new CD player, to provide a donation to charity, or perhaps to get fit.

A second type of choice involves **product competition**, where competitors offering different products attempt to satisfy the same consumer's needs and wants. For example, a person who wants to get fit can do so by joining a health club or by purchasing workout videos so they can work out at home. The third type of choice comes from **brand competition**, where competitors offering similar products or services vie for consumer dollars. So the consumer who decides to join a health club still must choose among competitors within this industry, such as GoodLife Fitness Centres versus the YMCA. Marketers who don't understand that they face all three types of competition can find they've lost out in the battle for customer dollars.

COMPETITION IN THE MACROENVIRONMENT

Marketers also need to consider competition in the macroenvironment, that is, the overall structure of their industry. This structure can range from one firm having total control to a situation in which numerous firms compete on an even playing field. Four structures de-

---

✳ ✳ ✳

competitive intelligence (CI)
The process of gathering and analyzing public information about rival firms.

✳ ✳ ✳

discretionary income The portion of income people have left over after paying for such necessities as housing, utilities, food, and clothing.

✳ ✳ ✳

product competition Very different products competing to satisfy the same consumer needs and wants.

✳ ✳ ✳

brand competition Similar products or services that compete based on the brand's reputation or perceived benefits.

scribe differing amounts of competition, ranging from complete domination of a market by one company to a situation in which no company has a strong advantage.

A **monopoly** exists when one seller controls a market. Because the seller is "the only game in town," it feels little pressure to keep prices low or to produce quality goods or services. Canada Post used to have a monopoly on the delivery of written documents, but now it battles fax machines, e-mail, and courier companies for market share. A recent advertising campaign by Canada Post to encourage letter writing is one part of their strategy to enhance their competitive position in an industry that used to be a monopoly.

In most Canadian industries , the government attempts to limit monopolies and even any move toward it by upholding Section 33 of the *Competition Act*, which prohibits the lessening of competition that will be against the interests of consumers. Sometimes these actions generate controversy, as in the federal government's recent consideration of mergers in the banking sector. While consumers and consumer lobby groups argued that the mergers of banks in Canada, though not creating a monopoly, would result in significantly reduced choice for consumers and a decline in customer service, the banks argued that to compete effectively in global markets, mergers were necessary.

In an **oligopoly** there is a relatively small number of sellers, each holding substantial market share, in a market with many buyers. Because there are few sellers in an oligopoly, each is very conscious of the actions of all other members. Oligopolies most often exist in industries requiring substantial investments in equipment or technology to produce a product, where only a few competitors have the resources to enter the game. For example, an entrepreneur with little start-up cash is not likely to be successful entering the auto industry. Instead, a few large firms such as General Motors, Ford, Chrysler, Toyota, and Honda dominate the market.

In **monopolistic competition**, many sellers compete for buyers in a market. Each firm offers a slightly different product, and each has only a small share of the market. In this type of market structure, Nike, Reebok, and Adidas vigorously compete with one another to offer consumers some unique benefit. For example, while every major athletic shoe manufacturer sells many types of basketball shoes, a consumer can obtain the Air Jordan only from Nike.

Finally, **perfect competition** exists when there are many small sellers, each offering basically the same good or service. In such industries, no single firm has a significant impact on quality, price, or supply. While true conditions of perfect competition are rare, agricultural markets where there are many individual farmers each producing the same wheat, corn, or soybeans come the closest. Even in the case of food commodities, though, there are opportunities for marketers to distinguish their offerings. In the Canadian dairy industry, the introduction of cold-filtered milk (see Exhibit 3.7) created a point of difference in the market with producers' claims that the cold filter process resulted in an improved taste and shelf life over regular milk products.

The Technological Environment

New Era firms see technology as an investment the firm can't afford *not* to make. Forward-looking managers see technology as the key to the future, even if it means a risky investment at the expense of short-term profits. Many of these exciting technological developments profoundly affect marketing activities. The Internet, computerized customer databases, and toll-free telephone numbers have made it possible for people to buy virtually anything they want (and even some things they don't want) without ever leaving their homes—simply by typing their orders into their computers or by placing a call to the Home Shopping Network. Physical distribution has improved due to automated inventory control afforded by such advancements as bar codes and computer light pens. We'll talk more about these technological advancements and their impact on the practice of marketing in later chapters.

Changes in technology can dramatically transform an industry—look at how transistors revolutionized data processing and consumer electronics. Successful marketers continuously scan the external business environment in search of ideas and trends to spark their

✳✳✳
monopoly A market situation in which one firm, the only supplier of a particular product, is able to control the price, quality, and supply of that product.

✳✳✳
oligopoly A market structure in which a relatively small number of sellers, each holding a substantial share of the market, compete in a market with many buyers.

✳✳✳
monopolistic competition A market structure in which many firms, each having slightly different products, offer consumer unique benefits.

✳✳✳
perfect competition A market structure in which many small sellers, all of which offer similar products, are unable to have an impact on the quality, price, or supply of a product.

Exhibit 3.7

The introduction of cold filtered milk created a point of difference in a food commodity business.

✳ ✳ ✳

patent Legal document granting an individual or firm exclusive right to produce and sell a particular invention.

own research efforts. They also monitor ongoing research projects in government and private research organizations. When inventors feel they have come across something exciting, they usually want to protect their exclusive right to produce and sell the invention by applying for a **patent**. A patent is a legal document that gives inventors—or individuals and firms—exclusive rights to produce and sell a particular invention. Sometimes companies monitor government patent applications registered at the Canadian Intellectual Property Office (www.strategis.ic.gc.ca/sc_mrksv/cipo) to discover innovative products they can purchase from the inventor.

And there are other ways marketers keep in touch with technology. Many important inventions are part of government-funded research grants. Clever marketers keep track of what government grant goes to whom for what research, hoping to be the first to identify and obtain exclusive rights to potentially profitable ideas.

The Legal Environment

The legal environment includes all laws—municipal, provincial, federal, and global—that affect businesses.

The main federal law governing business activity in Canada is the *Competition Act*, a comprehensive law that regulates most business activity in Canada. One main purpose of the Act is to promote competition and efficiency in the market by preventing business activities that would lessen competition (such as some mergers). The Act also restricts specific marketing practices that can be detrimental to both consumers and other businesses, such as misleading advertising or price-fixing.[49] While the *Competition Act* and other pieces of legislation, such as the *Broadcast Act*, cover all types of businesses, other federal legislation details regulations that apply to specific industries, such as food and drug products in the case of the

Table 3.1 Examples of Federal Legislation Affecting Marketing Decisions

Law	Purpose
Competition Act	Developed to promote free competition and encourage efficiency in the marketplace. Prohibits mergers that will lessen competition and specific marketing activities, such as misleading advertising, price-fixing, predatory pricing, and telemarketing and multilevel marketing fraud.
Consumer Packaging and Labelling Act	Controls the content of labelling used and stipulates that label information must appear in both English and French.
Textile Labelling Act	Regulates the labelling and advertising of consumer textile goods, such as clothing, bedding, carpets, and upholstered furniture coverings.
Food and Drugs Act	Sets requirements for the sale of food and drug products in Canada.
Canadian Environmental Protection Act	Prohibits activities that will damage the environment as a result of pollution and other toxic substances.
Motor Vehicle Safety Act	Regulates the manufacture and importation of motor vehicles and motor vehicle equipment, including setting emission standards and safety equipment requirements.
Trademarks Act	Protects and regulates brand names and trademarks.
Tobacco Act	Regulates the sale of tobacco products and requires health warnings on cigarette and other tobacco products.

Food and Drugs Act and cigarettes and other tobacco products in the *Tobacco Act.* Table 3-1 summarizes the *Competition Act* and other federal legislation that affect Canadian marketing decision making.

Provincial laws affecting marketing activities vary across the country, so marketers must be aware of those that may have an impact on their decisions. In the area of advertising, for example, Quebec is the only province that bans all TV advertising aimed at children. When the *Consumer Protection Law* (*Loi sur la protection du consommateur*) in Quebec came into effect in 1980, it was heavily influenced by parent groups' concerns about the impact of advertising on children. But now several other groups, including the Association Canadienne des Annonceurs in Montreal (the Quebec branch of the Association of Canadian Advertisers), have been lobbying the Quebec government to change this law in recognition that Quebec children are exposed to advertising in media not covered by the Act, such as on the Internet, through spill from specialty channels such as YTV and Teletoon, and from US stations.[50] Although television advertising directed at children is allowed in the rest of the country, it must be approved by Advertising Standards Canada, which has strict guidelines on how to advertise in an ethical manner to children.

THE WATCHDOGS OF BUSINESS: REGULATORY AGENCIES

The federal and provincial governments have also created a number of *regulatory agencies*, governmental bodies that monitor business activities and enforce laws. At the federal level, the most important of these is the Competition Bureau, the organization responsible for administering the *Competition Act.* The Bureau investigates and charges firms that violate the provisions of the Act. Often the fines levied against the offending organization and its owners are substantial. In a recent Competition Bureau ruling, three related companies—American Family Publishers, Publishers Central, and First Canadian Publishers—were fined $1 000 000 for engaging in deceptive telemarketing techniques.[51] The actions of the companies included promising valuable prizes to consumers if they purchased various items. The items that consumers purchased were sold at inflated prices, and consumers never received the "prizes" promised to them. In addition to the corporate fine, the president of the companies received a personal fine of $100 000.

ADAPTING TO A REGULATORY ENVIRONMENT

Many times, firms loudly object if a government or regulatory agency puts a stop to their marketing plans. Lysol, the cleaner and disinfectant, provides an example of how one firm,

Exhibit 3.8

Organizations such as Concerned Children's Advertisers engage in self-regulation of advertising.

Warner Lambert, coped a bit more creatively with government regulation. In 1966, the US government objected to Lysol's claim that it helped prevent the spread of colds, because the firm lacked data to substantiate the claim. The company stopped making this claim in its advertising, but it also funded research at a leading medical school on the topic. Warner Lambert used the resulting data to convince the government that Lysol does inhibit the spread of colds, and commercials making this claim began to appear again in 1983.[52]

New Era firms know that the best of all possible worlds is one of no government regulation—one in which firms work together to make sure everyone plays fair. As mentioned earlier, the advertising industry operates in a self-regulated environment through Advertising Standards Canada (ASC). As a voluntary, independent entity, the ASC has very little power to enforce its recommendations to advertisers. Most advertisers, however, comply because they believe it is in the best interest of all advertisers to clean their own house rather than having the government step in and do it for them. Another group represents Canadian companies that target advertising to children: Since advertising to children is a sensitive topic in Canada, Concerned Children's Advertisers works to ensure that its advertising not only complies with the law, but also, as the video still in Exhibit 3.8 indicates, is proactive in addressing such issues as children's self-esteem, by showing children making informed decisions on their own.

The Sociocultural Environment

In both consumer and business-to-business markets, an understanding of social and cultural factors is a must. The sociocultural environment is the characteristics of the society, the people who live in that society, and the culture that reflects the values and beliefs of the society. We'll focus on these issues in detail in Chapters 6 and 8.

The first step toward understanding the characteristics of a society is to look at its **demographics**. These are statistics that measure observable aspects of a population, such as birth rate, age distribution, and income. The information revealed in demographic studies, such as those conducted by Statistics Canada (www.statscan.ca), is of great interest to mar-

✳ ✳ ✳
demographics Statistics that measure observable aspects of a population, including age, gender, ethnic group, income, education, occupation, and family structure.

Real People, Real Decisions
How it worked out at Ethical Funds

Margaret Yee chose Option 2 and decided to run a hard-hitting, emotional campaign to raise the awareness of Ethical Funds. With the help of Glennie Stamnes Strategy, an ad agency in Vancouver, the new positioning of Ethical Funds was communicated in the tag line "Do the Right Thing," and was used in newspaper, radio, magazine, and television advertisements. The ads were definitely risky. They depicted environmental disasters and the exploitation of children as labourers. One especially controversial ad showed teenagers smoking to reinforce the anti-tobacco stance of Ethical Funds.

In addition to more traditional media, the Ethical Funds Web site (www.ethicalfunds.com) was an integral part of the brand building effort and included a downloadable screen saver showing the images used in the ads. To further strengthen their positioning and to promote a socially important cause, Ethical Funds also engaged in cause marketing through a strategic alliance with UNICEF. For every Ethical Funds Registered

Educational Savings Plan (RESP) sold, Ethical Funds committed to donating 25% of its revenues to UNICEF's educational efforts in less developed countries.

The "Do the Right Thing" campaign had the desired effects. In the first year of the campaign, Ethical Funds sales increased by 44%, while sales in the rest of the industry were down by 40%. Since then, Ethical Funds sales have been consistently above the industry average and awareness studies confirm that the awareness of the organization among mutual fund investors has increased significantly. Additionally, Web site hits are up to about 5400 per day during RRSP season, and the Web site was recognized by Netscape as being innovative. Ethical Funds is an organization that proves that ethical business can result in success.

Sources: Personal communication with Margaret Yee; Peter Ashman, "Mutual funds with a conscience," *Marketing*, 19 October 1998: 19.

keters for predicting the size of markets for many products, from investments in mutual fund products such as those offered by Ethical Funds to housing, clothing, and toys. In later chapters, we'll also focus on such related issues as consumer lifestyles and cultural differences that help marketers determine if a product will sell equally well in different regions of Canada and in international markets.

Understanding consumers' attitudes, beliefs, and ways of doing things in different parts of the country or the world is especially important when developing marketing strategy. The consequences of ignoring these issues became evident during the 1994 soccer World Cup, when both McDonald's and Coca-Cola made the mistake of reprinting the Saudi Arabian flag, which includes sacred words from the Koran, on disposable packaging used in promotions. Despite their delight at having a Saudi team in contention for the Cup, Muslims worldwide protested this borrowing of sacred imagery, and both companies had to scramble to rectify the situation.[53] Marketers can avoid making this type of mistake through better understanding consumer values and beliefs.

Chapter Summary

1. Explain why organizations have adopted a New Era marketing focus on ethics and social responsibility.

Firms in the New Era of marketing emphasize social profit as well as economic profit. This means that New Era companies practise business ethics—they behave according to basic values, respond to consumerism issues, and respect the rights of consumers, to avoid costs to both bottom line and reputation. Ethical marketing means making products safe, pricing products fairly, promoting products honestly, and treating channel members fairly.

Social responsibility means that New Era firms act in ways that benefit the public, the community, and the natural environment. New Era marketers assume social responsibility through environmental stewardship, in which the firm's actions either improve or do not harm the natural environment, and cause marketing, using marketing strategies that promote the public good. New Era firms also practise social responsibility by promoting cultural diversity—including people of different sexes, races, ethnic groups, and religions as customers, suppliers, employees, and distribution channel members.

2. Describe the New Era emphasis on quality.

Quality-focused firms in the New Era of marketing strive to provide goods and services that meet customer expectations and result in economic profit. Total quality management (TQM) is a management philosophy that emphasizes satisfying customers through such programs as continuous quality improvement, employee empowerment, and a team approach. Marketing activities in quality-focused firms narrow in on defining consumer perceptions of quality and developing superior marketing mix strategies that, along with other company programs, meet worldwide standards of quality.

3. Discuss some of the important aspects of an organization's internal environment.

Success in the New Era of marketing rests heavily on an organization's resources and competencies. This includes the corporate culture, the set of shared values, attitudes, and beliefs that influences its decisions and practices. New Era firms have more risk-taking and people-centred cultures. New Era firms place value on their relationships with suppliers, intermediaries, competitors, and various publics. Important publics include employees, shareholders, government, media, financial institutions, and consumers.

4. Explain why marketers scan an organization's external business environment.

Understanding the economic environment is essential to marketing planning. The business cycle (prosperity, recession, recovery, and depression) and inflation affect customer purchase behaviour and business activities. Consumer expectations about the general economy and their income can create changes in the business cycle.

In a firm's competitive environment, brand competition, product competition, and the more general competition for consumers' limited discretionary income affect the development of marketing strategies that give the firm a competitive advantage. The amount of competition within a specific industry is determined by whether that industry is a monopoly, an oligopoly, or perfect or "imperfect" monopolistic competition.

In the technological environment, marketers must be knowledgeable about changes, often monitoring government and private research findings.

The legal environment affects production, product development, pricing, distribution, and advertising activities. Municipal, provincial, and federal governments have enacted regulations and laws to protect both consumers and businesses.

Understanding the sociocultural environment helps marketers recognize important trends and predict consumer purchasing preferences. An understanding of consumer demographics assists marketers in segmenting a population according to such characteristics as age, gender, family structure, social class, race, and geography.

Chapter Review

Marketing Concepts: Testing Your Knowledge

1. What is meant by the New Era of marketing? What are business ethics? What are some ways that marketers practise ethical behaviour in the marketing mix?

2. What is consumerism? What rights can consumers expect in the marketplace?

3. What is social responsibility? What is cause marketing? How do marketers promote cultural diversity?

4. What is total quality management? How do marketers add quality to the marketing mix?

5. What is corporate culture? What are some ways that the corporate culture of one organization might differ from that of another? How does corporate culture affect decision making? How are relationships with a firm's publics an important part of its internal environment?

6. Describe the business cycle. What is consumer confidence? How do consumer expectations affect the business cycle?

7. What different types of competition do marketers face? What is competitive intelligence?

8. How do technological advances affect marketing?

9. Describe the important elements in marketing's legal environment.

10. What is the sociocultural environment? What are demographics?

Marketing Concepts: Discussing Choices and Issues

1. When New Era firms seek to create social profit, they practise environmental stewardship. This may mean taking some products off the market and changing other products. What products have a good chance of being removed from the market. What products are likely to be positively affected by environmental stewardship? What new products would be in tune with these trends?

2. Taking a firm's perspective, what do you think are the positive and negative aspects of social profit?

3. The Canadian government has been both criticized and praised for its efforts to regulate and control business practices. What is your stand on this issue as a consumer?

4. This chapter pointed out that business ethics needs to be a two-way street, that consumers as well as businesses must behave ethically in the marketplace. Give some examples of unethical consumer behaviour. What should businesses do to prevent these types of behaviour?

5. Consumer privacy has become an important ethical issue, as hundreds of firms maintain large databases that record numerous details about people's personal lives. Do you think that sharing this information abuses consumers' rights to privacy? Why or why not?

Marketing Practice: Applying What You've Learned

1. When you graduate and are hired by a business firm or non-profit organization, one of the first things you will need to do is learn about the organization's culture. Make a list of the elements of a corporate culture. Make suggestions for how you might develop a better knowledge and understanding of each of these elements.

2. You have recently been employed by the marketing department of a firm that disposes of hazardous waste. Your new boss believes in the New Era of marketing and feels that building relationships with customers and all of the organization's publics is important. She has asked you to prepare a report listing the various publics you see as important to the organization. She has also asked you to make suggestions for ways to develop better relationships with each of these groups. Develop that report.

3. As an employee of a business consulting firm that specializes in helping people who want to start a small business, you have been assigned a client who is interested in starting a video delivery service, in which customers call in their video orders for home delivery. As you begin thinking about the potential for success for this client, you realize that understanding the external environment for this business is essential. First, decide which environmental factors are most important to this client. Then choose one of these factors, and

use your library and the Internet to identify the current and future trends in this area. Finally, in a role-playing situation, present all of your recommendations to the client.

4. Assume that you are employed in the marketing department of a medium-sized firm in the furniture industry, a manufacturer of products such as end tables, entertainment units, and dining room chairs. Your firm has recently been purchased, and the new owner is very concerned about social responsibility. Every member of the marketing department has been asked to put together a report on how this firm can become a more socially responsible organization. Develop your report for the new owner of the firm.

5. Quality is defined in terms of what consumers expect to satisfy wants and needs. What is quality in a college or university education? How good a job does your college or university do of providing quality? What programs and processes are in place to improve quality? With a group of students in your class, discuss the role of quality in education with several members of your school's faculty, with administrators, and with other students. Report your findings to your class.

Marketing Mini-Project: Learning by Doing

This mini-project is designed to help you find out more about New Era of marketing focus on ethics and social responsibility.

1. With one or several other students in your class, select a demographic group of consumers to study. You may wish to study female university students, male university students, young professional people, retail employees, young mothers, older citizens, or a specific ethnic group.

   a. Develop a brief questionnaire that will allow you to obtain information from members of this group about their experiences with businesses. You might want to ask about some or all of the following:
      - Their best experience with a business
      - Their worst experience with a business
      - Opinions about the ethical behaviour of business in general
      - How businesses ought to behave
      - The responsibility of businesses to the environment
      - The responsibilities of businesses to promote cultural diversity
      - Such consumer behaviours as shoplifting and returning used merchandise
      - The ethical behaviour of retail employees

   b. Obtain responses to your questionnaire from members of your selected demographic group.

2. Analyze the responses to your survey and prepare a report for your class on what you have learned. In what ways might the unique perspectives or characteristics of the group you selected have influenced their responses?

3. Include in your report recommendations for marketers on ways to improve their dealings with this group. Also include in your report recommendations for government, consumers, retail stores, and your marketing instructors.

Real People, Real Surfers: Exploring the Web

There are a number of important not-for-profit organizations and government agencies in a firm's legal and ethical environment, including:

The Competition Bureau (www.strategis.ic.gc.ca/)
The Canadian Radio-television and Telecommunications Commission (CRTC) (www.crtc.gc.ca)
Advertising Standards Canada (www.canad.com)
The Canadian Council of Better Business Bureaus (www.bbb.org/bureaus/canada.html)
The Consumers Association of Canada (www.consumer.ca)
The Canadian Marketing Association (www.cdma.org)
The American Marketing Association (www.ama.org)

Spend some time investigating the Web sites of these organizations and agencies (or others that you identify yourself) and answer the following questions for each site.

1. What is the major purpose of the organization or agency? What services does it provide?

2. In what ways does the organization or agency influence the behaviour of marketers?

3. In what ways does the organization or agency benefit consumers? In what ways does it benefit marketers?

4. Consider the design of the Web site(s). Is the design conducive for consumer use? For business use? Does the Web site provide a way for consumers to voice complaints? If so, is the complaint vehicle easy to find and to understand?

Controversy over Genetically Modified Food

Recent advances in biotechnology have presented numerous opportunities for farmers and food processors. For example, genetically-modified (GM) seeds, such as Yieldgard and Roundup Ready, have produced bountiful, "bug-free" harvests of canola, soybean, corn, and wheat for Canadian farmers. Currently, most of the $3 billion a year canola harvest and one-quarter of the soybeans grown in Canada come from GM seeds. It is estimated that about 60% of all processed food sold in Canadian supermarkets contains genetically-engineered ingredients.

However, consumer backlash to genetically altered food has been fierce. Groups as diverse as Greenpeace, the Council of Canadians, and the Sierra Club of Canada have banded together to protest GM foods (which are also referred to as "Frankenfoods"). These groups argue that the effects of GM foods on humans have not been adequately examined. As one protester at a Toronto anti-GM demonstration explained, "They are putting plant genes into animals and animal [genes] into plants and they are changing nature, and we don't really know what will happen to us in the future."

A WAR FOR CONSUMER SUPPORT

So far, the war over GM foods has been an information war, in which pro- and anti-GM groups use a variety of sophisticated and grassroots marketing strategies to win public and political support.

Industry groups, including the Canadian Council of Grocery Distributors (CCGD), the Food and Consumer Products Manufacturers of Canada (FCPMC), and the Food Biotechnology Communication Network (FBCN) have championed a number of communication initiatives to provide consumers with more information about GM foods. These include launching a Web site about GM foods (www.foodbiotech.org), implementing a bilingual toll-free information line, and distributing two million pro-GM pamphlets and brochures at Canadian supermarkets.

In the spring of 2000, seven multinational biotechnology companies, including Dow Chemical and Novartis, spent $73 million on a three- to five-year North American television advertising campaign designed to communicate the positive aspects of biotechnology.

Anti-GM groups have countered with a series of grassroots consumer campaigns. For example, Greenpeace presented Loblaws, Canada's largest grocery retailer, with 15 000 anti-GM postcards signed by customers. Similarly, the Council of Canadians maintains their own informational Web site and is active in handing out anti-GM pamphlets outside grocery stores.

In response to consumer pressure, a number of multinational food processors—including McDonald's, McCain Foods, Nestlé, and Unilever—have either phased out GM foods or have made plans to do so. The European Union has banned GM beef from North America and voted to not approve any new GM seeds for two years.

The Canadian government established the Canadian Biotechnology Advisory Committee (www.cbac-ccb.ca) to advise the government on issues related to biotechnology, including issues related to GM food. In late 2001 the Committee recommended that standards for the labelling of GM food be set by the federal government so that consumers are given full information about what their food contains. Additionally, a study sponsored by the Committee showed that there is an increasing awareness of biotechnology issues among Canadians, but that 59% of those sampled would rather have the government rely on scientific experts as compared to public opinion when determining policy on this topic.

MARKETING IN ACTION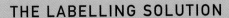

THE SCIENTIFIC PERSPECTIVE

In January 2000, 150 Canadian scientists issued a letter of support for GM foods. They argued that biotechnology has the potential to create more nutritious food with "improved fat and vitamin profiles." However, support for GM foods is by no means universal within the scientific community. Opponents suggest that GM foods are a threat to biodiversity. For example, insecticide-resistant genes developed for GM food products may spread to other plants and harm members of the food chain, such as the monarch butterfly or honey bee.

Both the US Food and Drug Administration (FDA) and Health Canada have classified GM products as equivalent to non-GM food. However, leaked documents indicate that FDA scientists had concerns about GM foods and were not convinced that they were safe.

THE LABELLING SOLUTION

As recommended by the Canadian Biotechnology Advisory Committee, one solution to the GM food issue is to have grocery chains and food processors identify GM and non-GM products. By seeing a clear distinction between the two, consumers will at least be able to choose to consume GM foods. However, GM supporters are opposed to labelling. They argue that labelling would unfairly stigmatize GM foods at a time when there is no clear scientific evidence to suggest that they are harmful to humans. In July 2001 Loblaws Supermarkets demanded that food marketers selling products in their grocery stores black out any non-GM labelling claims appearing on their food products, arguing that until standards were in place, providing such claims could be misleading to consumers.

The B.C. Vegetable Marketing Commission recently test marketed GM and non-GM-labelled potatoes at five Vancouver Island stores. Test results were inconclusive, since consumers did not show a strong preference for non-GM produce as expected. In a recent poll conducted in the United States, however, results showed that 93% of consumers support the labelling of GM food, and that 58% would not eat the food carrying that label. Additionally, recent focus groups commissioned by the US Food and Drug Administration revealed that "virtually all participants" wanted to know whether or not they are eating GM foods. As with most other aspects of the GM debate, more research is needed before it can be determined whether labelling has an impact on consumer behaviour.

Source: Jeff Fila wrote this case based on these sources: Peter Cook, "Europe's food stance would harm legitimate exports," *The Globe and Mail*, 19 January 2000; Angela Kryhul, "Fighting food fears," *Marketing Magazine*, 28 February 2000; Stuart Laidlaw, "Modified grains spark warning," *The Toronto Star*, 30 October 1999; Stuart Laidlaw, "University dismisses modified food study," *The Toronto Star*, 19 January 2000; Stuart Laidlaw and Laura Eggertson, "Modified food talks reach crucial stage," *The Toronto Star*, 18 January 2000; Lara Mills, "Customer service to the organics section," *Marketing Magazine*, 30 July 2001; Cynthia Reynolds, "Frankstein's Harvest," *Canadian Business*, 8 October 1999; Tanya Talaga, "Protesters want to squash genetically altered food," *The Toronto Star*, 23 January 2000; Lesley Young, "Report calls for GM labeling rules, *Marketing Magazine*, 3 September 2001; "The upside of GM foods," *Marketing Magazine*, 8 May 2000: 26; www.greenpeace.org, www.cbac-cccb.ca.

THINGS TO THINK ABOUT

1. Assume you work for a food company in Canada. Identify how aspects of the external business environment—economic, competitive, technological, legal, and sociocultural—determine whether your company should sell GM food.
2. What ethical issues does the GM food issue raise for food marketers? For environmentalists? For the Canadian government?
3. Based on the information in the case, do you think that foods sold in Canada should be labelled as GM or non-GM?
4. What impact would such labelling have on how foods are marketed in Canada?

4

Think Globally and Act Locally: Marketing in a Multinational Environment

When you have completed your study of this chapter, you should be able to

CHAPTER OBJECTIVES

1. Explain how complex relationships among firms, countries, and regions influence world trade.

2. Understand how political, legal, and cultural issues influence global marketing strategies and outcomes.

3. Explain the strategies a firm can use to enter global markets.

4. Understand the arguments for standardization versus localization of marketing strategies in global markets, and understand how elements of the marketing mix apply in international markets.

Real People, Real Decisions ✓ ✗

Meet Peter Einstein
A Decision Maker at MTV Europe

Peter Einstein is the person responsible for MTV's entrance into the European market. As director of marketing and network development for MTV Europe, he is a key decision maker in a campaign to shape the musical tastes of Europe's youth. Founded in 1987, MTV Europe transmits music-based programs for young adults across the continent. All of its shows are broadcast in English, and they are available to viewers throughout Europe. Based in London, MTV Europe was the first attempt by MTV Networks to take its music programming outside North America.

Einstein has overall responsibility for the growth and development of MTV Networks throughout Europe. He decides what markets to enter, and he helps to design the most appealing way for MTV Europe to win loyal viewers from Switzerland to Spain. He is also responsible for VH-1, which targets an older audience. Einstein began his career with MTV Networks in the United States, where he helped establish MTV, Nickelodeon, Nick at Nite, and VH-1 before joining MTV Europe in 1990. He holds a BSc in business administration and an MBA in marketing.

Let's Get Small

MTV Europe
www.mtveurope.com

Fans of MTV Europe would agree that the world is becoming a smaller place. Young adults in Berlin park themselves in front of the TV to check out "buzz clips" that their counterparts are watching in Paris, Rome, and Zurich. MTV Europe's basic format matches the North American version, but over 80% of the programs originate in Europe. And the MTV concept is spreading as new outposts continue to open in Asia, Australia, and Latin America. MTV is now the world's largest network, reaching 305 million households. Figure 4.1 illustrates the different forms MTV takes around the world and provides examples of places where the basic format has been tailored to the tastes of local fans.

MTV knows that the development of sophisticated transportation and communications systems around the world have led many firms to consider any market anywhere fair game. Even small, isolated firms are now a mouse-click away from customers in far-off places. As markets at home become saturated and opportunities for growth decline, it's natural to look elsewhere for customers. Honeydew Canada Foods, a manufacturer of frozen blended fruit drinks, for example, expanded into the US market in 1996, when the frozen juice category in Canada started to decline. Now 50% of the company's revenue comes from sales in the US market.[1]

However, the global game is not always easy to play: Competition comes from local and foreign firms, and differences in laws, customs, and consumer preferences across countries are significant. As the title of this chapter suggests, the smart marketer needs to think globally by considering diverse markets around the world, but act locally by being willing to adapt business practices to conditions in other parts of the globe.

For example, the athletic shoe giant Nike has had to adjust its thinking in the process of pursuing international markets. The company recently decided that appealing to soccer fans worldwide is a top priority and is actively pursuing new customers in countries from France to Chile (see Exhibit 4.1). In Canada, the company specifically targets Italian Canadian and Portuguese Canadian soccer fans using billboards featuring the soccer teams from Italy and Portugal.[2] This is a real change for a marketer that has made its mark in such "American" sports as basketball and football—the company virtually ignored the soccer market until the mid-1990s. Nike's president commented, "Once we set our sights on being a global company, we had to focus on soccer." Nike is facing fierce opposition from more entrenched companies such as Adidas, though, that are more familiar to soccer fans around the world. Nike paid $200 million to sponsor the Brazilian team in a recent World Cup.[3]

1. MTV Asia
Distribution: 31.3 million households, served by eight separate channels Heavy Rotation: half local (with no interregional crossover), half imports (Spice Girls, Mariah Carey, Celine Dion) What You Won't See: In Singapore, Janet Jackson's new album (banned by the government), in Malaysia *Singled Out* ("We wouldn't want to be seen encouraging young people to date," says an MTV Asia executive), anywhere on the continent, *Beavis and Butt-head* Local Hits: *TVMTV*, two guys run a pirate music channel out of a tree house Big Imports: *House of Style* Approximate Stage of Video Development: "I Want a New Drug" Beware of: *MTV Interactive*, a witless, American-style hyping of the Internet

2. MTV Australia
Distribution: 200,000 households Heavy Rotation: American R & B. German dance music (less than one quarter of programming is local) Local Hit: *Didge Indie*, an analog to our *Indie Outing* Big Import: *The Real World* (especially the season with the Australian cast member) Approximate Stage of Video Development: "Smells Like Teen Spirit" Beware of: Silverchair, an alarming number of bands that sound like Silverchair

3. MTV Brazil
Distribution: 16.3 million households Heavy Rotation: 60 percent local (pop, hard rock, reggae), 40 percent imports (Hanson, Spice Girls, miscellaneous classic rock) What You Won't See: R & B Local Hits: *Barraco*, a social-issues talk show, *Throat and Neck*, a "punk video-game" that viewers play over the phone Big Imports: *Beavis and Butt-head* (with subtitles) Failed Imports: *The Real World*, *Loveline* ("We don't have sexual problems," explains an MTV Brazil executive)

Approximate Stage of Video Development: "Rock You Like a Hurricane" Beware of: A remarkable fascination with Bon Jovi

4. MTV Latin America
Distribution: 8.3 million households served by separate North and South channels Heavy Rotation: in the North, local pop flavored by U.S. hip-hop: in the South, classic rock, European techno What You Will See: Bush and No Doubt on *Nacion Alternativa* Local Hit: *Rock and Goal*, a soccer show Big Import: *The Real World* Relative Stage of Video Development: "Jump Around" Beware of: nearly as much *Unplugged* refuse as in the U.S.

5. MTV Europe
Distribution: 57.7 million households served by four channels Heavy Rotation: in the U.K., bands that sound like Suede, elsewhere, bands that sound like Blackstreet Local Hits: Italy's *Stylissimo* fashion show Big Import: *Beavis and Butt-head* (in English) Beware of: David Hasselhoff

6. MTV India
Distribution: 7.7 million households Heavy Rotation: 70 percent local (mostly Hindi film music, some middle-aged crooners set to dance beats), 30 percent imports (Bryan Adams–style American rock) What You Won't See: heavy metal, any video in

which a cow is slaughtered (at least one has been nixed) Local Hits: *Party Zone* and *Mega Mix* (dance shows) Big Imports: their own version of *Club MTV*, taped in Bombay Failed Imports: *The Real World*, *Road Rules* Approximate Stage of Video Development: "The Safety Dance" Beware of: local pop stars' intermittent attempts to sing in English But at Least: No Spice Girls

7. MTV Japan
Distribution: 1.9 million households Heavy Rotation: 20 percent local, 80 percent imports. Either way, "The key to making a hit," says an MTV Japan executive, "is a song that can be sung by karaoke." What You Won't See: alt-rock ("In English is alternative enough," says the exec) Local Hits: *MTV Files*, a celebrity profile series Big Imports: *MTV Sports* Approximate Stage of Video Development: "Has Anybody Seen My Baby?" Beware of: a flotilla of Japanese teenybopper rap groups

8. & 9. MTV Mandarin & MTV Asia
Distribution: 24.7 million households, mostly in Taiwan Heavy Rotation: 70 percent local (primarily weepy ballads), 30 percent imports (groups featuring young boys, Michael Jackson) What You Won't See: hip-hop Local Hits: *MTV Campus*, which tours colleges; *Spotlight*, a karaoke show Big Import: *Singled Out* Approximate Stage of Video Development: any country music video Beware of: sporadic Kenny Rogers appearances

10. MTV New Zealand
Distribution: one million households Heavy Rotation: Coolio, Puff Daddy, Portishead Local Hit: *Wrekognize*, a hip-hop show Big Imports: *Loveline*, *The Grind* Beware of: rugby jokes

Figure 4.1 MTV Around the World
Source: Daniel Radosh, "¡Quiero Mi MTV!" *Spin*, February 1998: 42.

In this chapter, we'll look at the "big picture" of international marketing to understand the opportunities and challenges of doing business in a world that seems to be getting smaller by the minute. The major factors companies need to consider before entering international markets are summarized in Figure 4.2. First, we'll look at how today's world trade is influenced by a complicated set of interrelationships among countries and regions. Then we'll examine some of the environmental factors a marketer must consider before venturing into another country, including economic, political, and legal issues, and cultural differences. Finally, we'll get to the crucial questions for marketers: If a firm does decide to go global, how exactly can this be done? And what changes (if any) need to be made to the marketing mix of a product or service to compete effectively?

Exhibit 4.1

As this Chilean ad shows, Nike recently shifted its marketing focus to go after the worldwide soccer market.

World Trade

Many successful Canadian firms know that going global is an option they can't ignore. Trade is an important part of the Canadian economy, with exports accounting for 42% of GDP—the largest percentage of any G7 nation.[4] We export over $86 million of goods every year, and the value of trade is growing as Canada secures more free trade agreements. It is estimated that one in three jobs in Canada is related to exports.[5]

Many Canadian companies, both large and small, have benefited from globalization. Acadian Seaplants, a Nova Scotia harvester of seaweed, exports 90% of its production to over 55 countries. Weiss Advertising in Toronto produces TV commercials in Canada for customers in such international markets as France, Israel, Brazil and Spain. And large Canadian companies like Nortel Networks and McCain Foods realize the majority of their profits from activities in global markets.

HOW "WORLDLY" CAN A COMPANY BE?

We distinguish between types of companies by their definition of the scope of their market:

- A *domestic firm* confines its sales and marketing efforts to its home market.

- An *exporting firm* expands sales by offering its products for sale in other countries. Since exports to the United States account for 85% of Canada's total exports, many Canadian

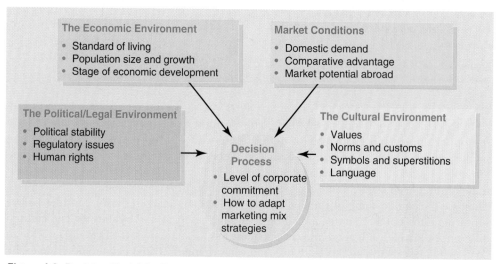

Figure 4.2 Decision Model for Entering Foreign Markets

Exhibit 4.2

Buckley's is an example of a Canadian firm that has successfully entered the US market.

To all those people who don't use Buckley's for their coughs:

Cowards.

Nasty cough? Try Buckley's Mixture. It's sugar and alcohol free. And it works fast and effectively to get rid of the worst coughs due to colds. So you'll have nothing to worry about, except the taste.

**Buckley's Mixture.
It tastes awful. And it works.**

Available at all RITE AID stores and Jewel OSCO, OSCO drug, Sav-On-Drug, and other fine pharmacies. 1-800-434-1034 www.buckleys.com

firms look to that market first for international expansion.[6] For example, Buckley's, the manufacturer of Buckley's Mixture cough syrup, is a good example of a Canadian company making serious efforts to expand into the US market. Using their successful Canadian advertising campaign, "It tastes awful. And it works," (see Exhibit 4.2) Buckley's is working toward establishing itself as the number-one competitor in the cough–cold product category in the United States.[7]

- A *multinational firm*, such as Kraft, operates in many foreign markets; it may modify the products it sells—Kraft adds lemon, egg, or mustard to its mayonnaise to please different European palates.[8] Though the firm's domestic market may account for even less than 50% of revenues, the company typically retains the business culture of its home country.

- A *global firm* views the world as its market, and it tends to operate the same way in many countries, adapting its basic strategy when necessary to conform to local conditions. As Gillette's CEO commented, "The most important decision I made was to globalize. We decided not to tailor products to any marketplace, but to treat all marketplaces the same. And it worked in most countries."[9] Global firms include McCain Foods, Bombardier, Nestlé, Coca-Cola, and Nortel Networks.

Buckley's Mixture
www.buckleys.com

COUNTERTRADE

Multinational and global firms must be able to accommodate the needs of trading partners. For example, often a foreign partner doesn't pay with cash for a firm's products. In many countries, sufficient cash or credit is not available, so elaborate deals are worked out whereby firms trade their products with each other (called *barter*), or even supply goods in return for tax breaks from the local government. This **countertrade**, in which goods are paid for with other items instead of with cash, accounts for about 25% of all world trade. For instance, a Russian textile plant that makes woollen socks pays its workers in socks rather than rubles.[10] These deals can get complicated. For example, PepsiCo has been selling its drinks in Russia for years in exchange for Stolichnaya vodka, which it then sells in other markets.[11]

❉ ❉ ❉
countertrade A type of trade in which goods are paid for with other items instead of with cash.

TRADE FLOWS

A **trade flow** is the pattern of economic interdependence among countries or regions. Understanding the "big picture" of who does business with whom is important to marketers when they devise global trade strategies. World trade activity is steadily increasing year by year. The volume of merchandise exported from one country to another is more than $6.2 trillion and grows by an average of six percent per year.[12] The Americas and Europe account for about 45% of total world trade in goods and services.[13] Among the most significant Canadian exports are automotive products, industrial machinery and equipment, consumer goods, agriculture and fishing products, and resource products, such as those from the energy and forestry sectors. The success of these industries internationally shows that a firm's prospects in other markets depend not only on its own abilities, but on the pros and cons of being based in a particular country.

❉ ❉ ❉
trade flow The pattern of economic interdependence among countries or regions.

Competitive Advantage

A company's success in both domestic and international markets depends on conditions in its home country that make it easier or harder to compete. Firms need to capitalize on their home country's assets and avoid competing in areas in which they are at a disadvantage. For example, German firms have trouble keeping production costs down due to the high wages, short workweeks, and long vacations that their skilled factory workers enjoy; so they compete better on high quality than on low price.

Canadian companies compete well internationally in the area of technology. For example, ATI Technologies of Ontario builds graphics chips that are installed in more than one-third of the desktop computers in the world; Montreal-based Optimal Robotics Corp. is the leading supplier in North America of self-checkout systems in grocery stores; and Sierra Wireless Inc. of Richmond, BC, holds 50% of the North American market for wireless data modems used in police cruisers, delivery trucks, and taxis.[14] Across all product categories, some business people contend that Canada has a built -in advantage in international operations because of the culturally diverse population in this country. As the chief strategy officer of BCE Inc. noted, "We have a critical mass of people of every language and culture on earth. In a global world, that has to be a huge plus."[15]

Professor Michael Porter proposed a model to explain which companies and industries are likely to become leaders or followers in the global market.[16] Porter showed that successful global firms were able to beat the competition at home—they were able to continuously innovate and improve, often by taking advantage of resources available in their home countries. Porter describes four keys to a nation's **competitive advantage** relative to other countries:

1. *Demand conditions:* The number and sophistication of domestic customers for a product. The French pride themselves on a long heritage of wine making, so they are very demanding when it comes to evaluating vintners. This forces the domestic wine industry to maintain a tradition of high quality that can then be exported to connoisseurs elsewhere.

2. *Related and supporting industries:* Companies must have access to other firms that provide the high-quality products and services they require to turn out competitive products. The Canadian automotive industry is helped by the large number of factories producing tires and other auto parts in close proximity to auto plants.

3. *Factor conditions:* The quality of a country's resources, including its infrastructure, the educational level of its people, and the availability of raw materials. Argentina is a leader in cattle production and leather goods, aided by its vast pampas, or plains, that are ideal for grazing.

4. *Company strategy, structure, and rivalry:* The way a country's businesses are organized and managed, and the intensity of competition that creates pressure to innovate. Many Japanese firms cooperate with one another in close-knit networks called *keiretsu* that make it difficult for foreign businesses to gain a foothold in Japan.

Borders, Roadblocks, and Communities

We like to think of the world as one big, open marketplace, where companies from every country are free to compete for business by meeting customers' needs better than the competition. Although the world seems to be moving toward such an ideal of *free trade*, in reality we're not there yet. Often a company's efforts to expand into foreign markets are hindered by roadblocks designed to favour local businesses over outsiders. As we've just seen, for example, Japan's *keiretsu* make it hard for foreigners to compete.[17] National borders do matter.

PROTECTED TRADE

In some cases, a government adopts a policy of **protectionism**, enforcing rules designed to give home companies an advantage. It may shield its own industries from foreign competition with red tape tactics, such as when South Korean customs officials delay approval of foreign shipments of fresh fruits and vegetables for up to four months (which definitely re-

Optimal Robotics Corp.
www.optimal-robotics.com

✳ ✳ ✳
competitive advantage The ability of a firm to outperform the competition, thereby providing customers with a benefit the competition can't.

✳ ✳ ✳
protectionism A government policy that gives domestic companies an advantage.

duces their freshness).[18] Western distillers saw huge potential in the Russian vodka market when the Soviet Union collapsed. However, the Russian government was determined to protect the local vodka industry. It allowed foreign companies only one percent share in the market by setting high import duties and banning alcohol advertising on Russian television.[19]

Many governments also set **import quotas** on foreign goods to reduce competition for its domestic industries. Quotas are limitations on the amount of a product allowed to enter or leave a country, and they can make goods more expensive to a country's citizens, because the absence of cheaper foreign goods reduces pressure on domestic firms to lower prices. Firms that look to the United States market, for example, need to be aware of US import quotas on sweetened candy, milk and cream, some types of cotton, and other products.[20]

An extreme quota is an **embargo**, which prohibits specified foreign goods completely. Over the past 30 years, Canada has imposed trade embargoes against several countries, including South Africa, Iraq, Haiti, and Libya, often for humanitarian or political reasons.[21] Governments also use **tariffs**, or taxes on imported goods, to give domestic competitors an advantage in the marketplace by making foreign competitors' goods more expensive than their own. For example, tariffs on rice in Japan prevent international rice growers from establishing a strong presence in that country.

The **General Agreement on Tariffs and Trade** (GATT) accords have done much to reduce the problems protectionism creates. This international treaty, initiated in 1948 under the United Nations, reduces import tax levels and trade restrictions among its 100 plus member nations. The cornerstone of GATT is a principle called *most favoured nation* (MFN), which states that a country should treat another as favourably as it deals with its best trading partners—what applies to one partner applies to all. Being designated an MFN is a coveted prize (often rewarded or revoked for political reasons, such as displeasure with a country's human rights policies) because it can result in a huge increase in business activity for companies at home. GATT's position is that the only reason to impose a tariff is to protect an infant industry, as when the shoe industry in Canada was granted protection by the federal government to allow it to get established.[22]

GATT addresses tariff issues but not other kinds of restrictions like quotas. In 1995, the **World Trade Organization (WTO)** formed to mediate trade disputes between nations to deal with cases in which unfair protectionism by one country is claimed by another. The WTO is tackling many thorny trade issues, including protection of copyright and patent rights to make it easier for firms to prevent pirated versions of their software, books, and music CDs from being sold in other countries. This is a serious problem for Canadian companies, as it results in an erosion of profits due to illegal sales. Brand piracy has been called "the crime of the 21st century."[23] As an attorney for Microsoft commented, "We refer to some countries in Asia as one-disk markets. More than 99% of the software is illegitimate copies."[24]

ECONOMIC COMMUNITIES

Groups of countries may also band together to promote trade among themselves and make it easier for member nations to compete elsewhere. These **economic communities** coordinate economic policies and ease restrictions on the flow of products and capital across their borders. Economic communities are important to marketers because they set policies in such areas as product content, package labelling, and advertising that influence strategic decisions when doing business in these areas. In South America, the economic community called MERCOSUR includes Argentina, Paraguay, Brazil, Uruguay, Chile, and Bolivia.[25] The Association of Southeast Asian Nations (ASEAN) includes six nations—Malaysia, Indonesia, the Philippines, Thailand, Singapore, and Brunei.[26] The economic communities in North America and Europe are NAFTA and the EU.

The **North American Free Trade Agreement (NAFTA)** formed the world's largest economic community, composed of Canada, the United States, and Mexico. Representing a market of 370 million consumers and a total $6.5 trillion in output, NAFTA became a unified trading bloc in 1994.[27] This extended the cooperative arrangement already established by Canada and the United States in 1989 under the Canada–US Free Trade Agreement. NAFTA is controversial. Some critics claim it diverts jobs from Canada to Mexico and the

✳✳✳
import quotas The limitations set by a government on the amount of a product allowed to enter or leave a country.

✳✳✳
embargo A quota completely prohibiting specified goods from entering or leaving a country.

✳✳✳
tariffs Taxes on imported goods.

✳✳✳
General Agreement on Tariffs and Trade (GATT) An international treaty to reduce import tax levels and trade restrictions.

✳✳✳
World Trade Organization (WTO) An organization that mediates trade disputes between nations and deals with cases in which one country claims unfair protectionism by another.

✳✳✳
economic communities Groups of countries that band together to promote trade among themselves and to make it easier for member nations to compete elsewhere.

✳✳✳
North American Free Trade Agreement (NAFTA) The world's largest economic community, composed of Canada, the United States, and Mexico.

US, where cheaper labour rates prevail, and results in Canadian plants closing and moving to the US, or in too much direct investment in the Canadian economy by US firms. However, the Agreement does appear to be stimulating economic growth in Canada. In the first five years of NAFTA, Canada's trade with the US increased by 80% and trade with Mexico doubled.[28]

Alternative Fuel Systems (AFS), a Calgary-based producer of alternatives to gasoline and diesel transportation systems, is one company that has benefited directly from NAFTA. AFS has a contract to convert 100 000 Mexican buses and taxis (Mexico City's entire public vehicle fleet) from gasoline to compressed natural gas. AFS vice-president Arie van der Lee says, "The Mexicans really want to deal with Canadian companies, but prior to NAFTA, there were trade obstacles...This project was certainly facilitated by the reduction in import duties through NAFTA."[29]

***
European Union (EU) An economic community that includes most of Western Europe.

The **European Union (EU)** began in 1957 as an agreement among six countries, and this community now includes most of Western Europe. This group represents about 350 million consumers from 15 countries.[30] The EU has begun many initiatives to improve the quality of products available to Europeans in member countries. These include standardizing regulations regarding information that must be shared with consumers, encouraging environmentally friendly consumption, and strengthening the rights of consumers who are dissatisfied with products and services.[31] In a controversial next step toward creating a united Europe, most member countries have abandoned their own currencies and converting to a common currency, the *Euro,* which will (it is hoped) unite a $6.4 trillion economy.[32]

Many companies are responding to this dramatic change by consolidating the different brands sold in individual countries into common *Eurobrands.* In the United Kingdom and France, for example, the Marathon candy bar sold by Mars is becoming the Snickers bar (a somewhat risky name change, considering that the British refer to women's underwear as "knickers").[33]

The Global Marketing Environment

Now we've seen something of the "big picture" of world trade that a firm must consider as it decides in which regions of the world it holds a competitive advantage. A firm's fortunes are affected by its country's policies and by those of other countries, which may make it easier or more difficult for foreign companies to compete. To complicate matters, the company needs to consider how to adapt to local environmental issues in a country or region. Environmental scanning is even more important in international markets. It may be a small world, but it's not a simple one. In this section, we'll see how economic, political, and cultural factors affect marketers' global strategies.

The Economic Environment

Countries vary in terms of their economic environment, including the level of economic development; therefore, a firm thinking about marketing its products or services in other countries needs to understand the economic circumstances influencing its potential customers. Great Canadian Bagel has experienced first-hand the impact that changing economic conditions in foreign markets can have. When the company opened its Canadski Bagel franchise in Moscow in the mid-1990s, the Russian economy was in the midst of a boom. But by 1999, Russia was experiencing high inflation rates and currency devaluations, which created price-sensitive consumers and rising costs for the company. It is expected that improvement in the Russian economy could take five to seven years, so Great Canadian Bagel has viewed its commitment in Russia as a long-term investment that will hopefully pay off in the future.[34]

INDICATORS OF ECONOMIC HEALTH

***
standard of living An indicator of the average quality and quantity of goods and services consumed in a country.

One way to gauge the market potential for a product is to look at a country's **standard of living**, which is an indicator of the average quality and quantity of goods and services consumed in a country. **Gross domestic product** is the total dollar value of goods and services produced in a nation in a year. It is also a benchmark of its wealth. But this indicator can be deceiving, because the money may be concentrated in the hands of a few, and the costs of the same goods and services may be much lower in a foreign market. For example, an income of $45 000 in Canada yields the same standard of living as an income of $5100 in Uganda.[35] Although $5100 may not sound like a lot of money to Canadians, it's good pay in Uganda—a reminder that we need to consider other factors when assessing a country's economic health.

A country's demographic characteristics also play an important role in determining its citizens' buying power and which products and services are likely to succeed. Birth rates and the size of different age groups are particularly important for forecasting market potential, because they tell us what types of products are likely to be in demand now and in the future. For example, the Canadian, American, and European populations are growing older—the population of Canadians aged 55 and older will grow from about 6.5 million people to over 10.5 million people by 2016, an increase of over 160%.[36] In contrast, about one-third of all Latin Americans and 40% of Africa's population are under 14 years old.[37] This difference means that great opportunities exist for products and services catering to young people in these regions.

Marketers also need to consider whether they can conduct "business as usual" in another country. The **economic infrastructure** is the quality of a country's distribution, financial, and communications systems. For example, Argentina boasts many modern conveniences, but its antiquated phone system is just starting to work properly after years of neglect by the government. If they are using the Internet to advertise and or sell to customers, marketers also need to be sure that adequate numbers of people in the markets they are considering will be online. For example, consumers in India have been relatively slow to adopt shopping online partly because of the non-convertibility of the Indian rupee, which means that consumers cannot order products from abroad.[38]

LEVEL OF ECONOMIC DEVELOPMENT

When marketers scan the world for opportunities, it helps if they consider a country's level of economic development to understand the needs of people who live there and the infrastructure conditions they must contend with. Economists describe three basic levels of development.

Less Developed Countries: A country at the lowest stage of economic development is a **less developed country (LDC)**. In most cases, the economic base is agricultural. Many nations in Africa and South Asia, such as Chad and Sri Lanka, are considered LDCs. Their standard of living is low, as are literacy levels. Opportunities to sell many products, especially luxury items, are minimal because most people grow what they need and barter for the rest. These countries are attractive markets for staples and inexpensive items. They may export important raw materials, such as minerals or rubber, to industrial nations.

Less developed countries can be attractive markets if a firm is willing to invest for the long haul. Africa, for example, was not considered an attractive market for many years. In 1996, sub-Saharan Africa attracted less than $1 of every $20 invested in the developing world. Now signs of change are in the air: Unilever, Nestlé, Eveready, and Coca-Cola are aggressively undertaking marketing efforts in Kenya; ITT Sheraton is planning two fancy hotels in Ghana; and the end of apartheid has brought many firms back to South Africa.[39] Weight Watchers is moving in, too—the company noticed that obesity-related diseases such as hypertension are rising with the influx of processed foods and fast-food restaurants.

Developing Countries: When economies shift their emphasis from agriculture to industry, standards of living, education, and the use of technology rise. These countries are **developing countries**. In such locales, there may be a visible middle class, often largely composed of small entrepreneurs.

Because 77% of the world's population lives in developing countries, the sheer number of potential customers and the presence of a skilled labour force attract many firms to these areas. Furthermore, the economy of the developing world is expanding at a healthy rate of five to six percent annually.[40] Throughout Latin America, Eastern Europe, and the Pacific

*** **gross domestic product** The total dollar value of goods and services that are produced in a nation in a year.

*** **economic infrastructure** The quality of a country's distribution, financial, and communications systems.

*** **less developed country (LDC)** A country at the earliest stage of economic development.

*** **developing country** A country in which the economy is shifting its emphasis from agriculture to industry.

Rim (generally Asia excluding Japan), new crops of consumers are interested in Western-style products.[41]

Eastern Europe, with its 300 million consumers, "needs it all," according to the general manager of an IKEA furniture store in Budapest, who claims that "basic needs satisfied in the West are not yet fulfilled here."[42] Eastern Europeans still are limited in what they can purchase, but their transition to a free market economy has brought with it a demand for Western goods that is expected to grow. Even now, consumers in Warsaw frequent posh boutiques that carry upscale merchandise, such as Christian Dior perfume and Valentino shoes.[43]

The countries of Latin America are emerging from decades of state control, and their economies are opening to foreign business.[44] Exports and imports are surging in this region—exports expanded by 13% in one year, with Mexico and Brazil being the two biggest traders.[45] A construction boom is also rebuilding roads, bridges, and other parts of the infrastructure required to move goods through these countries efficiently.

Global firms based in Europe have been moving rapidly into Latin America. European investment in the area has tripled in the last decade, partly fuelled by cultural similarities, such as the widespread use of the Spanish and Portuguese languages in both regions.[46] For example, Spain's Banco Santander spent $3.4 billion to buy banks in eight Latin American countries.[47]

The Pacific Rim countries of China (including Hong Kong), South Korea, Malaysia, Indonesia, Thailand, and Singapore are nicknamed the "Dragons of Asia" because of their tremendous economic growth, despite a serious tumble in the late 1990s. Most industries remain committed to investing in this corner of the world, and analysts predict continued demand for a broad range of consumer goods.[48] Many Canadian firms are very interested in the Chinese market—it's hard to ignore a potential market of over a billion people. Quebec's Lassonde, a juice maker producing such brands as Oasis, Rougemount, and Fruite, owns two plants in China, which produce juice for that market.[49] Inniskillin, the largest Canadian producer of icewine sells the majority of its product to Asian markets.[50]

Developed Countries: A **developed country** boasts sophisticated marketing systems, strong private enterprise, and bountiful market potential for many goods and services. Such countries are economically advanced and offer a wide range of opportunities for international marketers. Canada, the United States, the United Kingdom, France, Italy, Germany, and Japan are the most economically developed countries in the world.

Some of the most challenging marketing issues for Canadian companies arise when they compete for consumers' pocketbooks with Japanese firms—in Japan and elsewhere around the world. Japan's high level of affluence makes it an attractive market for foreign firms—if they can break into this difficult market. Japan imports close to $9.2 billion per year in products and services from Canada alone.[51] This track record puts Japan second only to the United States as the largest trading partner with Canada. Tourism is one of the Canadian industries that successfully targets Japanese consumers. The Canadian Tourism Commission recently spent $3 million on advertising in Japan in its "Colour of Canada" campaign (see Exhibit 4.3), which depicts the four seasons in Canada.[52]

The Political and Legal Environment

When entering an international market, a firm must carefully weigh political and legal risks. A company's fortunes often are affected by political and legal issues that may be beyond its control.

POLITICAL ISSUES

Political actions taken by a government can drastically affect the business operations of outsiders. At the extreme, when two countries go to war, the business environment changes dramatically. Short of war, though, a country may impose **economic sanctions** that prohibit trade with another country (as Canada does with Libya), so access to some markets may be cut off. Or internal pressures may prompt the government to take over the operations of foreign companies doing business within its borders. With **nationalization**, the domestic

---

❊ ❊ ❊
developed country A country that boasts sophisticated marketing systems, strong private enterprise, and bountiful market potential for many goods and services.

❊ ❊ ❊
economic sanctions Trade prohibitions imposed by one country against another.

❊ ❊ ❊
nationalization A domestic government's takeover of a foreign company for its assets with some reimbursement, though often not for the full value.

Exhibit 4.3

The Japanese market is important to the Canadian tourism industry.

government reimburses a foreign company (often not for the full value) for its assets after taking it over; with **expropriation**, a domestic government seizes a foreign company's assets without any compensation.

Companies perform *political risk assessment* to avoid such problems by identifying countries with relatively stable political environments. If they do operate in politically volatile environments, many Canadian companies purchase political risk insurance to insure the company against such things as war, civil strife, kidnapping, and expropriation.[53] Canadian Occidental, which has oil operations in such countries as Yemen, Indonesia, Columbia, and Nigeria, prefers not to purchase risk insurance, however, despite the fact that a car bomb blew the doors out of its office in Yemen in 1999. Instead, the company has developed a list of "ethical guidelines" and is trying to get other Canadian resource companies to do the same. The company believes that good business practices are often the best protection against political risk.[54]

REGULATORY ISSUES

Governments and economic communities impose numerous regulations about what products should be made of, how they should be made, and what can be said about them. Sometimes a company has no choice but to alter product content to comply with local laws. Heinz 57 Sauce tastes quite different in Europe, simply because of different legal restrictions on preservatives and colour additives.[55] Canadian food companies expanding to the US market often face an extensive set of regulatory requirements involving ingredient lists and nutrition guidelines, which mean that the companies have to create entirely new packaging for that market.[56]

Other regulations are less focused on ensuring quality and more focused on ensuring that the host country gets a piece of the action. **Local content rules** are a form of protectionism, stipulating that a certain proportion of a product must consist of components supplied by industries in the host country or economic community. For example, under NAFTA rules, cars built by Toyota in Ontario must have 62.5% of their components made in North America to be able to enter Mexico and the US duty-free.[57] That helps to explain why Japanese automakers such as Toyota have increased their local presence by opening manufacturing plants in Canada and hiring local workers to run them.[58]

Countries also regulate how products can be promoted. Many nations impose quotas on foreign TV programming, and, in some cases, television networks are state controlled and may not accept any advertising. In Russia, the Inspectorate for the Control of the Condition

❊ ❊ ❊
expropriation A domestic government's seizure of a foreign company's assets without any compensation.

❊ ❊ ❊
local content rules A form of protectionism stipulating that a certain proportion of a product must consist of components supplied by industries in the host country.

of Advertising and Artistic Decorations attempted to clamp down on the overabundance of Western marketing messages by requiring all stores to display promotional signs only in Russian.[59]

HUMAN RIGHTS ISSUES

Some governments and individual companies are especially vigilant about denying business opportunities to countries that mistreat their citizens. They are concerned about conducting trade with local firms that exploit their workers, or that keep costs down by employing young children or prisoners for slave wages.

Canadian firms that wish to expand their operations overseas often are enticed by the very low wages they can pay to local workers. Although they provide needed jobs, some companies have been criticized for exploiting workers by paying wages that fall below even local poverty levels, for damaging the environment, and for selling poorly made or unsafe items to foreign consumers.

Levi Strauss & Co. operates in more than 60 countries worldwide, and it has been singled out for its dedication to what CEO Robert Haas calls "responsible commercial success." This philosophy emphasizes the adoption of ethical business practices that encourage workforce diversity, honesty, and a concern for human rights. A company task force developed guidelines for doing business abroad, taking into account working conditions, the environment, and human rights. In Bangladesh, Levi Strauss grew concerned about child labour violations when it discovered that girls as young as 11 were working full-time sewing its Dockers pants. While allowing the children to keep their jobs to support their families, the company arranged to pay for their school tuition, books, and uniforms.[61] However, even Levi Strauss was the target of criticism when, in 1998, it reversed an earlier decision not to manufacture in China because of pervasive human rights violations there.[62]

A small Canadian business that is taking an ethical stance on human rights issues and trade is A Fine Balance Imports and Exports, a Whitehorse craft boutique run by Stefanie Konkin, a twentysomething entrepreneur. Konkin, who imports products mostly from developing countries, personally visits all of the plants that she purchases from to ensure that good working conditions are in place. She also puts 10% of her profits toward international development projects. Customers like her ethical practices as well. As Konkin contends, "People just feel better when they're responding with a conscience to global issues."[63]

The Cultural Environment

After a firm clears the political and legal issues that can hamper entry into foreign markets, it still needs to understand and adapt to the customs, characteristics, and practices of its citizens. Basic beliefs about such cultural priorities as the role of family or proper relations between the sexes affect people's responses to products and promotional messages. In the late 1970s, Procter & Gamble introduced Pampers diapers in Japan. Although successful in Canada and the United States, this product did not sell well in Japan, because P&G neglected some important cultural differences between North American and Japanese parents. One was that the typical Japanese mom changes her baby's diaper about 14 times a day, twice as often as her North American counterpart. Pampers were too expensive for a Japanese mother to use. The company also learned to promote a white unisex diaper in Asia despite the popularity of colour-coded ones in North America. When women chose a pink package, they admitted they had a daughter—but male children are much more desired in many Asian cultures.[64]

VALUES

cultural values A society's deeply held beliefs about right and wrong ways to live.

collectivist culture A culture in which people subordinate their personal goals to those of a stable community.

Every society has a set of **cultural values**, or deeply held beliefs about right and wrong ways to live, that it imparts to its members.[65] For example, cultures differ in their emphasis on collectivism versus individualism. In **collectivist cultures**, such as those found in Venezuela, Pakistan, Taiwan, Thailand, Turkey, Greece, and Portugal, people subordinate their personal goals to those of a stable community. In contrast, consumers in **individualist cultures**, such as those in Canada, the United States, Australia, Great Britain, and the Netherlands tend to attach more importance to personal goals. People in these cultures are more likely to change memberships when the demands of the group become too costly.[66] Consistent with this difference, a study by the research firm Wirthlin Worldwide found that the most important values to Asian executives are hard work, respect for learning, and group loyalty. In contrast, North American businesspeople emphasize the values of personal freedom, self-reliance, and freedom of expression.[67] It is vital that marketers understand these differences. For example, a perfume advertising slogan like "Cachet. As individual as you are," which successfully appeals to North American women, would not go over as well in a collectivist culture.

Values can show up in strange ways. For example, Japanese culture is well known for its emphasis on the value of cleanliness. When people give money as a wedding gift, they often iron the bills before placing them in the envelope. Some laundromats even allow customers to rinse out the inside of a machine before using it. As Exhibit 4.4 shows, Tokyo bus drivers and cab drivers wear immaculate white gloves while working.

The value of cleanliness has reached new proportions. Demand for products such as antiseptic bicycle grips and karaoke microphones and gauze masks is skyrocketing, and a plethora of sterilized products, ranging from stationery and floppy disks to telephones and dishwashers, is invading the market. Pentel makes a germ-free pen decorated with a medical blue cross; the popular brand is advertised with the slogan, "The pen is mightier than the bacterium." Japan's Sanwa Bank literally "launders money" for its customers in specially designed ATM machines, whereas Tokyo's Mitsubishi Bank opened a "total anti-germ branch" featuring ATMs with surfaces made of plastics saturated with chemicals that resist bacteria and fungus. A bank spokesperson noted that the branch is especially popular with young female customers, who say they "don't want to touch things handled by middle-aged men."[68]

NORMS AND CUSTOMS

Values are general ideas about good and bad behaviours. From these flow **norms**, or specific rules dictating what is right or wrong, acceptable or unacceptable. Specific types of norms include:[69]

- A **custom** is a norm handed down from the past that controls basic behaviours, such as division of labour in a household.
- A **more** is a custom with a strong moral overtone. A more often involves a *taboo*, or forbidden behaviour, such as incest or cannibalism. Violation of a more often meets with strong punishment from other members of a society.

✳ ✳ ✳
individualist culture A culture in which people tend to attach more importance to personal goals than to those of the larger community.

✳ ✳ ✳
norms The specific rules dictating what is right or wrong, acceptable or unacceptable.

✳ ✳ ✳
custom A norm handed down from the past that controls basic behaviours.

✳ ✳ ✳
more A custom with a strong moral overtone.

Exhibit 4.4

The Japanese emphasis on the value of cleanliness is evident in the white gloves that cab drivers wear.

✳ ✳ ✳
convention A norm regarding the conduct of everyday life.

• A **convention** is a norm regarding the conduct of everyday life. Conventions deal with the subtleties of consumer behaviour, including the "correct" way to furnish one's house, wear one's clothes, and host a dinner party.

All three types of norms may determine what behaviours are appropriate in different countries. For example, a more may tell us what kind of food is permissible to eat. A meal of dog may be taboo in Canadian culture, whereas Hindus would shun beef, and Muslims avoid pork products. A custom dictates the appropriate hour at which the meal should be served—many Europeans and Latin Americans do not begin dinner until around 9:00 p.m. Conventions tell us how to eat the meal, including such details as the utensils, table etiquette, and even the appropriate apparel to be worn at dinnertime.

A global marketer must learn about the characteristics of people in different countries and adapt to local practices to avoid insulting local business partners. A vice-president at Caterpillar, Inc., a company that exports over $3 billion in farm and industrial products per year, certainly demonstrated a willingness to understand unfamiliar customs. While toasting a new business relationship with a Saudi sheik, he was expected to eat what the Saudis regard as the choicest part of a lamb—its eyes. His reaction sums up what you sometimes must do to succeed in foreign cultures: "You just swallow hard and do it."[70]

Careful analysis of cultural differences can lead to success, even in foreign markets considered difficult to crack. Until 1995, Procter & Gamble didn't even sell dish soap in Japan, but now its Joy brand is the top seller (see Exhibit 4.5). P&G offered new technology and packaging (providing the soap in cylinders instead of fat-necked bottles that took up more space) that let crowded Japanese grocery stores make more money, and spent heavily on oddball commercials that created a buzz. The company even sent researchers to watch how Japanese homemakers wash their dishes. They found that most women squirted out more detergent than was needed—a clear sign of frustration with the weak products available—and P&G cornered the market by convincing consumers that Joy was more powerful than other soaps.[71]

Conflicting customs can be a problem when Canadian marketers try to conduct business in other countries where executives have different ideas about what is proper or expected. One small company Getting Through Customs Inc. (www.getcustoms.com) has developed a business to assist executives in understanding international business etiquette. Their PASSPORT database, which can be accessed through their Web site, will educate a traveller on such things as local customs, appropriate business gifts, conversation styles, and negotiating tactics. For example, their report on Columbia includes this advice: "Take the time to greet everyone formally. Give the person you are greeting your undivided attention. Men shake hands with each other and with women. Women choose whether or not to shake hands with other women; sometimes women will clasp each other's forearms instead. Friends are expected to hug and exchange kisses on the cheeks. When men hug each other, they often add a backslap or two."[72]

Exhibit 4.5

Procter & Gamble's Joy Liquid succeeded in Japan due to a careful analysis of cultural differences.

Country customs also differ in the area of bribery. In Japan, bribery is called *kuroi kiri* (black mist); in Germany, it's *schmiergeld* (grease money); whereas Mexicans refer to *la mordida* (the bite); the French say *pot-de-vin* (jug of wine); and the Italians speak of the *bustarella* (little envelope). They're all talking about *baksheesh*, the Middle Eastern term for tip or gratuity.

In many cultures, business success depends as much on *baksheesh* as on luck or ability. *Bribery* occurs when someone voluntarily offers payment to get an illegal advantage. *Extortion* occurs when payment is extracted under duress by someone in authority.[73] Bribes are given to speed up required work, to secure a contract, or to avoid having one cancelled, and they are a way of life in many countries. Canada is one of several countries that has signed an Organization of Economic Co-operation and Development (OECD) Convention to fight bribery. Under the Convention, members will impose criminal sanctions (such as fines or imprisonment) on someone caught trying to bribe a foreign public official.[74]

SYMBOLS AND SUPERSTITIONS

On the surface, many marketing images have virtually no literal connection to actual products. What does a dog named Fido have to do with a cell phone? How can a celebrity such as Wayne Gretzky enhance the image of a soft drink or pain reliever? The meanings we impart to these symbols are largely influenced by our culture, so marketers need to take special care that the symbol they use in a foreign market has the meaning they intended. Even the same product may be used quite differently and take on a different meaning to people. In parts of rural India, for example, the refrigerator is a status symbol, so people want a snazzy looking one that they can keep in the living room to show off to visitors.[75]

Faces, the Canadian cosmetics company that operates in several international markets including Singapore, realized that promotional material created for Valentine's Day had to include wording that was vague enough to be meaningful both in markets like Canada, where Valentine's Day is celebrated, and in markets like Singapore, where Valentine's Day is not celebrated. The final wording chosen for the special heart-shaped tent card was: "Heart and Soul. Care for the body you love."[76]

For help in understanding how consumers interpret the meanings of symbols, some marketers are turning to a field of study known as **semiotics**, which examines how meanings are assigned to symbols.[77] For example, although the cowboy on packs of Marlboro cigarettes is a well-known symbol of the frontier spirit in many countries, people in Hong Kong see him as a low-status labourer. Philip Morris has to make sure he's always pictured riding a white horse, which is a more positive symbol in that country. Even something as simple as a colour takes on very different meanings around the globe. Pepsodent toothpaste found this out when it promised white teeth to people in Southeast Asia, where black or yellow teeth are status symbols.

Marketers also need to be concerned about taboos and superstitions. For example, the Japanese are superstitious about the number four. *Shi*, the word for four, is also the word for death, so Tiffany sells glassware and china in sets of five in Japan. In Arab countries, alcohol and pork are forbidden to Islamic consumers (even stuffed pig toys are taboo), and advertisers can't show nudity or even the faces of women in photos, because these are outlawed by the government.[78]

LANGUAGE

Language barriers can be big obstacles to marketers breaking into foreign markets. These barriers affect product labelling and usage instructions, advertising, and personal selling. It's vital for marketers to work with local people who understand the subtleties of language to avoid the confusion that may result.

For example, the meaning of a brand name—one of the most important signals a marketer can send about the character and quality of a product—can get mangled as it travels around the world. Local product names often raise eyebrows to visiting Canadians, who may be surprised to stumble upon a Japanese coffee creamer called Creap, or a Mexican bread named Bimbo.[79]

✳ ✳ ✳
semiotics The field of study that examines how meanings are assigned to symbols.

ETHNOCENTRICITY

Even if a firm succeeds in getting its products into an international market, there's no guarantee that local consumers will be interested. Sometimes a willingness to try products made elsewhere comes slowly. In marketing, the tendency to prefer products or people of one's own culture over those from other countries is called **ethnocentrism**. For example, the French tend to be a bit finicky about their cuisine, and food products from other countries are evaluated critically. However, the upscale British department store Marks & Spencer is making inroads in France selling English-style sandwiches like egg and watercress on whole wheat bread and ethnic dishes such as chicken *tikka masala* that are not widely found in Paris. Viewed as convenience foods for young office workers, these foreign choices are less expensive than the traditional French loaf split down the middle and lathered with butter and ham or Camembert cheese. So, ethnocentrism can be overcome, but it does take time.

In addition, ethnocentric consumers are likely to feel it is ethically wrong to buy products from other countries because they want to support their domestic economy. Some consumers in the United States, for example, believe that purchasing products made outside the US is "un-American," an attitude that creates a potential challenge for Canadian marketers operating in that market.

However, it seems likely that ethnocentrism will become less of a problem in the US over time, as people get more accustomed to the idea of living in a global society. In fact, several Canadian products, such as Clearly Canadian beverages, Moosehead beer, and Eau Canada, a perfume, have been successful with US consumers by positioning themselves as distinctively Canadian (see Exhibit 4.6).

CULTURAL CHANGE

Marketers need to understand cultural differences, but they also must realize that the global landscape is constantly changing. Just as it's important to engage in political risk assessment, it's also imperative to monitor changes in cultural values and behaviours to ensure that marketing strategies are keeping up. For example, worldly consumers are increasingly interested in sampling foods and other products from around the globe.

Since 1978, the Europe-based Research Institute on Social Change (RISC) has conducted international measurements of social change in more than 40 countries. Surveys include questions on values and attitudes, behaviour, and media usage. This type of comprehensive, ongoing project provides a broad understanding of cultural currents, which makes it possible to anticipate changes in one country before these spread to others. For example, widespread concern for the environment first appeared in Sweden in the early 1970s, in France in the beginning of the 1980s, and finally in Spain in the early 1990s.

✳ ✳ ✳

ethnocentrism The tendency to prefer products or people of one's own culture.

they say that
purple represents vanity.
i have to agree.
i'm my own favourite flavour.

we both share a belief
in healthy living.
can i be part of your life?

clearly canadian.

seeclearlynow

Exhibit 4.6

The Canadian firm Clearly Canadian Beverage Corp. has found that being Canadian is an advantage in the US market.

SPOTLIGHT ON REAL PEOPLE *G.A.P. Adventures Inc.*

Bruce Poon Tip, the barely 30-year-old president and CEO of G.A.P. Adventures Inc. of Toronto (www.gap.ca), is an international marketer, who knows the importance of thinking globally and acting locally. In fact, to better understand local culture in the countries where he operates, he routinely travels the globe with his customers. G.A.P. Adventures arranges and operates international ecotours for people in 21 countries. Identified as one of the fastest growing businesses in Canada, the company has revenues of about $7.8 million per year and currently offers over 700 small-group tour packages to locations throughout North, Central, and South America, Asia, Africa, and Australia. Since knowledge of each tour location is critical to the success of the company, each trip is led by an experienced tour leader, who is a specialist in the local area's culture, language, and environment.

An important part of Poon Tip's business is ecotourism. He is currently a consultant on ecotourism for the World Bank and Conservation International and claims that "G.A.P. has become a model for sustainable tourism. We're starting some local community projects to teach communities to sustain themselves through tourism, giving them alternatives to logging or being involved in the drug trade. I couldn't have achieved anything without these communities; [they] made us successful. G.A.P. has proven that ecotourism can work hand in hand with conservation and be profitable at the same time."

The company's tours range in price from $1295 to $2395, and primarily target adventuresome, educated travellers who are looking for vacations where they can experience different cultures. As the company Web site states, "Great Adventure People come from all backgrounds and ages, but are like-minded in attitude and what they want out of their vacations. They are tired of the week-on-the-beach standard holiday, and uncomfortable with the luxury holidays which distance you from the full story—this is the attitude of a Great Adventure Person." The company has recently extended its products and introduced G.A.P. Plus, travel packages for people aged 55 and older, who may be looking for a less physically rigorous vacation than many of the tours offered to younger groups.

The promotional activities for G.A.P. Adventures' tours have included the use of their Web site and travel brochures, but perhaps their most powerful sales tool is their cross-Canada road show, set up in theatres and churches, featuring speakers from around the world and film and slide shows. To further extend these promotional activities and to increase his presence among US customers, Poon Tip is currently developing a television program with a production company in Atlanta, which will highlight the company's tours. Only about 10% of the company's revenues now come from the United States, but the company views this as an important growth market for the future.[80]

1. What are the benefits that G.A.P. Adventures Inc. offers its customers?
2. How can the company learn more about potential customers in the US?
3. Visit the G.A.P. Adventures Web site. Do you think that the company's promotional efforts, including the Web site, need to be different when targeting US versus Canadian customers? Why or why not?

Based on sophisticated statistical analyses, RISC places people into one of the 10 segments shown in Figure 4.3. Analysts can track changes in these clusters over time. For example, between 1989 and 1996, the British population moved in the direction of stability, ethics, and community, and began to hold a more globally-oriented view of the world. This helps explain why the British are more sympathetic to the idea of the European Union than they used to be, and it also highlights the need for marketers to be sensitive to environmental concerns the British may have about new products introduced there.[81]

G.A.P. Adventures Inc.
www.gap.ca

How "Global" Should a Global Marketing Strategy Be?

Understanding all the economic, legal, and cultural differences around the world can be a daunting task, not to mention understanding the complexity of world trade. But if a firm decides to expand beyond its home country, it must make important decisions about how to structure its business and also how to adapt its product marketing strategy to accommodate local needs.

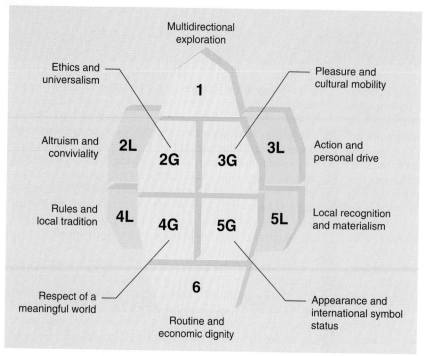

Figure 4.3 The Ten RISC Segments

Source: Michael R. Solomon, Gary Bamossy, and Søren Askegaard, *Consumer Behaviour: A European Perspective*, London: Prentice Hall Europe, 1999: 410; "RISC methodology," RISC International, Paris, 1997: 14.

First, the company must decide on the nature of its commitment, including whether it will partner with another firm or go it alone. Then it must make specific decisions about the marketing mix for a particular product or service. In this final section, we'll consider issues related to global strategy at these two levels: the company and the product.

Company-Level Decisions: Choosing a Market Entry Strategy

A firm deciding to go global must determine the level of commitment it is willing to make to operate in another country. This commitment can range from casual involvement to a full-scale "marriage." At one extreme, the firm can simply export its products; at the other, it can directly invest in another country by buying a foreign subsidiary or opening its own stores. The decision about the extent of commitment involves a trade-off between control and risk. Direct involvement gives the firm more control over what happens in the country, but risk also increases if the operation is not successful. Let's review four strategies representing increased levels of involvement: exporting, contractual arrangements, strategic alliances, and direct investment. These are summarized in Figure 4.4.

EXPORTING

If a firm chooses to export, it must decide whether it will attempt to sell its products on its own or rely on intermediaries to represent it in the target country. These representatives are specialists known as **export merchants**, who understand the local market and can find buyers and negotiate terms.[82]

An exporting strategy allows a firm to sell its products in global markets and cushions the firm against downturns in its domestic market. Because the exported products are produced at home, the firm is able to maintain control over design and production decisions.[83]

In some cases, however, these advantages may be offset by foreign barriers to entry, such as tariffs, or negated by local content laws requiring that the products have a proportion of components made in the importing country. For example, Japan's Nippon Telephone & Telegraph Company used product specifications as a trade barrier when it was forced to accept bids from foreign firms. The communications giant created specifications that fit only

✷ ✷ ✷

export merchant An intermediary that a firm uses to represent it in another country.

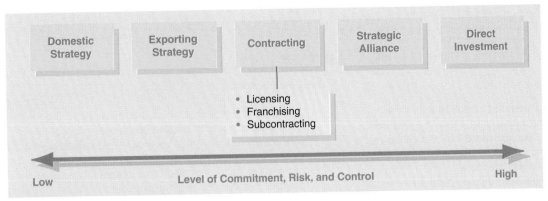

Figure 4.4 Market Entry Strategies

existing Japanese products—and neglected to provide details in any language but Japanese.[84] Exporting firms found it hard to meet that kind of challenge.

CONTRACTUAL AGREEMENTS

The next level of commitment a firm can make to a foreign market is a contractual agreement with a company in that country to conduct some or all of its business there. These linkages can take several forms. Two of the most common are licensing and franchising.

In a **licensing** agreement a firm (the licenser) gives another firm (the licensee) the right to produce and market its product in a specific country or region in return for royalties. Because the licensee produces the product in its home market, it can avoid many of the barriers to entry that the licenser would have encountered. However, the licenser also loses control over how the product is produced and marketed, so if the licensee does a poor job, the company's reputation may be tarnished.

Franchising is a form of licensing involving the right to adapt an entire way of doing business in the host country. Franchising is a particularly attractive market entry strategy for "soft service" businesses, such as restaurants or hotels, where the service provision requires the physical presence of both the consumer and the service provider.[85] Yogen Fruz World-Wide (www.yogenfruz.com), the Canadian frozen dessert company, has used franchising as its main mode of entry into international markets. The company currently has 4900 franchise locations in 80 countries and anticipates the opening of another 500 franchises in the German market alone over the next couple of years.[86] As with licensing, there is a risk to the parent company if the franchisee does not use the same quality ingredients or procedures, so firms like Yogen Fruz monitor these operations carefully. In fact, in several markets, Yogen Fruz has had to find or create local production to support its franchises.

STRATEGIC ALLIANCES

Firms seeking an even deeper commitment to a foreign market develop a **strategic alliance** with one or more domestic firms in the target country. These relationships often take the form of a **joint venture**, in which a new entity owned by two or more firms is created to allow the partners to pool their resources for common goals. Strategic alliances also allow companies easy access to new markets, especially as these partnerships often bring with them preferential treatment in the partner's home country. Telesat Canada, a satellite company based in Ottawa, has entered into a joint venture with InSight Telecommunications Corp. of Boston to distribute broadcasting and Internet services. The company is the first foreign company to offer US domestic satellite service, and their joint venture with a US firm helped in the struggle to get a license from the US government. The government has traditionally been reluctant to open that business up to foreign firms.[87]

DIRECT INVESTMENT

Another way a firm expands internationally is to make a direct investment in other countries, either by buying a business outright in the host country or building their own manufacturing or other operations. Ownership gives a firm maximum freedom and control over operations. McCain, one of the most global of Canadian firms with 85% of all sales coming

✳ ✳ ✳
licensing An agreement in which one firm gives another firm the right to produce and market its product in a specified location in return for royalties.

✳ ✳ ✳
franchising A form of licensing involving the right to adapt an entire system of doing business.

✳ ✳ ✳
strategic alliance The relationship developed between a firm seeking a deeper commitment to a foreign market and a domestic firm in the target country.

✳ ✳ ✳
joint venture A strategic alliance in which two or more firms form a new entity, allowing the partners to pool their resources for common goals.

Real People, Real Decisions
Decision Time at MTV Europe

MTV Europe's initial marketing objectives were to raise awareness and build viewership. Although promotional messages were sometimes translated into different languages, the basic approach was pan-European, reflecting MTV's slogan of "One World, One Music."

Marketing research revealed some problems, however. One was that the European teen audience was less homogeneous than MTV had presumed. Then local competition began to emerge. Several alternative local music channels started up, backed by large media groups and record labels. Competitors included Viva in Germany, Videomusic in Italy, MCM/Euromusique in France, and ZTV in Sweden.

These competitors had several advantages over MTV. They could tailor their programming to individual markets rather than to an entire continent. They could broadcast in their country's language: This gave them an edge in France and Italy, where relatively few young people speak English well enough to understand MTV. Finally, local channels were able to establish closer bonds with local advertisers and cable markets. As a result of all these factors, research revealed that many viewers felt MTV to be "foreign," with more of an American than a European identity. They had trouble bonding with MTV.

Peter Einstein faced a critical marketing mix decision regarding the best way to produce new programming for his core audience: Should MTV continue its pan-European strategy, or develop regional products? If it did adopt a regional approach, to what extent should its programming vary by country? Einstein considered three options:

Option 1. Stay with the pan-European strategy.

Option 2. Create different regional channels to compete head-to-head with local alternatives. For example, create an MTV France to compete with MCM/Euromusique.

Option 3. Maintain the pan-European entity but devote a few parts of the channel to certain regions. For example, broadcast Italian programming to the Italian audience for a few hours per day or produce local programming in English.

Now, join the MTV Europe decision team: Which option would you choose, and why?

---

from outside Canada, has invested heavily in operations in other countries. It has built plants in more than 10 countries and, for its expansion into the US in the late 1990s, it acquired a US french fry company Ore-Ida Foods Inc.[88]

Product-Level Decisions: Choosing a Marketing Mix Strategy

Marketers operating in two or more countries have a crucial decision to make: How necessary is it to develop a customized marketing mix for each country? This was the problem Peter Einstein faced as he pondered the fate of MTV Europe. As the French ad in Exhibit 4.7 shows, MTV did make some attempts to develop separate messages in each country, but its basic programming was the same across European markets.

The choice between standardization and localization can be difficult and complex. For example, as seen in Exhibit 4.8, Tower Records, the music store chain, has opened its own outlets in Taiwan, Hong Kong, and Singapore. Although Western musicians sell well in Asia, they are outsold 10 to 1 by local stars. The Chinese like sentimental love ballads, and snap up songs based on Western or Japanese tunes (Bee Gees hits sung with Chinese lyrics have gone over well).[89]

STANDARDIZATION VERSUS LOCALIZATION

Advocates of standardization argue that the world has become so small and tastes so homogeneous that basic needs and wants are the same everywhere.[90] A focus on the similarities among cultures certainly is appealing. After all, if no changes in a firm's marketing strategy had to be made to compete in foreign countries, it would realize large economies of scale, because it could spread the costs of product development and promotional mate-

Exhibit 4.7

As this French ad shows, some of MTV's messages are tailored to local markets.

rials over many markets. For example, Reebok created a new centralized product development centre to develop shoe designs that can easily cross borders.[91] Widespread, consistent exposure also helps create a global brand by forging a strong, unified image all over the world—Coca-Cola signs are visible on billboards in London and on metal roofs deep in the forests of Thailand.

In contrast, those in favour of localization feel that the world is not *that* small, and products and promotional messages should be tailored to local environments. These marketers feel that each culture is unique and that each country has a *national character*—a distinctive set of behavioural and personality characteristics.[92] Snapple failed in Japan, because consumers there didn't like the drink's cloudy appearance. Similarly, Frito-Lay Inc. stopped selling Ruffles potato chips (too salty) and Cheetos (the Japanese didn't appreciate having their fingers turn orange after eating a handful).[93]

PRODUCT DECISIONS

A firm seeking to sell a product in a foreign market has three choices. Sell the same product in the new market, modify it for the market, or develop a brand-new product for the foreign market. Let's take a closer look at each option.

- A *straight extension strategy* retains the same product for domestic and foreign markets. Coca-Cola sells the same formula in every country, and Gillette offers the same razor blades everywhere.

Exhibit 4.8

Tower Records had to localize its product selection when the music chain opened outlets in Asia.

- A *product adaptation strategy* recognizes that in many cases people in different cultures do have strong and different product preferences. Sometimes these differences can be subtle, yet important. That explains why Kellogg, which markets the identical version of its Corn Flakes and Rice Krispies brands in North America and Europe, had to remove the green "loops" from Froot Loops after research showed that Europeans felt they were too artificial looking.[94]

  In other cases, products must be adapted because varying living conditions or customs require different designs. When the Electrolux appliance company began selling refrigerators in Europe, it found that Northern Europeans want large refrigerators because they shop once a week in supermarkets, whereas Southern Europeans want them small because they shop daily in open-air markets. Northerners like freezers on the bottom, southerners on the top. And the British are avid purchasers of frozen foods, so they insist on a unit with 60% freezer space.[95]

- A *product invention strategy* means that a company develops a new product as it expands to foreign markets. Ford's "world cars," including the Probe model shown in the Dutch ad in Exhibit 4.9, are being sold around the globe. In some cases, a product invention strategy takes the form of *backward invention*. The firm may find it needs to offer a less complex product than it sells elsewhere, such as a manually operated sewing machine or a hand-powered clothes washer to people without access to a reliable source of electricity.

In India, Coca-Cola bought a local brand called Thums Up, after finding that this Coke imitator was actually outselling Coke by 4 to 1. Coca-Cola abandoned the Indian market in 1977, when the government ordered the company to turn over its secret formula. By the time it returned in 1993, Thums Up had become so entrenched that Coke decided in this rare case that it was better to market a local imitator than its own brand. Coca-Cola is now making plans to export Thums Up to other Asian countries with large Indian populations.[96]

Sometimes Canadian marketers develop and launch their products in other markets before launching them in Canada. Since launching its first beverage in the late 1980s, Clearly Canadian has always launched new products in major cities in the US before selling in the Canadian market. The company contends that if the product is successful in the US, the Canadian launch is made easier. As the vice-president of marketing, Jonathan Cronin, says, "If you're successful there, you draw attention to yourself, and that's the best advertising you can do."[97]

De Probe is er.

Exhibit 4.9

The Ford Probe was developed to be a "world car," an example of a product invention strategy.

PROMOTION DECISIONS

The marketer must also decide whether it's necessary to change product promotions in a foreign market. Some firms endorse the idea that the same message will appeal to everyone around the world. The advertising director for the Unisys Corporation, a company that specializes in computers, explained the decision to launch a standardized global campaign: "Now they are seeing the same message, the same company, the same look wherever they go. That really stretches my advertising dollars."[98]

Unisys's decision to adopt a global message illustrates one key to the success of a standardized strategy: It is more likely to work if there are not unique cultural factors affecting the purchase—computer buyers tend to have more in common than, say, perfume buyers. This "one world, one message" strategy also has a greater chance of success if the firm's target customers live in cosmopolitan urban areas where they regularly see images from different countries. The Swedish ad for Diesel jeans in Exhibit 4.10 includes imagery from North Korea to appeal to these "global consumers."

For such a campaign to succeed, the message should focus on basic concepts, such as romance or family ties, because these are likely to be understood everywhere. For example, Unilever promotes its Impulse Body Spray worldwide by employing the theme "boy meets girl," and Nescafé dwells on the warmth of a shared cup of coffee around the world.[99]

Fans of a localization strategy, on the other hand, feel that cultural differences translate into market differences, which may in turn call for different advertising strategies. When Tim Hortons moved into the US market, for example, it faced a completely undeveloped "morning market" in that country for coffee and baked goods. Many US customers were grabbing a cup of coffee at a local gas station on their way to work. Tim Hortons strategy became one of creating a morning market by using an advertising tag line: "Morning people. Where do they come from?" This strategy contrasted to their focus on lunch menu items, such as sandwiches and chili, in the Canadian market.[100]

PRICE DECISIONS

Costs associated with transportation, tariffs, and differences in currency exchange rates often make the product more expensive for a company to make or sell in foreign markets compared to its home country. Aside from cost factors, sometimes a higher price is charged in international markets because consumers there value the uniqueness of the product. Kokanee beer, for example, is sold for $1 more per six-pack than its American competitors, because their American consumers place a higher value on a product that is Canadian.[101]

Exhibit 4.10

Some promotions, such as this ad for Diesel jeans, are not tailored to specific foreign markets.

Real People, Real Decisions
How it worked out at MTV Europe

MTV Europe chose Option 3. The company retained its pan-European channel and, using digital compression technology, it was able to split its signal and transmit different channel feeds to different countries. This allowed some limited customization, including local advertising, for these countries while still retaining most of the international programming and positioning.

MTV Europe continues to believe that one of its major strengths is that it unites an entire continent of young people. Peter Einstein and his colleagues feel that teenagers in Oslo and Milan have more in common with each other than with their parents. By maintaining its pan-European strategy and introducing some local variations, the network can tailor the programming mix to each country. MTV has worked hard to build a strong brand image, and Einstein did not want to dilute its audience. The network still has the unique advantage of being able to bring international stars into the local

market by broadcasting such shows as the European Music Awards in Berlin, which is the premiere music award show in Europe.

Einstein broke MTV's marketing objectives into two areas that addressed the overall priorities of the channel as a "brand," and the needs of individual territories to counter local competition and satisfy local tastes. MTV "had its cake and ate it, too" by continuing to broadcast its pan-European programming across Europe, while developing local programming and off-air activities to build even greater loyalty. MTV frequently presents tours by local music groups. The tours are promoted through the local press and radio stations. MTV is now evaluating how well its decision worked to see if Europe views it as an international, cosmopolitan "brand," or as a local network. As the global landscape continues to change, companies like MTV continue to search for ways to think globally and act locally.

※ ※ ※
grey market The importing of products by an unauthorized party, who then sells them for a fraction of the price.

※ ※ ※
dumping Pricing products lower in a foreign market than they are offered in the home market.

One danger of pricing too high is that competitors will find ways to offer the product at a lower price, even if this is done illegally. A **grey market** exists when an unauthorized party imports products and then sells them for a fraction of the price. Goods such as watches, cameras, and perfumes often move through the grey market—Seiko estimates that one out of every four of its watches brought into the United States is unauthorized.[102]

A company can also run into trouble if it tries to price a product too low to establish it in a new market. Some countries outlaw a practice called **dumping**, in which a company tries to get a toehold in a foreign market by pricing its products lower than they are offered at home—often removing excess supply from home markets and keeping prices up there. In one case, Eastman Kodak accused Japanese rival Fuji Photo Film of selling colour photographic paper in the United States for as little as a quarter of what it charges in Japan.[103]

DISTRIBUTION DECISIONS

Getting the product to foreign consumers is half the battle. Marketers used to dealing with a handful of large wholesalers or retailers may have to rely instead on thousands of small stores, or they may run into problems finding a way to package, refrigerate, or store goods for long periods of time in less developed countries.

Sometimes similar distribution arrangements across countries are possible and present an advantage for companies. For McCain Foods, for instance, entering the South American market was made easier because of existing distribution arrangements with McDonald's restaurants in markets like North America. McDonald's started its expansion in the late 1990s into Brazil, Chile, Uruguay, Paraguay, and Argentina by building close to 400 McDonald's outlets. McCain, a supplier for McDonald's restaurants in North America, was asked to supply the 25 000 tonnes of frozen fries a year needed to supply the South American restaurants. To fulfill that need and keep up with the McDonald's expansion plans in the region, which meant opening a new restaurant about every four days until the year 2000, McCain built a plant in Argentina. Having established production and distribution in the region, McCain then began to explore other distribution arrangements for its products, namely the fast-growing frozen food grocery segment in South America. It is estimated that Argentina, Brazil, and Chile have the fastest-growing frozen food markets in the Western hemisphere.[104]

Establishing a reliable distribution system is essential if the marketer is to succeed in an international market. Establishing a reliable system might be especially difficult in developing countries where thousands of individual distributors (some who transport goods to remote rural areas on ox carts or bicycles) must be persuaded to take on the product. It's also essential in developed countries, where competition for shelf space may be fierce. For example, the British product Virgin Cola entered the United States market in 1998 and the Canadian market in 1999 after its successful launch in the UK in 1994. Although the product had also been successful in other European markets before coming to North America, it has not yet made a big impact in North America, partly because distribution is a key to success in the North American beverage business. With Pepsi and Coca-Cola controlling so much of the distribution in North America, new entrants like Virgin have a difficult time getting their product distributed in this market.[105]

Chapter Summary

1. Explain how complex relationships among firms, countries, and regions influence world trade.
A country's stage of economic development determines a global firm's marketing opportunities. In less developed countries, opportunities are usually limited to agricultural or mining products. In developing countries, such as those in Eastern Europe, Latin America, and the Pacific Rim, an industrial-based economy is evolving, and the rising middle class creates great demand for basic consumer goods. Developed countries, such as Japan, have highly sophisticated marketing systems and offer almost limitless marketing opportunities for goods and services. A company's prospects for success in both domestic and foreign markets are helped if it has a competitive advantage, which occurs when conditions in its home country make it easier to compete. In some areas of the globe, countries have banded together to form economic communities to promote international trade. These economic communities include the economic alliance established by the North American Free Trade Agreement (NAFTA) and the European Union (EU).

2. Understand how political, legal, and cultural issues influence global marketing strategies and outcomes.
In some cases a government adopts a policy of protectionism—it enforces rules designed to give home companies an advantage. It may shield its own industries from foreign competition with red tape tactics, impose tariffs that increase the costs of foreign goods, require that a certain percentage of goods sold in the country be made with domestically produced components, or set quotas on the amount of products it will allow to be imported. In addition, a firm may have to adapt to the country's values, customs, and language. A value is a strongly held belief that something is right or wrong, and products that appeal to people in one country because they promote one value may turn off those in another country.

3. Explain the strategies a firm can use to enter global markets.
Different foreign market entry strategies represent varying levels of commitment for a firm. Exporting goods entails little commitment but also allows the firm little control over how its products are sold. A greater commitment for a firm involves a contractual agreement strategy, such as licensing or franchising. An even greater commitment to a foreign market occurs when a firm forms a strategic alliance with one or more companies in the host country. Finally, the firm can choose to invest directly by buying an existing company or starting a foreign subsidiary in the host country.

4. Understand the arguments for standardization versus localization of marketing strategies in global markets, and understand how elements of the marketing mix apply in international markets.

Firms that operate in two or more countries can choose to standardize their marketing strategies by using the same approach in all countries, or to localize by adopting different strategies for each market. Proponents of the standardization perspective focus on similarities across countries. Supporters of the localization perspective seek to adapt to the national character of each country. The firm needs to decide if the product it currently sells can be sold in the new market, if it needs to be modified, or if a brand-new product must be developed. Similarly, in many cases, the promotional strategy must be tailored to fit the needs of consumers in another country, who may not be able to relate to the messages used at home. The product may need to be priced differently, especially if income levels are not the same in the new market. Finally, different methods of distribution may be needed, especially in countries lacking a solid infrastructure that provides adequate transportation, communications, and storage facilities.

Chapter Review

Marketing Concepts: Testing Your Knowledge

1. What are domestic firms, exporting firms, multinational firms, and global firms?

2. Describe the market conditions that influence a firm's decision to enter international markets.

3. How do governments develop policies and regulations that protect home companies? How have GATT and the WTO reduced protectionism?

4. What are economic communities? How have they changed global marketing opportunities?

5. How are countries classified according to their level of economic development? What marketing opportunities are available in countries in each stage of economic development?

6. What aspects of the political and legal environment influence a firm's decision to enter an international market?

7. What cultural factors in a country influence a foreign firm's ability to succeed there?

8. How is a firm's level of commitment related to its level of control in a foreign market? Describe the four levels of involvement that are options for a firm.

9. What are the arguments for standardization of marketing strategies in the global marketplace? What are the arguments for localization? What are some ways a firm can standardize or localize its marketing mix?

Marketing Concepts: Discussing Choices and Issues

1. Do you think Canadian firms should be allowed to use bribes to compete in countries where bribery is an accepted and legal form of doing business? Why or why not?

2. Some countries have been critical of the exporting of North American culture by such businesses as Coca-Cola. Do you think this attitude is reasonable? Explain your thinking.

3. Trade regulations and protectionism are important political issues in Canada. Do economic communities increase or decrease protectionism? What do you think are the positive and negative aspects of protectionist policies for Canadian firms?

4. Every society has its own unique cultural environment. People in developed countries such as Canada are often critical of some of the values and customs of less developed countries where, for example, it may be legal for children to work long hours in factories with health and safety hazards and where the rights of women and minorities are not protected. Do firms that wish to do business in these countries need to accept all such cultural differences without question, or should they work to change the culture? Should firms from Canada and other developed countries totally avoid markets in which there are human rights violations? What are the pros and cons of entering such markets?

Marketing Practice: **Applying What You've Learned**

1. Assume you are a marketing manager for a manufacturer of personal computers. Your company is considering strategic opportunities abroad, and your boss has asked you to assess the possibilities for entering the following countries: Kenya, Costa Rica, Poland, and France.

   a. Based on what you've read in this chapter, identify the pros and cons of marketing your products in each of the four countries.

   b. Tell which country you think should be the primary target for your company, and why.

2. Assume that your firm is interested in the global market potential for over-the-counter pain medicines in the following countries: South Africa, Japan, and Mexico.

   a. Prepare a summary of the demographic, economic, and cultural differences you expect to find in these countries.

   b. Tell how the differences might affect marketing strategies for over-the-counter medicines.

3. McDonald's fast food, Ford automobiles, and Pampers disposable diapers are very different products that are marketed globally.

   a. Outline the reasons each of these companies might choose to:

      1. standardize its product strategies

      2. localize its product strategies

      3. standardize its promotion strategies

      4. localize its promotion strategies

   b. Organize a debate in your class to argue the merits of the standardization perspective versus the localization perspective.

4. Although most large corporations have already made the decision to go global, many small- to mid-size firms are only now considering such a move. Consider a small firm that manufactures gas barbecue grills.

   a. What type of market entry strategy (exporting, contractual agreement, strategic alliance, or direct investment) do you feel would be best for the firm? Why?

   b. How would you recommend that the firm implement the strategy? That is, what type of product, price, promotion, and distribution strategies would you suggest?

Marketing Mini-Project: **Learning by Doing**

The purpose of this mini-project is to begin to develop an understanding of a culture other than your own and how customer differences lead to changes in the ways marketing strategies are implemented in that culture.

1. As part of a small group, select a country you would like to know more about and a product you think could be successful in that market. As a first step, gather information about the country. Many campuses have international students representing many countries. If possible, find students from the country and talk with them about the country. You will probably also wish to investigate other sources of information, such as books and magazines found in your library, or information from the Internet.

2. Prepare a summary of your findings, which includes the following:

   a. An overall description of the country, including such factors as its history, economy, and religions, that might affect marketing of the product you have selected.

   b. The current status of this product in the country.

   c. Your prediction for the future success of the product in the country.

   d. Your recommendations for a product strategy (product design, packaging, brand name, price, and so on).

   e. Your recommendations for promotional strategies.

3. Present your findings and recommendations to the class.

Real People, Real Surfers: **Exploring the Web**

For this exercise, you must first select a less developed or developing country of interest to you. Assume that you are the director of marketing for a firm that manufactures bicycles. You are considering entering the market in the country you have selected. You recognize that businesses must carefully weigh opportunities for global marketing. Use the Internet to gather information that would be useful in your firm's decision. The following Web sites may be useful to you as a starting point; however, there are other sites that would be helpful in gathering information on your chosen market.

The Department of Foreign Affairs and International Trade

www.dfait-maeci.gc.ca

InfoExport at the Department of Foreign Affairs and International Trade

www.infoexport.gc.ca

Strategis: Canada's Business Information Source

www.strategis.ic.gc.ca

Industry Canada Corporate Information Site

www.info.ic.gc.ca/cmb/welcomeic.nsf/icPages/Menu-e

CIA Guide to Country Profiles

www.odci.gov/cia/publications/factbook/country.html

International Monetary Fund

www.imf.org/

Write a report that answers the following questions:

1. What are the physical characteristics of the country (geography, weather, natural resources, and so forth)?

2. Describe the economy of the country.

3. What is the country's investment climate?

4. What trade regulations will your firm face in entering the country?

5. What is the country's political climate? Are there obvious political risks?

6. Based on this information, what overall strategy do you recommend for your firm—exporting, a contractual agreement, a strategic alliance, or direct investment?

7. What are your specific recommendations for implementing the strategy?

8. As a final part of your report, describe the Internet sites you used to gather this information. Which sites were most useful, and why?

MARKETING IN ACTION

Krispy Kreme Doughnuts Inc.

Serving hot, fresh doughnuts is the trademark of US-based doughnut chain Krispy Kreme. The company has developed a cult-like following in the US and is a favourite of many Hollywood celebrities. The Smithsonian Institution has even declared Krispy Kreme to be a national treasure. Until recently, the company only sold its doughnuts in the US market. Seeing an opportunity north of the border, however, the company has now expanded into Canada, with plans for 50 stores across the country.

The choice of Canada for the company's first international expansion was partly driven by the recognition that Canadians love doughnuts. Consumption of doughnuts per person is higher in Canada than in the US, and in fact it is higher than any other country in the world. However, competition is also intense. There are over 3200 doughnut shops in Canada and Tim Hortons, the leading doughnut seller, has become a Canadian cultural institution. With over 1900 Tim Hortons outlets in Canada, one of Krispy Kreme's main tasks will be to convince Canadians to switch from Tim Hortons.

Krispy Kreme, founded in 1937, has 154 outlets in the US and annual sales of over $300 million. The company has been engaged in aggressive expansion over the past decade, expanding from just a few stores in the eastern part of the country. It plans further US expansion over the next few years as it expands further into Canada.

Inside every Krispy Kreme store is a doughnut-making machine, visible to patrons, which can produce 3000 doughnuts per hour. As soon as a fresh batch of doughnuts is made, a neon sign in the window is lit announcing "Hot Doughnuts Now." That is the only advertising the company does in the US. Unlike the multimillion dollar advertising budgets of its competitors, Krispy Kreme relies on word of mouth when it opens a store in the US. For example, before a new store opens, the company puts out a sign that announces the new store and provides a phone number. If people call they are asked if they would like to become a Krispy Kreme ambassador. The ambassadors are sent T-shirts and coupons and are asked to hand them out to their friends and to convince them to visit the store. Currently there are 600 or 700 ambassadors in each market in the US where there is a Krispy Kreme store.

The company also places its products on TV shows in order to generate awareness and publicity. Krispy Kreme doughnuts and their characteristic white with green polka dot boxes have appeared on *Ally McBeal, ER, That 70's Show* and *The Rosie O'Donnell Show*. While some of these product placements are paid for, many occur simply because celebrities want to promote the product. The results of the Krispy Kreme marketing approach are clear. While larger US competitor Dunkin' Donuts sells four million doughnuts a day in 45 000 locations, Krispy Kreme sells thee million in approximately 154 stores.

Tim Hortons, Krispy Kreme's main Canadian competitor, practises a fairly traditional style of marketing. The company has achieved $1.1 billion in annual sales by spending $70 million a year on advertising and running successful promotions (such as the "Roll up the Rim" campaign). Tim Hortons has 13% of the quick service restaurant sales in Canada, and part of its success has been the broadening of its menu. One in every three bagels sold in Canada is now sold by Tim Hortons and the company also offers an expanded lunch menu including soups, sandwiches and chili. In contrast, Krispy Kreme stores only offer 22 different flavours of doughnuts and coffee.

In addition to improvements in menu, location of stores is a critical success factor for Tim Hortons. The company constantly upgrades its current outlets and establishes smaller outlets in places such as hospitals, universities and retail stores. The philosophy has been to bring the restaurant to the consumer, instead of expecting the consumer to search out the restaurant.

Krispy Kreme's initial entrance into the Canadian market was an unquestioned success. The first Canadian store opened in Mississauga, Ontario in December 2001 and in its first week broke the company's opening-week sales record by achieving $465 000 in sales. The marketing tactics used to launch the first Canadian store were different than those used in US launches.

MARKETING IN ACTION

There were no signs asking people to become Krispy Kreme ambassadors, and product placements and celebrity endorsements were not used, because such tactics have less impact with Canadian consumers. The main strategy for the Canadian store opening was a large-scale sampling of the product through a series of doughnut "drops" where a total of 60 000 doughnuts were given away throughout Mississauga and Toronto in the months leading up to the store opening. Some billboards and transit ads were also used, along with promotions such as the distribution of coupons for "buy one dozen, get one dozen for free," and toques and T-shirts (made by Roots) with the Krispy Kreme logo on them.

As Krispy Kreme continues its expansion in Canada and becomes less of a novelty product, it will inevitably be put into closer competition with Tim Hortons. In the US the "American" character of the Krispy Kreme brand has sustained its success. Judi Richardson, vice president of marketing and communications for KremeKo, claims that for the Canadian launch "…we have done, hopefully, everything we can to be as Canadian as we can with this very American brand." Since Tim Hortons is such a well-established Canadian brand, the challenge for Krispy Kreme will be to determine how to compete effectively with Tim Hortons "the Canadian way."

Sources: Based on Angela Kryhul, "The Krispy Cult," *Marketing Magazine*, 28 January 2002; "Kevin Libin, "Holey War," *Canadian Business*, 21 August 2000, 34–40; Peter Vamos, "Krispy Kreme comes to Canada," *Strategy Magazine*, 19 June 2000, 7; Scott Gardiner, "In praise of Saint Timmy", *Marketing Magazine*, 21 August 2000; www.timhortons.com, www.krispykreme.com.

THINGS TO THINK ABOUT

1. What are the elements of the Krispy Kreme brand that make it "American"? What are the elements of the Tim Hortons brand that make it "Canadian"?
2. Would you characterize Krispy Kreme's initial marketing strategy in Canada as being standardized or localized? Should Krispy Kreme continue to use the same strategy it used for the first store opening as it opens stores across Canada?
3. How should Krispy Kreme compete against Tim Hortons in the Canadian market?

PART I CASE

It's a Small World Market After All

Computer Friendly Stuff grapples to break into the North American market at the large retail chain level.

Note from CFS to students: As a student, I never bothered reading introductory material ("Is it going to be on the test?"), but trust us here. The cases at the end of each part of this text will make sense only if you read the background information on Computer Friendly Stuff on pages 115–117. Plus it's on the test—just kidding.

OK, We Need Some Seed Money...

By the middle of May 1996, it was pretty clear that I would be quitting my job and heading out on my own. I saw a market need I believed I could fill—making people's jobs more fun by creating computer toys that made their boring, beige, impersonal computers more attractive. The Original Computer Bug computer toy and screen savers were about to be born. I had tentative financing lined up, but I had to survive until then. Luckily, I had a couple of ideas. First, I remembered that Spike Lee had financed his first movie entirely on his credit cards. Second, I remembered that my sister Susie had credit cards.

After begging and promising stock options, I finally got my sister to join me in the business. We brainstormed about the future of the business, and Susie immediately pointed out that we might want to have sources of financing other than her Visa and MasterCard. "You're absolutely right," I said, reaching for her American Express. Actually, our financing came through fairly quickly. I decided early on to approach friends who were successful entrepreneurs. This was quick, and it allowed me to work with people I trusted. In exchange for 50% of the company, I raised $70 000. In retrospect, it was not enough, but I did get a brief understanding of what it feels like to be Bill Gates. Susie and I celebrated with our first brand-name canned food in six weeks. The investors' money meant that we could afford to pay for the expensive moulds required for making Computer Bug prototypes.

Look Mom, a Marketing Plan!

The prototypes took a long time to prepare, but finally we were ready to go to market. We didn't have a sales force, but we did have a marketing plan. It was one sentence long—a title. We called it "Starting at the Top." That meant we had to do most of the legwork at first. I remember walking home triumphantly from the post office after mailing out 18 samples to the 18 largest toy, gift, and computer retailers in North America, including Toys 'R' Us, CompUSA, and Wal-Mart. Confident that our product would sell itself, we sat back and waited for the first six or seven million orders to roll in. We were busy picking out interior leather from a BMW brochure one day, when Susie brought up the fact that we hadn't heard back from any of the retailers. Not to worry, I told her, snail mail is notoriously slow.

Bill and Rubeo Join the Team

It was during this period that one of our investors Bill Martens, quit his job also and joined CFS full time. Despite our slow start, Bill thought that our company had enormous potential and was attracted to its creative nature. Actually, I can honestly credit Bill with making us a company. He started by buying a filing cabinet. At about the same time, another friend, Chris Rubeo, joined us. In addition to his amazing "character voice" talent, Chris was an excellent carpenter, so he built us a shelf. We rewarded him by promoting him to bookkeeper. He had zero experience in accounting, but we took heart in the fact that our local bookstore has comfortable chairs in the small business self-help section.

'Tis the Season to Sell Bugs Anywhere You Can

Since the large retailers weren't breaking down our door, we decided to change our focus for Christmas

1997. We made cold calls to single-store retailers across the United States, using a *Yellow Pages* CD-ROM. Responses to the product concept were encouraging. I had been a sales rep for a large corporation and had never seen so many small retailers respond so well to a new product. We were in 50 stores by Christmas, but even that barely kept us afloat. So we decided to bypass retail stores and sell directly to consumers by renting a kiosk at a local mall. We also sold directly at large Christmas fairs.

Our schedule that Christmas was back-breaking, but we survived financially and learned an important lesson: Selling items one at a time stinks. No, I'm kidding: We learned that when we marketed directly to our customer, the product sold off the shelf. For example, at one Christmas show, we averaged one sale every three minutes for over ten hours! It was this type of customer response that kept us going during the rough times. But what we found even more invaluable was that we were getting to know our customer, up close and personal. We were meeting our market face to face.

We're Ready for the Big Time

During this period, we had been trying to rent space at the International Toy Fair, the largest and most important toy show in the world. Booths for new companies had been sold out two years in advance. However, just before Christmas, we found an older company willing to sublet space in its showroom. With just six weeks to prepare, we swung into action. If those mass retailers weren't going to write us back, we would go to them.

We didn't have a lot of money, which is what people say when they don't have *any* money. We decided to go the guerrilla route and focus on promotion. We spent $1000 and built our own seven-foot Computer Bug costume, which Rubeo volunteered to wear. We also had 10 000 catalogue sheets printed up. We were set to barnstorm the Toy Fair and take no prisoners.

But to take no prisoners, you have to actually meet the enemy. We arrived at the Toy Fair and discovered that our sublet was an eight-foot space with imitation wood veneer, located in the back of a decrepit model train company. The few customers that made it back our way had no interest in computer toys. We weren't having much luck with the costume either. According to show rules, Rubeo was limited to standing in our space or standing outside the building entrance on Fifth Avenue with about 25 other mascots in the freezing cold. Despite his noble efforts to throw his costumed body at anyone who was wearing a buyer's badge, we were getting nowhere. All the buyers were too eager to get inside where it was warm.

With just two days left at the Toy Fair and little to show for our time and money, we opted for an emergency strategy session. Susie pointed out that it was the day before Valentine's Day. She suggested we hand out chocolate—pure genius. I ran to a store across the street, bought out their supply of chocolate hearts. Armed with catalogue sheets and chocolate, we began walking the floors of the Toy Fair building behind Rubeo, who was in costume, being sure to stay one step ahead of building security. Whenever we ran into security guards, Rubeo would loudly proclaim to everyone in the immediate area, "Welcome to the 1997 International Toy Fair!" and they assumed that we were working for the show itself. At least, people were paying attention to us. But we still weren't close to getting a meeting with a large retail chain buyer.

International Sales 101

Finally, we hit pay dirt. A nice couple approached us and told us they were toy distributors from New Zealand. They covered more than 150 computer, toy, and gift stores and were interested in a $15 000 order. Playing it cool, we sat down and discussed details with them. As soon as they left, the high fives started flying. The Toy Fair was a success! By the next Christmas, they had upped the order to more than $20 000, and we had cemented a solid relationship. The New Zealanders even commissioned us to build a mascot costume for them to promote the Bug. The best part was the terms. Being an overseas distributor, they paid upon our shipping the product rather than after they received the product, meaning that we got crucial income up front. Suddenly, we were an international company. The bugs were selling well, and little kids all over New Zealand were sending us fan e-mail.

As it turned out, by Christmas, New Zealand wasn't our only foreign distributor, although it remained the largest. We had recreated our success story—and became global—with companies from England, the Middle East, and Asia. International sales seemed so simple. One distributor, money up front, and no returns. It was almost too good to be true. And in a way, it was. In the North American market, we were still limited to renting stalls in flea markets next to bikers selling leather Harley-Davidson Christmas stockings.

North America or Bust

We had to come up with a plan to sell in North America, or we were doomed. I knew that as much as we all believed in Computer Friendly Stuff, the company couldn't stand another flea market Christmas season. We took stock of what we had learned:

1. The first step is to find a need and fill it.
2. Even the best product doesn't sell itself—you have to market it.
3. International sales can play a significant role early on, even for small companies.
4. Good marketing creates its own luck.

Armed with that knowledge, we looked forward to 1998 and breaking into the much larger North American retail market.

Questions

1. What concepts from Chapters 1 to 4 apply to this case?
2. What is meant by "good marketing makes good luck"? Do you think CFS made its own luck at the International Toy Fair?

3. How would CFS's strategy change if the international sales had not occurred? What makes its product desirable to an international market?
4. English, in many ways, is the language of the Internet. What makes the Original Computer Bug a good product to sell online, especially in a global market? What are the pros and cons of selling this type of product over the Internet?

Marketing Plan Questions

Refer to the Sample Marketing Plan in Appendix A as you answer these questions about developing and modifying a marketing plan for CFS.

1. For this year's marketing plan, how would you define CFS's distinctive competency, which is its key strength and a critical component of its competitive strategy?
2. Looking ahead to next year's marketing plan, what additional information about global markets should CFS be gathering as it gets ready to expand distribution to more countries?

CBC ⬤ VIDEO CASE 1

Dirty Business Tricks

Entrepreneur Norman Paul, CEO of MediTrust, claims that Shoppers Drug Mart conspired to ruin his mail order pharmacy and is suing the corporate giant for $755 million. Competition is expected in business but at what point does competitive activity cross legal and ethical lines? Paul established MediTrust in 1992 as a mail order alternative to established in-store pharmacies, with a dispensing fee of about half what drugstores were charging. In 1993, he realized that someone was pressuring suppliers, telling them not to do business with MediTrust. Paul believes that his mail order concept was such a threat to the established pharmacies that Shoppers Drug Mart led an industry-wide conspiracy to destroy MediTrust. The Pharmacists Professional Association, for example, had distributed a video to managers of employee benefit programs explaining the risks of mail order and citing examples of medication being damaged in transit.

At the centre of Paul's conspiracy theory, however, is evidence of a defamatory letter that was produced by a fake organization, "the Society for Concerned Pharmacists," that reported to represent 6000 pharmacists. The letter, which challenged the credibility of MediTrust's business plan, was distributed to five reporters and three members of the financial community in 1996 when Paul was attempting to raise money for MediTrust through an initial public offering. Paul believes that the letter ruined his ability to raise the needed capital to sustain his business.

Paul hired a private investigator to find out who sent the letter. The Society's address turned out to be a rented mailbox located across the street from Shoppers Drug Mart's head office, which was rented by the executive secretary to the CEO of Shoppers Drug Mart, David Bloom, and vice-president of public affairs, Arthur Konviser. Although Konviser originally claimed no knowledge of the letter or the Society, Shoppers Drug Mart lawyers filed a statement of defence that indicated "Konviser was involved in the preparation and distribution of the letter."

Shoppers Drug Mart representatives claim that the letter had no impact on MediTrust, suggesting, "MediTrust's business imploded under its own weight, burdened by bad management and a business plan that was...perhaps doomed from the beginning."

The lawsuit has significant implications for business practice in Canada. A judgment against Shoppers would send a strong message about what is unacceptable business practice. If Shoppers is exonerated, companies may become even bolder in their attempts to undermine their competition.

Paul eventually sold MediTrust to Edmonton's Katz Group, a multibillion-dollar retail pharmacy organization that recently bought US-based Drug Emporium.

Questions

1. In your opinion, would the letter have had a devastating effect on Paul's business?
2. Proving that Konviser was involved in the preparation and distribution of the letter may have been difficult. Why would Shoppers Drug Mart want to "come clean" and admit to his involvement?
3. How can business people decide what is ethical and unethical competitive behaviour?

Source: Adapted from the transcript of "Trash Talks," *Venture* #760 (17 October 2000).

CBC ⊕ VIDEO CASE 2

Profiting from Philanthropy

Several Canadian corporations donate money to charities, but what is their motivation for doing so? Are these companies New Era firms, concerned with social as well as corporate profit? Or are these companies interested only in promoting their own bottom line? Increasingly, Canadian businesses are practising "strategic philanthropy," carefully choosing to support charity groups that are consistent with both the priorities of the company's target market and with their corporate image. Companies engaging in strategic philanthropy get involved in active partnerships with charities, and this provides good public relations opportunities. Many companies view such arrangements as a powerful marketing tool.

Proponents of strategic philanthropy argue that it provides a win–win situation for the company and for the charity. While the charity gets needed donations and publicity, the company boosts its own image and provides social value at the same time. For example, Kraft Foods sponsored a food drive and encouraged people to donate boxes of Kraft Dinner to be sent to food banks. The company received a lot of publicity from the food drive and increased sales of Kraft Dinner. The company then matched the consumer donations of Kraft Dinner box for box, which doubled the amount of food donated to the food banks.

When The Hudson's Bay Company opened its Outfitters store in Toronto, it partnered with two charitable organizations—The Canadian Canoe Museum and Trails, a charity that helps inner city kids by taking them on outdoor adventures. Part of the profits from products sold during the opening was donated to the two organizations. And representatives from both charities were at the store opening, which helped generate publicity for their own organizations as well as for The Bay. According to Linton Carter, The Bay donations manager, the company was interested in partnering with organizations that supported The Bay's corporate image and whose activities were consistent with the historic roots of the company and the outdoor positioning of Outfitters.

Critics of strategic philanthropy question the need to have corporations benefit from their charitable work. What happened to simply donating money for the sake of doing so? Why should a company receive a direct benefit from being a good corporate citizen?

Judith John, vice-president of marketing and communications at the United Way, claims that one of the main disadvantages of strategic philanthropy is that some good charities do not get supported. Strategic philanthropy promotes a matching process between companies and charities. This creates a lot of competition among charitable groups who vie for corporate dollars to make up for significant government cutbacks. John is concerned about those charities that do not match well with corporate agendas, but nevertheless provide important services to communities. Who will support those organizations?

Rob Moore, a public relations consultant with Edelman Canada, researched consumer attitudes toward corporate philanthropy and found that consumers are interested in finding out about corporate charitable work. Therefore, promoting good deeds through strategic philanthropy is not only acceptable to consumers but may also be expected by them. His findings also suggest that it is important for consumers to feel that a partnership between a company and a charity is equal. If consumers feel that the company is deriving more benefit than the charitable organization, they may develop negative attitudes toward the company.

Questions

1. What are the benefits of strategic philanthropy for corporations? For charities? For consumers?
2. What are the problems of strategic philanthropy for corporations? For charities? For consumers?
3. Can you name other Canadian companies that practise strategic philanthropy?
4. Overall, would you say that strategic philanthropy is an effective marketing tool?

Source: This case was prepared by Auleen Carson and is based on "Give and Take," *Undercurrents #112*, 24 January 1999.

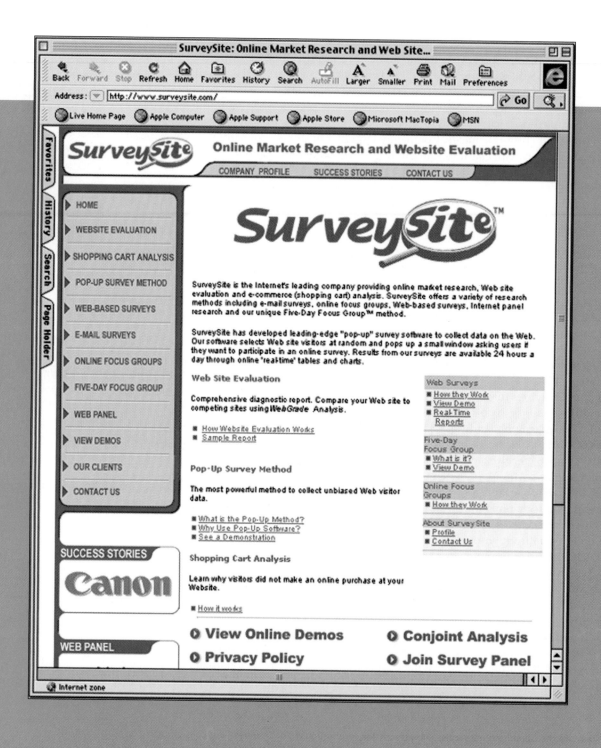

5 Marketing Information and Research: Analyzing the Business Environment

When you have completed your study of this chapter, you should be able to

CHAPTER OBJECTIVES

1. Describe the marketing research process.

2. Explain the differences between exploratory, problem-solving, and causal research, and describe some research techniques available to marketers.

3. Deal with the issues involved in making sense of research results.

4. Discuss how marketers implement research results.

Real People, Real Decisions ✓ ✗

Meet Dr. Marshall Rice
A Decision Maker at SurveySite

Dr. Marshall Rice is the founder of SurveySite, the Internet's leading provider of online market research. Located in Toronto, SurveySite conducts Web-based research for local, national, and international clients, including Microsoft, Ford Motor Company, Canadian Tire, The World Bank, Dell Computer Corporation, and Telus. Rice and his team at SurveySite use such research methods as online surveys and Web-based consumer panels to help clients better understand their Internet customers. Their research is used to support many different types of marketing decisions, including the look and design of a company's Web site, which products and services to offer to customers, how to provide better customer service, and what prices to charge for a company's products.

Rice has a BA from the University of Manitoba and a Masters and PhD in communications from the University of Illinois. In addition to his duties at SurveySite, he is a professor of marketing at the Schulich School of Business at York University in Toronto.

SurveySite
www.surveysite.com

❋ ❋ ❋
marketing research The process of collecting, analyzing, and interpreting data about customers, competitors, and the business environment to improve marketing effectiveness.

❋ ❋ ❋
marketing intelligence
Information about a firm's external environment, which allows marketers to monitor conditions that affect demand for existing products or create demand for new products.

Information for Decision Making

Firms succeed by knowing what consumers want, when they want it, where they want it, and what competing firms are doing about it. In other words, the better a firm's information, the better it will succeed. The Tetley Tea company knows this first hand. Since the company entered the Canadian tea market in the mid-1980s, it has done continuous market research with tea-drinking consumers to better understand their attitudes and motivations as well as their view of competitive products. The company's research efforts have certainly paid off. Since the product was introduced, the brand has gone from last place in the market to first, a feat the company attributes directly to having good consumer information.[1]

Sometimes firms gather their own information; sometimes they hire firms like SurveySite to collect it for them. This information gathering is called **marketing research**, the process of collecting, analyzing, and interpreting data about customers, competitors, and the business environment to improve marketing effectiveness. Virtually all companies rely on some form of marketing research, though the amount and type of research vary dramatically. Due to resource constraints, for instance, small businesses may limit their marketing research activities to searching out information from published sources, such as business magazines and government studies, and only rarely conduct research studies themselves. Large companies such as Ford Canada, on the other hand, might routinely conduct large consumer studies to understand what consumers want in their products, as the ad in Exhibit 5.1 suggests. In this chapter, we'll see how marketers conduct research and what kind of information it provides to marketing decision makers.

We can identify three types of information needed to make effective marketing decisions.

- *Ongoing Information*: Marketing managers watch daily or weekly sales data to analyze regional sales by brand or product line, and monthly sales reports to measure progress toward marketing's sales goals and market share objectives. For example, marketing managers in department stores like Zellers can use up-to-the-minute sales information obtained from store cash registers around the country so that they can detect problems with products, promotions, and even the firm's distribution system.

- *Monitored Information*: Marketing managers need information about the firm's external environment. Although marketers might need this information on an ongoing basis, too, they call it by another name—**marketing intelligence**—because this type of information allows the firm to monitor conditions that affect demand for existing products

BEFORE OUR DESIGNERS CREATE A CAR THEY TALK TO OUTSIDE *EXPERTS.*

SEVERAL times a year we invite people to come and brainstorm with Ford Motor Company designers and engineers. We talk about cars, sure. But often we talk about NON-CAR THINGS: computers, appliances, music, the environment, quality in very general terms. We know that to design cars and trucks with relevance and appeal, you have to LISTEN to your customers. It's part of the learning process that leads us to quality.

· FORD · FORD TRUCKS · *Ford* · LINCOLN · MERCURY ·

QUALITY IS JOB 1.

or create demand for new products. Marketing managers often use this intelligence on a regular basis to predict fluctuations in sales due to economic conditions, political issues, and events that heighten consumer awareness. St. John's–based Cable Atlantic estimates that their marketing research budget is four to five times higher than the national average because the company considers marketing intelligence to be so critical to marketing decision making. The company conducts large market research studies, using techniques such as phone surveys, about every 12 months to keep up with trends and events affecting consumer demand. The marketing intelligence activities have produced bottom-line results. Cable Atlantic has achieved a cable penetration rate among its customers that is 10% higher than the national average.[2]

- *Specific Information*: Sometimes marketing managers need more specific information, such as immediate feedback on a proposed change in pricing strategy or consumers' perceptions of a new advertising campaign.

Marketers might also use specific information to identify opportunities for new products or to provide data about the quality of their existing products, who uses them, and how. Most of the research conducted by market research companies such as SurveySite provides this type of specific information. For example, SurveySite helped Hewlett-Packard determine a name for their new scanning product by performing an online survey with over 4000 respondents.[3]

The Steps in Marketing Research

The collection and interpretation of strategic information is hardly a one-shot deal that managers engage in "just out of curiosity." Ideally, marketing research is an ongoing *process*, a series of steps marketers take to learn about the marketplace. Whether a company conducts the research itself or hires another firm to do it, the goal is the same—to help managers make informed marketing decisions. Figure 5.1 shows the steps in the research process.

Defining the Problem

Defining the research problem as precisely as possible allows marketers to search for the right answers to the right questions. Sometimes marketers cannot determine exactly what the problem is because they're focusing on symptoms, such as declining sales, and not on the underlying problem that's causing sales to drop. For example, a drop in sales of a sunscreen may be due to a new competitor, lack of cooperation from distributors, or even a fashion trend promoting a deep tan.

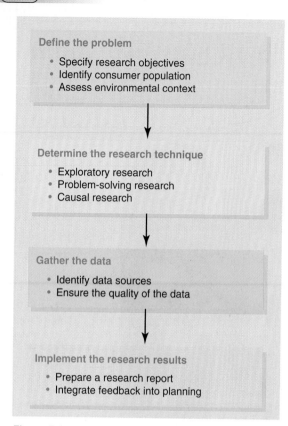

Figure 5.1 The Marketing Research Process

Define the problem
- Specify research objectives
- Identify consumer population
- Assess environmental context

Determine the research technique
- Exploratory research
- Problem-solving research
- Causal research

Gather the data
- Identify data sources
- Ensure the quality of the data

Implement the research results
- Prepare a research report
- Integrate feedback into planning

Mercedes-Benz
www.mercedes-benz.ca

✴ ✴ ✴
research design A plan that specifies what information marketers will collect and what type of study they will do.

Defining the problem has three components:

- *Specifying the research objectives*: What questions will the research attempt to answer?
- *Identifying the consumer population of interest*: What are the characteristics of the consumers involved in the problem situation?
- *Placing the problem in an environmental context*: What factors in the firm's internal and external business environment might be influencing the situation?

Providing the right kind of information for each of these pieces of the problem is not as simple as it seems. For example, suppose a luxury car manufacturer wants to find out why its sales have fallen off dramatically over the past year. The research objective could revolve around any number of possible questions: Is the firm's advertising failing to reach the right consumers? Is the right message being sent? Do the firm's cars have a particular feature (or lack of one) that is turning customers away? Is there a problem with the firm's reputation for providing quality service? Do consumers believe the price is right for the value they get? The particular objective chosen depends on a variety of factors, such as the feedback the firm is getting from its customers, the monitored information it receives from the marketplace, and sometimes even the intuition of the people designing the research. Often the focus of a research question surfaces during exploratory research. For example, Mercedes-Benz regularly monitors drivers' perceptions of its cars, partly through feedback from dealers. When the company started getting reports from its dealers that people were viewing the cars as "arrogant" and "unapproachable," even to the point where they were reluctant to sit in the models on display in the showroom, a research project was undertaken to better understand the reasons for this perception.[4]

The research objective determines the consumer population that will be studied. The research might focus on current owners to find out what they especially like about the car. Or it might study non-owners to understand their lifestyles, what they look for in a luxury automobile, or their beliefs about the company itself that keep them from choosing the cars. Research conducted for Mercedes-Benz showed that, although people rated its cars very high on engineering quality and status, many were too intimidated by the elitist Mercedes image to consider buying one. Mercedes dealers reported that a common question asked by visitors to showrooms was, "May I actually sit in the car?" Based on this research, Mercedes took steps to soften its image by changing the tone of its advertising to project a slightly more down-to-earth impression.[5]

Placing the problem in the context of the firm's environment helps researchers structure the research, determine the specific types of questions to ask, and identify factors they will need to take into account when measuring results. Environmental conditions also provide a valuable perspective. For example, when the economy is tight and sales of luxury cars are generally declining, the population to be studied might be narrowed down to a select group of consumers who are still willing and able to indulge in a luxury vehicle. Alternatively, consumers may be moving away from glitzy status-conscious materialism, so that the research question comes down to how promotional strategies can convey honest and basic values that go beyond "snob appeal."

Determining the Research Technique

Once marketers have isolated specific problems, the second step of the research process is to decide on a "plan of attack." This plan is the **research design**, which specifies what information marketers will collect and what type of study they will do. All marketing problems do not call for the same techniques, even though marketers can solve some problems

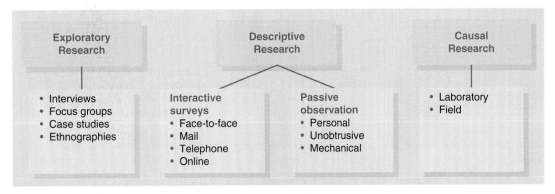

Figure 5.2 Marketing Research Techniques

effectively with a number of alternate techniques. Figure 5.2 summarizes many of the techniques used by market researchers.

Marketers may be able to find the information they need inside the organization, in the form of company reports, feedback received from customers, salespeople, or stores, or even in the memories of long-time employees.

Often, though, they also need to look outside their own organization for data. They can obtain reports published in the popular and business press, such as *The Globe and Mail Report on Business* or the *Financial Post*, and look at published research on the state of the industry conducted by trade organizations, such as the *Directory of Chains* published by *Canadian Grocer*. Marketers can also use research studies conducted by private research organizations or government agencies, such as Statistics Canada (www.statcan.ca). One data source used by many Canadian marketers is Statistics Canada's *Market Research Handbook*, which contains such demographic information as population size, average household income, and family structure for all provinces and 45 major cities across the country.[6] Because this information is available in many libraries across the country, it is an especially cost-effective resource for small businesses, as they try to better understand their markets.

The Internet is also a useful resource for obtaining external information. In addition to the Statistics Canada site, some other valuable sources of external information can be found at:[7]

- Bank sites, such as those of the TD (www.tdbank.ca/economics/index.html) and Royal Bank (www.royalbank.com/economics/index.html), provide useful information on the economy.

- NADBank (www.nadbank.com) provides data on Canadian newspaper readership and market data for several product and service categories.

- Blue Book of Canadian Business (www.bluebook.ca) includes profiles of Canada's top-performing companies and can be a very useful resource for business-to-business marketing activities.

- Strategy Magazine Online (www.strategymag.com) contains articles on marketing in Canada and has a search engine that searches the archives of the magazine.

- Marketing Tools (www.marketingtools.com), run by *American Demographics* magazine, lets users search for marketing books and articles.

- CompuServe (compuserve.com) provides full-text articles from more than 450 business and trade publications.

- Dun & Bradstreet Canada (www.dnb.ca/marketspectrum) provides customized market information to businesses by combining their database of market information with the information their customers have already collected. See Exhibit 5.2.

EXPLORATORY RESEARCH

Marketers use **exploratory research** to generate topics for future, more rigorous studies, ideas for new strategies and opportunities, or just to get a better handle on a problem they are experiencing with a product. Because the studies are usually small in scale and less costly to conduct than other techniques, marketers can use exploratory research to test their

* * *

exploratory research Technique that marketers use to generate insights for future, more rigorous studies.

Exhibit 5.2

Companies like Dun & Bradstreet Canada provide customized market research for businesses.

✳ ✳ ✳

consumer interviews One-on-one discussions between a consumer and a researcher.

✳ ✳ ✳

focus group A product-oriented discussion among a small group of consumers led by a trained moderator.

hunches about what's going on without too much risk. Exploratory studies often involve in-depth probing of a few consumers who fit the profile of the "typical" customer. Researchers may interview consumers, salespeople, or other employees about products, services, ads, or stores. They may simply "hang out" and watch what people do when choosing among competing brands in a store aisle. Or they may locate places where the consumers of interest hang out and ask questions in these settings. As Exhibit 5.3 shows, some researchers find that many young people are too suspicious or sceptical in traditional research settings, so they may interview young people waiting in lines to buy concert tickets or in clubs.[8]

Most exploratory research provides *qualitative data*, detailed verbal or visual information (for example, videotapes of people preparing dinner at home) about consumers' attitudes, feelings, and buying behaviours, that is summarized in words rather than numbers. Researchers for a manufacturer of Swiss chocolate, for example, interviewed consumers and found that many chocolate lovers hide secret stashes around their houses. The company used the results of this exploratory research to develop an advertising campaign built around the theme: "The True Confessions of Chocaholics."[9]

Exploratory research can take many forms. **Consumer interviews** are one-on-one discussions in which an individual shares his or her thoughts in person with a researcher.

In addition to interviewing actual users of their product, some marketers find it useful to interview people who may not themselves be consumers, but who may know a lot about the consumers. One Canadian ad agency working on an ad campaign for scotch interviewed bartenders to gain additional insight into scotch drinkers. Another agency in England, when they were working on an ad for a shoe company, talked to people who shined shoes and to prostitutes who had clients with foot fetishes.[10]

The **focus group** is the technique marketing researchers most often use for collecting exploratory data. Focus groups usually consist of eight to twelve recruited consumers, who sit together to discuss a product, ad, or some other marketing topic introduced by a discussion leader, or moderator. Typically, the moderator tapes these group discussions, which may be held at special interviewing facilities that allow for observation ("spying") by the client, who watches from behind a one-way mirror. As Exhibit 5.4 shows, focus groups don't *always* run smoothly, particularly if one or two opinionated members dominate the session.

Researchers screen focus group participants in advance to meet criteria that will make their opinions relevant. For example, participants may be recruited, not because they use the company's brand, but because they use a competitor's product. General Motors used focus groups to discover what features of competitors' cars appealed to drivers so that these could be incorporated into its own designs. One result was that GM followed Saab's example by putting fuses in the glove box.[11]

Many researchers use **projective techniques** to get at people's underlying feelings, especially when they feel that people will be unable or unwilling to express their true reactions. A projective test asks the participant to respond to some ambiguous object, often by telling a story about it. For example, the manufacturer of Brawny paper towels was locked in a struggle with ScotTowels for the number-two market position behind Bounty. The company decided to re-examine its brand identity, personified by a character named Brawny, a 60-foot man holding an axe. Managers were afraid Brawny was too old-fashioned, or that women were confused about why a man was selling paper towels in the first place. Women in focus groups were asked questions such as, "What kind of woman would he go out with?" "What is his home life like?" Then they were asked to imagine how he would act in different situations, and even to guess what would happen if they were locked in an elevator with him for 20 minutes. Responses were reassuring—the women saw Brawny as a knight in shining armour who would get them out of the elevator—a good spokesman for a product that's supposed to be reliable and able to get the job done. Brawny kept his job.[12]

The **case study** is a comprehensive examination of a particular firm or organization. In business-to-business marketing research in which the customers are other firms, for example, researchers may try to learn how one company makes its purchases. Their goal is to identify the key decision makers, to learn what criteria they emphasize when choosing between suppliers, and perhaps to learn something about any conflicts and rivalries among these decision makers that may influence their choices.

An **ethnography** is a detailed report on observations of people in their own homes or communities. Although a true ethnography, as conducted by anthropologists, can involve living with a group for months or years, marketing researchers usually devise shortcuts to get the information they need. True North Communications, for example, has devised an ethnographic research technique called "Mind and Mood," in which consumer interviews are conducted in a few hours in the respondent's home. As one advertising professional who uses the technique says, "You actually go into people's homes to talk to them. You meet

Exhibit 5.3

Researchers find it easier to collect data from young people on their own turf.

* * *

projective techniques Tests that marketers use to explore people's underlying feelings about a product, especially appropriate when consumers are unable or unwilling to express their true reactions.

* * *

case study A comprehensive examination of a particular firm or organization.

* * *

ethnography A detailed report on observations of people in their own homes or communities.

After spending hours with a focus group from Hell, we think you're entitled to a complete 5-minute breakdown.

Exhibit 5.4

A product designed to make focus groups easier.

SPOTLIGHT ON REAL PEOPLE *Growing Healthy, Inc.*

Marketers have many sophisticated research tools at their disposal, and one of the most effective is a form of observation that's about as low-tech as you can get: Go shopping. Many businesses hire "mystery shoppers" to visit stores, hotels, and restaurants. Posing as regular customers, they report back on how they were treated, how employees describe products to them, the cleanliness of the facilities, or even what other shoppers say in casual conversation about the choices available. The importance of seeing how consumers treat your products with your own eyes was not lost on 31-year-old Julia Knight. She quit her marketing job with a cosmetics firm to open Growing Healthy, Inc., a frozen baby-food company. To understand how parents shop for baby food, she abandoned her work clothes for blue jeans and sneakers and hung out in the aisles of local supermarkets. One tidbit she picked up: Some shoppers spend more on cat food than on baby food, even though they would never admit this to a researcher.

Because she didn't have children of her own, sometimes she enlisted friends to accompany her with their kids. This helped her to see first-hand why food shopping can be so stressful when one has to deal with screaming children who are constantly demanding candy or other treats. In between headaches, Julia learned an important lesson: Kids don't like to stay in the frozen-food section because it's too cold, so parents have a tendency to speed through icy aisles and not take the time to look at new products. She persuaded supermarket managers to put small freezers in the baby-food section instead. Sales of her frozen baby foods thawed out nicely.[14]

1. The chapter describes several ways to conduct marketing research. How would you classify the research technique used by mystery shoppers?
2. What are the advantages of mystery shopping over other forms of marketing research?
3. Mystery shopping can give the researcher a bird's-eye view of the sales floor. Why should a company be cautious about making decisions based on the reports of mystery shoppers?

them where they're most comfortable, see what they've got on their walls, what kind of furnishings they have, and you can get a sense of what's important to them."[13]

When the Ontario Ministry of Health was creating an anti-smoking campaign, ethnographic interviews were conducted with teenagers to understand their motivations for smoking as well as what was important to them. The researchers determined that a health message (such as the traditional "If you smoke, you will get cancer") was not going to convince teens to give up smoking. Instead the ads needed to touch on important issues for that age group. The final ads used messages such as "Smoking cigarettes will make you ugly" and showed images like a girl aging as she smoked.[15]

DESCRIPTIVE RESEARCH

descriptive research Tool that probes more systematically into the problem and bases its conclusions on large numbers of observations.

We've seen that marketers have many tools at their disposal, including focus groups and ethnographic techniques, to help them better define a problem or opportunity. These are usually modest studies involving a small number of people. In some situations, this information is all that the marketer needs to make decisions; but very often, the next step after exploratory research is to conduct **descriptive research**, which probes more systematically into the problem and bases its conclusions on larger numbers of observations. These observations typically are quantitative data that take the form of averages, percentages, or other statistics summarizing results from a large set of measurements. Quantitative data can be as simple as the number of large-screen TVs sold in a month in Future Shop locations in different regions of the country, or as complex as statistical analyses of responses to a survey mailed to thousands of consumers. In each case, analyses are conducted to answer a specific question in contrast to the "fishing expedition" that may occur in exploratory research.

cross-sectional design Type of descriptive technique that involves the systematic collection of quantitative information at one point in time.

The most common descriptive technique is **cross-sectional design**. This involves the systematic collection of quantitative information, such as responses to a survey or data from store register receipts, from one or more samples of respondents at one point in time. The data may be collected on more than one occasion but generally not from the same pool of respondents. Lever Pond's did a cross-sectional survey of dermatologists to determine which soap they recommend to their patients for mildness. Since 87% of the respondents recommended the Lever Pond's brand Dove, and only 13% recommended the competitive brand, the company turned the results of its survey directly into an advertising campaign. Outdoor billboards that showed the results of the survey were used in major centres across Canada.[16]

In contrast to the one-shot study, a **longitudinal design** tracks the responses of the same sample of respondents over time. Market researchers often create *consumer panels* to gather this kind of information; a sample of respondents representative of a larger market agrees to provide information about purchases on a weekly or monthly basis. When 3M wanted to find out how it should market its Buf-Puf Sponge facial scrub pads, the company recruited a teen advisory board by running ads in *Seventeen, Sassy,* and *'Teen.* 3M periodically consults these consumer panel members about their use of personal care products and their concerns about appearance.[17]

A lot of marketing research obtains data by using some form of *interactive instrument* in which the consumer responds to questions. These responses are then combined with those of other respondents to arrive at some general conclusions. The most common interactive instrument is a **survey**, a questionnaire asking participants about their beliefs or behaviours. For example, when Bayer wanted to determine how to improve the health care products it offers, including the Aspirin brand, it mailed out surveys to 10 000 health care professionals across Canada including doctors and pharmacists.[18]

Surveys can be administered in a variety of ways, each of which has its pros and cons. *Mail surveys,* such as the one done by Bayer, are easy to administer and offer a high degree of anonymity to respondents. On the downside, because the questionnaire is printed and mailed, researchers have little flexibility in the types of questions they can ask and little control over the circumstances under which the respondent is answering them. Mail surveys also take a long time to get back to the company and are likely to have a much lower response rate than other types of surveys because people tend to ignore them.

Telephone surveys usually consist of a brief phone conversation in which an interviewer reads a short list of questions to the respondent. One problem with this approach is that the growth of *telemarketing*, the sale of products and services over the phone, has eroded the willingness of many consumers to participate in phone surveys—especially when those telemarketers have pretended to be conducting marketing research (see Good or Bad Decision?). Another drawback of telephone surveys is that the respondent may not feel comfortable speaking directly to an interviewer, especially if the survey is about a sensitive subject. Finally, increasing numbers of people use answering machines and caller identification to screen calls, further reducing the response rate.

Face-to-face surveys, in which a live interviewer asks questions of a respondent by, for example, going door-to-door, used to be a common way to collect data. However, this practice has declined markedly in recent years due to escalating costs and security concerns—people just aren't willing to open their doors to strangers anymore. More typically, today's face-to-face interviews occur in a "mall-intercept" study in which researchers recruit shoppers in malls or other public areas. Mall-intercepts offer good opportunities to get feedback about marketing issues like new package designs or styles or even reactions to new foods or fragrances. However, because only certain groups of the population frequently shop at malls, a mall-intercept study does not provide the researcher with a representative sample of the population unless the population of interest is mall shoppers. In addition to the mall-intercept being more expensive than mail or phone surveys, respondents may be reluctant to answer questions of a personal nature in a face-to-face context. Rather than relying on face-to-face surveys, Staples Business Depot Canada decided to use automated kiosks in its stores to survey consumers about their satisfaction with the company. Because of the anonymity that the kiosk affords respondents, the company estimates that two out of three people take part in the kiosk surveys, compared with one out of three who are asked to do a face-to-face survey.[20]

good OR **bad** DECISION?

Sometimes telemarketers portray themselves as marketing researchers to get consumers to listen to their sales pitches. They ask consumers to answer a "survey" and then follow up with a sales offer. This practice, called *sugging*, is a concern of legitimate market researchers, who often find their own information gathering affected by the negative consumer reaction to this practice. The Canadian Marketing Association has taken a strong stance in its Code of Ethics against sugging, but many telemarketers continue using this technique, presumably because it is so effective. Do you think it is appropriate for telemarketers to engage in sugging?[19]

* * *
longitudinal design Technique that tracks the responses of the same sample of respondents over time.

* * *
survey A questionnaire that asks participants about their beliefs or behaviours.

Online surveys, such as those administered by SurveySite, are growing in popularity, as more consumers and businesses are getting hooked up to the Internet. The Carrier Corporation, which makes air conditioners, found respondents more willing to answer questions about its products via computer, perhaps because it's more interesting to take a survey this way.[21] Online surveys are a quick and cost-effective way to collect data. Unlike mail and phone surveys, online surveys can generate a large number of responses very quickly. However, it must be remembered that, like the people who visit malls, people who use the Internet are not representative of the total population. Online surveys are, therefore, useful only for those companies whose population of interest is people who are online. An additional concern about online surveys relates to the quality of responses the firm will receive—particularly because no one can be really sure who is typing in the responses.[22]

All these techniques require a response from the consumer, whether in the form of a verbal response to an interview question, a checkmark placed on a piece of paper, or a mouse click on a computer screen. Other forms of data collection use a *passive instrument* in which the consumer's behaviours are simply recorded—often without his or her knowledge. Researchers do this through personal observation, unobtrusive measures, and mechanical observation.

With *personal observation,* consumers in public settings are watched to understand how they react to marketing activities. After Frito-Lay found that shoppers spend twice as much time in the coffee aisle as in the snack foods section, it began to advertise its chips near the coffee cans.[23] Researchers for Rocky Mountain Railtours observed their customers' behaviour as they were travelling through the Canadian Rockies by train. They noticed that these travellers seemed to like the experience of the train trip itself as much as the beautiful scenery they were seeing. This led the company to change the theme of their advertising from just talking about the mountain scenery to talking about the train service experience. One of the ads claimed: "No one ever wrote a folk song about a minivan," and the overall slogan for the new ads was "The only way to see the Canadian Rockies." The company saw a 23% increase in their bookings as a result of the ads.[24]

Some companies have successfully used observation in combination with other methods, such as consumer interviews, in an effort to improve the quality of information gathered. To examine how consumers make milk brand decisions, researchers in Atlantic Canada observed over 200 consumers in 12 stores and followed up with brief interviews. In the interviews, consumers claimed that they bought a certain brand, even though the researcher knew from observation that they had bought a different one. Similarly, in interviews most consumers claimed that they checked the expiry date on the milk cartons, whereas observation showed that hardly anyone did so. All of this information allowed the researchers to conclude that milk is a low-involvement purchasing decision with weak loyalty levels. The consumers were not deliberately lying in the interviews; they simply did not pay that much attention to their milk buying behaviour.[25] As this example shows, sometimes it is wise to use multiple research methods when performing marketing research.

Researchers also use *unobtrusive measures* to check traces of physical evidence that remain after some action has been taken, when they suspect that people will probably alter their behaviour if they know they are being observed. For example, instead of asking a person to report on the alcohol products currently in his or her home, the researcher might go to the house and perform a "pantry check," recording the bottles found there. As seen in Exhibit 5.5, a few research firms have found that the road to marketing intelligence is strewn with garbage—literally. The company sifts through garbage, searching for clues about each family's consumption habits. The "garbologists" can tell, for example, which soft drink accompanied what kind of food. As one garbologist noted, "The people in this study don't know that we are studying their garbage so the information is totally objective."[26]

Mechanical observation relies on non-human devices to record behaviour. For example, some grocery stores use infrared sensors in their ceilings to track the movements of shopping carts.[27] Another application of mechanical observation is people meters, operated by such companies as Nielsen Media Research and BBM Bureau of Measurement. These boxes are attached to the television sets of selected viewers to record patterns of television

Rocky Mountaineer Railtours
www.rkymtnrail.com

Real People, Real Decisions
Decision Time at SurveySite

Marshall Rice was considering how to expand SurveySite's business. The company had traditionally focused on providing survey-based research on the Web, but Rice was interested in looking at different methodologies that could be adapted to the Internet environment. One product he considered offering to his customers was an on-line focus group, which would combine some elements of traditional focus groups (such as group discussion) with the flexibility of the Internet environment. He wanted to draw on the Internet chat room idea by inviting the group participants to a Web site that would allow them to participate in focus group discussions on their own time over a specified period, say three to five days. Like traditional focus groups, the on-line focus group would be led by a trained moderator, who would monitor the online discussion and keep participants on track.

Rice decided to conduct his own marketing research to determine whether his existing clients would be interested in online focus groups and, if they were, what features they would like to see. To conduct this exploratory research, he interviewed a small sample of his most important clients. During these interviews, respondents told him that one problem with traditional focus groups is that customers from only limited geographic regions and time zones can participate in the groups; this is a concern for companies like Microsoft, who have customers around the world. Conducting groups online would allow participants in different geographic areas to be involved in the same groups.

Another benefit that some clients mentioned was the ability to get results quickly. Because the participants in the online focus groups would be typing in their responses on their computers, the client would have the transcript from the focus group immediately after the group ended. Clients also liked the idea that they could observe the focus group while it was happening and "talk" to the moderator privately by typing in questions that they hadn't thought of before the focus group. Additionally, several clients mentioned that the anonymity of the online environment might encourage responses from individuals who may be shy in a group, and that this anonymity could also encourage all respondents to be more honest. Finally, several clients thought that the online environment may get rid of one of the most annoying

problems in "live" focus groups: the domination of the group by one or two loud, opinionated members. Those people who tried to dominate a group online could be more effectively dealt with by the moderator (perhaps through a private e-mail).

Not all of the clients were completely sold on the online focus group idea, though. Some clients were concerned that the anonymity provided by the online environment would detract from the reliability of the information. How could the researchers be sure that the person recruited for the group was actually the only one involved in typing in responses? Other clients were concerned with the inability to see nonverbal communication from the participants (such as facial expressions and body language) or to hear intonation, both of which can indicate a person's feelings and reactions better than simply words.

As Rice reviewed the responses of his clients, he began to wonder whether the online focus group product was worth introducing. Even traditional focus groups were losing some of their appeal for companies. If companies were not sold on the focus group concept generally, they would certainly not be interested in online groups. Rice was also considering the cost of organizational changes that would be necessary to support the introduction of the new product. Focus groups required people who could be moderators and analyze qualitative data. There would have to be some retraining of existing SurveySite employees and some new people hired to be able to offer this new technique.

In making his decision, Rice considered two options.

Option 1: Develop and introduce an online focus group product.

Option 2: Abandon the online focus group product idea for now and continue to focus the efforts of SurveySite on survey research techniques online. As a follow-up to the exploratory interviews with existing clients, plan to conduct more extensive research with both existing and potential clients to better determine the potential for online focus groups.

Now, join Marshall Rice and the SurveySite team. Which option would you choose, and why?

---

watching. These "television ratings" are how the networks determine how much to charge advertisers for commercials and which shows to cancel or renew. Nielsen also uses observation on the Internet to determine which Web sites are most popular on a daily and weekly basis. The Nielsen Web usage data can be viewed at the Nielsen Net ratings site (www.nielsen-netratings.com).

Exhibit 5.5

"Garbologists" search for clues about consumption activities, an unobtrusive measure.

CAUSAL RESEARCH

The descriptive techniques we've examined do a good job of providing valuable information about *what* is happening in the marketplace, but they can't tell us *why*. Sometimes marketers need to know if something they've done has brought about some change in behaviour. For example, does the layout and design of a store affect the amount people buy? This question can't be answered through simple observation.

For example, managers at a grocery chain notice from their sales data across a number of stores that purchases of produce are higher in those stores that are designed to resemble farmers' markets with free-flowing layouts and "stalls," where produce is displayed. Can we say that design of these stores caused the increased sales, or is the answer simply that these stores happen to be located in areas where people buy more produce no matter what the store looks like?

***

causal research Techniques that attempt to understand cause-and-effect relationships.

Causal research refers to techniques that attempt to understand cause-and-effect relationships. In causal research, marketers want to know if a change in something (for example, layout used in a store) is responsible for a change in something else (for example, an increase in produce sales). They call the factors that might cause such a change *independent variables* and the outcomes *dependent variables*. In this example, the layout of the store is an independent variable and sales data for produce are a dependent variable.

***

experiments Techniques that test prespecified relationships among variables in a controlled environment.

To rule out alternative explanations, researchers must carefully design **experiments** that test specified relationships among variables in a controlled environment. Because this approach tries to eliminate competing explanations for the outcome, respondents may be brought to a *laboratory* where the researcher can be sure that they are reacting to precisely what they should be and nothing else. For example, a study testing whether the layout in a grocery store influences the likelihood that shoppers will buy more produce might bring a group of people into a testing facility, where they are shown a "virtual store" on a computer screen and are asked to fill a grocery cart as they click through the "aisles." The experiment might vary the interior of the store as a market style layout or a more typical grid layout to see if this affects whether people put more produce into their carts.

Although a laboratory allows researchers to exert careful control over what test subjects see and do, marketers don't always have the luxury of conducting this kind of "pure" research. It is possible to conduct *field studies* in the real world, as long as care is taken to be sure that the variables are carefully controlled.

For example, the grocery chain could choose two grocery stores for which the demographics of the people who shop there are known to be the same. Then the company could vary the layouts in the stores, using the market style design in one store and the traditional design in the other, and record produce purchases made over a six-month period. If a lot more produce was bought in the first store than in the second (and the company was sure that nothing else was different between the two stores, such as discounted prices on produce offered by a competitor of one of the stores during the same time), the company might conclude that the presence of a market style layout in the store does indeed result in increased produce sales.

Gathering Data

At this point the researcher has determined the nature of the problem that needs to be addressed. He or she has decided on a research design that will specify how to investigate the problem and what kinds of information (data) will be needed to do so. Once these decisions have been made, the next task is to actually collect the data. The researcher can buy existing data, called *secondary data,* which have been collected by other organizations, such as Statistics Canada. Or can obtain *primary data,* collected for the specific purposes of the study. These data can be in the form of responses to questionnaires, simple observations of consumers where they shop and work, or even paying consumers to come to research facilities. As in the grocery store example, advances in technology even allow researchers to create simulations of real-world situations to gather feedback. For example, as seen in Exhibit 5.6, companies such as General Mills observe people's reactions to new products in virtual stores before they are actually introduced. These *simulations* allow the company to test the impact of price cuts, new packaging, or even the best location on store shelves to feature the product to ensure that people will look at it.[28]

Many people are concerned about potential violations of privacy, as firms continue to gather detailed data about their personal lives. The Blockbuster Entertainment Corp., for example, encountered a firestorm of criticism when it was accused of trying to sell information detailing customers' video rental habits.[29] Critics charged that people's movie preferences (whether for action movies, pornography, or cartoons) were their own business. Data gatherers need to ensure that the information collected will be used only for the stated purpose and that respondents are aware of their right to refuse to provide information.

GATHERING DATA INTERNATIONALLY

Conducting market research in other countries is important for Canadian firms operating in international markets. However, market conditions and consumer preferences vary widely in different parts of the world, and there are big differences in the sophistication of market research operations and the amount of data available to global marketers.

For these reasons, choosing an appropriate data collection method is difficult. In some countries, many people do not have phones, or low literacy rates may interfere with mail surveys. Local customs can be a problem as well. Offering money for interviews, a common practice in Canada, is considered rude in Latin American countries.[30] Focus groups are virtually impossible in Saudi Arabia, where gatherings of four or more people except for family or religious events are banned. Interviews are also difficult there since it is illegal to

Exhibit 5.6

Simulations allow companies to test the impact of marketing decisions before they are made in the real world.

stop strangers on the street or knock on the door of someone's house.[31] Cultural differences also affect responses to survey items. Both Danish and British consumers, for example, agree that it is important to eat breakfast, but the Danish sample may be thinking of fruit and yogourt, whereas the British sample is thinking of toast and tea. Sometimes these problems can be overcome by involving local researchers in decisions about the research design, but, even so, care must be taken to ensure that they fully understand the study's objectives and can relate what they find to the culture of the sponsoring company.

Language differences can also pose challenges for international marketing research. When SurveySite conducted an online survey for Microsoft across 13 countries, for example, the study had to be translated into seven different languages.[32] To ensure that surveys using many languages are translated properly, researchers often use a process called *back-translation*, which requires two steps. First, a questionnaire is translated into the second language by a native speaker of that language. Second, this new version is translated back into the original language to ensure that the correct meanings survive the process. Even with precautions such as these, however, researchers must interpret data obtained from other cultures with care.

SEARCHING FOR THE POT OF GOLD: SINGLE SOURCE DATA AND DATA MINING

One research issue that marketers have been trying to solve for years is knowing what impact each piece of their marketing mix has on their total marketing strategy. Short of moving in with a family for a few months, marketers have had no way to determine the effect of advertising or other promotional activities on consumer purchasing. Today, technology allows researchers to gather data from actual store transactions, which can be directly traced to marketing activities. For example, IRI (Information Resources Inc.) gets weekly cash register data from 20 000 grocery stores, which enable the firm to create a store-by-store picture of what is selling and where, so that manufacturers can restock the hottest-selling items on time and get immediate feedback about the effect of price changes or other promotions on sales.[33]

✳ ✳ ✳

single-source data Information that is integrated from multiple sources to monitor the impact of marketing communications on a particular customer group over time.

Single-source data refers to information that is integrated from multiple sources, such as in-store coupon redemptions, sales data, and household data, to monitor the impact of marketing communications on a particular customer group over time. Warner-Lambert, which makes Clorets chewing gum, is one company that believes in the value of single-source data. The company uses it to address these questions:[34]

- How often do consumers switch between buying mint and gum forms of Clorets?
- What are the best markets for chunk bubble gums?
- How effective is a 25-cent coupon attached to each pack of gum in increasing sales?

The revolution in single-source data is made possible by the widespread use of checkout scanners in stores, as seen in Exhibit 5.7. In addition to speeding up your checkout time, those machines are storing a record of just how many bags of munchies you bought and

Exhibit 5.7

Checkout scanners enable marketers to collect single-source data.

what brands you chose. Combined with records from the store's other customers (and buyers at other locations), this is a potential pot of gold for firms willing to invest in the research needed to track all those millions of transactions.

For retailers who can specifically identify individual consumers, perhaps because they have a loyalty card that links their purchases with demographic information, the data from scanners are especially useful. For example, the grocery chain Safeway tracks the purchases of regular customers who show a Savings Club card when they get to the register. Using this information, Safeway can more effectively tailor special offers, including coupons, to these customers. So heavy consumers of hot dogs might be sent cents-off coupons for mustard and ketchup.

Purchases made online are also continuously recorded, and the identity (username) of the consumer (as well as their virtual address) is always recorded along with their purchases. Thus, companies such as Chapters.indigo.ca can track the purchase habits of each consumer and use that information to tailor communication messages to individuals. If a consumer has ordered several gardening books, for example, they could be sent an e-mail when a new gardening book comes out and offered a special deal if they purchase the book. We'll be studying this style of database marketing in more detail in Chapter 16. To take advantage of the massive amount of transaction information now available, sophisticated analysis techniques called **data mining** are becoming a priority for many firms. Data mining uses supercomputers to combine different databases to explore relationships between buying decisions, exposure to marketing messages, and in-store promotions. These operations are so complex that often a *data warehouse* costing more than $10 million must be built simply to store the data and process them.[35]

* * *

data mining Sophisticated analysis techniques that take advantage of the massive amount of available transaction information.

Data mining is becoming big business. It's estimated that firms will spend $73 billion in 2001 just to sort customer data. Data mining has four important applications for marketers.[36]

- *Customer acquisition*: The firm can determine which of its current customers respond best to specific offers and send the same offers to non-customers matching those characteristics.

- *Customer retention*: The firm can identify big-spending customers and target them for special offers and inducements other customers won't receive.

- *Customer abandonment*: Sometimes a firm wants customers to take their business elsewhere because they actually cost the firm too much to service them. Data mining can identify which customers are not spending enough to justify keeping them.

- *Market basket analysis*: The firm can develop focused promotional strategies based on its records of which customers have bought certain products.

Ensuring the Quality of the Research: Garbage In, Garbage Out

A firm can gather data in many ways, including focus groups, ethnographies, observational studies, and controlled experiments. But how much faith should it place in what it finds?

A research project is only as good as the information it collects. All too often, marketers who have commissioned a study assume that because they have a massive report full of impressive-looking numbers and tables, they must have the "truth." Unfortunately, there are times when this "truth" is really just one person's interpretation of the facts. At other times, the data used to generate recommendations are flawed. As the expression goes, "Garbage in, garbage out."[37] Typically, three factors influence the quality of research results.

VALIDITY

Validity is the extent to which the research actually measures what it was intended to measure. This was part of the problem underlying the famous New Coke fiasco in the 1980s, in which Coca-Cola underestimated people's loyalty to its flagship soft drink after it replaced "Old Coke" with a new, sweeter formula. The company assumed that blind taste testers' preferences for one anonymous cola over another was a valid measure of consumers' preferences for a cola brand. Coke found out the hard way that only measuring taste is not the same as measuring people's deep allegiances to their favourite soft drink, and sales eventually recovered after the company brought back the old version as "Coca-Cola Classic."[38]

* * *

validity The extent to which research actually measures what it was intended to measure.

Figure 5.3 A Completion Test Designed for Children

Source: James McNeal, "Child's play," *Marketing Tools*, January–February 1998: 20.

✷ ✷ ✷
reliability The extent to which research measurement techniques are free of errors.

✷ ✷ ✷
representativeness The extent to which consumers in a study are similar to a larger group in which the organization has an interest.

✷ ✷ ✷
sampling The process of selecting respondents who statistically represent a larger population of interest.

RELIABILITY

Reliability is the extent to which the research measurement techniques are free of errors. Sometimes, for example, the way a researcher asks a question creates an error by biasing people's responses. Imagine that an interviewer working for Trojans condoms stopped male college students on campus and asked them if they used contraceptive products. Do you think their answers might change if they were asked the same questions on an anonymous survey they received in the mail? Most likely they would be different, because people are reluctant to disclose what they actually do when their responses are not anonymous. Researchers try to maximize reliability by thinking of several different ways to ask the same questions, by asking these questions on several occasions, or by using several analysts to interpret the responses.

Reliability is a problem when the researchers can't be sure the consumer population they're studying even understands what is being asked. For example, children are difficult subjects for market researchers, because they tend to be undependable reporters of their own behaviour, have poor recall, and often do not understand abstract questions.[39] In many cases, the children cannot explain why they prefer one item over another (or they're not willing to share these secrets with grown-ups).[40] For these reasons, researchers have had to be especially creative in designing studies involving younger consumers. In the example shown in Figure 5.3 (called a *completion test*), boys are told to write in the empty balloon what they think the boy in the drawing will answer when the girl asks, "What program do you want to watch next?" Reliability is increased because the children can respond to pictures depicting a familiar situation in their own words.

REPRESENTATIVENESS

Representativeness is the extent to which consumers in the study are similar to a larger group in which the organization has an interest. This criterion for evaluating research underscores the importance of **sampling**, the process of selecting respondents who statistically represent a larger population of interest.

Because a firm rarely has the resources to ask *everybody* in a market segment for their reactions, it often has to settle for some smaller group, or *sample*. The issue becomes how large or small should the sample be, and how are these people chosen? A variety of different sampling techniques is available.

Random sampling is the process of selecting names by chance from a list containing all names in a total population. Random sampling can be expensive and time-consuming, because a large number of people must be located who are willing to participate to ensure that the population is accurately represented.

A *quota sample* is the division of the total population into categories by age, income, marital status, or other demographic. The researcher draws a portion (quota) of names from those categories relevant to the study, ignoring those who belong to other categories.

In many cases, researchers obtain a less scientific (but also less expensive) *convenience sample* by using whoever is willing to participate in the study. You may even have been part of a convenience sample if you've ever responded to requests for volunteers for academic studies posted on campus bulletin boards. In our SurveySite case, Marshall Rice conducted interviews with a convenience sample of some of his best customers when he did his exploratory research.

Implementing the Research Results

We've gone over the process of choosing a research objective, designing a study, collecting the data, and ensuring that the results are accurate. Now what happens to the research? Sometimes marketers are content to let the information they've collected just lie there; they

Real People, Real Decisions

How it worked out at SurveySite

Marshall Rice decided to pursue Option 1 and introduce an online focus group product right away. Based on his exploratory research and his own experience, he felt that the focus group technique could be successfully adapted to the Internet environment and would provide clients with a value-added product. He also felt that timing was important. SurveySite operates in the online environment, where decisions need to be made quickly. SurveySite couldn't afford to take a wait-and-see attitude, because that would allow competitors to develop the product first.

Instead of developing just one type of focus group, Rice and the team at SurveySite developed two different versions. The Online Focus Group was developed as a direct alternative to live, face-to-face groups. These groups of eight to ten people get together in a chat room for about 90 minutes of moderated discussion. Exhibit 5.8 shows an example of an online focus group. The second product is unique to the Internet environment: FocusSite is a two-day focus group, which is held with 25 or more participants. Respondents participate in the discussion on their own schedule several times during the two days, which allows companies to gather extensive amounts of information about their customers, while providing the respondents with flexibility.

Both products have been very successful for SurveySite. Companies have used the online focus groups to better understand customer motivations and to gauge customer reaction to specific marketing tactics, such as Web sites and Internet banner ads. You can view a demonstration of the online focus group by visiting the SurveySite Web site at www.surveysite.com.

feel satisfied because they have accumulated piles of impressive-looking computer printouts. However, to use the information to make marketing decisions, the marketer must analyze and report it in a way that makes sense. Thus, the important final steps in the marketing research process are to prepare a report of the research results and to integrate these results into long-term planning.

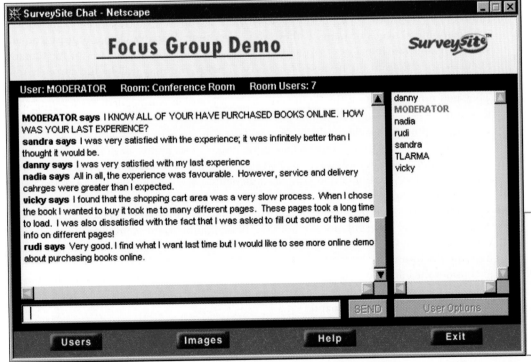

Exhibit 5.8

SurveySite online focus groups help clients understand consumers' buying behaviour on the Internet.

A good research report is intended as feedback to managers. For it to be useful, it should answer the following questions—in plain language.

- What is the problem being studied?
- What are the limitations of the study?
- What are the important findings?
- What are the recommendations for action based on the results?

INTEGRATING FEEDBACK INTO LONG-TERM PLANNING

Marketing research is an ongoing process of collecting and interpreting information that should be constantly referred to and updated as the company conducts long-term planning. At Hewlett-Packard, for example, every piece of customer feedback that the company receives is assigned to an "owner." This employee is responsible for acting on the information and informing the customer what was done to address the problem identified by the company's research.[41]

To make sense of research data, many firms develop a **marketing information system (MIS)** to continuously gather, sort, analyze, store, and distribute relevant and timely marketing information to its managers. A good MIS includes the internal data that marketing needs to detect problems in the firm's marketing effort and to evaluate the performance of specific marketing strategies. It also includes data on competition and other elements in the firm's business environment that affect its ability to compete, and it maintains data on demographic, cultural, and social trends that help identify marketing opportunities. Most MIS systems are designed to maintain up-to-date records of sales, orders, customer lists, inventories, costs, quality control, shipping and production schedules, and other activities in all functional areas that yield usable data for the firm's marketing decision makers. For example, Frito-Lay's MIS generates daily sales data by product line and by region that its managers use to evaluate the market share of different Frito-Lay products compared to each other and to competing snack foods in each region.[42]

PREDICTING THE FUTURE

Another interesting aspect of long-term planning is trying to anticipate marketplace conditions well into the future. Some marketing researchers, known as *futurists*, specialize in predicting the future. They try to forecast trends or changes in lifestyles that will affect the wants and needs of customers in the coming years. By understanding the possibilities of the future, marketers have the opportunity to shape their offerings to better meet and anticipate consumers' needs or wants as they evolve over time. Watts Wacker, a futurist who advises companies such as Coca-Cola and Samsung, had the following advice for Air Canada about its operations in the twenty-first century: "Energy, not time, will be the currency that you want to give back to travellers in the next century. Mobile ticket agencies in airports! They pull up to the gate if the flight you have just boarded is cancelled. Re-ticketing services in the air for changes in connecting flights." He also offered a more extreme suggestion: a soundproof capsule in which passengers can de-stress by screaming.[43]

One methodology futurists use is imagining different **scenarios**, or possible future situations, that might occur, and assigning a level of probability to each. Sometimes the future can be shaped by a limited number of key outcomes. For example, the future of the banking industry or the telecommunications industry can be shaped by laws that would deregulate the industries. It is possible to develop different scenarios that reflect different levels of deregulation—no deregulation, moderate deregulation, and complete deregulation. Creating scenarios is one of the most important techniques forecasters use in trying to understand the future. Each scenario can provide an image of the future that allows marketers to consider the impact of different marketing strategies. The farther we look into the future, however, the more difficult it is to develop distinct alternative scenarios, so forecasts get murkier as the time frame expands.

It is extremely unlikely that we can predict any one scenario with any certainty. We can, however, predict a range of scenarios that covers reasonable possibilities. Futurists call this

---

✳ ✳ ✳

marketing information system (MIS) Procedure developed by a firm to continuously gather, sort, analyze, store, and distribute relevant and timely marketing information to its managers.

✳ ✳ ✳

scenarios Possible future situations that futurists use to assess the likely impact of alternative marketing strategies.

a *scenario space*. The scenario space provides a strategic backdrop to consider alternative marketing strategies. It can help answer questions such as "What happens if I develop this product or technology and the world looks like scenario A?" "What happens if it looks like scenarios B or C or D?"

For example, Heublein developed a set of scenarios to try to predict consumers' preferences down the road for a variety of products. This approach helped the company to anticipate such trends as movement away from preferences for coloured liquors like scotch and bourbon in favour of wine, so it shifted its product emphasis in this direction, while rival Schenley did not and fell victim to changes in demand as this change indeed developed.[44]

One prominent futurist company, Brain Reserve, provides its clients with FutureScapes, which guide companies in understanding and anticipating consumer behaviour and show them how to leverage that insight by developing new products and services to meet the needs of their future customers. By tracking themes that show up in movies and other mass media, BrainReserve has predicted such trends as cocooning (staying home), cashing out (quitting the rat race), down-aging (acting youthful), and the surge of demand for such products as fresh food and four-wheel-drive cars.[45] Although many marketers disagree with these predictions, others eagerly retain the services of these futurists to help them prepare for the years ahead.

Chapter Summary

1. Describe the marketing research process.

   To make informed decisions, marketers either conduct their own research or hire an outside firm to do it for them. The research process begins with defining the problem and choosing the research technique that will provide the needed information. This results in a research design that specifies how data will be collected and what will be done with this information. The research tries to ensure that the data are valid and reliable and that responses are representative of the target market. The final step is to implement the results by integrating this feedback into long-term planning.

2. Explain the differences between exploratory, problem-solving, and causal research, and describe some research techniques available to marketers.

   Exploratory research typically uses qualitative data collected by individual interviews, focus groups, or observational methods such as ethnography. Problem-solving techniques rely on quantitative data generated by surveys and other interactive instruments that collect information on the phone, in the mail, in person, or on the Internet. Causal research goes a step further by designing controlled experiments to understand cause-and-effect relationships between marketing independent variables, such as price changes, and dependent variables, such as sales.

3. Deal with the issues involved in making sense of research results.

   When interpreting research results, the marketer must be aware of issues that may affect the quality of the data collected. Validity is the extent to which the research actually measures what it was intended to measure. Reliability is the extent to which the research measurement techniques are free of errors. Representativeness is the extent to which consumers in the study are similar to a larger group in which the organization has an interest.

4. Discuss how marketers implement research results.

   For research to be useful, it must be sorted, organized, and analyzed. Results should be clearly presented in a research report that specifies the problem being studied, the limitations of the study, the important findings, and recommendations for action based on the results. In some cases the results are combined with other information in a marketing information system that is used by decision makers on an ongoing basis.

KEY TERMS

case study (127)

causal research (132)

consumer interviews (126)

cross-sectional design (128)

data mining (135)

descriptive research (128)

ethnography (127)

experiments (132)

exploratory research (125)

focus group (126)

longitudinal design (129)

marketing information system (MIS) (126)

marketing intelligence (122)

marketing research (122)

projective techniques (127)

reliability (136)

representativeness (136)

research design (124)

sampling (136)

scenarios (138)

single-source data (134)

survey (129)

validity (135)

Chapter Review

Marketing Concepts: **Testing Your Knowledge**

1. Describe the types of information marketers need to make effective decisions.

2. What are the phases in the marketing research process? Why is defining the problem to be researched so important?

3. What is the goal of exploratory research? What techniques are used to gather data in exploratory research?

4. What is problem-solving research? What techniques are used in problem-solving research?

5. What ethical problems are associated with marketing research? What problems does a researcher encounter when conducting marketing research in global markets?

6. What are single-source data? What are some ways that marketers use single-source data?

7. What is meant by reliability, validity, and representativeness of research results?

8. What is a marketing information system (MIS)? What types of information are included in an MIS? What are some of the sources of data in an MIS?

9. What are futurists? How do futurists assist marketers in long-term planning?

Marketing Concepts: **Discussing Choices and Issues**

1. Do you think marketers should be allowed to conduct market research with young children? Why or why not?

2. Are you willing to divulge personal information to marketing researchers? How much are you willing to tell, or where would you draw the line?

3. What is your overall attitude toward marketing research? Do you think it is a beneficial activity from a consumer's perspective? Or do you think it merely gives marketers new insights on how to convince consumers to buy something they really don't want or need?

4. Sometimes firms use data mining to identify and abandon customers who are not profitable, because they don't spend enough to justify the service needed or because they return a large proportion of the items they buy. What do you think of such practices? Is it ethical for firms to prune out these customers?

Marketing Practice: **Applying What You've Learned**

1. Your firm is planning to begin marketing a consumer product in several global markets. You have been given the responsibility of developing plans for marketing research to be conducted in Eastern Europe, Western Europe, and China. In a role-playing situation, present the difficulties you expect to encounter, if any, in conducting research in each of these areas.

2. As an account executive with a marketing research firm, you are responsible for deciding on the type of research to be used in various studies conducted for your clients. For each of the following client questions, list your choices.

   a. What do consumers like and dislike about shampoo?

   b. What are the best media vehicles for a local insurance broker to use for its advertising?

   c. How much label information on cereal boxes do consumers read before they make a purchase?

   d. Are consumers more likely to buy brands that are labelled as environmentally friendly?

   e. How do women determine if a particular perfume is right for them?

   f. What types of people read the local newspaper?

   g. How frequently do consumers switch brands of soft drinks?

   h. How will an increase in the price of a brand of laundry detergent affect sales?

   i. How do the different members of a family participate in the purchase of a new car?

3. Your marketing research firm is planning to conduct surveys to gather information for a number of clients. Your boss has asked you and a few other new employees to do some pre-

liminary work. He has asked each of you to choose three of the topics that will be included in the project and to prepare an analysis of the advantages and disadvantages of mail surveys, telephone surveys, face-to-face surveys, or observation for each.

a. the amount of alcoholic beverages consumed in a city

b. young adults' use of illegal drugs

c. why a local convenience store has been losing customers

d. how heavily the company should invest in manufacturing and marketing home fax machines

e. the amount of money people spend on lottery tickets

f. reader recall of magazine advertisements

g. what local doctors would like to see changed in the hospitals in the city

h. consumers' attitudes toward several sports celebrities

Marketing Mini-Project: **Learning by Doing**

The purpose of this mini-project is to familiarize you with research techniques used by marketers and to help you apply these techniques to managerial decision making.

1. With a group of three other students in your class, select a small retail business or fast-food restaurant to use as a "client" for your project. Be sure to get the manager's permission before conducting your research. Then choose a topic from among the following possibilities to develop a study problem:

   · employee–customer interactions

   · the busiest periods of customer activity

   · customer perceptions of service

   · customer likes and dislikes about offerings

   · customer likes and dislikes about the environment in the place of business

   · the benefits customers perceive to be important

   · the age groups that frequent the place of business

   · the buying habits of a particular age group

   · how customer complaints are handled

2. Develop a plan for the research:

   a. Define the problem as you will study it.

   b. Choose the type of research you will use.

   c. Select the techniques you will use to gather data.

   d. Develop the mode and format for data collection.

3. Conduct the research.

4. Write a report or develop a class presentation that includes four parts.

   a. Introduction: a brief overview of the business and the problem studied

   b. Methodology: the type of research used, the techniques used to gather data (and why they were chosen), and the instruments and procedures used, the number of respondents, duration of the study, and other details that would allow someone to replicate your study

   c. Results: a compilation of the results (perhaps in table form) and the conclusions drawn

   d. Recommendations: a list of recommendations for actions management might take based on the conclusions drawn from the study.

Real People, Real Surfers: **Exploring the Web**

Monitoring changes in demographics and other consumer trends is an important part of the marketing intelligence included in an MIS. Today, much of this information is gathered by government research and is available on the Internet.

Statistics Canada provides tabled data for Canadian cities at their site, www.statcan.ca. Using both Statistics Canada data and any other data you can find on the Internet, develop a report on a Canadian city of your choice that answers these questions:

1. What is the total population of the city?

2. Describe the population of the area in terms of age, income, education, ethnic background, marital status, occupation, and housing.

3. How does the city compare to the demographic characteristics of the entire Canadian population?

4. What is your opinion of the different Web sites you used? How useful are they to marketers? How easy were they to navigate? Was there information that you wanted that was not available? Was there more or less information from the sites than you anticipated? Explain.

MARKETING IN ACTION

Pet Food Express

Donna Boyd and Tom Earl were designing a business they would start when they finished their business studies in three months. They were enthusiastic about the possibilities for their idea: a pet food delivery service (tentatively named Pet Food Express) for a medium sized city in Ontario. They knew no similar service was available in the city, and that most pet owners shopped for pet food either at grocery or pet stores. As dog and cat owners themselves, they felt there was a real need for this service: It would provide convenience to pet owners by offering a selection of popular pet foods that could be ordered over the phone or via e-mail. The delivery aspect of the service would provide real benefits for people who like to shop in bulk for their pet food, but who don't like the hassle of transporting the food. Tom and Donna also thought that they would be able to offer better discounts than stores because they wouldn't incur the large overhead that stores do. They also anticipated that the service would especially appeal to pet owners who were seniors and those who did not have a vehicle of their own.

To assess demand for their idea, Donna and Tom decided to conduct some market research. They decided to do a phone survey with people randomly chosen from the local phone directory. They designed the following questionnaire:

Hello, my name is _____ and I am conducting a survey. May I have a moment of your time to ask you a few questions?

1. Do you own a dog or a cat? Yes___ No___
2. Do you have more than one pet? Yes___ No___
3. Do you do the purchasing of the pet food? Yes___ No___ (If no, may I please speak with the person who does the purchasing?)
4. Do you buy canned or dry food for your pet? Canned___ Dry___
5. What brand of pet food do you buy?
   If they purchase dry food ask this:
6. Which one of these size/price combinations do you prefer?
   a) 10 lb. bag for $15   b) 20 lb. bag for $25   c) 40 lb. bag for $40
7. What do you find most unappealing about buying a large quantity of pet food?
8. On a scale of 1-5, with 1 being Not at all Important and 5 being Very Important, how important are the following to you when you purchase your pet food?
   Brand   Price   Size of Package   Nutrition Quality
   Selection   Store Location   Pet's Preference   Delivery Service
9. At which store do you buy the bulk of your pet food?
10. How often do you prefer buying your pet food: Weekly, Biweekly, Monthly, Other
11. If a delivery service for your pet food was available, would it appeal to you? Yes___ No___
12. What radio station do you normally listen to?
13. Which of the following age groups do you belong to?
    Less than 18   18-25   25-45   45-64   65 and over
14. Which of the following groups would your total household income fall under?
    Less than $20 000 $20 000–$45 000 $45 000–$60 000   over $60 000
15. Do you ever purchase products over the Internet? Yes___ No___

THINGS TO THINK ABOUT

1. Evaluate Tom and Donna's proposed research technique (telephone survey). Develop a more comprehensive market research plan based on the first two stages of the marketing research process.
2. What changes would you make to the questionnaire? Rewrite it, incorporating your changes.
3. What other sources of information would be useful to them as they develop their business idea?

6

Why People Buy: Consumer Behaviour

When you have completed your study of this chapter, you should be able to

CHAPTER OBJECTIVES

1. Explain why understanding consumer behaviour is important to organizations.

2. Explain the prepurchase, purchase, and postpurchase activities consumers engage in when making decisions.

3. Describe how internal factors influence consumers' decision-making processes.

4. Describe how situational factors at the time and place of purchase may influence consumer behaviour.

5. Describe how consumers' relationships with other people influence their decision-making processes.

Real People, Real Decisions ✔ ✘
Meet Robert Barnard
A Decision Maker at d~Code

Robert Barnard is one of the founders of d~code, a company that researches the needs, wants, and behaviours of the Nexus generation Canadians: 18 to 34 year olds. The Nexus generation accounts for approximately one-third of the Canadian adult population, making it an attractive target segment for many companies. The insights that Barnard and other members of the d~Code team can provide about the behaviour of this consumer segment are, therefore, in great demand by organizations who consider Nexus consumers to be one of their target markets.

Robert Barnard began his entrepreneurial career early. At the age of 19, he created a clothing company and, at the same time, formed Generation 2000, an innovative national youth organization, which encouraged young Canadians to get involved in the development of Canada. In 1994,

Barnard and others formed d~Code to provide strategies and ideas to organizations seeking to connect with the Nexus Generation. d~Code is the only company in Canada that focuses exclusively on understanding the Nexus Generation.

Barnard has a BA in Geography from the University of Western Ontario and, in addition to his work at d~Code, has served on several not-for-profit boards of directors. He was named as one of the "100 Canadians to Watch For" by *Maclean's* magazine in 1993 and as one of Canada's "Top 40 Under 40" in 1997.

Sources are R. Barnard, D. Cosgrave, and J. Welsh, *Chips & pop: Decoding the Nexus generation*, Toronto: Malcolm Lester Books, 1998; personal interview with Robert Barnard.

d~Code
www.d-code.com

✳ ✳ ✳
consumer behaviour The process individuals or groups go through to select, purchase, and use goods, services, ideas, or experiences to satisfy their needs and desires.

Decisions, Decisions

New products, clever packaging, and creative advertising surround us, clamouring for our attention—and our money. But consumers don't all respond in the same way to marketing activities. Each consumer is a unique person, with unique reasons for choosing one product over another. Recall that the focus of the marketing concept is to satisfy consumers' wants and needs. These wants and needs can be satisfied only to the extent that marketers understand why and how people buy products. Robert Barnard helps Canadian marketers understand Nexus consumers by answering such questions as: what are the attitudes and lifestyles of Nexus consumers, why do they prefer certain products, which ads do they respond to, and how do they purchase products? **Consumer behaviour** is the process individuals or groups go through to select, purchase, and use goods, services, ideas, or experiences. Marketers recognize that consumer behaviour is an ongoing process—it is more than what happens at the moment a consumer hands over money and, in turn, receives a good or service.

Although it seems as if some purchases are made spontaneously (and we may regret our rashness later), in reality, we make these buying decisions only after we have undergone a series of steps—problem recognition, information search, evaluation of alternatives, product choice, and postpurchase evaluation—summarized in Figure 6.1.

Traditionally, researchers have tried to understand how consumers make decisions by assuming that people carefully collect information about competing products, determine which products possess the characteristics or product attributes important to their needs, weigh the pluses and minuses of each alternative, and arrive at a satisfactory decision. But how accurate is this picture of the decision-making process?

Although it does seem that people undergo these steps when making an important purchase, is it realistic to assume that they do this for everything they buy? Researchers now realize that consumers actually possess a set of decision approaches, ranging from painstaking analysis to pure whim, depending on the importance of what is being bought and how much effort the person is willing to put into the decision.[1] Researchers have found it convenient to think in terms of an "effort" continuum, which is anchored on one end by *habit-*

ual decision making (such as deciding to purchase a can of pop) and at the other end by *extended problem solving* (such as deciding to purchase a computer). Many decisions fall somewhere in the middle and are characterized by *limited problem solving*, which means that consumers do work to make a decision, but most likely rely on simple rules of thumb instead of learning about and considering all the ins and outs of every product alternative. As the ad for Sympatico.ca in Exhibit 6.1 implies, some Internet marketers believe that the Internet can reduce the effort needed to make product decisions by offering so many products and services in one place.

Involvement determines the extent of effort a person puts into deciding what to buy. **Involvement** is the importance of the perceived consequences of the purchase to the person. As a rule, we are more involved in the decision-making process for products that we perceive as risky in some way (regardless of whether they really are). **Perceived risk** may be present if the product is expensive, complex, and hard to understand, or if the purchase of the wrong product could result in embarrassment or social rejection. For instance, some people perceive clothing purchases as risky because they feel a wrong choice could lead to negative social consequences. Perceived risk can also be a factor in the buying process itself for certain products. A study of condom buying among Canadian university students, for example, found that 66% of men and 60% of women report that they are embarrassed when buying condoms and, therefore, do not buy them at all. As one researcher put it, "Approaching the cashier is the moment of truth. There is also the worry that a 'price check on a 12-pack of Durex condoms' will be announced to the entire store."[2]

When perceived risk is low, as in buying a pack of gum, the consumer feels *low involvement* in the decision-making process—the consumer is not overly concerned about which option he or she chooses because it is not especially important or risky. In low-involvement situations, the consumer's decision is often a response to environmental cues, such as deciding to try a new type of chewing gum because it is prominently displayed at a store checkout counter. Under these circumstances, managers must concentrate on how products are displayed at the time of purchase to influence the decision maker. For example, a chewing gum marketer may decide to spend more money to be sure its gum stands out at a checkout display or to change the colour of the gum wrapper to a bright pink to be sure it gets noticed among the other gums.

For *high-involvement* purchases, such as a house, car, computer, or interview suit, the consumer is more likely to carefully process all of the available information and to have thought about the decision well before buying the item. The consequences of the purchase are important and risky, especially because a bad decision can result in significant financial losses, aggravation, decreased performance, or embarrassment. So for high-involvement products, managers must start to reduce perceived risk by educating the consumer about why their product is the best choice well in advance of the time that the consumer is ready to make a decision. To understand what goes on during each of the steps in the decision-making process, in the next section, we'll follow the fortunes of one consumer, a student named Emma, who is in the market for a new notebook computer. This is a highly involving purchase decision for her because of the cost of the product and because the performance of

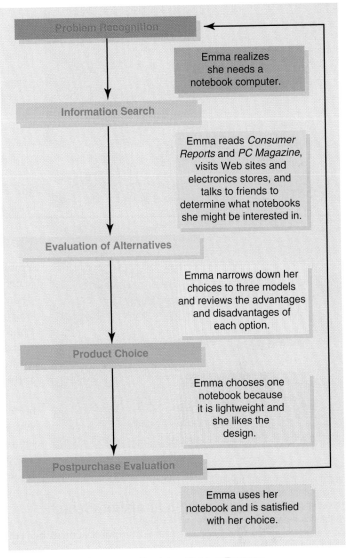

Figure 6.1 The Consumer Decision-Making Process

✳ ✳ ✳
involvement The relative importance of perceived consequences of the purchase to a consumer.
✳ ✳ ✳
perceived risk The belief that use of a product has potentially negative consequences, either financial, physical, or social.

Exhibit 6.1

Some companies believe that buying online simplifies consumer decision making.

the computer will have an important impact on her own performance in courses and, perhaps, in future jobs.

Problem Recognition

Problem recognition occurs whenever the consumer sees a significant difference between their current state of affairs and some desired or ideal state. The consumer needs to solve a *problem*, which may be small or large, simple or complex. A student like Emma, who needs to have a computer for writing papers, doing research on the Internet, and sending e-mail, has a problem. Although she can use the computers provided on campus, she realizes that often when she needs a computer the most, such as at the end of term, so does every other student. Emma also wants her computer to be portable so that she can use it to take notes in classes and take it to the library while she researches her assignments. Thinking about the future, Emma realizes that, in her job, she will probably have a lot of work to do after hours. Having a notebook computer will allow her to do the work in the comfort of her own apartment.

✳ ✳ ✳

problem recognition The process that occurs whenever the consumer sees a significant difference between his or her current state of affairs and some desired or ideal state. This recognition initiates the decision-making process.

✳ ✳ ✳

information search The process whereby a consumer searches for appropriate information needed to make a reasonable decision.

Information Search

Once Emma recognizes her computer problem, she needs adequate information to resolve it. During the **information search** part of the decision-making process, the consumer checks their memory and surveys the environment to identify what options exist to solve the problem. The ad shown in Exhibit 6.2 reminds us that some information sources, such as advertisements or the Yellow Pages, often provide valuable guidance during this step. Emma might rely on ads she has seen for notebook computers, recommendations from friends, and additional research she might do by reading *Consumer Reports* and *PC Magazine*, or by signing onto Web sites for companies, such as Dell Computers Canada (www.dell.ca) and Apple Canada (www.apple.com/ca). She also might visit some electronics stores, like the Future Shop, where she can discuss her purchase with salespeople and try out some computers.

Evaluation of Alternatives

Once the alternatives have been identified, the consumer must decide which are preferable. There are two components to this stage of the decision-making process. First, a consumer, armed with information, identifies the set of products they are interested in. Then they narrow down their choices by deciding which of all the possibilities are feasible and comparing the advantages and disadvantages of each remaining option. Emma might want a top-of-the-line notebook, like a Dell Inspiron, but realizes that her student budget doesn't allow for such a purchase. As she looks around, she decides that the notebooks she likes in her price range are the Apple iBook, the Compaq Presario, and the Gateway Solo. She has narrowed down her options by considering only affordable notebooks.

Now, Emma has to choose. It's time for her to look more systematically at each of the three possibilities and identify the important characteristics, or **evaluative criteria**, she will

✳ ✳ ✳

evaluative criteria The dimensions that consumers use to compare competing product alternatives.

Exhibit 6.2

Sources such as the Yellow Pages may be used by consumers during their information search.

use to decide among them. These may be the power of the computer, its weight, the size of the monitor, the battery life, the warranty offered, or even the computer's design or colour options. Keep in mind that marketers often play a role in educating consumers about *which* product characteristics should be used as evaluative criteria—usually, they emphasize the dimensions in which their product excels. For example, ads for the Apple iBook focus on its light weight and ease of use, whereas ads for the Compaq Presario may focus on price, because it is one of the least expensive notebook computers available.

Product Choice

Deciding on one product and acting on this choice is the next step in the decision-making process. Emma has spent several weeks thinking about the alternatives, and she's finally ready to take the plunge and buy! After agonizing over her choice, she decides that, even though the Gateway Solo was rated the best by *Consumer Reports,* the Apple iBook has the features she is looking for. She feels it offers similar technical features to the other options, but has the best design. The recent advertising slogan she has seen for Apple, "Think different," appeals to her sense of individuality, and the iBook is the lightest of all the options and will easily fit in her backpack. She signs onto the Apple Canada Web site and buys her notebook computer. A few days later the computer arrives at her door.

Choices often are complicated because it's hard to juggle all of the different product characteristics. One notebook computer may offer better memory, another is $500 cheaper, whereas another is lighter in weight. How do consumers make sense of all these characteristics and arrive at a decision?

Consumers often rely on decision guidelines when weighing the claims made by different companies. These **heuristics**, or rules, help simplify the process. One such heuristic is "price = quality," so many people willingly buy the more expensive brand because they assume that if it costs more, it *must* be better.

Perhaps the most common heuristic is **brand loyalty**, which assumes that people buy from the same company over and over because they believe that the company makes superior products. Consumers feel that it's not worth the effort to consider competing options. The creation of brand loyalty is a prized goal for marketers. People form preferences for a favourite brand and then may literally never change their minds in the course of a lifetime, making it extremely difficult for rivals to persuade them to switch.

Postpurchase Evaluation

In the last stage of decision making, the consumer evaluates the quality of the decision made. After mulling over the alternatives and picking one, they evaluate just how good a choice it was. Everyone has experienced regret after making a purchase, and (hopefully) we have all been pleased with something we've bought. The evaluation of the product results in a level of **consumer satisfaction/dissatisfaction**, which is determined by the overall feel-

✳ ✳ ✳
heuristics A mental rule of thumb that leads to a speedy decision by simplifying the process.

✳ ✳ ✳
brand loyalty A pattern of repeat product purchases, accompanied by an underlying positive attitude toward the brand, which is based on the belief that the brand makes products superior to its competition.

✳ ✳ ✳
consumer satisfaction/dissatisfaction The overall feelings or attitude a person has about a product after purchasing it.

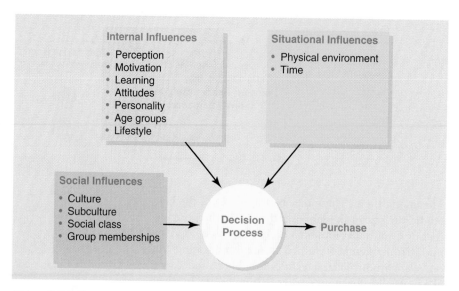

Figure 6.2 Influences on Consumer Decision Making

ings, or attitude, a person has about a product after purchasing it. In this case, fortunately, Emma's feelings couldn't be better. Her computer is reliable and easy to use, and its light weight means that she can easily carry it to her classes.

Just how do consumers decide if they are satisfied with their purchases? One answer would be, "That's easy. The product is either wonderful, or it isn't." However, it's a little more complicated than that. When consumers buy a product, they have some *expectations* of product quality. How well a product or service meets or exceeds these expectations determines customer satisfaction. In other words, consumers assess product quality by comparing what they have bought to a *performance standard* created by a mixture of information from marketing communications, informal information sources such as friends and family, and their own experience with the product category.

So, even though Emma's new iBook is not as powerful as some of the other options she considered, she's happy with her purchase because it meets or exceeds her own expectations. Emma has completed the consumer decision-making process by recognizing a problem, conducting an information search to resolve it, identifying the feasible alternatives, making a product choice, and then evaluating the quality of her decision.

As well as understanding the mechanics of the consumer decision-making process, marketers try to ascertain what influences in consumers' lives affect this process. There are three main categories: internal, situational, and social influences. In Emma's case, for example, the evaluative criteria she used to compare notebook computers and her feelings about each computer may have been influenced by such internal factors as her desire to be unique and how the iBook suited that, such situational factors as her satisfaction with the information and service provided on the Apple Canada Web site, and such social influences as her prediction that her friends would be impressed when they saw her taking notes in class on a new notebook computer. Figure 6.2 shows the influences in the decision-making process and emphasizes that all of these factors work together to affect the ultimate choice each person makes. Let's consider how each of these three types of influence work, starting with internal factors.

Internal Influences on Consumer Decisions

In certain advertisements for Gillette razor blades, a "macho" man is shown in a rugged, outdoor setting. This imagery is bound to appeal to male consumers, right? Not necessarily. When rival company Schick studied how men were reacting to Gillette's ads, it found that these images called up an unpleasant association men had learned to make with this kind of harsh environment. They felt like "lone wolves" rather than people who like to be touched.[3] Because many men today like to be a bit more "touchy-feely" than the rough, tough "macho" masculine type depicted in the Gillette ad, this wasn't the feeling they wanted to have after shaving. Based on this research, Schick devised an ad for its razors showing a woman gently stroking a man's face—a very different approach from Gillette's ad. Let's see how internal factors relating to the way people absorb and interpret this kind of information influence the decision-making process.

Perception

Perception is the process by which people select, organize, and interpret information from the outside world. We receive information in the form of *sensations*, the immediate response of our sensory receptors—eyes, ears, nose, mouth, and fingers—to such basic stimuli as light, colour, and sound. Our impressions about products often are based on their physical qualities. We try to make sense of the sensations we receive by interpreting them in light of our past experiences. For example, Emma chose the Apple notebook computer partly because of its distinctive design, which she associates with style and individuality.

The perception process has important implications for marketers because, as consumers absorb and make sense of the vast quantities of information competing for their attention, it is likely that they won't notice any one marketing message. And, if they do notice it, there's no guarantee that the meaning they give it will be quite the same one the marketer intended. The issues that marketers need to understand during this process include exposure, perceptual selection, and interpretation.

- *Exposure:* The stimulus must be within range of people's sensory receptors to be noticed. For example, the lettering on a billboard must be big enough for a passing motorist to read easily, or the message will be lost. As Exhibit 6.3 shows, many people believe (falsely) that even messages they can't see will persuade them to buy advertised

✳ ✳ ✳
perception The process by which people select, organize, and interpret information from the outside world.

GORDON'S AND TONIC

GORDON'S
EST 1769
SPECIAL
LONDON
DRY GIN

EXPERIENCE THE MIX

Exhibit 6.3

Many people believe in subliminal advertising, even when the images are clearly visible.

products. Although claims about subliminal advertising involving messages hidden in ice cubes among other places have been surfacing since the 1950s, little evidence supports their existence or claims that this technique would work even if it were used. The British ad shown here reflects this belief, although in this case the characters are clearly visible.

- *Perceptual Selection*: Consumers choose to pay attention to some stimuli but not to others. Consumers are more likely to be aware of messages that speak to their current needs. A newspaper ad for a fast-food restaurant that would go unnoticed after lunch may grab your attention if you sneak a glance at the paper during a class that ends at lunchtime.

- *Interpretation*: Meaning is assigned to the stimulus. This meaning is influenced by prior associations the person has learned. The Benetton ad shown in Exhibit 6.4 is a great example of how these assumptions alter our interpretations. Although the ad shows two men handcuffed to each other, some people assumed that the black man was cuffed to the white man, and the company was the target of many complaints about racism after the ad appeared.

Motivation

Motivation is an internal state that drives us to satisfy needs. Once we activate a need, a state of tension exists that *drives* the consumer toward some *goal* that will reduce this tension by eliminating the need.

For example, Emma began to experience a gap between her present state—having to rely on the computers on campus—and a desired state—having a computer that allows her to work at home and on campus. The need for a new notebook computer is activated, which motivates Emma to test and learn about different models, to talk with friends about their experiences with notebook computers, and finally to buy a new notebook computer.

Psychologist Abraham Maslow developed an influential approach to motivation.[4] Maslow formulated a **hierarchy of needs**, which categorizes motives according to five levels of importance, the more basic needs being on the bottom of the hierarchy and the higher needs at the top. The hierarchy suggests that before a person can meet needs in a given level, they must first at least partially meet the needs in the levels below. As illustrated in Figure 6.3, this approach shows individuals starting at the lowest level with basic needs for food, cloth-

---

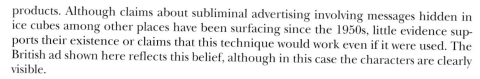

Benetton
www.benetton.com

✳ ✳ ✳

motivation An internal state that drives us to satisfy needs by activating goal-oriented behaviour.

✳ ✳ ✳

hierarchy of needs An approach that categorizes motives according to five levels of importance, the more basic needs being on the bottom of the hierarchy and the higher needs at the top.

Exhibit 6.4

People's prior assumptions coloured their interpretations of this controversial ad.

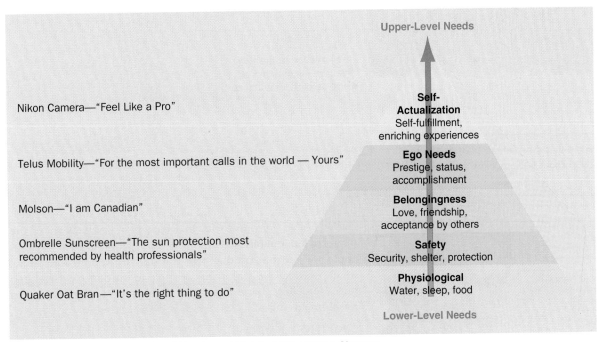

Figure 6.3 Maslow's Hierarchy of Needs and Related Advertising Slogans

ing, and shelter and then progressing to higher levels to satisfy more complex needs, such as the need to be accepted by others or to feel good about themselves. Ultimately, people can reach the highest-level needs, and they will be motivated to attain such goals as spiritual fulfillment. As the figure shows, if marketers understand the particular level of needs that is relevant to consumers in their target market, they can tailor their products and messages to point out how these needs can be satisfied.

Learning

Learning is a change in behaviour after gaining information or experience. Learning about products can occur deliberately, as when we set out to gather information about different CD players before buying one brand. We also learn even when we are not trying. Consumers recognize many brand names and can hum many product jingles, for example, even for products they themselves do not use. Psychologists who study learning have advanced several theories to explain the learning process, and because a major goal for marketers is to "teach" consumers to prefer their products, these perspectives are important. In this section, we'll briefly review the most important perspectives on how people learn.

BEHAVIOURAL LEARNING

Behavioural learning theories assume that learning takes place as the result of connections that form between events perceived by the individual. In one type of behavioural learning, **classical conditioning**, a person perceives two stimuli at about the same time. After a while, the person transfers his or her response from one stimulus to the other. For example, an ad shows a product and a breathtakingly beautiful scene, so that (the marketer hopes) you will transfer the positive feelings you get from looking at the scene to the advertised product. Another common form of behavioural learning is called **operant conditioning**, which occurs when people learn that their actions result in rewards or punishments. This feedback influences how they will respond in similar situations in the future. Just as a rat in a maze learns the route to a piece of cheese, consumers who receive a reward, such as a prize in the bottom of a box of cereal, will be more likely to buy that brand again. That feedback acts as a *reinforcement* for the behaviour.

The learned associations in classical and operant conditioning also have a tendency to transfer to other similar stimuli in a process called **stimulus generalization**. This means that

✲ ✲ ✲
learning A relatively permanent change in behaviour caused by acquired information or experience.

✲ ✲ ✲
behavioural learning theories Theories of learning that focus on how consumer behaviour is changed by external events or stimuli.

✲ ✲ ✲
classical conditioning Learning that occurs when a stimulus eliciting a response is paired with another stimulus that initially does not elicit a response on its own but will cause a similar response over time because of its association with the first stimulus.

✲ ✲ ✲
operant conditioning Learning that occurs as the result of rewards or punishments.

✲ ✲ ✲
stimulus generalization Behaviour caused by a reaction to one stimulus that occurs in the presence of other similar stimuli.

Since the program's inception in 1981, over one million Esso Medals of Achievement have been awarded to young boys and girls.

"Good sportsmanship and fair play are the two best goals to shoot for in hockey and in life."

Wayne Gretzky

The medals are not for the best, fastest or strongest hockey players, but for those who give their best, who love the game and who exhibit good sportsmanship.

Any minor league team is eligible to receive three medals and 17 Certificates of Participation. See your local Esso-branded retailer, visit www.imperialoil.ca or contact the Canadian Hockey Association for an enrollment form.

Honorary Chairman
Esso Medals and Certificates of Achievement Program

Imperial Oil
CANADA **Esso**

*Trademarks of Imperial Oil Limited. Imperial Oil, licensee.
®Official Mark of the Canadian Hockey Association.

Exhibit 6.5

Observational learning can be encouraged by using celebrity endorsers.

✳ ✳ ✳

cognitive learning theory A theory of learning that stresses the importance of internal mental processes and that views people as problem solvers, who actively use information from the world around them to master their environment.

✳ ✳ ✳

attitude A learned predisposition to respond favourably or unfavourably to stimuli based on relatively enduring evaluations of people, objects, and issues.

✳ ✳ ✳

personality The psychological characteristics that consistently influence the way a person responds to situations in the environment.

the good or bad feelings associated with a product will "rub off" on other products that resemble it. For example, some marketers create *product line extensions*, in which new products share the name of an established brand so that people's good feelings about the current product will transfer to the new one. Dole, which is associated with fruit, was able to introduce refrigerated juices and juice bars; Sun Maid branched out from raisins to raisin bread.

COGNITIVE LEARNING

In contrast to behavioural theories of learning, **cognitive learning theory** views people as problem solvers, who do more than passively react to associations between stimuli. Supporters of this viewpoint stress the role of creativity and insight during the learning process. One type of cognitive learning theory is *observational learning*, which occurs when people watch the actions of others and note what happens to them as a result. They store these observations in memory and, at some later point, use the information to guide their own behaviour, especially when they admire or identify with these people in some way. Many promotional strategies, such as the ad featuring Wayne Gretzky in Exhibit 6.5, centre around endorsements by athletes, movie stars, and music idols whose fans have observed their successes.

Attitudes

An **attitude** is a lasting evaluation of a person, object, or issue.[5] Consumers have attitudes toward very product-specific behaviours, such as using Crest toothpaste rather than Colgate, as well as toward more general consumption-related behaviours, such as how often to brush one's teeth.

A person's attitude has three components: affect, cognition, and behaviour. In a marketing context, *affect* is the overall feeling a person has about a product. *Cognition* is the beliefs and knowledge the person has about the product. *Behaviour* is what happens when the person takes action by buying or using the product.

Depending on the nature of the product, one of these three components—feeling, knowing, or doing—will be the dominant influence in creating an attitude toward a product. Affect is usually dominant for expressive products, which we use to say something about ourselves, such as perfume, in which the way the product makes us feel determines our attitude toward it. Cognition may be more important for complex products, such as computers, which require us to process technical information. Behaviour often determines attitudes for commonly purchased, low-involvement items, such as chewing gum, for which we often form an attitude based simply on how the product tastes or performs.

Personality

Personality is the set of unique psychological characteristics that consistently influences the way a person responds to situations in the environment. One adventure-seeking consumer

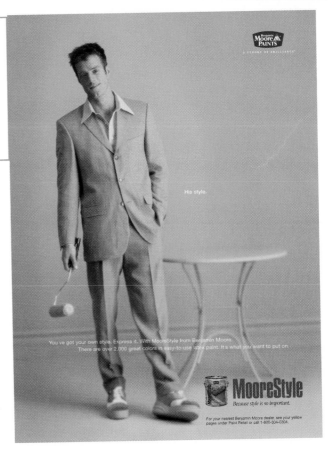

Exhibit 6.6

Personality and style can influence product choice.

may always be on the lookout for new experiences and cutting-edge products, whereas another is happiest in familiar surroundings, using the same brands over and over. To appeal to thrill seekers who like to break the rules, Isuzu positioned its Rodeo sport-utility vehicle as a car that lets a driver break the rules. Advertising was created to support this idea by showing kids jumping in mud puddles, running with scissors, and colouring out of the lines.[6] For marketers, identifying differences in personality contribute value to crafting marketing strategies. Some specific characteristics, called personality traits, relevant to marketing strategies include innovativeness, self-confidence, and sociability.

- *Innovativeness*: The degree to which a person likes to try new things. Cutting-edge products, such as radical new hairstyles and fashions, might appeal to an innovative woman.

- *Self-confidence*: The degree to which a person has a positive evaluation of his or her abilities, including the ability to make good product decisions. People who don't have much self-confidence are good candidates for such services as those of image consultants, who assist in making the right choices.

- *Sociability*: The degree to which a person enjoys social interaction. A sociable person might, for example, respond to entertainment-related products that claim to bring people together or make parties more fun.[7]

The notion that consumers buy products that are extensions of their personality traits makes sense. Marketers try to create *brand personalities* to appeal to different types of consumers. The ad for Benjamin Moore paints in Exhibit 6.6, for example, positions their brand of paint as a way of expressing personality and style.

How we feel about our own personalities strongly influences our purchasing decisions. We may buy a certain type of clothing or drink a particular brand of beer because we think it makes a statement about who we are. A person's **self-concept** is his or her attitude toward the self. The self-concept is composed of a mixture of beliefs about one's abilities, observations of one's own behaviour, and feelings (usually both positive and negative) about one's personal attributes, such as body type or facial features. The extent to which a person's self-concept is positive or negative can influence the products he or she buys.

In developing a new line of snack cakes, Sara Lee found that consumers who had a negative self-concept preferred portioned snack items because they felt they lacked the self-control to regulate how much they ate.[8] On the more positive side, *self-esteem advertising* attempts to stimulate positive feelings about the self.[9] This technique is used in ads for Kellogg's Special K cereal, such as the one shown in Exhibit 6.7, which attempt to counter negative self-esteem by encouraging their female consumers to "look good on your own terms."

✳ ✳ ✳

self-concept An individual's self-image that is composed of a mixture of beliefs, observations, and feelings about personal attributes.

Age Groups

d~Code is a company that recognizes the value of understanding the characteristics and behaviours of consumers in different age groups. A person's age is an important determinant

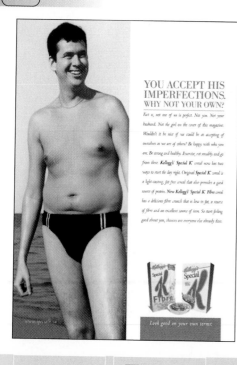

YOU ACCEPT HIS IMPERFECTIONS. WHY NOT YOUR OWN?

Fact is, not one of us is perfect. Not you. Not your husband. Not the girl on the cover of this magazine. Wouldn't it be nice if we could be as accepting of ourselves as we are of others? Be happy with who you are. Be strong and healthy. Exercise, eat sensibly and go from there. Kellogg's Special K cereal now has two ways to start the day right. Original Special K cereal is a light-tasting, fat free cereal that also provides a good source of protein. New Kellogg's Special K Fibre cereal has a delicious fibre crunch that is low in fat, a source of fibre and an excellent source of iron. So start feeling good about you, chances are everyone else already does.

Look good on your own terms.

Exhibit 6.7

Self-esteem advertising encourages consumers to have a positive self-concept.

of his or her needs and wants. Many of us feel we have more in common with those of our own age, because we share a common set of experiences and memories about cultural events, whether these involve World War II or Edgefest. Indeed, marketers of products from cookies to cars are banking on *nostalgia* to draw in customers, as people are attracted to products and services that remind them of past experiences. Winnipeg-based K-Tel International has successfully introduced several products that appeal to consumer nostalgia. Their online music store (www.ktel.com) offers such '70s music classics as

Real People, Real Decisions

Decision Time at d~Code

During their first year of operation, Robert Barnard and the team at d~Code defined their business as helping organizations to better understand, attract, and retain Nexus generation consumers. Using focus groups, interviews, and consumer panels, the team at d~Code researched the Nexus generation to determine the significant influences on their behaviour as consumers. This research revealed some important distinguishing characteristics of Nexus buying behaviour. For example, these consumers are experimental and describe themselves as being less brand loyal than other people. However, they do seem to develop loyalty to brands that can offer a strong identity that is consistent with Nexus values. Volkswagen's "Drivers Wanted" and Molson's "I am Canadian" advertising campaigns are two campaigns that appeal to Nexus consumers, because they provide a core brand identity, while still leaving room for individualism and diversity, two important Nexus values.

Nexus consumers have grown up with media and are, therefore, expert at gathering information about consumer goods. They view buying as fun, but only when it is done on their own terms. In retail environments, for instance, they are confident with their abilities as shoppers and would rather be left alone to make purchase decisions, not followed around by salespeople. Their confidence also leads them to want a two-way relationship, or dialogue, with companies that they buy from. They believe "you

shouldn't trust anyone trying to sell you something," so Nexus consumers are wary of flashy marketing campaigns and prefer authenticity in products, such as that displayed by the slogan used in Sleeman beer ads: "We brew good beer—we hope you like it."

The research that d~Code conducted also identified lifestyle elements that distinguish Nexus consumers from other segments of the population. For example, Nexus consumers are more interested in leisure activities, such as movies and amusement parks, compared to other Canadians. People in the Nexus generation have embraced extreme sports, including skateboarding, rock climbing, and snowboarding, and they are also the most well-travelled young generation to date.

The expertise and insight into the Nexus consumer that the d~Code team developed during their first year of operation, meant that they were well positioned for consulting with organizations who wanted to appeal to this generation of consumers. As experts in the buying behaviour of a particular market segment, they could provide insight into marketing issues, ranging from new product development to advertising strategy and the design of retail environments. But despite their success with some clients, during the first year of operation the company went two months without a contract. Although many small businesses face similar situations in their initial years of operation, Barnard was getting worried about the long-term viability of the firm.

K.C. and the Sunshine Band and ABBA. Because of numerous calls from nostalgic consumers, the company also recently re-introduced one of their most successful products from the 1970s: the Patty Stacker, a plastic tube that helps consumers make perfect hamburger patties.[10] Many marketing strategies appeal to a specific age group, such as children, Nexus consumers, the middle-aged, or the elderly. As we age, our needs change. The young adult, who spends a lot of time in bars, clothing stores, or perhaps backpacking across Europe, grows into the newlywed, who must focus on setting up house—and perhaps anticipating the time when a baby's diapers and toys will fill it up.

And so the process goes, until a person reaches old age, at which time his or her priorities may shift from saving for the kids' education to buying a retirement home. Therefore, our purchase preferences depend on our current position in the **family life cycle**—the stages through which family members pass as they grow older. It's important to note that dramatic cultural changes affecting people's living arrangements have forced marketers to change their concept of the traditional family life cycle. This updated view tries to take into account such alternative situations as single-parent families, childless couples, and homosexual relationships, and to consider the unique needs of each living situation when developing new products and communicating with these consumers. For example, Xtra! publishes magazines and newspapers targeting Canada's gay and lesbian consumers. As the ad in Exhibit 6.8 shows, Xtra! also sponsors an annual gay and lesbian

✳ ✳ ✳
family life cycle A means of characterizing consumers based on the different family stages they pass through as they grow older.

At the end of those two months without work, Barnard was approached by a large, multinational packaged goods company that was interested in a project with d~Code. This company thought that d~Code should just focus on consumer packaged goods, thereby developing expertise not only on Nexus consumers, but on a particular industry. Since the company giving this advice was the largest client d~Code had ever dealt with, and the project in mind would have been the largest one for d~Code to date, the advice was intriguing.

But Barnard also saw other options for d~Code. His continuing interest in public affairs meant that he was interested in applying his knowledge of Nexus consumers to government and not-for-profit marketing issues, which would allow d~Code to be involved in developing programs to help society, not just individual companies. He was also convinced that the knowledge of the Nexus generation could be used effectively to better understand Nexus employees, as well as consumers.

Barnard saw three main options for the future of d~Code:

Option 1. Continue to operate as they had during their first year. Continue researching the buyer behaviour of the Nexus consumer to provide marketing advice to a variety of clients. During the first year of operation, Barnard had been eager to accept any business that became available, whether it was with a consumer goods firm or a firm that did business-to-business marketing. By continuing to look for business across a wide range of organizations, this option would allow the organization to get a broad base of experience, which could then lead to the development of a more defined positioning later on.

Option 2. Take a broader approach to the knowledge base that d~Code has about the buyer behaviour of the Nexus generation. This option would keep the company focused on the Nexus segment of the population, but would broaden the applications of this knowledge to include different functional areas in business (such as human resources strategy). Additionally, d~Code would apply this knowledge to a diverse group of clients including private sector, government, and not-for-profit organizations.

Option 3. Reposition d~Code to become specialists in how a particular industry, consumer packaged goods, can connect with Nexus consumers. This more-focused strategy would allow d~Code to concentrate resources and, given the interest shown by the one firm that approached them, this could be the most profitable option in the short run. Given the number of consumer packaged goods companies in Canada producing a range of goods from food products to cosmetics, this strategy also had a lot of potential in the long run.

Now, join the d~Code decision team. Which option would you recommend, and why?

Exhibit 6.8

Xtra! helps Canadian marketers better understand the needs and characteristics of gay and lesbian consumers.

consumer show, which helps companies better understand the consumer behaviour of gay and lesbian consumers.

Lifestyles

✳✳✳
lifestyle The pattern of living that determines how people choose to spend their time, money, and energy and that reflects their values, tastes, and preferences.

A **lifestyle** is a pattern of tastes as expressed in a person's preferences for activities such as sports, interests such as music, and opinions on politics and religion. *Lifestyle marketing* is a strategy that recognizes that people can be grouped into common market segments based on similarities in lifestyle preferences.[11] Consumers often choose products, services, and activities that are associated with a certain lifestyle. As the d~Code researchers found out, there are some unique lifestyles that characterize Nexus consumers and lead to product preferences.

✳✳✳
psychographics Information about the activities, interests, and opinions of consumers that is used to construct market segments.

Psychographics, which groups consumers according to similarities in their activities, interests, and opinions (known as AIOs), is often used by marketers as a way of making demographic information, such as age and income, more meaningful. As d~Code found in researching Nexus consumers, AIOs are based on preferences for such things as vacation destinations, club memberships, hobbies, political and social attitudes, and tastes in food and fashion. As d~Code did with Nexus consumers, marketers use psychographics to create profiles of customers who resemble each other in terms of their activities and patterns of product usage.[12] For example, marketers at the beginning of the walking-shoe craze assumed that all purchasers were just burned-out joggers. Subsequent psychographic research that examined the activities, interests, and opinions of these walkers showed that there were actually several psychographic segments within the larger group of walkers, who engaged in the activity for very different reasons, including walking for fun, walking to save money, and walking for exercise. This research resulted in the creation of walking shoes aimed at different segments, from Footjoy JoyWalkers to Nike Healthwalkers.

Situational Influences on Consumer Decisions

We've seen that such internal factors as how people perceive marketing messages, their motivation to acquire products, and their unique personalities influence the decisions they will make. In addition, when and where consumers shop influences their purchase choices. Important cues include people's physical surroundings, as well as the amount and type of other consumers also present in that situation. Dimensions of the physical environment, such as decor, smells, the "feel" of natural fabrics like wool versus synthetic ones like polyester, and even temperature, can significantly influence consumption. One study found that pumping certain odours into a casino actually increased the amount of money patrons fed into slot machines.[13]

The Physical Environment

It's no secret that people's moods and behaviours are strongly influenced by their physical surroundings. Despite all their efforts to pre-sell consumers through advertising, marketers know that the store environment influences many purchases. For example, consumers decide on about two of every three supermarket product purchases in the aisles. Therefore, the messages they receive at the time and their feelings about being in the store are important influences on their decisions.[14]

Two dimensions, *arousal* and *pleasure*, determine if a shopper will react positively or negatively to a store environment. In other words, the person's surroundings can be either dull or exciting (arousing), and either pleasant or not. Just because the environment is arousing doesn't necessarily mean it will be pleasant—we've all been in crowded, hot stores that are anything but. Maintaining an upbeat feeling in a pleasant context is one factor behind the success of theme parks such as Disney World, which try to provide consistent doses of carefully calculated stimulation to patrons.[15]

The importance of these surroundings explains why many retailers are combining two favourite consumer activities, shopping and eating, into elaborate *themed environments*. Eating out is an important form of out-of-home entertainment for many consumers, and innovative firms are scrambling to offer customers a chance to eat, buy, and be entertained all at once. The West Edmonton Mall, the largest shopping and entertainment complex in the world, provides its customers with a themed environment including over 800 stores, 110 restaurants, 26 movie theatres, a casino, and a large indoor amusement park. A lot of the appeal of these themed environments is that there are plenty of interesting things to look at while eating a meal or shopping. In addition to visual stimuli, other sensory cues can influence consumers— one reason why the Rainforest Cafes in Vancouver and Toronto offer simulated thunder and lightning storms in addition to rainforest scenery in their restaurants. Research supports the assertion that sounds and music can affect eating behaviour—one study found that diners who listened to loud, fast music ate more and faster than those who listened to classical music.[16]

West Edmonton Mall
www.westedmall.com

Indeed, a growing recognition of the important role played by a store or restaurant's audio environment has created a new market niche, as some companies now are selling musical collections tailored to different activities. These include RCA Victor's "Classical Music for Home Improvements" and Sony Classics' "Cyber Classics," which are billed as music specifically for computer hackers to listen to while programming. Sony's "Extreme Classics," packaged just for bungee jumpers, is claimed to be the "loudest and most dangerous music ever written."[17]

In-store displays, such as the one in Exhibit 6.9, are a commonly used device to attract attention in the store environment. Although most displays consist of simple racks that dispense the product or related coupons, some include elaborate performances and scenery.[18] For example:

- *Quebec Frozen Food Association*: A cardboard display showing a man peering around the corner plays the following message when a consumer is in front of it: "Psst! Yes, you. You've got to taste our frozen foods. They're so good. They're so fresh. And they're really practical."[19]
- *Timex*: A still-ticking watch sits in the bottom of a filled aquarium.
- *Kellogg's Corn Flakes*: A button with a picture of Cornelius the Rooster is placed within the reach of children near the corn flakes. When a child presses the button, they hear the rooster cock-a-doodle-do.

Advertisers also are being more aggressive about hitting consumers with their messages, wherever they may be. *Place-based media* is a growing specialized medium that targets consumers in places such as airports, doctors' offices, campuses, or health clubs. Montreal-based Zoom Media targets the 18–34 age group with washroom ads, including ones that "speak" a taped message when someone stands in front of the ad.[20]

Time

Another important situational factor is how much time one has to make a decision. Time is one of consumers' most limited resources. We talk about "making time" or "spending time,"

Exhibit 6.9

Dramatic point-of-purchase displays often influence people's buying decisions once in the store.

CDPlus
www.cdplus.com

and we are frequently reminded that "time is money." Many consumers believe they are more pressed for time than ever before.[21] This sense of time poverty makes consumers responsive to marketing innovations that allow them to save time, including such services as one-hour photo processing, bagged salads and other prepared foods in supermarkets, and ordering products on the Internet.[22] CDPlus is a Canadian company that sells music over the Internet. The company has been successful because consumers can log on to the CDPlus Web page, browse through thousands of titles, listen to selections from many of them, and order and pay for them—all without setting foot inside a store. This saves the customer time, and the "store" is always open. Emma, our decision maker buying a notebook computer, appreciated the fact that she was able to save time by searching the Internet for product information and actually buying her computer online.

Social Influences on Consumer Decisions

Our discussion of consumers so far has focused on factors that influence us as individuals, such as the way we learn about products. Although we are all individuals, we are also members of many groups that, whether we realize it or not, influence our buying decisions. Families, friends, and classmates often influence our decisions, as do larger groups with which we identify, such as ethnic groups and political parties. Now let's consider how social influences such as culture, social class, and influential friends and acquaintances affect the consumer decision-making process.

Culture

✳ ✳ ✳
culture The values, beliefs, customs, and tastes that a group of people value.

Culture is a society's personality. It is the values, beliefs, customs, and tastes, as well as the products and services produced or valued by a group of people. As we saw in Chapter 4, cultural values are deeply held beliefs about right and wrong ways to live.[23] Canadian values include freedom and autonomy, mixed with a strong sense of community that is expressed through social institutions, such as our medical system.[24] Canadians also value education, and the bilingual and multicultural nature of Canada has made Canadians respectful of differences between people.

A consumer's culture influences his or her buying decisions, and a renewed sense of nationalism has led many marketers to recognize the value of identifying their products specifically with Canada and Canadian cultural symbols.[25] For example, when Zellers introduced Martha Stewart products in Canada for the first time, ads showed Martha with a Mountie saying, "I think I'm going to like Canada." Post used a Canadian flag with a Shreddie in the middle instead of a maple leaf when the company introduced Maple Crunch Shreddies, and Molson used a moose in its ads to introduce Miller Lite beer to the Canadian market.[26] Another Molson product, Canadian, not only builds on national pride with its brand name, but also has consistently been promoted with culturally based, patriotic ads—such as the "I am Canadian" campaign that featured a young man ranting about how being Canadian is different than being American. The ad for Canoe.ca in Exhibit 6.10 also tries to appeal to the Canadian identity.

As the Canoe.ca ad shows, identifying and understanding differences between Canadian and American consumers is often an important issue for Canadian marketers, especially those working in US-owned companies. US management may favour using a US marketing strategy in Canada, assuming that cultural differences are small and that Canadian consumers will respond the same way that American consumers do. In many ways, Canadian and American consumers are similar. However, as Lever Pond's found out in marketing its Degree deodorant product, Canadian consumers can be sometimes be quite different from their US counterparts—their successful, humorous US advertising campaign was not seen as funny by Canadian consumers. Apparently Canadians react better than Americans to a self-deprecating and low-key humour approach, so Lever Pond's used this style of humour in new ads designed specifically for the Canadian marketplace. The "Stress" campaign that they eventually ran in Canada showed stressful situations and a meter on the screen registering the stress levels. One ad showed a man in a bar, who is approached by a number of people who ask, "Remember me?"; when a pregnant woman asks the question, the stress meter gives a maximum reading.[27]

Many American multinational companies operating in Canada have chosen to create separate Canadian Web sites, despite the fact that the Internet is a global medium. The reasons why companies such as Microsoft, Nabisco, Kellogg, Kraft, and Pepsi-Cola have Canadian Web sites include a need to serve consumers in both English and French, the existence of different products or models (as in the case of the car company Ford), and the desire to cater to the unique needs of Canadian consumers. The manager of Microsoft's Canadian Web site argues that "to properly service this environment, we feel it necessary to have a Web site representative of Canada's uniqueness."[28]

Molson Canadian
www.iam.ca

Canoe Network
www.canoe.ca

Exhibit 6.10

The use of cultural symbols can be an effective way to connect with consumers.

Canadian marketers also need to understand differences in culture between French Canadians and English Canadians and how these differences have an impact on marketing strategies. For instance, Bell Mobility found out that there were differences between French and English consumers with respect to their cell phone behaviour. Whereas English Canadians liked certain practical aspects of the cell phones, French Canadian consumers were much more interested in being able to use the phones in minor emergency situations. Bell had originally used the same campaign in both French and English Canada, with the only difference being language. But after the English campaign did poorly in Quebec, they hired a Quebec ad agency to do a uniquely French ad, and consumers responded well to it.[29] Similarly, Wampole Canada launched maple-flavoured vitamin C tablets in Quebec only. The company has found that Quebec consumers prefer sweeter products and that they are more willing to try something new.[30]

Subcultures

❋ ❋ ❋
subculture A group within a society whose members share a distinctive set of beliefs, characteristics, or common experiences.

A **subculture** is a group coexisting with other groups in a larger culture, whose members share a distinctive set of beliefs or characteristics. Each of us belongs to many subcultures. These include religious groups, ethnic groups, and regional groups, as well as those that form around media creations such as Trekkies, fans of *Star Trek*.

For Canadian marketers, some of the most important subcultures to consider are racial and ethnic groups, because Canada is such a diverse society. Many Canadian consumers identify strongly with their heritage and are influenced by products that appeal to this aspect of their identities. Additionally, the actual needs and wants of consumers in different subcultures may be very different. For example, 87% of Chinese Canadian homes have an automobile, compared to 72% of other Canadians. Seventy-one percent of Chinese Canadians prefer to buy new cars over used, and 81% pay with cash when purchasing a car.[31] These are some of the reasons why automakers, such as Ford Canada, have recognized the importance of the Chinese Canadian market. Several Canadian firms are now practising **multicultural marketing** by successfully targeting consumers in several subcultures. For example, Burger King Canada has successfully targeted marketing efforts to Italian Canadians and Chinese Canadian consumers, and Bell Canada, Procter & Gamble, and Midas Canada have all designed marketing strategies to appeal to various ethnic subcultures.[32] We'll look at more examples of multicultural marketing activities in Canada when we discuss target marketing in Chapter 8.

❋ ❋ ❋
multicultural marketing The practice of recognizing and targeting the distinctive needs and wants of one or more ethnic subcultures.

In a country as large as Canada, regional subcultures also exist and influence consumer behaviour. For Tim Hortons, regional differences can be important in deciding what products to offer in their restaurants. Sugar pies, baked beans, and toast are available only in Quebec; Ontarians love fritters; and in some communities in BC, chocolate croissants are a popular menu item.[33]

Social Class

❋ ❋ ❋
social class The overall rank or social standing of groups of people within a society according to the value assigned to such factors as family background, education, occupation, and income.

Social class is the overall rank of people in a society. People within the same social class work in similar occupations, have similar income levels, and usually share common tastes in clothing, decorating styles, and leisure activities. These people also share many political and religious beliefs, as well as ideas about valued activities and goals.[34]

Many products and stores are designed to appeal to people in a specific social class.[35] Working-class consumers tend to evaluate products in more utilitarian terms, such as sturdiness or comfort, rather than in style or fashionability. They are less likely to experiment with new products or styles, such as modern furniture or coloured appliances, because they tend to prefer predictability to novelty.[36]

❋ ❋ ❋
status symbols Products that consumers purchase to signal membership in a desirable social class.

Luxury goods often serve as **status symbols**, visible markers that provide a way for people to flaunt their membership in higher social classes (or at least to make others believe they do). Although ostentatious products fell out of favour in the 1990s, we are witnessing a resurgence of consumer interest in luxury goods. Companies such as Hermès International, LVMH Hennessy, Louis Vuitton, and Baccarat are enjoying sales gains of

SPOTLIGHT ON REAL PEOPLE *Parasuco Jeans*

Salvatore Parasuco started selling jeans out of his Montreal high-school locker in 1975. Now his company, Parasuco Jeans, annually sells about 1.5 million pairs of jeans and 500 000 other denim products, including jackets and skirts. How does a medium-size Canadian firm compete with global denim giants like Levi Strauss? Close attention to consumer behaviour has allowed Parasuco Jeans to develop a distinct positioning in the North American jeans market. The company combines a focus on a particular age group (youth) with multicultural marketing, specifically targeting its products to consumers who are part of visible minority subcultures.

The company successfully caters to the youth market by producing fashionable, club-wear products. It has cultivated an image of innovation and distinction by producing controversial ads with sexual content (see Exhibit 6.11) and by using techniques such as moving billboards that depict a woman blowing a kiss. Natalie Bibeau, the communications and marketing di-

rector for Parasuco claims, "We're edgier than the competition and it shows in our advertising. People expect to find something different from Parasuco and are prepared to pay for it." To add to their difference, in the Parasuco flagship store in Montreal, the change rooms feature see-through glass doors that get clouded with a gas and become opaque only when the customer turns on a switch.

The company practises multicultural marketing by featuring models from various ethnic subcultures in their print ads and on their Web site and by distributing through retail outlets that cater to consumers from those subcultures. The company also attributes part of their success with ethnic subcultures to the Parasuco brand name, which sounds exotic. The company has a large Hispanic following in the US and estimates that, of the 70% of sales that come from the US, 75% are to Hispanic and African-American consumers.[37]

1. Describe the decision-making process that buyers of Parasuco jeans probably go through.
2. In addition to age and subculture, what other internal and social influences may influence the consumers of Parasuco jeans?
3. Go to the Parasuco Web site (www.parasuco.com) and view the pictures of their New York and Montreal stores. How are situational factors used to encourage jeans purchases in these stores? What other situational factors could be used effectively by Parasuco in these stores?

Parasuco Jeans
www.parasuco.com

Exhibit 6.11

Parasuco targets youth and ethnic subcultures with their jeans products.

from 13 to 16%, as affluent consumers are once again indulging their desires for the finer things in life.[38]

Group Behaviour

Most of us enjoy belonging to groups, and we may even derive comfort from knowing what others are thinking or doing as we try to make up our own minds. Group membership has entered cyberspace, as "netizens" around the world rapidly are forming virtual communities.[39] Communities such as Tripod (www.tripod.com) and Geocities (www.geocities.com) allow people to chat about their mutual interests, help one another with inquiries and suggestions, and, perhaps most importantly from a marketer's perspective, get suggestions for new products and services.

Anyone who has ever "gone along with the crowd" knows that people act differently in groups than they do on their own. There are several reasons for this. With more people in a group, it becomes less likely that any one member will be singled out for attention, and normal restraints on behaviour may be reduced. Decisions made by groups differ from those made by each individual. In many cases, group members show a greater willingness to consider riskier alternatives following group discussion than they would if each member made his or her own decision with no discussion.[40]

Even shopping behaviour changes when people do it in groups. For example, people who shop with at least one other person tend to make more unplanned purchases, buy more, and cover more areas of a store than those who go alone.[41] Group members may be convinced to buy something to gain the approval of the others, or they may simply be exposed to more products and stores by pooling information with the group. For these reasons, retailers are well advised to encourage group shopping activities.

REFERENCE GROUPS

A **reference group** is a set of people a consumer wants to please or imitate. Unlike a larger culture, the "group" can be composed of one person, such as your spouse, or someone you've never met, such as a rock singer like Sarah McLachlan. The group can be small, such as your immediate family, or it could be a large organization, such as Greenpeace.

Consumers often change their behaviour to gain acceptance into a particular reference group. **Conformity** is at work when a person changes as a reaction to real or imagined group pressure. For example, someone preparing to go out to a club with a new group of friends may choose to wear clothing similar to what they think the others will be wearing to be sure they'll be accepted by them.

Home shopping parties, epitomized by the Tupperware party, capitalize on group pressures to boost sales.[42] A company representative makes a sales presentation to a group of people, who have gathered in the home of a friend or acquaintance. Participants model the behaviour of others who can provide them with information about how to use certain products, especially since the home party is likely to be attended by a relatively homogeneous group (for example, neighbours or co-workers). Pressures to conform may be particularly intense and may escalate as more and more group members begin to "cave in" (a process sometimes termed the *bandwagon effect*). Canadian companies such as Kids Only and Weekenders have no doubt benefited from the bandwagon effect by using home shopping parties to distribute their products.

Some of the strongest pressures to conform come from our **sex roles**, society's expectations of the appropriate attitudes, behaviours, and appearance for men and women. These assumptions about the proper roles of women and men, flattering or not, are deeply ingrained in marketing communications.[44] Many products take on masculine or feminine attributes, and consumers often associate them with one sex or the other.[45] For example, for many years, hardware stores were seen as "masculine," so much so that Home Hardware of St. Jacobs, Ontario, had the advertising slogan, "Home of the

---

✳ ✳ ✳

reference group An actual or imaginary individual or group that has a significant effect on an individual's evaluations, aspirations, or behaviour.

✳ ✳ ✳

conformity A change in beliefs or actions as a reaction to real or imagined group pressure.

✳ ✳ ✳

sex roles Society's expectations about the appropriate attitudes, behaviours, and appearance for men and women.

good OR bad DECISION?

Marketers can play an important role in teaching us how society expects us to act as men and women. For example, children's toys, including dolls for girls and soldiers for boys, play an important role in shaping their preferences. The Barbie doll has been criticized for reinforcing unrealistic ideas about what women's bodies should look like. Recently, Mattel introduced a shopping-themed Barbie doll called Cool Shoppin' Barbie. The doll comes with all the equipment kids need to pretend Barbie is shopping—including a Barbie-sized MasterCard. Although Mattel includes a warning about sticking to a budget, some critics fear the doll sends the wrong message to girls about the desirability of shopping.[43] Do you agree with this criticism? Do toy manufacturers have a greater responsibility for presenting positive sex role portrayals than other companies? Why or why not?

Handyman." But at the end of the 1990s, Home Hardware replaced its slogan of 25 years when it was realized that the company had equal numbers of male and female customers in their stores. Their new slogan, "Help is close to home," avoided any sex role references.[46]

OPINION LEADERS

Some individuals are particularly likely to influence others' product decisions. An **opinion leader** is a person who influences others' attitudes or behaviours.[47] Opinion leaders are valuable information sources, because they are usually knowledgeable about a product category and, unlike commercial endorsers who are paid to represent the interests of just one company, they have no "axe to grind." In addition, opinion leaders often are among the first to buy new products, so they absorb much of the risk. This experience reduces uncertainty for others who are not as courageous. And, although company-sponsored communications tend to focus exclusively on the positive aspects of a product, this hands-on experience makes opinion leaders more likely to impart *both* positive and negative information about product performance.

Think about the people you know on campus who may be opinion leaders when it comes to setting trends in fashion or being the first to get a new CD. One study identified a group of male students who were opinion leaders for fashion products on campus. These men shared some important characteristics:[48]

- They were socially active.
- They were appearance conscious and narcissistic (that is, they were quite fond of themselves and self-centred).
- They were involved in rock culture.
- They were heavy readers of magazines, including *Playboy* and *Sports Illustrated*.
- They were likely to own more clothing in a broader range of styles than other students.

❈ ❈ ❈
opinion leader A person who is frequently able to influence others' attitudes or behaviours by virtue of their active interest and expertise in one or more product categories.

Exhibit 6.12

d~Code's expertise about Nexus consumers was used to develop ads like this one for Royal Mutual Funds.

Real People, Real Decisions
How it worked out at d~Code

Robert Barnard and the team at d~Code chose Option 2, what Barnard terms the "diversity" approach to business. d~Code broadened the type of consulting they were doing, believing that this was the best long-term approach. They changed their focus from trying to understand Nexus as just consumers and moved to a study of them as people—as customers, employees, and citizens. Barnard believed that this diversity perspective would actually allow d~Code to better understand the behaviour of Nexus consumers, since the internal, situational, and social influences on consumer decisions are affected by their roles as employees and citizens. This broader perspective is also very consistent with the values of Nexus, an important consideration since all of the employees of d~Code, including Barnard, are also members of the Nexus generation.

Today d~Code (www.d-code.com) is a successful consulting organization that works with profit, not-for-profit, and government organizations. Barnard and the team at d~Code are continuously researching the Nexus generation and helping organizations to better understand, attract, and retain Nexus customers, employees, and citizens.

In the last part of this chapter, we've seen how other people, such as friends or even casual acquaintances, influence our purchase decisions. We've considered how our preferences are shaped by our group memberships, by our desire to please or be accepted by others, even by the way we think we're "supposed" to act as men or women. We've explored why some people are more influential than others in affecting our product preferences. In addition to the influences exerted on each of us by virtue of being members of a culture, a social class, and several subcultures, it's easy to see that group affiliations exert a powerful pull on us as we make marketplace decisions. It's clear that people truly are "social animals," and to understand consumer behaviour we need to consider internal factors such as personality, situational factors such as the amount of time available to decide, and social factors such as group identity to get a handle on what we *thought* was the relatively simple business of making a decision.

Chapter Summary

1. Explain why understanding consumer behaviour is important to organizations.

   The marketing concept focuses on satisfying consumers' wants and needs. For organizations to succeed at this, they need to understand the processes that occur before, during, and after the selection of goods or services.

2. Explain the prepurchase, purchase, and postpurchase activities consumers engage in when making decisions.

   Consumer decisions differ greatly, ranging from habitual, almost mindless, repeat (low-involvement) purchases to complex, extended problem-solving activities for important, risky (high-involvement) decisions. First, consumers recognize that there is a problem to be solved. The search for information in memory and in the marketplace reduces the risk of making a wrong choice. The set of alternatives, those which will be actively considered, are judged based on various dimensions or evaluative criteria. Consumers may simplify the process by using mental shortcuts or heuristics. Following the purchase, consumer perceptions of product quality lead to satisfaction or dissatisfaction.

3. Describe how internal factors influence consumers' decision-making processes.
A number of internal factors influence consumer decisions. Perception is how consumers select, organize, and interpret stimuli. Consumers must first be exposed to the marketing communications. To prevent sensory overload, consumers practise perceptual selectivity; that is, they are selective in their attention by focusing on stimuli. Consumers differ in interpretation of stimuli, because the meaning assigned is based on individuals' prior experiences or beliefs. Marketers should also understand that consumers act because they are motivated to achieve goals, which may depend on which level of needs is currently satisfied. Learning is a change in behaviour that results from information or experience. Behavioural learning results from external events such as rewards, punishments, or the previous pairing of stimuli. Behavioural learning may result in stimulus generalization in which attitudes toward a brand or company may be transferred to other products, such as product line extensions. Cognitive learning refers to internal mental activity and includes observational learning in which behaviour results from imitation of the observed behaviour of socially attractive others.

An attitude is a lasting evaluation of a person, object, or issue. There are three components to attitudes: affective, cognitive, and behavioural. Marketers design products consistent with consumer attitudes or seek to change attitudes, frequently focusing on one of the three components.

Marketing strategy should also consider consumers' psychological makeup or personality. Personality traits, such as innovativeness, self-confidence, and sociability, may be used to develop market segments. Marketers seek to understand a consumer's self-concept to develop product attributes that match some aspect of the consumer's self.

Both the age of consumers and their family life cycle classification are strongly related to consumption preferences. Consumer behaviour may also differ based on lifestyles, thus creating different marketing segmentation opportunities. Similarly, the use of psychographics in which people are grouped according to activities, interests, and opinions may explain reasons for purchasing products.

4. Describe how situational factors at the time and place of purchase may influence consumer behaviour.
The physical and social environments at the time of purchase create differences in consumer behaviour. Retailers often create themed environments and in-store displays to influence customers to make purchases. Time (or the lack of it) influences which products are selected and characteristics of the decision process.

5. Describe how consumers' relationships with other people influence their decision-making processes.
Consumers' overall priorities for products and activities are determined by the culture of the society in which they live. Consumer decisions may be influenced by cultural values, or the enduring beliefs of the culture. In Canada, differences between French Canadian and English Canadian consumers often influence marketing strategies. Consumers within the same culture may also be members of different religious, ethnic, or regional subcultures. Many Canadian companies practise multicultural marketing by targeting their marketing strategies to consumers from various ethnic subcultures.

Social class and reference groups are other types of social influence that have an impact on product and store choices. One way social influences are felt is in the expectations of society regarding the proper roles for men and women, which have led to many sex-typed products. Consumers are motivated to please or imitate people they know or whom they respect. Purchases often result from conformity to real or imagined group pressure. Opinion leaders are especially influential people.

KEY TERMS

attitude (154)

behavioural learning theories (153)

brand loyalty (149)

classical conditioning (153)

cognitive learning theory (154)

conformity (164)

consumer behaviour (146)

consumer satisfaction/ dissatisfaction (149)

culture (160)

evaluative criteria (148)

family life cycle (157)

heuristics (149)

hierarchy of needs (152)

information search (148)

involvement (147)

learning (153)

lifestyle (158)

motivation (152)

multicultural marketing (162)

operant conditioning (153)

opinion leader (165)

perceived risk (147)

perception (151)

personality (154)

problem recognition (148)

psychographics (158)

reference group (164)

self-concept (155)

sex roles (164)

social class (162)

status symbols (162)

stimulus generalization (153)

subculture (162)

Chapter Review

Marketing Concepts: Testing Your Knowledge

1. What is consumer behaviour? Why is it important for marketers to understand consumer behaviour?

2. How does the decision process differ under conditions of high involvement and low involvement? What are the steps in the decision process, and what activities occur in each?

3. What is perception? For marketers, what are the implications of each component of the perceptual process?

4. How are consumers motivated to buy certain products over others? How has Maslow's hierarchy of needs contributed to an understanding of consumer behaviour?

5. What behavioural and cognitive learning theories are important to marketers? How do these perspectives differ when applied to consumer behaviour?

6. How do the three components of attitudes account for consumer decision making and purchasing behaviour?

7. What is personality? How is consumer behaviour influenced by an individual's personality and self-concept?

8. Why is self-concept such an important personal influence on purchasing behaviour? How do age and the family life cycle influence consumers? What is the significance of lifestyles in understanding consumer behaviour and purchasing decisions?

9. Why is an understanding of social influences such as culture and subculture important to marketers? What is the significance of social class to marketers? What are reference groups, and how do they influence consumers?

10. What are the situational influences on consumer purchasing behaviour? How does each affect purchasing decisions?

Marketing Concepts: Discussing Choices and Issues

1. Some consumer advocates have criticized marketing messages that link products to idealized people and situations and encourage the belief that the products will change consumers' lives in the portrayed direction. Tell whether you agree and explain why or why not.

2. This chapter raised the question, "Do we buy what we are?" What answer would you give based on your experience? Provide examples that support your opinion.

3. A number of current demographic or cultural trends are important to marketers. What are some important trends that may affect marketing of the following products?

   a. housing

   b. home health care

   c. newspapers

   d. education

   e. travel and tourism

4. Affect, cognition, and behaviour are three components that can be used by marketers to shape people's attitudes about products. Identify the product categories you think are most likely to be affected by each component, and discuss the merits of trying to change people's attitudes about them.

5. Culture is not static—it continues to change. What values, beliefs, and customs of Canadian culture do you see changing? How are these changes affecting marketing? What products will be affected by these changes?

6. Consumers often buy products because they feel pressure from reference groups to conform. Does conformity exert a positive or negative influence on consumers? How do consumer demographics, psychographics, and lifestyles affect their readiness to conform? With what types of products is conformity more likely to occur?

Marketing Practice: **Applying What You've Learned**

1. Assume that you are the director of marketing for a chain of camping and outdoor gear stores. Your firm is expanding, and it is your job to develop general recommendations for store design. Prepare a summary of your recommendations for store design elements that you believe will provide the best shopping environment for your customers.

2. Assume that you are an account executive with an advertising agency. Your current client is a firm that makes swimwear. You know that swimwear purchases are often influenced by a variety of social or "other people" factors. Write a report that lists these social influences, explain why each is important, and outline how you might use these influences in developing an advertising campaign.

3. This chapter indicated that consumers go through a series of steps (from problem recognition to postpurchase evaluation) as they make purchases. Write a detailed report describing what you would do in each of these steps when deciding to purchase one of the following products:

   a. an automobile

   b. a suit

   c. a vacation

4. Sometimes advertising or other marketing activities cause problem recognition to occur by showing consumers how much better off they would be with a new product or by pointing out problems with products they already own. For the following product categories, what are some ways in which marketers might try to stimulate problem recognition?

   a. cell phone

   b. toothpaste

   c. vitamins

   d. fast food

5. You work for a firm that markets frozen foods and are concerned about the effects of current consumer trends, including the increasingly diverse ethnic make-up of the population, changing roles of men and women, increased concern for time and for the environment, and decreased emphasis on owning status goods. Others in your firm do not understand or care about these changes. They believe that the firm should continue to do business just as it always has. Develop a role-playing exercise with a classmate to discuss these two different points of view for your class. Each of you should be sure to include the importance of each of these trends to your firm, and your suggestions for marketing strategies to address these trends.

Marketing Mini-Project: **Learning by Doing**

The purpose of this mini-project is to increase your understanding of the roles of personal, social, and situational factors in consumer behaviour.

1. With several other members of your class, select one of the following product categories (or some other product of your choice):

   a. perfume

   b. computers

   c. women's or men's shoes

   d. automobiles

2. Visit three stores or locations where the product may be purchased. (Try to select three that are very different from each other.) Observe and make notes on all the elements of each retail environment.

3. At each of the three locations, observe people purchasing the product. Make notes about their characteristics (for example, age and sex) and their actions in the store in relation to the product.

4. Prepare a report for your class describing the situational variables and individual consumer differences you discovered and how they relate to the purchase of the product.

5. Present your findings to your class.

Real People, Real Surfers: Exploring the Web

Visit the Web site for d~Code (www.d-code.com). Answer the following questions about the information at the site:

1. What research methods that d~Code uses to understand Nexus consumers are described on the site? What do you think are the advantages and disadvantages of using these methods to understand consumer behaviour?

2. What information about Nexus consumer behaviour is described on the site?

3. Identify five Canadian companies that you think would be interested in information on Nexus consumers. How might these companies use information about Nexus consumers in designing their marketing strategies?

MARKETING IN ACTION

Airborne Entertainment

CraniumCrank, WeGotGames, TheFunniest and Hollywood Buzz are examples of some of the wireless content channels produced for cell phones by Montreal based Airborne Entertainment (www.pocketboxoffice.com). Airborne's channels are a strong contrast to the first wave of wireless content that provided stock quotes, news and weather information to cell phone users. The Airborne brand, PocketBoxOffice, provides 13 unique channels of entertainment content (ranging from comedy to games and astrology) to all of the major wireless carriers in North America. Andy Nulman, one of the co-founders of Airborne and the former CEO of the Montreal Just for Laughs Comedy Festival, believes that there is tremendous potential for wireless content in the future: "We feel like the early pioneers of television did in the early days of kinescopes. That's where the wireless industry is right now."

Although wireless content is in its early stages in Canada, it is already well established in markets such as Europe and Japan. In Japan, 53% of air time usage of web-enabled cell phones is for entertainment content. Despite this international success, North American consumers may not be as accepting of wireless content, mainly because they are faced with other choices for Internet content. For example, outside of North America it is often cheaper to pay for content on a cell phone than it is to pay for Internet access at home, whereas in North America the cost of Internet access is relatively affordable for most consumers. This has meant that many North American consumers have developed a preference for receiving content on their computers, not their cell phones. To increase the trial and adoption of wireless content, many Canadian mobile carriers initially offered the content to their cell phone subscribers for free. Now, however, most carriers have introduced a pricing model similar to cable television where customers pay for particular channels that they choose.

One of the main target groups for Airborne's wireless content is the youth market. Penetration of that market in Canada is already strong, partly because of the comfort that this group has with cell phones. Consumers in this age group have grown up with cell phones, are used to carrying them all the time, and are used to the small screens. For many older consumers who are used to using large monitors on desktop computers, the small screen poses a potential barrier to subscribing to wireless content. Additionally, the state of wireless technology currently only allows for text-heavy, mainly black and white content, but as technology improves colour graphics, audio and video will also be available in the wireless format.

Airborne's marketing activities have so far been focused on convincing the major wireless carriers in North America, such as Rogers AT&T, Bell Mobility and Telus in Canada, to offer the PocketBoxOffice channels to consumers. These wireless carriers, in turn, have marketed the channels to consumers through direct mail advertising, radio and in-store promotions, and through Internet advertising and promotions. However, because Airborne's business is tied to consumer acceptance of wireless content, it may have to begin consumer based advertising, perhaps in partnership with the mobile carriers, in order to stimulate consumer acceptance. In the meantime, Airborne is entering the Latin American and German markets by teaming up with carriers there, and is working on further content development through partnerships with companies such as Disney Interactive, MuchMusic, and National Lampoon.

Sources: Danny Kucharsky, "Unplugged humour," *Marketing Magazine*, 28 January 2002, 10; www.pocketboxoffice.com.

THINGS TO THINK ABOUT:

1. In addition to the youth market, what other groups of consumers would be primary target groups for Airborne's channels in Canada? What are the main benefits of wireless content for each target group?
2. For each target group, identify the important social, internal and situational influences that affect a consumer's decision to purchase wireless entertainment content.
3. Should Airborne engage in consumer based advertising? Who should be their target group(s) for such advertising in Canada? What type of advertising would be most appropriate for each group?

7

Why Organizations Buy: Business-to-Business Markets

When you have completed your study of this chapter, you should be able to

CHAPTER OBJECTIVES

1. Describe the general characteristics of business-to-business markets and business buying practices.

2. Explain how marketers classify business and organizational markets.

3. Explain the business buying situation and describe business buyers.

4. Explain how e-commerce is dramatically changing business-to-business marketing.

5. Summarize the main stages in the business buying decision process.

Real People, Real Decisions ✓ ✗

Meet Michel Bendayan
A Decision Maker at Ritvik Holdings Inc.

Michel Bendayan is the international sales and marketing manager for Ritvik Holdings Inc., the Montreal based producer of Mega Bloks, the second largest construction toy manufacturer in the world after Lego. Founded in 1967 by Victor J. Bertrand and his wife Rita, Ritvik Holdings started as a toy distribution agency. By the early 1980s, the Bertrands had focused on the construction toy niche market. In 1985, they launched Mega Bloks, a line of building blocks and accessories, in Canada and the United States. The company began international sales in 1989 and is now a worldwide organization with operations in eight countries, employing over 3000 people, and selling a line of 75 to 100 items in four sizes in 100 countries. Sales of Mega Bloks have grown exponentially in the past five years and the products are now the world's market share leader in the pre-school construction toy segment.

Michel Bendayan has been in his current position since April 2001, after working in Belgium for two and a half years with Ritvik's vice president of international. There he helped open a European subsidiary, did business development for the Eastern Europe, Italian and Spanish markets, and managed the European distribution, warehousing, and freight operations. Before joining Ritvik in 1998, Bendayan worked for Hasbro Canada as product manager for the Parker Brothers and Milton Bradley brands. Prior to that he completed a B.Com degree from McGill University in 1994.

As international sales and marketing manager, Bendayan works with other international marketing and sales managers to determine worldwide international marketing strategy and product launch tactics. He is also directly responsible for market development in Eastern Europe, Spain, Italy, and the Middle East—identifying new distributors, working on getting product listings, understanding retail and consumer preferences and trends, and working directly with retailers to grow the sales of Mega Bloks products.

Business Markets: Buying and Selling when Stakes Are High

You might think most marketers spend their days dreaming up the best way to promote cutting-edge Web browsers or funky shoes. Not so. Many marketers know that the "real action" is more likely to be found in lead pipes, office supplies, safety shoes, meat lockers, or machine tools. In fact, some of the most interesting and most lucrative jobs for young marketers are in industries which you probably have never heard of.

An individual consumer may decide to buy two or three T-shirts at one time, each emblazoned with a different design. Large companies such as Canadian Tire, Petro-Canada, Pepsi-Cola, and McDonald's buy hundreds, even thousands, of employee uniforms embroidered with their corporate logos in a single order. Like an end consumer, a business buyer makes decisions—with an important difference. The purchase may be worth millions of dollars, and both the buyer and seller have a lot at stake in making a wise decision.

In this chapter, we'll look at the big picture of the business marketplace, in which the fortunes of business buyers and sellers can hang in the balance of a single transaction. Then we'll examine how marketers categorize businesses and organizations to develop effective business marketing strategies. Finally, we'll look at business buying behaviour and the business buying decision process.

To begin, consider these transactions: Bombardier (owners of de Havilland, Canadair, Lear, and Short PLC) makes business jets, such as the one in Exhibit 7.1, to sell to corporate customers. Procter & Gamble sells cases of Tide to RC Distributors, a Northern Ontario wholesaler. The Stratford Festival buys costumes, sets, and programs. Ford Motor Company plans to purchase 350 000 Hewlett-Packard computer systems for employee home use. BC Gas buys advice from Anderson Consulting. The Winnipeg Public Library decides to buy a Canon copier. Home Depot buys drywall from the Canadian Gypsum Company.

All of these market activities have one thing in common—they are part of **business-to-business marketing**. This is the marketing of goods and services that businesses and other

***

business-to-business marketing
The marketing of goods and services that business and organizational customers need to produce other goods and services for resale or to support their operations.

Exhibit 7.1

Bombardier is a Canadian firm that builds business jets for corporations and individuals.

organizational customers buy for some purpose other than for personal consumption. Firms may resell these goods and services, or they may use them to produce still other goods and services to sell to other businesses or to support their own operations. Business-to-business customers include manufacturers, wholesalers, retailers, and a variety of other organizations, such as hospitals, colleges and universities, and government agencies. Another name for business-to-business markets is organizational markets.

Business customers create vast opportunities for marketers. When measured in dollars, the market for business and organizational goods and services is *four* times larger than the consumer market.[1]

To put the size and complexity of business markets into perspective, let's consider a single product—a pair of jeans. A consumer may browse through several racks of jeans and ultimately purchase a single pair, but the store at which the consumer shops has purchased many pairs of jeans in different sizes, styles, and brands from different manufacturers. Each of these manufacturers purchases fabrics, zippers, buttons, and thread from other manufacturers, which in turn purchase the raw materials to make these components. In addition, all of the firms in this chain need to purchase equipment, electricity, labour, computer systems, office supplies, packing materials, and countless other goods and services. So, even a single purchase of the latest style of Diesel jeans is the culmination of a series of buying and selling activities among many organizations—many people have been keeping busy while you're out shopping.

Characteristics That Make a Difference in Business Markets

In theory, the same basic marketing principles hold in both consumer and business markets—firms identify customer needs and develop a marketing mix to satisfy those needs. For example, take the company that made the desks and chairs in your classroom. Just like a firm that markets consumer goods, the classroom furniture company first must create an important competitive advantage for its target market of colleges and universities. Next the firm develops a marketing mix strategy beginning with a product—classroom furniture that will withstand years of use by thousands of students while providing a level of comfort required of a good learning environment (and you thought those hard-backed chairs were intended just to keep you awake during class). The firm must offer the furniture at prices the schools will pay. Then the firm must develop a sales force or other marketing communication strategy to make sure your school (and hundreds of others) consider—and hopefully choose—its products when furnishing classrooms. Although marketing to business customers does have a lot in common with consumer marketing, there are differences that make this basic process more complex.[2] Figure 7.1 looks at some of these differences. Let's review them.

MULTIPLE BUYERS

In business markets, products often have to do more than satisfy an individual's needs. They must meet the requirements of everyone involved in the company's purchase decision. If you decide to buy a new chair for your room or apartment, you're the only one who has to be satisfied. For your classroom, the furniture must satisfy not only students but faculty,

Organizational Markets	Consumer Markets
• Purchases made for some purpose other than personal consumption	• Purchases for individual or household consumption
• Purchases made by someone other than the user of the product	• Purchases usually made by ultimate user of the product
• Decisions frequently made by several people	• Decisions usually made by individuals
• Purchases made according to precise technical specifications based on product expertise	• Purchases often made based on brand reputation or personal recommendations with little or no product expertise
• Purchases made after careful weighing of alternatives	• Purchases frequently made on impulse
• Purchases made based on rational criteria	• Purchases made based on emotional responses to products or promotions
• Purchasers often engage in lengthy decision process	• Individual purchasers often make quick decisions
• Interdependencies between buyers and sellers; long-term relationships	• Buyers engage in limited-term or one-time-only relationships with many different sellers
• Purchases may involve competitive bidding, price negotiations, and complex financial arrangements	• Most purchases made at "list price" with cash or credit cards
• Products frequently purchased directly from producer	• Products usually purchased from someone other than producer of the product
• Purchases frequently involve high risk and high cost	• Most purchases are low risk and low cost
• Limited number of large buyers	• Many individual or household customers
• Buyers often geographically concentrated in certain areas	• Buyers generally dispersed throughout total population
• Products: often complex; classified based on how organizational customers use them	• Products: consumer goods and services for individual use
• Demand derived from demand for other goods and services, generally inelastic in the short run, subject to fluctuations, and may be joined to the demand for other goods and services	• Demand based on consumer needs and preferences, is generally price elastic, steady over time and independent of demand for other products
• Promotion emphasizes personal selling	• Promotion emphasizes advertising

Figure 7.1: Differences between Organizational and Consumer Markets

administrators, campus planners, and the people at your school who actually do the purchasing. Instead of simply deciding on an appropriate price for the product, business-to-business marketers frequently must submit written quotations stating their prices and then hope a competitor doesn't submit a lower quote.

NUMBER OF CUSTOMERS

Compared to consumers, organizational customers are few and far between. In Canada, there are about 10 million consumer households but fewer than 50 000 businesses and organizations. But unless your name is Bronfman or Gates, each organizational buyer has more to spend than you do as an individual consumer. Business marketers have a narrow customer base and a small number of buyers. Kodak's business division that markets sophisticated medical products to hospitals and other medical groups has a limited number of potential customers compared with its consumer film division.

SIZE OF PURCHASES

Business-to-business products can dwarf consumer purchases, both in the quantity of items ordered and in the price of individual purchases. A company that supplies uniforms to other businesses, for example, buys hundreds of large drums of laundry detergent each year in contrast to a consumer household that buys a box of detergent every few weeks. Organizations purchase some products, such as a highly sophisticated piece of manufacturing equipment or computer-based marketing information systems, that can each cost a million dollars or more. For example, the Nortel Networks telecommunications switch shown in Exhibit 7.2 sells for about $80 000. Recognizing such differences in the size of purchases allows marketers to meet business customers' needs. Although it makes perfect sense to use mass-media advertising to sell laundry detergent to consumers, selling thousands of dollars worth of laundry detergent or a million-dollar computer is best handled by a strong personal sales force.

GEOGRAPHIC CONCENTRATION

Another difference between business markets and consumer markets is geographic concentration—many business customers are located in a small geographic area rather than being spread out across the country. Whether they live in the heart of Toronto or in a small

Exhibit 7.2

Telecommunications switches made by Nortel Networks are usually considered large purchases by organizations.

fishing village in PEI, consumers buy and use toothpaste and televisions. Not so for business-to-business customers, who may be almost exclusively located in a single region of the country. In Canada, much of the industrial buying power is concentrated in Toronto, Montreal, and Calgary, where major Canadian corporations have their head offices.

Business-to-Business Demand

Demand in business markets differs from consumer demand. Most demand for business-to-business products is derived, inelastic, fluctuating, and joint. Understanding these differences in business-to-business demand is important for marketers in forecasting sales and in planning effective marketing strategies.

DERIVED DEMAND

Consumer demand is a direct connection between a need and the satisfaction of that need. Business customers don't purchase goods and services to satisfy their own needs. Business-to-business demand is **derived demand**, because a business's demand for goods and services comes either directly or indirectly from consumers' demand. For example, the demand for building products such as Canadian Gypsum's drywall or even the Jacuzzi Whirlpool tubs shown in Exhibit 7.3 is derived from the demand for new homes. Retailers buy goods to resell in response to consumer demand, whereas other organizations and firms buy products that are used to produce still more goods and services that consumer markets demand.

✳ ✳ ✳
derived demand The demand for business or organizational products that is derived from demand for consumer goods or services.

Exhibit 7.3

For Jacuzzi, demand for tubs goes up and down with the economy and the number of new homes being built.

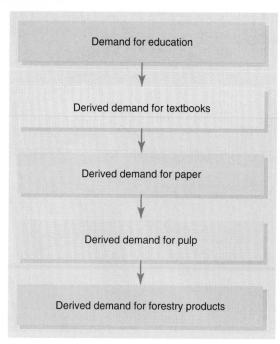

Figure 7.2 Derived Demand

* * *
inelastic demand The demand for products does not change because of increases or decreases in price.

Consider Figure 7.2. Demand for forestry products comes from the demand for pulp to make paper used to make textbooks. The demand for textbooks comes from the demand for education. As a result of derived demand, the success of one company may depend on another company in a different industry. The derived nature of business demand means that marketers must be constantly alert to changes in consumer trends that ultimately will have an effect on business-to-business sales.

INELASTIC DEMAND

The demand for business or organizational products is generally *inelastic*. **Inelastic demand** means that regardless of whether the price of a business-to-business product goes up or down, customers will still buy the same quantity. (We shall talk more about price elasticity in Chapter 12.) We see inelastic demand in business-to-business markets, because an individual business product is usually just one of the many parts and materials that go into producing the consumer product. It is not unusual for a large increase in price for a single business product to have little effect on the price of the final consumer product. For example, the BMW in Exhibit 7.4 sells for about $50 000. To produce the car, BMW purchases thousands of different parts. If the price of tires, batteries, or stereos goes up—or down—BMW will still buy enough to meet consumer demand for its cars. As you might imagine, increasing the price of a $50 000 car by $30 or $40 or even $100 won't change consumer demand.

But business-to-business demand isn't always inelastic. Sometimes producing a consumer good or service relies on only one or a few materials or component parts. If the price of the part increases, demand may become elastic if the manufacturer of the consumer good passes the increase on to the consumer. Steel, for example, is a large component of auto-

SPOTLIGHT ON REAL PEOPLE *Worldbid.com*

Roy Berelowitz is president of Worldbid.com, a global business-to-business web portal headquartered in Victoria, B.C. WorldBid.com offers a global business-to-business marketplace for small and medium sized companies. In addition to providing access to over $1 trillion in buy and sell leads in over 1100 industries, its services include a worldwide business directory, company showrooms, online auctions, document posting, shipping, international payments, and online email access. More than 80 000 companies are currently registered with the service and about 90 companies and 1500 buy or sell leads are added each day.

Worldbid.com has more than 60 country and vertical sites in an interactive trade network. Local partners build country sites in local languages and handle marketing and membership sales in that country. A common look and feel to the websites and translation services facilitate business trade across borders and around the world. Its strategy is to combine this international reach with service innovation, low overhead, an aggressive growth plan, and proprietary software (patents pending) to become the leading global B2B portal. Recent partnerships with Microsoft in Canada and Forbes.com in the United States may help the company attain that goal. It is not yet cash flow positive and Worldbid.com faces significant country focused competition such as BCE's BellZinc.ca, which boasts upwards of 250 000 Canadian members. The company's key challenges are finding appropriate partners and raising capital to finance growth.[3]

1. **What services do Worldbid.com and BellZinc.ca provide their customers?**
2. **What challenges do you foresee as Worldbid.com tries to implement their strategy?**

Exhibit 7.4

The final sticker price of the BMW convertible depends on the price BMW has to pay for thousands of parts.

mobiles. Automobile manufacturers will need to pay a lot more for steel should the price of steel go up. An increase in the price of steel can drive up the price of automobiles so much that consumer demand for the automobiles drops, decreasing the demand for steel.

FLUCTUATING DEMAND

Considering that demand coming from the end consumer, even small changes can create large increases or decreases in business demand. The **acceleration principle** (also called the multiplier effect) explains how a small percentage change in consumer demand can create a large percentage change in total industrial or business demand. Take, for example, a small—say, five percent—increase in consumer demand for air travel. If the airlines are already filling their flights, they may decide they need new planes to meet the increased consumer demand. For Boeing or Bombardier Aerospace, these orders for new planes may double or even triple the normal demand.

A product's *life expectancy* is another reason for fluctuating demand. Business customers tend to purchase certain products, such as large machinery used in the manufacture of goods, infrequently, perhaps only every 10 or 20 years. Thus, demand for such products fluctuates; it may be very high one year when many customers' machines are wearing out but low the following year because everyone's old machinery is working fine.

Changes in a company's inventory policies can also create demand fluctuations. Consider a firm that has historically kept a 30-day supply of parts. Operations managers may decide instead to keep only a 14-day supply of parts to reduce costs. Demand for the part will first go down because the manager will be placing a smaller order (for 14 days) and then level off at that 14-day quantity.

JOINT DEMAND

Joint demand is the result of two or more goods being necessary to create a product. For example, General Motors requires tires, batteries, and spark plugs. If the supply of one of these decreases, General Motors will be unable to manufacture as many automobiles and so will not buy as many of the other items. Therefore, the sale of B.F. Goodrich tires to General Motors partly depends on the availability of batteries and spark plugs, even though the tire manufacturer has nothing to do with these products.

Classifying Business-to-Business Markets

Many firms buy products in business markets so that they can produce other goods in turn. A lot of the Canadian Gypsum Company's customers are contractors, who build homes and offices and sell them to families and organizations. Other business-to-business customers resell, rent, or lease goods and services. Still others, such as the Red Cross,

✳ ✳ ✳
acceleration principle (multiplier effect) A marketing phenomenon in which a small percentage change in consumer demand can create a large percentage change in business-to-business demand.

✳ ✳ ✳
joint demand The demand for two or more goods that are used together to create a product.

provincial governments, and local churches, serve the public in some way. As Figure 7.3 shows, these distinctions lead to broad categories: producers, resellers, and organizations. For business marketers, the classification of firms is significant, because it identifies firms that purchase similar products and that have similar buying practices. This identification helps marketers in developing strategies that effectively target different organizational customers.

One tool firms use is the **North American Industry Classification System (NAICS)**. This is a numerical coding system for classifying industries, which was developed jointly by the United States, Canada, and Mexico. NAICS replaced the US Standard Industrial Classification (SIC) system in 1997 so that the North American Free Trade Agreement (NAFTA) countries could compare economic and financial statistics.[4] Like the SIC system, the NAICS is used to collect and report data on business activity, such as the number of firms, the total dollar amount of sales, the number of employees, and the growth rate for industries, all broken down by geographic region. These reports have become an essential tool for classifying business-to-business customers. Many firms use them to assess potential markets and to determine how well they are doing compared to their industry group as a whole.

The NAICS uses a different six-digit numerical code for each industry. At its inception, the system included 20 major sectors identified by two-digit numbers, which Figure 7.4 shows. This may change, however, because the new system will be updated every five years, so that classifications can keep up with changes in the economy. For example, the number 51 identifies the information industry. The major sectors are further broken down into sub-sectors (three digits), industry groups (four digits), industries common to Canada, the US, and Mexico (five digits), and specific country industries (six digits – "0" for Canada).

To use the NAICS to find new customers, a marketer might first determine the NAICS groups of current customers and then evaluate the sales potential of the overall NAICS groups or particular segments based on the number of employees of firms in the groups. For example, a firm that supplies employee uniforms could evaluate the sales potential of firms having 150 and 1000 employees in an NAICS category and set its sights on attractive firms in that category. In other cases, a firm might choose to target firms in a cross-section of categories, as Sprint did in its campaign, dubbed "Real Solutions," aimed at all companies that employ 100 to 500 people.[5] Let's take a closer look at the four major categories into which organizations fall.

✳ ✳ ✳

North American Industry Classification System (NAICS) The numerical coding system that the United States, Canada, and Mexico use to classify firms into detailed categories according to their business activities and shared characteristics.

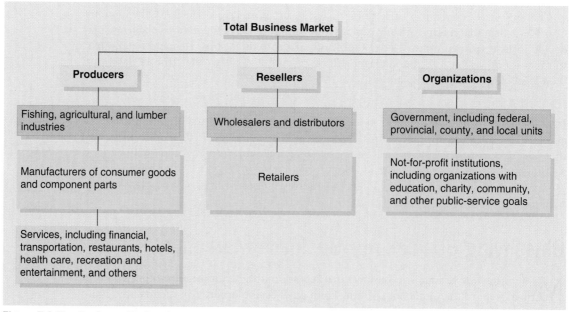

Figure 7.3 The Business Marketplace

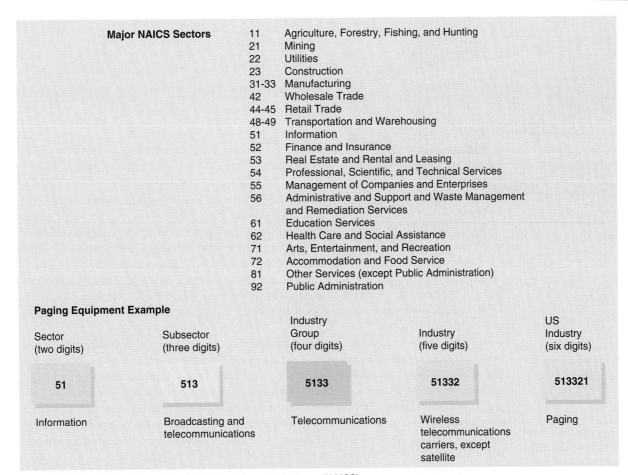

Figure 7.4 North American Industrial Classification System (NAICS)

Producers

Producers purchase products for use in the production of other goods and services that they in turn sell to make a profit. Producers are customers for a vast number of products from raw materials to goods manufactured by other producers. For example, DuPont buys resins and uses them to manufacture insulation material for sleeping bags. Ontario mould maker ProtoPlast buys aluminum ingots, which it turns into industrial moulds. Auto manufacturers, such as Ford, buy a variety of component parts—from transmissions to carpet—and use them in the cars they ship to consumers. Service producers buy linens, furniture, and food to produce the quality accommodations and meals their guests expect.

Resellers

Resellers buy finished goods for the purpose of reselling, renting, or leasing to other businesses. Resellers include retailers and wholesalers. Bestfoods, for examples, sells its food products to the distribution arms of giant resellers such as Loblaws, IGA, and Westfair, who then distribute the food to their retail stores. Although resellers do not produce goods, they do provide their customers with the time, place, and possession utility we talked about in Chapter 1 by making the goods available to consumers when and where they want them.

Governments

Government markets make up the largest single business or organizational market in Canada. The Canadian government market includes more than 6000 government agencies and organizations, more than 740 municipal and local governments, 10 provincial governments,

※ ※ ※
producers
The individuals or organizations that purchase products for use in the production of other goods and services.

※ ※ ※
resellers The individuals or organizations that buy finished goods for the purpose of reselling, renting, or leasing to others to make a profit and to maintain their business operations.

※ ※ ※
government markets Federal, provincial, and local governments that buy goods and services to carry out public objectives and to support their operations.

Exhibit 7.5

Governments are the only customers for certain products.

3 territory governments, and a federal government that collectively spent more than $371 billion in 1998.[6] The federal government alone has more than 225 separate institutions[7] that typically procure through a tendering process $5 to $6 billion worth of goods and services each year.[8]

Governments are just about the only customers for certain products, such as snow plows, garbage trucks, and transit buses like the one illustrated in Exhibit 7.5. But a lot of government expenditures are for more familiar and less expensive items, such as printer toner, pens, and Post-it Notes.

For business marketers, selling goods and services to governments is different from selling to producer or reseller markets. Taking a prospective buyer to lunch may be standard practice in the corporate world, but in government markets, this practice may be in conflict with ethical (and legal) standards for government personnel. Because governments make purchases with taxpayer money, laws require them to adhere to strict regulations. Generally, government buyers must develop detailed specifications and obtain **competitive bids** for even the simplest purchases. With competitive bids, potential suppliers must submit detailed proposals including price and associated data for a proposed purchase. The firm making the best offer gets the bid. Government agencies are usually required by law to accept the lowest bid from a qualified vendor.

Governments regularly publish information on upcoming bidding opportunities to let possible vendors know about purchases they are about to make. In Canada, the federal government's tendering process is managed by a private company called MERX, which offers a Web site for searching and submitting tenders for government procurement opportunities with a value of $25 000 or more (www.merx.ca). MERX also gives companies access to thousands of other procurement opportunities from provincial and municipal governments as well as hundreds of colleges, universities, hospitals, and school boards across Canada.

✳ ✳ ✳

competitive bids A business buying process in which two or more suppliers submit proposals (including price and associated data) for a proposed purchase and the firm providing the better offer gets the bid.

Not-for-profit Institutions

Not-for-profit institutions are organizations with charitable, educational, community, and other public service goals—such as hospitals, churches, colleges, universities, museums, and nursing homes—that buy goods and services to support their functions. The institutional market also includes charitable and cause-related organizations, such as the Salvation Army and the Red Cross. Not-for-profit institutions tend to operate on low budgets, and in all but the largest ones, non-professional part-time buyers who have other duties—or who are volunteers—normally make the purchases. Such customers often rely on marketers to provide more advice and assistance before and after the sale than professional business buyers require.

✳ ✳ ✳

not-for-profit institutions Organizations with charitable, educational, community, and other public service goals that buy goods and services to support their functions and to attract and serve their members.

The Nature of Business Buying

So far we've talked about how business-to-business markets are different from consumer markets and about the different types of customers that make up business markets. In this section, we'll discuss some of the important characteristics of business buying.

To be successful in business-to-business markets means developing marketing strategies that meet the needs of organizational customers better than the competition. To do this, marketers must understand business buying behaviour. Armed with this knowledge, marketers are able to participate in the buyer's decision process from the start. Take a firm that sells equipment to hospitals. Understanding that physicians (rather than buyers) who practise at the hospital often initiate decisions to purchase new equipment means that the firm's salespeople will make sure the physicians know about new technologies and improved equipment. In this section, we'll first look at the different types of buying situations found in business markets. Then we'll examine the role of professional purchasers and buying centres in business buying.

The Buying Situation

Like end consumers, business buyers spend more time and effort on certain purchases than on others. Devoting such effort to a purchase decision often depends on the complexity of the product and how often the decision has to be made. A **buy class** identifies the degree of effort required of the firm's personnel to collect information and make a purchase decision. These classes are straight rebuys, modified rebuys, and new-task buys.

STRAIGHT REBUY

Buyers are only human—when a purchase has low risk, they often rely on strategies that simplify the process, such as using a fixed set of trusted suppliers for routine purchases.[9] Products like computer paper, shipping cartons, and cleaning compounds are low risk. Being successful in such markets means keeping prices down and developing selling policies to keep the buying process as simple as possible. A **straight rebuy** is the purchase of items that a business-to-business customer regularly needs. The buyer has purchased the same items many times before and routinely reorders them when supplies are low, often from the same suppliers. Reordering takes little time. Buyers typically maintain a list of approved vendors that have demonstrated their ability to meet the firm's criteria for pricing, quality, service, and delivery.

Because straight rebuys can mean a steady income to a firm, many business marketers go to great lengths to cultivate and maintain relationships with customers that will lead to straight rebuys. Salespeople, for example, regularly call on these customers to personally handle orders and to see if there are additional products the customer needs. They may attempt to obtain long-term contracts. Rebuys keep a supplier's sales volume up and selling costs down.

MODIFIED REBUY

Straight rebuy situations do not last forever. A **modified rebuy** occurs when a firm wants to shop around for suppliers with better prices, quality, or delivery times. A modified rebuy can also occur when the organization has new needs for products it already buys. A buyer who has purchased many copying machines in the past, for example, may have to evaluate several lines of copiers, such as the digital copier in Exhibit 7.6, if the firm has a new need for digitized office equipment.

Exhibit 7.6

The Mita copier/printer combo: Changing technology makes purchasing for the digitized office a modified rebuy.

Real People, Real Decisions

Decision Time at Ritvik Holdings Inc.

From 1989 to 1999 Ritvik's international marketing strategy was to take a successful North American product line and export it to Europe and other countries worldwide. While this approach had moderate success, sales growth in North America had increased exponentially while sales in Europe grew at a much lower rate.

Perhaps accounting for this slower sales growth, Bendayan and others in the new European office received feedback from large European retailers that the North American product line, particularly the packaging, did not have the clean and simple look and feel that appealed to European customers. Bendayan and his colleagues commissioned focus group and survey research in Europe with mothers of small children, which confirmed this difference in consumer preferences. Most European consumers liked simple and compact box packaging, similar to that of Lego or Playmobil, that showed a picture of the product or the product in use, and had little writing. In North America, most consumers were influenced either by the flashiness of the packaging—bolder colours, graphic callouts, and bold text that highlighted product benefits—or the size of the packaging, bigger or more interesting being better. Consequently Mega Bloks packaged their products in either bulk bags, or shaped theme packaging such as a set of Bloks that came in a dump truck or in a container shaped like a puppy. With respect to box packaging, North American consumers tend to like detailed information on the packaging that explains who the product is for and how it is used. Such detailed text makes European packaging very cluttered as it has to be presented in multiple languages, which makes it hard for customers to find and focus on their own language.

Ritvik managers also observed that European retailers had different buying behaviour than their North American counterparts. In Europe Mega Bloks is perceived to be foreign brand, only slightly lower in price and of similar quality to that of Lego, which most retailers carry as their premium brand. Having limited shelf space, buyers in European retail organizations have to justify carrying Mego Bloks over less expensive but lower quality blocks made by local block manufacturers. Most European countries have at least one local construction block manufacturer. North American retailers perceive Mega Bloks to be a high quality domestic brand that is less expensive than Lego and priced competitively. In short, Mega Bloks is a quality value brand in North America but a near premium brand in Europe.

In late 1999, Ritvik had developed a new line of theme sets called "Maxiland," which consisted of boxed building blocks and play accessories relating to farming, trains, and the police, and other themes targeting the 2–5 age category in which Ritvik was wanting to build market share, both in

Modified rebuys require more time and effort than straight rebuys. The buyer generally knows the purchase requirements and a few potential suppliers; for example, many professional contractors think of Windsor doors as a "household name." Marketers know that modified rebuy situations can mean that some vendors get added to a buyer's approved supplier list whereas others may be dropped. Astute marketers routinely call on buyers to detect and define problems that can lead to winning or losing in such situations. For example, salespeople will want to find out when modified rebuys are going to occur. They try to identify the major criteria that will be used for the purchase decision, that is, whether price, delivery, product features, or something else will determine who gets the order. Armed with that information, the salesperson will be able to persuade the buyer that his or her firm can do a great job of satisfying the buyer's needs.

NEW-TASK BUYING

✳ ✳ ✳

new-task buy A new business-to-business purchase that is complex or risky and that requires extensive decision making.

A first-time purchase is a **new-task buy**. Uncertainty and risk characterize buying decisions in this classification, and they need the most effort because the buyer has no previous experience on which to base a decision. Your college or university, for example, may decide (if it hasn't done so already) to go into the "distance learning" business, which is delivering courses to off-site students. Buying the equipment to set up classrooms with two-way video transmission, as shown in Exhibit 7.7, will be an expensive and complex new-task buy for your school. The buyer has to start from scratch to gather information on purchase specifications, which may be highly technical and complex and require detailed input from others. In new-task buying situations, buyers not only lack experience with the product, but

North America and in Europe. As part of the launch team, Bendayan and his colleagues needed to decide what strategy would be most appropriate. They considered the following options:

Option 1   Develop standard packaging for the North American market and export it worldwide. This alternative was an extension of Ritvik's current product strategy. It would be much less expensive to produce one standardized package and easier to manage the distribution of fewer stock keeping units (SKUs). On the other hand, research had shown that North American packaging was not as appealing to most European consumers, which would negatively affect European market development.

Option 2.   Develop different packaging for the European and North American markets. This option would respond to European consumer preferences and help Mega Bloks achieve growth targets for the European market. Large retailers such as Argos in the UK and El Corte Ingles in Spain would not list a product unless the manufacturer customized it to meet their needs. European style packaging would also support Mega Bloks' positioning in Europe. On the other hand, producing two versions of the packaging for each product in a relatively small volume line would be expensive, with extra graphic design costs, printing costs, production set-up costs, warehousing and physical distribution costs, all of which could increase the variable cost of the European product by as much as 10%.

Option 3.   Develop standard packaging for the European market and sell it worldwide. This alternative would allow Ritvik to develop market share in Europe and compete with Lego head-on in Lego's own back yard. On the other hand, North American consumers and retailers may not like the "European" look and feel of the packaging and that look and feel would not be consistent with other Mega Bloks products. The North American market currently represents 60% of Mega Bloks sales and Ritvik usually accommodates the preferences of larger retailers who control access to the large value minded consumer segment. On the other hand this packing might allow Mega Bloks to make inroads with specialty North American retailers that sell higher end, European toys.

Now, join the Ritvik Mega Bloks decision team: which option would you choose, and why?

Exhibit 7.7

For colleges and universities, the equipment necessary to equip distance-learning classrooms is a new-task purchase.

often are unfamiliar with firms that supply the product. This combines to make supplier choice critical, and buyers gather much information about quality, pricing, delivery, and service from several potential suppliers.

For suppliers, new-task buying represents both a challenge and an opportunity. Although a new-task buy can be significant in itself, many times the chosen supplier gains the added advantage of becoming an "in" supplier for more routine purchases that will follow. A growing business that needs an advertising agency for the first time, for example, may seek exhaustive information from several firms before selecting one and will continue to use the chosen agency's services for future projects without exploring other alternatives. Marketers know that to get the order in a new-task buy situation, they must develop a close working relationship with the business buyer. Such relationships mean that buyers can count on business marketers to help develop product specifications and terms for the purchase that are in the best interests of the customer's organization and its needs.

The Professional Buyer

Just as it is important for marketers of consumer goods and services to understand their customers, it is essential that business-to-business marketers understand who handles the buying for business customers. Trained professional buyers typically carry out buying in business-to-business markets. These professional buyers can go by the titles *purchasing agents, procurement officers,* or *directors of materials management.* Unlike consumers who may spend only a few hours a month making purchase decisions, professional purchasers do it all day, every day.

Professional buyers have a lot of responsibility. They spend the company's money and buy the products that keep it running. These buyers tend to focus on economic factors beyond the initial price of the product, including transportation and delivery charges, accessory products or supplies, maintenance, and other ongoing costs. They select suppliers and negotiate for the lowest prices and are responsible for selecting quality products and ensuring their timely delivery. Their purchases can range in price and significance from paper clips to multimillion-dollar computer systems.

Sometimes, like consumers, business buyers make decisions based on emotions, brand loyalty, long-term relationships they have established with particular salespeople, or aesthetic concerns. Even the buyer's age, income, education, personality, and attitudes can affect his or her decisions. Marketing communications play a big role in the buyer's decision process. For example, most buyers depend on vendors' salespeople to keep them informed about new products.

A key factor in many purchase decisions is whether the buyer perceives the purchase to be risky.[10] Some buyers are more risk averse than others. Successful business marketers try to develop strategies that help the buyer avoid risk. These include providing samples of a new product for a business customer or placing a new piece of equipment in the customer's facility to try for a few weeks.

Big firms with many facilities in different locations often practise **centralized purchasing**. This means that, even when others in the organization participate in the decision of what to buy, one department does all the buying for the company.[11] With centralized purchasing, a firm has more buying power and can get the best prices. Wal-Mart can offer its customers lower prices than other stores (see Exhibit 7.8), because its centralized purchasing department buys large quantities of items and can demand volume discounts from suppliers. For sellers such as Kraft Foods, centralized purchasing means they only need to make a single sale to have their peanut butter in IGA locations across the country.

The professional buyers who work in centralized purchasing offices often become expert at the ins and outs of certain types of products, and each may have a specialized role in the purchasing function. In the buying departments of retail chains, for example, an individual buyer (and several assistant buyers) may be responsible for buying only women's sleepwear or junior tops or children's size 2 to 6X and, thus, develop even greater expertise in their specific area.

✳ ✳ ✳

centralized purchasing A business buying practice in which an organization's purchasing department does the buying for all of the company.

Exhibit 7.8

Centralized purchasing is one way Wal-Mart keeps "dropping" prices for its customers.

The Buying Centre

Whether or not a firm's buying is a centralized process—whether the purchase situation calls for a modified or new-task buying situation—several people may need to work together to reach a decision. Depending on what they need to purchase, these participants may be production workers, supervisors, engineers, secretaries, shipping clerks, and/or financial officers. In a small organization, everyone may have a voice in the decision. The group of people in the organization who participate in the decision-making process is the **buying centre.**

THE FLUID NATURE OF THE BUYING CENTRE

Although the term *buying centre* may conjure up an image of offices buzzing with purchasing activity, it usually is a cross-functional team of decision makers. Generally, the members of a buying centre have some expertise or interest in the particular decision, and they are able as a group to make the best decision.

Hospitals, for example, frequently make purchase decisions through a large buying centre. When making a decision to purchase disposable oxygen masks, one or more physicians, the director of nurses, and purchasing agents may work together to determine quantities and select the best products and suppliers. A separate decision regarding the types of pharmaceutical supplies to stock might need a different cast of characters to advise the purchasing agent. This means that marketers must continually identify which of a firm's employees are involved in every purchase and develop relationships with them all.

ROLES IN THE BUYING CENTRE

Buying centre participants have unique roles in the decision process. In some cases, the purchasing agent or professional buyer who makes the purchase may also make the decision. In other cases, the buyer's chief role is to gather information for users of the product or a top manager who will ultimately make the final decision.

For suppliers, the buying centre concept complicates the marketing process. A salesperson, for example, may have to provide different types of information to satisfy the interests of all participants. For example, a customer's engineers may want to know about the technical specifications of the product, whereas managers who will have to oversee the use of the product are interested in the safety of the product or in what types of in-service training the supplier is willing to provide. The salesperson also has to determine who has the most influence on the decision, who plays the key role of decision maker, and who actually makes the purchase. Take, for example, the hospital purchase of oxygen masks. The purchasing

* * *
buying centre The group of people in an organization who influence and participate in purchasing decisions.

department's major concerns will likely centre on price and delivery schedules, the nursing staff may be interested in packaging that is easy to open, and the physicians will be concerned with product design and that there will be few, if any, faulty masks. The salesperson must convince each one of these people that his or her product will satisfy their needs better than that of the competition.

Depending on the complexity of the purchase and the size of the buying centre, a participant may assume one, several, or all of the six roles shown in Figure 7.5. Let's review them.

The *initiator* begins the buying process by first recognizing that the firm needs to make a purchase. A production employee, for example, may notice that a piece of equipment is not working properly and notify a supervisor. At other times, the initiator may suggest purchasing a new product because it will improve the firm's operations. Depending on the initiator's position in the organization and the type of purchase, the initiator may or may not influence the actual purchase decision. For marketers, it's important to make sure individuals who might initiate a purchase are aware of improved products they offer.

The *user* is the member of the buying centre who needs the purchased product. The user's role in the buying centre varies. For example, an administrative assistant may give his or her input on the features needed in a new copier that the assistant will be "chained to" for several hours a day. Marketers need to inform users of their products about ease of use and other user benefits their products provide over those of competitors.

The *gatekeeper* is the member who controls the flow of information to other members. Typically the gatekeeper is the purchasing agent who gathers information and materials from salespeople, schedules sales presentations, and controls suppliers' access to other participants in the buying process. For salespeople, developing and maintaining strong personal relationships with gatekeepers is critical to their being able to offer their products to the buying centre.

An *influencer* affects the buying decision by dispensing advice or sharing expertise. By virtue of their expertise, engineers, quality control specialists, and other technical experts in the firm generally have a great deal of influence in purchasing equipment, materials, and component parts used in production. The influencers may or may not wind up using the product. Marketers need to identify key influencers in the buying centre and work to persuade them of their product's superiority.

The *decider* is the member of the buying centre who makes the final decision. This person usually is the person with the greatest power within the buying centre and often has power within the organization to authorize spending the company's money. For a routine purchase, the decider may be the purchasing agent. If the purchase is complex, a manager or CEO may be the decider. The decider is key to a marketer's success and deserves a lot of attention in the selling process.

The *buyer* is the person who has responsibility for executing the purchase. Although the buyer often has a role in identifying and evaluating alternative suppliers, this person's primary function is handling the details of the purchase. The buyer obtains competing bids,

Role	Potential Player	Responsibility
• Initiator	• Production employees, sales manager, almost anyone	• Recognizes that a purchase needs to be made
• User	• Production employees, secretaries, almost anyone	• Individual(s) who will ultimately use the product
• Gatekeeper	• Buyer/purchasing agent	• Controls flow of information to others in the organization
• Influencer	• Engineers, quality control experts, technical specialists, outside consultants	• Affects decision by giving advice and sharing expertise
• Decider	• Purchasing agent, managers, CEO	• Makes the final purchase decision
• Buyer	• Purchasing agent	• Executes the purchase decision

Figure 7.5 Roles in the Buying Centre

negotiates contracts, and arranges delivery dates and payment plans. Once a firm makes the purchase decision, marketers turn their attention to negotiating the details of the purchase with the buyer. Successful marketers are well aware that providing exemplary service in this stage of the purchase can be key to future sales.

Electronic Business-to-Business Commerce

While we are still talking about the nature of business buying, let's discuss electronic commerce, which is the most important change in organizational buying in recent years. **Electronic commerce**, or e-commerce, is the buying and selling of products electronically, usually via the Internet (discussed in more detail in Chapter 15). We typically think of e-commerce in relation to consumer markets—sites such as Chapters.ca that sell books or Futureshop.com that sells consumer electronics. Here we're concerned with e-commerce in business markets.

For several decades, firms have used electronic data interchange (EDI) systems to communicate with business partners. EDI allows for limited communication through the exchange of computer data between two companies. But EDI is expensive and transmits only rigidly formatted electronic documents such as purchase orders and invoices.

Today, many firms have replaced their EDI systems with Internet tools that allow them to electronically transfer all kinds of data—even engineering drawings—as well as to make EDI-type exchanges. Ford, General Motors, and DaimlerChrysler, for example, established a huge automotive-parts exchange on the Internet linking 60 000 suppliers around the world to bid on more than US$240 billion worth of auto-part purchases.[12] For sellers, too, e-commerce provides remarkable advantages. Boeing, for example, received orders for $100 million in spare parts in the first year that its Web site was in operation.[13] The Internet also allows businesses to reach new markets: Saskatoon-based Point2.com, for example, is able to coordinate via the Internet the sale of used mining equipment that would otherwise have been discarded because of the cost of an individual seller finding a buyer for their specialized equipment.[14]

Using the Internet for e-commerce allows business marketers to link directly to suppliers, factories, distributors, and customers, radically reducing the time necessary for order and delivery of goods, tracking sales, and getting feedback from customers. Experts anticipate that, by 2003, Canadian businesses will exchange an estimated $56 billion via the Internet, up from $6.6 billion in 1999.[15] John Roth, president and chief executive officer of Nortel Networks Corp., Canada's largest information technology company, suggests that "the Internet changes everything—everyone {big or small} can now become a global competitor and supplier."[16] One implication of this is that all firms, big and small, will need to have an international orientation as well as a source of competitive advantage to compete successfully. This is what WorldBid.com hopes to facilitate.

Although the Internet is the primary means of e-commerce, some companies have used similar computer technology to develop more secure means of conducting business. **Intranets** are in-house computer connections an organization creates to distribute information internally. City workers in Mississauga, Ontario, for example, use the intranet "WebBoard" to communicate all official announcements, new policies, technology implementations, staff appointments, and most recently, smog alerts.[17] Intranets are more secure than Internet connections, because they are protected by electronic firewalls that prevent access by unauthorized users.

When the intranet is opened to authorized external users, it is called an *extranet*. With extranets, marketers allow suppliers, distributors, and other authorized users to access data that the company makes available. Toronto-based 3Com Canada Inc., for example, uses extranet technology as a way to connect to branch offices, keep in touch with partners, and offer employees better ways of getting their jobs done.[18]

In addition to saving companies money, extranets allow business partners to collaborate on projects (such as product design) and to build better relationships. Hewlett-Packard and Procter & Gamble, for example, swap marketing plans and review ad campaigns with their advertising agencies through extranets. Extranets are also used by public service organizations

✳✳✳
electronic commerce The buying and selling of products electronically, usually via the Internet.

Nortel Networks
www.nortelnetworks.com

✳✳✳
intranet The internal computer connections that organizations use to distribute information among their different offices and locations.

to coordinate their resources and ability to serve the public. Ontario hospitals, for example, have an emergency patient referral system called CritiCall which allows admitting clerks, hospital administrators, and even physicians (by calling CritiCall) to track beds, emergency department status, and other medical resources. This allows them to direct patients to facilities that can help them quickly.[19]

Buying Groups

✷ ✷ ✷

buying group The coordination of purchasing among member organizations to realize economies of scale and other efficiencies.

Onvia.com Inc.
www.onvia.com

Buying groups reflect a cooperative purchasing effort among organizations that individually may be too small to command volume discounts or enjoy other economies of scale. By pooling their purchases with other companies, buying group members can cut overall procurement costs by as much as 10%.[20]

Gold Leaf Office Products Ltd. is a Canadian buying group that has 11 member companies, with combined annual sales of about $180 million. In addition to handling their bulk buying, the staff at Gold Leaf's office publishes catalogues for members, prints advertising flyers, and runs a group-wide private brand of supplies—all of better quality and at a lower cost to the firms than they could manage on their own.[21] Onvia.com Inc., founded in Vancouver in 1996 and now operating out of Seattle, combines the purchasing power of more than 400 000 small business owners and gives them access to the goods and services of about 700 manufacturers and 25 wholesale distributors at reduced prices.[22]

The Business Buying Decision Process

We've seen a number of players in the business buying process, beginning with an initiator and ending with a buyer. To make matters more challenging to marketers, members of the buying team go through several stages in the decision-making process. The business buying decision process, as Figure 7.6 shows, is a series of steps similar to those in the consumer decision process (discussed in Chapter 6). The business buying process is more complex than the consumer decision-making process, however, and each step can mushroom into several additional steps.

Problem Recognition

As in consumer buying, the first step in the business buying decision process occurs when someone sees that a purchase can solve a problem. For straight rebuy purchases, this step may be a result of the firm running out of paper, pens, or garbage bags. In these cases, the buyer places the order and the decision-making process ends. Recognition of the need for modified rebuy purchases often comes from wanting to replace outdated existing equipment, from changes in technology, or from an ad, brochure, or other form of marketing communications that offers the customer a better product at a lower price. The need for new-task purchases often arises because the firm wants to enhance its operations in some way, or a smart salesperson tells the business customer about a new product that will increase the efficiency of the firm's operations.

Information Search

In the second step of the decision process for purchases other than straight rebuys, the buying centre searches for information about products and suppliers. Members of the buying centre may individually or collectively refer to reports in trade magazines and journals, seek advice from outside consultants, and pay close attention to marketing communications from different manufacturers and other

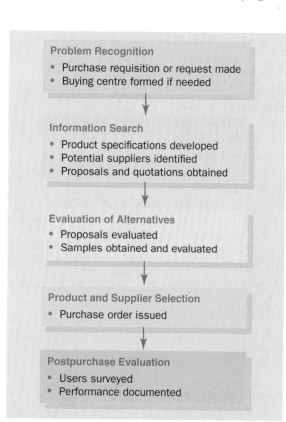

Figure 7.6 Steps in the Business Buying Decision Process

Problem Recognition
- Purchase requisition or request made
- Buying centre formed if needed

Information Search
- Product specifications developed
- Potential suppliers identified
- Proposals and quotations obtained

Evaluation of Alternatives
- Proposals evaluated
- Samples obtained and evaluated

Product and Supplier Selection
- Purchase order issued

Postpurchase Evaluation
- Users surveyed
- Performance documented

suppliers. As in consumer marketing, it's the job of marketers to make sure that information is available when and where business customers want it—by placing ads in trade magazines, by mailing brochures and other printed material to prospects, and by having a well-trained, enthusiastic sales force regularly calling on customers.

DEVELOPING PRODUCT SPECIFICATIONS

Business buyers often find it's a good idea to develop product specifications, a written description laying out their exact product requirements—the quality, size, weight, colour, features, quantities, warranty, service terms, and delivery and training requirements for the purchase. When the product needs are complex or technical, engineers and other experts are the key players in identifying specific product characteristics and determining whether standardized, off-the-shelf or customized, made-to-order goods and services will do.

OBTAINING PROPOSALS

Once the product specifications are in hand, the buyer's next step is to obtain written or verbal proposals, or *bids*, from one or more potential suppliers. For standardized or branded products in which there are few, if any, differences in the products of different suppliers, this may be as simple as an informal request for pricing information, including discounts, shipping charges, and confirmation of delivery dates. At other times, the request is in the form of a formal written *request for proposal* or *request for quotation*, which requires suppliers to develop detailed proposals or price quotations for supplying the product.

Evaluation of Alternatives

In this stage of the business buying decision process, the buying centre assesses the proposals. Total spending for goods and services can have a major impact on the firm's profitability, so all other things being equal, price is the primary consideration. Pricing evaluations take into account discount policies for certain quantities, returned goods policies, the cost of repair and maintenance services, terms of payment, and the cost of financing large purchases. For capital equipment, cost criteria also include the life expectancy of the purchase, the expected resale value, and disposal costs for the old equipment. In some cases the buying centre may negotiate with the preferred supplier to match the lowest bidder. Although a bidder often is selected because it offers the lowest price, sometimes the buying decision is based on other factors. For example, American Express wins bids for its travel agency business by offering extra services such as a corporate credit card and monthly reports that detail the company's total travel expenses.

American Express
www.americanexpress.com

The more complex and costly the purchase, the more time spent searching for the best supplier—and the more marketers must do to win the order. For example, marketers often make formal presentations and product demonstrations to the buying centre group. In the case of installations and large equipment, marketers sometimes arrange for buyers to speak with or even visit other customers to see for themselves how the product performs.

Product and Supplier Selection

Once buyers have assessed all proposals, the next step in the buying process is the purchase decision—the selection of the best product and supplier to meet the firm's needs. Although price is usually a factor, in firms that have adopted a total quality management approach (discussed in Chapter 3), the quality, reliability, and durability of materials and component parts are paramount. Reliability and durability rank high for equipment and systems that keep the firm's operations running smoothly without interruption. For some purchases, warranties, repair service, and regular maintenance after the sale are important.

A supplier's ability to make on-time deliveries is the critical factor in the selection process for firms that have adopted an inventory management system called **just in time (JIT)**. JIT systems reduce inventory and stock to very low levels or even zero and ensure a constant supply through precisely timed deliveries just when needed. For both manufacturers and resellers, the choice of supplier may come down to one whose location is nearest. To win a

* * *
just in time (JIT) Inventory management and purchasing processes that manufacturers and resellers use to reduce inventory to very low levels and ensure that deliveries from suppliers arrive only when needed.

Like most decisions, outsourcing is not without risk. In 1995, the Canadian government outsourced the Canada Student Loans Program to some of the country's major banks. The banks were convinced that they could manage the loans better than Ottawa, reduce the default rate, and show a profit from the program. However, in 1999, the banks realized that the default rate had increased by seven percent since they began managing the program. The banks demanded $155 million in risk protection from the government, up from $75 million, to cover defaulted loans. Students were also complaining about the heavy-handed background checks and collection methods employed by the private banks. In July 2000, the federal Human Resources Department began administering the $1 billion-a-year program, with promises to run it more efficiently.

Do you think the government should pay the banks the larger risk protection demanded? Do you think there are certain kinds of firms for which outsourcing is a good idea? What firms? For what kinds of firms might outsourcing not be advantageous?

* * *
single sourcing The business practice of buying a particular product from only one supplier.

* * *
multiple sourcing The business practice of buying a particular product from many suppliers.

* * *
reciprocity A trading partnership in which two firms agree to buy from one another.

* * *
outsourcing The business buying process of obtaining outside vendors to provide goods or services that otherwise might be supplied in-house.

* * *
reverse marketing A business practice in which a buyer firm shapes a supplier's products and operations to satisfy its needs.

large customer, a supplier organization may even have to be willing to set up production facilities close to the customer to guarantee JIT delivery.[23]

One of the most important functions of a buyer is deciding how many suppliers can best serve the firm's needs. Sometimes one supplier is more beneficial to the organization than multiple suppliers. **Single sourcing**, in which a buyer and seller work quite closely, is particularly important for a firm that needs frequent deliveries or specialized products. But reliance on a single source means that the firm is at the mercy of the chosen supplier to deliver the needed goods or services without interruption. **Multiple sourcing** is buying a product from several suppliers. With multiple sourcing, suppliers are more likely to remain price competitive. And if one supplier has problems with delivery, the firm has others to fall back on.

Using one or a few suppliers rather than many has its advantages. A firm that buys from a single supplier becomes a large customer with a lot of clout when it comes to negotiating prices and contract terms. Having one or a few suppliers also lowers the firm's administrative costs, because it has fewer invoices to pay, fewer purchase orders to put into the system, and fewer salespeople to see than if it used many sources.

Sometimes supplier selection is based on **reciprocity**, which means that a buyer and seller agree to be each other's customers by saying essentially, "I'll buy from you and you buy from me." For example, a firm that supplies parts to a company that manufactures trucks would agree to buy trucks from only that firm. Consumer and Corporate Affairs Canada frowns on reciprocal agreements and often determines that such agreements between large firms are illegal because they limit free competition—new suppliers simply don't have a chance against the preferred suppliers. In other countries, reciprocity is a practice that is common and even expected in business-to-business marketing.

With **outsourcing**, firms obtain outside vendors to provide goods or services that might otherwise be supplied in-house. For example, the federal government could have managed its own electronic tendering system but found it more cost effective and efficient to outsource this service to MERX.

Yet another type of buyer–seller partnership is **reverse marketing**. Instead of sellers trying to identify potential customers and then "pitching" their products, buyers try to find suppliers capable of producing specific products they need and then attempt to "sell" the idea to the suppliers. The seller works to satisfy the buying firm's needs while assuring themselves of product quality, sufficient supply, and reasonable terms. This is why Big Grocer approached Bestfoods about a preferred vendor agreement.

Postpurchase Evaluation

Just as consumers evaluate purchases, an organizational buyer assesses whether the performance of the product and the supplier is living up to expectations. The buyer surveys the users to determine their satisfaction with the product as well as with the installation, delivery, and service provided by the supplier. By reviewing supplier performance, a firm decides whether to keep or drop the supplier. Many suppliers recognize the importance of conducting their own performance reviews on a regular basis. Measuring up to a customer's expectations can mean winning or losing a big account.

Real People, Real Decisions
How it worked out at Ritvik Holdings Inc.

Ritvik decision makers chose Option 3: to develop standard packaging for the European market and sell it worldwide. They felt that the extra costs involved in developing two different packages could not be supported with the forecasted production volumes. There would not be enough units to amortize the costs. Because North American sales were doing extremely well, there was not perceived as strong a need for the new line in North America. On the other hand, a more customized product might help build sales in Europe. Before launching the European style packaging in North America, Ritvik management tested the new product with North American consumers and retailers. They sent prototypes of the new product with its new packaging to their largest retail customers, took samples to toy fairs, and conducted focus groups with mothers. Feedback was generally positive. Since the product investment had already been made they decided to try it in the North American market to see what the retail and consumer response would be.

The new product line was launched in Europe and North America in the fall of 2000 in time for the pre-Christmas sales period, which accounts for 70% of all toy buying. In the first year the new product achieved listings of roughly 75% of the outlets in the most mature Mega Bloks European markets such as France, Belgium and the UK. In North America the new product achieved listings of roughly half that in the first year. In the second year listings and sales continued to meet expectations in Europe and the line was refreshed to maintain and build sales in Europe. Second year North American sales fell sharply and the product line was pulled from the North American market. Ritvik is now reconsidering its international product strategy and revisiting the three options considered for the Maxiland decision.

Chapter Summary

1. Describe the general characteristics of business-to-business markets and business buying practices.

Business-to-business markets include business and organizational customers that buy goods and services for purposes other than for personal consumption. Business and organizational customers are usually few in number, may be geographically concentrated, and often purchase higher-priced products in larger quantities. Business demand is derived from the demand for another good or service, is generally not affected by price increases or decreases, is subject to great fluctuations, and may be tied to the demand and availability of some other good.

2. Explain how marketers classify business and organizational markets.

Business customers include producers, resellers, governments, and not-for-profit organizations. Producers purchase materials, parts, and various goods and services needed to produce other goods and services to be sold at a profit. Resellers purchase finished goods to resell at a profit, as well as other goods and services to maintain their operations. Governments and other not-for-profit organizations purchase the goods and services necessary to fulfill their objectives. The North American Industry Classification System (NAICS), a numerical coding system developed by NAFTA countries, is the most widely used classification system for business and organizational markets.

3. Explain the business buying situation and describe business buyers.

The business buy class identifies the degree and effort required to make a business buying decision. Purchase situations can be straight rebuy, modified rebuy, and new-task buying. Business buying is usually handled by trained professional buyers. A buying centre is a group of people who work together to make a buying decision. The roles in the buying centre are initiator, user, gatekeeper, influencer, decider, and buyer. The most important recent change in business buying is the growth of electronic commerce, or e-commerce, in which firms buy and sell products using the Internet, intranets, or extranets.

KEY TERMS

acceleration principle (179)

business-to-business marketing (174)

buy class (183)

buying centre (187)

buying group (190)

centralized purchasing (186)

competitive bids (182)

derived demand (177)

electronic commerce (189)

government markets (181)

inelastic demand (178)

intranet (189)

joint demand (179)

just in time (JIT) (191)

modified rebuy (183)

multiple sourcing (192)

new-task buy (184)

North American Industry Classification System (NAICS) (180)

not-for-profit institutions (182)

outsourcing (192)

producers (181)

reciprocity (192)

resellers (181)

reverse marketing (192)

single sourcing (192)

straight rebuy (183)

4. Explain how e-commerce is dramatically changing business-to-business marketing.

Every company, big or small, can now become a global competitor and supplier. This means that all firms need to have an international orientation and some source of competitive advantage. The Internet allows business marketers to link directly to suppliers, factories, distributors, and customers, radically reducing the time necessary for the order and delivery of goods, for tracking sales, and for getting feedback from customers. It also means companies can get access to a worldwide supply of goods and services, putting pressure on both pricing and quality.

5. Summarize the main stages in the business buying decision process.

The stages in the business buying decision process are similar to, but more complex than, the steps in consumer decision making. These steps include problem recognition, information search during which buyers develop product specifications and obtain proposals from prospective sellers, proposal evaluation, supplier selection, and formal evaluation of the performance of the product and the supplier. A firm's purchasing options include single or multiple sourcing. In outsourcing, firms obtain outside vendors to provide goods or services that otherwise might be supplied in-house. Other business buying activities are reciprocity and reverse marketing.

Chapter Review

Marketing Concepts: Testing Your Knowledge

1. What are some general characteristics of business-to-business markets? What is one primary difference between business customers and consumers?

2. How is business-to-business demand different from consumer demand? What are some of the factors that cause business demand to fluctuate?

3. How are business-to-business markets generally classified? What types of purchases do the major types of organizations make?

4. What is the NAICS? What purpose does it serve? Of what use is it to business marketers?

5. Describe the three buy class situations.

6. What is the role of electronic commerce in business-to-business marketing?

7. What are the characteristics of business buyers?

8. What is a buying centre? What are the roles of the various people in a buying centre?

9. What are buying groups, and how is the Internet facilitating rapid growth in these groups?

10. What are the stages in the business buying decision process? What happens in each stage?

11. What is single sourcing? Multiple sourcing? Outsourcing? Explain how reciprocity and reverse marketing operate in business-to-business markets.

Marketing Concepts: Discussing Choices and Issues

1. Do you agree with the idea that business-to-business marketing is more important to a country's economy than consumer marketing? Which one do you think provides better career opportunities for new college and university graduates? Explain your answers.

2. A number of business buying practices may be criticized as being unfair to one or more suppliers. What are the benefits of reciprocity to business firms? Is anyone hurt by reciprocity?

3. The practice of buying business products based on sealed competitive bids is popular among all types of business buyers. What are the advantages and disadvantages of this practice to buyers? What are the advantages and disadvantages to sellers? Should companies always give the business to the lowest bidder? Why or why not?

4. When firms engage in outsourcing, they relinquish control over how goods and services are produced. What are the advantages of outsourcing to a firm? What are some of the hazards of outsourcing? What can firms do to make sure that outsourcing benefits both them and the outsourcing firm?

Marketing Practice: **Applying What You've Learned**

1. You are looking for a part-time job and being considered by a small, weekly newspaper. Knowing that you are a marketing student, the editor has asked you to provide a sample article that explains business demand in a way that will be interesting to the owners of small local shops and other businesses. Write that article and circulate it among three classmates, asking each to provide brief written comments and suggestions.

2. You've just been hired by a small consulting company that services small- to medium-sized firms. One of the company's clients produces custom-imprinted T-shirts for local sports teams and other groups and is thinking about switching to a JIT inventory control system. The client, who has 10 employees, currently buys the T-shirts in bulk and keeps large quantities of stock imprints and other supplies on hand. Your boss has asked you to prepare a list of issues the owner has to consider. Prepare the list and discuss each point with a classmate who assumes the client's role.

3. As a new director of materials management for a textile firm that manufactures sheets and towels, you are hoping to simplify the buying process where possible, thus reducing costs for the firm. You have first examined each purchase and classified it as a straight rebuy, a modified rebuy, or a new-task purchase. Your next job is to outline the procedures or steps in the purchasing process for each type of purchase. Indicate the type of purchase and outline the steps that must be taken in the purchase of each of the following items.

   a. computer paper

   b. textile dyes for this year's fashion colours

   c. new sewing robotics

   d. new software to control the weaving processes

Marketing Mini-Project: **Learning by Doing**

The purpose of this mini-project is to gain knowledge about one business-to-business market using the NAICS codes and other government information.

1. Select an industry of interest to you and use the NAICS information found on the Internet (www.statcan.ca/english/Subjects/Standard/standard_classifications.htm) or in your library.

   a. What are the codes for each of the following classifications?
      NAICS Sector (two digits)
      NAICS Subsector (three digits)
      NAICS Industry Group (four digits)
      NAICS Industry (five digits)
      Canadian Industry (six digits)

   b. What types of products are or are not included in this industry?

2. Find out what information Industry Canada has on your industry. Go to the Strategis Web site (strategis.ic.gc.ca/scecnmy/sio/homepage.htmllibrary) to review Canadian industry statistics. Note that Strategis still uses SIC codes instead of NAICS codes, so you will have to look up your industry again using the "Search For SIC Code" button on the page.

   Statistics Canada is the country's national statistical agency with a mandate to collect, compile, analyze, abstract and publish statistical information on virtually every aspect of the nation's society and economy. Go to the Statistics Canada Web site (www.statcan.ca/english/search) and enter the name of your industry into the search engine. What information does Statistics Canada have on your industry?

3. Canadian Industry Norms & Key Business Ratios is a CD-ROM resource available in many libraries, that has data useful for analyzing trends and assessing the strengths and weaknesses of the agriculture, mining, construction, transportation, wholesaling, utilities, retailing, finance, insurance, real estate, and services industries. Information on specific companies is also available. See what information is available on one of these industries.

4. *The Blue Book of Canadian Business* provides detailed profiles of leading Canadian companies (public, private, crown, and cooperatives) in terms of sales, assets, net income, and stock trading volume. The Canadian Key Business Directory profiles the top 20 000 public and private companies. Look up one of the companies in your industry and find their net sales, gross profits, and income before tax.

Real People, Real Surfers: Exploring the Web

Mega Bloks Ritvik Holdings isn't the only company that makes construction toy products. Visit Mega Bloks' Web site (www.megabloks.com) and that of their main competitor, Lego (www.lego.com), and other speciality toy producers such as Rokenbok (www.rokenbok.com) or K'nex (www.knex.com).

Based on your experience, answer the following questions:

1. In general, how do the Web sites compare? Which are easier to navigate, and why? Which are more innovative and attractive, and why?

2. Evaluate each site from the perspective of a toy store buyer. What features in each site would be useful? What information is available that a buyer might need? Which site would be most useful for a buyer? Why?

3. Evaluate each site from the perspective of a parent. What features in each site would be useful? What information is available that a parent might need? Which site would be most useful for a parent? Why?

MARKETING IN ACTION

Venture 4th

Venture 4th provides office space, secretarial services, technology services, and marketing, accounting, and other business expertise for start-up ventures in Halifax, Nova Scotia. The brain trust of four commerce graduates—Sean O'Connor, Sarah Brown, Rick Styles, and Paul Rainer—Venture 4th currently has six clients, ranging from a fledgling e-tail business to a profitable specialty food importer.

NEED FOR CHANGE

Ever since Venture 4th opened its doors two years ago, office technology has been a major headache. The four partners had started their service business on a shoe-string budget—using their own computers and desktop printers, purchasing an inexpensive fax machine and scanner, and renting a low-end photocopier for general use. (Clients with special computer and high-speed Internet access needs provided those resources for themselves). Unable to afford a more elegant Ethernet solution, they ran a "sneaker net" system, where users brought disks to a central computer to use the laser printer, colour inkjet printer, and scanner. This system was adequate for the first year, when there were only two clients. With greater demand on the resources, however, and differences in computer speeds, software versions, and printer drivers, the system was driving everyone crazy—particularly Rick Styles, who was responsible for keeping this hodgepodge of equipment operating. The issue came to a head when the e-tail client said he couldn't continue to run his business out of the Venture 4th office space without more reasonable office technology support.

When this was discussed at the next weekly partners' meeting, Sarah Brown, the partner primarily responsible for new business development, indicated that she thought she could land two more clients and another $40 000 a year revenue if they had more modern and higher-capacity office equipment linked in a network solution. With this to motivate them, the Venture 4th team began in June to investigate the purchase of an Ethernet office network linked to high-speed Internet access and a digital imaging system comprising an integrated network printer, copier, scanner, and fax machine.

PRELIMINARY INVESTIGATIONS

It took Styles three weeks to do a preliminary investigation of the options. He called Copies Plus, from which Venture 4th was renting its Rocket copier, and Iain Carver, their small business representative, came the following day to do a needs analysis. Based on current and projected printing and copying volume, Carver recommended a digital imaging system that could make at least 10 000 copies a month. This ruled out the "all in one" desktop solutions Styles had been looking at the last time he was in Future Shop. Carver recommended the Rocket 3000E system, left a brochure, and promised to follow up with a price quote. During the visit, Carver "tuned up" the rental unit and left some samples of a new brand of laser printer paper that Copies Plus was carrying.

The next day, a Xena representative called, asked for Styles, and made an appointment for the following week to discuss Xena document solutions. The rep, Peter Smith, having overheard Sarah Brown talking about their need for a new copier one evening at a downtown bar, had approached her with a funny "pick-up" line, engaged her with polite conversation, and then returned (to her relief) to his friends. Later he approached one of Brown's friends and found out where she worked. When he met with Styles, he marveled at his ability to keep the current system running and promised to return with a system recommendation and prices.

About a week after Styles had received a faxed Rocket quote and a couriered envelope with Smith's recommendation and pricing for a Xena 33DT system, Sean O'Connor mentioned that he had seen a Cambon digital imaging system in the law firm used by Venture 4th. O'Connor

MARKETING IN ACTION

had been quite impressed with the system and had talked with one of the secretaries about it while waiting to see the firm's lawyer. The secretary said that the system had been in place for about a year and had made a big difference in the law firm's ability to produce and manage the receipt of thousands of documents. This recommendation prompted Styles to call a Cambon distributor, who faxed him the specifications of the Cambon DC330.

PRESENTATIONS

At Venture 4th, strategic decisions and those involving more than $10 000 had to have unanimous approval by the partners. Therefore, Styles invited Carver, Smith, and a representative from the Cambon distributor to the July 6 partners' meeting to present the merits of their systems. At the end of each presentation, Styles asked the reps whether the presented price was the best they could do. In a "Regis" parody, Paul Rainer followed this with, "Is that your final answer?" Only the rep from the Cambon distributor responded with a last-minute price reduction, taking $200 off the price of the system.

The Rocket system had the fastest copying—35 pages per minute versus 33 for the Cambon and 32 for the Xena—and it was rated for the greatest volume—20 000 to 60 000 copies per month versus 10 000 for the other two. While the Rocket system was the least expensive at $14 500, its printing technology was not PostScript compatible without adding an optional $1500 feature. PostScript compatibility is important for desktop publishing applications—which some of Venture 4th's clients might want.

The Xena system, priced at $19 200, came with a PostScript printing capability but did not have a stapling feature. Xena had a strong reputation for product quality and support, and its history of copying innovation impressed the partners.

The rep from the Cambon distributor arrived late but did a creditable job explaining the benefits of his system. The Cambon system, priced at $18 100 (after the $200 reduction) had been awarded a "recommended buy" by the US-based Buyers Laboratory, a product testing and rating organization. Although the Cambon product took longer to warm up than the others, it had the highest printing resolution at 1200×600 dpi (dots per inch) versus 600×600 for the other two and the greatest paper capacity at 3500 sheets compared to 2000 sheets for the others. The Xena rep, presenting before the Cambon rep, had explained that there were more important factors than dpi for print quality and that the Xena system had the crispest image.

At the end of the partners' meeting, Styles summarized the advantages and disadvantages of each system. The partners agreed that they should purchase one of the systems. O'Connor liked the Cambon solution best, having been impressed on his visit to the law firm, and noted that the Cambon distributor had lowered his price once and might do so again if pressed. Brown liked the idea of saving some money by buying the Rocket, then upgrading later if anyone wanted to get the PostScript option. Styles and Rainer leaned toward the Xena solution, considering company's reputation; they also noted that the rep from the Cambon distributor came late and questioned what kind of support they might get from him. The partners decided that they should all go to see each of the systems in action.

The next day, Styles called the reps and arranged a visit to one of their installations. When they visited the company with a Rocket system, the paper had just jammed on the system and a technician had to be called. The staff who used the system said that this didn't happen very often and that they were generally happy with the system. Both the Xena and Cambon solutions were working when the Venture 4th partners came to see them, and the staff who used the systems raved about them.

NEGOTIATIONS

On July 10, Styles called the three reps to say that he and his partners were going to make a purchase decision at 4:00 that afternoon. He told them that if they wanted to reconsider

MARKETING IN ACTION

their pricing and submit a lower quote, they could do so before 3:00. At 1:00, the Rocket rep faxed in a new price of $14 000 and a one-year option to buy the PostScript upgrade at $1300. At 2:00, the Cambon rep faxed in a new price of $17 900 and offered free installation and three hours of staff training. Styles called the Rocket rep back, confirmed that his price included installation, and got a verbal commitment to three hours of staff training. At 2:45, Styles called Smith at Xena and was told that the original price of $19 200 was the best he could do and that the price included installation and three hours of training. At 4:15, during the partner deliberations, the Xena rep called back. He told Styles that Xena was going to announce a price reduction on the 332DC system the next day and that his manager had authorized a $500 price reduction for Venture 4th. Armed with this new information, Styles went back into the partner meeting to get a consensus decision.

Source: This case was written by Professor Brock Smith of the University of Victoria.

THINGS TO THINK ABOUT

1. If you were a partner of Venture 4th, which system would purchase, and why?
2. How does this purchase process compare with the model illustrated in Figure 7.6?
3. Where was the most time spent in this purchase process? Why?
4. Assuming that this decision process is typical, what are the implications for sales and marketing organizations?

8

Sharpening the Focus: Target Marketing Strategies

CHAPTER OBJECTIVES

1. Understand the three steps of developing a target marketing strategy.

2. Understand the need for market segmentation in today's business environment.

3. Know the different dimensions marketers use to segment consumer markets.

4. Understand the bases for segmentation in business-to-business markets.

5. Explain how marketers evaluate and select potential market segments.

6. Explain how marketers develop a targeting strategy.

7. Understand how a firm develops and implements a positioning strategy.

Real People, Real Decisions ✓ ✗

Meet Candace Fochuk-Barey
A Decision Maker at Ford Motor Company of Canada

As Marketing Manager, Special Markets at the Ford Motor Company of Canada, Candace Fochuk-Barey is responsible for overseeing the positioning of Ford brands and services to specific target markets. Currently one of Ford's priority special markets is women, especially those 24 to 54 years old. While many automotive marketing activities have traditionally targeted men, recently Ford has been proactive in targeting women, recognizing that women represent a large and potentially profitable target segment for car and truck sales. To facilitate the effective targeting of Ford products to Canadian women, Fochuk-Barey participates in various new product launch teams at Ford and was instrumental in founding the Ford of Canada's Women's Council and the

Canadian Chapter of the Women's Automotive Association International.

Fochuk-Barey, who has a degree from McMaster University, began her career at Ford in 1979 and has held a variety of positions since then in general marketing, vehicle sales, and customer service. She is also active in her community, helping to organize the Canadian Woman Entrepreneur of the Year Awards and sitting on the Career Assessment and Planning advisory board of the YWCA of Toronto.

Sources: Lesley Daw, "Female-friendly Ford," *Marketing Magazine*, 17 August 1998: 2–22; Liza Finlay, "Mom power," *Marketing Magazine*, 19/26 July 1999; personal interview with Candace Fochuk-Barey.

Ford Motor Company of Canada
www.ford.ca

✳ ✳ ✳

market fragmentation Creation of many consumer groups due to a diversity of distinct needs and wants in modern society.

Selecting and Entering a Market

The goal of the marketer is to satisfy needs, but in our complex society, it is naive to assume that everyone's needs are the same. Candace Fochuk-Barey and her colleagues at Ford Canada know that different types of consumers have different priorities when it comes to buying a car. So when Ford designs and markets its cars, it needs to consider the different needs that exist in the marketplace. Understanding these needs is especially complex today, because technological and cultural advances have created a condition of market fragmentation. **Market fragmentation** occurs when people's diverse interests and backgrounds have divided them into different groups with distinct needs and wants. Because of this diversity, the same product or service will not appeal to everyone.

Consider, for example, the effects of fragmentation in the fast-food industry. When a McDonald's hamburger was still a novelty (with under a million sold), people were happy to order just a plain hamburger, fries, and drink. Today's consumers would be very unhappy if salads, chicken, or wraps disappeared from the menu. But how many menu items do McDonald's, Harvey's, or Pizza Hut need to offer? Why is it that kids insist on a Happy Meal, whereas their parents prefer to grab a pita at Wendy's or a veggie burger at Harvey's?

Marketers must balance the efficiency of serving the same items to everyone with the effectiveness of offering each individual exactly what he or she wants. Mass marketing is certainly the most efficient plan. It costs much less to offer one product to the entire market, because that strategy eliminates the need for distinct marketing activities, such as separate advertising campaigns and packages, for each item. From the consumer's perspective, the best strategy would be one that offers the perfect product for each individual. However, that degree of customization is often not possible for companies to provide.

Fortunately, some groups of customers tend to want the same kinds of offerings; and in many situations, it is possible to identify such a group and develop products, services, or specialized stores for them. For example, there are many small businesses in Canada: About 99% of Canadian businesses have fewer than 100 employees.[1] Recognizing the potential in this large group of customers, who have similar needs, Grand & Toy launched The Stockroom, an Internet-based office supplies store (www.thestockroom.ca) that targets small businesses. While the Grand & Toy Web site (www.grandandtoy.com) is geared to the

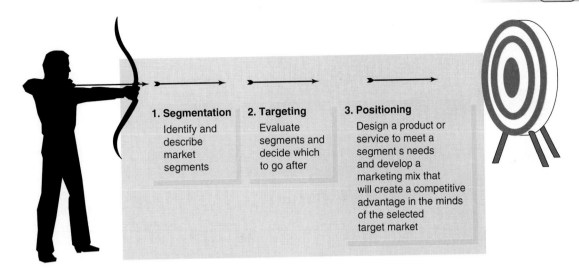

Figure 8.1 Steps in the Target Marketing Process

needs of large businesses (offering benefits like large volume discounts), The Stockroom site caters to small businesses with its products and pricing policies. The general manager of The Stockroom describes the company's approach this way, "...we felt it was important to take a very aggressive, focused stance, purely aimed at the small business segment."[2] Instead of trying to sell the same thing to all customers, marketers like Grand & Toy often select a **target marketing strategy**, in which they divide the total market into different segments based on customer characteristics, select one or more segments, and develop products to meet the needs of those specific segments. The three-step process of segmentation, targeting, and positioning is illustrated in Figure 8.1. Let's start with the first step—segmentation.

Segmentation

Segmentation is the process of dividing a larger market into smaller pieces, based on one or more meaningful, shared characteristics. Segmentation is a fact of marketing life. You can't please all the people all the time, so you need to take your best shot. Just how do marketers segment a population? Segmenting the market is often necessary in both consumer and, as we saw in the case of Grand & Toy, business markets. In each case, the marketer must decide on one or more useful **segmentation variables** that divide the total market into fairly homogeneous groups, each with different needs and preferences. In this section we'll look at how this is done, beginning with the types of segmentation variables used to divide up consumer markets.

Dimensions for Segmenting Consumer Markets

At one time, it was sufficient to divide the sports shoe market into athletes versus non-athletes. Today, a walk through any sporting goods store will reveal that the athlete market has fragmented in many directions, and includes shoes designed for jogging, basketball, tennis, cycling, cross-training, and skateboarding. Some manufacturers of athletic footwear geared to young boarders, such as Vans (see Exhibit 8.1), Airwalk, and DC, chalked up annual sales gains of 20 to 50% in the past few years. Known to their peers as shredders, riders, or skaters, the youth who wear these shoes can be seen riding skateboards down the handrails and steps of city parks. They coast downhill and shoot into the air on snowboards. During mud season, they twist their stunt bikes down slippery hills and, in summer, they flip and glide on wakeboards pulled by powerboats. Over the next few years, sports marketers expect the skateboard and snowboard populations to double and wakeboarders to soar six-fold. To cash in on this trend, PepsiCo Inc.'s Mountain Dew began to feature snowboarding in its advertisements and was rewarded with a hefty increase in sales.[3]

***

target marketing strategy
Dividing the total market into different segments based on customer characteristics, selecting one or more segments, and developing products to meet the needs of those specific segments.

***

segmentation The process of dividing a larger market into smaller pieces, based on one or more meaningful, shared characteristics.

***

segmentation variables Bases for dividing the total market into fairly homogeneous groups, each with different needs and preferences.

All these sports require segmentation. Several segmentation variables can slice up the market for all the shoe variations available today. First, not everyone is willing or able to pay $150 on the latest running shoe, so marketers consider income. Second, some men may be more interested in basketball shoes, whereas some women may want the latest aerobics styles, so marketers also consider gender. Not all age groups are going to be equally interested in buying specialized athletic shoes, and some kids may be more inclined to risky "extreme" sports than others. As this example shows, the larger consumer "pie" can be sliced into smaller pieces in a number of ways, including demographic differences, psychological differences, and behavioural differences.

SEGMENTING BY DEMOGRAPHICS

Demographics are vital for identifying the best potential customers for a product or service because objective characteristics like a person's sex or age are (usually) easy to identify, and information about the demographics of a consumer market are easily obtained from government sources like Statistics Canada (www.statcan.ca). IBM uses demographics to segment its consumer markets and then develops separate marketing messages to appeal to various groups, including Aboriginal, visible minority, disabled, gay and lesbian, and senior citizen consumers. Each message uses copy and spokespeople likely to appeal to members of a specific segment. So, ads for IBM's VoiceType software that allows users to control the PC by voice, feature Curtis Mayfield, a Grammy award-winning soul singer and musician who is now a quadriplegic. As IBM's vice president for market development observed, "When you pay attention to people, you increase the chance of them buying from you."[4]

Important demographic dimensions for segmenting consumer markets include age, gender, family structure, income and social class, ethnicity, and geography. We have already spoken about many of these dimensions in Chapter 6, when we introduced them as factors that influence consumer behaviour. Now let's see how each of them can be used to divide up consumer markets.

Age. Consumers in different age groups have very different needs and wants. Members of a generation tend to share the same outlook and priorities. As we saw in Chapter 6, for example, Nexus consumers (those consumers aged 18 to 34 years) share certain characteristics and product preferences that distinguish them from other age groups.

Canadian demographer David Foot has identified several segments of Canadian consumers based on age. These include the Baby Boom (those people born in 1947–1966), The Baby Bust (those born in 1967–1979), the Baby Boom Echo (those born in 1980–1995), and the Millennium Busters (those born in 1996–2010).[5] While each of these groups of consumers presents needs that some marketers are interested in, the largest demographic segment in Canada, the **baby boomers**, accounts for about one-third of the Canadian population and is, therefore, a segment of prime importance to many marketers. Several companies have achieved success by monitoring the changing needs of this group of consumers. Coca-Cola, for example, can attribute part of its success in North America to the fact that boomers drank a lot of pop when they were young. Coke has now modified its marketing efforts to keep up with the changing tastes of the boomers. They changed their prod-

✳ ✳ ✳
baby boomers The largest age segment in Canada, it includes people who were born between 1947 and 1966.

uct line to include juice and bottled water to cater to the concerns that aging boomers have for their health.[6]

The President's Choice private label products, sold through Loblaws and affiliated stores, also appeal to the needs of the baby boom segment. These products include the Decadent chocolate-chip cookie, which offers indulgence, low-fat foods that are "Too Good to Be True" and help boomers stay healthy, and ready made frozen meals that offer a meal solution for time-starved boomers.[7]

The baby boom echo are the children of the baby boomers. The youngest part of the baby boom echo, who are now children and youth, represent a large and potentially lucrative group of consumers. The youth market in Canada is estimated to be worth over $13.5 billion, and teens are the second fastest growing segment in Canada.[8] These consumers tend to spend their money on items such as clothing, personal grooming, entertainment, sports, and eating out. Montreal-based La Senza has successfully targeted teen and tween (aged 5 to 13) girls with their La Senza Girl stores, and banks such as the Royal and CIBC have savings programs and debit cards specifically aimed at kids.[9]

The older part of the baby boom echo, those people born in the early to mid-1980s are moving away from their families for the first time and starting to make major purchases on their own. This age group includes a subsegment of consumers who attend university or college, an important target group for companies like DirectProtect, which sells insurance to students, and brewers such as Moosehead (www.moosehead.ca), Molson (www.molson.com), and Labatt (www.labatt.ca), who realize that many of the heavy users of their products can be found on campuses across Canada.

Older consumers, most of whom are the parents of the baby boomers, are another age segment of interest to Canadian marketers. Twenty-two percent of the Canadian population is 55 years of age or older.[10] Since many people are now retiring younger than age 65, these consumers are enjoying increased leisure time, making them an ideal target for travel and other leisure products. Health is also a major concern for these consumers; some of them may be experiencing failing health, and others are simply interested in maintaining good health as they age. The Healthwatch service provided by Shoppers Drug Mart, which provides advice from pharmacists, a database of individualized health information, and a health magazine, is a good example of a service targeted to the needs of these consumers.

Gender. Many products, including fragrances, clothing, and footwear, are designed to appeal to men or women, either because of the nature of the product or because the marketer chose to appeal to one sex or the other. Segmenting by sex starts at a very early age—even diapers come in pink for girls and blue for boys. As proof that consumers take these differences seriously, market researchers report that most parents refuse to put male infants in pink diapers.[11] Ford Canada recognizes that women and men may have different needs when it comes to purchasing and servicing cars and trucks, which is why the company is now focusing efforts on trying to better understand and serve the needs of Canadian women. Similarly, companies such as Home Depot Canada, Marriott Hotels, and Mr. Lube, which have traditionally focused on marketing to men, have started developing products and messages specifically targeting Canadian women.[12] In the past, clothing retailer Banana Republic has sold clothes for both men and women in the same store, but the company recently decided to begin differentiating their stores by gender by opening their first Banana Republic for Men in the Toronto Eaton's Centre.

Family Structure. Because family needs and expenditures change over time, one way to segment consumers is to consider the stage of the family life cycle they occupy (see Chapter 6). Not surprisingly, consumers in different life cycle segments are unlikely to need the same products, or at least in the same quantities.[13] For example, many food companies cater to the needs of people who live alone by providing single portion frozen and prepared foods, but also offer "jumbo" packs for those people who live in larger households.

As we age and move into new life situations, different product categories ascend and descend in importance to us. Young singles and newlyweds are the most likely to exercise, to go to bars, concerts, and movies, and to consume alcohol. Young families are heavy users of disposable diapers and toys and games for children. They are also interested in household appliances, furniture, and such vehicles as minivans. Older couples and singles are more likely to use maintenance services, and older people are a prime market for retirement communities and golf products. Condominiums that are built in Canadian cities are often designed with different family structures in mind. Some target single divorced men and women; others go after young families and include amenities such as on-site day care; and still others target vacation-home buyers.[14] Canadian department stores also consider family life cycle by specifically targeting brides and grooms to be with their wedding registry services.

Income and Social Class: The distribution of wealth is of great interest to marketers, because it determines which groups have the greatest buying power: Many marketers are interested in capturing the hearts and wallets of high-income consumers. In Canada, the average family income is about $62 000, but 9.5% of the population has a household income above $100 000.[15] These high-income consumers are a good target market for such luxury products as expensive jewellery, as well as financial services of brokers and investment products. The Wealthy Boomer Inc. (www.thewealthyboomer.com) is a Canadian company that targets high-income baby boom consumers with its magazine, *The Wealthy Boomer*. At the same time, other marketers target average- and lower-income consumers—the majority of Canadian consumers. The Hudson's Bay Company successfully targets these income groups with its Bay and Zellers department stores.

Sometimes, it is possible for a company to appeal to both average- and higher-income consumers. Leon's Furniture, a company that has successfully appealed to average-income consumers in the past, decided to expand its customer base in 2000 by appealing to a more upscale target market. The company revised its product line to include more upscale furniture and renovated stores to appeal to a higher-end market. The challenge for the company, though, was trying to convince the new target consumers that Leon's actually was upscale. In a series of TV ads, a high-income couple is shown having success shopping at Leon's, but they are wearing a fake nose and glasses disguise so that their friends won't see them shopping there. The campaign was a success with the new upscale market, and was also a hit with the current, average-income consumers.[16]

Ethnicity: As discussed in Chapter 6, many Canadian marketers are adopting a multicultural approach to their marketing activities in recognition of the ethnic diversity of the Canadian population. Ethnicity can have a strong impact on a consumer's preferences for products and services, such as magazines or television shows, foods, apparel, and choice of leisure activities

French Canadian consumers, who account for 20 to 30% of Canadians, are the second largest ethnic market in Canada (after those people of British origin) and are, therefore, an important segment for marketers.[17] Most French Canadian consumers live in Quebec, but there are also large segments of French Canadian consumers in New Brunswick and Ontario. As discussed in Chapter 6, national marketers often decide to specifically target the French Canadian market through the development of different products to suit the needs of this group and the use of French language advertising. For example, MusiquePlus and MusiMax are the French language music video TV stations owned by CHUM, the same company that operates MuchMusic and MuchMoreMusic in the English Canadian market. While MusiquePlus and MusiMax show many of the same videos as on the English stations, they mainly feature French music and programming to appeal to the music tastes of the French Canadian consumers. As the vice president of sales for CHUM Specialty Television, observes, "They are not MuchMusic and MuchMoreMusic in French. They have an identity of their own with a more regional than national focus."[18] So when Procter & Gamble was looking for a French Canadian spokesperson for Cover Girl cosmetics, they chose Genevieve Borne, a MusiquePlus VJ, because of her appeal to female French Canadian teens.

Over one million people in Canada are of Aboriginal origin, and they are located in various regions throughout the country.[19] Half of the Aboriginal people in Canada are under the age of 30, and the income of Aboriginal consumers is rising faster than that of other Canadians.[20] One company that targets Aboriginal consumers is Dinawo Sportswear and Casuals (www.dinawo.com), a native-owned clothing business located on the Six Nations Reserve in Ontario, that produces clothing incorporating native art and symbols.[21] The banking sector in Canada has also been proactive in targeting both Aboriginal consumers

CHUM Limited
www.chumlimited.com

and business owners. All of the major Canadian banks operate branches in Aboriginal communities with services targeted to meet their needs, as the ad for the Royal Bank in Exhibit 8.2 shows.[22]

Other than people of British, French, and Aboriginal origins, the three largest ethnic groups in Canada are German, Italian, and Chinese. Of these three, the fastest growing is the Chinese Canadian community.[23] Tropicana Products Ltd. considers the Chinese Canadian community to be one of the most important target markets for its orange juice product. It communicates with this target with Chinese language print ads placed in Chinese Canadian newspapers and promotions such as coupons for 68 cents (both 6 and 8 are considered to signify prosperity in the Chinese culture). The company is careful to avoid the use of the number four (which means death) in any of their pricing and advertising.[24]

Other large ethnic groups in Canada include the South Asian community, which accounts for 2.4% of the population, and the Black community, which is 2% of the Canadian population.[25] Bell Canada provides customer service representatives who speak Hindi, Punjabi, Urdu, and Tamil, so that they can better serve their South Asian customers.[26] To reach the over 351 000 people in Canada of Jewish origin, companies such as Baskin-Robbins offer kosher food products, Hallmark offers cards and festive products targeted to Jewish holidays, and the Liquor Control Board of Ontario offers 80 different types of kosher wines.[27]

Targeting ethnic groups is especially important in urban centres in Canada. In Toronto and Vancouver, visible minorities make up over 30% of the total population. In Ottawa, Montreal, Edmonton, and Calgary, they make up between 10 and 12% of the population.[28] The composition of ethnic markets is different across these cities, however. For example, in Montreal, 30% of the visible minority population, the single largest group, is Black; whereas in Vancouver and Toronto the largest ethnic group is Chinese.[29] Targeting ethnic markets is accomplished through the use of ethnic media, such as *Sing Tao Daily*, a newspaper for Chinese Canadians, or *The Weekly Gleaner*, a Caribbean Newspaper, and such television stations as CFMT-TV (see Exhibit 8.3) which targets a variety of ethnic groups including Italian, Portuguese, Greek, and South Asian. Other methods of reaching these markets include sponsorships of ethnic cultural and community events, such as Bell Canada's sponsorship of the Chinese New Year Festival at the SkyDome in Toronto.

Geography: People's preferences for products and services often depend on which region of the country they live in. For example, a recent study of how upper-income people across Canada spend their money showed significant regional differences. Compared to the average Canadian, those upper-income people living in Edmonton were more likely to spend their money on skiwear and snowmobile suits, those in Saskatoon were more likely to purchase home exercise equipment, those in Montreal were more likely to purchase leather and fur coats and jackets, those in Halifax were more likely to purchase art goods and decorative ware, those in St. John's were more likely to buy snow blowers, and those in the north were more likely to purchase outboard motor boats.[30] Similarly, a study of snacking

BRINGING YOU THE WORLD AT HOME

ROGERS MEDIA

Contact Melanie Farrell at (416) 260-3619
mfarrell@rci.rogers.com

cfmt international

Real People, Real Decisions
Decision Time **at Ford Motor Company of Canada**

In the late 1990s, management at Ford Canada realized that they were not getting a large share of the women's market. Ford had captured almost 23% of the Canadian car market by 1998, but it had less than 15% share of the total car sales to women. Candace Fochuk-Barey's research of the market highlighted the importance of women consumers to Ford: Women influence 80% of all vehicle purchases. If Ford did not do a better job of understanding and targeting women, they were going to have a hard time improving their overall share of the market.

Fochuk-Barey identified some characteristics of the women car buyer segment. Of those women who are involved in vehicle purchases, 44% are between the ages of 25 and 54 and half of them do not have a spouse. These characteristics had some important implications for Ford's target marketing activities. For example, communicating with these consumers by showing a happy nuclear family in ads, which Ford had done in the past, was probably not connecting with a large part of this segment. Research also showed

that women take more time than men to search for information before making a car purchase (six to nine months, compared to less than three months for men), and that women like to purchase from a company that they feel cares about their customers and their community. With respect to the actual product, women car buyers are looking for a reliable car that is durable, offers good value, is easy to handle, and has a good warranty.

With these characteristics of the segment in mind, Fochuk-Barey formulated some marketing activities designed specifically for better serving the needs of women: Ford offered their dealers a course on "Service—Responding to a Woman's Perspective"; recruited more women as salespeople; began sponsoring the Run for the Cure, a national fundraiser for breast cancer research; and ran seminars for women on such topics as car maintenance and car seat safety.

After achieving some success with these initial targeting efforts, Fochuk-Barey wanted to expand Ford's focus on women customers. She felt there was an opportunity to tar-

behaviour found that Maritimers consume more potato chips than consumers in other regions (almost double the national average), and Quebec consumers eat less than half of the average amount of corn chips that consumers in other regions do.[31]

A recognition of these kinds of regional differences can lead marketers to focus efforts on one or more regions, or to have different marketing strategies in different regions. When marketers want to segment regional markets even more precisely, they sometimes combine geography with demographics by using a technique called **geodemography**. A basic assumption of geodemography is that "birds of a feather flock together": People who live near one another share similar characteristics. Sophisticated statistical techniques identify geographic areas that share the same preferences for household items, magazines, and other products. This allows marketers to construct segments consisting of households with a common pattern of preferences, so that a company can hone in on those customers who are most likely to be interested in its specific offerings—in some cases so precisely that families living on one block will be included in a segment whereas those on the next block will not.

One Canadian geodemographic system, PSYTE, is a large database developed by Compusearch Micromarketing Data and Systems. This system classifies Canadian consumers into 60 clusters, based on postal code and demographic information. The resulting clusters include Boomers and Teens, Conservative Homebodies, Young City Singles, Brie and Chablis, and Suburban Nesters.[32] The PSYTE system is used by Canada Post in their GeoPost Plus program, which allows marketers to target direct mail to clusters of consumers that match their target segment. For

good OR bad DECISION?

Calvin Klein has been accused of using adolescent sexuality to sell products since 1980, when a then-teenaged Brooke Shields proclaimed, "Nothing comes between me and my Calvins." More recently, Klein ran ads that featured very young-looking male and female models. In one spot, an old man with a gravelly voice says to a scantily-clad young boy, "You got a real nice look.... You think you could rip that shirt off you? That's a real nice body. You work out? I can tell." The campaign generated a lot of controversy and was finally shelved—but not before the company got a lot of free publicity.[33] Should marketers be allowed to craft sexual appeals targeted to young people?

＊＊＊

geodemography Segmentation technique that combines geography with demographics.

---

get a specific vehicle—the Ford Windstar—to women. The Windstar made sense for a couple of reasons. First, one-third of all trucks sold in Canada were sold to women, and the majority of these vehicles were minivans. So women, especially mothers, were interested in minivan products. Second, the Windstar made sense from an internal point of view. Ford wanted to improve its performance in the minivan product category since they ranked fifth out of the five largest automakers in that market. The Windstar had achieved a five-star safety rating, the top safety rating for any minivan. This was a potential selling point to mothers who were concerned for the safety of their children.

Fochuk-Barey recognized that there were potential risks for Ford in focusing the marketing efforts for one vehicle so strongly on one target group. Were women a large enough group to make the product profitable? Would Ford alienate some male customers for the product by focusing their efforts so strongly on women? Fochuk-Barey considered two options:

Option 1. The first option was to identify women, and mothers specifically, as the primary target market for the Windstar. This would involve changing every aspect of the marketing for the Windstar, starting with the design of the vehicle through to the ads and sales efforts, to meet the needs of mothers. With this option, it would be the first time that women would be considered the primary target segment for a Ford car or truck.

Option 2. The second option was to target the Windstar to women, but with a less substantial effort. Women would be just one of the target markets for the product, so the design of the vehicle would not be changed to specifically meet the needs of mothers. Instead, the target marketing efforts would primarily be reflected in advertising decisions.

Now, put yourself in Candace Fochuk-Barey's shoes: Which option would you choose, and why?

example, the Boomers and Teens segment is described as "late middle-aged consumers who are university and college educated with children over the age of 6. Mostly double income families who live in their own homes." The cluster Young City Singles are "young singles and some couples who rent predominantly newer, downtown apartments and other dwellings." Using a geodemographic system like GeoPost Plus, a marketer of home improvement products like outdoor paint and fencing, can identify precisely which postal codes will be the best prospects for direct mail advertising for their product, while avoiding other postal codes where residents aren't likely to be interested.

SEGMENTING BY PSYCHOGRAPHICS

Demographic information is useful, but it does not always provide enough information to divide consumers into meaningful segments. For example, we can use demographic variables to discover that the female college and university student segment uses a lot of perfume, but not necessarily to know whether different women in this segment prefer perfumes that allow them to express a self-image that is, say, sexy versus athletic. Psychographic data are useful to understand differences between consumers, who may be demographically similar to one another but whose needs vary.

Although demographic segmentation divides the market in terms of objective characteristics, psychographics gets beneath the surface to segment the market in terms of shared attitudes, interests, and opinions.[34] Psychographic segments usually include demographic information such as age or sex, but the richer descriptions that emerge go well beyond these characteristics. While some advertising agencies and manufacturers develop their own psychographic techniques to classify consumers, others choose to subscribe to larger services that divide the population into segments and sell pieces of this information to clients for specific strategic applications. The most well known of these systems is **VALS™ (Values and Lifestyles)** developed by SRI International (www.future.sri.com). VALS divides people into eight groups, which are determined by both psychological characteristics, such as willingness to take risks, and "resources," which include such factors as income, education, energy levels, and eagerness to buy. As shown in Figure 8.2, three self-orientations are key to the system. Consumers with a principle orientation base decisions on abstract, idealized criteria rather than on feelings or a desire for societal approval. People with a status orientation strive for a clear social position and make decisions based on the perceived opinions of a valued social group. Action-oriented individuals are motivated by a desire to make an impact on the physical world or to affect others and resist social controls on their behaviour.

The VALS system helps identify consumers who are most likely to be interested in certain types of products, services, or experiences. For example, people who tend to fall into the experiencer category are likely to agree with statements like "I like a lot of excitement in my life" and "I like to try new things." VALS helped Isuzu market its Rodeo sport-utility vehicle by focusing on experiencers, many of whom believe it is fun to break rules in ways that do not endanger others. The car was positioned as a vehicle that lets a driver break the rules by going off-road, and sales increased significantly.[35]

VALS is one of the most comprehensive psychographic systems available, but because its conclusions are based on residents of the US, many Canadian firms prefer to use Canadian psychographic systems, such as the

✳ ✳ ✳
VALS™ (Values and Lifestyles) Psychographic system that divides people into eight segments.

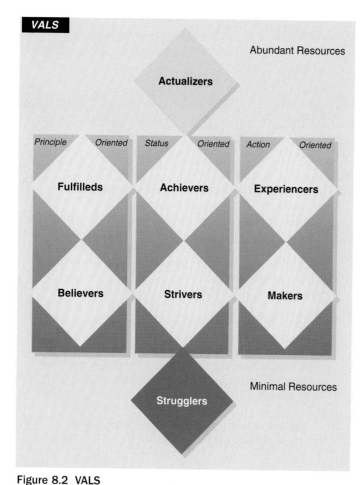

Figure 8.2 VALS

Source: SRI International, Menlo Park, CA.

one developed by the Environics Research Group (www.environics.net). Like VALS, Environics segments people on the basis of attitudes, values, and lifestyles. The 12 "tribes" identified by Environics range from the Rational Traditionalists (who are motivated by financial independence, security, and stability, and whose key values include respect for authority, duty, and delayed gratification) to the Social Hedonists (who are motivated by experience seeking, and who value hedonism, immediate gratification, and sexual permissiveness).[36] While the Rational Traditionalists may be a good target market for certain financial and insurance services, the Social Hedonists would probably be a prime target for *Tribe Magazine* and such leisure activities as snowboarding.

SEGMENTING BY BEHAVIOUR

People may use the same product for different reasons, on different occasions, and in different amounts. So, in addition to demographics and psychographics, it is useful to study what consumers actually do with a product. **Behavioural segmentation** divides up consumers on the basis of how they act toward, feel about, or use a product or service. For example, Peachtree Network, a company that operated online grocery stores across Canada, originally segmented its market into three segments, based on why consumers used the service: busy people, people with mobility difficulties, and nerds.[37]

One common way to segment based on behaviour is to divide the market into users versus non-users of a product or service (users have acted to make a purchase, which is a behaviour). Then marketers can reward current users (as Air Canada does with frequent flyer miles) or try to win over new ones. For example, the Prudential insurance company found that about 40% of its policy sales are initiated by customers rather than by its agents. Therefore, the company segments the market in terms of whether people are currently Prudential policy owners or non-owners. When the company deals with current policy owners, it focuses on making it easier for them to buy additional policies when they decide they're ready to do so; when communicating with non-owners, it uses a different focus to persuade them to take the plunge and buy that first policy. Indeed, two-thirds of Prudential's new insurance policies sales are to existing policyholders.[38]

In addition to distinguishing between users and non-users, marketers can further segment current customers into groups of heavy, moderate, and light users. Many marketers abide by a rule of thumb called the **80/20 rule**: 20% of purchasers account for 80% of the product's sales (this ratio is just an approximation). Therefore, it often makes more sense to focus on the smaller number of people who are heavy users of a product rather than on the larger number who are just casual users. Kraft Foods began an advertising campaign to remind its core users to not "skip the zip," after its research showed that indeed 20% of households account for 80% of the usage of Miracle Whip. These heavy users consume 17 pounds of Miracle Whip a year.[39]

Another way to segment a market based on behaviour is to look at **usage occasions**, or when consumers use the product most. Many products are associated with specific occasions, including time of day, holidays, business functions versus casual situations. Greeting cards, for example, are a product associated with specific occasions. Carlton cards, Canada's leading greeting card marketer, experiences peak demand related to four special occasions: Christmas, Valentine's Day, Mother's Day, and Easter.[40] In addition to meeting the demand for these occasions with specialized cards, advertising, and in-store promotions, Carlton also engages in marketing efforts designed to encourage the giving of cards on other occasions, such as Earth Day. Similarly, ski resorts like Mont Tremblant, that experience heavy demand during vacation periods, might offer great bargains during the off-season to tempt vacationers who would otherwise just visit the resort during Christmas vacation.

Being strongly associated with an occasion can be a mixed blessing for a product. On the one hand, sales can be almost guaranteed at that time (think about how many people cook a whole turkey on Thanksgiving); on the other hand, a product can become locked into an occasion. Ocean Spray is working hard to expand cranberry consumption beyond the holiday season. By introducing new cranberry foods like cranberry bagels and a line of drinks called Refreshers, the company has tripled sales over a 10-year period.[41] This strategy reflects a desire to make cranberries more of an "everyday" product.

✳ ✳ ✳
behavioural segmentation
Technique that divides consumers into segments on the basis of how they act toward, feel about, or use a product or service.

✳ ✳ ✳
80/20 rule A marketing rule of thumb that 20% of purchasers account for 80% of a product's sales.

✳ ✳ ✳
usage occasions Indicator used in one type of market segmentation based on when consumers use a product most.

Dimensions for Segmenting Business Markets

We've reviewed the segmentation variables marketers use to divide up the consumer market, but how about all the business-to-business marketers? Segmentation also helps them to divide up business and organizational customers. Though the specific variables may differ, the underlying logic of dividing the larger market into manageable pieces that share relevant characteristics is the same.[42]

ORGANIZATIONAL DEMOGRAPHICS

Demographic data help business marketers to understand the needs and characteristics of their potential customers. For example, a manufacturer of work uniforms needs to know which industries currently provide uniforms for their employees. For each industry that uses uniforms, from chemical processing to pest control, a marketer needs to know how many companies are potential customers, the number of employees in each, what types of uniforms are needed, and so on. That information enables the manufacturer to offer its services to the prospects that are most likely to be interested in outfitting employees in its protective clothing.

Many industries use the North American Industry Classification System (NAICS), discussed in Chapter 7, to obtain information about the size and number of companies operating in a particular industry. Other government information sources, such as Statistics Canada and Strategis (www.strategis.gc.ca), provide valuable business demographic information.

COMPANY-SPECIFIC CHARACTERISTICS

Just as individual consumers who share demographic characteristics still differ in important ways, business-to-business segmentation must take into account that each firm has characteristics that influence the types of products and services it needs. Marketers need to do their homework on an individual level by classifying companies within an industry in terms of the unique way each operates.

Operating variables include the production technology used, the business customer's degree of technical, financial, or operations expertise, and whether the prospect is a current user or non-user of the product. Business marketers should understand the characteristics of their best customers and try to locate other firms that match this profile. Companies track past purchasing history to develop loyalty among repeat customers, who are in a different segment than those who currently use competing firms. For example, in our earlier example of The Stockroom, which serves the office supplies needs of small businesses, Grand & Toy can analyze the purchase behaviour of various types of small businesses to better understand the needs of these businesses. They could then use this information to develop promotions (such as large discounts on the most popular items) to attract new business customers. In addition, they can use the information on purchase history to develop meaningful rewards for their existing customers to promote loyalty.

Business marketers also must consider how different customers will use their products or services. They must focus on identifying different end-use applications for these offerings. The personal computer industry is a good example of how firms can segment a market based on end use. Some major PC manufacturers have divided the market into three user segments: corporate, small business, and home. Apple tailors its Quadra, Classic, and Performa lines to the needs of each user group, whereas Compaq sells separate models it calls Deskpro/m, Deskpro/i, and Prolinea.[43] The Dell Canada Store Web site (www.dell.ca) divides the market into consumer, business, and government users.

Targeting

We've seen that the first step in target marketing is segmentation, in which the firm divides the market into smaller groups that share certain characteristics. The next step is targeting, in which marketers evaluate the attractiveness of each potential segment and decide which of these groups they will try to turn into customers. The customer group or groups selected are the firm's **target market**.

✳✳✳
operating variables The production technology used, the business customer's degree of technical, financial, or operations expertise, and whether the prospect is a current user or non-user of the product.

Dell Canada Store
www.dell.ca

✳✳✳
target market Group or groups that a firm selects to turn into customers as a result of segmentation and targeting.

Exhibit 8.4

SoyaWorld targets the mainstream dairy market with the So Good soy beverage.

SoyaWorld, a Canadian soy beverage marketer, has attained 60% of the dairy alternative market by carefully considering specific target markets. Soy beverages is the fastest-growing beverage category in Canada, and SoyaWorld has identified three main targets in the total market: the mainstream dairy market, the Asian market, and the organic market. For the mainstream dairy segment, SoyaWorld introduced So Good, a soy beverage with an improved taste that comes in several flavours. Since the product was being promoted as an alternative to milk, So Good was packaged to look like milk and was placed in the dairy cases of major supermarkets. Billboards, TV, and magazine ads, such as the one shown in Exhibit 8.4, were all used to reach the mainstream market. SoyaWorld targets Asian consumers with their Sunrise brand, a product that has a more traditional soy taste. For the organic target segment, they offer So Nice, a soy beverage, and Rice Choice, a fortified rice beverage. To reach the organic and Asian segments, the SoyaWorld products are distributed through specialty retailers, such as Chinese grocery stores and health food stores, in addition to selected larger grocery stores.[44] In this section, we'll review how marketers like SoyaWorld assess the customer groups in the market, and what selection strategies they use for effective targeting.

SoyaWorld Inc.
www.soyaworld.com

Evaluate Market Segments

Because a marketer identifies a segment does not necessarily mean that it's a useful one to target. A viable target segment should satisfy these requirements.

1. Members of the segment must be similar to each other in their product needs and wants and, at the same time, different from consumers in other segments. Without real differences in consumer needs, firms might as well use a mass-marketing strategy. For example, it's a waste of time to develop two separate lines of skin care products for working women and non-working women, if both segments have the same needs with respect to skin care.

2. The segment must be measurable. Marketers must know something about the size and purchasing power of a potential segment before deciding if it is worth their efforts.

3. The segment must be large enough to be profitable now and in the future. When the Beef Information Centre, whose goal is to increase beef consumption in Canada, was considering the BC market, they evaluated the Chinese Canadian community as a possible segment. Based on available statistical information, they estimated the segment to be close to 300 000 people; they knew that food was important to this group, since they spend more money on food than any other ethnic group. If the Beef Information Centre could convince just 25% of these consumers to eat one more beef meal a month, sales of beef would increase by 170 000 pounds per year. This analysis led the organization to target the Chinese Canadian segment in Vancouver through magazine ads like the one in Exhibit 8.5, recipes distributed at grocery stores, and the sponsorship of a Chinese cooking show on TV.[45]

Exhibit 8.5

Chinese Canadian consumers were identified as a profitable segment for the Beef Information Centre of BC.

4. Marketing communications must be able to reach the segment. It is easy to select television programs or magazines that will efficiently reach older consumers, consumers with specific levels of education, certain ethnic groups, or residents of major cities, because the media they prefer are easy to identify. It is unlikely, however, that marketing communications can reach only left-handed blonde people with tattoos who listen to the band Savage Garden. Therefore, it may not make sense to target that segment.

5. The marketer must be able to adequately serve the needs of the segment. Does the firm have the expertise and resources to satisfy the segment better than the competition? Some years ago, Exxon made the mistake of trying to enter the office products business, a growing segment. The company's expertise at selling petroleum products did not transfer to copying machines, and the effort was unsuccessful.

Develop Segment Profiles

✳ ✳ ✳
segment profile A description of the "typical" customer in a segment.

Once a marketer has identified a set of usable segments, it is helpful to generate a profile of each to understand segment members' needs and to look for business opportunities. This **segment profile** is a description of the "typical" customer in that segment. A segment profile might include customer demographics, location, lifestyle information, and a description of how frequently the customer buys the product.

When Toyota introduced the Echo subcompact car into the Canadian market, the target segment was described demographically as "60/40 male/female, 40% married, median age 32, 48% university educated with an average household income $42 000." In addition, the segment displayed the following psychographic traits: idealistic, experimental, independent, educated, urban, and not brand loyal.[46]

✳ ✳ ✳
market potential The maximum demand expected among consumers in a segment for a product or service.

The firm's goal at this point is to take a hard look at each possible segment, and determine which (if any) will be profitable to enter. To do this, the firm tries to forecast each segment's **market potential**—the maximum demand expected among consumers in that segment for a product or service. To determine market potential, the firm must identify the number of consumers in the segment and how much they spend in the product category. Then it must determine the sales potential for its product or service if it targets this segment. To predict this, the firm needs to estimate the number of consumers in the segment and how much they spend in the product category. This number is the total dollar potential. The firm then projects its market share. Multiplying total dollar potential by market share gives the likely actual dollar amount the firm might make.

This decision process underscores the idea that the sheer size of a potential market segment is not the only determinant of whether to target that segment—a large segment can also be attracting a lot of other competitors. For example, a manufacturer of industrial uniforms is deciding whether to develop a line of protective clothing for chemical workers or to focus on developing new business by persuading banks, real estate offices, and other service businesses to outfit their employees in "career apparel." The market potential for the chemical industry may be several times larger, because most people in that industry require uniforms. However, there are also a few established industrial uniform manufacturers, which have already cornered much of the business and command a great deal of loyalty. If the company feels that realistically it can expect to grab only a tiny market share in the protective clothing category, it may decide it is better off going after the newer career apparel segment, in which loyalties have yet to be established. It may be better to be a "big fish in a small pond."

Choose a Targeting Strategy

A basic targeting decision is how finely tuned the target should be: Should the company go after one large segment or perhaps focus on meeting the needs of one or more smaller segments? Let's look at four strategies for deciding which market segment(s) to pursue. Figure 8.3 summarizes these strategies.

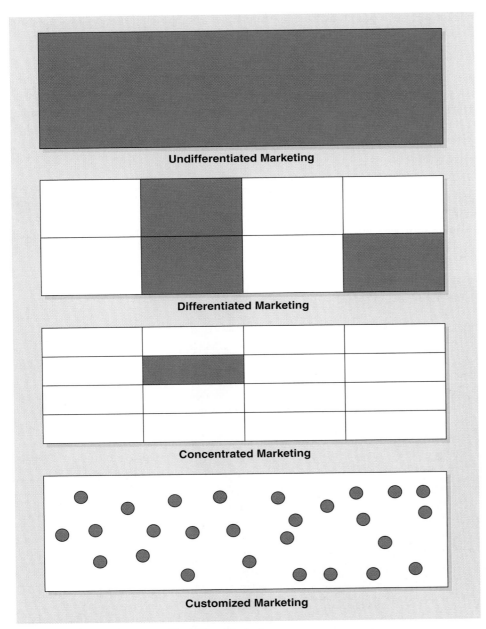

Figure 8.3 Choosing a Target Marketing Strategy

UNDIFFERENTIATED MARKETING

✳ ✳ ✳
undifferentiated targeting strategy Appealing to a broad spectrum of people.

A company that selects an **undifferentiated targeting strategy** is appealing to a broad spectrum of people. If successful, this type of operation can be very efficient, especially because production, research, and promotion costs benefit from economies of scale—it's cheaper to develop one product or one advertising campaign than to choose several targets and create separate products or messages for each. But the company must be willing to bet that people have similar needs, or that any differences among them will be so trivial that they will not matter, so that the same product and message will appeal to many customers.

DIFFERENTIATED MARKETING

✳ ✳ ✳
differentiated targeting strategy Developing one or more products for each of several distinct customer groups and making sure these offerings are kept separate in the marketplace.

A company that chooses a **differentiated targeting strategy** develops one or more products for each of several distinct customer groups and makes sure these offerings are kept separate in the marketplace. A differentiated strategy is called for when consumers are choosing among well-known brands, when each has a distinctive image in the marketplace, and when it's possible to identify one or more segments that have distinct needs for different types of products. The cosmetics company L'Oréal uses a differentiated targeting strategy. The company has the resources to offer several product lines at a variety of prices. It targets the luxury market with such brands as Lancôme and Helena Rubinstein, whereas less expensive offerings such as Elsève and L'Oréal target large department stores and discounters.[47]

CONCENTRATED MARKETING

✳ ✳ ✳
concentrated targeting strategy Focusing a firm's efforts on offering one or more products to a single segment.

When a firm focuses its efforts on offering one or more products to a single segment, it is using a **concentrated targeting strategy**. A concentrated strategy is often useful for smaller firms that do not have the resources or the desire to be all things to all people. For example, the cosmetics company Hard Candy, shown in Exhibit 8.6, sells its funky line of nail polish and other products only to twentysomething women (or to those who wish they still were).

CUSTOM MARKETING: A "SEGMENT OF ONE"

Ideally, marketers should be able to define segments so precisely that they can offer products and services that exactly meet the needs of every individual or firm. In business markets, an individualized strategy is often used by companies, such as aircraft manufacturers like Bombardier, with few customers who spend a lot of money to make sure their individual

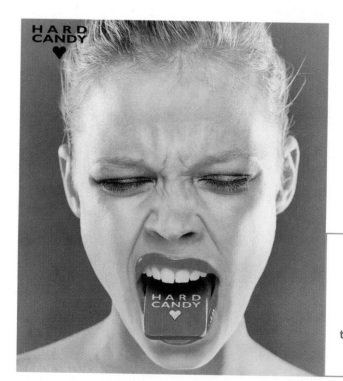

Exhibit 8.6

Hard Candy uses a concentrated targeting strategy as the company targets twentysomething women.

SPOTLIGHT ON REAL PEOPLE *Pita Boys*

Understanding their consumer segment's characteristics and practising target marketing have led to success for two young entrepreneurs Stephen Vail and David Fullerton, founders of the Pita Boys restaurants in Halifax. Although the four Pita Boys restaurants attract 18- to 45-year-old consumers, the focus of marketing efforts has been on the younger end of that range, namely university and college students. While the older customers are professionals, who view the meat and vegetable pita offerings at Pita Boys as a healthy lunch alternative, the younger customers are students, who not only like the food but also respond to the Pita Boys advertisements that appear in student and entertainment newspapers. The ads are simple (black and white) but feature creative, memorable slogans such as "We serve drunks," "Crazy, Dancin' Pita Rollin Machines," and

"Because Size Does Matter." Sponsorship of movie premieres and concerts has also been effective at reaching the student market. As Fullerton says, "The student market is easy. I know people that age, and I know what it feels like to be them."

The success of the targeting activities of the Pita Boys restaurants has grabbed the attention of much larger, more experienced marketers. Coca-Cola, for example, pays for ads on a local Halifax radio station, which feature both Coke and the Pita Boys, simply because it wants to be associated with the popular restaurants. Two beer companies are also involved in marketing activities with the Pita Boys to enhance their own profile among students, even though the restaurants do not serve beer.[48]

1. What dimensions, in addition to age, can be used to segment the market for Pita Boys restaurants?
2. The Pita Boys restaurants currently use a concentrated targeting strategy. Evaluate the pros and cons of the company switching to a differentiated targeting strategy.

needs are met. In consumer markets, this level of concentration shows up in personal or professional services, by doctors, lawyers, and hair stylists, for example. In most consumer markets, individualized marketing strategies are neither practical nor possible when mass-produced products such as cars or computers enter the picture. However, advances in technology, coupled with the new emphasis on building solid relationships with customers, have focused managers' attention on devising a **custom marketing strategy** in which specific products and the messages about them are tailored to individual customers. Online retailers, such as HMV.com, for example, are able to send customized messages to users regarding the status of their orders, upcoming promotions that may be of interest based on the products they have bought in the past, and announcements of new releases.

Some other companies are able to practise **mass customization**—modifying a basic product or service to meet the needs of an individual.[49] Calgary-based Critical Mass has worked with Nike to develop NIKEiD, an interactive part of the Nike Web site (www.Nike.com), where consumers can design and purchase their own running shoes.[50]

✳ ✳ ✳
custom marketing strategy
Approach that tailors specific products and the messages about them to individual customers.

✳ ✳ ✳
mass customization Approach that modifies a basic product or service to meet the needs of an individual.

Positioning

The final, crucial stage of the target marketing process is providing consumers in a targeted market segment with a product or service that meets their unique needs and expectations. **Positioning** means developing a marketing strategy aimed at influencing how a particular market segment perceives a product or service in comparison to the competition. Developing a positioning strategy entails gaining a clear understanding of the criteria target consumers use to evaluate competing products, and then convincing them that your product will meet those needs. This can be done in many ways. Sometimes, it's a matter of making sure that cool people are seen using your product—that's why designer Tommy Hilfiger provides free clothes to rap singers.[51] Hilfiger makes it look easy, but, in reality, an effective positioning strategy requires the marketer to coordinate all of the elements of the marketing mix to be sure that the target customers think of the product the way they're supposed to.

✳ ✳ ✳
positioning Developing a marketing strategy aimed at influencing how a particular market segment perceives a product or service in comparison to the competition.

Develop a Positioning Strategy

The success of a target marketing strategy hinges on a marketer's ability to identify and select an appropriate market segment. Then the marketer must devise a marketing mix that will effectively target the segment's members, by positioning the product to appeal to that segment. Let's review the four steps necessary to complete the positioning process.

ANALYZE COMPETITORS' POSITIONS

Marketers must understand how their competitors are perceived by the target market. Aside from direct competitors in the product category, are there other products or services that provide the same benefits people are seeking? For example, when a company such as Coca-Cola develops a new drink, it must consider how to compete against many alternatives in addition to those offered by archrival Pepsi. The surprise success of Jolt, which is fortified with caffeine, led Coca-Cola to develop Surge to target students, athletes, and people who don't like the taste of coffee but who need to "Feed the Rush."[52]

IDENTIFY COMPETITIVE ADVANTAGE

The next task is to offer a product or service with a competitive advantage, to provide a reason why consumers will perceive the product as better than the competition. If the company offers only a "me-too product," it can induce people to buy for a lower price. Other forms of competitive advantage offer a superior image such as status or luxury (Rolex), a unique product feature (Levi's 501 button-fly jeans), or better service ("At Speedy, You're a Somebody").

FINALIZE THE MARKETING MIX

Once a positioning strategy is set, marketers must put all of the pieces of the marketing mix into place. The elements of the marketing mix must match the selected segment. This means that the product or service must deliver benefits that the segment values, such as convenience or status. Furthermore, marketers must price this offering at a level these consumers will pay, make the offering available at places consumers are likely to go, and correctly communicate the offering's benefits in locations where consumers are likely to take notice.

EVALUATE THE TARGET MARKET'S RESPONSES AND MODIFY THE STRATEGY

The target marketing process is ongoing. Over time the firm may find that it needs to change which segments it targets, and the needs of people in these chosen segments may change as well. Marketers need to monitor these changes and adjust their positioning strategies when necessary. Sometimes marketers redo a product's position to respond to marketplace changes.

✳ ✳ ✳
repositioning Redoing a product's position to respond to marketplace changes.

An example of such a makeover, a strategy called **repositioning**, was undertaken by Adults Only Video, a Canadian video chain that specializes in the sale and rental of pornographic movies. The company decided to reposition itself to appeal to couples aged 25 to 54. The company's traditional target market was males 18 to 25; but increased competition for this segment from Internet providers caused the company to reassess its position. The management at Adults Only Video described their repositioning as a move from a "sleazy" image to a "softer" one. The repositioning was accomplished by changing the product mix in the stores (to include products like candles, books, and magazines) and changing their advertising strategy to include female voice-overs in their radio ads and the placement of print ads in mainstream newspapers. The company also ran a large promotion, the "Millionaire Kiss-off," in which couples could win $1 million by breaking the world's record for the longest kiss.[53]

Positioning Dimensions

There are many dimensions marketers use to establish a brand's position in the marketplace. These include:

- Lifestyle image: Grey Poupon mustard is a "higher-class" condiment.
- Price leadership: Buy.com is "Canada's Low Price Internet Superstore."

- Attributes: Dare Bread Bites have "A bit of the bakery in every bite."
- Product class: The Mazda Miata is a sporty convertible.
- Competitors: The Pepsi Challenge claims "More people prefer the taste of Pepsi over Coke."
- Occasions: Wrigley's gum is an alternative at times when smoking is not permitted.
- Users: Sunny Delight is the "Goodness kids go for."
- Quality: Lexus promises "The Relentless Pursuit of Excellence."

BRINGING A PRODUCT TO LIFE: THE BRAND PERSONALITY

Brands, like people, can be described in terms of personality traits. These descriptions might include words like cheap, elegant, sexy, bold, or wimpy. A positioning strategy often tries to create a **brand personality** for a product or service—a distinctive image that captures its character and benefits. When the Mark Anthony Group was developing a name for its lemonade-based alcohol product, they did research with consumers to determine what name would communicate the right brand personality. The "person" they chose for their hard lemonade, "Mike," is described as a "fun, party, happy-go-lucky guy who is infatuated with lemons."[54]

Products as people? Marketing researchers find that most consumers have no trouble describing what a product would be like "if it came to life." People often give clear, detailed descriptions, including what colour hair the product would have, the type of house it would live in, and even whether it would be thin, overweight, or somewhere in between.[55] If you don't believe us, try doing this yourself.

PERCEPTUAL MAPPING

Creating a brand personality as part of a positioning strategy is one way of developing an identity for the product that the target market will prefer over competing brands. How do marketers determine where their product actually stands in the minds of consumers? One solution is to ask consumers what characteristics are important and how competing alternatives would rate on these attributes. Marketers use this information to construct a **perceptual map**, a picture of where products or brands are "located" in consumers' minds.

For example, suppose you want to construct a perceptual map of women's magazines as perceived by Canadian women to give you some guidance while developing an idea for a new magazine. After interviewing a sample of female readers, you determine questions women ask when selecting a magazine: Is it "service oriented," emphasizing family, home, and personal issues; or is it "fashion forward," oriented toward personal appearance and fashion? Is it for "upscale" women, who are older and established in their careers; or for relatively "downscale" women, who are younger and just starting out in their careers?

The perceptual map in Figure 8.4 illustrates how these ratings might look for certain major women's magazines. The map provides some guidance as to where your new women's magazine might be positioned. You might decide to compete directly with either the cluster of "service magazines" in the middle left or the fashion magazines in the upper right. In this case, you would have to determine what benefits your new magazine might offer that these existing magazines do not. *Chatelaine*, for example, repositioned itself in 1999 from a service-type magazine to a more urban, contemporary and youth and fashion-oriented publication.[56] This repositioning moved *Chatelaine* further away from its nearest Canadian competitor, *Canadian Living*.

To introduce a new magazine, you might try to locate an unserved area in this perceptual map. *Elm Street*, a relatively new entrant to the Canadian women's magazine scene, has tried to position itself for the upscale woman who is interested in articles on a broad range of topics, a part of the market that they felt was unserved. An unserved segment is a potential opportunity for marketers: With luck, they can move quickly to capture a segment and define the standards of comparison for the category. According to Figure 8.4 there may be room for a magazine targeted to "cutting-edge" fashion for younger women.

Creating a positioning strategy is the last step in the target marketing process. We can summarize this sequence of the target marketing process by looking at the strategy developed by Montreal-based G.I. Energy Drinks, when they introduced the Guru energy drink.

✳ ✳ ✳
brand personality A distinctive image that captures a product or service's character and benefits.

✳ ✳ ✳
perceptual map A picture of where products or brands are "located" in consumers' minds.

Chatelaine
www.chatelaine.com

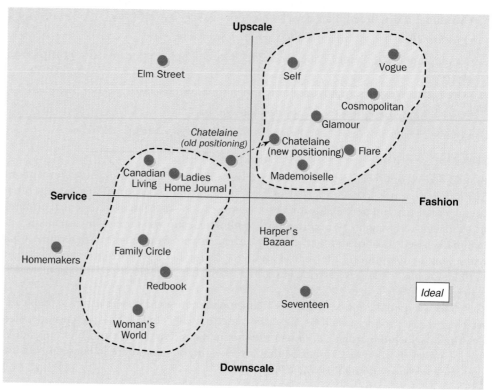

Figure 8.4 Perceptual Map

The company segmented the market in terms of age and psychographics, and then targeted a segment of 16 to 24 year olds, whose profiles indicated they were into "new-age" beverages that would give them a feeling of energy without unhealthy additives. The company reached these consumers by selling their drinks at raves in Montreal and Toronto (see Exhibit 8.7), advertising in club culture magazines, and sponsoring events like snowboarding demonstrations. A company spokesperson describes the Guru positioning strategy this way: "We really feel the best way to reach people is through trial and onsite promotions.... We want to provide the consumer with a drink that will enhance the activity they are already participating in."[57]

Exhibit 8.7

Many Canadian energy drinks, such as Generator and Guru, reach their target segment by being sold at raves.

Real People, Real Decisions
How it worked out at Ford Motor Company

Candace Fochuk-Barey and her colleagues chose Option 1: They decided to target the Ford Windstar van primarily to mothers. In addition to researching the needs of mothers, the company put together an internal design team, which was made up of 30 female employees who were also moms. The redesigned Windstar included such "mom friendly" features as sleeping baby lights (that don't come on and wake the baby when the van doors are opened), a personal audio system for children riding in the back, a conversation mirror (so that mothers driving can see the road and their kids riding in the back), a storage area for diapers under the radio, a larger fuel tank so that the driver would have to fill up less frequently, and smart locks so kids can't be locked in.

The design team also became an integral part of the advertising for the new van. That the redesigned Windstar was a success for Ford clearly illustrates the power of understanding the needs of a particular segment and addressing those needs through a targeted marketing strategy.

Fochuk-Barey has continued to target other Ford products and services to women. For example, Ford runs a Web site (www.ford4women.com), which encourages women to learn more about car ownership, and Ford offers free seminars "Car Smarts—Seminars for Women" at dealerships across the country.

Chapter Summary

1. Understand the three steps of developing a target marketing strategy.

The first step, market segmentation, involves dividing a large market into a set of smaller markets that share important characteristics. The second step is targeting, in which marketers select one or more of these groups to serve as their target market. The third step, called positioning, is developing a clear and positive image to communicate to members of the target market.

2. Understand the need for market segmentation in today's business environment.

Market segmentation is often necessary in today's marketplace because of market fragmentation—the splintering of a mass society into diverse groups due to technological and cultural differences. Most marketers can't realistically do a good job of meeting the needs of everyone, so it is more efficient to divide the larger pie into slices, or segments, whose members share some important characteristics and tend to exhibit the same needs and preferences.

3. Know the different dimensions marketers use to segment consumer markets.

Marketers frequently find it useful to segment consumer markets based on demographic characteristics including age, gender, family life cycle, social class, ethnic identity, or place of residence. A second dimension, psychographics, uses measures of psychological and social characteristics to identify people with shared preferences or traits. Consumer markets may also be segmented based on how consumers behave toward the product, for example, their brand loyalty, usage rates (heavy, moderate, or light), usage occasions, product type purchased, and reasons for using a product.

4. Understand the bases for segmentation in business-to-business markets.

Categories similar to those in the consumer market are used for segmenting business markets. Business demographics include industry or company size, North American Industry Classification (NAICS) codes, and geographic location. Business markets may also be segmented based on operating variables and end-use applications.

5. Explain how marketers evaluate and select potential market segments.

To choose one or more segments to target, marketers examine each segment and evaluate its potential for success as a target market. Meaningful segments have wants that are different from those in other segments, can be identified, can be reached with a unique marketing mix, will respond to unique marketing communications, are large enough to be profitable, have future growth potential, and possess needs that the organization can satisfy better than the competition.

6. Explain how marketers develop a targeting strategy.

After they have identified the different segments, they estimate the market potential of each segment. The relative attractiveness of segments also influences the firm's selection of an overall marketing strategy. The firm may choose an undifferentiated, differentiated, concentrated, or custom strategy, based on the company's characteristics and the nature of the market.

7. Understand how a firm develops and implements a positioning strategy.

After they have selected the target market(s) and overall strategy, marketers must determine how they wish the brand to be perceived by consumers relative to the competition: Should the brand be positioned like, against, or away from the competition? Through positioning, a brand personality is developed. Brand positions can be compared using such research techniques as perceptual mapping. In developing and implementing the positioning strategy, firms analyze the competitors' positions, determine the competitive advantage offered by their product, tailor the marketing mix in accordance with the positioning strategy, and evaluate responses to the marketing mix selected. Marketers must continually monitor changes in the market that might indicate a need to reposition the product.

Chapter Review

Marketing Concepts: Testing Your Knowledge

1. What is market segmentation and why is it an important strategy in today's marketplace?

2. List and explain the major demographic characteristics frequently used in segmenting markets.

3. Describe the major ethnic groups in Canada and tell how they provide unique market segments for many products.

4. Explain consumer psychographic segmentation.

5. How can consumer behaviour be used for segmenting consumer markets?

6. What are the major dimensions used for segmenting business markets?

7. List the criteria used for determining whether a segment may be a good candidate for targeting.

8. Explain undifferentiated, differentiated, concentrated, custom, and mass-customization marketing strategies.

9. What is product positioning? Describe the three approaches marketers use to create product positions.

10. List the steps in developing and implementing a positioning strategy.

Marketing Concepts: Discussing Choices and Issues

1. Some critics of marketing have suggested that market segmentation and target marketing lead to an unnecessary proliferation of product choices, which wastes valuable resources. These critics suggest that if marketers didn't create so many different product choices, there would be more resources to feed the hungry, house the homeless, and provide for the needs of people around the globe. Are the results of segmentation and target marketing harmful or beneficial to society as a whole? Should these criticisms be of concern to firms? How should New Era firms respond to these criticisms?

2. One criterion for a usable market segment is its size. This chapter suggested that to be usable, a segment must be large enough to be profitable now and in the future, and that some very small segments get ignored because they can never be profitable. How large should a segment be? How do you think a firm should go about determining if a segment is profitable? Have technological advances made it possible for smaller segments to be profitable? Do firms ever have a moral or ethical obligation to develop products for small, unprofitable segments?

3. Some firms have been criticized for targeting unwholesome products to certain segments of the market—the elderly, ethnic subcultures, the disabled. What other groups deserve special concern? Should a firm use different criteria in targeting such groups? Should the government oversee and control such marketing activities?

4. Marketers are always looking for a better way to segment consumer markets. In the past, they used demographics, lifestyles, geodemographics, and product-related behaviour. With a group of classmates, brainstorm to see if you can come up with other possible means for segmenting markets that might be useful to some firms.

Marketing Practice: **Applying What You've Learned**

1. Assume that you have been hired to develop a marketing plan for a small regional brewery. In the past, the brewery produced and sold a single beer to the entire market—a mass-marketing strategy. As you begin your work for the firm, you feel that the firm could be more successful if it developed a target marketing strategy. The owner of the firm, however, is not convinced. Write a memo to the owner outlining:

   a. the basic reasons for target marketing.

   b. the specific advantages of a target marketing strategy for the brewery.

2. Assume that you are the director of marketing for a company that markets personal computers to business and organizational customers. You feel that if your market is segmented, you will be able to satisfy your customers' needs more efficiently and effectively. You must first decide what bases to use for segmenting the market.

   a. Develop a list of the potential segmentation variables you might use.

   b. Include your thoughts on how useful each might be to your marketing strategy.

   c. What are your final recommendations for the bases for segmenting the market?

3. As the marketing director for a company that is planning to enter the business market for photocopy machines, you are attempting to develop an overall marketing strategy. You have considered the possibility of using mass-marketing, concentrated marketing, differentiated marketing, and custom marketing strategies.

   a. Write a report explaining what each type of strategy would mean for your marketing plan in terms of product, price, promotion, and distribution channel.

   b. Evaluate the desirability of each type of strategy.

   c. What are your final recommendations for the best type of strategy?

4. You are an account executive for a marketing consulting firm, and your newest client is an educational institution—the one you are currently attending. With a group of classmates, develop an outline of your ideas for positioning the institution, including the following:

   a. Who are your competitors?

   b. What are the competitors' positions?

   c. What target markets are most attractive for your client?

   d. How will you position your client for those segments relative to the competition?

   Present your results to your class.

Marketing Mini-Project: **Learning by Doing**

This mini-project will help you develop a better understanding of how target marketing decisions are made. The project focuses on the market for automobiles.

1. Gather ideas about different dimensions useful for segmenting the automobile market. You may use your own ideas and those mentioned in the Real People, Real Decisions case on

Ford Motor Company of Canada. You probably will also want to examine advertising and other marketing communications developed by different automobile manufacturers; read articles in newspapers and magazines; look at Internet automobile sellers; and talk with salespeople at local automobile dealerships about different types of consumers and the cars that they buy.

2. Based on the dimensions for market segmentation you have identified, develop a questionnaire and conduct a survey of consumers. You will have to decide which questions should be asked and which consumers should be surveyed.

3. Analyze the data from your research and identify the different potential segments.

4. Develop segment profiles that describe each potential segment.

5. Generate several ideas for how the marketing strategy might be different for each segment based on the profiles.

6. Develop a presentation (or write a report) outlining your ideas, your research, your findings, and your marketing strategy recommendations.

Real People, Real Surfers: Exploring the Web

In this chapter, you learned about psychographic segmentation systems, such as VALS and the Environics "tribes." To learn more about these systems, visit the SRI (the creators of VALS) Web site (www.future.sri.com) and the Environics Web site (www.environics.net). When you follow the VALS links, you will discover that SRI has also developed three other segmentation systems: Geo-VALS, Japan-VALS, and iVALS.

1. Based on the Environics site, describe all of the Environics tribes. For each tribe, identify what companies might be interested in targeting them. What tribe do you identify with?

2. From the information on the SRI Web site, describe Geo-VALS, Japan-VALS, and iVALS. What are some ways these segmentation systems might be used by organizations?

3. You can determine your own VALS type by taking the survey on the SRI Web site. Although the segments are based on people who live in the United States, the questions are also relevant for Canadians. When taking the survey, simply omit the zip code question. After you determine which segment you belong to, assess whether you think this VALS type accurately portrays you.

4. What is your opinion of the SRI and Environics Web sites? Whom do you think they are targeting with their sites? Do you think the sites are an effective way to promote their products to potential customers? What suggestions do you have for improving the Web sites?

5. Write a report of your findings.

MARKETING IN ACTION

Youtopia.com

Youtopia.com, an Ottawa-based company, operates a Web site targeting North American teens. The purpose of the site is to gather information about teens, which can then be used by such sponsoring companies as Clearasil, Pringles, Blockbuster, HMV, Sony, and Durex to better reach the teen market segment. This segment in Canada alone spends about $10 billion on goods and services; however, it is known for being fickle. Companies who target the teen segment are interested in gaining a better understanding of this group of consumers through sites such as Youtopia.com, so that they can engage in marketing efforts that will promote loyalty among teen consumers.

Youtopia is set up as a games site, where teens participate in games, contests, surveys, and focus groups sponsored by various advertisers. Each visitor gets 500 virtual Youdollars for registering and collects between 5 and 100 Youdollars for participating in the various online activities. Participants can then trade in their Youdollars for prizes. For example, to get a $5 gift certificate for Cineplex Odeon, participants redeem 1000 Youdollars.

Durex Canada sponsors the "Play It Safe" virtual dating game on the Youtopia site. One activity participants do while playing the game is select condom style preferences while getting prepared to go out on a date, thereby providing valuable market research for Durex. Sonya Agnew, director of marketing for Durex Canada, says that Durex is always looking for new and innovative ways to reach young people and it saw Youtopia as a good option for doing so.

The launch of the Youtopia site in June 2000 included a virtual Britney Spears, who is a shareholder in the company, as the official spokesperson on the site. Youtopia also sponsored the Spears 2000 tour, and she starred in TV ads for the site. To generate hits on their site, Youtopia sent e-mail targeted to teens, generated from e-mail lists purchased from hotmail.com and yahoo.com, asking them if they wanted to shop for free and play games online. The launch was a success. On its first weekend, Youtopia received over a million hits. Within a week, the company had a database of 200 000 registered teens and was working toward a database of one million within two months of the launch.

Not everyone is sold on the Youtopia concept, though. Some argue that research has shown that teens are not comfortable providing personal information over the Internet, so the site will have limited appeal to sponsors in the long run. Some companies are also worried that, because the site is designed to look like a game site to obscure its true purpose as a market research site, sponsoring companies are going to be seen as manipulative by some teens. Youtopia.com's challenge, therefore, is to continue to provide value added to both teens and sponsoring companies with its Web site.

Sources: Liz Adams, "Doing what comes naturally," *Strategy Magazine*, 17 July 2000: D5; Andrea Zoe Aster, "Game site doubles as focus group," *Marketing Magazine*, 12 June 2000: 4; Carey Toane, "Smells like teen research," *Marketing Magazine*, July 2000.

THINGS TO THINK ABOUT

1. What are some of the problems facing Youtopia.com?
2. What factors are causing the problems?
3. What are the alternatives?
4. What are your recommendations for solving the problems?
5. How could your recommendations be implemented?

Different Keystrokes for Different Folks

After discovering who its primary customer is, CFS enters the business-to-business market and learns about market segmentation.

Know Thy Customer

During the end of our first year, a big department store in the American Midwest asked to have the Computer Bug mascot make an appearance. Rubeo and I were excited about it. We had visions of happy kids taking pictures with the Bug, while their parents spent their life savings buying hundreds of Bugs. We even showed up early to make sure that every kid got the chance to get a picture. A few hours later, as we were standing completely alone in our allotted spot between ladies' lingerie and infants' clothing, Rubeo made an observation: We were wasting our time. "Sure," I replied, "but look at this great little jumper I got for my nephew Timmy." On our five-hour drive home, we reflected on how mismatched we were for that location. We started to see the wisdom behind target marketing.

Fortunately, after a year of trade shows, Christmas shows, fan mail, and in-store appearances (good and bad), we had a clear understanding of whom we were marketing to. This feedback replaced formal marketing research, since our budget was limited. Although the product appealed to many types of people, we found that the primary buyers for the Original Computer Bug were made up of two groups: professional women aged 20 to 50, and boys and girls aged 7 to 14.

The "professional women" market segment wasn't surprising. Studies show that women buy more gifts than men do. The children's marketing segment came as a bigger surprise. We had no idea that our character would appeal so much to kids. We noticed their reactions at trade shows and we began to see it in our fan mail. At one point, an entire fourth-grade class sent us a giant poster, on which each of them had drawn pictures of what they would look like if they were computer bugs. Luckily, we had developed a product with a wide appeal. We used the Simpsons as a humour guideline: sophisticated enough for adults, yet goofy enough for kids. And lots of bodily functions—kids never get enough of burping.

Initially we thought our market was "everyone." In fact, we developed a saying early on: "At CFS, we don't sell just to computer users. We sell to anyone who knows anyone with a computer—which is everyone." The reality, however, was different. The product may appeal to all computer users, but the buyers are a much more limited segment of the market.

Reach Thy Customer

The frustrating thing was that we couldn't afford to target even the two primary buying segments directly. Mass advertising was too expensive for a small firm with limited resources: We realized that our future lay in business-to-business marketing.

To reach these customers, we had several options. In addition to computer stores, which were a given, we decided to target gift stores for women and toy stores for children. Being able to target three such diverse retail sectors made us realize that we had a unique product. This versatility has been a big factor in our success.

As manufacturers, selling in the business-to-business market meant that we sold to two groups: wholesalers such as Globel Distribution and retailers (including stores, catalogues, and online storefronts) such as Radio Shack Canada. These were our new customers now, not the women and children. Our focus was on creating brand awareness. Although we had obtained trademark protection, concepts such as ours can be stolen fairly easily (since you can't trademark an idea), and we were concerned with getting our products to market first. We want people to want the Original Computer Bug. (After all, kids want Beanie Babies, not Beanie rip-offs.) As of this writing, we admit to looking forward a little to being ripped off: People don't rip off loser products, only smash hit products.

Initially, when we sold to wholesalers and retailers, we used the same marketing strategy: We'd lug our

booth to trade shows and sell to anyone who'd buy. It didn't take too long to realize that this strategy often caused us to get lost in the crowd. In the computer market, we knew that exhibitors spent a lot of money on elaborate and flashy exhibits. So, when we did our first Comdex, the world's largest computer trade show, Chris Rubeo converted a big-screen TV into a giant computer, complete with an oversized keyboard, mouse, and styrofoam Computer Bug. It looked just like a computer and didn't cost much because we built it ourselves.

However, as nice as our booth was, it was still small next to Goliaths like Netscape and Microsoft. How could we establish a presence and stand out from the big guys? We simply didn't have enough money to compete. Large companies would offer expensive giveaways, such as colourful shopping bags, which cost more than our entire show budget. We needed something inexpensive but effective. We worked with Creative Solutions International, a consulting firm, and came up with nine different small cards that adhered to the side of the badges attendees had to wear at the show. Each card showed the Computer Bug pointing up at the badge-holder, saying things like: "This person stole towels from the hotel room" or "Badges? We don't need no stinkin' badges!" or "This person will take 2000 of whatever you're selling." They worked perfectly. They were cheap, they made use of vacant real estate, and everyone noticed them, because the badge is the first place you look when you meet someone.

You would think that this idea would carry over to Toy and Gift Trade Shows. Not so. Computer trade shows have a fun, irreverent atmosphere, so our badge cards fit in well. Toy shows and gift shows are a bit more reserved, with many buyers in suits. Thus, people aren't as open to having something goofy attached to their badges. To compensate, we began to stress the Computer Bug mascot much more. At gift shows, we had a bigger problem: the booth itself. The giant computer was a big hit at Comdex, but the technology emphasis seemed to intimidate some buyers at gift shows. They were used to stuffed animals and carved driftwood. We eventually ditched the big monitor in favour of a normal monitor, and we began showcasing the actual bug figure and stuffed animal bugs we were developing. We also made greater use of Rubeo in costume, as we did at toy shows. Although these were relatively

minor changes, they resulted in significantly more sales in the three diverse markets.

One Is the Loneliest Number

We were finally on our way to cracking our primary markets. With every show, we learned more about marketing in the business-to-business world. For now, we had another problem on our hands: We couldn't survive forever as a one-product company. Profit margins were too thin and existing customers like the New Zealanders were already clamouring for something new. It was time to look at product development.

Questions

1. At the consumer level, CFS makes products that appeal to a wide demographic—computer users. Within that demographic, CFS thought its products appealed most to professional women aged 20 to 50 and children aged 7 to 14. Do you think the "professional women" category can be refined even more into distinct subgroups? Do you think there are other primary segments of consumers that CFS may have overlooked?

2. CFS decided to use an undifferentiated target marketing strategy when launching its first product. Was this a good decision? Describe a scenario in which they would want to move to a differentiated approach: A custom approach.

3. From a target marketing perspective, what are some difficulties in developing a product that must appeal to all age groups?

4. A company always does market research when it observes and talks to its customers, as CFS did at trade shows. Can you think of other inexpensive yet effective methods that start-up companies can use to obtain market research?

Marketing Plan Questions

Refer to the Sample Marketing Plan in Appendix A as you answer these questions about developing and modifying a marketing plan for CFS.

1. For this year's marketing plan, what brand personality should CFS develop for each of its products? Is there a positioning strategy that runs through all of its products?

2. Looking ahead to next year's marketing plan, how can CFS use behavioural segmentation to identify additional subgroups within the overall market for its products?

CBC ◉ VIDEO CASE 1

Researching with Focus Groups

Focus groups are a popular but controversial marketing research technique. The traditional focus group consists of a small group of consumers brought together for two to three hours to discuss topics ranging from strategic issues like trying to identify consumer needs and consumer perceptions of brands, to tactical issues like what is the best brand name for a product. Focus groups are facilitated by a moderator, who ensures that the right questions are asked and that the discussion doesn't go off topic or become dominated by one or two vocal members of the group.

The simplicity of the focus group technique is appealing for marketing decision makers. The participants in focus groups speak about the product and company in language that is meaningful to them, which in itself is useful for companies who are trying to better understand their consumers and how to communicate with them.

However, focus groups present some problems. It is a research technique that relies on people's ability to express their opinions and describe their reasons for making purchase decisions. One concern about the use of this technique is that consumers are increasingly unable or unwilling to provide clear reasons for the purchase decisions they make. After all, consumers make many of their shopping decisions unconsciously. Therefore, market researchers need to become more creative with the focus group method to gain an understanding of consumer attitudes and motivations.

When the Happy Planet Beverage Company of Vancouver ran focus groups, the moderator used a variety of techniques in addition to asking direct questions to better understand consumer attitudes. Participants played a shopping game, in which they were assigned themes (such as fresh, economical) and asked to find juices in the "store" that fit those themes. Participants drew pictures of what they thought the typical Happy Planet consumer looks like. They were also given several bottles of juice and asked to move them around a table to categorize them according to characteristics like quality and price. The results of the focus group were useful for Happy Planet and raised issues that the company had not previously considered.

Other companies are not as successful in their use of focus group results. When Enbridge Home Services Inc. used focus groups to test an ad for gas fireplaces, which showed a couple making love on a rug, the participants liked the ad. When the company ran the ad on television, though, there were so many complaints that the ad had to be taken off the air. Steve Letwin, president of Enbridge Home Services claimed that, "Most of the complaints came from people in that older age group. The focus groups that we used probably didn't get that kind of sample in there."

Deciding who should be in a focus group is critical for producing useful results. One problem faced by many companies who run focus groups is the participation of focus group "regulars," people who are professional focus group participants. One regular participant who does six to eight groups a year and is paid $50 to $100 per group says that most "regulars" don't give their true opinions. Since they are getting paid by the company doing the research, they say flattering things about the company's product, no matter what their true opinions are. Screening for focus group participants tries to get rid of "regulars" by asking participants before the group is set up whether they have done groups in the past. Additional screeners reject people who know too much about a product, work in companies that make similar products, or work in market research.

Some companies believe that the results of focus groups can be enhanced with results from other market research techniques. Alison Findlay, a partner at In-Sync research in Toronto, has had some success setting up focus groups as arguments, where one group of people are assigned the role of advocates for the company's brand: They have to argue on behalf of the brand and convince the other participants to use it. These groups are good at getting people to articulate all of the benefits and disadvantages of a brand. In-Sync has recently hired an anthropologist and is exploring the use of such ethnographic techniques as observing people in their own homes as a way of understanding the unconscious behaviours and motivations of consumers.

Questions

1. What types of research questions are most suited to the use of the focus group technique?
2. What types of research questions are not at all suited to the use of focus groups?
3. How can ethnographic techniques be used in conjunction with focus groups?
4. How confident would you be in making marketing decisions based on the results of focus groups?

Source: This case was prepared by Auleen Carson and is based on "Focus Groups," *Venture #734* (11 January 2000).

CBC ● VIDEO CASE 2

The Ultimate Exam Pants

Exam Pants. That is what Steve Debus had in mind for his product when he created a line of clothing to fulfill a university entrepreneurship course business plan assignment. As Debus recalls, "I had the idea to design these pants for student life. You could eat, sleep, drink, party, get up the next day and go to class in them and still look good." After graduating from university, Debus worked for a specialty sports clothing company, which he approached with his exam pants idea. The company's reception was not enthusiastic, so Debus quit his job and, in 1996, set up Modrobes Saldebus Lounge Clothing Inc. in Toronto and started designing and producing his pants.

Debus has always targeted young people with his product, especially those in colleges and universities across Canada. Currently 75% of his customers are young women. His product designs are similar to the original exam pants idea. He produces casual clothing and avoids the use of denim, which he sees as fading in popularity because it is not suited to the current needs of people. He claims that people working at desks in front of computers all day need clothing that is comfortable. The Modrobes clothing is designed with this need in mind and is positioned as "funky urban sportswear."

To reach his target customers, Debus has followed a direct to consumer approach, with the objectives of generating initial sales and creating awareness of the product that will build future sales through retail outlets. To accomplish these objectives, he takes his clothing where his target market is. Initially, he set up tables of pants at universities and offered his customers a guarantee: "If these aren't the most comfortable pair of pants you've had in your life, return them and I'll give you your money back."

After finding success on campuses, he started broadening his focus to events such as concerts. In the summer of 1999, Modrobes travelled to all eight of the Edgefest Concert Tour locations, which attracts about 30 000 people a day. In that same summer, Debus sold his product in the US for the first time by setting up a booth at Woodstock '99. With a total audience of 225 000 people and competition from 2000 other vendors, Woodstock was the largest event Debus had attended. His presence there cost $10 000 ($6000 for the booth itself and $4000 in travel costs), but it was also his most successful event for sales. He made $35 000 at the festival.

For long-term distribution of his product line, Debus has opened two of his own retail operations in Toronto and has established relationships with over 350 stores across Canada, including the 33 stores in the Athletes World chain. While such exposure is an advantage from a distribution perspective, Debus is concerned about oversaturation, which could result in negative consumer attitudes. His target consumers want a brand that is unique and "cool." To stay that way, Modrobes has started customizing their product for individual retailers, at no extra cost to them. For Athletes World, for example, Debus produces an exclusive version of the product with unique styling so that the brand image is kept fresh. Additionally, Debus runs ads in youth targeted magazines such as *Vice* and *Tribe*, using the tag line "I want you in my pants" and showcasing the company as a small, independent company to appeal to the anti-corporate sentiment that he has seen among members of his target market.

So far, Modrobes has not experienced any decline in popularity; however, keeping up with sales and growth is difficult. The company has grown from first year sales of $70 000 to over $3 million in sales in year four. As Debus says, "Our biggest challenge for the future is being able to maintain that level of energy doing all those events as well as being able to maintain the operation of business having the supply flow out to the stores.... I'd rather not be a traditional company. I'd rather do all those things or nothing."

Questions

1. Develop a complete segment profile for the typical Modrobes customer. Should Debus consider other segments for the future? Why or why not?
2. How can Debus keep up with the changing needs of his target consumers?
3. Describe the brand personality that Debus is trying to build for Modrobes. How can the company use other marketing activities to further develop and strengthen the Modrobes brand personality?

Source: This case was prepared by Auleen Carson and is based on "Modrobes: Capitalizing on Cool," *Venture #724* (12 October 1999), and "Targeting yourself," by Astrid Van Den Broek, *Marketing Magazine*, 2 August 1999: 9–10.

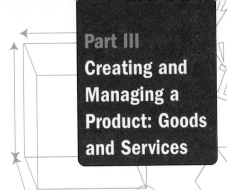

9

Creating the Product

When you have completed your study of this chapter, you should be able to

CHAPTER OBJECTIVES

1. Explain the layers of a product.

2. Describe the classifications of products.

3. Explain the importance of new products.

4. Describe how firms develop new products.

5. Explain the process of product adoption and the diffusion of innovations.

Real People, Real Decisions ✓ ✗
Meet Marshall Myles
A Decision Maker at Roots

Marshall Myles is executive vice-president at Roots, where he oversees all of the retail, wholesale, and real estate operations of the company. His career at Roots began in 1976, when he worked at the first Roots store located in Toronto. Later, he became responsible for all Roots retail store openings, further developing skills he had gained at Dylex, where he had also been involved in the development of retail stores. Myles is currently in charge of the develop-ment and opening of every Roots store and is constantly assessing new product and retail concepts to keep the company on the leading edge of the Canadian fashion and retail scene. Myles studied business at York University.

Sources: Personal interviews with Roots personnel; the Roots Web site www.roots.com; and Geoff Pevere, *Team Spirit*, Toronto: Doubleday Canada, 1998.

Roots Canada
www.roots.com

Build a Better Mousetrap ...

"Build a better mousetrap and the world will beat a path to your door." Although we've all heard that adage, the truth is: Just because a product is better, there is no guarantee it will succeed. For decades, the Woodstream Company built wood mousetraps. Then the company decided to build a better one. Woodstream's product development people researched mouse eating, crawling, and resting habits. They built prototypes of different mousetraps to come up with the best possible design, and tested them in homes. Finally, the company unveiled the sleek-looking "Little Champ," a black plastic miniature inverted bathtub with a hole (see Exhibit 9.1). When the mouse went in and ate the bait, a spring snapped upward, and the mouse was history.[1]

Sounds like a great new product (if you're not a mouse), but the "Little Champ" failed. Woodstream studied mouse habits, *not* consumer preferences. The company later discovered that husbands set the trap at night, but wives were left to dispose of the trap holding the dead mouse in the morning. Unfortunately, wives thought the "Little Champ" looked too expensive to throw away, so they felt they should empty the trap for reuse. This was a task most women weren't willing to do—they wanted a trap they could happily throw away.

Woodstream's failure underscores the importance of creating products that provide benefits people seek. It also tells us that any number of products, from low-tech cheese to high-tech traps, potentially deliver these benefits. In this case, cheese and a shoebox could trap a mouse as well as a high-tech trap. So, in developing new products, marketers need to take a close look at whether those products successfully satisfy consumers' needs better than the alternatives.

As defined in Chapter 1, a product is anything tangible or intangible that, through the exchange process, satisfies consumer or business customer needs. Products can be physical goods, services, ideas, people, or places. A good may be a sweatshirt, pack of cookies, digital camera, house, or pair of jeans. A **good** is a tangible product, something that we can see, touch, smell, hear, taste, or possess. In contrast, intangible products—services, ideas, people, places—are products that we can't always see, touch, taste, smell, or possess. Banking services, a concert, convincing people to recycle or vote for a particular political candidate, and getting people to visit a particular province on their next vacation are all examples of intangible products. We'll discuss intangible products in Chapter 11.

Marketers think of the product as more than just a *thing* that comes in a package. They view a product as a *bundle* of attributes, including packaging, brand name, benefits, and supporting features in addition to a physical good. In this chapter, we'll first examine what

✳ ✳ ✳
goods Tangible products we can see, touch, smell, hear, or taste.

Exhibit 9.1

A better mousetrap? Only if it satisfies customer needs.

a product is and how marketers classify consumer and business-to-business products. Then we'll look at new products, how marketers develop new products, and how markets accept them.

Layers of the Product Concept

A product is *everything* that a customer receives in an exchange. As Figure 9.1 shows, the product has three distinct layers—the core, actual, and augmented layers. In developing product strategies, marketers need to consider how to satisfy customers' wants and needs at each of these three levels.

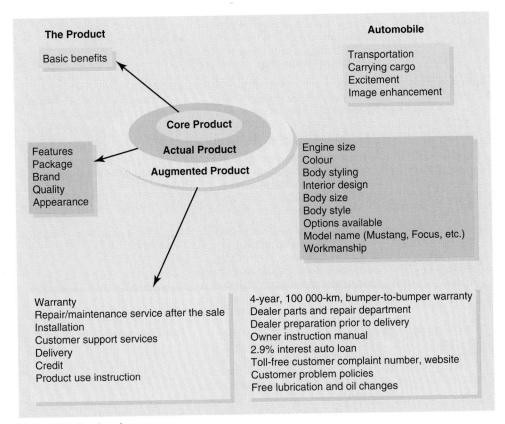

The Product

Basic benefits

Automobile

Transportation
Carrying cargo
Excitement
Image enhancement

Core Product

Actual Product

Augmented Product

Features
Package
Brand
Quality
Appearance

Engine size
Colour
Body styling
Interior design
Body size
Body style
Options available
Model name (Mustang, Focus, etc.)
Workmanship

Warranty
Repair/maintenance service after the sale
Installation
Customer support services
Delivery
Credit
Product use instruction

4-year, 100 000-km, bumper-to-bumper warranty
Dealer parts and repair department
Dealer preparation prior to delivery
Owner instruction manual
2.9% interest auto loan
Toll-free customer complaint number, website
Customer problem policies
Free lubrication and oil changes

Figure 9.1 Product Layers

THE CORE PRODUCT

The *core product* consists of all the benefits the product will provide for consumers or business customers. As noted in Chapter 1, a benefit is an outcome that the customer receives from owning or using a product. Wise old marketers (and some young ones, too) will tell you, "A marketer may make and sell a 1/20 drill bit, but a customer buys a 1/20 hole." This time-worn saying tells us that people are buying the core product, in this case, the ability to make a hole. If a new product, such as a laser, comes along that provides that outcome in a better way or more cheaply, the drill-bit maker has a problem. Marketing is about supplying benefits, not products. Table 9.1 illustrates how some marketers rigorously test their products "in action" to be sure they deliver the benefits they promise.

Many products actually provide multiple benefits. For example, the primary benefit of a car is transportation—all cars (in good repair) provide the ability to travel from point A to point B. But products also provide *customized benefits*—benefits customers receive because manufacturers have added specific features to win customers. Different drivers seek different customized benefits in a car. Some want economical transportation; others want a top-of-the-line, all-terrain vehicle; and still others look for psychological benefits such as self-confidence, pride, and excitement.

Table 9.1 Product Testing

Product	Testing Procedure	Benefit
Fruit of the Loom men's briefs	Worn by male members of a symphony orchestra.	Comfortable fit, even when sitting for long periods.
Chrysler cars	Cars face gale-force, blizzard conditions (snow included). If the car passes that test, it is subjected to simulated desert heat the next day.	Reliable transportation even under the worst weather conditions.
Sherwin Williams paint	40,000 panels, painted with both Sherwin Williams and competitors' paints, are subjected to the weather for up to 15 years (the length of the warranty on some paint).	A house paint that remains attractive throughout the warranty period.
Apple computer Powerbooks	To simulate real-life conditions, computers are drenched with pop, smeared with mayonnaise, and baked in ovens (to mimic the trunk of a car in the summer heat).	Computing power that is impervious to normal wear and tear—and more.
Shaw Industries carpet products	Workers pace up and down rows of carpet samples eight hours a day. One worker reads three books a week and has lost 40 pounds in three years as a carpet walker.	Carpeting that is attractive and durable after years of wear.
Mattel Barbie	Scuba-diving Barbie must swim and kick for 15 straight hours to make sure she would last up to a year. Other tests make sure her skin won't crack and create unsafe sharp edges and that pieces of the doll can't be bitten off and swallowed by children.	A toy that is both fun and safe for children.
Procter & Gamble hair care products	P&G pays $1200 for mannequin heads with realistic hair for testing new hair care products. Each of P&G's 15 "heads" has a name. When the hair begins to get thin, the "head" is retired.	Attractive, healthy hair.

Source: Faye Rice, "Secrets of Product Testing," *Fortune*, 28 November 1994, 166–72.

THE ACTUAL PRODUCT

The second level of the product, the *actual product*, is the physical good or the delivered service that supplies the desired benefit. For example, with a washing machine, the core product is the ability to get clothes clean, but the actual product is a large, square, metal apparatus. With a medical exam, the core product is maintaining your health, but the actual product is a lot of annoying poking and prodding. The actual product also includes the unique features of the product, such as its appearance or styling, the package, and the brand name. Roots makes many different types of clothes from leather jackets to sweatshirts to footwear—all offering the same core benefit of relaxed, comfortable (Canadian) style.

THE AUGMENTED PRODUCT

Finally, marketers offer customers an *augmented product*—the actual product plus other supporting features such as a warranty, credit, delivery, installation, and repair service after the sale. Marketers know that adding these supporting features to a product is an effective way for a company to stand out from the crowd. For example, Enterprise Rent-a-Car provides short-term use of vehicles (the actual product) to customers who need a temporary means of personal transportation (the core product). Enterprise has competed successfully with industry giants Avis and Hertz by offering an augmented service the other companies do not offer: free customer pickup service—a product strategy that's paid off handsomely for Enterprise with increased sales and market share.[2]

Enterprise Rent-a-Car
www.enterprise.com

Classifying Products

We've learned that a product can be a tangible good or an intangible service or idea, and that there are different layers to the product. Now, we'll look at how products differ from one another. Marketers classify products into categories, which represent differences in how consumers and business customers feel about products and how they purchase them. Such an understanding helps marketers develop new products that satisfy customer needs. Figure 9.2 summarizes the classification of consumer and business products.

Generally, products are either *consumer products* or *business products*, although some of the same products—such as toilet paper, vacuum cleaners, and light bulbs—are bought by consumers and businesses. However, consumer and business purchasers differ in how they make the purchase decision. We'll first consider differences in consumer products based on how long the product will last and on how the consumer shops for the product. Then we'll discuss the general types of business-to-business products.

Consumer Product Classes Defined by How Long a Product Lasts

Marketers classify consumer goods as durable or nondurable, depending on how long the product lasts. You expect a refrigerator to last a few years, but a litre of milk will last only a week or so until it's a science project. **Durable goods**, such as cars, furniture, and appliances, are consumer products that provide benefits over a period of months, years, or even decades. In contrast, **nondurable goods**, such as newspapers and food, are consumed in the short term.

Durable goods are more likely to be purchased under conditions of high involvement (as discussed in Chapter 6), whereas purchases of nondurable goods are more likely low-involvement decisions. When consumers buy a computer or a house, they spend a lot of time and energy on the decision process. For these products, marketers need to understand consumers' desires for different product benefits and features and the importance of warranties, service, and customer support. This highlights the need for marketers to ensure that consumers can find the information they need when, where, and how they want it. Today's marketers recognize that they can provide quick information to consumers of durable goods through the Internet. On the Dell Web site (www.dell.ca), for example, detailed descriptions of all of the computer products available for sale on the site are presented, as well as information about the servicing of those products.

✳ ✳ ✳
durable goods Consumer products that provide benefits over a period of time, such as cars, furniture, and appliances.

✳ ✳ ✳
nondurable goods Consumer products that provide benefits for a short time because they are consumed (such as food) or are no longer useful (such as newspapers).

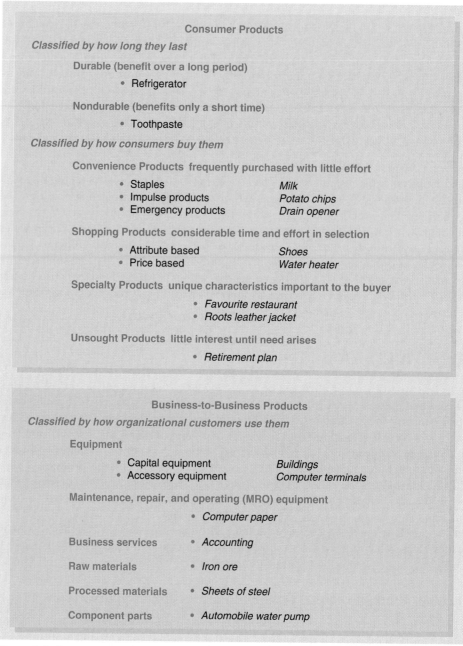

Figure 9.2 Classification of Products

In contrast, customers usually don't "sweat the details" so much when choosing among nondurable goods. There is little, if any, search for information or deliberation. Sometimes, this means that consumers buy whatever brand is available and reasonably priced. In other instances, the purchase of nondurable goods is based largely on past experience. Because a certain brand has performed satisfactorily in the past, customers see no reason to consider other brands and choose the same one out of habit. For example, some consumers buy the familiar orange box of Tide laundry detergent again and again. In such cases, marketers can probably be less concerned with developing new product features to attract customers and should focus more on pricing and distribution strategies.

Consumer Product Classes Defined by How Consumers Buy the Product

Marketers also classify products based on where and how consumers buy the product. Both goods and services can be convenience products, shopping products, specialty products, or unsought products. A **convenience product** is typically a nondurable good or service, which consumers purchase frequently with a minimum of comparison and effort. As the name implies, consumers expect these products to be convenient and will buy whatever brands are easy to obtain. In general, convenience products are low priced and widely available. You can buy a litre of milk or a loaf of bread at grocery stores, at convenience stores, and at many gas stations. Consumers generally know all they need or want to know about a convenience product, devote little effort to purchases, and willingly accept alternative brands if their preferred brand is not available in a convenient location. What's the most important thing for marketers of convenience products? Making sure the product is available where it's convenient for customers.

All convenience product purchases aren't alike, though. You may stop by a local market on your way home from school or work to pick up a litre of milk—a convenience product—because milk is something you always keep in the refrigerator. As long as you're there, why not grab a bag of potato chips for the drive home? Later that night, you dash out to buy something to unclog your kitchen drain—also a convenience product. Marketers classify convenience products as staples, impulse products, and emergency products.

Staples, such as milk, eggs, bread, and gasoline, are basic or necessary items that are available almost everywhere. Most consumers consider them basic necessities and don't perceive differences between brands. With staples, marketers must offer customers a product that consistently meets their expectations for quality and make sure it is available at a price comparable to the competitions'.

Consider this situation: You are standing in the checkout line at the supermarket and notice a copy of *People* magazine featuring a photo of Drew Barrymore with a provocative headline. You've got to read that article. This magazine is an *impulse product*—something people often buy on the spur of the moment. With an impulse product, marketers have two challenges—to create a product or package design that is enticing, that "reaches out and grabs the customer," and to make sure their product is highly visible, for example, by securing prime end-aisle or checkout lane space. On the Internet, online shopping malls such as Norstar (www.norstarmall.ca) use 3D technology to increase the purchase of impulse products. In the Indigo store in the mall, for example, a book on the shelf may open and close to attract the attention of a consumer who is browsing in a particular section of the store.[3]

Emergency products are those products you purchase when you're in dire need. Bandages, umbrellas, and something to unclog the kitchen sink are examples of emergency products. Because you need the product badly and right now, price and sometimes product quality may be irrelevant to your decision to purchase. For example, if you're caught out in a sudden downpour of rain, any umbrella at any price will do. What are the challenges to marketers of emergency products? Like any other product, emergency products are most successful when they meet customer needs—you won't sell a drain cleaner that doesn't unclog a drain more than once. And emergency products need to be offered in the sizes customers want. If you cut your finger in the mall, you don't want to buy a box of 100 bandages—you want a box of 5 or 10. And making emergency products available when and where an emergency is likely to occur is the real key to success.

In contrast to convenience products, a **shopping product** is a good or service for which consumers spend time and effort gathering information on price, product attributes, and product quality, and compare alternatives before making a purchase. Consumers often have little prior knowledge about these products. Because they gather new information for each purchase occasion, consumers are only moderately brand loyal and will switch whenever a different brand offers new or better benefits. They may visit several stores or Web sites and devote considerable effort to comparing products. For most consumers, a pair of shoes, a big-screen television, and a house-cleaning service are examples of shopping products.

Some of the latest entrants into the computer category are wireless hand-helds, such as the ones produced by Canadian company Research in Motion (see Exhibit 9.2). These communication devices are a good example of a shopping product—because they are relatively new to the market, consumers don't know a lot about the different models and features. Consumers shopping for them may ask, "How does it allow me to send and receive e-mail? How large is the keyboard? Will it need accessories?" Designing successful shopping prod-

---

✳ ✳ ✳
convenience product A consumer good or service that is usually low priced, widely available, and purchased frequently with a minimum of comparison and effort.

✳ ✳ ✳
shopping product A good or service for which consumers spend considerable time and effort gathering information and comparing alternatives before making a purchase.

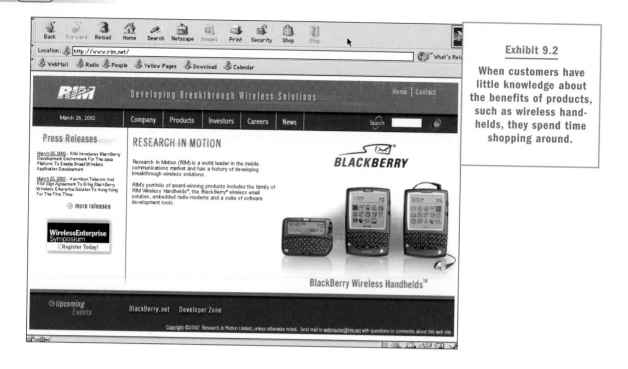

Exhibit 9.2

When customers have little knowledge about the benefits of products, such as wireless handhelds, they spend time shopping around.

ucts means making sure they have the attributes that customers want. And product packaging that points out those features helps consumers make the right decisions.

Some shopping products have different characteristics. For these *attribute-based shopping products*, such as a new party dress or a pair of designer jeans, consumers spend time and energy finding the best possible product selection. Other times, when choices available in the marketplace are just about the same, products are considered shopping products because of differences in price. For these *price-based shopping products*, determined shoppers visit numerous stores or Web sites in hopes of saving an additional $10 or $20. Whether dealing with new or with existing products, understanding how customers evaluate shopping products tells marketers if their strategies should focus more on product characteristics or on keeping prices lower than the competition.

Specialty products are such items as a Roots leather jacket, a Big Bertha golf club, a Rolex watch, or a favourite brand of perfume. A specialty service could be a favourite restaurant—one where you're willing to stand in line for an hour before being served. Specialty products and their unique characteristics are important to the buyer. For this reason, a consumer will devote significant effort to acquire a single item. Consumers usually know a good deal about specialty products, are loyal to specific brands, and spend little, if any, time comparing alternatives. For specialty products, firms create marketing strategies that make their product stand apart from the rest. For example, advertising for Roots clothes typically shows such entertainment celebrities as Deborah Cox and Jason Priestley and such sports celebrities as Elvis Stojko wearing the clothes in an attempt to differentiate the Roots brand from other clothing companies.

A fourth category of consumer products is the *unsought product*. Unsought products are goods or services (other than convenience products) for which a consumer has little awareness or interest until a need arises. For graduates with their first "real" jobs, retirement plans and disability insurance are unsought products. It requires a good deal of advertising or personal selling to interest people in unsought products—just ask any life insurance salesperson. Marketers are challenged to find convincing ways to interest consumers in unsought products. The London Life insurance company, for example, designed a life insurance product called Freedom 55 and advertised with appealing images of retired people enjoying beaches to convince consumers of the benefits of insurance. Another solution is to make pricing more attractive; for example, reluctant consumers may be more willing to buy an unsought product for "only pennies a day" than if they have to think about their yearly or lifetime cash outlay.

* * *

specialty product A good or service that has unique characteristics, that is important to the buyer, and for which the buyer will devote significant effort to acquire.

London Life
www.londonlife.com

Business-to-Business Products

Although consumers purchase products for their own use, organizational customers purchase products to use in the production of other goods and services or to facilitate the organization's operation. Marketers classify business-to-business products based on how organizational customers use them. As with consumer products, when marketers know how their business customers use a product, they are better able to design products and the entire marketing mix to meet customer demands.

The goods an organization uses in its daily operations are **equipment**. Heavy equipment, sometimes called *installations* or *capital equipment*, includes buildings and robotics used to assemble automobiles. Installations are big-ticket items and last for a number of years. Computers, photocopy machines, and water fountains are examples of *light* or *accessory equipment*. Accessory equipment is movable, costs less, and has a shorter life span than capital equipment. Equipment marketing strategies usually emphasize personal selling and may mean custom designing products to meet a customer's specific needs. For example, Kinetic Services Inc. (www.kinetic.bc.ca), a Canadian robotics equipment manufacturer, custom designs its robotics products for such clients as the Canadian Space Agency.

Maintenance, repair, and operating (MRO) products are goods that a business customer consumes in a relatively short time. MRO products do not become a part of other goods and services. *Maintenance products* include light bulbs, mops, and cleaning supplies. *Repair products* are such items as nuts, bolts, washers, and small tools. *Operating supplies* include computer paper and oil to keep machinery running smoothly. Although some firms use a sales force to promote MRO products, others rely on catalogue sales, the Internet, and telemarketing to keep prices as low as possible.

Raw materials are products of the fishing, lumber, agricultural, and mining industries that organizational customers purchase to use in their finished products. For example, SoyaWorld uses soybeans as raw materials and transforms them into a finished product, So Good soy beverage; a steel manufacturer takes iron ore and changes it into large sheets of steel used by other firms in the manufacture of automobiles, washing machines, and lawn mowers.

Processed materials are produced when firms transform raw materials from their original state. Organizations purchase processed materials to manufacture their own products. Cement used in the manufacture of cement blocks and aluminum ingots used to make aluminum pop cans are examples of processed materials.

Some business customers purchase **specialized services** from outside suppliers. Services may be technical, such as equipment repair, or non-technical, such as market research and legal services. These services are essential to the operation of an organization but are not part of the production of a product.

Component parts are manufactured goods or subassemblies of finished items that organizations need to complete their own products. For example, a computer manufacturer needs silicon chips to make a computer, and an auto manufacturer needs batteries, tires, and fuel injectors. As with processed materials, marketing strategies for component parts usually involve nurturing relationships with customer firms and on-time delivery of a product that meets the buyer's specifications.

We now understand what a product is. We also know how marketers classify consumer products based on how long they last and how they are purchased, and we've seen how they classify business-to-business products according to how they are used. In the next section, we'll discuss the importance of new products or innovations.

It's "New and Improved!" Understanding Innovations

"New and improved!" What exactly do we mean when we use the term *new product?* From a marketing standpoint, a new product or an **innovation** is anything that customers *perceive* as new and different. Innovations may be a cutting-edge style such as body

---

❊ ❊ ❊
equipment Expensive goods an organization uses in its daily operations that last for a long time.

❊ ❊ ❊
maintenance, repair, and operating (MRO) products Goods that a business customer consumes in a relatively short time.

❊ ❊ ❊
raw materials Products of the fishing, lumber, agricultural, and mining industries that organizational customers purchase to use in their finished products.

❊ ❊ ❊
processed materials Products created when firms transform raw materials from their original state.

❊ ❊ ❊
specialized services Services purchased from outside suppliers that are essential to the operation of an organization but are not part of the production of a product.

❊ ❊ ❊
component parts Manufactured goods or subassemblies of finished items that organizations need to complete their own products.

❊ ❊ ❊
innovation A product that consumers perceive to be new and different from existing products.

Exhibit 9.3

The Nehru suit of the 1960s: Not all innovations are successful.

piercings, a fad such as Beanie Babies, a new communications technology such as wireless communication, or a new product such as DVD players. It may be a completely new product that provides benefits never available before, or it may simply be an existing product with a new style, in a different colour, or with some new feature. If an innovation is successful, it spreads through the population. First, it is bought and used by only a few people, and then more and more consumers adopt it.

Not all innovations are successful. Take, for instance, the Nehru jacket shown in Exhibit 9.3. In the 1960s, men's fashion designers felt men were ready for a dramatic and exciting change. Enter the Nehru jacket, fashioned after the traditional clothing worn by leaders of Indian society and named after a former prime minister of India. The suit was 100% polyester, a popular fabric in the 1960s. The problem was that polyester was also hot and uncomfortable and never seemed to fit the body just right. Whether it was the fabric or the look, men overwhelmingly rejected the Nehru style. Manufacturers and retailers lost millions of dollars, because they introduced the suit without first understanding their customers—just because fashion designers thought it was a great idea to radically change the way men dressed didn't mean the average guy would agree. Years later, it was rumoured that there were warehouses in which thousands of unsold Nehru jackets were still being stored. Let the buyer beware—they may resurface.

The Importance of Understanding Innovations

Understanding innovations can be critical to the success of firms for at least two reasons. First, technology is advancing at a dizzying pace. Products are introduced and become obsolete faster than ever before. In many industries, firms are busy developing another new-and-better product before the last new-and-better product even hits store shelves. Nowhere is this more obvious than with personal computers, for which a steady change in technology makes consumers want a bigger, better machine before the dust even settles on the old one. One company, Gateway, offers consumers a purchase plan that gives them the option of trading the machine in for a newer model every two years to make sure customers have what they want—and that they get it from Gateway.

Another reason why understanding new products is important is the high cost of developing them and the even higher cost of new products that fail. In the pharmaceutical industry, the cost of bringing each new drug to market is between $200 and $500 million.[4] Even the most successful firms can't afford many product failures with that kind of price tag.

Marketers must understand what it takes to develop a new product successfully; they must do their homework and learn what it is about existing products consumers find less than satisfactory and what exactly it will take to do a better job satisfying customer needs. Savvy marketers know they'll waste a lot of investment money if they don't.

Finally, new product development is an important contribution to society. We would never suggest that *everything* new is good, but many new products allow us to live longer, happier lives of better quality than before. Although there are some who disagree, most of us feel that our lives are better because of telephones, televisions, CD players, microwave ovens, and computers—except when these items break down. We're not saying that firms create new products because they want to make our lives better—businesses create new products that make our lives better because that's how they make profits and keep their stockholders happy.

Types of Innovations

Innovations differ in their degree of newness, and this helps to determine how quickly the products will be adopted by many members of a target market. Because innovations that are more novel require greater effort and more changes in behaviour, they are slower to spread throughout a population than new products that are similar to what is already available.

Marketers classify innovations into three categories based on their degree of newness; however, it is better to think of these three types as ranges along a continuum. The three types of innovations are based on the amount of disruption or change they bring to people's lives. For example, when the first automobiles were produced, they caused tremendous changes in the lives of their owners, far greater changes than when auto manufacturers introduced "new and improved" autos with automatic transmissions, air conditioning, and driving directions provided via satellite.

CONTINUOUS INNOVATIONS

A **continuous innovation** is a modification to an existing product, such as Kraft Canada's Easy Mac, the microwave version of its Kraft Dinner (see Exhibit 9.4). This type of modification can set one brand apart from its competitors. Roots has used continuous innovation in many of its product lines, adding a new style of leather jacket or a new neckline for a shirt. Most product innovations are continuous innovations. The term *continuous* tells us that the changes are evolutionary rather than revolutionary. Small changes reposition the product or allow a manufacturer to offer new product options. For example, phone manufacturers such as Panasonic now offer 900 MHz cordless phones in addition to older, less powerful models.

With a continuous innovation, the consumer doesn't have to learn anything new to use the innovation. From a marketing perspective, this means that it is far easier to convince consumers to adopt the innovation. A typewriter company, for example, many years ago modified the shape of its product to make it more "user friendly" to secretaries. One simple change was curving the tops of the keys, as we see on today's computer keyboards, because secretaries complained that flat surfaces were hard to use with long fingernails. Today, computer manufacturers have gone a step farther by building ergonomic keyboards that are less likely to cause painful wrist ailments.

How different does a new product have to be from existing products? It is said that "imitation is the sincerest form of flattery," and decisions regarding how much (if at all) one's product should resemble those of competitors often are at the centre of marketing strategy development. Sometimes, marketers feel that the best strategy is to follow the competition. For example, the packaging of "me-too" or look-alike products, such as store brand versions of national brands, can create instant market success, because consumers assume that similar packaging means similar products. A **knock-off** is a new product that copies with slight modification the design of an original product. Firms deliberately create knock-offs of clothing, jewellery, or other items, often with the intent to sell to a larger or different market. For example, companies may copy the haute couture clothing styles of top designers and sell them at lower prices to the mass market. It is difficult to legally protect a design (as opposed to a technological invention), because it can be argued that even a very slight change—different buttons or a slightly wider collar on a dress or shirt—means the knock-off is not an exact copy. However, industry pressure is building for legal protection of designs. Manufacturers argue that a design element, say, a distinctive curve on a car bumper, is as important to the integrity of the car as a mechanical innovation.[5]

DYNAMICALLY CONTINUOUS INNOVATIONS

A **dynamically continuous innovation** is a pronounced modification to an existing product that requires a modest amount of learning or change in behaviour to use it. The history of audio equipment is a series of dynamically continuous innovations. For

* * *

continuous innovation A modification of an existing product that sets one brand apart from its competitors.

* * *

knock-off A new product that copies with slight modification the design of an original product.

* * *

dynamically continuous innovation A change in an existing product that requires a moderate amount of learning or behaviour change.

Exhibit 9.4

The introduction of KD for the microwave was an example of a continuous innovation.

Real People, Real Decisions
Decision Time **at Roots**

There are few Canadian brand names as well known as Roots. In Canada and around the world, Roots has become synonymous with an outdoor, Canadian lifestyle, and this brand personality has been reinforced by the fact that Roots is the official outfitter for the Canadian Olympic teams. The Roots company, founded by Don Green and Michael Budman, started in 1973 with a single product, the Roots negative-heel shoe, and a single retail outlet in Toronto. After over 25 years of new product innovation, the company now has a broad product line ranging from sweatshirts, leather jackets, and poor-boy hats to home furnishings, a lodge in Ucluelet, BC, and vitamins. In addition the Roots organization operates over 150 exclusive Roots stores in 5 countries.

Marshall Myles and the team at Roots are well aware of the need to constantly innovate to remain competitive. They have created such new retail concepts as the Roots Home store, alongside innovations in their products. A major new product initiative that the company undertook was the introduction of a line of children's clothing in the early 1980s. The children's products, similar in type and style to the adult clothing, were sold in Roots stores. However, by 2000, the children's line had become so popular that about 30% of the space in Roots stores was dedicated to children's clothes; and customer demand was increasing. Demographically, the baby boomers were having children, thereby increasing demand for children's clothes. Roots customers were requesting more product line for children and, at the same time,

Myles was realizing that space was limited in the existing stores. He identified two options:

Option 1. The first option was to expand the Roots children's line of clothing by adding new products, but to continue to sell these products through existing Roots stores. This option would help to satisfy the demand for increased product from parents and reach parent purchasers where they were already buying their own clothes. One concern with this option was the ability of existing stores to handle more kids product, especially in light of the expansion of other Roots clothing lines.

Option 2. The other option was to design an entirely new retail concept, Roots Kids, which would also require an expanded product line of Roots children's clothing. In addition to making changes to the clothing offered, the new retail outlets would be customized to the children's market and would include in-store interactive video games and play stations for kids. Myles was not sure whether 30% of the existing store business was enough to justify the costs of building and maintaining the new retail outlets. Since companies like Gap and Guess already had retail stores dedicated to children's clothes, he also wondered whether the market could sustain another store of this type.

Now join Marshall Myles and the decision team at Roots. What option would you choose, and why?

---

many years, consumers enjoyed listening to their favourite songs on record players. Then in the 1960s, that same music became available on a continuous-play eight-track tape, requiring the purchase of an eight-track tape player. Then came cassette tapes, requiring a cassette player. In the 1980s, consumers could hear songs digitally mastered on compact disks; that required the purchase of a new CD player. In the 1990s, recording technology moved one more step forward with digital video disk (DVD) technology. Even though each of these changes required learning how to operate new equipment, consumers were willing to buy the new products because of the improvements in music reproduction, the core product benefit.

DISCONTINUOUS INNOVATIONS

* * *
discontinuous innovation A totally new product that creates major changes in the way we live.

A **discontinuous innovation** creates major changes in the way we live. To use a discontinuous innovation, consumers must engage in a great amount of learning, because no similar product has ever been on the market. Such major inventions as the airplane, car, and television have radically changed lifestyles. Another discontinuous innovation, the personal computer, is changing the way we shop and is allowing more and more firms' employees to work out of their homes.

Recognizing the degree of newness of innovations is important in developing marketing strategies. For example, if marketers know that consumers may resist adopting a new and radically different product, they may offer consumers free product trial or place heavier emphasis on a personal selling strategy to convince consumers that the new product offers benefits worth the hassle. Business-to-business marketers of technology products such as software, for instance, often provide in-service training for employees of their customers who invest in new products.

Developing New Products

Building on our knowledge of different types of innovations, we'll now examine how firms go about developing new products. Product development doesn't simply mean creating totally new products never before on the market. Many companies do that; but for many other firms, product development is a continuous process of looking for ways to make an existing product better or finding just the right shade of green for this year's bath fashions.

Not all new products are important. Consider what happened when a man named Lonnie Johnson walked into the slick conference room of Larami Corporation. He smiled mischievously at the assembled executives. Then he opened his pink, battered Samsonite suitcase and took out a gizmo that looked a bit like a phaser from *Star Trek*. Holding out this combination of a hand-held pump apparatus, PVC tubing, Plexiglas, and plastic pop bottles, Johnson aimed and fired. A giant stream of water shot across the room. Within a year, the Super Soaker (see Exhibit 9.5) had become one of the most successful water toys in retail history.[6]

The successful introduction of new products is getting tougher for entrepreneurs to accomplish. Even for large corporations, successful new product introductions are becoming more and more difficult. First, the costs of research and development are often so huge that firms must limit the number of new products in development. The fast pace of technological change means that products are outdated faster than ever, giving firms less time to recover their research and development costs. And, with so many products competing for limited shelf space, retailers often charge manufacturers exorbitant fees to stock a new product, increasing manufacturers' costs even more.[7] Firms must reduce the time it takes to get good products to market and increase the speed of adoption to quickly recover these costs.

New product development occurs in three phases, as Figure 9.3 shows. In the *visionary phase*, a firm generates and screens ideas to identify those that will work best for it. The *planning and development phase* means turning those ideas into a product. The *test and improve phase* means trying out marketing strategies in test markets to improve the marketing plan and product, if needed, before full commercial launch.

The Visionary Phase

In the visionary phase of product development, marketers generate new product ideas, screen new product concepts, and complete a business analysis. Marketers use a variety of sources to come up with great new product ideas that provide important customer benefits and are compatible with the

SuperSoaker
www.supersoaker.com

Exhibit 9.5

Entrepreneur Lonnie Johnson with his invention, the Super Soaker.

Phase of Development	Outcome
Visionary	
• Idea generation.	Identify product ideas that will provide important customer benefits compatible with company mission.
• Product concept screening.	Estimate potential technical and commercial success of product ideas.
• Perform business analysis.	Estimate potential for profit. What is the potential demand, what expenditures will be required, and what is the cost of marketing the product?
Planning and Development	
• Begin commercial development.	Develop a marketing plan.
• Begin technical development.	Design the product and the manufacturing and production process.
Test and Improve	
• Test complete marketing plan.	Develop evidence of potential success in the real market.
• Marketing mix adjustments.	Make improvements in marketing mix as needed.
• Launch product.	Implement full-scale marketing plan.

Figure 9.3 Phases in New Product Development

CanWest Global
www.canwestglobal.com

company mission. Ideas can come from customers, as well as salespeople, service providers, and others who have direct customer contact. Often firms use such marketing research activities as focus groups for new product *idea generation*. For example, a company like CanWest Global Communications that operates TV stations might hold focus group discussions to get ideas about types of programs not currently available.

Although ideas for products initially come from a variety of sources, it is up to marketers to expand these ideas into more complete product concepts. Product concepts describe what features the product should have and the benefits those features will provide for consumers. The second step in developing new products is screening product concepts. In *screening*, marketers and researchers examine the chances that the product concept might achieve technical and commercial success, thereby weeding out concepts that have little chance of success. Estimating *technical success* is assessing whether the new product is technologically feasible—is it possible to build this product? Estimating *commercial success* is deciding whether anyone is likely to buy the product. The marketing graveyard is littered with products that sounded interesting but that failed to catch on, including jalapeño pop, aerosol mustard, microwavable ice cream, aerosol toothpaste, and edible deodorant.[8, 9]

The marketers of Fit® (see Exhibit 9.6) had to first determine that producing a fruit and vegetable wash product would be possible—technical success. Researchers then had to interview consumers to see if they thought a fruit and vegetable cleaning product was something that they would purchase.

Exhibit 9.6

Marketers must make sure that consumers will buy unique product concepts such as Fit®, or risk heavy losses.

SPOTLIGHT ON REAL PEOPLE *The NRG Group*

The Internet is one of the most important innovations in recent business history, and it has become the birthplace of many other new product innovations. The Internet business environment changes daily, which means that the new product development process for Internet based businesses must be short and focused. One company that specializes in the development of new product ideas for the Internet is The NRG Group of Toronto.

Originally formulated as a dot-com "incubator" that provided assistance to young entrepreneurs during the idea generation phase of product development, The NRG Group now invests "upstream" in the product development process: when a company is in the early to middle stages of product development. For example, a company that approaches the NRG Group for assistance might already be at the business analysis or planning and development stages of product development.

The NRG Group focuses on supporting technology companies (especially those focused on infrastructure, personalization and wireless technologies) and tries to ensure that these companies bring their new products to market quickly. Unlike traditional venture capital firms that simply invest money, The NRG Group provides expertise in the form of consulting in such areas as product management, strategic sales and marketing. The NRG Group Web site describes their approach like this: "Utilizing a hands-on approach to manage our portfolio, our mandate is to advise, support and accelerate growth.... The goal of The NRG Group is to help outstanding technology companies bring better products to market faster with less risk." Typically The NRG Group provides financing of up to $1 million to a given company. In total, The NRG Group manages a portfolio of technology companies worth about $15 million. The NRG Group has supported the launch of such products as Medcomsoft (www.medcomsoft. com), a health care software company; Streetviews. com, a financial investment information centre; and Youthography (www.youthography.com), a marketing consulting company that provides assistance to companies targeting consumers who are 13-29 years old.[10]

1. How is each phase of the new product development process different for Internet-based new products compared to more traditional new products?
2. Go to The NRG Group Web site (www.thenrggroup.com) and look at the companies and products currently in The NRG Group's portfolio. Are these companies developing continuous, dynamically continuous, or discontinuous innovations?
3. How can The NRG Group most effectively reach young entrepreneurs who are developing Internet based businesses?

Once a product concept passes the screening stage, marketers conduct a *business analysis*. Even if they have evidence that there is a market for the product, they still must find out if the product can be a profitable contribution to the organization's product mix. How much potential demand is there for the product? Does the firm have the resources that will be required for successful development and introduction of the product?

The business analysis for a new product begins with assessing how the new product will fit into the firm's total product mix. Will the new product increase sales, or will it cannibalize sales of existing products? Are there possible synergies between the new product and the company's existing offerings that may improve visibility and the image of both? What is the probable customer demand for the new product? An equally important part of the business analysis is estimating the marketing costs necessary to stimulate demand and achieve desired distribution levels. This estimation may include the costs of training a sales force, recruiting distributors, advertising, conducting sales promotions, and communicating through press releases and direct mail.

The NRG Group
www.thenrggroup.com

Planning and Development

If it survives the scrutiny of a business analysis, a new product concept then undergoes commercial and technical development. *Commercial development* means putting together a marketing plan that builds on the initial projections made during product screening and business analysis. Forecasts are adjusted to fit more precise information about the market and how customers will respond to the product. Marketers also plan pricing, advertising, and distribution strategies. Prospective customers are again involved in the planning and development process—the better a firm understands how customers will react to a new product, the better its chances of commercial success.

In *technical development*, a firm's engineers work with marketers to refine the design and production process. Those involved in the technical development process must, for example, determine which parts of a finished good the company will make and which ones will be bought from other suppliers. If goods are to be manufactured, the company may have to buy new production equipment or modify existing machinery. Someone has to develop work instructions for employees and train them to produce the product. In developing service processes, technical development includes such decisions as which activities will occur within sight of customers and whether parts of the service can be automated to make delivery more efficient.

Technical development sometimes requires applying for a patent. Because patents legally prevent competitors from producing or selling the invention, a patent can reduce or eliminate competition in a market for many years, allowing a firm "breathing room" to recoup investments in technical development. For example, for many years, G.D. Searle Pharmaceuticals (now owned by Monsanto) held the patent for its NutraSweet brand of artificial sweetener. This exclusive right to make and sell the product allowed the company to reap huge profits, because no other company had a similar product. Now that the patent has expired, Searle faces competition in this market.

Testing and Improving the Product

test marketing Testing the complete marketing plan in a small geographic area that is similar to the larger market the firm hopes to enter.

The final phase of new product development includes test marketing, making final adjustments to the marketing mix, and commercial launch. In **test marketing**, the firm tries out the complete marketing plan—the distribution, advertising, sales promotion—but in a small geographic area that is similar to the larger market it hopes to enter. Test marketing can be conducted in an area as small as one city or as large as a country. For example, Vancouver has become a popular test market for innovative products, because Vancouverites have a reputation for being interested in new and unconventional things. Kera Vision, a US optical company, chose Vancouver as a test market for Intacs, a product that attaches to the eye to reshape the cornea and improve vision.[11] LG Electronics, a Korean appliance manufacturer, used all of Canada as a test market for the North American launch of its "smart" appliances, including an Internet fridge which allows users to surf the Web, send e-mail, or watch TV on a monitor built into the fridge, and a washing machine that automatically measures the detergent, determines water level, and sets the speed.[12]

There are pluses and minuses to test marketing. On the negative side, test marketing is extremely expensive. It can cost over a million dollars to conduct a test market even in a single city. A test market also gives the competition a free look at the new product, its introductory price, and the intended promotional strategy—and an opportunity to foil the test market by increasing their own promotion or get to the market first with a competitive product.

Because of the problems with test marketing, marketers sometimes conduct *simulated test markets*. Simulated test markets imitate the introduction of a product into the marketplace using computer software. These simulations allow the company to test the impact of price cuts, new packaging, or even where on store shelves to feature the product. The process entails gathering basic research data on consumer perceptions of the product concept, the physical product, the advertising, and other promotional activity. The test market simulation model uses that information to predict the product's success much less expensively (and more discreetly) than a traditional test market. As this simulated test market technology improves, traditional test markets may become a thing of the past.

On the positive side, by offering a new product in a limited area of the market, marketers can evaluate and improve the marketing program. Sometimes, test marketing uncovers a need to improve the product itself; sometimes, it indicates product failure, allowing the firm to save millions of dollars by "pulling the plug."[13]

The last step in new product development is the *product launch*. Launching a new product requires full-scale production, distribution, advertising, sales promotion—the works. For this reason, full-scale introduction of a new product cannot happen overnight. A launch requires planning and careful preparation. Marketers must implement trade promotion plans, which offer special incentives to encourage dealers, retailers, or other members of the channel to stock the new product so that customers will find it on store shelves the very first time they look. They must also develop consumer promotions, such as coupons. Marketers may arrange to have point-of-purchase displays designed, built, and delivered to retail outlets. If the new product is especially complex, customer service employees must receive extensive training and preparation.

As launch time nears, preparations gain a sense of urgency. Sales managers explain special incentive programs to salespeople. Soon, the media announce to prospective customers why they should buy and where they can find the new product. All elements of the marketing program—ideally—come into play like a carefully planned lift-off of the space shuttle.

Adoption and Diffusion Processes

We've presented the steps marketers take to develop new products from generating ideas to launch. Now, we'll look at what happens after that new product hits the market—how an innovation spreads throughout a population.

New products do not satisfy customer wants and needs until the customer uses them. **Product adoption** is the process by which a consumer or business customer begins to buy and use a new good, service, or an idea. The term **diffusion** describes how the use of a product spreads throughout a population.

After months or even years spent developing a new product, a firm faces the challenge of getting consumers to buy and use the product—and to do so quickly—so that it can recover the costs of product development and launch. To accomplish this, marketers must understand the product adoption process. In this section, we'll discuss the stages in this process. We'll also see how consumers and businesses differ in their eagerness to adopt new products and how the characteristics of a product affect its adoption rate—an important consideration for the introduction of new products.

* * *
product adoption The process by which a consumer or business customer begins to buy and use a new good, service, or an idea.

* * *
diffusion The process by which the use of a product spreads throughout a population.

Stages in a Customer's Adoption of a New Product

Whether the innovation is a new type of retail store or a better mousetrap, individuals and organizations pass through six stages in the adoption process. Figure 9.4 shows how a person goes from being unaware of an innovation through the stages of awareness, interest, evaluation, trial, adoption, and confirmation. At every stage, people drop out of the process, so the proportion of consumers who wind up using the innovation on a consistent basis is a fraction of those who are exposed to it.

AWARENESS

Learning that the innovation exists is the first step in the adoption process. To make consumers aware of a new product, marketers often conduct a massive advertising campaign, or media blitz. This was the case when McDonald's introduced its Arch Deluxe sandwich. At this point, some consumers will say, "So there's a new sandwich out there. So what?" and they will fall by the wayside, out of the adoption process. But this strategy works for new products when consumers see a new product as something they want and need and just can't live without.

INTEREST

For some of the people who become aware of a new product, a second stage in the adoption process is *interest*—a prospective

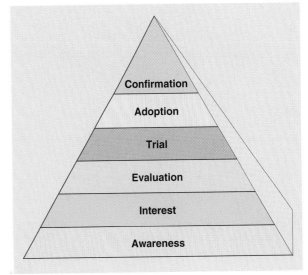

Figure 9.4 Adoption Pyramid

Confirmation
Adoption
Trial
Evaluation
Interest
Awareness

adopter begins to see how a new product could satisfy an existing or newly realized need. Interest also means that consumers look for and are open to information about the innovation. Marketers often design teaser advertisements to give prospective customers just enough information about the new product to make them curious and stimulate their interest. Despite the marketers' best efforts, though, some consumers drop out of the process at this point.

EVALUATION

In the evaluation stage, a prospect weighs the costs and benefits of the new product. For complex, risky, or expensive products, people think about the innovation a great deal before trying it. For instance, a firm will carefully evaluate buying a $6000 video conferencing system before purchase.[14] Marketers for such products help prospective customers see how such products can benefit them—holding video conferences means a company doesn't have to pay travel costs for employees to attend central location meetings.

However, little evaluation may occur with an impulse purchase. For example, consumers may do very little thinking before buying a chewing gum such as Trident Advantage, shown in Exhibit 9.7. For these products, marketers design the product and packaging to be eye-catching and appealing to get consumers to notice the product quickly.

Some potential adopters will evaluate an innovation positively enough to move on to the trial stage. Those who do not think the new product will provide adequate benefits drop out.

TRIAL

The next stage in the adoption process is *trial*—the potential adopters will actually experience or use the product for the first time. Often marketers stimulate trial by providing opportunities for consumers to sample the product. For example, when Barq's Root Beer (see Exhibit 9.8) was introduced into the Canadian market, they used a sampling team, the Barq's Brigades, to give consumers free samples in stores and at sports events to ensure that they got a chance to try the product for the first time.[15]

Based on the trial experience, some potential buyers move on to adoption of the new product. Sometimes prospective customers will not adopt a new product because it costs too much. This was the case with the digital camera. When first on the market, they were simply high-priced toys. A year later, when prices had dropped to below $1000, consumers were more willing to buy, and sales took off.[16]

ADOPTION

At the *adoption* stage, a prospect chooses a product. If the product is a consumer or business-to-business good, this means buying the product and learning how to use and maintain it. If the product is an idea, this means that the individual agrees with the new idea. For example, consumers who have adopted the idea that recycling helps protect our natural resources will carefully sort and recycle their glass, aluminum, plastic, and paper products.

This does not mean that all individuals or organizations that first choose an innovation are permanent customers, although

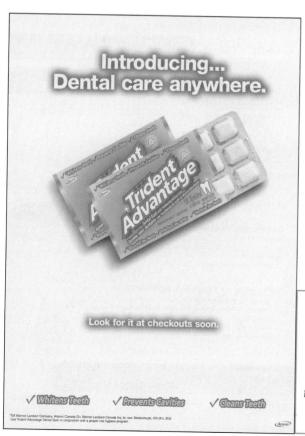

Exhibit 9.7

Consumers aren't likely to spend much time evaluating new impulse products like chewing gum before buying them.

Exhibit 9.8

When Barq's was introduced in Canada, sampling teams, the Barq's Brigades, made sure that people tasted the product.

many firms make this mistake. Some potential customers, even after initial adoption, do not go on to the final stage of confirmation. Marketers need to provide follow-up contacts and communications with adopters to ensure that they are satisfied and remain loyal to the new product over time.

CONFIRMATION

With initial adoption of an innovation, a customer weighs expected versus actual benefits and costs. Favourable experiences contribute to new customers becoming loyal adopters, as their initially positive opinions result in *confirmation*. Nothing lasts forever, however. Even loyal customers may decide that a new product is not meeting expectations and reject it. Some marketers feel that *reselling* the customer in the confirmation stage is important. They provide advertisements, sales presentations, and other communications to reinforce a customer's choice.

The Diffusion of Innovations

Diffusion describes how the use of a product spreads throughout a population. Marketers would prefer that their entire target market immediately adopt a new product; but this does not happen. Consumers and business customers differ in how eager or willing they are to try something new, lengthening the diffusion process by months or even years. Based on adopters' roles in the diffusion process, experts have classified them into five different categories.

ADOPTER CATEGORIES

Some people like to try new products. Others are so reluctant, you'd think they're afraid of anything new. As Figure 9.5 shows, there are five categories of adopters: innovators, early adopters, early majority, late majority, and laggards.[17] To understand how these differ, we'll study the adoption of one product—the microwave oven.

Innovators are roughly the first 2.5% of adopters. This segment is extremely adventurous and willing to take risks with new products. Innovators are typically well educated, younger, better off financially than others in the population, and worldly. Innovators who were into new technology knew all about microwave ovens before other people were aware they existed. Because innovators pride themselves on trying new products, they probably purchased microwaves when they were first introduced to the market in the mid-1970s.

Early adopters, approximately 13.5% of adopters, buy product innovations early in the diffusion process, but not as early as innovators. Unlike innovators, early adopters have greater concern for social acceptance. Typically, they

✳ ✳ ✳
innovators The first segment (roughly 2.5%) of a population to adopt a new product.

✳ ✳ ✳
early adopters Those who adopt an innovation early in the diffusion process but later than the innovators.

good OR bad DECISION?

When a new product is hot, it's hot—but the burning desire to get hold of it can make it too hot to handle. Athletic shoe manufacturers compete fiercely to produce dynamically continuous innovations that kids want. For example, Nike introduces new models of its Michael Jordan sneaker every year, and with each new version, the product becomes more and more desirable to young kids. News of one new model's arrival date in stores caused a frenzy. Students went so far as to skip school—with permission from their parents—to be the first in line to buy the Air Jordan for $140. One store employee observed, "Most of the students were with their parents."[18] Do you think Nike's marketers should feel good or bad about kids being so anxious to buy their new products?

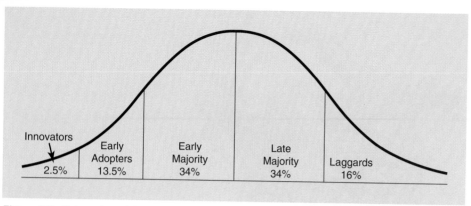

Figure 9.5 Categories of Adopters

❊ ❊ ❊

early majority Those whose adoption of a new product signals a general acceptance of the innovation.

❊ ❊ ❊

late majority The adopters who are willing to try new products when there is little or no risk associated with the purchase, when the purchase becomes an economic necessity, or when there is social pressure to purchase.

are heavy media users and often are heavy users of a new product category. Others in the population often look to early adopters for their opinions on various topics, making them key to a new product's success. For this reason, marketers often target early adopters in developing advertising and other communications efforts. For example, early adopters of the Bioré pore-cleaning strips (see Exhibit 9.9) were young, 18- to 34-year-old women who were heavy readers of fashion magazines. Bioré targeted this group with heavy advertising for the strips in fashion magazines and by giving out free samples at the Lilith Fair Tour.[19] After reading articles in *Consumer Reports* and other sources of information on new products, early adopters of the microwave made their first purchase in the late 1970s.

The **early majority**, about 34% of adopters, avoid being either first or last to try an innovation. They are typically middle-class consumers and are deliberate and cautious. Early majority consumers have slightly above-average education and income levels. When the early majority adopts a product, it is no longer considered new or different—it is, in essence, already established. Early majority microwave owners made their purchase in the early and mid-1980s, by which time there were 10 to 15 brands of microwaves sold by a wide variety of retailers.

Late majority adopters, about 34% of the population, are older, more conservative, and typically have lower-than-average levels of education and income. The late majority adopters avoid trying a new product until it is no longer risky. By that time, the product has become an economic necessity, or there is pressure from peer groups to adopt. Late majority homes did not have a microwave until their friends began asking, "How can you survive without a microwave?" By that time, the price of the ovens had gone down, and the innovators, early adopters, and even many of the early majority were purchasing a second or even a third microwave. To attract late majority buyers, marketers may offer lower-priced models of a product.

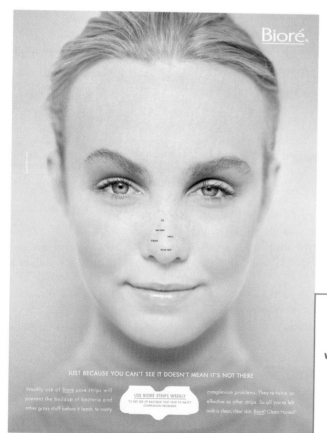

Exhibit 9.9

Most consumers were willing to try clean pore strips only after early adopters made recommendations.

Laggards, about 16% of adopters, are the last in a population to adopt a new product. Laggards are typically lower in social class than other adopter categories and are bound by tradition. By the time laggards adopt a product, it may already be superseded by other innovations.

By understanding these adopter categories, marketers are better able to develop strategies to speed the diffusion or widespread use of their products. For example, early in the diffusion process, marketers may put greater emphasis on advertising in special-interest magazines to attract innovators and early adopters. Later they may lower the product's price or come out with lower-priced models with fewer features to attract the late majority. We'll discuss the strategies for new and existing products in the next chapter.

PRODUCT FACTORS AFFECTING THE RATE OF ADOPTION

If you could predict which new products will succeed and which will fail, you'd quickly be in high demand as a consultant by companies worldwide. That's because companies make large investments in new products; but failures are all too frequent. Estimates of new product success rates range from 46 to 65%.[20] Much research is devoted to making us smarter about new product successes and failures.

Researchers have identified five characteristics of innovations that affect the rate of adoption. Figure 9.6 summarizes these factors: relative advantage, compatibility, complexity, trialability, and observability.[21] Whether a new product has each of these characteristics affects the speed of diffusion. As we've discussed, it took many years for the microwave to diffuse or spread throughout the Canadian population—from the mid-1970s to the early 1990s.[22] Examining these five factors helps understand both why the new product was not adopted during its early years and why adoption sped up later.

Relative advantage is the degree to which a consumer perceives that a new product provides superior benefits. In the case of the microwave oven, consumers in the 1960s and early 1970s did not feel that the product provided important benefits that would improve their lives. But by the late 1970s, that perception had changed, primarily because more women had entered the workforce. The 1960s' woman had all day to prepare the evening meal— she didn't have a need for the microwave. But in the late 1970s, when many women left home for work at 8:00 a.m. and returned home at 6:00 p.m., an appliance that would "magically" defrost a frozen chicken and cook it for dinner in 30 minutes provided a genuine advantage.

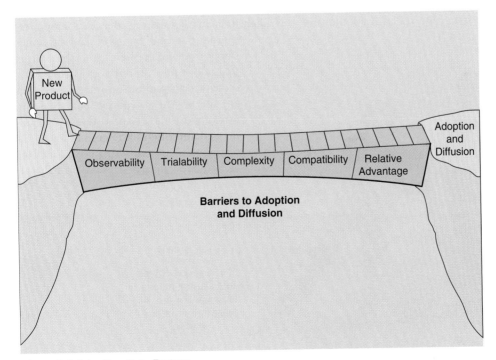

Figure 9.6 Adoption Rate Factors

Compatibility is the extent to which a new product is consistent with existing cultural values, customs, and practices. Did consumers see the microwave oven as being compatible with existing ways of doing things? No. Cooking on paper plates? If you put a paper plate in a conventional oven, you'd likely get a visit from the fire department. By anticipating compatibility issues early in the new product development stage, marketing strategies can address such problems in planning communications programs, or there may be opportunities for altering product designs to overcome some consumer objections.

Complexity is the degree to which consumers find a new product or its use difficult to understand. Many microwave users today haven't a clue about how a microwave oven cooks food. But when the product was introduced, consumers asked and marketers answered—microwaves cause molecules to move and rub together, creating friction, which produces heat—cooked pot roast. But that explanation was complex and confusing for consumers of the 1960s.

Trialability is the ease of sampling a new product and its benefits. Marketers took a very important step in the 1970s to speed up adoption of the microwave oven—product trial. Just about every store that sold microwaves invited shoppers to visit the store and see and sample an entire meal cooked in the microwave.

Observability is how visible a new product and its benefits are to others who might adopt it. The ideal innovation is easy to see. For example, in-line skates gained instant attention, because walkers, runners, and bikers saw bladers (see Exhibit 9.10) zip by them on bike and jogging paths. The microwave was moderately observable. Only close friends and acquaintances who visited someone's home could see whether the household had a microwave. Although marketers can't do much about the observability of new products—consumers are likely to keep their mattresses away from public viewing no matter what marketers do—they do recognize that marketing strategies for new products that are not observable face difficult challenges. They must develop a marketing mix that convinces consumers to invest in the product, even though no one else will know.

Organizational Differences Affect Adoption

Just as there are differences among consumers in their eagerness to adopt new products, businesses and other organizations are not alike in their willingness to buy and use new industrial products.[23] Firms that welcome product innovations are likely to be younger companies, in highly technical industries, with younger managers and entrepreneurial corporate cultures. Early adopter firms are likely to be market-share leaders that adopt new innovations and try new ways of doing things to maintain their leadership. Firms that adopt new products only when they recognize they must innovate to keep up are in the early majority. Late majority firms tend to be oriented toward the status quo and often have large financial investments in existing production technology. Laggard firms are probably already losing money.

Exhibit 9.10

The observability of in-line skating helped to increase the rate of adoption of in-line skates.

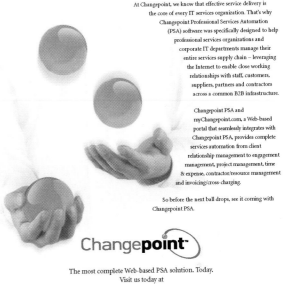
Business-to-business products, like consumer products, can possess characteristics that will increase their likelihood of adoption. Organizations are likely to adopt an innovation that helps them increase gross margins and profits. It is unlikely that firms would have adopted new products like voice mail unless they provided a way to increase profits by reducing labour costs. Organizational innovations are attractive when they are consistent with a firm's ways of doing business. Cost is also a factor in the new products firms will adopt. Firms are more likely to accept a new product if they perceive the improvement to be large in relation to the investment they will have to make. Changepoint Corporation of Ontario (see Exhibit 9.11), for instance, determined that their Professional Services Automation Software, which helps businesses manage their information technology activities, provides customers with a positive return on their investment after only 19 days of using it. Providing this proof of effectiveness allowed the company to gain even more widespread adoption of their product among business customers.

Real People, Real Decisions
How it worked out at Roots

Marshall Myles and the team at Roots decided to go with Option 2. A new retail product, Roots Kids, was launched with the opening of four Roots Kids stores across the country. The stores featured a new, expanded line of Roots Kids clothing and an interactive, entertainment-style retail environment that included the use of fibre optics in the front windows to attract attention to the new retail format. Bright colours and animal characters—frogs, snails, and turtles—were used in the decor of the

stores, along with the wood characteristic of other Roots retail outlets. Given the success of the new stores, Roots has plans to open several other Roots Kids stores over the next five years.

Chapter Summary

1. Explain the layers of a product.

   A product may be anything tangible or intangible that satisfies consumer or business-to-business customer needs. Products include goods, services, ideas, people, and places. The core product is the basic product category benefits and customized benefit(s) the product provides. The actual product is the physical good or delivered service, including the packaging and brand name. The augmented product includes both the actual product and any supplementary services, such as warranty, credit, delivery, and installation.

2. Describe the classifications of products.

   Marketers generally classify goods and services as either consumer or business-to-business products. They further classify consumer products according to how long they last and by how they are purchased. *Durable goods* provide benefits for months or years, whereas *nondurable goods* are used up quickly or are useful for only a short time. Consumers purchase *convenience products* frequently with little effort. Customers carefully gather information and compare different brands on their attributes and prices before buying *shopping products. Specialty products* have unique characteristics and are important to the buyer. Customers have little interest in *unsought products* until a need arises. Business products are for commercial uses by organizations. Marketers classify business products according to how they are used—equipment, maintenance, repair, and operating (MRO) products, raw and processed materials, component parts, and business services.

3. Explain the importance of new products.

   Innovations are anything consumers perceive to be new. Understanding new products is important to companies because of the fast pace of technological advancement, the high cost to companies for developing new products, and the contributions to society that new products can make. Marketers classify innovations by their degree of newness. A *continuous innovation* is a modification of an existing product, a *dynamically continuous innovation* provides a greater change in a product, and a *discontinuous innovation* is a new product that creates major changes in people's lives.

4. Describe how firms develop new products.

   New product development includes a visionary phase and a planning and development phase followed by testing and improvement. In the visionary phase, marketers generate new product ideas, assess their potential technical and commercial success, and conduct a business analysis to estimate the profitability of the new product. Planning and development includes developing a marketing program, planning how the product will be manufactured, and possibly obtaining a patent. The effectiveness of the new product may then be assessed in an actual or a simulated test market. Finally, the product is launched, and the entire marketing plan is implemented.

5. Explain the process of product adoption and the diffusion of innovations.

   Product adoption is the process by which an individual begins to buy and use a new product, whereas the diffusion of innovations is how a new product spreads throughout a population. The stages in the adoption process are awareness, interest, trial, adoption, and confirmation. To better understand the diffusion process, marketers classify consumers according to their readiness to adopt new products as innovators, early adopters, early majority, late majority, and laggards.

   Five product characteristics that have an important effect on how quickly (or if) a new product will be adopted by consumers are relative advantage, compatibility, product complexity, trialability, and observability. Similar to individual consumers, organizations differ in their readiness to adopt new products based on characteristics of the organization, its management, and characteristics of the innovation.

Chapter Review

Marketing Concepts: Testing Your Knowledge

1. What is a product?

2. What is meant by the core product, the actual product, and the augmented product?

3. List and give examples of the different classifications of consumer products.

4. What types of products are bought and sold in business-to-business markets?

5. What is a new product? Why is understanding new products so important to marketers?

6. List and explain the steps in developing new products.

7. Explain the different types of innovations based on their degree of newness.

8. List and explain the stages in an individual's adoption of an innovation.

9. List and explain the categories of adopters.

10. Describe the product factors that affect the speed of adoption.

Marketing Concepts: Discussing Choices and Issues

1. This chapter discussed the core product, actual product, and augmented product. Does this mean that marketers are simply trying to make products that are really the same seem different? When marketers understand these three layers of the product and develop products with this concept in mind, what are the benefits to consumers? What are the hazards of this type of thinking?

2. The phrase "new and improved" has been used so many times that, for many people, it is meaningless. Why has this occurred? What challenge does this present to marketers?

3. Discontinuous innovations are totally new products—something seldom seen in the marketplace. What are some examples of discontinuous innovations introduced in the past 50 years? What do you think the future holds for new products?

4. This chapter explained that knock-offs are slightly modified copies of original product designs. Should knock-offs be illegal? Who is hurt by knock-offs? Is the marketing of knock-offs good or bad for consumers in the short run? In the long run?

5. It is not necessarily true that all new products benefit consumers or society. What are some new products that have made our lives better? What are some new products that have actually been harmful to consumers or to society? Should there be a way to monitor new products that are introduced to the marketplace?

Marketing Practice: Applying What You've Learned

1. Assume that you have recently been hired by a firm that markets a new low-calorie, fat-free chocolate candy bar. Because of your knowledge of new product adoption, you know that consumers go through a series of stages in adopting a new product—awareness, interest, and so on. You also realize that it is important for marketers to "help" customers move from one stage to the next. Develop your recommendations for marketing activities that would be appropriate for each stage in the adoption process.

2. As a member of a new product team with your company, you are working with engineers in developing the world's first practical, battery-powered automobile. You know that different product characteristics (relative advantage, compatibility, and so on) influence the speed of adoption of the product. Considering such product characteristics, make a list of suggestions for the engineers (or for the marketing department) that will speed the adoption of the new product when it is introduced.

3. Assume that you are employed in the marketing department of the firm in the preceding example. In developing this product, you realize that it is important to provide a core product, actual product, and augmented product that meets the needs of customers. Develop an outline of how your firm might provide these three product layers in the battery-powered car.

4. Firms go to great lengths to develop new product ideas. Sometimes new ideas come from brainstorming, in which groups of individuals get together and try to think of as many different, novel, creative—and hopefully profitable—ideas for a new product as possible. With

a group of other students, participate in brainstorming for new product ideas for one of the following (or some other product of your choice).

a. an exercise machine

b. computer software

c. a new type of college or university

Then, with your class, screen one or more of the ideas for possible further product development.

Marketing Mini-Project: **Learning by Doing**

What product characteristics do consumers think are important in a new product? What types of service components do they demand? And most important, how do marketers know how to develop successful new products? This mini-project is designed to let you experience making some of these decisions.

1. Create (in your mind) a new product item that might be of interest to students like yourself. Develop a written description and possibly a drawing of this new product.

2. Show this new product description to a number of your fellow students who might be potential users of the product. Ask them to tell you what they think of the product. Some of the questions you might ask them are:

   a. What is your overall opinion of the new product?

   b. What basic benefits would you expect to receive from the product?

   c. What about the physical characteristics of the product? What do you like? Dislike? What would you add? Delete? Change?

   d. What do you like (or would you like) in the way of product packaging?

   e. What sort of services would you expect to receive with the product?

   f. Do you think you would try the product? How could marketers influence you to buy the product?

3. Develop a report based on what you found. Include your recommendations for changes in the product and your feelings about the potential success of the new product.

Real People, Real Surfers: **Exploring the Web**

Visit the Web site for three fashion retailers: Roots (www.roots.com), the Gap (www.gap.com), and Le Chateau (www.lechateau.ca). After you have visited the company Web sites, explore the Internet for additional information on each firm. Based on your experience on the Internet, answer the following questions:

1. Describe the number and variety of consumer and business-to-business products each company produces. Based on the classifications of products listed in the chapter, how would you classify these products?

2. Is an emphasis on product development evident in the description of the companies from their Web sites?

3. Does the Web site provide opportunities for consumers to purchase products? To provide input about existing products? To offer new product ideas?

4. What can you find out about each firm's new product development process? How does the process lead to extraordinary new products?

5. What is your evaluation of each Web site? Does the Web site focus more on the company's products or on some other aspect of the company? Does it provide easy access to important information about the company's products? What visitors would be attracted to the Web site? Is the Web site designed in such a way to encourage visitors to return again and again to the site?

MARKETING IN ACTION

Microsoft Xbox

The 2001 North American launch of the Microsoft Xbox was one of the most successful product launches in the history of the video game industry, with 1.5 million units sold in the month and a half following the launch. The Canadian launch, directed by Ryan Mugford, marketing manager of Xbox Canada, used a mixture of traditional advertising and grassroots marketing activities to target Canadian gamers. With the successful launch behind them, sustaining the sales momentum and increasing the adoption and diffusion of their game system are now the key marketing objectives for the Canadian Xbox team.

Microsoft has positioned Xbox as "the future of gaming," a theme that was featured in advertising that preceded the launch and was shown on MuchMusic. A Microsoft press release claims that the Xbox "empowers game artists by giving them the technology to fulfill their creative visions as never before...." One of the key product features that differentiates the Xbox is the ability to play games online.

The Xbox faces intense competition from established game producers Sony and Nintendo. Sony holds 61% of the market in North America. While the Nintendo GameCube is priced at $299, the more technologically powerful games produced by Sony and Microsoft sell for at least $150 more, reflecting their different target market. Sony and Microsoft are going after the 17- to 24-year-old hard core gaming segment. But, although Microsoft claims technological superiority, it can't match Sony in game availability, at least in the short run. Sony has over 1000 games available, while Microsoft launched Xbox with well under 50 titles.

To better understand gamers and their needs, Microsoft conducted over 1600 focus groups worldwide, and in Canada conducts continuous research with English and French speaking gamers. According to Mugford, the objective of researching gamers is to find out about their attitudes, habits and lives generally, not just their attitudes toward gaming.

The Canadian launch plan built on many of the insights from research. For example, knowing that many gamers are also avid music fans, one tactic was to launch a CD, "Xbox Soundtrack One," as a retail promotion to highlight an Xbox feature that allows music to be downloaded to replace existing game music. The CD features Canadian acts such as rock band Shocore and was so successful in Canada that it was adopted by other Microsoft divisions internationally.

The Xbox tour bus was part of the grassroots marketing approach used during the Canadian launch. The bus travelled across the country outfitted with 15 game consoles connected to the Internet and visited retail stores. Microsoft also developed a campus program following the model of beer reps, by introducing "game reps" who held Microsoft events and contests, such as the search for the ultimate gamer, at campuses across Canada on an ongoing basis.

Finally, to reach gamers online during the product launch and beyond, Microsoft launched the Xbox site (www.xbox.com) that, in addition to providing marketing information, offers an online community for Xbox adopters to discuss gaming strategies.

Sources: Chris Daniels, "Xbox's inner workings," *Marketing Magazine*, 19 November 2001; "Prophet heralds Xbox campaign," *Marketing Magazine*, 17 September 2001; Microsoft Press Release, "Xbox launch one of most successful in video game history," 8 January 2002; "Microsoft Canada celebrates the Xbox launch with several bashes across the country," *XboxWeb.com*, 13 November 2001; Kristopher Abel, "How the Xbox learned to be a Canadian console—a discussion with Ryan Mugford," www.gg8.com/news.

THINGS TO THINK ABOUT

1. Describe the core, actual and augmented layers of the Xbox product.
2. What type of innovation (continuous, dynamically continuous or discontinuous) is the Xbox? What implications does this have for the future marketing of Xbox?
3. Using the five characteristics that affect a product's rate of adoption, are there any factors that will act as barriers to the adoption of Xbox? What marketing activities can Microsoft engage in to overcome these barriers?
4. How can Microsoft best market the Xbox to the various categories of adopters?

INTRODUCING
"THE CHEF'S CADDY"™

THE PERFECT WAY TO STORE, CARRY AND USE YOUR IRREPLACEABLE TOOLS.

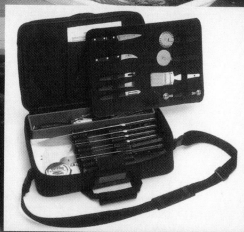

10

Managing the Product

CHAPTER OBJECTIVES

1. Explain the different product objectives and strategies a firm may choose.

2. Explain how firms manage products throughout the product life cycle.

3. Discuss how branding creates product identity and describe different types of branding strategies.

4. Explain the roles packaging and labelling play in developing effective product strategies.

5. Describe how organizations are structured for new and existing product management.

Real People, Real Decisions
Meet Mary Louise Huebner
A Decision Maker at Canada Cutlery Inc.

Mary Louise Huebner is co-owner and vice-president of marketing at Canada Cutlery Inc. (www.canadacutlery. com). A supplier of high-quality, professional knives, cooking tools, and other cutlery primarily to chefs in the restaurant and hotel industries, the Scarborough, Ontario-based company began operations in 1954, importing quality European cutlery into the Canadian market. In 1993, Canada Cutlery expanded into the United States with its product line. Currently, 70% of the company's sales are through food service distributors in Canada, and 30% of the sales come through distributors in the US.

Before joining Canada Cutlery, Huebner, who has an honours BBA from Wilfrid Laurier University, held marketing positions at several packaged goods companies, including Colgate-Palmolive and Campbell Soup, and worked in advertising at the Leo Burnett advertising agency. In addition to her duties at Canada Cutlery, Huebner is a marketing instructor at Seneca College in Toronto.

Sources: Personal interview with Mary Louise Huebner, Canada Cutlery literature, and Web site at www.canadacutlery.com.

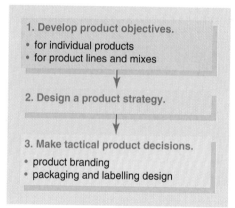

1. Develop product objectives.
- for individual products
- for product lines and mixes

2. Design a product strategy.

3. Make tactical product decisions.
- product branding
- packaging and labelling design

Figure 10.1 Steps in Managing Products

Creating and Nurturing Quality Products

What makes one product fail and another enjoy great success? It's worth repeating what we said in Chapter 2: Firms that plan well succeed. Product planning plays a big role in the firm's *tactical marketing plans*. The strategies outlined in the product plan tell how the firm expects to develop a product that will meet marketing objectives. In Chapter 9, we discussed what a product really is and how new products are developed and introduced into the marketplace. In this chapter, we'll finish the product part of the story by discussing how companies like Canada Cutlery manage products and examine the steps in product planning (see Figure 10.1). This will include developing product objectives and the strategies required to successfully market products as they evolve over time. We'll also discuss branding and packaging, two of the more important tactical decisions product planners make, and examine how firms organize for effective product management.

Using Product Objectives to Decide on a Product Strategy

When marketers develop product strategies, they are making decisions about product benefits, features, styling, branding, labelling, and packaging. But what do they want to accomplish? Clearly-stated product objectives provide focus and direction. Product objectives should support the broader marketing objectives of the business unit in addition to supporting the overall mission of the firm. For example, if the objectives of the firm focus on return on investment, its marketing objectives may then focus on market share and/or unit or dollar sales volume necessary for the firm to attain that return on investment. Product objectives need to specify how product decisions will support or contribute to reaching a desired market share or level of sales.

To be effective, product-related objectives must be measurable, clear and unambiguous, and feasible, and must specify a time frame. Consider, for example, how a frozen-entrée manufacturer might state its product objectives:

- "In the upcoming fiscal year, modify the product's fat content to reflect the trend toward low fat foods."

- "Introduce three new items to the product line to take advantage of increased consumer interest in ethnic foods."

- "During the coming fiscal year, improve the chicken entrées to the extent that consumers will rate them better tasting than the competition."

Planners must keep in touch with consumers or business customers, so that their objectives accurately respond to customer needs. Equally important in developing product objectives is an up-to-date knowledge of competitive product innovations. Above all, product objectives should consider the *long-term implications* of product decisions. Planners who sacrifice the long-term health of the organization to reach short-term sales or financial goals are being irresponsible. Product planners may focus on one or more individual products at a time, or they may look at a group of product offerings as a whole. In this section, we examine these different strategies. We also look at one important product objective: product quality.

Objectives and Strategies for Individual Products

The Volkswagen Beetle is an interesting story of a product that triumphed over great obstacles. When the product was first introduced in North America in the 1960s, dealers complained that the car was too ugly to sell. Many of those dealers were soon kicking themselves; dealers who did accept the challenge sold over 21 million Beetles to true believers who adored the car's simple engineering and funky image. The Beetle was a tremendously successful product in the 1960s and '70s despite its poor image. In the late 1990s, Volkswagen decided to capitalize on baby boomers' warm memories of the Beetle by introducing a "concept car" model reminiscent of the original (see Exhibit 10.1). Volkswagen's product strategy worked again. In the first months that the new Beetles were on the market, dealers couldn't keep enough on their lots to satisfy nostalgic customers. Sales of the new Beetle continue to be strong in Canada, and marketers of other products ranging from pop to condos are trying to capitalize on the Beetle success by using the car as a prize in their own promotions.[1]

Volkswagen
www.volkswagen.com

Exhibit 10.1

Volkswagen created customer excitement with its new Beetle.

Some product strategies, including those used in introducing the new VW Beetle, focus on a single new product. However, strategies for individual products may be quite different for new products, for regional products, and for mature products.

For new products, the objectives relate to successful *introduction*. Warner-Lambert Canada worked hard to introduce Dentyne Ice gum to youth across Canada in 2000.[2] After a firm has experienced considerable success with a product in a local or regional market, however, it may consider it time to grow the business by introducing the product nationally. Big Rock Brewery, a Calgary microbrewery, used their success in the Alberta beer market to introduce their beer into Ontario and British Columbia.[3]

For mature products, product objectives may focus on breathing new life into a product long taken for granted while holding onto the traditional brand personality. In the case of Habitant soups, for instance, the positioning of the soup as homemade, wholesome, and traditionally Canadian has been maintained over the more than 60 years that the brand has been selling. However the soup's packaging has been changed, most recently in the late 1990s, to update the image of the soup and attract new users.[4]

Objectives and Strategies for Multiple Products

Although a small firm might focus on one product, a larger company usually markets a set of related products. This means that some strategic decisions affect two or more products at once. Thus, the firm must think in terms of its entire *portfolio* of products (see Chapter 2). Product planning means developing *product line* and *product mix* strategies that encompass multiple offerings. Figure 10.2 illustrates these concepts, using some Procter & Gamble products as examples.

PRODUCT LINE STRATEGIES

A **product line** is a firm's total product offering designed to satisfy a single need or desire of a group of target customers. For example, Procter & Gamble's line of fabric and home-care products includes four different types of laundry soap: Tide, Cheer, Gain, and Ivory Snow.

Procter & Gamble
www.pg.com

❋ ❋ ❋
product line A firm's total product offering designed to satisfy a single need or desire of target customers.

←	Width of Product Mix			→
Paper Products	**Fabric and Home-Care Products**	**Health Care Products**	**Beauty Care Products**	**Food and Beverage Products**
Pampers	Bounce	Metamucil	Cover Girl	Crisco
Always	Cascade	Pepto Bismol	Max Factor	Folgers
Tampax	Ivory Liquid	Crest	Old Spice	Pringles
Bounty	Downy	Scope	Secret	Sunny Delight
Royale	Swiffer	Vicks	Head & Shoulders	Jif
	Mr. Clean		Pantene	
	COMET		Pert	
	Spic and Span		Vidal Sassoon	
	Tide		Camay	
	Cheer		Clearasil	
	Gain		Noxema	
	Ivory Snow		Coast	
	Dryel		Ivory soap	
	Febreze		Zest	
			Oil of Olay	

(Length of Product Line — vertical axis label)

Figure 10.2 Product Line Length and Product Mix Width

Exhibit 10.2

Bombardier added the Traxter ATV to its recreational product line, which already included Ski-Doo and Sea-Doo.

To do an even better job of meeting varying consumer needs, each of the brands comes in several different formulations. For example, in addition to regular Tide, there is Tide with bleach and Ultra Tide. The number of separate items offered within the same category determines the length of the product line

When a firm has a large number of variations in its product line, it is said to carry a *full line*. With a full-line strategy, it is possible to please many customer segments, thus increasing total sales potential. A company that adopts a *limited-line strategy* markets a smaller number of product variations. Sometimes, having a limited product line can improve the image of a firm, because it is perceived to be a specialist and has a clear, specific position in the market. Rolls-Royce motor cars, for example, makes only expensive, custom-built automobiles and, for years, has maintained a unique position in the automobile industry.

In developing product strategies, organizations may decide to extend their product lines by adding more brands or models. As we saw in Chapter 9, Roots extended their product line by adding children's clothing. Bombardier Inc., the manufacturer of Sea-Doos and Ski-Doos, recently extended their recreational product line with the introduction of their ATV Traxter (see Exhibit 10.2).

Bombardier Inc.
www.bombardier.com

When a company stretches its product line, it must decide on the best direction in which to go. If a firm's current product line includes middle- and lower-end items, an *upward line stretch* would add new items—those with a higher price, better quality, or more features. Folgers and Maxwell House took this route by adding such new coffee varieties as Gourmet Supreme, Columbian Supreme, French Roast, and Italian Espresso Roast.

Conversely, a *downward line stretch* completes a line by adding items at the lower end. Here the firm must be careful that the lower-end items don't blur the images of higher-priced, upper-end offerings. A firm like Godiva may not want to run the risk of cheapening its image, for example, by creating a new, less expensive chocolate bar to compete with products like Mr. Big and Sweet Marie.

In some cases, a firm may decide that its existing product line is meeting the needs of only a small portion of the market and that there is more than one opportunity for growth. Then the product strategy may call for a *two-way stretch*, that is, adding items at both the upper and lower ends. Marriott Hotels, for example, has added Fairfield Inns and Courtyard at the lower end and Marriott Marquis Hotels at the upper end.

A *filling-out* strategy may mean adding sizes or styles not previously available in a product category. Quebec's Lassonde did this when it was the first juice company in North America to use aseptic plastic bottles for its Fruite drinks. It also introduced the first refrigerated vegetable juice in North America, Vegetable Delight.[5] Sometimes the best strategy may be to *contract a product line*, particularly when some of the items are not profitable. For example, when sales for the once-popular Chevrolet Chevelle slowed in the 1980s, Chevrolet dropped the mid-size car from its line.

As we have seen, there are many ways a firm can modify its product line to meet the competition or take advantage of new opportunities in the marketplace. To further explore these strategic decisions, we return to Procter & Gamble. What does P&G do if the objective is to increase market share in the fabric-care market? One possibility would be to expand its line of laundry detergents. If the line extension meets a perceived consumer need not being addressed currently, this would be a good strategic move. But, whenever a product line or a product family is extended, there is the danger of **cannibalization**, which occurs when sales of an existing brand are eaten up by the new item, as the firm's current customers switch to the new product. This explains why P&G has created a whole new product line with its Dryel product to achieve growth in fabric care. The Dryel product (see Exhibit 10.3) is not cannibalizing sales from detergents such as Tide and Ivory Snow.[6]

PRODUCT MIX STRATEGIES

Product planning can go beyond a single product item or a product line to entire groups of products. A firm's **product mix** is its entire range of products. For example, in addition to a deep line of shaving products, Gillette makes toiletries such as Dry Idea and Right Guard deodorant, Paper Mate and Flair writing instruments, Oral B toothbrushes, Braun small appliances, and Duracelle batteries.

In developing a product mix strategy, planners usually consider the *width of the product mix,* the number of product lines produced by the firm. By developing several different product lines, firms can reduce the risk associated with "putting all their eggs in one basket." Normally, firms develop a mix of product lines that have some similarities, for example, products that can share distribution channels or manufacturing facilities. Sometimes, firms expand into new product lines to take advantage of a strong brand reputation with an existing target market. Above all, the planners should consider the wants and needs of customers. Because a firm is successful with one product is no guarantee people will buy just anything it puts on the market.

Quality as a Product Objective

More often, product objectives focus on product quality, the overall ability of the product to satisfy customers' expectations and to provide the benefits they seek. Quality is tied to how customers *think* a product will perform and not necessarily to some technological level of perfection. Product quality objectives coincide with marketing objectives for higher sales and market share and to the organization's objectives for increased profits.

As we saw in Chapter 3, quality depends on the product being evaluated. In some cases, product quality may mean:

- durability: Athletic shoes can't develop holes after their owner runs in them for only a few weeks.
- reliability: Maytag has established this important aspect of product quality with its lonely repairman.

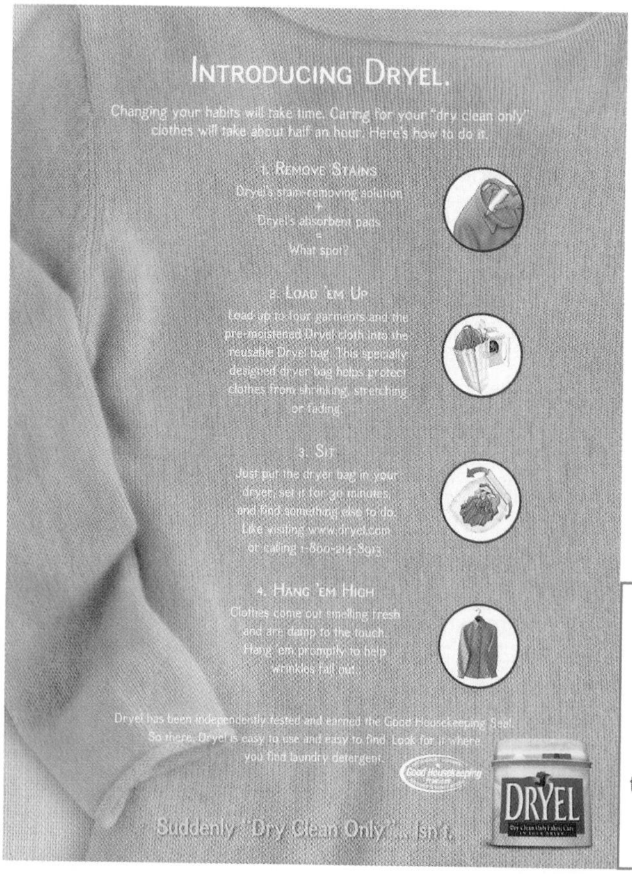

* * *

cannibalization The loss of sales of an existing product when a new item in a product line or product family is introduced.

* * *

product mix The total set of all products a firm offers for sale.

INTRODUCING DRYEL.

Changing your habits will take time. Caring for your "dry clean only" clothes will take about half an hour. Here's how to do it.

1. REMOVE STAINS

2. LOAD 'EM UP

3. SIT

4. HANG 'EM HIGH

Suddenly "Dry Clean Only"... Isn't.

DRYEL

Exhibit 10.3

By introducing a new product line with Dryel, Procter & Gamble was able to meet new customer demands and avoid cannibalizing laundry detergent brands.

- precision: High-tech audio equipment promises clearer music reproduction with less distortion.
- versatility: Some toothpastes satisfy different needs, offering cavity protection and fresh breath.
- ease of use, maintenance, and repair: This is especially important in business-to-business products.
- product safety: Volvo cars have a strong reputation for safety.
- degree of aesthetic pleasure they provide: The quality of products such as a painting, a movie, or even a wedding gown relates to this. Evaluations of aesthetic quality differ dramatically between people—to one person, high-quality television may mean *Masterpiece Theatre*, while to another, it's *South Park*.

Marketing planners often focus product objectives on one or both of two key aspects of quality: level and consistency. Customers often determine the *level of quality* of a product by comparing it with other brands in the same product category. A handcrafted Rolls-Royce boasts higher quality than an assembly-line Toyota Celica, but this may be irrelevant to Celica buyers who are more inclined to compare their sports car to a Mazda Miata than to an elite luxury car.

Consistency of quality means that customers receive the same level of quality in a product time after time. This is also a strong guarantee of repeat business and free word-of-mouth advertising for the producer that is able to deliver on this promise. Consistent quality is also one of the major benefits of organizations adopting total quality management practices. Consumer perceptions can change overnight with a single instance of inconsistent product quality. Ask anybody who has ever bought a new car that turned out to be a lemon: Most would be willing to walk before they would consider buying the same make or model again.

Marketing Throughout the Product Life Cycle

The zipper, a Canadian invention, is an example of a humble, low-tech product that has managed to live an exceptionally long life. Although the zipper was invented in the 1800s, it was not used in men's clothing until the 1930s. These "hookless fasteners," as they were once called, were originally intended for use on high buttoned shoes. It took time for them to be used in men's trousers, because competitors argued that this "newfangled gadget" could result in serious injuries. In 1936, the Prince of Wales adopted the zipper and was the first monarch to "sit on a throne bezippered."

Like the zipper, many products have very long lives. The **product life cycle** is a useful way to look at how product features change over the life of a product. In Chapter 9, we discussed how marketers introduce new products; but launching a product is only the beginning. Product marketing strategies must evolve as they continue through the product life cycle.

The concept of the product life cycle does not relate to a single brand but to the generic product. Thus, we talk about the life cycle of personal computers, not Compaq computers, of automobiles, not the Focus. Some individual brands have short life expectancies: Who remembers the Bricklin car or Evening in Paris perfume? Others seem almost immortal: A Boston Consulting Group study found that 27 of 30 brands that were number one in 1930 are still number one today—these include Ivory soap and Campbell's soup.[7]

✳ ✳ ✳
product life cycle Concept that explains how products go through four distinct stages from birth to death: introduction, growth, maturity, and decline.

The Introduction Stage

We can divide the life of a product into four separate stages. The first stage of the product life cycle, shown in Figure 10.3, is **introduction**—customers get their first chance to purchase the good or service. During this early stage, a single company usually produces the product. If the product is accepted and profitable, competitors will follow with their own versions.

During the introduction stage, the goal is to get first-time buyers to try the product. Sales (hopefully) increase at a steady but slow pace. Evident in Figure 10.3, the company does not make a profit during this stage, due to research and development (R&D) costs and heavy spending for advertising and other promotion.

✳ ✳ ✳
introduction The first stage of the product life cycle, in which slow growth follows the introduction of a new product in the marketplace.

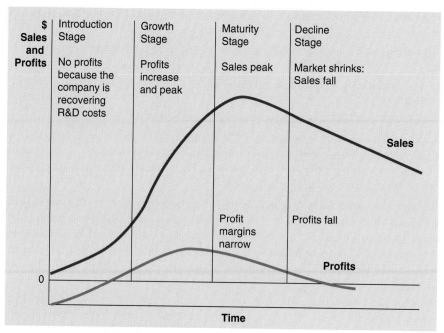

Figure 10.3 The Product Life Cycle

Pricing may be high to recover the R&D costs (demand permitting) or low to attract large numbers of consumers. The Samsung DVD player, shown in Exhibit 10.4, has a suggested retail price that is about double that of Samsung's VCRs and is designed to appeal to consumers who are willing to pay for the latest technological advances. The high cost helps Samsung recover its R&D costs.

Exhibit 10.4

Samsung DVD players are targeted at consumers who are willing to pay for the latest innovations.

For a new product to be successful, consumers must first know about it and believe that it is something they need. Thus, marketing during the introduction stage often focuses on informing consumers about the product, how to use it, and its benefits.

How long does the introduction stage last? As we saw in the Chapter 9 microwave oven example, it can be several years. How long the introduction stage lasts depends on a number of factors, including marketplace acceptance and producer willingness to support the product during its start-up. In the case of the microwave, sales in countries such as Japan were much stronger, because the companies supported the product through its long introduction stage.

Not all products make it past the introduction stage. In fact, the failure rate for new products has been cited to be as high as 90%.[8] One of the most noted examples of products that never got past the introduction stage is the Ford Edsel automobile. Introduced in 1957 and named after the only son of Ford's founder, the Edsel was designed to compete with such cars as the Chrysler New Yorker. It boasted high horsepower, tail fins, three-tone paint jobs, wraparound windshields, a "horse-collar" grille, and a push-button gearshift. The problem was that consumers didn't like the Edsel. Only 110 847 Edsels were made before Ford abandoned the car, making the word *Edsel* synonymous with product failure.[9]

The Growth Stage

The second stage in the product life cycle, the **growth stage**, sees a rapid increase in sales while profits increase and peak. Marketing's goal here is to encourage brand loyalty by convincing the market that this brand is superior to others in the category. In this stage, marketing strategies may include the introduction of product variations to attract market segments and grow market share. When competitors appear, marketers must use heavy advertising and other types of promotion. Price competition may develop, driving profits down. Some firms may seek to capture a particular segment of the market by positioning their product to appeal to a certain group.

***

growth stage The second stage in the product life cycle, during which the product is accepted and sales rapidly increase.

The Maturity Stage

The **maturity stage** of the product life cycle is usually the longest. Sales peak and then begin to level off and even decline while profit margins narrow. Competition grows intense when remaining competitors fight for a piece of a shrinking pie. Because most customers have already accepted the product, sales are often to replace a worn-out item or to take advantage of product improvements. For example, almost everyone owns a television, so companies typically sell new TVs to consumers whose sets have broken down. During the maturity stage, firms try to sell their product through all suitable retailers, because product availability is crucial in a very competitive market. Consumers will not go far to find one brand when others are closer at hand.

To remain competitive and maintain market share during the maturity stage, firms may tinker with the marketing mix, coming out with new versions of the product that include new features. For example, television manufacturers are hoping to invigorate sales with flat-screen TVs. Warner-Lambert Canada introduced Listerine oral care strips, the first product extension of Listerine mouthwash (see Exhibit 10.5). The strips offer the same breath

***

maturity stage The third and longest stage in the product life cycle, in which sales peak and profit margins narrow.

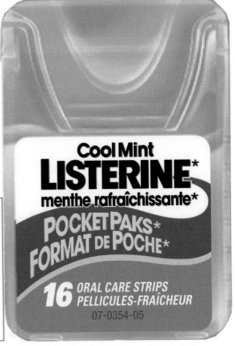

Exhibit 10.5

By introducing Listerine in a new format to meet customer needs for convenience, Warner-Lambert Canada gave a mature product new life.

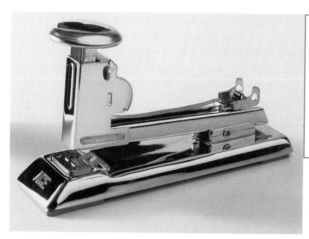

Exhibit 10.6

The venerable Pilot stapler may be in decline, but it's not dead. Loyal fans have kept this niche product on the market.

freshening benefit of the original Listerine, but are small and dissolve in the mouth, thereby making the Listerine product portable and offering consumers a new benefit.[10]

Attracting new users of the product is another strategy used in the maturity stage. Market development, as discussed in Chapter 2, means introducing an existing product to a market that doesn't currently use it. Many Canadian firms are finding new markets for their products in countries around the world. To find new users for their products, firms in the Canadian wine industry, for example, have been actively pursuing markets in Pacific Rim countries such as Korea and China.

The Decline Stage

✳ ✳ ✳

decline stage The final stage in the product life cycle, in which sales decrease as customer needs change.

The **decline stage** of the product life cycle is characterized by a decrease in product category sales. This is often because new technology has made the product obsolete, as when computers caused the decline of the typewriter. Although a single firm may still be profitable, the market as a whole begins to shrink, profits decline, and suppliers pull out. In this stage, there are usually many competitors with no one having a distinct advantage.

A firm's major product decision in the decline stage is whether to keep the product. Once the product is no longer profitable, it drains resources from the firm—resources that could help develop newer products. If the decision is to drop the product, elimination can be handled in two ways: Phase it out by cutting production in stages and letting existing stocks run out, or drop the product immediately. If the established market leader anticipates that there will be some residual demand for the product for a long time, it may make sense to keep the product on the market. The idea is to sell a limited quantity of the product with little or no support from sales, merchandising, advertising, and distribution, and let it "wither on the vine." Some classic products have been able to hang on with little or no marketing support. For example, the Pilot stapler (see Exhibit 10.6) has been on the market for over 70 years: Despite sleeker and less costly competitors, the Pilot maintains its reputation as *the* heavy-duty stapler.[11]

Creating Product Identity: Branding Decisions

Knowing the stage of their product in the product life cycle helps marketers successfully manage the product. Equally important is giving that product an identity: Branding is an extremely important (and expensive) element of product strategies. In this section, we examine what a brand is and how certain laws protect brands. And we discuss the importance of branding and how firms make branding decisions.

What's in a Name (or a Symbol)?

How do you identify your favourite brand? By its name? By the logo (how the name appears)? By the packaging? By some graphic image or symbol, such as Canadian Tire's red

SPOTLIGHT ON REAL PEOPLE *The Body Blocker Company*

Lila Lewandoski and Shashi Behl decided, while studying together at the University of Saskatchewan, that they wanted to be business partners. They now operate The Body Blocker Group, a company that makes and sells UV-protective clothing for kids and adults. The idea for their clothes came from Lewandoski's concern about sun damage to her skin after working for many summers as a lifeguard. After researching the physics of ultraviolet rays and checking out the other manufacturers of UV-protective clothing, the pair developed a business plan, including the product strategy for the company. Their business plan was so strong that it won an award from the Canadian Youth Business Foundation and secured a business loan, which allowed them to develop a prototype for their clothing: a high-necked, knee- and elbow-length, one-piece suit for children.

To test their product, Lewandoski and Behl did "market research" for an entire summer at a wading pool in Calgary by talking with parents and allowing kids to try on the suits. They studied the response to the suits and found out that kids did not like the high neck and that people wanted a sportier, more colourful suit. With the results of this research, Behl and Lewandoski revised the product in line with the quality objectives of their company. Behl describes the overall product quality objective of the company this way: "We aim to create tough, long-lasting clothes."

The two entrepreneurs have worked with a fashion designer to refine their product line even further. Now they have kids' suits available in purple or blue with stripes in multiple colours. They have also added other products to their line—shirts, hats, skirts, and sarongs for adults; hats and dresses for kids. Their product mix has also been expanded to include sunscreen products and a laundry product for swimsuits.[12]

1. In what stage of the product life cycle is UV-protective clothing?
2. Visit The Body Blocker Web site. Would you say that the entrepreneurs are creating a unique brand identity for their product on the Web site? What suggestions would you make for the development of an even stronger brand identity?
3. What are some other potential product line and product mix expansion strategies for The Body Blocker company?

The Body Blocker
www.bodyblocker.com

✳ ✳ ✳
brand A name, term, symbol, or any other unique element of a product, which identifies one firm's product(s) and sets them apart from the competition.

triangle and green maple leaf? A **brand** is a name, term, symbol, or any other unique element of a product, which identifies one firm's product(s) and sets it apart from the competition. Consumers easily recognize the Coca Cola logo, the pink Energizer bunny (a *trade character*), and the triangular blue Nabisco logo (a *brand mark*) in the corner of the box. Branding provides the recognition factor products need to succeed in regional, national, or international markets.

CHOOSING A BRAND NAME, MARK, OR CHARACTER

There are several important considerations in selecting a brand name, brand mark, or trade character. It must have a positive connotation and be memorable. Consider Toro's experience when it introduced a lightweight snow thrower called the "Snow Pup." Sales were disappointing, because "pup" conveyed a small, cuddly animal, not a desirable image for a snow thrower. Renamed the "Snow Master," its sales went up markedly.[13]

A brand name is probably the most used and most recognized form of branding. Kool-Aid, a word that most kids know, has been used to maintain a long-term relationship with consumers. Kool-Aid now markets iced tea versions of its beverages to appeal to adult tastes (see Exhibit 10.7).

A good brand name can position a product by conveying a certain image or personality (Molson Canadian) or describing how it works (Drano), or else it may be ambiguous, such as Exxon, Ajax, and Lotus. Brand names sometimes need to change over time. For example, Kentucky Fried Chicken became KFC when "fried" went out of style, the Canadian Imperial Bank of Commerce became CIBC to avoid the use of "imperial," and for similar reasons the Toronto Dominion bank became TD.[14] Changing a brand name isn't always the right strategy, though. The Hudson's Bay Company found out the importance of its brand name, which has been used in Canada for over 330 years, when it considered changing its

Exhibit 10.7

Kool-Aid has used its long-standing popularity with kids to make new iced tea products aimed at adults who drank Kool-Aid as kids.

✳ ✳ ✳

trademark The legal term for a brand name, brand mark, or trade character; a trademark legally registered by a government obtains protection for exclusive use in that country.

✳ ✳ ✳

family brand A brand that a group of individual products or individual brands share.

name to HBC in 1999. Consumer outcry against the new name was so intense that the company decided to stick with "The Bay." [15]

How does a firm select a good brand name? Good brand designers say there are four "easy" tests: *easy to say, easy to spell, easy to read,* and *easy to remember.* Consider P&G's Tide, Cheer, Gain, Downy, and Ivory Snow. And the name should also "fit" four ways: *fit the target market, fit the product's benefits, fit the customer's culture,* and *fit legal requirements.* When the Mutual Life Assurance Company of Canada decided to change its brand name in the late 1990s, it chose a very non-traditional name for the insurance market: Clarica. A multimillion-dollar advertising campaign supported the name change, but the name was criticized by many marketers for, among other things, sounding more like skin cleanser than an insurance company. Clarica responded with the humorous ad in Exhibit 10.8, which it hoped would further increase the awareness of its brand name.[16]

When it comes to graphics for a brand symbol, name, or logo, the rule is: it must be recognizable and memorable. No matter how small or how large, the triangular Nabisco logo in the corner of the box is a familiar sight. And it should have visual impact. This means that from across a store or when you are quickly flipping the pages in a magazine, the brand will catch your attention. One product that made the wrong kind of visual impact with its brand name was a snack product called HITS. It was only on the shelves for a short time, because the manufacturer realized that when the packages were put end to end on store shelves, the logos produced an unintended effect: HitsHitsHitsHitsHits.[17]

Some marketers enhance brand recognition by creating a *trade character,* such as the Pillsbury Dough Boy, the Jolly Green Giant, or Mr. Clean. A&W uses the Root Bear to strengthen brand recognition (see Exhibit 10.9).

TRADEMARKS

The legal term for a brand name, brand mark, or trade character is **trademark**. Marketers can legally register brands as trademarks to make their use by competitors illegal in Canada. However, it is possible for a firm to have protection for a brand even if it has not legally registered it. Common law protection exists if the firm has used the name and established it over a period of time. Although a registered trademark prevents others from using it on a similar product, it may not bar its use for a product in a completely different type of business.

The Importance of Branding

Marketers spend vast amounts of money on new product development, advertising, and promotions to develop strong brands. If successful, the investment creates **brand equity**, which is a brand's value to its organization. Brand equity means that a brand has high customer loyalty, perceived quality, and brand name awareness. For a firm, brand equity provides a competitive advantage, because it gives the brand the power to capture and hold onto a larger share of the market and to sell at prices with higher profit margins. Some of the most valuable brands in the world are BMW, Nike, Apple, and Ikea.[18]

Exhibit 10.8

Clarica used this humorous ad to help make its brand name more memorable.

Exhibit 10.9

The A&W Root Bear is an example of a trade character.

* * *
brand equity The value of a brand to an organization.

* * *
brand extension A new product sold with the same brand name as a strong existing brand.

When brands possess strong brand equity, they provide important opportunities for a firm. A firm may leverage a brand's equity with **brand extensions**, new products sold with the same brand name, such as the Listerine oral care strips and Dentyne Ice mentioned earlier. If existing brand equity is high, the firm is able to sell the brand extension at a higher price than if it had given it a new brand, and the brand extension will attract new customers immediately. However, if the brand extension does not live up to the quality or attractiveness of the original brand, brand equity will suffer, reducing brand loyalty and sales.

Branding Strategies

As Mary Louise Huebner at Canada Cutlery knows, brands are important to a marketing program's success, so decisions about branding strategies are a major part of product decision making. Marketers have to determine whether to create individual or family brands, national or private-label brands, or be involved in co-branding.

INDIVIDUAL BRANDS VERSUS FAMILY BRANDS

Part of developing a branding strategy is deciding whether to use a separate, unique brand for each product item—*an individual brand strategy*—or market multiple items under the same brand name—a **family brand**—an umbrella brand strategy. Individual brands may do a better job of communicating clearly and concisely what the consumer can expect from the product, whereas family brands allow a firm to develop a brand for an entire product line. Thus, the decision to use an individual or family branding strategy often depends on characteristics of the product and whether the company's overall product strategy calls for introduction of a single, unique product or for the development of a group of similar products. Pillsbury Canada uses family branding with its Green Giant, Pillsbury, Old El Paso, Underwood, and Accent family brands. Under the Old El Paso name are such Mexican foods as salsa

good OR bad DECISION?

Pharmaceutical marketers in Canada face a difficult challenge in trying to develop strong brand equity through advertising. Under the *Food and Drugs Act,* pharmaceutical advertisers can mention either their product's brand name or its use, but they cannot mention both in the same ad. Wyeth-Ayerst Canada decided to push these regulations to the limit with ads for their birth-control pill Alesse that aired on MuchMusic. The ads, titled "Lessons Learned," showed young women discussing lessons they had learned about relationships and men. Consistent with the regulations, the company did not mention the brand name in an ad that talks about contraception, but one woman in the ad says, "Less may be more for you," a phrase that sounds very much like "Alesse may be more for you." Do you think Wyeth-Ayerst Canada is adhering to the *Food and Drugs Act* legislation regarding pharmaceutical advertising? Health Canada is reviewing legislation with respect to pharmaceutical advertising, since the US and other countries now allow pharmaceutical marketers to be more aggressive in their branding efforts. Do you think the existing Canadian legislation is fair? What should be the Canadian government's objectives in regulating advertising for pharmaceutical products?[19]

Real People, Real Decisions
Decision Time at Canada Cutlery Inc.

In the late 1990s, Mary Louise Huebner was considering how to best manage the branding of Canada Cutlery's product lines. Canada Cutlery has eight different product lines: four lines of knives designed to meet the needs of chefs at different stages of their careers (from apprentice to professional chef), a line of knife sharpeners, two lines of specialized tools such as cleavers and spatulas, and a line of cutlery carrying cases. Canada Cutlery is a niche player in the professional cutlery market. Dominant players, such as J.A. Henckels (which also sells knives and kitchen tools in the consumer market) and Victorinox (which also makes the Swiss Army Knife), have much larger market share overall. However, one of Canada Cutlery's strengths has been its focus and success in the educational market: Canada Cutlery is a supplier to chef training schools, a strategy which Huebner views as an excellent way to build the company's business. Once chefs have worked with a brand of knife, they tend to stay with it for their entire career. By introducing apprentice chefs to Canada Cutlery products, the potential for long-term brand loyalty was significant.

For 20 years, Canada Cutlery had practised a co-branding strategy with its European supplier. Since quality is important to Canada Cutlery's professional chef customers, the co-branding strategy that highlighted not only the Canada Cutlery name but also that of a respected European cutlery manufacturer, enhanced the quality image of Canada Cutlery's products. Since chefs purchase products across all of Canada Cutlery's product lines, Huebner knew that it was important to have the same brand name and logo on all of the products, so the co-branding strategy was used across all product lines.

In the late 1990s, Canada Cutlery's supplier decided that it was no longer interested in being involved in a co-branding strategy. Instead, the supplier wanted to use its own name exclusively on the products that Canada Cutlery would sell. Since branding is so central to Canada Cutlery's product management strategy, Huebner carefully considered her branding options in light of the supplier's decision to stop the co-branding strategy.

Option 1. Canada Cutlery could stay with its existing supplier, stop using the Canada Cutlery name for branding purposes, and market its products under the supplier's name. The advantage of this strategy was that the company could keep the same supplier relationship that had been developed over 20 years with a company that it knew provided quality products. However, there were potential problems with this option. The supplier's name was not easy to pronounce, and Huebner had noticed that this was a problem, especially for some US customers who were not familiar with European names. The other concern had to do with the loss of control over the brand name. The supplier intended to sell its trademark to other distributors, which could potentially affect the quality perceptions of the product.

Option 2. Canada Cutlery could start using its own brand name on its products, a strategy that would also require identifying a new supplier. Finding another supplier that could provide the high-quality product that Canada Cutlery wanted could be difficult. An additional problem would be the promotional costs associated with establishing a new brand name with customers. The advantage of this option, though, was that it gave Canada Cutlery complete control of its branding strategy, which could allow the company to develop a stronger relationship with its customers. Huebner felt that by using its brand name across all product lines, the company would not only create stronger awareness but could also possibly realize some promotional economies of scale.

Option 3. Canada Cutlery could follow the same kind of co-branding strategy it had used in the past, but with a new supplier. Following this option would allow Canada Cutlery to share the promotional costs needed to establish the new co-branded name with its new supplier. As with Option 2, a potential challenge was finding an acceptable supplier.

Now, join Mary Louise Huebner and the Canada Cutlery team: Which option would you choose, and why?

---

and Nachips; under its Green Giant name are frozen and canned vegetables and other frozen products; and under the Pillsbury name are Pizza Pops, Toaster Strudel, and refrigerated baked goods.[20]

NATIONAL AND STORE BRANDS

Retailers today are often in the driver's seat when it comes to deciding what brands to sell. In addition to choosing from producers' brands like those from Pillsbury Canada, called **national or manufacturer brands**, retailers decide whether to offer their own versions. **Store**

✳ ✳ ✳
national or manufacturer brands Brands that the manufacturer of the product owns.

✳ ✳ ✳
store or private-label brands Brands that are owned and sold by a specific retailer or distributor.

brands, also called **private-label brands**, are the retail store's or chain's exclusive trade name. Loblaws, for example, sells its President's Choice private-label brand along with national brands.

Retailers choose a private-label branding strategy, because they generally make a larger profit than on national brands. Private-label strategies are also important when retailers seek to maintain a consistent store image; for example, clothing retailers such as the Gap and Holt Renfrew protect their image by offering store brands.[21] The BC company Private Reserve Water produces private-label water for such companies as Holiday Inn Express, Clearnet Communications, and several golf clubs, restaurants and catering companies across North America. Many of the companies that buy from Private Reserve Water use the private-label product in promotions, as Clearnet did when it gave away the water to support its slogan, "Try us, we're refreshing and new."[22]

LICENSING

Some firms choose to use **licensing** to brand their products. A licensing agreement typically means that one firm sells another firm the right to use a brand name for a specific purpose and for a specific period of time. Firms choose a licensing strategy for a variety of reasons: Sometimes it provides instant recognition and consumer interest in a new product; at other times licensing is important to positioning a product for a certain target market. For example, bourbon maker Jack Daniels licensed its name to T. Marzetti for producing Jack Daniels bourbon-flavoured mustard. Much better known, however, is the licensing of entertainment names. Movie producers license their properties to manufacturers of a seemingly infinite number of products: When Disney movies hit the screens, such licensed merchandise as figures, toys, and clothing are sold through stores and distributed through other retail outlets such as McDonald's.

CO-BRANDING

Starbucks cafés in Chapters stores and McDonald's outlets in Wal-Mart stores are both examples of **co-branding**. Co-branding, which some call one of the "pre-eminent marketing strategies" today, joins two brands in partnership to market new or existing products.[23]

Co-branding ideally benefits both partners—in combination, the two brands can enjoy more recognition power than either would alone. Starbucks and Chapters products, for example, are complementary and appeal to the same target group, so by co-branding, both brands are strengthened.[24]

Creating Product Identity: Packaging and Labelling Decisions

How do you know if the pop you are drinking is "regular" or "caffeine free"? How do you keep your low-fat grated cheese fresh after you have used a little of it? Why do you always leave your bottle of Calvin Klein Obsession perfume out on your dresser so that everyone can see it? The answer to all these questions is effective packaging and labelling. In this section, we discuss the strategic functions of packaging and some of the legal issues of package labelling.

Packaging Functions

A **package** is not simply the covering or container for a product. Marketers who want to create great packaging that meets and exceeds consumers' needs and that creates a competitive advantage must understand all the things a package does for a product. Figure 10.4 shows how packaging serves a number of different functions.

First, packaging protects the product. Packaging for computers, televisions, and stereos protects the units from damage during shipping, storage, and life "on the shelf" before purchase. Cereal, potato chips, or grated cheese wouldn't be edible for long if packaging didn't

---

❊ ❊ ❊

licensing An agreement in which one firm sells another firm the right to use a brand name for a specific purpose and for a specific period of time.

❊ ❊ ❊

co-branding An agreement between two brands to work together in marketing new or existing products.

❊ ❊ ❊

package The covering or container for a product, which provides product protection, facilitates product use and storage, and supplies important marketing communication.

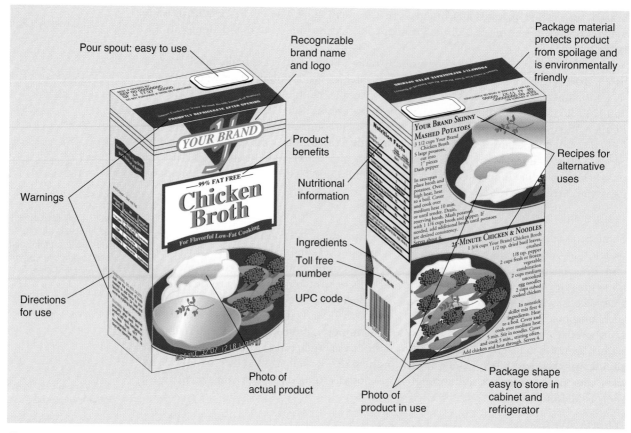

Figure 10.4 Functions of Packaging

provide protection from moisture, dust, odours, and insects. The chicken broth in Figure 10.4 is protected (before opening) from spoilage by a multilayered, soft box.

In addition to protecting the product, effective packaging makes it easy for consumers to handle and store the product. For example, when Clearly Canadian redesigned their bottle, one of the considerations was the bottle shape. While other beverages were packaged in large, bulbous shapes, they chose to make the Clearly Canadian bottle slender so that it would fit easily into the consumer's hand.[25]

Beyond these utilitarian functions, the package plays an important role in marketing communication. Effective product packaging uses colours, words, shapes, designs, and pictures to provide brand and name identification for the product. For years, Toronto-based M•A•C Cosmetics had distinct black packaging that was very successful with consumers. Competitors, eager to cash in on some of this success, began copying the packaging, which prompted M•A•C to completely redesign their packaging, including putting lipstick in bullet-shaped containers, to regain a distinctive image.[26]

Packaging can also provide specific information consumers want and need, about the specific variety, flavour or fragrance, directions for use, suggestions for alternative uses (e.g., recipes), product warnings, and product ingredients. Packaging often includes warranty information and gives a toll-free telephone number and a Web site address so that consumers can communicate with the company.

A final communication element is the Universal Product Code (UPC), the set of bars or lines printed on the side or bottom of most items sold in grocery stores and other mass-merchandising outlets. The UPC is a system of product identification. Each product has a unique 10-digit number assigned to it. These numbers supply specific information about the type of item (grocery item versus meat, produce, drugs, or a discount coupon), the manufacturer (a five-digit code), and the specific product (another five-digit code). At checkout counters, electronic scanners read the UPC bars and automatically transmit

MAC Cosmetics
www.maccosmetics.com

data to a computer controlling the cash register, allowing retailers to track sales and control inventory.

Designing Effective Packaging

Designing effective packaging involves many decisions. Should the package have a zip-lock closing, have an easy-to-pour spout, be compact for easy storage, be short and fat so it won't fall over or tall and skinny so it won't take up much shelf space?

Planners must consider the packaging of other brands in the same product category. For example, dry cereal usually comes in tall rectangular boxes. Quaker, however, introduced a line of cereal packaged in reclosable plastic bags; it offers these at prices that are 25 to 35% less than well-known brands packaged in boxes. Not all customers are willing to accept a radical change in packaging, though, and retailers may be reluctant to adjust their shelf space to fit the new item.

The choice of packaging material has functional, aesthetic, cost, and environmental considerations. Enclosing a fine liqueur in a velvet or silk bag may enhance its image; and the image of masculinity is often evoked when wood is the packaging material. Firms seeking to act in a socially responsible manner also consider the environmental impact of packaging. Shiny gold or silver packaging transmits an image of quality and opulence, but some metallic inks are not biodegradable and are harmful to the environment. Some firms are developing innovative *green packaging* that is less harmful to the environment than traditional materials. However, there is no guarantee that consumers will accept such packaging. They didn't take to plastic pouch refills for certain spray bottle products, even though the pouches took up less space in landfills: They didn't like pouring the refill into their old spray bottles. But customers have accepted smaller packages of concentrated products such as laundry detergent, dishwashing liquid, and fabric softener.

What about the shape? Square? Round? Triangular? In the shape of an hourglass? Like an old-fashioned apothecary jar so consumers can reuse it as an attractive storage container? What colour should it be? White to communicate purity? Yellow because it reminds people of lemon freshness? Brown because the flavour is chocolate? Sometimes these decisions are based on personal factors: The familiar Campbell's soup can was produced in red and white, because a company executive liked the football uniforms at a US university.

Finally, what graphic information should the package show? Should there be a picture of the product on the package? Should cans of green beans always show a picture of green beans? Should there be a picture of the results of using the product, such as beautiful hair? Should there be a picture of the product in use, perhaps a box of crackers showing the crackers with delicious-looking toppings arranged on a silver tray? Should there be a recipe or coupon on the back? All of these decisions rest on a marketer's understanding of consumers and perhaps a little creative genius. Vancouver-based Urban Juice and Soda Co., the makers of Jones Soda, decided to offer personalized packages to their customers. Customers can upload a picture on the company's Web site that is then used to produce 12 personalized bottles of Jones Soda.[27]

Jones Soda Company
www.jonessoda.com

Labelling Regulations

The *Consumer Packaging and Labelling Act* controls most package communications and labelling in Canada. One of the objectives of this Act is to make labels more helpful to consumers by providing useful information. The federal government is reviewing this legislation to make labels, especially on food products, more effective. For example, nutritional labelling (such as information on calories, fat, and vitamins) of food products is currently voluntary in Canada, but this may be made mandatory in the near future.

Other legislation affecting the labelling of products in Canada is included in the *Textile Labelling Act*, the *Food and Drugs Act*, and the *Tobacco Act*. In 2000, Canada became the first country in the world to require tobacco manufacturers to include graphic health warning messages on cigarette packages and to require that information on smoking-related diseases be included inside the cigarette packages.[28]

Organizing for Effective Product Management

Firms don't create great packaging, brands, or products—people do. Like all elements of the marketing mix, the effectiveness of product strategies depends on marketing managers and the decisions they make. In this section, we discuss how firms organize for the management of existing products and for the development of new products.

Management of Existing Products

In small firms such as The Body Blocker Group, the marketing function may be handled by a single marketing manager, who is responsible for new product planning, advertising, making Web site decisions, marketing research, and just about everything else. The Body Blocker simply is not big enough—and doesn't need—a large marketing management team.

In larger firms with many products, a number of managers are responsible for different brands, product categories, or markets. Depending on the organization, product management may include brand managers, product category managers, and market managers.

BRAND MANAGERS

❋ ❋ ❋
brand manager A manager who is responsible for developing and implementing the marketing plan for a single brand.

Sometimes a firm has different brands within a single product category. For example, General Foods produces several brands of coffee, including Brim, Maxim, Maxwell House, International Coffees, Sanka, and Yuban. In such cases, a separate **brand manager** may be responsible for each brand.

Procter & Gamble brand managers once acted independently and were responsible for coordinating all marketing activities for a brand: positioning, identifying target markets, research, distribution, sales promotion, packaging, and evaluating the success of these decisions. Today, P&G's brand managers are more like team leaders. They still are responsible for positioning of brands and developing brand equity, but they are likely to work with sales, finance, and logistics staff members as a part of customer business teams working with major retail accounts.[29]

The brand management system has its problems. Acting independently, brand managers may fight for increases in short-term sales for their own brand. They may push too hard with coupons, cents-off packages, or other price incentives to a point where customers will refuse to buy the product without them. That can hurt long-term profitability.

PRODUCT CATEGORY MANAGERS

❋ ❋ ❋
product category manager A manager who is responsible for developing and implementing the marketing plan for all of the brands and products within a product category.

❋ ❋ ❋
market manager A manager who is responsible for developing and implementing the marketing plans for products sold to a specific customer group.

Some larger firms have such diverse product offerings that there is a need for extensive coordination. Eastman Kodak is best known for its cameras, film, and other photography supplies; however, it also markets X-ray film and equipment, health products like Bayer Aspirin, Phillips Milk of Magnesia, and Midol, household products such as Lysol and Minwax, and printers, optical disks, and photocopiers. In such cases, organizing for product management may include **product category managers**, who coordinate the mix of product lines within the more general product category and who consider the addition of new product lines. In recent years, both Procter & Gamble and Lever Brothers have consolidated brands under product category managers, who are responsible for profit and losses within the category.[30]

MARKET MANAGERS

Some firms have developed a **market manager** structure, in which different managers focus on specific customer groups rather than on the products the company makes. This type of organization can be useful for firms that offer a variety of products serving the needs of a wide range of customers. For example, Raytheon (see Exhibit 10.10), which specializes in consumer electronics products, special-mission aircraft, and business aviation, sells some products directly to consumer markets, others to manufacturers, and still others to government.[31]

Organizing for New Product Development

In Chapter 9, we discussed the importance of new products to the long-term health of an organization. Because launching new products is so important, the management of launch-

Exhibit 10.10

Firms such as Raytheon that offer products to a wide variety of customers need marketing managers to focus on different markets.

ing them is, too. In some instances, one person handles new product development. However, in larger organizations, new product development almost always needs many people working under the new product manager. Often, the people who are assigned to manage new product development are especially creative people with entrepreneurial skills.

The challenge in large companies is to get specialists in different areas to work together in **venture teams**, in which members focus exclusively on the new product development effort. The venture team may be located away from traditional company offices, perhaps in a separate building, called a *skunk works*. This odd term suggests that the group avoids opponents of change within the firm who might stop a project that challenges the status quo. Often having team members with different areas of knowledge, for example, design, engineering, and marketing, contributes to creativity.

Whirlpool, the appliance company, can thank its venture team for winning $30 million in a nationwide save-energy refrigerator design contest sponsored by a group of electric utilities. The seven-person Whirlpool team developed a refrigerator that was 25% more energy

✳ ✳ ✳

venture teams Groups of people within an organization who work together focusing exclusively on the development of a new product.

Real People, Real Decisions
How it worked **out at Canada Cutlery Inc.**

Mary Louise Huebner chose Option 2 and began developing a unique branding strategy for Canada Cutlery. The first task was to find a new supplier: It took the company a year to find another acceptable European supplier, but the wait was well worth it. The new supplier provides the same or higher quality than the previous supplier and at a better price.

The new family brand name chosen for Canada Cutlery products was "CCI Superior Culinary Master," which Canada Cutlery trademarked in both Canada and the US. "Culinary master" is a term used to describe a chef who has achieved the highest status possible in the culinary field. By using this name, Huebner aimed to reinforce to customers that the brand offered high quality. For each of their product lines, sub-brands were developed—the Masterpiece Series, the Apprentice Series, and the Superior Classic Series.

Canada Cutlery also made some product design changes, including the addition of ergonomic handles and colour-coded handles (such as blue for poultry, red for meat, green for produce) to help chefs prevent cross-contamination, an increasingly important issue in food preparation.

To put their brand name on their products, Canada Cutlery also invested in an etching machine. This major purchase has opened up yet another branding opportunity for the company. Now it is possible for Canada Cutlery to provide private-label products for food retailers and other companies, who may want to put their own brand names on knives and kitchen tools. Additionally, Canada Cutlery was granted patents for its products in several other countries, so Mary Louise Huebner is now beginning to seek out potential licensing arrangements with distributors in those countries to further build the CCI Superior Culinary Master Brand.

efficient and did not use ozone-depleting chlorofluorocarbons.[32] Runner-up Frigidaire also used a team approach and discovered that the time they needed for new product development was cut in half.[33]

Chapter Summary

1. Explain the different product objectives and strategies a firm may choose.

Objectives for individual products may be related to introducing a new product, expanding the market of a regional product, or rejuvenating a mature product. For multiple products, firms may decide on a full- or a limited-line strategy. Companies often decide to extend their product line with an upward, downward, or two-way stretch, with a filling-out strategy, or they may decide to contract a product line. Firms that have multiple product lines may choose a wide product mix with many different lines or a narrow one with few. Product quality objectives refer to the durability, reliability, degree of precision, ease of use and repair, or degree of aesthetic pleasure.

2. Explain how firms manage products throughout the product life cycle.

The product life cycle explains how products go through four stages from birth to death. During the introduction stage, marketers seek to get buyers to try the product and may use high prices to recover research and development costs. During the growth stage, characterized by rapidly increasing sales, marketers may introduce new product variations. In the maturity stage, sales peak and level off. Marketers respond by adding desirable new product features or with market development strategies. During the decline stage, firms must decide whether to phase a product out slowly, to drop it immediately, or, if there is residual demand, to keep the product.

3. Discuss how branding creates product identity and describe different types of branding strategies.

A brand is a name, term, symbol, or other unique element of a product used to identify a firm's product. A brand should have a positive connotation and be recognizable and memorable. Brand names need to be easy to say, spell, read, and remember, and it should fit the target market, the product's benefits, the customer's culture, and legal requirements. To protect a brand legally, marketers obtain trademark protection. Brands are important, because they help maintain customer loyalty and because brand equity or value means a firm is able to attract new customers. Firms may develop individual brand strategies or market multiple items with a family or umbrella brand strategy. National or manufacturer brands are owned and sold by producers, whereas private-label or store brands carry the retail or chain store's trade name. Licensing means a firm sells another firm the right to use its brand name. In co-branding strategies, two brands form a partnership in marketing a new or existing products.

4. Explain the roles packaging and labelling play in developing effective product strategies.

Packaging, the covering or container for a product, protects a product and allows for its easy use and storage. The colours, words, shapes, designs, pictures, and materials used in package design communicate a product's identity, benefits, and other important information. Package designers must consider cost, product protection, and communication in creating a package that is functional, aesthetically pleasing, and not harmful to the environment. Product labelling in Canada is controlled by a number of federal laws aimed at making package labels more helpful to consumers.

5. Describe how organizations are structured for new and existing product management.

To successfully manage existing products, the marketing organization may include brand managers, product category managers, and market managers. Large firms, however, often give new product responsibilities to new product managers or to venture teams, groups of specialists from different areas who work together for a single new product.

KEY TERMS

brand (270)

brand equity (272)

brand extension (273)

brand manager (278)

cannibalization (266)

co-branding (275)

decline stage (270)

family brand (273)

growth stage (269)

introduction (267)

licensing (275)

market manager (278)

maturity stage (269)

national or manufacturer brands (274)

package (275)

product category manager (278)

product life cycle (267)

product line (264)

product mix (266)

store or private-label brands (274)

trademark (272)

venture teams (279)

Chapter Review

Marketing Concepts: Testing Your Knowledge

1. List and explain some popular objectives and strategies used for individual and multiple products.

2. Explain what is meant by a full-line strategy and a limited-line strategy. How might a firm stretch or expand its product line?

3. What is a product mix? What is meant by the width of a product mix?

4. Why is quality such an important product strategy objective? What are the important dimensions of product quality?

5. How are products managed during the different phases of the product life cycle?

6. What is a brand? What are the characteristics of a good brand name? How do firms protect their brands?

7. List and explain some of the different branding strategies.

8. What are the functions of packaging? What are some important elements of effective package design?

9. What should marketers know about package labelling?

10. Describe some ways firms organize the marketing function to manage existing products. What are the ways firms organize for the development of new products?

Marketing Concepts: Discussing Choices and Issues

1. Quality is an important product objective, but quality can mean different things for different products, such as durability, precision, or aesthetic appeal. What does quality mean for the following products?

   a. automobile

   b. pizza

   c. running shoes

   d. hair dryer

   e. deodorant

   f. post-secondary education

2. Firms often take advantage of a popular, well-known brand by developing brand extensions, because they know that the brand equity of the original or parent brand will be transferred to the new product. However, the transfer can go the other way. If a new product is of poor quality, it can damage the reputation of the parent brand; whereas a new product that is of superior quality can enhance the parent brand's reputation. What are some brand extensions that have either damaged or enhanced the parent brand equity?

3. Marketers sometimes seem to stick with the same packaging ideas year after year, regardless of whether they are the best possible design. Following is a list of products. For each one, discuss what, if any, problems you have with the package. Then think of ways the package could be improved. Why do you think marketers don't change the old packaging? What would be the results if they adopted your package ideas?

   a. dry cereal

   b. laundry detergent

   c. frozen orange juice

   d. litre of milk

   e. potato chips

   f. loaf of bread

Marketing Practice: Applying What You've Learned

1. You may think of your college or university as an organization that offers a line of different educational products. Assume that you have been hired as a marketing consultant by your college or university to examine and make recommendations for extending its product line. Develop alternatives that the organization might consider:

   a. an upward line stretch

   b. a downward line stretch

   c. a two-way stretch

   d. filling-out strategy

   Describe how each might be accomplished. Evaluate each alternative.

2. Assume you are the vice-president of marketing for a firm that markets a large number of specialty food items, such as gourmet sauces, marinades, and relishes.

   a. Your firm is interested in improving its marketing management structure. You are considering several alternatives: a brand manager structure, having product line managers, or focusing on market managers. Outline the advantages and disadvantages of each type of organization. What is your recommendation?

   b. Your firm is also interested in aggressively pursuing the development of a number of new products. You have been asked to develop recommendations for organizing this new product development. Prepare a report that outlines your recommendations for organizing the new product development.

3. Assume you are working in the marketing department of a major manufacturer of athletic shoes. Your firm is introducing a new product, a line of disposable sports clothing. You wonder if it would be better to market the line of clothing with a new brand name or use the family brand name, which has already gained popularity with your existing products. Make a list of the advantages and disadvantages of each strategy. Develop your recommendation.

4. Assume you have been recently hired by Kellogg, the cereal manufacturer. You have been asked to work on a plan for redesigning the packaging for Kellogg's cereals. In a role-playing situation, present the following report to your marketing superior:

   a. discussion of the problems or complaints customers have with current packaging.

   b. several different package alternatives.

   c. your recommendations for changing packaging or for keeping the packaging the same.

Marketing Mini-Project: Learning by Doing

In any supermarket, you will find examples of all of the different types of brands discussed in this chapter: individual brands, family brands, national brands, store brands, and co-branded and licensed products. This mini-project is designed to give you a better understanding of branding as it exists in the marketplace.

1. Go to a supermarket in your community.

2. Select two product categories of interest to you, for example, ice cream, cereal, laundry detergent, soup, or paper products.

3. Make a list of the brands available in each product category. Identify what type of brand each is. Count the number of shelf facings (the number of product items at the front of each shelf) for each brand.

4. Arrange to talk with the store manager at a time that is convenient for them. Ask the manager to discuss:

   a. how the store decides which brands to carry.

   b. whether the store is more likely to carry a new brand that is an individual brand versus a family brand.

   c. what causes a store to drop a brand.

   d. the profitability of store or private-label brands versus national brands.

   e. other aspects of branding that the store manager sees as important from a retail perspective.

5. Present a report to your class on what you learned about the brands in your two product categories.

Real People, Real Surfers: **Exploring the Web**

As we discussed in this chapter and in Chapter 9, companies protect their products by obtaining patents, copyrights, and legal protection for their brands with trademarks. The Canadian Intellectual Property Office oversees all of these forms of protection. Visit the Intellectual Property Office Web site at www.strategis.ic.gc.ca/sc_mrksv/cipo/welcome/welcome-e.html. Use the Internet site to answer the following questions.

1. What is a patent? What can be patented?

2. Who may apply for a patent? Can foreign individuals or companies obtain a Canadian patent? Explain.

3. What happens if someone infringes on a patent?

4. What is a copyright? Who owns a copyright?

5. What is copyright infringement? Give some examples.

6. What is a trademark?

7. Who may file a trademark application? Do firms have to register a trademark? Explain.

8. What are the benefits of trademark registration?

9. Can a person's name be registered as a trademark?

10. How long do trademarks, patents, and copyrights last?

11. How would you evaluate the Canadian Intellectual Property Office Web site? Was it easy to navigate? Was it useful? What recommendations do you have for improving the Web site?

MARKETING IN ACTION

Krave's Candy Company

Winnipeg based Krave's Candy Company (www.clodhoppers.tv) produces Clodhoppers, a small candy made of cashews, graham wafer and white chocolate. Started in 1995 by entrepreneurs Chris Emery and Larry Finnson, the company has already gone through a complete brand image makeover, packaging redesigns and a major international expansion in its short history. All of these changes have been aimed at increasing the company's sales and capturing more of the total market for boxed chocolates, a market that is currently valued at between $160 million and $200 million in Canada alone. The company has had considerable success. With annual sales in the millions, the company was named as one of Canada's top ten food companies by the magazine *Food in Canada*. The key to maintaining success in the future will be the ability of Emery and Finnson to effectively manage both the brand's identity and the company's growth through both product line extensions and increased geographic distribution.

The original Clodhopper brand identity was built around the fictitious Krave family, which even had its own coat of arms. The first page of the original Krave's Web site claimed, "From their secluded castle high in the European Alps, secret recipes have been handed down from generation to generation." The "family" was used to help establish an image of quality for the Clodhopper product, which, according to the "Krave's family" tradition, was made "using only the finest ingredients from around the world." In reality, the recipe for Clodhoppers does have some family tradition behind it, since it originated with the grandmother of one of the partners.

Emery and Finnson learned the importance of packaging in establishing a brand identity early in the company's history when the original 300 gram transparent plastic jar that they used for the candy created problems with retailers. Based on the packaging, retailers tended to place the product in the snack aisles, near the popcorn products. Since Clodhoppers were priced at close to $6 a jar, the price didn't compare favourably against the lower priced snacks. Additionally, the plastic jar made the product look cheap and because the product would settle over time, a four centimetre gap would appear at the top of the jar, making the jar look half empty to customers. To address these packaging problems, Emery and Finnson repackaged the product so that it would fit into the upscale boxed chocolate product category, which includes competitors such as Black Magic and Pot of Gold. The quality image of the candy was reinforced by using a black package with gold and red trim that included an image of the Alps (to tie in with the Krave family) in the background. Consistent with the high quality image, a gold foil bag was used on the inside of the package, which also helped to establish the product as being appropriate as a gift. While this upscale packaging was consistent with other boxed chocolate competitors and got the product placed on the right shelves in stores, it did not do a good job of differentiating the Clodhopper brand.

Searching for a more distinctive identity, Emery and Finnson revised the entire positioning of the brand. The fictitious Krave family was replaced by the entrepreneurs themselves as the trade characters for the product. The brand is now called "Chris and Larry's Clodhoppers," and both the "retro" style packaging and the Web site feature cartoon characters of Chris and Larry.

A large part of the success of Krave's Candy has been its ability to sell the brand to important distributors who would then stock Clodhoppers in their stores. Clodhoppers are now available in large national retail chains such as Wal-Mart, Shoppers Drug Mart, Zellers, and Loblaws, as well as in regional grocery stores such as Sobeys, Safeway and Save-on-Foods. However, one of the most important distribution arrangements for the future growth of Krave's was their expansion into the US market. During a trade show in Toronto in 2000, Emery and Finnson met Wal-Mart USA president and CEO Lee Scott, and secured a deal that expanded their distribution into Wal-Mart stores in the United States. Chris and Larry are trying to achieve large volume in the US market by practising very aggressive pricing. The 212-gram box sells at Wal-Mart USA stores for $1.97, as compared to its current retail price in Canada of $5.87 for a 300-gram box.

MARKETING IN ACTION

Christmas is the most important time of year for Krave's since 85% of the company's sales occur at this time. To reinforce their brand at Christmas, the company runs a sampling program, giving consumers free samples in stores. In the future Finnson and Emery would like to reduce the seasonality of their business by engaging in efforts to reinforce the brand name at other times of the year. They have only used a small amount of paid advertising in the past, partly because of limited budgets, but they are now considering how it might be used in the future.

In addition to their international launch of Clodhoppers, the company also introduced two new Clodhopper flavours to their product line: chocolate fudge and peanut butter. The original flavour was also renamed "vanilla fudge" to give it a more candy-like name and to create consistency with the chocolate introduction. The chocolate flavour was an especially important product introduction since chocolate flavoured candies account for all of the top 10 products in the boxed chocolate market. As an additional modification to the product line, in April 2001 Krave's launched a Clodhopper flavoured Blizzard at more than 500 Dairy Queens across Canada.

While Finnson and Emery hope these brand and product modifications will help the company gain more sales, they are also considering the introduction of other flavours, the introduction of new product lines, and further packaging changes that could help them achieve even more growth for their company.

Sources: Krave's Web site (www.clodhoppers.tv); Myron Love, "Winnipeg candy manufacturer scores major Wal-Mart sale," *Food in Canada*, March 2001; Casey Mahood, "Madeover Clodhoppers stepping out," *The Globe and Mail*, 7 January 2000, M1; Judy Waytiuk, "Constant Kraving," *Marketing Magazine*, 29 March 1999, 14; Brend Sedo, "Krave something sweet?" *Realm*, (www.realm.net/net/7/wild-e.html).

THINGS TO THINK ABOUT

1. In what stage of the product life cycle is the boxed chocolate industry? What implications does this have for marketing management at Krave's?
2. What are the advantages and disadvantages of the rebranding of Clodhoppers as "Chris and Larry's Clodhoppers"? What opportunities does this brand image present for the future?
3. Visit the Krave's Web site (www.clodhoppers.tv) and evaluate both the site and the packaging shown on the site. Does the Krave's Web site reinforce the branding of the product? Can you suggest any improvements to the site?
4. What objectives, product line extensions, branding and packaging alternatives should Krave's Candy consider for its future product decisions?

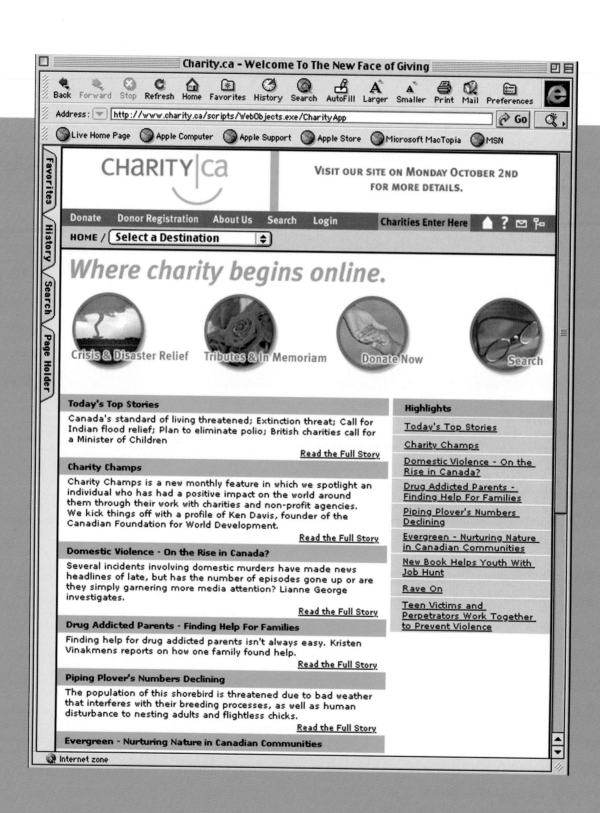

11

Broadening the Product Focus: Marketing Intangibles and Services

When you have completed your study of this chapter, you should be able to

CHAPTER OBJECTIVES

1. Explain the marketing of people, places, and ideas.

2. Describe the four characteristics of services, and understand how services differ from goods.

3. Explain how marketers measure service quality.

4. Explain marketing strategies for services and not-for-profit organizations.

Real People, Real Decisions ✓ ✗
Meet Vaughn McIntyre **and** Susan Brekelmans
Decision Makers at Charity.ca

Charity.ca is a Canadian Internet-based company whose purpose is to market an idea: responsible giving to charities. Through their Web site, the company focuses on educating Canadians about charitable giving by presenting news stories about individual charities and about the process of giving to charity. The site also acts as a link between donors and charitable organizations. Charities can register on the Charity.ca Web site and receive donations directly online from registered donors.

Vaughn McIntyre, CEO, and Susan Brekelmans, charity liaison officer, have been with Charity.ca since the company

started in January 2000. McIntyre has over 30 years of experience in the technology sector, having held executive positions in both computer hardware and software firms. Brekelmans, who holds a BA from McGill University, worked in radio at the CBC and as a fundraiser and events manager for ABC CANADA Literacy Foundation before joining Charity.ca.

Sources: Interviews with Vaughn McIntyre and Susan Brekelmans, and information on the Charity.ca Web site www.charity.ca.

Marketing What Isn't There

✳ ✳ ✳
intangibles Experience-based products that cannot be touched.

This chapter considers some of the challenges and opportunities facing marketers like Vaughn McIntyre and Susan Brekelmans, whose primary offerings are **intangibles**, experience-based products that cannot be touched. Charity.ca markets the idea (an intangible) of giving money to charity, and it also provides services (also intangibles) to donors and charitable organizations. Charity.ca provides donors with an easy way to donate to charities online and charities with a new way to reach donors. A post-secondary education, a hockey game, a political candidate, a tourist destination, and a meal in a restaurant are other examples of intangibles, all of which, like Charity.ca, can be marketed effectively using the methods that have been discussed in previous chapters. However, the marketer whose job it is to sell these intangibles must also deal with some issues that are different from those faced by marketers whose products are tangible.

The main focus of the chapter will be on services, a type of intangible that also happens to be the fastest-growing sector in our economy. As we'll see, all services are intangible, but not all intangibles are services. We start by considering different types of intangibles before moving into the nuts and bolts of services marketing.

Does Marketing Work for Intangibles?

The marketing activities of sports teams such as those in the NHL, CFL, and NBA (see Exhibit 11.1) illustrate the extent to which the marketing concept is applicable to experiences. Marketing activities, including pricing strategies and advertising, are involved in convincing people to attend games. Once fans are at the game, the atmosphere (including shows presented when the game is not being played) and offerings (such as food and drink) are designed to provide entertainment for fans. Individual players, like Raptor Vince Carter, are marketed to enhance the appeal of the team. And teams are often involved in marketing ideas, supporting charity work in their communities, or individual players encouraging young people to stay in school. All of this shows that we need to expand the marketing concept and recognize that it applies to many types of products, even those we can't put in our shopping carts.

Even the intangible electric power, formerly considered a commodity, is now branded and marketed directly to consumers. As deregulation takes place in the energy sector across

The McMichael Gallery
www.mcmichael.com

Exhibit 11.1

Sports teams use the marketing concept to attract fans to their games.

Canada, many consumers are now in a position to choose among suppliers of energy. This means that hydro companies have increased their marketing activities to convince consumers to purchase their energy services over those of competitors. The former Ontario Hydro, for example, launched a new brand name, Hydro One, with TV, newspaper, magazine, and radio ads using the Who song "I Can See for Miles" and the tag line "Connecting at the speed of life."[1]

Not-for-profit organizations, including symphonies, charities, zoos, museums, and youth organizations, are also increasingly thinking about branding and image building, as the ad for the McMichael gallery in Exhibit 11.2 shows. There are more than 80 000 charitable organizations in Canada, so competition for customers and donors is fierce.[2] For example, Goodwill wanted to increase donations to its clothing bins, so the group's smiling face logo was redesigned and a new headline, "Helping Create a Better Community," was added. Clothing donations have increased by 10% since the change.[3]

Still, some producers of intangibles have been slow to accept the idea that what they do can or should be marketed. Many people who work in health care, the legal profession, or the arts, for example, resist the notion that the quality of what they produce and the demand for their services are affected by the same market forces driving the fortunes of paper producers, food canners, or even power utilities. For example, the idea of advertising professional services has always been controversial in Canada. Until recently, law firms were allowed to promote themselves only through business cards and the *Yellow Pages*. When these restrictions were loosened, a

Exhibit 11.2

Art galleries and other not-for-profit organizations are increasingly concerned with such marketing issues as branding.

few law firms began experimenting with large-scale advertising campaigns. The Quebec firm Langlois Gaudreau developed a campaign that cost over $1 million and included seven print ads, each featuring a different partner wearing a different hat. One ad showed a partner in a surgical cap and the headline, "When it comes to finances, we operate." An ad showing a partner in deep-sea diving gear had a headline, "We always go in-depth." The objective of the campaign was to differentiate the firm from its competitors and position it as a youthful, energetic firm that takes a fresh approach to legal problems.[4]

Although there are similarities in the marketing activities for intangibles and tangible products, important differences also exist in the types of marketing strategies appropriate for some kinds of intangibles—it's not appropriate to run a "Midnight Madness" sale for a divorce hearing. Still, basic steps can ensure that any organization satisfies its patrons, and that's what the marketing concept is all about.

As the ad for the Charlottetown Festival in Exhibit 11.3 shows, marketing can be used effectively in the promotion of performing arts organizations. To see how some other basic marketing concepts apply to an artistic product, let's suppose that a local theatre company wants to increase attendance at its performances. Remembering the basics of developing a strategic plan discussed in Chapter 2, here are some marketing actions the organization might take to realize its goals.[5]

- The organization could develop a *mission statement*, as well as some concrete objectives, such as: "Increase the number of season ticket holders by 20% over the next two years."

- A *situation analysis* could include an assessment of environmental threats and opportunities. The arts marketer is, after all, competing for the consumer's discretionary dollar against other theatre groups. The marketer is also up against other forms of entertainment the consumer might desire instead of going to a play at all, from attending a concert to a movie to a pro wrestling match.

- The arts organization's goals must consider which part of the *product life cycle* it is in. For example, after audience levels have stabilized for the plays the company puts on

Exhibit 11.3

Marketing can be used effectively to promote performing arts organizations, such as the Charlottetown Festival.

(mature stage), the organization should consider developing new markets for its performances. It might even make product modifications, as some opera companies do when they project English translations above the stage to draw new patrons who may be unfamiliar with Italian, German, and other languages used in performance.

Marketing People, Places, and Ideas

As we've discussed, even a small theatre company can benefit by applying some basic marketing principles to its activities. In addition to the arts, people, places, and ideas often need to be "sold" by someone and "bought" by someone else. Let's consider how marketing is relevant to each of these.

MARKETING PEOPLE

As we saw in Chapter 1, people are products, too. Many of us find it distasteful to equate people with products. In reality, though, a sizeable number of people hire personal image consultants to devise a marketing strategy for them, and others undergo plastic surgery, physical conditioning, or cosmetic makeovers to improve their "market position" or "sell" themselves to potential employers, friends, or lovers.[6]

Politicians are created and marketed by sophisticated consultants, who "package" candidates and compete for "market share" of votes. A political campaign is really a marketing campaign. Politicians and their "brand managers" identify voters' needs through phone surveys and focus groups, and then "test market" campaign positions. They use advertising and public relations to maximize awareness and sway evaluations, and they work hard to establish a better position than their opponents. The political process is like other marketing exchanges, except that votes are the currency.[7]

From actors and musicians to superstar athletes and supermodels, the famous and near-famous jockey for market position in popular culture. Celebrities like Shania Twain are carefully packaged by agents, who try to get them positive exposure in the media, recording contracts, or product endorsements, such as Twain's endorsement for Revlon.[8]

Revlon
www.revlon.com

Like other products, celebrities often craft a "brand identity" using the same strategies marketers use to ensure that their products make an impression on consumers. In the case of a singer like Shania Twain, the cover of her CDs, her appearance in magazines and on TV shows, and her music videos are all important marketing tools in establishing her brand identity. In addition to these branding efforts, there are other strategies marketers use to "sell" a celebrity.[9] One is the *pure selling approach*, in which agents present their clients' qualifications to potential "buyers" until they find one who is willing to act as an intermediary. An agent might send a singer's tapes to talent scouts at record companies, or photos of an aspiring model to beauty magazines. In this case, the celebrity is sold to distributors, just as the representative of a snack food company tries to get grocery retailers to give their product adequate shelf space. Another strategy is the *product improvement approach*, in which the agent works with the client to modify certain characteristics that will increase market value. This means changing the person's repertoire or image to conform to whatever is currently in demand. For example, Madonna's image changes have included East Village punk to lacy virgin to Marilyn Monroe clone, and she continues to change with each succeeding release.[10]

Yet another strategy is the *market fulfillment approach*. The agent scans the market to identify needs that have not been met. After identifying a need, the agent finds a person or a group that meets a set of minimum qualifications and develops a new "product." These "manufactured stars" are common, for example, in the music world in which groups including the Monkees, the New Kids on the Block, and the Spice Girls were successfully formed by auditioning hundreds of photogenic young singers and musicians until developing the right combination of teen idols.

MARKETING PLACES

In business-to-business marketing, local chambers of commerce mount intensive campaigns to attract new companies to their towns. An ad for Moncton, New Brunswick, in *Canadian Business* encourages companies to "Share the Success" of being located in the Greater

Moncton area. In tourism marketing, organizations try to attract visitors (and their dollars) to a site, whether a resort, theme park, city, or, as shown in Exhibit 11.4, a province like Ontario.

Countries and major cities around the world go to great lengths to attract visitors, as they compete for their share of the tourism market. Here is how some Canadian places are competing for tourists' dollars:

- Nunavut, Canada's newest territory, specializes in offering adventure tours ranging from dog sled trips to boating and ecotours where tourists can observe wildlife. Cultural heritage tours are also offered where tourists can learn and observe traditions and lifestyles of the people of Nunavut.[11]

- British Columbia is one of the most successful Canadian tourist destinations. It offers everything from sightseeing tours through the mountains, to fishing and whale watching to skiing and snowboarding vacations. One of the newest tourist products in BC is a gardening theme vacation, targeted at high-income Japanese women with a strong interest in gardening. The participants visit large public gardens such as the Butchart Gardens in Victoria as well as some private backyard gardens and take workshops to learn how to arrange plants in hanging baskets.[12]

- Northern Ontario ran a very unusual, humorous tourism campaign to increase visitors to that region. Unlike most tourism advertising that features photos of scenery and happy people, their campaign had as its theme "So Beautiful, It's Hard to Share." The campaign reflected the love–hate relationship that Northern Ontario residents have with tourists.[13]

MARKETING IDEAS

You can see people. You can stand in a place. So how do you market something, like the idea of giving money to charity, that you can't see, smell, or feel? **Idea marketing** seeks to gain market share for a concept, philosophy, belief, or issue. As we saw in Chapter 3, this

idea marketing Marketing activities that seek to gain market share for a concept, philosophy, belief, or issue by using elements of the marketing mix to create or change a target market's attitude or behaviour.

Exhibit 11.4

Tourism marketing is used to attract visitors to places like Ontario.

INSURANCE FOR WHEN THE ROBOTS TAKE OVER ALL THE BORING JOBS.

MAJOR IN ARTS AND SCIENCES
THINK FOR A LIVING

Exhibit 11.5

Idea marketing here seeks to influence students' opinions about getting a general science or arts degree.

means using elements of the marketing mix to create or change a target market's attitude or behaviour. For example, the ad shown in Exhibit 11.5 reflects an attempt by one university to attract students (customers) to its College of Arts and Sciences.

Social marketing is also aimed at trying to sell ideas. The Health Canada ad shown in Exhibit 11.6, for example, illustrates how marketing can be used to convince people to live healthier lives. The Canadian government, through Health Canada, runs several social marketing campaigns every year—trying to convince people to stop smoking, live more active lives, and practise sexual responsibility.

Many companies feel that the best way to bring about social change is through *cause marketing*, in which commercial marketing efforts are linked to a charitable cause. This strategy is constructive, but it also makes good business sense. By having a good match between the company and the cause it supports, the company can build stronger relationships with existing customers. Shoppers Drug Mart, for example, sponsors the annual charity walk for the Juvenile Diabetes Foundation of Canada. People with diabetes are an important target group for Shoppers Drug Mart, so by sponsoring the walk and by supporting diabetes research, the company is building a stronger relationship with this customer group.[14] Other examples of cause marketing are Bell Canada's sponsorship of the Kids Help Phone and Web site (kidshelp.sympatico.ca), the collection of used books by Starbucks in support of literacy, and the support of AIDS and breast cancer awareness by shoe retailer Aldo Group.[15]

Even religious organizations market ideas about faith and desirable behaviour by adopting secular marketing techniques to attract young people to the Church. Evangelists use the power of television to convey their messages. So-called "megachurches" are huge steel and glass structures, with acres of parking, and slickly produced services complete with live bands and professional dancers to draw huge audiences. Some even offer aerobics classes, bowling alleys, and multimedia Bible classes to attract

Health Canada
www.hc-sc.gc.ca

Exhibit 11.6

Health Canada practises social marketing in its efforts to get people to stop smoking.

Exhibit 11.7

Professional service organizations, including law firms, use marketing techniques to attract clients.

"customers" turned off by traditional approaches to religion.[16] Not all religious leaders endorse the use of such marketing techniques: One official at a divinity school rejected the marketing concept by stating, "Church is not supposed to be a place where everybody's needs are met. It's supposed to be a place where we're transformed by God's grace into something we're not."[17]

What Is a Service?

We have seen that marketing can help sell all kinds of intangibles, from theatre performances to the idea of giving money to charity. Now that (hopefully) you are convinced that marketing is as important for a dance company as it is for a com-

Real People, Real Decisions
Decision Time **at Charity.ca**

From the inception of Charity.ca, a key concern for Vaughn McIntyre and Susan Brekelmans was which group of donors to target. The goal of the company was to build a new community of donors to increase the amount of donations given to Canadian charitable organizations. Rather than redirecting donations that would go to charities anyway, they wanted to find new sources of donations. This was also an important point in convincing charities to register on the Charity.ca site. Charitable organizations did not want to cannibalize their other avenues of donations. They would only be interested in registering on the site if they were convinced that overall donations would increase.

The Charity.ca team was also convinced that the more they could target the content on the Web site to the needs and concerns of a specific group of consumers, the more effective it would be in convincing them to give. Content manager Tina Pittaway pointed out the contextual difference in this way: If one of their registered charities was an organ-

ization that raises money to support research on prostate cancer, the story presented on the site and the overall message they wanted to communicate would depend on the type of consumers they were speaking to. If their chosen target market was men 40 and older, then the story might begin "You've just been diagnosed with prostate cancer..." and proceed to discuss the disease and how giving to the charity can help people with the disease. If, on the other hand, the target market was people in their 30s, the story might begin "Your father has just been diagnosed with prostate cancer."

The traditional target market for many charities in Canada is people over the age of 45 with moderate to high disposable incomes. McIntyre and Brekelmans assumed that because this group constituted the current donor group for charities, they were not a primary group of interest for Charity.ca. Instead they considered three other target segments for Charity.ca.

pany that sells ballet slippers, it's time to look more specifically at an important type of intangible.

Services are acts, efforts, or performances exchanged from producer to user without ownership rights. Like other intangibles, a service satisfies needs by providing pleasure, information, or convenience. About 74% of the Canadian population is employed in the services sector in such industries as banking, insurance, professional services (see Exhibit 11.7), education, health care, hotels, restaurants, and recreational services.[18] If you pursue a marketing career, it's likely that you will work in some aspect of services marketing.

✳ ✳ ✳
services Intangible products that are exchanged directly from the producer to the customer.

Characteristics of Services

Services come in many forms, from those done *to* you, such as a massage or a teeth cleaning, to those done *for* you, such as having your CD player repaired, getting a new paint job on your car, or having an organization like Charity.ca ensure that your money gets to the charity of your choice. Regardless of whether they affect our bodies or our possessions, *all* services share four characteristics that make them distinct from physical products: intangibility, perishability, inseparability, and variability.

INTANGIBILITY

Service intangibility means that customers can't see, touch, or smell good service. Unlike the purchase of a good, they cannot inspect or handle services before they purchase them. Because they're buying something that isn't there, consumers look for reassuring signs before purchasing, and marketers must ensure that these signs are available when consumers look for them. That's why the service provider's appearance and the "look" of the facility can make or break a service business. When we talk about how customers decide if a service is giving them what they want, marketers overcome the problem of intangibility by providing

Option 1: Young people, aged 20 to 30, represented an interesting target segment for Charity.ca, because this market was largely untapped by charitable organizations. These people also tend to be experienced in the Internet environment and might, therefore, be more comfortable donating online. Some concerns about these consumers related to whether they had enough disposable income to be considered a worthwhile segment, and whether they were at a point in their life when they would be motivated to give money to charities.

Option 2: Another segment of consumers, those aged 30 to 54 who had relatively high levels of education and income, seemed to have an interest in giving to charities, but lacked the time to research them and develop a good donating strategy. These consumers were time pressed: They were developing their careers and probably had children as well. These consumers are comfortable on the Internet and interested in making an informed choice about giving. A key concern for these consumers, however, would be privacy online.

Option 3: A third group that Charity.ca was considering was "surfing seniors," people aged 65 and over, who have started to use the Internet to search for information and e-mail friends and relatives. This group had potentially the most disposable income of the three groups under consideration, and they were probably convinced that giving to charity was a good idea. Although a concern with this group was that they were perhaps being reached by charities through other means, Charity.ca could focus on increasing the amount these consumers are currently giving.

Now join Vaughn McIntyre and Susan Brekelmans and the Charity.ca decision team. Which option would you choose, and why?

physical cues to reassure the buyer. These cues include uniforms, brand logos, and carefully designed Web sites.

PERISHABILITY

Service perishability means that a firm can't store its services—it's a case of use it or lose it. When rooms go unoccupied at a ski resort, there is no way to make up for the lost opportunity to exchange a product for money. Marketers try to avoid these problems by using the marketing mix to encourage demand for the service during times when it would otherwise be low. **Capacity management** is the process by which organizations adjust their services in an attempt to match demand. In the summer, for example, Whistler combats its perishability problem by opening its lifts to mountain bikers, who tear down the sunny slopes.

* * *
capacity management The process by which organizations adjust their offerings in an attempt to match demand.

VARIABILITY

Service variability is the inevitable differences in a service provider's performances from one day to the next: An NHL goalie may be "hot" one game and ice cold the next. Even the same service performed by the same individual for the same customer can vary. It's rare that you get exactly the same cut from a hair stylist.

It is difficult to standardize services, because service providers and customers vary. Your experience in courses is an example. A university or college can standardize its offerings to some degree—course calendars, course content, and classrooms are fairly controllable. Professors, however, vary in their training, life experiences, and personalities, so there is little hope of being able to make teaching uniform (not that this would necessarily be desirable anyway). And because students with different backgrounds and interests vary in their needs, the lecture that one finds fascinating might put another to sleep.

INSEPARABILITY

Although a firm can manufacture goods before sale, a service can take place only at the time the service provider performs an act on either the customer or the customer's possession. It's hard to take notes on a lecture when the professor doesn't show. In some cases, the service can be sold before delivery, such as a ticket to a concert months before the event.

Still, the expertise, skill, and personality of a provider, or the quality of a firm's facilities and equipment, cannot be detached from the offering itself. The central role played by employees in making or breaking a service underscores the importance of the **service encounter**, or the interaction between the customer and the service provider.[19] The most expertly cooked meal is ruined if a surly or incompetent waiter brings it to the table. Our interactions with service providers can range from the most superficial, such as buying a movie ticket, to telling a psychiatrist (or bartender) our most intimate secrets. In each case, though, the quality of the service encounter can play a big role in determining how we feel about the service we receive.

* * *
service encounter The actual interaction between the customer and the service provider.

To minimize the potentially negative effects of bad service encounters and to save on labour costs, some service businesses are experimenting with **disintermediation**, which eliminates the need for customers to interact with people. Examples are self-service gas stations, Internet banking, and ATM machines. Even salad and dessert bars reduce reliance on a waiter or waitress.

* * *
disintermediation The process of eliminating interaction between customers and service providers.

The Goods–Services Continuum

In reality, most products are a *combination* of goods and services. The purchase of a "pure good" like a car still has service components, such as bringing it to the dealer for maintenance work. The purchase of a "pure service" like a makeover at a department store has product components, for example, lotions, powders, and lipsticks the cosmetologist uses to create the "new you."

The goods–services continuum in Figure 11.1 shows that some products are dominated by either tangible or intangible characteristics—for instance, salt versus teaching—whereas others tend to include a mixture of goods and services—such as flying in an airplane. A product's placement on this continuum gives some guidance as to which marketing issues are likely to be most relevant. As the product approaches the tangible pole of this continuum,

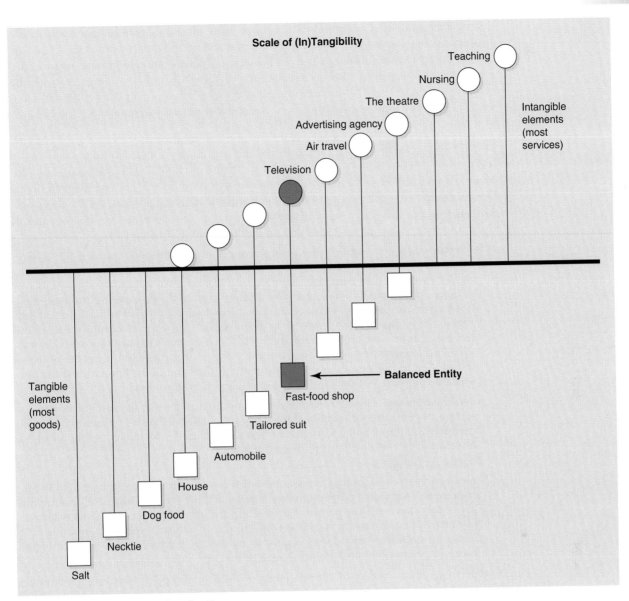

Figure 11.1 The Goods–Services Continuum

there is fairly little emphasis on service; the physical product itself is the focal point, and people will choose one over others based on the product's function or image. As the product gets near the intangible pole, the physical product shrinks in importance, and the service encounter plays a key role in shaping the service experience. In the middle of the continuum, however, both goods and services contribute substantially to the quality of the product, because these products rely on people to satisfactorily operate equipment that will deliver quality service. Let's consider each of these three positions as we move from products dominated by tangibles to those dominated by intangibles.

GOOD-DOMINATED PRODUCTS

Many tangible products are accompanied by supporting services, even if this means only that the company maintains a toll-free telephone line or Web site for questions or provides a 30-day warranty against defects. Including a service with the purchase of a physical good is termed **embodying**.[20] This is becoming an increasingly popular option in the computer industry, especially for companies that are trying to break into international markets saturated with cheap products but with insufficient guidance in their use. As millions of people buy their first computers, they are apt to find it difficult to navigate the maze of set-up

✳ ✳ ✳

embodying The inclusion of a service with a purchase of a physical good.

instructions, and next to impossible to cope with machines that unexpectedly crash. Indeed, a recent survey by *PC Magazine* found that 28% of its readers needed technical support in the first year of owning a personal computer. What's more, in grading manufacturers' service performance, they gave two-thirds of them Cs and Ds. Companies with the resources to do so find that embodying follow-up service is a potent marketing tool when competing with "clone" manufacturers. As an executive at Compaq observed, "The bad guys give us an opportunity to differentiate."[21]

EQUIPMENT- OR FACILITY-DRIVEN SERVICES

As Figure 11.1 shows, some products require a mixture of tangible and intangible elements. Many hospitals and restaurants fall in the middle of the continuum, because they rely on expensive equipment or facilities and skilled personnel to deliver a product. *Facility-driven services*, such as automatic car washes, amusement parks, museums, movie theatres, health clubs, and zoos, must be concerned with these three important factors:[22]

- *Operational factors:* Technologies must move customers smoothly through the service: Clear signs and other guidelines must show customers how to use the service. In particular, firms need to minimize waiting times. Marketers have developed a number of tricks to give impatient customers the illusion that they aren't waiting too long. One hotel chain, responding to complaints about the long wait for elevators, installed mirrors in the lobby: People's tendency to examine their appearance occupied them until the elevators arrived, and protests declined.[23] Burger King's research showed that multiple lines create stress in customers—especially if one moves faster than the others— so it shifted to single lines in which customers at the head of the line order at the next available register. McDonald's is now experimenting with the same technique.[24]

- *Locational factors:* These are especially important for frequently purchased services, such as dry cleaning or retail banking, that are obtained at a fixed location. Fast food restaurants, such as Subway, try to have several restaurants, all in convenient locations, to satisfy their customer's need for convenience.

- *Environmental factors:* Service managers who operate a storefront service requiring people to come to their location realize they must create an attractive environment to lure customers. That's why sports venues such as the Saddledome in Calgary offer plush luxury suites, where wealthy patrons can watch sports events in style. The Calgary Flames, like many Canadian sports franchises, tries to provide all fans with a fun, exciting environment when they attend their games by including such features as between-period contests, promotions, and other fun events.[25]

One trend is for services to adopt a more retail-like philosophy, borrowing techniques from clothing stores or restaurants to create a pleasant environment. Banks, for example, are creating signature looks for their branches through the use of lighting, colour, and art. When ING Direct, a Netherlands-based bank, opened in Canada, they didn't open traditional bank branches at all. The company, which specializes in Web- and telephone-based banking transactions, decided to open cafés instead of branches, where banking services were sold along with Starbucks and other brands of coffee.[26]

ING Direct
www.ingdirect.ca

PEOPLE-BASED SERVICES

At the intangible end of the continuum are people-based services. In the Great American Backrub store, for instance, customers sit in a specially designed chair and, for $7.95, get a massage that lasts exactly eight minutes (no appointment necessary). The owner of the store explained, "To get Americans to buy massages, I realized you had to solve three problems. You had to come up with something that was quick, inexpensive and most important, you had to find a way to do it without asking people to take their clothes off."[27]

Because people have less and less time to perform various tasks, the importance of people-based services is increasing. Personal concierge services, such as Toronto-based Orderly Lives, is a growing industry, because they help consumers meet obligations despite time pressures by doing almost anything for them, from organizing a party to doing the grocery shopping to planning a vacation.[28] Self-improvement services such as those offered by wardrobe consultants and personal trainers also are popular and, in some cities, even professional dog walkers do a brisk business.

Core and Augmented Services

Another important issue in defining a service is understanding that when we buy a service, we may be buying a set of services. The **core service** is a benefit that a customer gets from the service. For example, H&R Block stresses the benefit of the peace of mind you'll get by letting the company prepare your tax return, so peace of mind is the core service. In most cases, though, the core service alone just isn't enough. To attract customers, a services firm often tries to offer **augmented services**, which are actions it takes to differentiate itself from the competition by adding benefits to the core service.

For example, the core service bought with an airline ticket is safe transportation. Yet airlines rarely stress the basic benefit of arriving at your destination. Instead, they emphasize augmented services (see Figure 11.2) such as frequent flyer miles, speedy checkout, and on-site hotels. In addition, augmented services may be necessary to deliver the core service. In the case of air travel, airports are adding attractions to encourage flyers to choose to fly to one site over another.[29] These are some augmented services now available at airports around the world:

- London Gatwick: Internet café, Planet Hollywood restaurant, personal shopper services
- Amsterdam Schiphol: casino, airport television station, sauna, dry cleaner, grocery store
- Frankfurt International: supermarket, disco, sex shop
- Singapore Changi: fitness centre, karaoke lounge, putting green

If differentiation is so important, how can a service stand out? One way to compete by offering superior augmented services is to develop innovations competitors lack. Some airlines have started offering buffet service rather than prepackaged meals on their flights. American Airlines and British Airways offer showers for passengers in the arrival lounge.[30]

Another strategy for standing out is by finding a better way to deliver the core service to customers, so the benefit of the augmented service is added convenience. Some service entrepreneurs operate mobile units that allow them to come to your house to change the oil in your car or even to groom your pet. A Chicago funeral home even began to offer drive-through service to its clients, so that viewers can see a deceased loved one on a screen without leaving their cars.[31]

✳ ✳ ✳
core service The basic benefit of having a service performed.

✳ ✳ ✳
augmented services The core service plus additional services provided to enhance value.

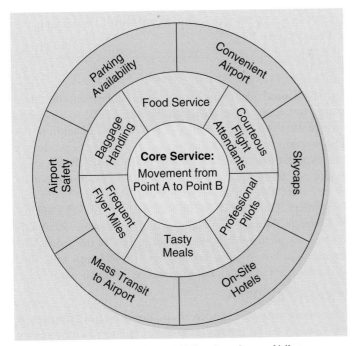

Figure 11.2 Core and Augmented Services for an Airline

SPOTLIGHT ON REAL PEOPLE *MBA Consulting Alliance (MBAC*

The MBA Consulting Alliance (MBACA) is a business consulting service staffed by business students at the University of Calgary. The company was started by Jeanne Shaw and Olivia Woo, who were MBA students at the time and were looking for employment in the summer between their first and second years of study. Since then, the business has expanded to be a year-round operation that employs up to 35 students a year to perform business consulting activities, including reviewing business plans, conducting market research, and performing financial and operational analyses.

One of MBACA's competitive advantages is the ability to offer quality services for a reasonable cost. The company charges $50 an hour for services, for which a large consulting organization would charge $200 to $300 an hour. As one MBACA board member argues, "You know you are going to get some brains, but it is not going to cost you a lot." As a result, many of MBACA's clients are small companies for whom cost is an important consideration. One client who was looking for help expanding her small business said of the service, "They had a lot of bright ideas, a lot of up-to-date knowledge."

MBACA provides a valuable service to its service providers as well. In addition to their pay ($35 per hour), the student consultants get the opportunity to try out some of the theories and techniques they have learned in school. Several people who have worked for MBACA over the years have used the experience they gained to start their own businesses or to continue into a career of consulting with a larger organization.[32]

1. Where do consulting services fit on the goods–services continuum in Figure 11.1?
2. What is the core service offered by MBACA? Are there augmented services that MBACA could offer to its clients to further differentiate its services?
3. How can MBACA ensure that their student consultants provide a quality service to clients?

Bank of Montreal
www.bmo.com

Providing Quality Service

If a service doesn't provide quality, then it could be a disservice. The Bank of Montreal launched a controversial advertising campaign in the late 1990s, which highlighted the poor service provided by Canadian banks, including themselves. The campaign, titled a "Sign of the Times," asked "Can a bank change? It is possible." As Exhibit 11.8 shows, one of the ads showed a sign saying, "Banks only help the rich." The bank wanted to differentiate itself by recognizing some of the negative service quality perceptions of Canadian banking customers and then promising to be a different bank.[33]

Judging Service Quality

The Bank of Montreal's "Sign of the Times" ads highlight the power of expectations. Many of us have come to expect nothing but aggravation when dealing with banks, so a pleasant experience comes as a nice surprise that can leave a lasting impression. Satisfaction or dissatisfaction, then, is more than a reaction to the actual performance quality of a product or service. It is influenced by prior expectations regarding the level of quality.[34] When an offering is as we expected it, we may not think much about it. If it fails to live up to our expectations, however, we will not be happy. And, on those rare occasions when it is better than we expect, we turn into loyal customers. Think about watching a young sports team such as the Toronto Raptors. In its first few years, fans may be delighted if stronger teams don't blow the team out of the water, and when the team actually has a winning season, this scores a lot of points with its followers. In contrast, a Los Angeles fan might not be so happy with "just" a winning season but rather wants the team to win championships on a regular basis.

QUALITY IS ABOUT EXCEEDING EXPECTATIONS

Quality service ensures that customers are satisfied with what they paid for. However, as we've seen, satisfaction is relative, because the service recipient compares the current experience to some prior set of expectations. That's what makes delivering quality service tricky. What may seem like excellent service to one customer may be mediocre to another

person "spoiled" by earlier encounters with an exceptional service provider. Thus, marketers must identify customer expectations and then work hard to exceed them.

The Canadian hotel chain Delta Hotels (www.deltahotels.com) has worked on improving the aspect of its service for which guests most often expect to have problems: check-in time. Delta has developed a frequent customer program called Delta Privilege, through which it collects pertinent information about guests, such as the guest's room preferences and credit card number. This advance preparation allows the company to promise one-minute check-in to its Privilege members, which exceeds most guests' expectations. Meeting or exceeding expectations is not easy. These expectations can be influenced by stories people hear from friends and acquaintances, and they are not always realistic in the first place.[35] In some cases, there is little marketers can do to smooth ruffled feathers. Exaggerated customer expectations, such as providing a level of personal service impossible for a large company to accomplish, account for about 75% of the complaints reported by service businesses. However, providing customers with logical explanations for service failures and compensating them in some way can reduce dissatisfaction substantially.[36]

Ironically, the employees who have the greatest impact on service perceptions are among the lowest-ranking individuals in the company. This makes it especially important for management to engage in **internal marketing**, selling the firm's own employees on the idea that they work for a superior company of which they can be proud. If the service provider doesn't believe in the job and the company, this attitude will quickly be apparent to the customer.

The Ritz-Carlton hotel chain is legendary for anticipating guests' desires, and one reason is the company's extensive internal marketing efforts. New employees receive an intensive two-day orientation, 100 additional hours of training, plus a daily appearance inspection. To ensure that attentiveness to guests' needs remains at a peak, the company regularly surveys customers and even hires outside auditors to pose as guests.[37]

EVALUATIVE DIMENSIONS OF SERVICE QUALITY

Because services are inseparable, in that they are not produced until the time they are consumed, it is difficult to make a prepurchase evaluation of quality. Most service businesses cannot offer a free trial. Because services are variable, it is hard to predict consistency of quality, and there is little or no opportunity for comparison shopping. The selection process for services is somewhat different than with goods, especially for services that are highly intangible, such as those on the right end of the continuum in Figure 11.1.[38] Services marketers need to clearly communicate the benefits their service will provide, as illustrated in the ad for Telus in Exhibit 11.9.

It is helpful for marketers to understand the criteria consumers use to judge a service, especially when these standards vary among different target

✳ ✳ ✳
internal marketing Marketing activities aimed at employees to inform them about the firm's offerings and their high quality.

Sometimes a company lowers expectations of service quality, so that it's sure to exceed them. That's why Disney would rather overestimate than underestimate waiting times at each attraction, and people are "pleasantly surprised" when they take a trip on Space Mountain sooner than they had planned.[39] Is it true that "ignorance is bliss"; that is, should companies bend the truth in this way to satisfy their customers?

good OR bad DECISION?

Exhibit 11.9

This Telus ad tries to clearly identify the benefits its service provides.

markets. In general, marketers think about the following three dimensions that customers use to assess quality.

Search qualities are the attributes that the consumer can examine before purchase. These include colour, style, price, fit, smell, and texture. Tangible goods are more likely to have these characteristics, so services need to build them in by paying attention to such details as the style of flight attendants' uniforms or the decor of a hotel room. The "Service Experience Blueprint" shown in Figure 11.3 illustrates how one design firm tried to build in such cues for a grocery chain. The company planned an upgraded, freshly painted parking lot that included a special preferred parking space for expectant mothers (complete with a stork logo) to signal that the company cares.[40] Attention to detail makes a difference.

Experience qualities are product characteristics that customers can determine during or after consumption. For example, we can't predict how good a vacation we'll have until we have had it, so marketers need to reassure customers before the fact that they are in for a positive experience. A travel agency may invest in a slick presentation complete with alluring images of a tropical resort, and perhaps even supply enthusiastic recommendations from other clients who had a positive experience.

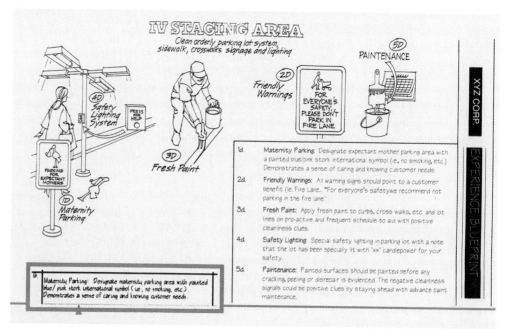

Figure 11.3 Service Experience Blueprint

Credence qualities are attributes we find difficult to evaluate even *after* we've experienced them. For example, most of us don't have the expertise to know if our doctor's diagnosis is correct.[41] Evaluations here are difficult and, to a great extent, the client must trust the service provider. That is why tangible clues of professionalism, such as diplomas or an organized office, count toward purchase satisfaction.

Measuring Service Quality

Because the customer's experience of a service is crucial to determining future patronage, service marketers feel that measuring positive and negative service experiences is important in services industries. Indeed, one-third of the business of marketing research firms is now devoted to measuring customer satisfaction *after* the sale.[42]

Marketers can gather consumer responses in a variety of ways (see Chapter 5). For example, some companies hire "mystery shoppers" to check on hotels and airlines and report back. These shoppers usually work for a research firm, although some airlines reportedly recruit "spies" from the ranks of their most frequent flyers. Some firms also locate "lost customers," former patrons, to find out what turned them off the service provider so that they can correct the problem.

GAP ANALYSIS

Gap analysis is a measurement tool that gauges the difference between a customer's expectation of service quality and what actually occurred. By identifying specific places in the service system where there is a wide gap between what is expected and what is received, services marketers can get a handle on what needs improvement. These are some major gaps discovered.[43]

* The firm doesn't understand what its customers' expectations are. Many service organizations have an operations orientation rather than a customer orientation. For example, a bank may close its branches early in the day to balance transactions, because that's more efficient, even though it's not convenient for customers who want to go to the bank after work.

* The firm fails to establish a quality control program. Successful service firms, such as American Express and McDonald's, develop written quality goals. American Express found that customers complained most about its responsiveness, accuracy, and timeliness. The company established 180 specific goals to correct these problems, and it now monitors how fast employees answer phones in an effort to be more responsive.

* Employees do not deliver the service at the level specified by the company. Teamwork is crucial to service success. Unfortunately, many companies don't clearly specify what they expect of employees. Merrill Lynch addressed this problem by assembling its operations personnel into quality groups of 8 to 15 employees to foster teamwork among workers and clarify its expectations for how the workers should interact with clients.

* The firm makes exaggerated promises or does not accurately describe its service to customers. When the Holiday Inn hotel chain developed an advertising campaign based on the promise that guests would receive "No Surprises," many operations personnel opposed the idea, saying that *no* service organization, no matter how good, can anticipate every single thing that can go wrong. Sure enough, the campaign was unsuccessful. A services firm is better off communicating exactly what the customer can expect, and what will happen if the company doesn't deliver on its promises.

THE CRITICAL INCIDENT TECHNIQUE

The **critical incident technique** is another way to measure service quality.[44] The company collects and closely analyzes very specific customer complaints. It can then identify *critical incidents*, specific contacts between consumers and service providers that result in dissatisfaction.

Some critical incidents involve situations in which the expectations of customers cannot be met by the service organization. For example, it is impossible to satisfy a passenger who says to a flight attendant: "Come sit with me. I don't like to fly alone." In other cases, though, the firm is capable of meeting these expectations but fails to do so. For example,

✳ ✳ ✳

gap analysis A marketing research methodology that measures the difference between a customer's expectation of a service quality and what actually occurred.

✳ ✳ ✳

critical incident technique A method for measuring service quality in which marketers use customer complaints to identify critical incidents, specific face-to-face contacts between consumers and service providers that cause problems and lead to dissatisfaction.

the customer might complain to a flight attendant, "My seat won't recline." A potentially dissatisfied customer can be turned into a happy one if the problem is addressed, or perhaps even if the customer is told why the problem can't be solved at this time. Customers tend to be fairly forgiving *if* they are given a reasonable explanation for the problem. Unfortunately, that doesn't occur very often.

Strategies for Developing and Managing Services

What can the firm do to maximize the likelihood that a customer will choose its service and become a loyal customer? With services differing from goods in so many ways, decision makers struggle to market something that isn't there. However, many of the same strategic issues apply. Table 11.1 illustrates how three different types of health care practitioners can devise marketing strategies to improve their practices. In this section, we'll review ways that a service business can determine its best prospects and design a service experience that will be distinctive.

Services as Theatre

One way to develop a services strategy that lets the firm stand out from the competition is to think about a service as a show put on for an audience. Whether it's a visit to a doctor's office or a meal at a fine restaurant, each service contact can be thought of as a dramatic performance, complete with actors, props, and costumes. A *service performance* often takes place in two areas, the *back stage* and the *front stage*. The back stage is where the service is produced, and the front stage is where it gets delivered to the customer.

Table 11.1 Health Care Marketing Strategies

	Psychologist	Orthodontist	Chiropractor
Marketing Objective	Add ten billable hours per week	Attract five new adult patients; increase awareness of practice in community to generate referrals	Increase new patients by 50% within one year
Target Markets	Inactive clients	Primary market: Women 25–55, middle income and above Secondary market: Male executives over 40	25–50-year-olds, 65% blue collar, 60% female within a 6–km radius of my office
Benefits Offered	Feel happy Solve problems	Beauty Professional self-confidence	Relief of back, neck, shoulder, head pain; convenience
Strategy	Write a letter to former patients; remind them that if they have learned the basics of turning their lives around, they may just need some short-term assistance now	Talk to 200 people in two days at a local health fair; position myself as the community specialist in cosmetic dentistry	Change location to a new shopping centre—locate between a supermarket and a fitness centre that attracts a large female clientele. Give seminars at the health club and place articles in its newsletter

Source: Adapted from Alan L. Bernstein, *The Health Professsional's Marketing Handbook* (Chicago: Year Book Medical Publishers, 1988).

Think of the activities that occur in a fancy restaurant. On the front stage, waiters, wine stewards, and the maître d' "perform" for diners by reciting daily specials, opening bottles with a flourish, or even bringing flaming delicacies to the table without burning down the restaurant. The fine restaurant will take great care to set its tables elegantly and play appropriate music softly in the background. Back stage in the kitchen is another story. The kitchen may be a much more chaotic environment where the chefs and waiters work hard to get the meals just right. In addition, like the scenes in a play, a service usually happens in steps so that service marketers can anticipate the points at which problems may arise. A look at the flowchart of a hotel service in Figure 11.4 shows the many different operations on stage and behind the scenes.

Targeting and Positioning Strategies for Services

Like any other product, perhaps the most crucial strategic decisions for a service revolve around its definition in the market: Who are the target customers, and how do they perceive the service? As we saw in Chapter 8, the target marketing process is an essential part of many marketing strategies. Let's see how these concepts apply to service businesses.

TARGETING: DEFINING THE SERVICE CUSTOMER OR AUDIENCE

Just as there are few (if any) physical goods that appeal to everyone, it is also true that not all people or organizations are interested in receiving a particular service. Residents of a nursing home probably won't be good candidates for body piercing, a small retailer probably can't afford to hire a sophisticated management consultant, and high-school students may not line up to buy tickets to a Pavarotti concert.

Most services can identify a target customer that they can serve well. In some cases, an organization may develop a separate strategy for multiple segments. To understand how this process works, consider how a local theatre might go about identifying desirable market segments and targeting them.

The theatre can usually identify a small, hard-core group of supporters and a larger group of occasional attendees. It should classify the audience by light, medium, and heavy attendance, and determine if these groups differ in terms of psychographics, demographics, and benefits sought, so that it can tailor its marketing mix to each. Depending on the strategic goal of the arts organization, these are some targeting actions it might take:[45]

- *Audience maintenance:* If the goal is to encourage current customers to deepen their commitment to the organization, the theatre company could develop newsletters for subscribers or send letters thanking them for their patronage.

- *Audience enrichment:* If the goal is to enhance the experience of attendees to ensure their ongoing loyalty to the organization, the company can improve augmented services, such as parking, lighting, or temperature control in the auditorium.

- *Audience expansion:* If the goal is to increase the number of theatre lovers who attend performances, the organization can conduct research to generate a profile of the people who now attend and target others with similar characteristics. For example, they can attach a postage-paid survey to the back of a play program and encourage audience members to complete and return it.

- *Audience development:* If the goal is to convince non-attenders who don't normally go to the theatre that the productions are something they would enjoy, expose people to productions by encouraging the development of school programs, corporate events, and group sales. The Canadian Opera Company went a step further by running racy ads to entice people to try the opera. An ad for a production of Strauss's *Elektra* went so far as to suggest that the troubled characters from the Greek tragedy would be at home on the *Jerry Springer* show.[46]

The Canadian Opera Company
www.coc.ca

POSITIONING: DEFINING THE SERVICE TO CUSTOMERS

Chapter 8 explained how positioning is a process of creating a specific image for a product that differentiates it from competitors. Researchers have identified five dimensions that successfully position a service, whether it's a theatre, bank, baseball team, or auto repair shop.[47]

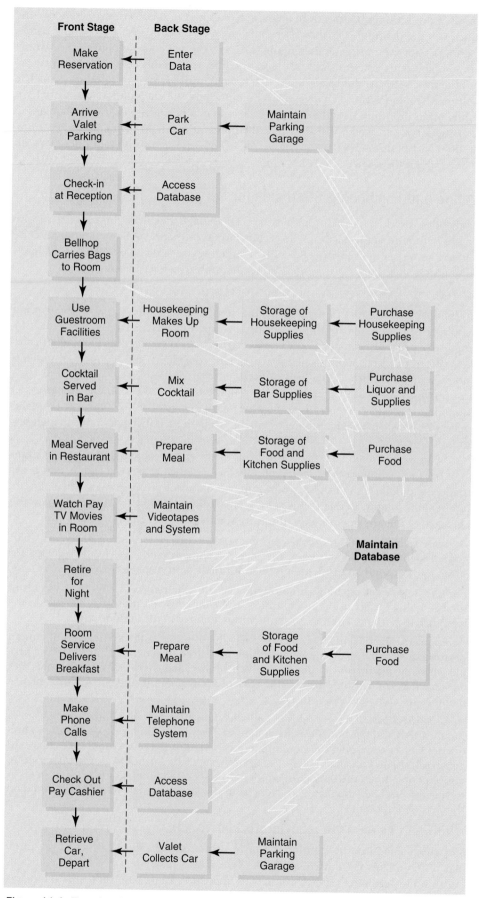

Figure 11.4 Flowcharting a Hotel Visit

Real People, Real Decisions
How it worked out at Charity.ca

The Charity.ca team was strengthened with the addition of a new vice-president of marketing, Rosanne Caron, formerly with Canoe.ca, who brought in a wealth of marketing, advertising, research, and Internet experience. The team chose Option 2 and targeted their Web site to consumers, aged 30 to 54, with some post-secondary education, high credit card use, and access to and comfort with the Internet. They developed stories for the site with the needs of this group in mind, such as "Donor Driven—You're in Control" and "How Much Should I Give?" Although age and psychographic variables had been used to define this group, the team realized that their initial consideration of it was missing an important variable: gender. Studies were showing that women take the lead in household decision making with respect to charitable giving. Additionally, the population of women on the Internet was growing quickly. The Charity.ca marketing team gave consideration to refining their target segment and developing content on the Web site that would specifically appeal to women in the 30 to 54 age group.

They also identified a secondary target market for Charity.ca: The consumers identified in Option 1, people aged 20 to 30, were an important, secondary segment, that represented a lot of potential for donations in the future. These consumers were brand-new donors who had no affiliation with a particular cause. The objective with these consumers would focus on "training" them about issues in charitable giving, with the hope that they would give when they are financially able. In support of the choice of this secondary target segment, Charity.ca used an innovative method to promote their Web site during the summer before their main media launch—a crew of university students called Goodwill Hunters (see below). These young people visited charities and participated in events across Canada to create a community-level awareness of Charity.ca's services. It was also hoped that these students would help spread the word about Charity.ca among their peer group when they returned to school.

As the team considered the future of Charity.ca, they realized that targeting would become even more significant and complex in the future. Their vision was a Web site that would eventually service six or seven major segments of consumers and would include many other features, possibly even merchandising. Visit the Charity.ca Web site. Can you identify segments that the site should be targeting in the future?

Tangibles: Services often rely heavily on **physical evidence**, such as apparel, facilities, graphics on a Web site, and other visible signals of product quality, to communicate a desired position. Such cues as the facility (modern decor versus traditional), distinctive colours (the dependable dark brown of UPS versus the bright purple and orange of Federal Express), and logos (the tiger of AGF versus the bull of Merrill Lynch) all communicate the underlying characteristics of the service organization. One of the most powerful ways to create physical evidence for a service is to adopt a *branding strategy*, much as a marketer of a tangible product would do. Such services marketers as Tim Hortons, Cirque du Soleil, and real estate company Century 21 have branded their services to create a unique identity for themselves. By developing a clear image for a brand name, consumers feel as if they "know" the service.

Responsiveness: Some services emphasize the speed and care with which they respond to customers' requests. For example, print shops such as Kinko's promote their 24-hour service and their preservation of their clients' valuable documents. Domino's Pizza was known for its promise to deliver a pizza within 30 minutes—until a jury awarded more than $78 million to a woman who was hit by a driver rushing to make a delivery.[48]

Empathy: An organization that says it understands its customers' needs and genuinely cares about their welfare often gains an edge on the competition. A Toronto-based funeral home successfully promoted itself with the slogan, "Where every service is special."[49]

✳ ✳ ✳
physical evidence A visible signal that communicates not only a product's quality but also the product's desired market position to the consumer.

Assurance: An organization can emphasize the knowledge or competence of its employees. This is a good strategy for minimizing risk, especially for services in which the customer finds it difficult to evaluate the quality of service received. The financial services company Standard Life Mutual Funds (www.standardlife.ca) proclaims in its ads, "Profit from our knowledge."

Chapter Summary

1. Explain the marketing of people, places, and ideas.

People, especially politicians and celebrities, are often packaged and promoted. Place marketing aims to create or change the market position of a particular locale, whether a city, province, country, resort, or institution. Social marketing, the promotion of causes and ideas, includes cause marketing, in which corporations use advertising, public service, and publicity to link themselves with a good cause in hopes of boosting sales. Not-for-profit organizations also develop marketing strategies to "sell" social services, cultural experiences, ideas such as environmental protection, or a political or religious philosophy. The marketing of religion, aimed at both increasing primary demand and at individual "brand" choice, has gained in popularity as evidenced by the increased use of religious broadcasts and religious advertising.

2. Describe the four characteristics of services, and understand how services differ from goods.

Services are products that are intangible and that are exchanged directly from producer to customer without ownership rights. Generally, services are acts that accomplish some goal and may be directed toward either people or an object. Important service characteristics are intangibility (they cannot be seen, touched, or smelled), perishability (they cannot be stored), variability (they are never exactly the same from time to time), and inseparability from the producer (most services are produced, sold, and consumed at the same time). In reality, most products are a combination of goods and services. Some services are product related: Tangible products are marketed with supporting services. Some are equipment or facility based: Elaborate equipment or facilities are required for creation of the service. Other services are people based: People are actually a part of the service marketed.

3. Explain how marketers measure service quality.

Customers' perceptions of service quality are related to their prior expectations. Because services are intangible, evaluation of service quality is more difficult than for products, and customers often look for cues to help them decide whether they received satisfactory service. Gap analysis measures the difference between customer expectations of service quality and what actually occurred. Using the critical incident technique, service firms can identify the specific contacts between customers and service providers that create dissatisfaction.

4. Explain marketing strategies for services and not-for-profit organizations.

Not-for-profit organizations need to focus on defining strategic objectives, understanding who competes with them for people's dollars or beliefs, and developing a target marketing strategy. Some tactics focus on enhanced satisfaction of current customers, whereas others emphasize developing new markets for the organization. In developing strategies for services, marketers focus on both the core service, or the basic benefit received, and on augmented services, which include innovative features and convenience of service delivery. As with strategies for marketing physical goods, service strategies include targeting segments of service customers and positioning the service to differentiate it from competitors' offerings. This can be done by emphasizing such dimensions as tangibles (including employee appearance, design of facilities, and company logos), responsiveness, empathy, and assurance.

Chapter Review

Marketing Concepts: Testing Your Knowledge

1. What are intangibles? How do basic marketing concepts apply to the marketing of intangibles?

2. What do we mean by marketing people? Marketing places? Marketing ideas?

3. What is a service? What are the important characteristics of services that make them different from goods?

4. What is the goods–services continuum? What are product-related services, equipment- or facility-based services, and people-based services?

5. How do marketers create augmented services to increase market share?

6. How do consumers evaluate service quality? How do marketers work to create service quality?

7. Describe some of the ways marketers measure service quality.

8. How may services marketing strategies be compared to directing a theatre performance?

9. How does target marketing apply to the marketing of services?

10. What are the five dimensions that successfully position a service?

Marketing Concepts: Discussing Choices and Issues

1. Sometimes service quality may not meet customers' expectations. What problems have you experienced with quality in the delivery of the following services? What do you think is the reason for the poor quality?

   a hotel accommodations

   b dry cleaning

   c a haircut

   d your education

2. There has been much criticism of the way politicians have been marketed in recent years. What are some of the ways marketing has helped our political process? What are some ways the marketing of politicians might have an adverse effect on our government?

3. Many not-for-profit and religious organizations have found that they can be more successful by marketing their ideas. What are some ways that these organizations market themselves that are like and different from the marketing by for-profit businesses?

Marketing Practice: Applying What You've Learned

1. Because of increased competition in their community, you have been hired as a marketing consultant by a large group of family dentists. You know that the characteristics of services—intangibility, perishability, variability, and inseparability from the producer—create unique marketing challenges. You also know that these challenges can be met with creative marketing strategies. Outline the challenges each of the four characteristics of services create for marketing the dentists. List your ideas for what might be done to meet each of these challenges.

2. As an entrepreneur, you plan to open a car wash. You feel that you have the best chance of success if you can create a product that is superior to that offered by competing businesses. Put together a list of ways in which you can augment the basic service offering (features, delivery, and so on) to develop a better product. List the advantages and disadvantages of each.

3. You are a customer for a post-secondary education, a very expensive service product. You know that a service organization can create a competitive advantage by focusing on how the service is delivered after it has been purchased—making sure the service is efficiently and comfortably delivered to the customer. Develop a list of recommendations for your college or university for improving the delivery of its service. Consider both classroom and non-classroom aspects of the educational product.

4. Assume that you have been hired as a campaign manager for a local candidate for mayor. Your job is to create and manage a plan for marketing a person. Prepare an outline for your marketing plan. First list the special problems and challenges associated with marketing a person rather than a physical product. Then outline your ideas for product, price, and promotion strategies.

5. You have been recently hired by your city government to head up a program to create 100% compliance with recycling regulations. Develop a presentation for the city council in which you will outline the problems in "selling" recycling. Develop an outline for the presentation. Be sure to focus on each of the four Ps.

Marketing Mini-Project: Learning by Doing

1. Select a service that you will purchase in the next week or so.

2. As you experience the service, record the details of every aspect, including people, physical facilities, location, waiting time, hours, transaction, other customers, tangible aspects, search qualities, credence qualities.

3. Recommend improvements to the service encounter.

Real People, Real Surfers: Exploring the Web

Fast-food restaurants fall in the middle of the goods–services continuum—half goods and half services. To be successful in this highly competitive market, fast-food chains must carefully develop targeting and positioning strategies. Visit the Web sites of the some fast-food chains: Harvey's (www.harveys.ca), McDonald's (www.mcdonalds.ca), and Wendy's (www.wendys.com), which links to Tim Hortons.com. Thoroughly investigate each site.

1. How is each Web site designed to appeal to each restaurant's target market?

2. How does each restaurant position its product? How is this positioning communicated through the Web site?

3. What changes or improvements would you recommend for each Web site?

MARKETING IN ACTION

Cineplex Odeon

The market for cinemas in Canada hit bottom in 1991, when consumers were more likely to rent videos or seek out other entertainment options. Cinema operators responded by trying to make movie going a total entertainment experience that would offer benefits that home movie watching couldn't. In particular, large theatre chains like Famous Players (www.famousplayers.com) and AMC Theatres of Canada embarked on huge expansion plans in the late 1990s, which have redefined the experience of movie going.

Cineplex Odeon (www.loewscineplex.com/canada), the company that pioneered the multiplex concept in Canada in 1979 with the opening of a 10-screen theatre in Toronto, just started its expansion plans in 2000. Management problems at Cineplex in the 1990s stalled expansion plans, but in 1998 Cineplex merged with Loews Theaters, a US subsidiary of Sony Corporation, and gained the capital needed to try to regain market share. Speaking of their delayed expansion Allen Karp, president of Cineplex Odeon, said, "Famous was able to get out of the box first and make a big boom, and there's a secondary boom with AMC. We're the echo."

Famous Players led the movie theatre expansion by building mega-theatres under three different brand names: Silver Screen, Colossus, and Coliseum. All of these theatre complexes offered bigger screens, more comfortable stadium seating with cup-holder armrests, and entertainment extras in the lobbies, including interactive game centres and expanded food and drink options. The company also expanded its offerings on its screens by showing live concerts and live pay-per-view wrestling events at their theatres. AMC entered the movie market in Toronto in 1998 with the same entertainment style complexes offered by Famous Players, but with the addition of "love seats," chairs that had retractable arm rests, to appeal to the date segment. In describing the transformation of the movie theatre environment, Dennis Kucherway, vice-president of public relations for Famous Players stated, "We needed to bring the market back, but we wanted to create something that would make people come to the theatre and stay longer."

Cineplex began its expansion program in 2000 with plans to add 12 new megaplexes, resulting in 164 new screens and 40 000 additional seats. The company is trying to differentiate itself from Famous Players by targeting a different market. While Famous Players targets consumers aged 12 to 24, Cineplex is trying to appeal to an older audience with a more sophisticated and understated environment. Instead of the loud, theme-park atmosphere of most Famous Players locations, Cineplex will offer a less cluttered lobby area and a café called Alan Smithee's.

Just as Cineplex embarked on its expansion to regain market share, a new entrant to the market, Galaxy, allied with Famous Players, announced plans to enter the market with 20 new theatres across Canada. Their theatres will include Playdium Interactive arcades and such fast food outlets as Pizza Pizza and New York Fries. Galaxy is also engaging in innovative and aggressive marketing activities to build its presence in the market. When it opened its first theatre in the summer of 2000 in Peterborough, Ontario, the company distributed 25 000 videos to households in the area. The 30-minute video, which promoted the Galaxy theatre and showed trailers from 12 blockbuster movies, met with enthusiastic response from customers.

The entrance of yet another large competitor in the movie theatre market raises questions about how Cineplex Odeon should compete in this market. Can the Cineplex Odeon theatre experience be improved so that it is differentiated from its competitors?

Sources: Peter Vamos, "Cineplex Odeon fights back," *Strategy Magazine*, 31 July 2000: 1; Astrid Van Den Broek, "FP breaks out of movie house mould," *Marketing Magazine*, 17 January 2000, www.marketingmag.ca; David Carr, "Luring audiences back to the cinema," *Marketing Magazine*, 18 January 1999, www.marketingmag.ca; Carey Toane, "Direct video drop lures moviegoers," *Marketing Magazine*, 17 July 2000: 4; Joe Chidley, "Attack of the monster cinemas," *Canadian Business*, 11 December 1998: 26–34.

THINGS TO THINK ABOUT

1. What is the problem facing Cineplex Odeon?
2. What factors are important to understanding this problem?
3. What alternatives might Cineplex Odeon consider?
4. What are your recommendations for solving the problem and how would they be implemented?

Maybe You Can Judge a Bug by Its Cover

Computer Friendly Stuff learns the benefits of expanding its product line and the benefits of good packaging.

So What Do You Have for an Encore?

As Computer Friendly Stuff completed its first year in business, we realized that we could not survive with only one product. The toy industry is always hungry. What's popular one Christmas is old news the following year. As a result, a company is only as good as its last product. Hence, last year's "Tickle-Me" Elmo breeds this year's "Walking-Talking" Elmo, which will probably breed "Oops, Somebody Made a Stinky" Elmo, and so on. Now, we were far from peaking with Computer Bug (Beanie Babies were around for four years before making it big), but already we had numerous customers asking for additional CFS products. We also discovered that large retailers don't like dealing with one-product companies. In many cases, bringing in a new vendor requires them to complete a massive amount of paperwork. Having multiple products makes the effort more worthwhile to them. Also, if a company has multiple products, the retailer has more confidence that the company is going to be around for a while.

The first question we faced was whether we should develop additional Computer Bug characters or an entirely new product line. We decided to move ahead in both directions, though our main focus was on developing a new product line. We did this for two reasons. First, we felt that the Computer Bug had not yet reached maturity as a brand: The demand wasn't great enough to warrant follow-on products. Second, we decided that by launching an entirely new product, we could spread out our risks and increase our overall chances of success.

New Product Development at CFS

Computer Friendly Stuff develops new products in a fairly unsophisticated manner. We come up with ideas while in the shower, in the car, or at the movies; then we write them down and put them in a file marked "ideas that we got in the shower, car, or movies." Every now and then, we open the file and discuss the ideas or, if we are bored, the movies. Fortunately, this haphazard method has worked quite well for us so far and we have more ideas than we have the time to develop them.

In general, when we began, we limited ourselves to ideas that make computers more fun to use—products that had the same core benefit. As we grow, we are expanding into other areas, such as non-computer–related toys. In each case, however, our ideas stem from what we perceive to be market needs.

Monitor Morphs is an idea that I had fairly early on. This product consists of two bendable arms that attach to a computer, plus a CD-ROM containing screen savers. The arms stick out from the side of the monitor to hold pens or paper. The screen savers are giant faces that perform distinct functions, including falling asleep, and, of course, barfing onto the monitor screen (when we get stuck for ideas, we go with barf). The total effect of the product is that it makes your computer look like a giant head with arms.

We sat on the Monitor Morph concept for a while because we couldn't agree on a good name. Product names are incredibly important to us. Good names help move a product. "Cabbage Patch Kids" works much better than "Maternity Ward Newborns." "GI Joe" works much better than "GI Fred." We also feel that good names improve our day-to-day working conditions. If they are fun to say, they will be fun to describe to our customers and vendors. We spend a lot of time working on the names for our products and divisions, because we want something that is goofy, descriptive, and easy to say, spell, read, and remember. We have applied this line of thought to all of our names, including Computer Friendly Stuff, the Original Computer Bug, Monitor Morphs, Corporate Friendly Stuff (a new division), and Chubby Stubbies (another new product—cute chubby stuffed animals with stubby little legs).

Although Monitor Morphs serve the same need as the Computer Bug, there is a major difference between the two. Simply put, we feel that the Computer Bug is a strong concept: We look at the Bug as a potential fran-

chise. We would like to grow it in several ways, including pitching a TV show around it, licensing the characters, and developing offshoot products. We look at the Monitor Morphs as more of a one-time fad product that may or may not generate a degree of licensed offshoot products. But you never can tell. Monitor Morphs may ultimately be more popular. Warner Brothers, for example, has already expressed interest in creating Monitor Morphs with us for their characters. If this deal goes through, and they are produced and sell well, the Monitor Morph concept may prove to have a longer product life cycle than we originally planned.

Fortunately, product development for the Morphs was much easier than product development for the Computer Bug. Looking back on the development of the Computer Bug, we realize that we were in the Stone Age. My first go at product development was to build the prototypes myself. ("Susie, I need more Elmer's Glue.") I quickly realized that retail buyers weren't interested in toys that looked like their third grader's art project, so I turned to outside suppliers. Working with North American suppliers turned out to be expensive due to labour costs, so we gradually developed solid ties with overseas companies. The large number of suppliers in Asia works to our advantage. Most companies are willing to develop products for free in exchange for the rights to manufacture them. We are now at the point where we can submit sketches, prototypes, or mock-ups to our overseas supplier and receive finished prototypes in a matter of weeks. It usually takes two or three revisions to get things perfect, but the process is very cost effective.

Packaging 101

You would think that new product development is the key to success and that packaging and distribution are relatively minor issues. Not so. The best product in the world will fail if a supposedly simple thing like packaging is done incorrectly. We found this out the hard way. We actually went through three different types of packages for the Computer Bug in our first year. Had we used focus groups or a professional package design firm in the beginning, we probably would not have experienced these problems.

Our first package design suffered from the "It's a dessert/It's a floorwax" problem. We tried to do too much. We began with putting the Bug in a plastic lab beaker so it would look like some type of lab experiment. The rubber stopper on top of the beaker had a coin slot so that the beaker could double as a bug piggy bank. Sadly, this was my idea. I obviously wasn't subscribing to the "less is more" theory.

The beaker/bank idea was wrong in so many ways for us. First, the round shape took up too much valuable shelf space: Retailers hate anything that wastes space and doesn't stack neatly. Second, shoppers couldn't see the CD-ROM. We found that the buyer noticed the toy figure, but often missed the main concept: The CD allows you to "see" the Bug living inside your computer. Third, the package design didn't work. Once assembled, the Bug wouldn't stay in place. On one trip to a small toy store, we discovered that all the bugs had spun around in the beakers so that they had their backs to the customer. Summing up, our first packaging was a disaster. On the upside, my mom keeps hers on the kitchen counter and has saved $12 in it.

Our second attempt at packaging was more conservative. We threw out the beaker concept and developed a small box with a plastic window. The box was designed to look like a computer. When you looked inside the computer screen, you saw the Bug smiling out at you with the CD-ROM behind it. It was a good package. Overseas customers loved its compact size. However, we realized it wasn't a great package, because customers still had trouble seeing the CD-ROM in the back. Also, the package was ugly, because it was the colour of a computer. Always a sure way to attract customers: "Hey, buy our dull grey product!"

With our third attempt, we called in the experts. For a larger firm, this would mean hiring a design consultant. We sort of did this. We cooked a big spaghetti dinner for a British package designer who lived in our building. Then we locked the door and piped in Winston Churchill's Battle of Britain speech until he came up with something we could use. The plan worked. He came out with his hands in the air holding a workable blister pack. A blister pack is a flat piece of cardboard with a piece of clear moulded plastic covering the product. It is fairly common, but our design was unique in that it had "legs" that allowed the product to stand alone as well as hang on a peg. Also, the bright yellow package clearly showed the CD-ROM along with the Bug. The only downside was that it took up more shelf space than the second packaging.

One terrific bonus of this design was that we could adopt it for our other products. Christmas 1998 featured the redesigned packages, and we saw immediate results in the number of reorders. The lesson we took from the painful packaging process was that we can't always reinvent the wheel. When we first began, we thought that we'd get more attention by using really unusual packaging (the beaker). What we learned is that some ideas are popular (square stacking boxes), because they are the best ways to do things. Now, we have enough piggy banks in our warehouse to use as Christmas gifts through the year 2037.

If you thought our product and packaging decisions required a lot of rethinking, wait until you read our next case on pricing.

Questions

1. CFS chose to develop a new product before building on the Computer Bug line. Do you think this was a good decision? The obvious way to develop this product is to develop additional Computer Bug characters. Can you think of other ways to develop this product? Describe other possible characters. What do they build on and how do they extend the line?

2. CFS developed Monitor Morphs after developing the Original Computer Bug. Do other new products come to mind? Describe them.

3. Can CFS set up a regular process to ensure that it develops new products on a regular basis?

4. Are Monitor Morphs a fad, as CFS claims, or a potential franchise? If Warner Brothers is interested, who else might be? What would you like to see as a Monitor Morph product?

5. How does one establish a brand with a toy that is easy to copy? What does branding mean here?

6. Develop your own package for Monitor Morphs. Draw a prototype. What is most important in this package?

Marketing Plan Questions

Refer to the Sample Marketing Plan in Appendix A as you answer these questions about developing and modifying a marketing plan for CFS.

1. For this year's marketing plan, identify the current location of the Computer Bug, Monitor Morphs, and Chubby Stubbies within the product life cycle.

2. Looking ahead to next year's marketing plan, describe the screening methods and business analysis CFS should use as part of its new product development process.

CBC 🔴 V I D E O   C A S E   1

Shifting to the US

Shift (www.shift.com) is a Canadian-based magazine for "living in a digital culture." It features articles on such topics as music, technology, politics, and sex. After operating for seven years in Canada, Shift was preparing to enter the US market in the fall of 1999. While a launch of any new product is a difficult process, Shift would be one of about 1000 new magazines that are launched in the US market every year, only half of which would make it to their second year.

Andrew Heinzman, the founder and publisher of Shift, believes that despite the competitive environment, there is an opportunity for the magazine to do well in the US market. The US-based Wired magazine used to be very similar in content to Shift. However, Wired has been repositioned as a business technology magazine and now targets an older reader, averaging 43 years of age. Heinzman hopes to fill the niche in the US that Wired used to occupy and attract 25- to 35-year-old urban, computer-literate consumers.

Preparing for the US launch required US $5 million to cover the rent for a New York office and the salaries of several employees and consultants who would help Heinzman with the launch. He had four months to prepare for it. Heinzman was hoping to attract 100 000 readers with the launch issue and then build readership in the US to 290 000 by the end of five years.

Even though Shift was going to be the same in the Canadian and US markets, product modification in this industry is continuous. After each issue is published, the Shift editorial team, who view their role as just as much marketing as journalism, discuss the details of the issue and how the next one could improve on it. They continued this type of product development during the preparation for the US launch and also began considering what type of articles and cover might sell best in the US market.

Heinzman hired a direct mail specialist to help develop a US marketing plan. The consultant presented several different types of magazine covers that he thought would work in the US and recommended that the team go with one featuring a beautiful woman in a suggestive pose. The editorial staff was initially concerned that this was not consistent with the philosophy of Shift, but they eventually went with the recommended cover, because they felt it would attract attention in the crowded US magazine market.

To further attract attention of both advertisers and readers, Heinzman hired PR specialists. They ensured that Shift got some coverage in the New York Post and planned a launch party for 1000 people, including media representatives and potential advertisers. The Shift team was disappointed that no US TV network attended the party, but they were still hopeful that their magazine would cut through the clutter and be successful in the US market.

Questions

1. In addition to the methods discussed in the case, what else could Shift do to increase awareness and interest among potential readers in the US? What could they do to increase awareness and interest among potential advertisers in the US?

2. Visit the Shift Web site (www.shift.com) and view the sample issues online. What kinds of articles are included in the magazine? Have any other new products been added to complement the printed magazine? Is there any opportunity to provide feedback on Shift? Do you think the Web site is effective?

3. Based on the adoption rate factors described in Chapter 9, do you think Shift has a good chance of surviving? Why or why not?

Source: This case was prepared by Auleen Carson and is based on "Shift USA," Venture #725 (19 October 1999).

CBC ◉ VIDEO CASE 2

Battle of the Brands

Many marketing decision makers consider brand management to be one of the most important components of marketing management. From the company's perspective, branding is critical for both creating a unique identity in the marketplace and establishing credibility and loyalty. Successful branding leads to the development of brand equity, or the value of the brand. Since strong brand equity can allow companies to charge higher prices for their products, developing brand equity is a goal of many marketing programs. Similarly, strong brand equity can pave the way for the company to introduce brand extensions, new products that leverage the existing brand equity by using the same brand name.

With so many companies striving to create brand equity, consumers are faced with a clutter of brands in the marketplace, which is often confusing and frustrating. One response to this clutter is a trend, especially among younger consumers, to reject branding and brand extensions. The dilemma for companies, therefore, is how to brand effectively without alienating consumers. Three Canadian companies that have found different ways to respond to this problem are Roots, Greens Plus, and Jones Soda.

The strong equity of the Roots brand has provided that company with multiple opportunities for brand extensions. Roots is putting their brand name on more and more products, from fragrances to home decor to pet accessories to an airline. Don Green, co-founder of Roots, admits that he is concerned about overextending the brand and recognizes that consumers place their trust in it. He is, therefore, cautious about which products he puts the Roots brand name on and always strives to maintain the high quality of the Roots products that consumers expect from the brand.

Stewart Brown is the inventor of Greens Plus, a brand of vitamins that started out as a niche brand distributed mainly through health food stores. Recently, he had to decide whether to revise his brand's identity and make it a mass market brand. Since only 15% of people who buy vitamins shop in health food stores, Brown knew that reaching the other 85% of the market through supermarkets and pharmacies would open up the potential of the brand. Although marketing consultants were telling the entrepreneur that the brand should be in the mass market, Brown hesitated to revise its positioning. He felt that the patrons of health food stores, who knew his brand as an exclusive health food store brand, would feel alienated from a mainstream brand. Ultimately, Brown decided to make Greens Plus a mainstream brand, hoping that he could do so while still maintaining the loyalty of the health food store consumers.

Peter Van Stolk of Jones Soda has developed a strong brand identity for his line of beverages in a somewhat untraditional way. Jones Soda does not run paid advertising; instead it uses the company's Web site and word of mouth to promote the brand. Van Stolk's distribution arrangements are unconventional, steering clear of major grocery chains in favour of places like laundromats and small independent convenience stores. Unpaid publicity has also played a role in building the Jones Soda brand identity. The novel anti-corporate brand positioning of Jones Soda has resulted in several articles being written about the company in the Canadian press as well as *People* magazine. Jones Soda even put their label, considered a cornerstone of traditional branding activities, into consumers' hands by running a photo contest, with the winning photo appearing on the label. The low-key but innovative approach to branding followed by Jones Soda appeals to consumers like the "anti-brand kids," who reject such branding activities as logo clothing, claiming that they don't want to be anyone's billboard.

Naomi Klein, author of *No Logo*, a book that is highly critical of brands and branding activities, claims that one pitfall of branding is that having a strong brand name is like "holding up a target saying 'kick me'." While strong branding can create opportunities for brands, it also exposes them to potential criticism. One company that has experienced this criticism is Nike. Overextension of the Nike brand name has led some consumers to rebel against it: The name was appearing on so many different types of products that consumers began to question what Nike stood for. This led first to criticisms of the company for exploiting labour in less developed countries to produce the multitude of products, and then to a decline in sales for Nike products. With branding lessons like Nike in mind, marketing managers need to think clearly about branding decisions to ensure that their brand positioning is meaningful to consumers.

Questions

1. Is the role of branding different in different industries and in consumer versus business to business markets? Can you identify industries where branding is critical and industries where it is less important?
2. Compare the Roots, Greens Plus, and Jones Soda examples from the video. What does the brand name mean to consumers in each of these cases? What implications does this have for branding decision making?
3. What recommendations would you make to Roots, Greens Plus, and Jones Soda regarding future brand extensions?

Source: This case was prepared by Auleen Carson and is based on "Overbranding," *Venture* #705 (24 November 1998).

12

Pricing the Product

CHAPTER OBJECTIVES

When you have completed your study of this chapter, you should be able to

1. Explain the importance of pricing and how prices can take both monetary and non-monetary forms.

2. Understand the pricing objectives that marketers typically have in planning pricing strategies.

3. Explain how customer demand influences pricing decisions.

4. Describe how marketers use costs, demands, and revenue to make pricing decisions.

5. Understand some of the environmental factors that affect pricing strategies.

Real People, Real Decisions ✔ ✘

Meet Astrid De Bruyn
A Decision Maker at Palliser Furniture Ltd.

Astrid De Bruyn's job is to increase sales and profitability at Palliser Furniture Ltd. Palliser, established by A.A. DeFehr in 1944, is Canada's largest household furniture manufacturer (thirteenth largest in North America) with 4200 employees; manufacturing facilities in Manitoba, Alberta, North Carolina, Mexico, and Indonesia; and international sales offices in the US, Germany, and Mexico. Palliser manufactures wood and laminated bedroom, home office, and entertainment furniture (casegoods, shipped in boxes) and leather upholstered furniture (sofas, chairs, and recliners). US sales, having doubled in each of the past few years, represent 60% of total sales of over $325 million per year.

De Bruyn is the merchandising manager for the Logic Division of Palliser Furniture Ltd., which manufactures entry-priced bedroom, home office, and entertainment furniture. She has spent seven years with Palliser in a variety of sales and marketing positions. A graduate of the University of Manitoba MBA program, she was recruited by Palliser as director of special marketing projects. After working in two sales positions—export sales manager and sales representative for Missouri, Iowa, Nebraska, and Kansas—she moved back to Winnipeg in the Spring of 1999 to assume her current position. As merchandising manager, De Bruyn is responsible for managing the product line, merchandising new introductions, and acting as a liaison between operations and sales.

Palliser Furniture Ltd.
www.palliser.com

"Yes, But What Does It Cost?"

That's certainly a top-of-mind issue for De Bruyn—in managing Palliser product lines, she is concerned with both the cost to the consumer and the cost of bringing the furniture to market. She needs to set prices that make Palliser products attractive to customers while also profitable for her organization.

The question of what to charge for a product is a central part of marketing decision making. In this chapter, we'll tackle the basic question, " What is price?" Then we'll see how marketers begin to determine pricing strategies by developing pricing objectives and by looking at the role of demand, costs, revenues, and the environment in the pricing decision process. Chapter 13 builds on this knowledge by explaining how the pricing decision process leads to pricing strategies.

Monetary and Non-monetary Prices

❋ ❋ ❋
price The value that customers give up, or exchange, to obtain a desired product.

"If you have to ask how much it is, you can't afford it!" We have all heard that, but how often do you buy something without asking the price? If we weren't concerned about price, we'd all drive dream cars, take trips to exotic places, and live like royalty. Most of us, however, need to consider a product's price before buying. **Price** is the value that customers give up, or exchange, to obtain a desired product. Payment may be in the form of money, goods, services, favours, votes, or anything else that has *value* to the other party. We'll examine the concept of price from various perspectives and discuss how pricing strategies are important to the success of an organization, and then see how price works with the other Ps of the marketing mix.

As Chapter 1 explained, marketing is the process that creates exchanges of things of value. We usually think of this exchange as people trading money for a good or a service. Often, the monetary value of a product is called something other than price, sometimes to hide the idea that you are being charged a price or perhaps to assume an air of greater respectability. For example, colleges and universities charge *tuition* for an education, a lawyer or accountant charges a *professional fee*, and students who join a chapter of the American Marketing Association pay *dues*. No matter what it is called, it's still a price.

But in some marketplace practices, price can mean exchanges of non-monetary value. Long before societies minted coins, people exchanged one good or service for another.

This practice of **bartering** was the basis for the economic development of Canada, with the Hudson's Bay Company trading goods to Northwest trappers for furs. Bartering still occurs today, and with advances in Internet technology, is increasing at more than 20% per year.[1] Canadian organizations such as Nation Wide Barter (www.nationwidebarter.com) and Barter Plus Systems Inc. (www.barterplus.com) have established large barter networks, where organizations can exchange goods and services for barter credits. Someone who owns a home at a mountain ski resort, for example, may exchange a weekend for barter credits to spend in a restaurant or for car repairs. No money changes hands, but as the Canada Customs and Revenue Agency understands well, there is an exchange of value: Taxpayers are supposed to report as income the value of goods or services received in exchange for other goods or services.

Non-monetary costs are also important for marketers to consider. When evaluating purchase alternatives, consumers take into account other economic costs such as **operating costs**, **switching costs**, and **opportunity costs**. Operating costs are those involved in using the product, such as toner in a printer. Switching costs are involved in moving from one brand to another, such as getting new cheques printed if you switch banks. Opportunity costs are the benefits and value you give up, or miss out on, by engaging in one activity or buying one product and not another, such as the income you forgo while in school.

Sometimes the lowest priced product isn't the lowest cost product over time. The personal investment consumers make in buying and using products is also a cost. Convenience-store operators, such as Mac's or 7-11, and Internet companies, such as Indigo.com, among other marketers, focus on minimizing the time, energy, and effort consumers have to expend to satisfy their needs and wants. As discussed in Chapter 6, consumers also experience psychological costs—such as stress, hassle, cognitive difficulty, and cognitive dissonance—when trying to buy and use products. (Have you ever tried to assemble a bike or gas barbecue?) Many marketers, auto-malls and courier companies, for example, focus on making it as easy as possible to buy and use their products. Psychological costs are particularly challenging when marketing ideas, such as not drinking and driving (see Exhibit 12.1). Some people perceive the social costs of not drinking to be higher than the value of reducing what

bartering The practice of exchanging a good or service for another good or service of like value.

operating costs Costs involved in using a product.

switching costs Costs involved in moving from one brand to another.

opportunity cost The value of something that is given up to obtain something else.

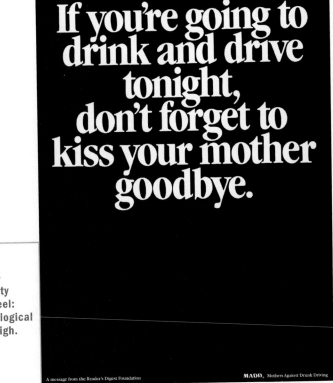

Exhibit 12.1

Selling sobriety behind the wheel: Sometimes psychological costs are too high.

they think is an already low risk of having a serious or possibly fatal accident. Sometimes, as one author put it, it's a lot more difficult to sell "brotherhood than soap."[2]

The Importance of Pricing Decisions

How important are good pricing decisions? Pricing is probably the least understood and least appreciated element of the marketing mix. Marketers like to talk about advertising and other communication elements. It's fun to think about changing technology and how firms invest in new-product development. Even decisions about channels of distribution seem to be more exciting than setting the right price. Yet, as Astrid De Bruyn realizes, price has a major strategic impact on the firm—it determines the net value received by the customer in an exchange (benefits minus costs) versus the net value (profit) received by the firm.

The plight of US airlines is a good example of how bad pricing decisions can hurt an entire industry. During the decade before 1992, companies in the airline industry engaged in a fierce price war. The per-mile fare was lowered nearly 25% (accounting for inflation of the dollar), while costs such as labour and fuel more than doubled.[3] As a result, from 1990 to 1992, the airlines lost over $10 billion, more than they had earned since the start of commercial air travel. Sometimes it's not advantageous for a firm to cut its prices.

Good pricing decisions are critical to a firm's success in the marketplace. For most organizations, the only source of profit is through the price charged for products. If customers are not willing to pay the price asked for a firm's product, the firm will not make a profit and will have failed its shareholders.

Even during the best economic times, most consumers rank "reasonable price" as the most important consideration in a purchase. In addition, reasonable prices count most when consumers decide where to shop.[4] Price is even more important during recessions, when consumers have less to spend and count their pennies carefully. Marketers try to come as close to reasonable as possible when deciding on a price.

Individual consumers aren't the only buyers who focus on price. As we saw in Chapter 7, purchasing agents for firms often put a high priority on getting the best price. At least one study has found that price may be second only to quality in these decisions. Buying professionals know that when all else is equal, getting a low price keeps costs down and helps make their firm's product competitive.[5]

Pricing and the Marketing Mix

Pricing decisions, like product decisions, are interrelated with all other marketing mix decisions. Let's take a look at each relationship.

PRICE AND DISTRIBUTION

We must study pricing decisions from the viewpoint of each member of the channel of distribution—the manufacturers, wholesalers, and retailers—that help get the product to consumers. Will the pricing plan allow each channel member to be successful in reselling the product to end customers? Is the **margin** a wholesaler or retailer earns—the difference between their cost and their selling price—too low to cover their costs?

Manufacturers usually want channel partners to perform marketing, selling, and physical distribution tasks. By taking their costs into account, channel members can figure out the margin they need to operate at a profit; a margin that covers the channel member's shipping costs, inventory costs, customer credit, overhead, and marketing and selling costs. Marketers must take these margins into consideration in deciding on a final selling price for a product. In any case, manufacturers are legally restricted from forcing channel partners to resell a product at a given price, for such control would hamper competition and hurt consumers. So, a pricing plan must appeal to channel partners on its own merits.

Consider the plight of such Canadian magazine wholesalers as Metro News or The News Group, who are intermediaries between publishers and magazine retailers. Traditionally, publishers received 50% of the retail price, distributors (who take the magazines from the publishers and deliver them to the wholesalers) 10%, and wholesalers 40%, which was split evenly with retailers. Retailers, in an attempt to increase their own profitability and combat

***
margin The difference between the cost of the product and the selling price of the product.

price discounters, have recently sought relationships with wholesalers outside their sales region and have demanded an additional four to eight percent of the split.[6] To win contracts in this more competitive marketplace, wholesalers have increased their marketing costs, cut prices, and engaged in mergers and acquisitions. They are now seeking better terms from the publishers, who are already facing financial pressures from new media and international competitors. The publishers now need to rethink their channel and pricing strategy.

The relationship between place and price also means that marketers select retail channels that match their product's price and image. For example, a shopper would not expect to find a Rolex watch in Sears or Wal-Mart, nor expect to see Timex watches on display at Birks.

PRICE AND PRODUCT

The price of the product must cover the costs of doing business, but price also sends a *signal* about product quality. For example, the prices of Rolex and Gucci watches, such as the one in Exhibit 12.2, tell consumers much about the products—that they're made from durable, precision parts—and that those who can afford them are probably in an upper-income class. And although experts and the media often try to tell women that most makeup and skin care products have identical ingredients and are pretty much the same, the premium prices charged for certain brands continue to convince consumers that higher price means a better product. Sometimes it does, and sometimes it doesn't.

The stage of the product's life cycle also affects pricing. Early in the life cycle, a single firm may be the only producer of a highly desirable product. This firm is a *monopoly supplier*, so it's able to charge a premium price. Later, as competitors enter the market, prices often go down. For example, Novell Inc. sold Netware 4.0 to business customers. The product, which links up to 1000 PCs into a common network, sold for as much as $48 000 early in the growth phase. But, as the market grew, Microsoft decided to enter with a product similar to Novell's but priced $35 000 less.[7]

PRICE AND COMMUNICATION

Pricing is strongly related to communication activities, if for no other reason than the firm needs to be sure it has enough revenue to pay for their advertising and promotion. It is just as important that the advertising strategies justify the cost of the product. For example, an ad for an expensive fragrance should project luxury, quality, and status imagery to convince shoppers that they are getting "quality" for their money. Even ads for high-end building materials, such as the Corian countertops in Exhibit 12.3, create a luxury appeal through advertising.

PRICE AND RELATIONSHIP MANAGEMENT

Pricing is also strongly tied to relationship management. High-priced products often have sufficient margins to support a closer and more responsive relationship with customers. SMED, a Calgary-based builder of office interiors, for example, entertains key clients and prospective clients at a $14-million alpine retreat and takes them salmon fishing in the

Gucci
www.gucci.com

SMED
www.smed.ca

Exhibit 12.3

Even for building materials such as Corian countertops, advertising must justify the cost of high-end products.

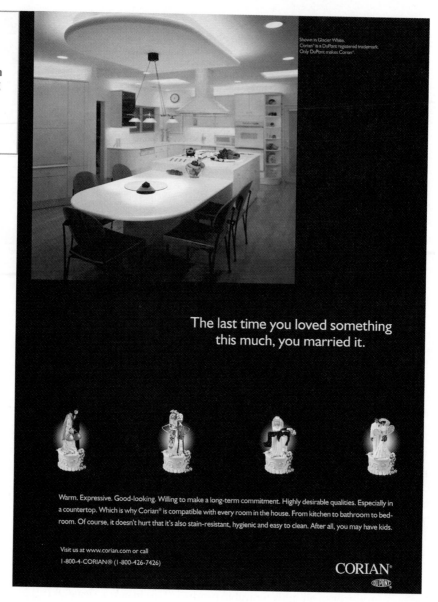

Shown in Glacier White.
Corian® is a DuPont registered trademark.
Only DuPont makes Corian®.

The last time you loved something this much, you married it.

Warm. Expressive. Good-looking. Willing to make a long-term commitment. Highly desirable qualities. Especially in a countertop. Which is why Corian® is compatible with every room in the house. From kitchen to bathroom to bedroom. Of course, it doesn't hurt that it's also stain-resistant, hygienic and easy to clean. After all, you may have kids.

Visit us at www.corian.com or call
1-800-4-CORIAN® (1-800-426-7426)

CORIAN®
DUPONT

Queen Charlotte Islands to build relationships and gain client trust.[8] Individualized attention on such a grand scale is not possible when lower margins or purchase volumes result in less profit per customer.

Developing Pricing Objectives

Taking the importance of price and its relation to other marketing mix elements into consideration, we can now start to learn how marketers focus on price. Figure 12.1 shows the steps in price planning, beginning with developing pricing objectives.

Pricing objectives must support the broader objectives of the firm, such as maximizing shareholder value, as well as its overall marketing objectives, such as increasing market share. Consider, for example, the different pricing decisions of the three major rivals in the breakfast cereal market.

From 1983 to 1988, major cereal producers increased net prices more than six percent per year. Then came the low-priced supermarket brands, which, by 1994, had captured nine percent of the market. In 1993, the top two makers of ready-to-eat cereals announced very different pricing strategies. General Mills *cut* prices on three of its major brands in the large sizes in an effort to increase its market share. Kellogg's response, however, was a 2.6% price *increase* on its cereals; they planned to soften the impact with discount coupons, the idea being to hold customers and to increase profits with frequent price-oriented promotions.[9] Three years later, in 1996, Post announced it was "changing the way the entire cereal category works" with an across-the-board price rollback, and, at the same time, initiating a new advertising campaign.[10] Each of these pricing strategies had an objective: General Mills sought to increase market share, Kellogg tried to increase profits, and Post hoped to increase consumers' total consumption of cereal. Table 12.1 provides examples of different types of pricing objectives, which we also discuss later.

Sales or Market Share Objectives

A **sales** or **market share objective** involves setting prices at a level that will maximize sales, in either dollars or units, or will attain a desired level of sales or market share. Does setting a price to increase unit sales or market share (*sales objectives*) simply mean pricing the product lower than the competition? Sometimes this is the case. The telephone industry provides a good example: Suppliers such as Telus, Sprint, and AT&T constantly make rate adjustments to keep them ahead in the "telephone wars." Lowering prices is not always necessary to increase market share. If a company's product has an important competitive advantage over competitors' offerings, keeping the price at the same level as other firms do may satisfy sales objectives.

Profit Objectives

A **profit objective** focuses on a target level of profit growth or a desired net profit margin. A profit objective is important to firms that believe that profit motivates shareholders and bankers to invest in a company. Coca-Cola recently announced a change in North American pricing strategy—to a premium pricing strategy designed to increases profits instead of a market share strategy that had achieved eight percent annual sales growth but declining profits.[11]

Figure 12.1 Steps in Price Planning

1. Develop Pricing Objectives
2. Estimate Demand
3. Determine Costs
4. Evaluate the Pricing Environment
5. Choose a Pricing Strategy (see Chapter 13)
6. Develop Pricing Tactics (see Chapter 13)

✳ ✳ ✳
sales or market share objective Pricing products to maximize sales or to attain a desired level of sales or market share.

✳ ✳ ✳
profit objective Pricing products with a focus on a target level of profit growth or a desired net profit margin

Table 12.1 Pricing Objectives

Type of Objective	Example
Sales or Market Share	Institute pricing strategy changes to support a five percent increase in sales.
Profit	During the first six months, set a price to yield a target profit of $200 000. Or Set prices to allow for an eight percent profit margin on all goods sold.
Competitive Effect	Alter pricing strategy during first quarter of the year to increase sales during introduction of new product. Or Maintain low-end pricing policies to discourage new competitors from entering the market.
Customer Satisfaction	Simplify pricing structure to simplify decision process for customers. Or Alter price levels to match customer expectations.
Image Enhancement	Alter pricing policies to reflect the increased emphasis on the product's quality image.

Although profits are an important consideration in pricing all goods and services, they are critical when the product is assumed to be a fad. Fad products can expect a rather short market life, making a profit objective essential to allow the firm to recover its investment in a short period of time. In such cases, the firm must harvest profits before customers lose interest and move on to the next electronic pet, troll doll, or cartoon idol.

Competitive Effect Objectives

✳ ✳ ✳
competitive effect objective
Pricing that is intended to have an effect on the marketing efforts of the competition.

A pricing plan with a **competitive effect objective** is intended to have a certain effect on the marketing efforts of the competition. Sometimes, a firm deliberately seeks to pre-empt or reduce the effectiveness of one or more competitors.

Recently, Toys 'R' Us sought to cut into the Christmas toy sales of Wal-Mart and Kmart. It launched an early-November program offering nearly $500 worth of price-off coupons. The move gave Wal-Mart and Kmart too little time to react. This "Christmas surprise" enabled Toys 'R' Us to generate a significant portion of its holiday-time sales from one single price-off coupon program.[12]

Customer Satisfaction Objectives

✳ ✳ ✳
customer satisfaction objective
Pricing to offer the maximum value to the customer.

Many quality-focused firms believe that profits result from making customer satisfaction the primary objective. Firms that have **customer satisfaction objectives** set prices to offer the maximum value to the customer, believing that by focusing solely on short-term profits, a company loses sight of keeping customers for the long term.

Saturn
www.saturnbp.com

Events in the auto industry illustrate this difference between short-term and long-term pricing philosophies. Many people hate to buy a new car because they feel the dealers are untrustworthy hucksters and there is no way they can win in the auto marketplace. Not so with Saturn, where the objective is to satisfy customers. With Saturn's value pricing strategy, customers get one price and one price only—no haggling, no negotiation, no "deals." As Exhibit 12.4 shows, customers can even go to Saturn's Web site to get detailed price information without needing a salesperson. This objective has worked for the company, and it is generating a new breed of car salespeople at dealerships, who use low-pressure sales tactics and promise customer satisfaction and service after the sale.

The negative side of value pricing for car dealers is that it reduces margins, making each sale less profitable. Dealers must be convinced that customer-satisfying pricing will, in the long term, sell more cars and increase profits.

Image Enhancement Objectives

✳ ✳ ✳
image enhancement objective
Pricing to communicate product quality and establish a desired image to prospective customers.

Organizations that make pricing decisions based on **image enhancement objectives** recognize that consumers often use price to make inferences about the quality of a product. In fact, marketers know that price is often an important means of communicating not only quality but also image to prospective customers.

interactive pricing
CENTER
SATURN.

SATURN

Welcome to the Interactive Pricing Center, where you can do lots of useful things. You can build your own Saturn, starting with a base car, then adding any options you might like. You can calculate an estimated monthly payment based on the Manufacturer's Suggested Retail Price (MSRP). You can begin the GMAC credit application process. You can even do all your research online.

If this is your first time here or you have a question, please review the Frequently Asked Questions **on the bottom of this page.**

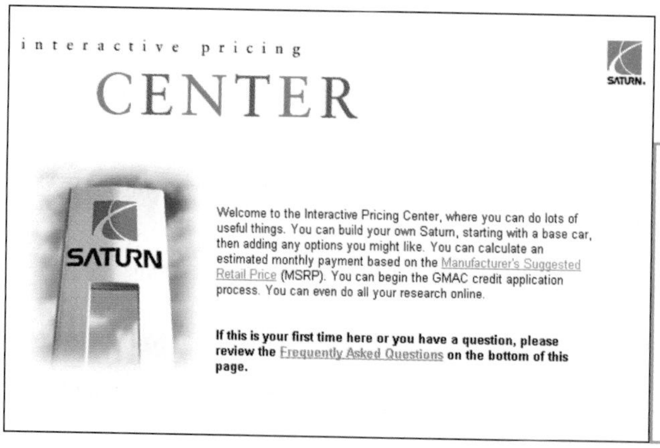

Exhibit 12.4

Saturn uses a pricing strategy designed to please customers: no "dealing," no hassle, no razzle-dazzle.

The image enhancement function of pricing is particularly important for prestige or luxury products like Ekati diamonds. While the high price tag on a Rolex watch or a Rolls-Royce car reflects the higher production costs, it is also vital to shaping an image of an extraordinary product with ownership limited to only wealthy consumers.

Another example of image pricing comes from Calgary-based Nevada Bob's Golf Inc., the world's largest chain of golf speciality retail stores. Backed by cross-Canada market research, they have begun moving their image upmarket—starting by taking "discount" out of the store brand name (it was "Nevada Bob's Discount Golf"). They are now offering a broader and more upscale range of golf products, a more comfortable customer-friendly storefront and improved customer service, while still offering a best-price guarantee.[13]

A low price is just as important in communicating a different image, say, for a Timex watch. In other instances, the desire is to communicate the image of a good-quality product that is reasonably priced.

Ekati Diamonds
www.ekati.ca

Nevada Bob's Golf Inc.
nevadabobs.com

Flexibility of Price Objectives

It is important that pricing objectives be *flexible*. Often, it is necessary to develop pricing objectives (and strategies) tailored to different geographic areas and time periods. There may be varying levels of competition in different parts of the country, making it necessary to lower prices in the areas with the heaviest competition. Some geographic regions may have greater sales potential, making it wise for firms to develop pricing objectives aimed at obtaining a larger market share in those areas. Mortgage lenders may do this by offering lower rates in areas where new housing starts are booming.

Market conditions can change during the year, requiring price adjustments for seasonal and other reasons. Accommodation rental rates in Whistler, BC are much higher during the winter than during the summer; rates in Summerside, PEI, or Grand Bend, Ontario, are higher during the summer vacation months.

Pricing objectives are only one part of price planning. Before any prices can be set, marketers must understand two very important factors: demand and costs. In the next two sections, we will examine these factors.

Estimating Demand: How Demand Influences Pricing

Demand is customers' desire for products. How much of a product consumers want and are willing to buy changes according to the price of the product. Therefore, one of the earliest steps that marketers take in price planning is to estimate demand for their products.

Demand Curves

The effect of price on the quantity demanded is often illustrated by a **demand curve**. The demand curve, which can be a curved or straight line, shows the quantity of a product that customers will buy in a market during a period of time at various prices if all other factors remain the same.

Figure 12.2 shows demand curves for normal and prestige products. The vertical axis for the demand curve represents the different prices that a firm might charge for a product (P). The horizontal axis shows the number of units or quantity (Q) of the product. The demand curve for most goods (shown on the left side of Figure 12.2) slopes downward and to the right. As the price of the product goes up (P_1 to P_2), the number of units that customers are willing to buy goes down (Q_1 to Q_2). If prices decrease, customers will buy more. This is known as the *law of demand*. For example, if the price of bananas in the grocery store goes up, a customer will probably buy fewer of them. If the price increases too much, the customer will eat his or her cereal without bananas.

Although this type of price–quantity relationship is typical, there are exceptions. There are situations in which otherwise rational people desire a product more as it *increases* in

✳ ✳ ✳
demand curve A plot of the quantity of a product that customers will buy in a market during a period of time at various prices if all other factors remain the same.

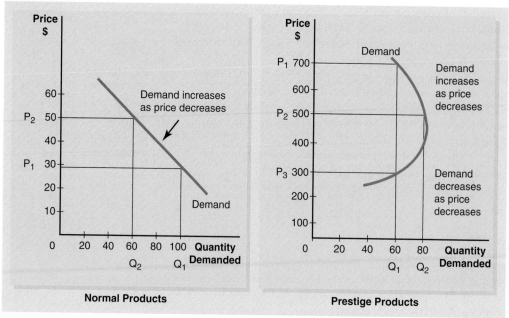

Figure 12.2 Demand Curves for Normal and Prestige Products

price. For *prestige products*, such as luxury cars or jewellery or even some business diplomas and degrees, an increase in price may actually result in an *increase* in the quantity demanded, because consumers see the products as more valuable. In such cases, the demand curve slopes upward. If the price decreases, consumers perceive the product to be less desirable and demand may decrease. Figure 12.2 shows the "backward-bending" demand curve associated with prestige products. Still, the higher-price–higher-demand relationship has its limits. If the firm increases the price too much, making the product simply out of range for buyers, demand will begin to decrease, as shown by the backward direction taken by the top portion of the backward-bending curve.

SHIFTS IN DEMAND

The demand curves we've shown assume that all factors other than price stay the same. But what if they don't? What if the product is improved? What happens when there is a new advertising campaign? What if a stealthy photographer catches Leonardo DiCaprio or Molson "rant" icon Jeff Douglas (Joe Canadian) using the product at home? Any of these things could cause an *upward shift* of the demand curve. An upward shift means that, at any given price, demand is greater than before the shift occurs. Figure 12.3 shows the upward shift of the demand curve as it moves from D_1 to D_2. At D_1, before the shift occurs, customers will be willing to purchase the quantity Q_1 at the given price, P. For example, customers at a particular store may buy 80 barbecue grills at $60 a grill. But then the store runs a huge advertising campaign, featuring a celebrity on her patio using this barbecue grill. The demand curve shifts from D_1 to D_2. (The store keeps the price at $60.) Take a look at how the quantity demanded has changed to Q_2. In our example, the store is now selling 200 barbecue grills. From a marketing standpoint, this shift is the best of all worlds. Without lowering prices, the company can sell more of its product. As a result, total revenues go up and, unless the new promotion costs as much as the increase in revenues it triggers, so do profits.

In the real world, factors other than the price and other marketing activities influence demand. If it rains, the demand for

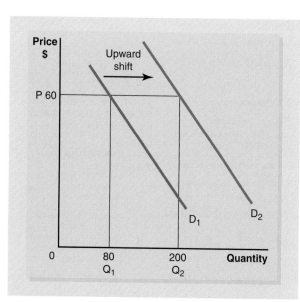

Figure 12.3 Shift in Demand Curve from Changes in Advertising

umbrellas increases, and the demand for tee times on a golf course is a wash. There is little demand for garden tools and fertilizer in the winter, and the demand for houses and furniture decreases during a recession. In addition, the development of new products may influence demand for old ones. Even though some firms may still produce and sell phonographs, the introduction of the cassette tape and the compact disc all but eliminated the demand for new vinyl records. These are examples of **derived demand**—the demand for a product that is influenced or affected by environmental, economic, sociocultural, and other factors outside of the control of marketers.

Changes in the economy also affect demand. For example, starting in 1990, the recession and rising new car prices combined to boost demand for used cars at the time when people were holding onto their cars longer. As a result, the price of used cars, such as those in Exhibit 12.5, went up 8.6%, compared to 2.5% for new cars and 2.7% for consumer prices overall.

ESTIMATING DEMAND

Understanding and estimating demand is extremely important. One reason is that a firm's production scheduling is based on anticipated demand—ideally the firm will avoid making too many items that people won't want. In addition, all marketing planning and budgeting must be based on reasonably accurate estimates of potential sales.

The first step in estimating demand for a particular product is to identify demand for an entire product category in the markets that the company serves. Pepsi-Cola, for example, will estimate the entire demand for soft drinks in domestic and international markets. A small business, such as a start-up premium coffee supplier, will estimate demand only in markets that it expects to reach. Marketers predict total demand by first identifying the number of buyers or potential buyers and then multiplying that estimate by the average amount each member of the target market is likely to purchase. For example, the coffee entrepreneur may estimate that there are 10 000 consumer households in his market who would be willing to buy his premium coffee and that each household would purchase approximately 25 pounds of coffee a year. Thus the total annual demand for the product is 250 000 pounds.

Once the marketer has estimated total demand, the next step is to predict what the company's market share is likely to be. The company's estimated demand is its share of the whole (estimated) pie. In the coffee example, the entrepreneur may feel that he can gain five percent of this market, or 12 500 pounds, or about 1000 pounds a month—not bad for a startup business. Such projections need to take into consideration other factors that can affect demand, such as new competitors entering the market, the state of the economy, and changing consumer tastes.

❋ ❋ ❋
derived demand Demand for a product that is influenced or affected by environmental, economic, socio-cultural, and other factors outside of the control of marketers.

Pepsi-Cola
www.pepsi.com

Exhibit 12.5

When a recession slows the sales of new cars, consumers often find lower-priced used cars attractive.

The Price Elasticity of Demand

In addition to understanding the relationship between price and demand, marketers also need to know how sensitive customers are to *changes* in the price. In particular, it is critical to understand whether a change in price will have a large or a small impact on demand. How much can a firm increase or decrease its price before seeing a marked change in sales? If the price of a pizza goes up $1, will people switch to subs or burgers? What would happen if the price goes up $2? $3? $5? **Price elasticity of demand** is a measure of the sensitivity of customers to changes in price: If the price changes by 10%, what will be the percentage change in demand for the product? The word *elasticity* reminds us that changes in price usually cause demand to stretch or retract like a rubber band.

Price elasticity of demand is calculated as follows:

$$\text{Price elasticity of demand} = \frac{\text{percentage change in quantity demanded}}{\text{percentage change in price}}$$

ELASTIC AND INELASTIC DEMAND

Sometimes customers are very sensitive to changes in prices, and a change in price results in a substantial change in the quantity demanded. In such cases, demand is said to be **elastic**. In other situations, a change in price has little or no effect on the quantity that consumers are willing to buy, and demand is said to be **inelastic**.

For example, using the formula, suppose the pizza maker finds (from experience or from marketing research) that lowering the price of her pizza by 10% (from $10 per pie to $9) will cause a 15% increase in demand. She would calculate the elasticity of demand as 15 divided by 10. The price elasticity of demand would be 1.5. If the price elasticity of demand is greater than 1, demand is elastic; that is, consumers respond to the price decrease by demanding more. Or, if the price increases, consumers will demand less.

When demand is elastic, changes in price and in total revenues (total sales) work in opposite directions. If the price is increased, revenues decrease. If the price is decreased, there will be an increase in total revenues. With elastic demand, the demand curve shown in Figure 12.4 is more horizontal. For the pizza maker, with an elasticity of demand of 1.5, a decrease in price will increase her total sales.

In some instances, demand is inelastic so that a change in price results in little or no change in demand. For example, if the 10% decrease in the price of pizza resulted in only a 5% increase in pizza sales, then the price elasticity of demand calculated would be 5 divided by 10, which is 0.5 (less than 1), and our pizza maker faces *inelastic demand*. When demand is inelastic, price and revenue changes are in the same direction; that is, increases in

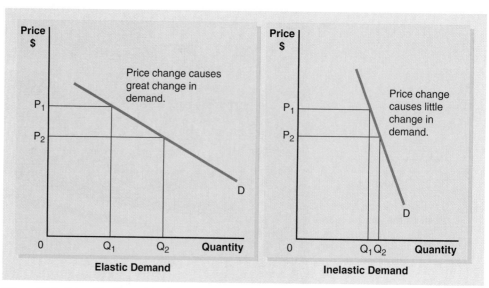

Figure 12.4 Price Elastic and Inelastic Demand Curves

Exhibit 12.6

Because demand for gasoline was price elastic, competing service stations fought for valuable customers with low, low prices in the 1960s.

price result in increases in total revenue, whereas decreases in price result in decreases in total revenue. With inelastic demand, the demand curve shown in Figure 12.4 becomes more vertical. Generally, the demand for necessities is inelastic. Even large price increases do not cause us to buy less food or to give up our telephone.

If demand is price inelastic, can marketers keep raising prices so that revenues and profits will grow larger and larger? And what if demand is elastic? Does it mean that marketers can never raise prices? The answer to these questions is "no." Elasticity of demand for a product often differs for different price levels and with different percentages of change. In the 1950s and 1960s, the price of gasoline was less than 12 cents a litre (54 cents an imperial gallon). There were the rare "gas wars" (see Exhibit 12.6), when the price of gas was less than 9 cents a litre (40 cents a gallon). In those years, if the price of gasoline had increased 10 or 20 cents a gallon (an increase of 20% or more), demand would have decreased as consumers refused to pay the higher prices and simply stayed home—demand was elastic at the low price. If the price of gasoline dropped 10 cents, many consumers would decide to take more trips, drive across the country and see Victoria, PEI, or Niagara Falls. Today, gasoline prices are seldom less than 60 cents a litre (about $2.70 an imperial gallon!), and consumers have become used to changes in gasoline prices of 5 to 10 cents a litre or more. Now a 20% price change is a common occurrence, making gasoline demand *price inelastic*.

As a general rule, oil companies and pizza makers can determine the *actual* price elasticity only after they have tested a pricing decision and calculated the resulting demand. Only then will they know whether a specific price change will increase or decrease revenues. To estimate what demand is likely to be at different prices for new or existing products, marketers often conduct research. One approach is to conduct a laboratory study in which consumers tell marketers how much of a product they would be willing to buy at different prices. For example, researchers might ask participants if they would rent more movies if the price were reduced from $4.50 to $3.50, or how many bags of their favourite chocolate chip cookies they would buy at $3, $4, or $5. At other times, researchers conduct field studies in which they vary the price of a product in different stores and measure how much is actually purchased at the different price levels.

Procter & Gamble once learned about price elasticity the hard way. In 1993, it launched a price war for its disposable diapers. The strategy was to grow market share for Luvs, P&G's lower-price brand, which it had repositioned as a middle-price, no-frills brand. The idea was to stem the growth of private-label disposable diapers. It succeeded; but in the process, Luvs also cut into sales of P&G's premium brand, Pampers.[14] Because of the sensitivity of customers to price changes—that is, the elasticity of demand—firms such as P&G that have more than one item in a product line must be careful that pricing strategies don't cannibalize sales of other company products.

INFLUENCES ON DEMAND ELASTICITY

Other factors can affect price elasticity and sales. Consider the availability of *substitute* goods or services. If a product has a close substitute, its demand will be elastic; that is, a change in price will result in a change in demand, as consumers move to buy the substitute product. For example, Coke and Pepsi may be considered close substitutes by all but the most die-hard cola fans. If the price of Pepsi goes up, many people will buy Coke instead. Marketers of products with close substitutes are less likely to compete on price, recognizing that doing so could result in less profit for everyone as consumers switch from one brand to another.

Price elasticity also depends on the time period marketers are considering. Demand that is inelastic in the short term, may become elastic in the long term. In general, the longer the time period, the greater the likelihood that demand will be more elastic. Here again, the role of substitutes matters because longer time periods make it possible for substitutes to enter the market. If the price of oil increases, there may not be much immediate change in the quantity demanded. However, in the long term, demand will build for alternatives for home heating, such as gas, electric, and solar power. Utilities may build more electric power plants, and auto manufacturers will develop viable electric cars and buses, such as the one powered by the Ballard fuel cell shown in Exhibit 12.7.

There is also an *income effect* on demand. This means changes in income affect demand for a product, even if its price remains the same. For *normal goods,* such as clothing and housing, and for luxury goods, demand is income elastic. This means that as income increases, the amount purchased increases. For necessities such as salt, toilet tissue, and toothpaste, demand is income inelastic, because changes in income do not have much impact on demand. Consumers can't do without these products. For some *inferior goods,* as income increases, demand decreases; if, in a period of economic recession, household income decreases, there is likely to be an increase in sales of dried beans, an inexpensive source of protein, whereas the number of steaks consumed goes down. But if the economy improves and incomes rise, consumers will be able to afford and demand steaks instead of beans.

Finally, the changes in prices of *other* products affect the demand for an item, a phenomenon called *cross-elasticity of demand.* When products are substitutes for each other, an increase in the price of one will increase the demand for the other. For example, if the price of bananas goes up, consumers may instead buy more strawberries, blueberries, or apples. However, when products are complements—that is, when one product is essential to the use of a second—then an increase in the price of one decreases the demand for the second. For example, if the price of gasoline goes up, consumers may drive less and, thus, demand for tires will also decrease.

Exhibit 12.7

In the long run, the price of gasoline may become elastic again as better-performing electric cars and buses hit the market.

Real People, Real Decisions
Decision Time **at Palliser**

The Logic Division of Palliser had recently adopted and adapted a kitchen cabinet technology, called "membrane press," to make an innovative new product line of entertainment and home office furniture. This technology, not previously used in furniture manufacturing, allows the manufacturer to apply a vinyl covering to medium density fibreboard and fashion a variety of textures, colours, and designs onto the board. Palliser required significant equipment purchases and time to adopt this technology to its production process.

In April 1999, they launched their first three collections of home office furniture. These featured two finishes and four configurations, contemporary styling with strong design elements and colours. Palliser made major placements with two national Canadian and US retailers and various regional independent retailers, and supported them with extensive marketing and communications materials and sales support.

A year into the launch, the new products were not generating expected sales levels for the retailers or for Palliser. The retailers and Palliser sales representatives raised numerous concerns: The series offered was too contemporary for the current retailer base; the product required some limited assembly, unlike previous Palliser introductions, and retailers were positioning it in the ready-to-assemble (RTA) areas of their stores; and Palliser's price points were higher than their RTA competitors'.

In April 2000, De Bruyn was preparing to attend the semi-annual High Point furniture show in North Carolina. This is the largest home furnishing show in the world, with over 8 million square feet of showroom space, 2500 manufacturers, and an attendance of over 100 000 buyers and retailers. There was internal pressure to have Palliser's membrane press technology accepted by retailers and consumers, and key decisions had to be made about the membrane press product line.

Option 1. Leave pricing as is and see if the product line can hold its own. Palliser cannot dictate to its retailers where the product will be positioned within their stores and must accept that the product will be placed in the RTA area and compared to other RTA products. De Bruyn could refocus her marketing strategy to support an enhanced value positioning relative to other RTA products and to justify its higher price point. This task would be made easier if other RTA manufacturers increased their price points, as expected, in the near future. However, it would take time to implement and see the effects of a refocused marketing strategy. The Logic Division cannot wait too long to remove a line that is not performing, since production capacity could be used for collections that are performing well.

Option 2. Change pricing immediately. De Bruyn could match the pricing of the other RTA manufacturers. Retailers like the quality and craftsmanship of Palliser. A lower price would provide an extra boost to encourage new retailers to carry this product line, and an increase in sales volume could make up for a decrease in profitability per unit However, there are a number of disadvantages to this option: Retailers who previously purchased the product will need to be given discounts for the inventory they hold; these preceding retailers may feel they were being overcharged previously and they may start to question all of Palliser's pricing; Palliser will be giving up gross margin on the sale of this product which might not be recovered in volume.

Option 3. Develop new products using this technology. De Bruyn could encourage Palliser to develop a new product or products incorporating the membrane press technology that would address either the styling or RTA issues or both. The development of any new products would take about one year, during which time the equipment and staff associated with the new technology would likely remain idle. While new products could find better acceptance in the marketplace, there is also the possibility that they would not.

Option 4. Sell the machinery. De Bruyn could recommend that Palliser consider the new products a failure, limit its losses, and sell the equipment. This would open up manufacturing capacity for more profitable product lines. The downside to this option is that Palliser might be prematurely giving up on an opportunity that just requires more time for market acceptance. The new technology does differentiate their products and gives Palliser a presence in the RTA market.

Now, join the Palliser team. Which option would you choose, and why?

Determining Cost

Estimating demand helps marketers develop possible prices to charge for a product. It tells them how much they think they'll be able to sell at different prices. Knowing this brings them to the next step in determining a product's price—making sure the price will cover costs. Before marketers can determine price, they must understand the relationship of cost, demand, and revenue for their product. In this section, we'll present different types of costs that marketers must consider in pricing and two types of analyses that they use in making pricing decisions.

Types of Costs

The cost of a product is important in determining what to charge for it. If a firm prices a product lower than the cost to produce it, it will lose money. How much the price exceeds the cost determines the amount of profit the firm may earn, everything else being equal. Before looking at how costs influence pricing decisions, it is necessary to understand the different types of costs that firms incur. Palliser, for example, must buy wood, adhesives, hardware, and fabrics or leather to make their furniture. If a college student wants to build a bookcase in her dorm, the only costs would be for the lumber, nails, and paint. If, after graduation, she decides to make a business of producing and selling bookcases in competition with Palliser, this young entrepreneur would have to worry about costs for other things, including renting a factory, hiring employees, utilities, and insurance. How would these costs affect pricing decisions?

VARIABLE COSTS

✳ ✳ ✳
variable costs The costs of production (raw and processed materials, parts, and labour) that are tied to, and vary depending on, the number of units produced.

A firm incurs **variable costs** in producing a product. These are the per-unit costs of production that will fluctuate depending on how many units or individual products a firm produces. If it takes 25 cents worth of nails, a variable cost, to build one bookcase, it will take 50 cents worth for two, 75 cents worth for three, and so on. For the production of bookcases, variable costs would also include the cost of lumber and paint, and there would also be the cost of factory workers (unless you get your roommates to work for free). Table 12.2 shows some examples of the variable cost per unit or *average variable cost* and the total variable costs at different levels of production (for producing 100, 200, and 500 bookcases). If the firm produces 100 bookcases, the average variable cost per unit is $50 and the total variable cost is $5000 ($50 × 100). If production is doubled to 200 units, the total variable cost now is $10 000 ($50 × 200).

In reality, calculating variable costs is usually more complex. As the number of bookcases the factory produces increases or decreases, average variable costs may change. For example, if the company buys just enough lumber for one bookcase, the lumber yard will charge top dollar. If it buys enough for 100 bookcases, it will get a better deal. And if it buys enough for thousands of bookcases, it may cut variable costs even more. Even the cost of labour goes down with increased production, as manufacturers are likely to invest in labour-saving equipment that allows workers to produce bookcases faster. This is the case in the example in Table 12.2. By purchasing wood, nails, and paint at a lower price because of a volume discount and by providing a means for workers to build bookcases more quickly, the cost per unit of producing 500 bookcases is reduced to $40 each.

Variable costs don't always go down with higher levels of production. Using the bookcase example, at some point the demand for the labour, lumber, or nails required to produce the bookcases may exceed the supply. The bookcase manufacturer may have to pay employees overtime to keep up with production. The manufacturer may have to buy additional lumber from a distant supplier that will charge more to cover the costs of shipping. The cost per bookcase rises.

FIXED COSTS

✳ ✳ ✳
fixed costs Costs of production that do not change with the number of units produced.

Fixed costs are those that do *not* vary with the number of units produced—the costs remain the same whether the firm produces 1000 bookcases this month or only 10. Fixed costs include rent or the cost of owning and maintaining the factory, utilities to heat or cool the factory, and the costs of equipment such as hammers, saws, planers, and paint sprayers used in the production of the product. The salaries of a firm's executives (and marketing managers such as Astrid De Bruyn) are also fixed costs. All these costs are constant, no matter how many items are manufactured.

Table 12.2 Variable Costs at Different Levels of Production

Variable Costs for Producing 100 Bookcases		Variable Costs for Producing 200 Bookcases		Variable Costs for Producing 500 Bookcases	
Wood	$13.25	Wood	$13.25	Wood	$9.40
Nails	0.25	Nails	0.25	Nails	0.20
Paint	0.50	Paint	0.50	Paint	0.40
Labour (3 hours × $12/hr)	$36.00	Labour (3 hours × $12/hr)	$36.00	Labour (2.5 hrs × $12/hr)	$30.00
Cost per unit	$50.00	Cost per unit	$50.00	Cost per unit	$40.00
Multiply by number of units	100	Multiply by number of units	200	Multiply by number of units	500
Cost for 100 units:	$5000	Cost for 200 units:	$10 000	Cost for 500 units:	$20 000

One bookcase = one unit.

Average fixed cost is the fixed cost per unit produced, that is, the total fixed costs divided by the number of units (bookcases) produced. Although total fixed costs remain the same no matter how many units are produced, the average fixed cost will decrease as the number of units produced increases. For example, a firm's total fixed costs of production are $30 000. If it produces one unit, the total $30 000 is applied to the one unit. If it produces two units, $15 000, or half of the fixed costs, is applied to each unit, and so on. As it produces more and more units, average fixed costs go down and so does the price we must charge to cover fixed costs.

Like variable costs, in the long term, total fixed costs may change. For example, the firm may find that it can sell more of a product than it has manufacturing capacity to produce, so it builds a new factory, its executives' salaries go up, and more money goes into manufacturing equipment.

Combining variable costs and fixed costs yields **total costs** for a given level of production. As a company produces more and more of a product, both average fixed costs and average variable costs may decrease. Average total costs may decrease, too, up to a point, that is. As we said, as output continues to increase, average variable costs may start to increase. These variable costs ultimately rise faster than average fixed costs decline, resulting in an increase to average total costs.

As total costs fluctuate with differing levels of production, the price that producers have to charge to cover those costs changes. Therefore, is it useful for marketers to calculate the minimum price necessary to cover all costs—the break-even price.

Break-Even Analysis

Break-even analysis is a technique marketers use to examine the relationship between cost and price and to determine what sales volume must be reached at a given price before the company breaks even. The break-even point is the point at which the company doesn't lose any money and doesn't make any profit; all costs are covered, but there isn't a penny extra. A break-even analysis allows marketers to identify how many units of a product they will have to sell at a given price to be profitable.

Figure 12.5 uses our bookcase manufacturing example to demonstrate break-even analysis. The vertical axis represents the amount of costs and revenue in dollars, and the horizontal axis shows the quantity of goods produced and sold. In this break-even model, we assume that there is a given total fixed cost and that variable costs do not change with the quantity produced.

In this example, the total fixed costs (for the factory, the equipment, electricity) are $200 000, and the average variable costs (for materials and labour) are constant. The figure shows the total costs (variable costs plus fixed costs) and total revenues if varying quantities are produced and sold. The point at which the total revenue and total costs lines intersect

✳ ✳ ✳
total costs The total of the fixed costs and the variable costs for a set number of units produced.

✳ ✳ ✳
break-even analysis A method for determining the number of units that a firm must produce and sell at a given price to cover all its costs.

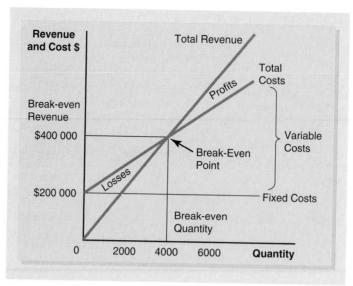

Figure 12.5 Break-Even Analysis

is the *break-even point*. If sales are above the break-even point, the company makes a profit. Below that point, the firm suffers a loss.

To determine the break-even point, the firm first needs to calculate the *contribution per unit*, or the difference between the price the firm charges for a product (the revenue per unit) and the variable costs. This *contribution margin* is the amount the firm has after paying for the wood, nails, paint, and labour to contribute to meeting the fixed costs of production. For our example, assume that the firm sells its bookcases for $100 each. Using the variable costs of $50 per unit that we had before, contribution per unit is $100 − $50 = $50. Using the fixed cost for the bookcase manufacturing of $200 000, we can now calculate the firm's break-even point in units of the product.

$$\text{Break-even point (in units)} = \frac{\text{total fixed cost}}{\text{contribution per unit to fixed costs}}$$

$$\text{Break-even point (in units)} = \frac{\$200\ 000}{\$50} = 4000 \text{ units}$$

Thus, the firm must sell 4000 bookcases at $100 each to meet its fixed costs and to break even. In a similar way, we can calculate the break-even point in dollars. This shows us that to break even, the company must sell $400 000 worth of bookcases.

$$\text{Break-even point (in dollars)} = \frac{\text{total fixed cost}}{1 - \dfrac{\text{variable cost per unit}}{\text{price}}}$$

$$\text{Break-even point (in dollars)} = \frac{\$200\ 000}{1 - \dfrac{\$50}{\$100}} = \frac{\$20\ 000}{1 - 0.5} = \frac{\$20\ 000}{0.5} = \$400\ 000$$

After the firm's sales have met and passed the break-even point, it begins to make a profit. How much profit? If the firm sells 4001 bookcases, it will make a profit of $50. If it sells 5000 bookcases, the profit would be calculated as follows:

$$\begin{aligned} \text{Profit} &= \text{quantity above break-even point} \times \text{contribution margin} \\ &= 1000 \times \$50 \\ &= \$50\ 000 \end{aligned}$$

Often a firm will set a *profit goal*, which is the dollar profit figure it desires to earn. The break-even point may be calculated with that dollar goal included in the figures. This is not really a "break-even" point because it includes profits; it's more of a "target amount." If the bookcase manufacturer feels it is necessary to realize a profit of $50 000, her calculations would be as follows:

$$\text{Break-even point (in units with target amount included)} = \frac{\text{total fixed cost + target profit}}{\text{contribution per unit to fixed costs}}$$

$$\text{Break-even point (in units)} = \frac{\$200\ 000 + \$50\ 000}{\$50} = 5000 \text{ units}$$

Sometimes the target return or profit goal is expressed as a *percentage of sales.* For example, a firm may say that it wants to make a profit of at least 10% on sales. In such cases, this profit is added to the variable cost in calculating the break-even point. In our example, the company wants to earn 10% of the selling price of the bookcase, or 10% × $100 = $10 per unit. We add this $10 to the variable costs of $50 and calculate the new target amount as we calculated the break-even point before. The contribution per unit becomes:

$$\text{Contribution per unit = selling price } - \text{ (variable costs + target profit)}$$

$$= \$100 - (\$50 + \$10) = \$40$$

$$\text{Break-even point (in units)} = \frac{\text{total fixed cost}}{\text{contribution per unit to fixed costs}}$$

$$\text{Break-even point (in units)} = \frac{\$200\ 000}{\$40} = 5000 \text{ units}$$

Break-even analysis does not provide an easy answer for pricing. It provides answers about how many units the firm must sell to break even and to make a profit; however, without knowing whether demand will equal that quantity at that price, companies can make big mistakes. It is, therefore, useful for marketers to estimate the demand for their product and then perform a *marginal analysis.* Palliser, for example, needs to consider its demand in deciding whether to maintain current pricing.

Marginal Analysis

Marginal analysis provides a way for marketers to look at cost and demand at the same time. It examines the relationship of **marginal cost**, the increase in total costs from producing one additional unit of a product, to **marginal revenue**, the increase in total income or revenue that results from selling one additional unit of a product. Marginal analysis allows marketers to identify the output and the price that will generate the maximum profit.

Figure 12.6 shows the various cost and revenue elements considered in marginal analysis. As in Figure 12.5, the vertical axis in Figure 12.6 represents the cost and revenues in dollars, and the horizontal axis shows the quantity produced and sold. Figure 12.6 shows the average revenue, average cost, marginal revenue, and marginal cost curves. Note that the average revenue curve is also the demand curve. Table 12.3 presents the data that might result from a marginal analysis that considers profits at different price levels. If only one unit is produced, the average total cost per unit is the same as the marginal cost per unit. However, after the first unit, the marginal cost at first decreases and then increases in response to the decrease and subsequent increase in total costs discussed in our bookcase example.

* * *
marginal analysis
A method that uses cost and demand to identify the price that will maximize profits.

* * *
marginal cost
The increase in total cost that results from producing one additional unit of a product.

* * *
marginal revenue
The increase in total revenue (income) that results from producing and selling one additional unit of a product.

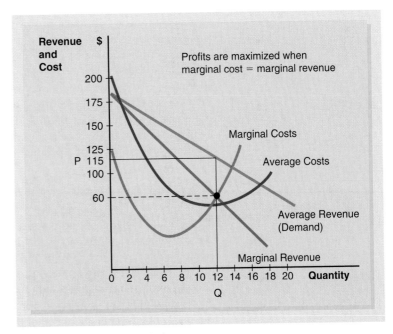

Figure 12.6 Marginal Analysis

Table 12.3 Profit Maximization with Marginal Analysis

1	2	3	4	5	6	7	8	9	10	11
Quantity (Q)	Total Fixed Costs	Total Variable Costs	Average Variable Cost (3) (1)	Total Cost (2) + (3)	Average Total Cost (5) (1)	Marginal Cost	Price	Total Revenue (1) × (8)	Marginal Revenue	Total Profit (9) – (5)
0	$300	$ 0	$ 0	$ 300	——					
1	300	170	170	470	$470	$470	$170	$ 170	$170	–$300
2	300	282	141	582	291	112	165	330	160	–252
3	300	348	116	648	216	66	160	480	150	–168
4	300	396	99	696	174	48	155	620	140	–76
5	300	425	85	725	145	29	150	750	130	25
6	300	438	73	738	123	13	145	870	120	132
7	300	441	63	741	106	3	140	980	110	239
8	300	448	56	748	94	7	135	1080	100	332
9	300	468	52	768	85	20	130	1170	90	402
10	300	500	50	800	80	32	125	1250	80	450
11	300	528	48	828	75	28	120	1320	70	492
12	300	588	49	888	74	60	115	1380	60	492
13	300	689	53	989	76	101	110	1430	50	441
14	300	938	67	1238	88	249	105	1470	40	232
15	300	1200	80	1500	100	262	100	1500	30	0

As the price of a product goes down, the amount that will be sold (demand) increases (assuming that demand does not track the prestige product curve discussed earlier). Thus, total revenues increase even though prices decrease. Notice, however, that the amount of added revenue for each additional unit sold (marginal revenue) decreases at each lower price level. If the price is decreased far enough, total revenue will start to fall.

Profit is maximized at the point at which marginal cost is *exactly* equal to marginal revenue. To find the selling price at which profit will be maximized, look in Table 12.3 to see the point at which marginal cost equals marginal revenue. In this example, both marginal cost and marginal revenue are $60 at the 12-unit level. Based on the demand in this example, the firm will sell 12 units if the price per unit is set at $115. Given these costs and this demand, the firm will maximize profits at that point. If the firm continues to lower the price, more units of the product will be sold, but total profits will decrease.

One word of caution in using marginal analysis: Although the procedure is straightforward, things seldom are in the real world. Production costs may vary unexpectedly due to shortages, inclement weather, unexpected equipment repairs, and other mishaps. Revenues may also unexpectedly move up and down due to the economy, what the competition is doing, or a host of other reasons. Predicting demand, an important factor in marginal analysis, is never an exact science, making marginal analysis a less-than-perfect way to determine the best price for a product.

Evaluating the Pricing Environment

In addition to demand and costs, it is important to consider factors in the firm's external environment to make successful pricing decisions. Thus, our fourth step in developing pricing strategies is to examine and evaluate the pricing environment. Whether they are pricing clothes at Army & Navy, furniture at Palliser, or that expensive Rolex, marketers need to understand what's going on in the marketplace. Only then can they develop pricing that not only covers costs but also provides a competitive advantage—pricing that meets the needs of customers better than the competition. This section will discuss some impor-

SPOTLIGHT ON REAL PEOPLE *General Motors*

Even before the terrorist attacks on the World Trade Center and the Pentagon the big three North American carmakers—GM, Ford, and DaimlerChrysler—were facing large financial losses and slumping retail sales. Sales plummeted in the immediate aftermath of the September 11th attacks, and John Devine, chief financial officer of General Motors, faced the daunting prospect of low US consumer confidence and a deepening recession. In response he cut prices drastically in both the United States and Canada—offering 0% financing on both 2001 and 2002 models, effectively cutting prices by as much as $3000. Ford and Chrysler quickly matched the strategy for their 2001 models and some of their 2002s.

The incentives worked and car sales rose more than 10% over the previous October. GM, the first mover, was the biggest beneficiary. In Canada GM truck sales increased 34.8% and total sales increased 19%. Ford's sales fell 10% and Chrysler's fell 7.5%. Devine was so pleased with the results that he extended the promotion through November.

Although GM's sales skyrocketed and their dealers made a lot of money, there was a price to be paid for the price cuts. GM's profit fell 58% in the fourth quarter to $255 million—but that was better than Ford, which lost $860 million during this period. Industry analysts suggest that the incentives didn't increase car consumption—they merely accelerated sales that would have been made in 2002 at a higher price. They also caution that those price conscious consumers are not very loyal, so the long-term benefit is dubious. Incentives can also cheapen the image of brand and erode resale values, which makes leases more expensive in the long run.

Devine acknowledges that the pricing strategy cost GM some money, but suggests that overall "it was the right thing to do." Only time will tell, but relative to the other North American auto manufacturers, he just might be right—the price cuts may have hurt the industry but at least GM got the sales.[15]

1. Given the potential problems with cutting prices, why did John Devine pursue his price cutting strategy?
2. What pricing strategy would you recommend for GM in 2002?

---

tant external influences on pricing strategies—the economic environment, competition, consumer trends, and some unique aspects of international trade.

General Motors
www.gm.com

The Economy

Economic trends have an important role in directing pricing strategies. The business cycle, inflation, economic growth, and consumer confidence all help to determine whether one pricing strategy or another will succeed. But the upswings and downturns in a national economy do not affect all product categories or all regions equally. Devaluation of the Canadian dollar relative to the US in the 1990s made American imports relatively expensive but made Canadian exports inexpensive for American consumers. Marketers need to understand how economic trends will affect their particular business.

TRIMMING THE FAT: PRICING IN A RECESSION

During recessions, consumers grow more price sensitive. They switch to generic brands to get a better price and patronize discount stores and warehouse outlets. Even wealthy households, relatively unaffected by recession, tend to cut back on conspicuous consumption, if for no other reason than to avoid attention. As a result, during periods of recession, many firms find it necessary to cut prices to levels at which costs are covered but the company doesn't make a profit to keep factories in operation. Unfortunately, price sensitivity tends to persist for a time even when a recession ends.[16] During such periods, marketers need to consider what pricing policies will be helpful in regaining pre-recession sales and profit levels.

Recession had an even greater impact on Japanese consumers in the early 1990s. Unlike Canadian consumers, the Japanese were used to paying high prices all the time to satisfy an inefficient, multilayered distribution system. However, this recession opened the door to discount retailing. Specialty retailers bought directly from manufacturers and were able to sell goods at least a third below department stores' prices. The trend has gained momentum, and bargain hunting is becoming a consumer sport in Japan.[17]

INCREASING PRICES: RESPONDING TO INFLATION

Economic trends also influence a firm's ability to increase prices, because they affect what consumers see as an acceptable or unacceptable price range for a product. For example, inflation accustoms consumers to price increases; but they can grow fearful for the future and whether they will have enough money to meet basic needs. In such a case, they may cut back on purchases. Then, as in periods of recession, inflation may cause marketers to lower prices and temporarily sacrifice profits to maintain sales levels. On the other hand, hyperinflation of 30 to 40% a month, such as Brazil experienced in the 1990s, causes consumers to spend all of their money as fast as they receive it. Pricing is particularly challenging in a hyperinflation environment.

The Competition

Decision makers must always consider how the competition will respond to their pricing actions. They know that consumers' expectations of what constitutes a fair price depends on what the competition is charging. The Marriott hotel chain, for example, monitors the room rates of Hilton, Hyatt, and other chains.

In the cut-throat fast-food industry, when Burger King trotted out its 99-cent Whopper, McDonald's retaliated with a 55-cent Big Mac (see Exhibit 12.8), and third-place Wendy's increased promotion of its 99-cent chicken nuggets and Double-Stack cheeseburgers.[18] It's not always a good idea to fight the competition with lower and lower prices. Pricing wars, like those in the fast-food industry, can change consumers' perceptions of what is a "fair" price, leaving them unwilling to buy at previous price levels. This will be a challenge in Coke's new premium pricing strategy as years of discounting have conditioned consumers to expect to pay less than $2.99 for a two-litre bottle. In addition, when firms focus on price competition, they often ignore the need to satisfy other customer wants. For instance, many consumers have become dissatisfied with traditional burgers at any price and are looking for restaurants that offer better-tasting meals.

The type of competitive environment in which an industry operates—whether it's an oligopoly, monopolistic competition, or pure competition—also influences price decisions. Generally, firms that do business in an oligopoly, in which the market has few sellers and many buyers, are more likely to adopt *status quo* pricing objectives, in which the pricing of all competitors is similar. Such objectives are attractive to oligopolistic firms because

Exhibit 12.8

In a price war strategy, McDonald's reduced the Big Mac's price to 55 cents when part of a Meal Deal.

avoiding price competition allows all players in the industry to remain profitable. The Canadian gasoline industry is an oligopoly, in which a few large petroleum refiners, such as Irving Oil, Shell, and Petro-Canada, control most of the market.

In a state of monopolistic competition, in which there are many sellers each offering a slightly different product, it is possible for firms to differentiate products and to focus on non-price competition. Thrifty Foods, the Vancouver Island grocery chain introduced in Chapter 1, for example, faces competition from Canada Safeway, the Real Canadian Superstore (Loblaw's), Save-On-Foods, Costco, other warehouse clubs, and other independent food retailers. This level of competition makes it difficult for Thrifty Foods to compete on price. Instead they focus on being competitively priced with superior quality, choice, service, and retail innovation. To combat consumer perceptions that their prices were higher than others, they introduced a new tag line in 1998, "We never lower our standards—just our prices," and have experienced increased market share despite increased competition from big-box discounters.

As we discussed in Chapter 3, firms in a purely competitive market have little opportunity to raise or lower prices. Rather, the price of soybeans, corn, or fresh peaches is directly influenced by supply and demand. When bad weather hurts crops, prices go up. And prices for almost any kind of fish have increased dramatically since health-conscious consumers began turning away from beef and other red meat.

Consumer Trends

Another environmental influence on price is consumer trends. Culture and demographics determine how consumers think and behave and so have a large impact on all marketing decisions. Marketers who continuously monitor the consumer environment are in a position to make better pricing decisions. These are some current trends:

- Consumers have grown disinterested in fancy stores with big markups. Grey Advertising agency calls these consumers "precision shoppers." They are more choosy, less inclined to shy away from lesser-known brands, and drawn to warehouse stores that offer inexpensive self-serve products.[20] Marketers of everything from autos to suits are scrambling to find ways to offer value and build bonds with customers who are weary of glitzy promotions and overpriced merchandise.

- Consumers want to be able to afford tokens of success. In the last decade, sales of products such as Lee Valley tools (see Exhibit 12.9), Calvin Klein fragrances, and BMW cars soared because they offered consumers a unique prestige product image—driving a BMW tells other drivers that "you've made it." Much of the success Starbucks has enjoyed is a result of their gourmet coffee being an "affordable luxury."

- Many of the women who opted for a career in their twenties are hearing the ticking of their biological clocks as they enter their late thirties and early forties. But couples having babies later in their lives are often better off financially than younger parents, and they are far more willing to spend whatever it costs to give their babies the best. For producers of products for babies and children, this means that price resistance is rather low within the group. Such parents have no problem spending $50 or more for a Beatrix Potter musical crib mobile and don't even flinch at the $75 price tag on a Wedgwood china Peter Rabbit cereal bowl and mug.

International Environmental Influences

Different situations influence pricing decisions by firms conducting international trade, including the *currency exchange rate*. Japanese auto sales in Canada soared by 36% in 1997, and total Japanese imports doubled.[21] This increase in market share was fuelled by a lower yen and higher US dollar that made North American models more expensive for Canadian consumers.

In 1999, the World Trade Organization (WTO) ordered Canada to cut subsidized dairy exports and increase foreign access to Canadian markets. The WTO supported the position of New Zealand and the United States that the Canadian government provides illegal export subsidies by having marketing boards that set milk prices and production volumes, exporting milk at less than the domestic price and paying the difference to the producers.[19] Part of Canada's system for limiting milk imports was also deemed to be in violation of international trade agreements. Ironically, the ruling came just before the Seattle WTO talks, when Canada led a delegation seeking to reduce the European Union's US$7 billion annual export subsidies on farm industries and to convince the United States to soften its tough anti-dumping trade laws. What do you think? Should companies be allowed to sell their excess inventory of products at any price they choose? Are marketing boards appropriate, or should market forces determine supply and demand? Should there be an organization like the WTO that initiates and enforces international trade agreements?

World Trade Organization
www.wto.org

Exhibit 12.9

Lee Valley tools have a prestige image among woodworking and gardening hobbyists.

✳ ✳ ✳

price subsidies Government payments made to protect domestic businesses or to reimburse them when they must price at or below cost to make a sale. The subsidy can be a cash payment or tax relief.

In international markets, national or local government policies can lead to differences in the prices competitors charge for products in global markets. Government **price subsidies** to domestic industries, in the form of either an outright payment or a tax relief, allow some firms to sell their products at prices often below production costs. Prairie farmers face this situation as low grain prices and US and European subsidies have combined to put Canadian farmers at a severe competitive disadvantage; they are seeking as much as one billion dollars in federal and provincial aid to make up for lost revenue.[22] American forest companies claim that Canada's software lumber is unfairly subsidized and have successfully lobbied for import restrictions.[23]

Want to take a luxury cruise? There'll be plenty of room thanks to European taxpayers. Between 1997 and 2000, European shipbuilders built over 30 new cruise ships. Cruise ship prices are low because of European Union government subsidies (up to nine percent of the price of the vessels) designed to keep ship-building labour on the job.[24]

In the price planning process, marketers first decide on pricing objectives and examine the pricing environment. Based on that and on an understanding of demand and costs, marketers can finally devise pricing strategies, which we will read about in the next chapter.

Real People, Real Decisions
How it worked out at Palliser

Astrid De Bruyn announced a price cut of $100 per configuration, at the High Point furniture show, matching the RTA manufacturers' price points. The reasons for her decision were: The sales and marketing team favoured a price decrease as they wanted to gain market share in the RTA area; the Logic Division, wanting to expand its scope of production, would eventually need to compete with RTA manufacturers at the entry price level, and this was a good opportunity for Logic to test itself against these producers; and Logic Division management believed that this new technology would find acceptance and that increased sales volume would likely lead to lower unit costs and higher margins.

Retailers who were carrying the existing product did complain that they had stock at the old prices. On a case-by-case basis, De Bruyn provided credit to the retailer's cooperative advertising for the difference. The retailer could then use the money to advertise the new prices.

For more information about the Palliser company and its products, visit their Web site at: www.Palliser.com.

Chapter Summary

1. Explain the importance of pricing and how prices can take both monetary and non-monetary forms.

   Price, the amount of outlay of money, goods, services, or deeds given in exchange for a product, can be monetary or non-monetary. Bartering occurs when consumers or businesses exchange one product for another. Pricing is important to firms, because it creates profits and influences customers to purchase. Pricing decisions are tied to decisions about the rest of the marketing mix. Prices must allow channel members to cover their costs and make a profit. Prices vary during stages in the product life cycle. Prices must cover the cost of promotions, and promotions must justify the product price.

2. Understand the pricing objectives that marketers typically have in planning pricing strategies.

   Effective pricing objectives are designed to support corporate and marketing objectives and are flexible. Pricing objectives often focus on sales (to maximize sales or to increase market share), or they may specify a desired level of profit growth or profit margin. At other times, firms may develop pricing objectives for competitive effect, to increase customer satisfaction, or to communicate a certain image to prospective customers. Pricing objectives need to be flexible to adapt to different geographic areas and time periods.

3. Explain how customer demand influences pricing decisions.

   For most products, lower prices increase demand; but with some prestige products, demand increases as price goes up. External influences or company efforts can create a shift in the demand curve. Price elasticity of demand is the sensitivity of customers to changing prices. With elastic demand, price changes create large changes in demand; with inelastic demand, price changes have little effect on demand.

4. Describe how marketers use costs, demands, and revenue to make pricing decisions.

   Marketers often use break-even analysis and marginal analysis to help price a product. Break-even analysis uses fixed and variable costs to identify how many units have to be sold at a specific price to begin making a profit. Marginal analysis uses both costs and estimates of product demand to identify the price that will maximize profits. In marginal analysis, profits are maximized at the point at which the revenue from producing one additional unit of a product equals the costs of producing the additional unit.

5. Understand some of the environmental factors that affect pricing strategies.

   Like other elements of the marketing mix, pricing is influenced by a variety of external environmental factors. These include economic trends, such as inflation and recession, and the firm's competitive environment, such as the number and size of competing firms. Pricing can also be influenced by changing consumer trends, product production costs, and differences in international market environments.

KEY TERMS

bartering (321)

break-even analysis (335)

competitive effect objective (326)

customer satisfaction objective (326)

demand curve (327)

derived demand (329)

fixed costs (334)

image enhancement objective (326)

margin (322)

marginal analysis (337)

marginal cost (337)

marginal revenue (337)

operating costs (321)

opportunity cost (321)

price (320)

price elastic (330)

price elasticity of demand (330)

price inelastic (330)

price subsidies (342)

profit objective (325)

sales or market share objective (325)

switching costs (321)

total costs (335)

variable costs (334)

Chapter Review

Marketing Concepts: Testing Your Knowledge

1. What are some examples of monetary and non-monetary prices?

2. Explain how pricing decisions are important to firms.

3. How are pricing decisions interrelated with other elements of the marketing mix?

4. How is demand influenced by price? What is elastic demand? What is inelastic demand?

5. What external influences affect demand elasticity?

6. Explain variable costs, fixed costs, average variable costs, average fixed costs, and average total costs.

7. What is break-even analysis? How do marketers use break-even analysis?

8. What is marginal analysis? How do marketers use marginal analysis?

9. What are some of the more frequently used pricing objectives?

10. What are some ways in which changes in the business cycle, the competitive environment, and consumer trends affect price planning?

Marketing Concepts: Discussing Choices and Issues

1. Governments sometimes provide price subsidies to specific industries; that is, they reduce a domestic firm's costs so that they can sell products on the international market at a lower price. What reasons do governments (and politicians) use for these government subsidies? What are the benefits and disadvantages to domestic industries in the long run? To international customers? Who would benefit or lose if all price subsidies were eliminated?

2. As the scope of marketing expands from producers of goods and services to marketing of such intangibles as ideas and people, the concept of pricing must also be expanded. What is the "price" for a political candidate, keeping your cholesterol level down, donating blood to the Red Cross, or wearing a seat belt? Why do marketers sometimes find it more difficult to sell these "products" than to sell a pair of sneakers?

3. Agricultural price subsidies are often hotly debated in Parliament. Farmers say they can't get along without them. Opponents say that agricultural prices need to be left to the natural pressures of supply and demand. In what ways are price supports good for farmers? For consumers? For our country? What are some ways they hurt us?

4. Critics of business often accuse marketers of taking advantage of consumers by setting prices that are far above the cost of producing the good or service—sometimes 10 or 20 or more times the cost. How do you feel about this? What reasons might a manufacturer of luxury products have for setting very high prices? Why might a pharmaceutical firm set the prices of its life-saving medicines higher than the cost of production requires?

Marketing Practice: Applying What You've Learned

1. Assume that you are the director of marketing for a large Rocky Mountain ski resort. It is essential that the resort maintain a high occupancy rate during the skiing season. Pricing is an important part of your marketing strategy, because the demand for rooms at your resort is very price elastic. For this reason, you feel that you should develop contingency pricing plans for use during changes in the economic environment (inflation and recessions, for example). List the economic conditions that might warrant changes in the pricing strategy, and give your recommendations for each possibility.

2. Assume that you are the assistant director of marketing for a firm that manufactures a line of hair-care products (for example, shampoos, conditioners). This morning, your boss came into your office and announced that she is going to recommend a dramatic price increase. You respond by saying, "Well, I guess that means we need to totally revamp our marketing plan." To this, she replies, "No, all we're going to do is to raise the price. We're not going to mess with anything else." After she leaves you think, "I've got to convince her that we can't make pricing decisions without considering the other elements of the marketing mix. It's all interrelated."

   In a role-playing situation with one of your classmates, explain to your boss why you think the marketing department should consider the implications of the price increase on the other marketing mix elements, what you feel these implications are, and what recommendations for change might be suggested.

3. Again, assume that you are the assistant director of marketing for a firm that manufactures a line of hair-care products. This morning, your boss came into your office and announced that she is going to recommend a dramatic price decrease. "If we decrease the price, we should be able to sell a lot more of our products and actually increase our total revenue and our bottom line as well." You respond by asking, "That's true if indeed our demand is elastic. But do we know that? Demand for our product may be fairly inelastic." To this your boss replies, "Elastic-ballistic. What difference does it make? Everyone knows that if you cut prices, you sell more and you make more money." After she leaves you think, "I've got to convince her that we have to know the effects of price changes on demand before we can make a move that could be a disaster."

   Again, in a role-playing situation with one of your classmates, explain elastic and inelastic demand to your boss. Discuss your recommendations for measuring the elasticity of demand for your product.

4. Assume that you and your friend have decided to go into business together manufacturing wrought iron birdcages. You know that your fixed costs (rent on a building, equipment, for example) will be $60 000 a year. You expect your variable costs to be $12 per birdcage.

   a. If you plan on selling the birdcages to retail stores for $18, how many must you sell to break even, that is, what is your break-even quantity?

   b. Assume that you and your partner feel that you must set a goal of achieving $10 000 profit with your business this year. How many units would you have to sell to make that amount of profit?

   c. What if you feel that you will be able to sell no more than 5000 birdcages? What price will you have to charge to break even? To make $10 000 in profit?

Marketing Mini-Project: **Learning by Doing**

Organizations develop pricing strategies to meet pricing objectives. These objectives may be related to sales, profit, the competition, customer satisfaction, or the image of the product. The purpose of this mini-project is to help you understand how different pricing objectives are important in marketing planning.

Many universities are having trouble filling up their existing dormitory space, as more and more students choose to live off campus in houses or in apartments. Identify your university's existing pricing objectives and developing recommendations for changes.

1. First, with two or three of your classmates, interview someone who participates in your university's pricing of dormitory space. It may be the vice-president for student affairs, the dean of students, the director of student life, or the vice-president for business and finance. Try to find out:

   a. The current prices charged for dormitory space.

   b. What the pricing objectives for dormitory space are.

   c. How the prices are calculated.

   d. The part that costs, demand, customer satisfaction, and competitive housing prices play in setting the dorm prices.

2. Next talk with students in your school to find out:

   a. Students' attitudes toward the prices charged for dormitory space.

   b. What a customer-pleasing price would be for dormitory space.

   c. The type and price of alternative housing used by students.

   d. Any other relevant student attitudes toward dormitory housing.

3. Develop a report that includes your findings and the recommendations you would make to your university. Be sure to focus on the pricing objectives currently in use and the alternative objectives that might be considered. What pricing strategies do your findings suggest? Present your results to your class.

Real People, Real Surfers: **Exploring the Web**

Barter exchanges are organizations that facilitate barter transactions between buyers and sellers. Many of the Canadian exchanges are members of the International Reciprocal Trade Association (IRTA) or the American National Association of Trade Exchanges (NATE).

First, visit the IRTA (www.irta.net) or NATE (www.nate.org) Web pages. Using links from those home pages to member exchanges or using an Internet search engine, locate and explore several barter exchange Web pages. Based on your Internet experience, answer the following questions:

1. What are the benefits to a business of joining a barter exchange?

2. What types of products are bartered?

3. How does a trade actually work with a barter exchange?

4. How does the exchange make its money? Who pays the exchange, and how much is charged?

5. Assuming the goal of barter exchange Web sites is to attract new members, evaluate the different Web sites you visited. Which Web site do you think was best? What features of the site would make you want to join if you were the owner of a small business? What features of the other sites made them less appealing than this one?

Ekati Diamonds

Australia's BHP Billiton Diamonds and two Canadian geologists own the Ekati diamond mine in Canada's Northwest Territories (NWT), 300 kilometres northeast of Yellowknife. Opened in 1998 and now producing around $600 million of rough diamonds annually, this single mine accounts for about 6% of the world's diamond supply.

Ekati is also the brand name of the highest quality diamonds produced by the mine, accounting for about 1% of the production or about 3700 diamonds. Ekati branded diamonds are a third of a carat or larger and receive a "Triple Ideal" grade from the American Gem Society (AGS). They are laser engraved with a serial number and have a unique fingerprint guaranteeing authenticity. The diamonds come with a certificate from the AGS verifying specifications, a certificate from the Ekati Diamond Mine™ guaranteeing origin, and another from the government of the NWT validating Canadian origin. This is the first time that a diamond's origin has been branded.

The Canadian origin of the diamonds is central to the marketing strategy of Ekati and BHP Billiton has adopted a maple leaf logo for the brand to help establish its Canadian identity internationally. Using imagery such as snow, ice, northern lights, and rugged terrain and words such as "pristine," "true north," "beauty," and "dependable," BHP Billiton is trying to link their diamonds to a romanticized vision of the Canadian North generated from the mystique of the Yukon gold rush. Although they would never say it because of the potential consumer and industry backlash, Canadian diamonds are also recognized as being "conflict free"—they are produced with North American human rights standards and are not the funding base for civil wars.

While most of the premium Ekati diamonds are sold uncut, about 10% are precision cut and polished in Canada and sold through about 35 high-end jewellery stores across Canada. Rather than try to directly target the large US market (50% of world sales), BHP Billiton thought it prudent to first test their marketing strategy in Canada where consumers may have greater

MARKETING IN ACTION

attachment to the North and may have patriotic motivation to buy premium priced Canadian diamonds. BHP Billiton's main communication vehicle has been their interactive website (www.ekati.ca). Other communication vehicles involved high-end print ads, point-of-sale material, brochures, charity events and trade kits.

While sales have met expectations for the pilot project, consumers have had difficulty justifying the price difference to "buy Canadian." Retailer Norbert Brinkhaus suggests that "there is still a tremendous lack of education out there...it's not that an Ekati diamond is that much more expensive, it's because they are cut to a standard that is unmatched by anybody."[25] Graham Nicholls, vice-president of external affairs for BHP Billiton, observes that there is great interest in Canadian diamonds, but only within a narrow niche of consumers. He and others at BHP Billiton are just not sure why.

Before setting sights on new markets such as the United States, BHP Billiton is conducting comprehensive market research. In order to present comprehensive marketing strategy packages to new retailers they want to know what motivates consumer purchase behaviour and how different target markets respond to various affective (image based) and informative (quantitative or verification based) appeals. They also need to understand differences between Canadian and American diamond consumers.

As BHP Billiton prepares for the expansion of the Ekati diamond marketing effort, their marketing staff is examining their current strategy to see if minor modifications are needed for entry into the US market.

THINGS TO THINK ABOUT

1. How is the Ekati diamond pricing strategy supported by product, distribution, and communication strategies?
2. What other information would you want to collect before expanding the marketing program for Ekati diamonds? How would you get that information?
3. How might the Ekati strategy need to be adapted for entering the US market?

It's all here...

Victoria, a paradise of spectacular

views, impressive mountain

ranges and the bold Pacific

Ocean. Nestled on the southern

most tip of British Columbia and

Vancouver Island, Victoria

balances bustle and busy with

serenity and softness.

Clarion Hotel
Grand Pacific

Overlooking Victoria's Inner Harbour and with

views of the Olympic Mountains, the Clarion Hotel

Grand Pacific boasts a superior location, luxurious

accommodation and Four Star Service. The hotel is

adjacent to the Provincial Legislature and just steps

away from The Victoria Conference Centre,

shopping, parks, and the many marine adventures

available in this garden city by the sea.

13

Pricing Methods

ISBN 0-13-014420-7

$9.99

9 780130 144201

SALE
SARICE
PRICE

When you have completed your study of this chapter, you should be able to

CHAPTER OBJECTIVES

1. Understand key pricing strategies.

2. Explain pricing tactics for individual and multiple products.

3. Describe the psychological aspects of pricing.

4. Understand some of the legal and ethical considerations in pricing.

Real People, Real Decisions ✓ ✗

Meet Stephen Webb
A Decision Maker at Clarion Hotel Grand Pacific

Stephen Webb has been general manager of the Clarion Hotel Grand Pacific in Victoria, British Columbia, for the past five years. Since moving to Canada from England in 1982, he has held numerous positions in the hospitality industry, including executive positions with the Delta Hotel chain in Toronto. As general manager, Webb is involved in the daily operations and overall focus of two hotels: the well-appointed Clarion Hotel Grand Pacific and the more modest Quality Inn, adjacent properties in Victoria's downtown Inner Harbour. He is the key decision maker in business planning, brand positioning, and program design. The 145-room Grand Pacific is one of the top three hotels in Victoria. It is consistently the industry leader in yearly occupancy rates and has the city's second highest average room rate. The 86-room Quality Inn, conveniently located across from car- and foot-passenger ferry terminals, commands the highest summer room rate in the city for its class of hotel, but has much lower annual occupancies than its sister property.

Clarion Hotel Grand Pacific
www.hotelgrandpacific.com

Price Planning: Move and Countermove

For both individual consumers and corporate travellers, the selection of a hotel depends very much on perceived value—what you get for what you pay. That's why Stephen Webb and Clarion managers constantly look for ways to improve their pricing strategies and keep Clarion ahead of the competition.

An old Russian proverb says: "There are two kinds of fools in any market. One doesn't charge enough. The other charges too much."[1] This underscores the strategic decision behind pricing—how much value to offer the customer versus how much value to retain in terms of profit for the firm. Today's marketers may ponder the message. In modern business, there seldom is a one-and-only, now-and-forever, best pricing strategy; pricing today has more of the continuous decision-making character of a chess game. The organization must think two or three moves ahead. And no pricing decision is set in stone. Costs increase. Sales decline. The competition changes its prices. Price reductions can discourage new competitors or at least sabotage competitors' product introductions.

In the 1990s, The Bay decided to shift toward a higher-price designer fashion image, abandoning its hard goods such as electronics and sporting goods. This strategy put them in direct competition with Eaton's, leaving Sears alone in the mid-price market. The Bay's pricing resulted in sagging sales and plummeting profits. A price war with Eaton's during the 1998 Christmas season caused both companies to lose millions of dollars. Eaton's eventually declared bankruptcy. The Bay, under the direction of new president, Marc Chouinard, decided to return to a pricing strategy that focused on more moderate price points.[2] The Bay realized that having a successful pricing strategy is often a continuous process of evaluation and re-evaluation.

This chapter looks at how companies develop and manage pricing strategies, and discusses some of the specific tactics that put pricing strategies in action. It concludes with an examination of the psychological and ethical issues in pricing strategy.

Pricing Strategies

Chapter 12 presented the first four steps in price planning. We've repeated Figure 12.1 here as Figure 13.1. Marketers first develop pricing objectives that support the overall corporate and marketing objectives. Then they examine demand, costs, and the pricing environment before moving on to our fifth step in price planning—choosing a pricing strategy.

Marketers whose responsibility it is to develop pricing strategies will consider a number of alternative strategies and try to anticipate the outcomes. The break-even analysis and marginal analysis procedures explained in Chapter 12 are almost always included in this process. In large firms, pricing analysts may conduct research to estimate demand and demand elasticity. Using costs and demand data, they estimate the revenues and profits that are likely to result from each possible strategy.

Figure 13.2 shows some common pricing strategies—strategies based on costs, demand, the competition, and customer needs—and strategies for new products.

Pricing Strategies Based on Cost

Marketing planners often choose one of several pricing strategies based on the cost of producing the product. Marketers use *cost-based strategies*, because they are simple to calculate and relatively safe. They ensure that the price will cover the costs the company incurs in producing and marketing the product.

Cost-based pricing methods, however, have drawbacks. They do not consider such factors as the nature of the target market, demand, competition, the product life cycle, and the product's image. In addition, although the calculations for setting the price may be simple and straightforward, it may be difficult to estimate costs accurately. Think about such firms as Nortel, Bombardier, and McCain, which produce many products. How does cost analysis allocate the costs for the plant, equipment, design engineers, maintenance, and marketing personnel, so that the pricing plan accurately reflects the cost of production for any particular product? For example, how do you allocate the salary of a marketing executive who deals with many different products? Should the cost be divided equally among all products? Should costs be based on the actual number of hours spent working on each product? Or should costs be assigned based on the revenues generated by each product? There is no one right answer. Even with these limitations, cost-based pricing strategies are often a marketer's best choice.

COST-PLUS PRICING

The most common cost-based approach to pricing a product is **cost-plus pricing**, in which a marketer totals the costs for the product and then adds the desired profit per unit. The goal of this approach is to set a price that will ensure the revenue received from selling the product will not only cover all the costs associated with the product but will also provide the desired profit or return on investment.

The most frequently used type of cost-plus pricing is straight markup pricing. The price is calculated by adding a set percentage to the cost. Most retailers and wholesalers use markup pricing exclusively because of its simplicity. Calculating markup pricing requires two steps: estimating the cost per unit of output and adding a markup.

The first step requires that the unit cost can be estimated reasonably well and that the level of output will not change much. For this and the other examples, we will consider how a small manufacturer and a retailer price a line of jeans. Assume that the jeans manufacturer has a fixed cost of $200 000 for producing 40 000 pairs of jeans, or $5 per pair. Variable costs for the jeans are $20 per pair. Total costs to make the jeans are $25 per pair, or $1 million for the 40 000 pairs.

The second step is to calculate the markup. There are two methods for calculating the markup percentage: markup on cost and the more popular markup on selling price. In *markup on cost pricing*, just

Figure 13.1 Steps in Price Planning

✳ ✳ ✳

cost-plus pricing A method of setting prices in which the seller totals all the costs for the product and then adds the desired profit per unit.

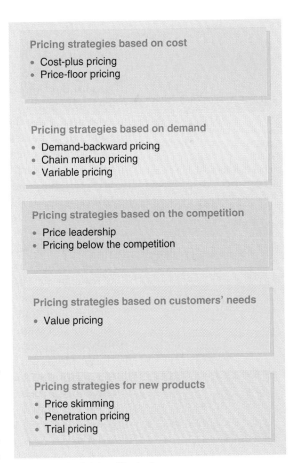

Figure 13.2 Pricing Strategies

as the name implies, a percentage of the cost is added to the cost to determine the selling price.

Markup on cost: For markup on cost, the calculation is:

$$\text{Price} = \text{total cost} + (\text{total cost} \times \text{markup percentage})$$

In our jeans example, if the manufacturer wants a profit of $200 000, what markup percentage would it use? The $200 000 is 20% of the $1 million total cost. To find the price, the calculation would be:

$$\text{Price} = \$25 + (\$25 \times 0.20) = \$25 + \$5 = \$30$$

(Note that in the calculations, the markup percentage is expressed as a decimal; that is, 20% = 0.20.)

Markup on selling price: As we noted, sometimes firms use a different calculation method—markup on selling price. Wholesalers and retailers more frequently use markup on selling price in pricing their products because the markup percentage becomes the seller's gross margin. For example, if a retailer knows it needs a 40% margin to cover overhead and profits, the retailer will calculate its price as a 40% markup on selling price.

Let's say a retailer buys the jeans from the manufacturer for $30 per pair. If the retailer requires a 40% markup on selling price, we would calculate the retailer's price as follows.

$$\text{Price} = \text{cost} / (1 - \text{markup percentage})$$

(Note that you always begin with 1.00 in the denominator.)

$$\text{Price} = \$30 / (1.00 - 0.40) = \$30 / (0.60) = \$50$$

Just to compare the difference in the final prices of the two markup methods, let's see what would happen if the retailer uses a markup on cost method. Using the same product cost and price with a 40% markup on cost would yield:

$$\text{Price} = \$30 + (\$30 \times 0.40) = \$30 + \$12 = \$42$$

PRICE-FLOOR PRICING

***

price-floor pricing A method for calculating price in which, to maintain full plant operating capacity, a portion of a firm's output may be sold at a price that covers only marginal costs of production.

These cost-based pricing methods do not take into account any factors except costs and profits. But there are times when firms need to consider other factors, such as the advantage of having a plant operating at its peak capacity, which keeps a skilled workforce fully employed. **Price-floor pricing** is a method for calculating price that considers both costs and what can be done to ensure that a plant can operate at its capacity.

Price-floor pricing has limited use, usually when the state of the economy or other temporary market conditions make it impossible for a firm to sell enough units of its product at a price that covers fixed costs, variable costs, and profit goals to keep its plants operating at full capacity. In such circumstances, it may be possible to sell part of the units produced at a lower price, one that covers only the marginal costs of production. If the price-floor price can be set above the marginal costs, then the firm can use the difference to increase profits or to help cover its fixed costs.

For example, assume the jeans firm, operating at full capacity, can produce 50 000 pairs of jeans a year. The average variable costs per unit are $20; the price that covers fixed costs, variable costs, and a desired level of profits is $30 per pair. Due to a downturn in the economy, the firm finds that it can sell only 40 000 units at this price. Using price-floor pricing, the firm can sell the additional 10 000 pairs of jeans at a price as low as $20 and maintain full-capacity operations.

If it adopts this approach, the firm will not make anything on the additional units, but it will not lose anything either. If it sells the additional 10 000 pairs at $25, then it will not only cover the variable costs but will also increase its total profits—10 000 × $5 or $50 000—not a bad deal. But several risks accompany price-floor pricing. Selling the additional 10 000 pairs of jeans at a lower cost might cannibalize full-price sales, and if the lower price is offered to some retailers and not others, it might anger those not included and undermine customer loyalty.

Exhibit 13.1

Price-floor pricing is a method for calculating price that considers both costs and what can be done to ensure that a plant can operate at its capacity.

Firms that produce their own national brands as well as manufacture private-label brands sold through various retailers and distributors may use price-floor pricing for the private-label end of the business. Thus, Frigidaire may sell 70% of its refrigerators under the Frigidaire name and the rest to Sears for sale under its own Kenmore brand name. The consumers in Exhibit 13.1 look at specifications to compare models of different prices.

Pricing Strategies Based on Demand

Demand-based pricing is basing the selling price on an estimate of volume or quantity that a firm can sell at different prices. To use any of the pricing strategies based on demand, firms must research demand—they must learn what quantities of a product different target markets are willing to buy at different prices. Often marketers use customer surveys in which consumers reveal whether they would buy a certain product and how much of it they would buy at various prices. More accurate estimates can be obtained by some type of field experiment. For instance, a firm might actually offer the product at different price levels in different test markets and gauge the results.

One strength of demand-based pricing strategies is that their use assures a firm that it will be able to sell what it produces at the determined price, because the price is based on research findings about customer demand rather than on the seller's costs. A major disadvantage is the difficulty of estimating demand accurately.

DEMAND-BACKWARD PRICING

Demand-backward pricing starts with determining what customers are willing to pay for a product and then working *backward* to determine if the product can be produced at a cost that generates an acceptable profit at this price.

Boeing is a firm that has used demand-backward pricing. The airplane manufacturer sought to persuade the major airlines to replace their aging fleets. Boeing calculated a demand-driven price by considering not only its asking price, but also the savings in operating costs customers would get with the newer, more efficient airliners. Boeing concluded that its manufacturing costs would have to drop about 30% per plane to get customers to replace their older jets. Boeing scaled down operations and reduced the costs of materials and labour so that it could produce a new plane at this lower price.[3]

Demand-backward pricing is more likely to be found at firms that produce high-ticket goods, in industries in which there are several companies competing for customer business or in which customers may simply do without the product if prices are too high. For example,

✳ ✳ ✳
demand-based pricing A price-setting method based on estimates of demand at different prices.

✳ ✳ ✳
demand-backward pricing Pricing strategy that starts with what customers are willing to pay, followed up with cost-management strategies to hold costs to a satisfactory level.

Boeing
www.boeing.com

many computer companies in the late 1990s recognized that they could attract large numbers of new computer owners if they kept prices below $1000. Many consumers simply were unwilling to go above that price for a family computer. It was then up to the companies to figure out how to manufacture their computers at low enough costs that would still allow a profit.

CHAIN-MARKUP PRICING

Chain-markup pricing extends the logic of demand-backward pricing from the ultimate consumer back through the distribution channel to the manufacturer. A manufacturer first determines the maximum end-user price that the market will bear, based on estimates of demand. Next, the manufacturer estimates the percentage margins that the retailer, wholesaler, and distributor will require to cover overhead and profits. The manufacturer then obtains the required cost of manufacturing. We'll discuss how prices to channel intermediaries are determined later in this chapter.

VARIABLE PRICING

Variable pricing, or custom pricing, is a strategy of tailoring the price of a product to reflect variability in market demand and what different customers are willing to pay. The price of gasoline, for example, is often set higher during periods of peak demand—like long weekends. Variable pricing is common in business-to-business marketing contexts where prices are typically negotiated in new buy or modified re-buy situations like the digital imaging system purchase described in the Venture 4th case at the end of Chapter 7, or submitted as sealed bids (typical of government purchases). Coca-Cola has been experimenting with the concept of variable pricing in vending machines—with the price determined by the ambient temperature outside the machine—and a rationale that consumers may be willing to pay more for a cold Coke when it is hot outside.[4]

Pricing Strategies Based on the Competition

Sometimes, a firm develops pricing strategies based on the competition—it prices its product at the same or similar level as the competition, below the competition, or above the competition.

Before Wal-Mart came to Canada, Zellers was clearly the price leader in discount stores. Other discount stores would price their products similar to Zellers.[5] A firm that chooses a **price leadership** strategy either is the industry leader or follows the industry leader by setting the same or similar prices. Usually, firms practise a price leadership strategy when they're in an oligopoly with relatively few producers—such as the Canadian petroleum industry. In such an industry, it is in the best interest of all firms to minimize price competition for everyone to make a profit. Price leadership strategies are popular, because they provide an acceptable and legal way for firms to agree on prices without ever talking with each other.

Even when there isn't a single industry price leader, firms may adopt a parity pricing strategy—they try to keep their price about equal to key competitors' prices. Gasoline retailers attempt to maintain a parity pricing structure by responding quickly to competitive price moves; this rapid response is often viewed by consumers as *price fixing*. Numerous national and provincial investigations of gasoline prices have found no evidence of price fixing, and the petroleum companies are spending millions of dollars educating consumers about the cost structure of gasoline.[6, 7]

Sometimes firms choose to price their products below the competition. By using rock-bottom prices on popular CDs, electronics stores, such as the Future Shop, have been able to get shoppers into their stores, where many will buy the high-profit electronics equipment sold by the retailer. Umbrella pricing is a strategy of ducking under the competition's price by a standard percentage. Corel Corp., for example, consistently prices its office software suite at least 20% below that of Microsoft. Coca-Cola is counting on its market leadership position, brand equity, and customer loyalty to support a new premium pricing strategy, pricing Coke products above the competition, in an attempt to increase margins and profits.[8]

Exhibit 13.2

Sanyo bases its pricing on customer needs using a cost-of-ownership strategy.

Pricing Strategies Based on Customers' Needs

When firms develop pricing strategies that cater to the needs of customers, they are less concerned with short-term successes than with keeping customers for the long term. Firms truly dedicated to customer satisfaction look at the wants and needs of customers in developing pricing strategies.

Sanyo, for example, bases pricing of its rechargeable batteries on customer needs by using a cost-of-ownership strategy (see Exhibit 13.2). The *cost of ownership* is the price consumers pay for a product, plus the cost of maintaining and using the product, less its resale (or salvage) value. Because Sanyo's batteries are reusable, consumers may see the initial high price in a more favourable light. Consumers will save money in the long run, because it costs them less to recharge the batteries than to buy new ones.

Firms such as Zellers or Wal-Mart that practise **value pricing**, or **every day low pricing (EDLP)**, develop a pricing strategy that promises ultimate value to consumers. As discussed in Chapter 1, customer v*alue* is the benefits received by a customer relative to the costs and sacrifices necessary to obtain those benefits—what this really means is that, in the customers' eyes, the product's price is justified by what they receive.[9]

When firms base price strategies on cost, they are operating under the old production orientation and not a marketing orientation. Value-based pricing begins with customers, then considers the competition, and then determines the best pricing strategy. Smart marketers know that the firm that wins is not necessarily the one with the lowest prices but rather the one that delivers the most value.

This has been the strategy behind the success of WestJet Airlines. Modelled after Southwest Airlines, WestJet focuses on everyday low fares, short distances, and good customer service to attract budget-conscious leisure travellers throughout Canada. They started with understanding their target market—what it would take to get people out of their cars for short-haul trips—then they made marketing mix decisions to deliver the value bundle sought by those customers: no-frill, direct flights, at rock-bottom prices, to and from under-utilized airports, using standard aircraft, serviced by personable staff, offering fun and light-hearted (perhaps even irreverent) customer interactions.

In practice, when marketers use EDLP strategies, consumers feel they get more for their money. Marketers hope that will make them see the price as reasonable and encourage them to remain loyal rather than snapping up whatever happens to be on sale. Deal-oriented consumers, however, have been conditioned to choose products because they are "on special" rather than because they are superior to others. The problem with "deals" or frequent price promotions is that consumers learn to wait for sales or stock up on products when they are on sale, thus making it difficult for companies to maintain "regular" margins and production volumes. Procter & Gamble tried to establish an EDLP strategy in the early 1990s for such products as Tide and Pampers, but abandoned this strategy in face of competitors continuing to offer sales, coupons, and other price promotions.[10]

✲ ✲ ✲

value pricing or **every day low pricing (EDLP)** A pricing strategy in which a firm sets prices that provide ultimate value to customers.

SPOTLIGHT ON REAL PEOPLE *Casket Royale*

A coffin is usually the most expensive item in a funeral. Until recently, Canada's funeral homes had a monopoly on coffins, so prices were high enough to kill you. Not anymore. Casket Royale is one of the first discount coffin outlets in Canada. Owned by brothers Natale and Joe Roda, the company is taking advantage of laws that allow a mourner to take his or her own casket to a funeral parlour, and they are using price as a competitive strategy. Customers select a discounted coffin, and men wearing suits and gloves deliver it to the funeral home. The brothers offer a wide selection, including some embroidered with pink rosebuds, and others with real spring mattresses. One model, called the Bubba Box, comes sheathed in denim. The discounters mark up their products by 100%, which seems like a lot until you realize that funeral parlours jack up wholesale prices by 300 to 500%. For example, the Basilica, a steel model lined with white velvet and pictures of the Last Supper, sells for $6000 at a funeral home, but it's yours from Casket Royale for $2325 Canadian—or less if you're willing to haggle. Casket Royale features an 800 number and 24-hour service, and is planning sales presentations at senior citizen homes. They considered, but rejected, this slogan: "Quality, affordability and service to die for."[11]

1. What kind of pricing strategy does Casket Royale use?
2. What other pricing strategies might Casket Royale consider?

New-Product Pricing

Chapter 9 showed how new products are vital to the growth and profits of a firm. And new products also present unique pricing challenges. When a product is new to the market or when there is no established industry price norm, marketers may use a skimming price strategy, a penetration pricing strategy, or trial pricing for a short introductory period of time.

SKIMMING PRICE

* * *
skimming price A very high, premium price that a firm charges for its new, highly desirable product.

Skimming means taking the top or best part of something—like the cream that separates and rises to the top of non-homogenized milk and is used for making ice cream and whipped cream. In pricing, setting a **skimming price** means that the firm charges a high, premium price for its new product, seeking to attract the top spending, least price sensitive, target market. For example, when Top-Flite introduced its new Strata golf balls with a new dimple design and more solid core for better flight with metal clubs in 1996, the price was three times that of regular balls. Pro shops still couldn't keep them in stock.[12]

If a product is highly desirable and offers unique benefits, demand is price inelastic during the introductory stage of the product life cycle. In such cases, a skimming pricing policy allows a firm to recover research, development, and promotion costs. Firms focusing on profit objectives in developing their pricing strategies often set skimming prices for new products.

A skimming price is more likely to succeed when a product provides such important benefits to the target market that customers feel they must have the product, no matter what the cost. When introduced in the late 1960s, hand-held calculators were such a product (see Exhibit 13.3)—they provided so much value over doing math by hand that they commanded prices as high as $200.

Second, for skimming pricing to be successful, there should be little chance that competitors can get into the market quickly. With highly complex, technical products, it may be quite a while before competitors can develop and test new products and get them into production. This is the case for patented pharmaceutical products that have a lock on the market.

Finally, a skimming pricing strategy is most successful when the market consists of several customer segments with different levels of price sensitivity. There must be a substantial number of initial product customers who have very low price sensitivity. After a period of time, the price can go down, and a second segment of the market with a slightly higher level of price sensitivity will purchase, and so on. The calculators that once commanded $200 can now be bought for less than $2—accessible to almost everyone.

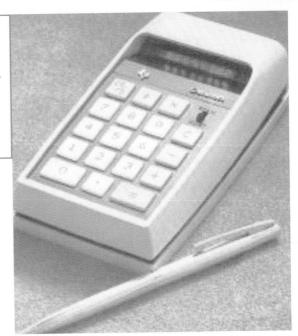

Exhibit 13.3

When first introduced, calculators had a price-skimming strategy.

PENETRATION PRICING

Penetration pricing is the opposite of skimming pricing. A new product is introduced at a very low price, as Intel did with its Pentium chip. Intel's pricing of its 486 microprocessor computer chip and its successor, the Pentium chip, illustrates the importance of a new product's price in determining its chances for success in the marketplace.[13] Because rivals were way behind in developing competitive chips, Intel set a high price for its 486 CPU. When the Pentium chip, which more than doubled the speed of the 486, was introduced, Intel knew that Motorola was working with IBM and Apple to develop comparable chips. Thus, it set a low price to sell more in a short period of time and derail Motorola's debut.[14] This strategy worked well for Intel. The low price encouraged demand and sales in the early stages of the product life cycle. If the marketing objective is to beef up market share, penetration pricing makes sense.

Another reason marketers use penetration pricing is to discourage competitors from entering the market. The firm first out with a new product has an important advantage. Experience has shown that a *pioneering brand* often is able to maintain dominant market share for the life of the product. Competitors looking at the market may feel that the potential for developing a profitable alternative is not good. Bayer aspirin and Hoover vacuum cleaners are examples of brands that were first to market, kept their leads for decades, and still dominate their fields. These pioneering brands don't need to do much talking to tell consumers who they are. Keeping prices low may even act as a *barrier to entry* to potential competitors, because the cost of developing and manufacturing a new similar product prevents a satisfactory return.

✳ ✳ ✳
penetration pricing A pricing strategy in which a firm introduces a new product at a very low price to encourage more customers to purchase it.

TRIAL PRICING

With **trial pricing**, a new product carries a low price for a limited period of time to lower the risk for a customer.[15] In trial pricing, the idea is to win customer acceptance first and make profits later. A low-enough introductory price may be an acceptable alternative to free samples.

Telus, for example, is conducting a $65 million experiment to bring digital TV, movies on demand, Internet, e-mail, and phone service into homes for one monthly bill. After the trial offer, Telus will decide how widely the services will be offered and whether there is an opportunity to increase prices.[16] Microsoft introduced the Access database program at the short-term promotional price of $99, when the suggested retail price was $495. Trial pricing assumes that the strong benefits of using a product will create loyal customers, who will spread favourable word-of-mouth communications to other prospective users. Trial pricing also works for services. Health clubs and other service providers frequently offer trial memberships or special introductory prices. They hope that customers will try the service at a low price and be converted to a regular-price customer.

✳ ✳ ✳
trial pricing Pricing a new product low for a limited period of time to lower the risk for a customer.

Developing Pricing Tactics

Once marketers have developed pricing strategies, the last step in price planning is to implement them. The methods companies use to set their strategies in motion are their pricing tactics, as Figure 13.3 shows.

Real People, Real Decisions
Decision Time at Clarion Hotel Grand Pacific

When Stephen Webb joined the Grand Pacific, it was clear that one of his main challenges would be in positioning and differentiating the two properties. Having two brands on adjacent properties had advantages. The company could appeal to different guest segments and implement a differential pricing strategy aimed at maximizing occupancy. Operating costs were lower than those of two separate hotels, because they could share management resources, share facilities such as the athletic club and swimming pool, and make more efficient use of laundry, cleaning, and other external services.

Webb, however, was concerned about the ability to keep the positioning of the two brands distinct. To some extent, guests of the Quality Inn received access to amenities far in excess of the room rate charged, which made it more difficult to "sell" the premium pricing at the Grand Pacific. The Quality Inn, built in 1958, was clearly in need of some structural renovations and detracted from the upscale image and ambience of the Grand Pacific. Some amenities, such as air-conditioning, expected by even budget-minded visitors, were not available in the Quality Inn. The Quality Inn, under-utilized during the off-season, could not command the same room rates of the Grand Pacific during the peak summer months. Occupancy rates for the Quality Inn were typically over 85% in May through August; about 70% in the shoulder seasons in March, April, September, October; and less than 40% in the off-season November to February. Occupancy rates at the Clarion brand were over 95% May through September; March, April, and October averaged 80%; and the low season November to February averaged 65%. Because the former owners of the Grand Pacific had originally planned on expanding the hotel with a phase two project, the current hotel was lacking the meeting room and restaurant space to take full advantage of corporate retreats and larger tour groups. Webb considered his options for a redesign of the Quality Inn that would enable the space to generate more revenue and better fit the desired product image:

Option 1. Renovate the existing Quality Inn—make the rooms larger and address structural concerns. With a significant electrical upgrade, air-conditioning and such amenities as hairdryers and coffee makers could be added to the rooms to make them more attractive to travellers. Renovations of this type were estimated at approximately six million dollars. With its excellent location and new look, the 86-room Quality Inn could continue to hold its market share. This level of renovation would be required at a minimum and was considered the status quo option.

Option 2. Webb investigated tearing down the Quality Inn and building an addition to the Grand Pacific, at an estimated cost in excess of $20 million. The renovations would include 8000 extra square feet of meeting space and expanded restaurant facilities. This option would give the Grand Pacific a total of 308 rooms, at an average annual room rate of about $148. Higher occupancy rates would also be expected in the shoulder and off-seasons under this option, due to larger group bookings. Also, the tourism industry was increasing in British Columbia; if the Clarion expanded immediately, it would be ahead of any competition that were thinking about expanding their room supply. Fewer rooms, however, would be available to budget-minded tourists in Victoria's Inner Harbour.

Now, join the Clarion team. Which option would you choose and why?

Pricing for Individual Products

How marketers present a product's price to the market can make a big difference in the attractiveness of the offering. These are two tactics:

- With *two-part pricing*, two separate types of payments are required to purchase the product. For example, golf and tennis clubs charge yearly or monthly fees plus fees for each round of golf or tennis. Cellular phone and Internet service providers offer customers a set number of minutes usage for a monthly fee plus a per-minute rate for extra usage.

- *Payment pricing* makes products appear more attainable by breaking up the total price into smaller amounts payable over time. For example, many customers now opt to lease rather than buy a car. The monthly lease amount is an example of payment pricing, which tends to make people less sensitive to the total price of the car.[17]

Pricing for Multiple Products

A firm may sell several products that consumers typically buy together. When people buy a burger, pizza, or taco for lunch, they often purchase a drink, fries, or salad as well. Similarly, when someone buys a personal computer, a box of diskettes is usually not far behind. These are some tactics marketers use for pricing multiple products.

PRICE BUNDLING

Price bundling is selling two or more goods or services as a single package for one price. A music buff can buy tickets to an entire concert series for a single price. A PC typically comes bundled with a monitor, keyboard, and software. A movie ticket may include a drink and popcorn. Even an all-you-can-eat special at the local diner is an example of price bundling. Price bundling is an increasingly popular pricing tactic for consumer electronics, small and large appliances, and even automobiles where the tangible product is bundled with an extended warranty package. The tangible product is priced near cost while more significant margins are made on the extended warranty.

From a marketing standpoint, price bundling makes sense. If products are priced separately, it is likely that customers will buy some but not all of the items. They might choose to put off some purchases until later, or they might buy from a competitor. Whatever revenue a seller loses from the reduced prices, it makes up in increased total purchases. Exhibit 13.4 for Malaysia Airlines shows price bundling for flights within Malaysia for the purchase of a flight to Kuala Lumpur.

CAPTIVE PRICING

Captive pricing is a tactic a firm uses when it has two products that work only when used together. The firm sells one item at a very low price and then makes its profit on the second high-margin item. Gillette has used captive pricing to sell its shaving products. In 1998, the company introduced the Mach3, a triple-bladed razor. Gillette spent about $1 billion on developing and introducing the new product, but anticipated that the razor would generate annual revenues of $1 billion by 2001.[18] While the razor sold for the low price of $6.99, blades for the Mach3 carried a high price of $1.50 or more per blade. The typical American man buys 30 blades a year. If he uses the Mach3 razor, it costs him $45 annually to replenish his supply of blades, compared to the $9 annual cost of generic blades. Although the blade and razor business generates only a third of corporate revenues for Gillette, the company's use of captive pricing tactics in this category delivers two-thirds of its profits.

Geographic Pricing

Geographic pricing is a tactic that establishes how firms handle the cost of shipping products to customers near, far, and wide. Characteristics of the product, customers, and competition may make it advisable to charge all customers the same price, or it may make better sense to vary the prices charged to customers in different locations, regardless of the overall pricing strategy selected.

F.O.B. PRICING

Often, pricing is stated as f.o.b. factory or f.o.b. delivered—f.o.b. stands for *free on board*, which means the supplier will pay to have the product loaded onto a truck or some other carrier. Also—and this is important—title passes to the buyer at the f.o.b. location. Thus, *f.o.b. factory* or **f.o.b. origin** means that the cost of transporting the product from the factory to the customer's location is the responsibility of the customer; **f.o.b. delivered** means that the seller pays both the cost of loading and transporting to the customer, which is included in the selling price.

The f.o.b. origin pricing creates many different prices, because the purchase price for each customer changes with shipping costs. But with f.o.b. delivered pricing, every customer pays the same price. Another option combines f.o.b. origin and f.o.b. delivered—sometimes,

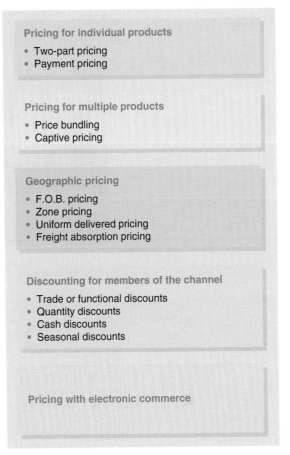

Pricing for individual products
- Two-part pricing
- Payment pricing

Pricing for multiple products
- Price bundling
- Captive pricing

Geographic pricing
- F.O.B. pricing
- Zone pricing
- Uniform delivered pricing
- Freight absorption pricing

Discounting for members of the channel
- Trade or functional discounts
- Quantity discounts
- Cash discounts
- Seasonal discounts

Pricing with electronic commerce

Figure 13.3 Pricing Tactics

✳ ✳ ✳
price bundling Selling two or more goods or services as a single package for one price.

✳ ✳ ✳
captive pricing A pricing tactic for two items that must be used together; one item is priced very low and the firm makes its profit on another, high-margin item essential to the operation of the first item.

✳ ✳ ✳
f.o.b. origin pricing A pricing tactic in which the cost of transporting the product from the factory to the customer's location is the responsibility of the customer.

✳ ✳ ✳
f.o.b. delivered pricing A pricing tactic in which the cost of loading and transporting the product to the customer is included in the selling price, paid by the manufacturer.

a seller's terms indicate that title to the product is transferred at the seller's location, but the seller will pay the freight. This plan is called *f.o.b. factory, freight prepaid.*

Sellers often prefer *f.o.b factory* pricing because of its simplicity. The marketer doesn't have to take into account the costs of shipping to different customers at varying distances from the factory. It also allows flexibility in how a product gets shipped, because pricing does not depend on a particular shipping method. In addition, the fact that the title is transferred before shipping shifts the risk of damage to the transit company and the customer.

ZONE PRICING

Another geographic pricing tactic is **zone pricing**. Like f.o.b. factory pricing, zone pricing means that distant customers pay more than customers who are close to the factory. However, in zone pricing, there are a limited number of different prices charged, based on geographic zones established by the seller. All customers located in each zone pay the same transportation charge.

Zone pricing simplifies geographic cost differences, which is important in certain markets. It would be nearly impossible for Canada Post's Express courier service to charge one price if a package shipped from Winnipeg went to Toronto, a different price if it went to Mississauga, another if it went to Don Mills, Ontario. Therefore, Express Post charges different rates for shipping packages from any single location to different zones across the country.

UNIFORM DELIVERED PRICING

With **uniform delivered pricing**, an average shipping cost is added to the price, no matter what the buyer's location or distance from the manufacturer's plant—within reason. Catalogue sales, home television shopping, e-commerce, and other types of non-store retail sales usually use uniform delivered pricing.

FREIGHT ABSORPTION PRICING

Freight absorption pricing means the seller takes on part or all of the cost of shipping. This policy is good for high-ticket items, when the cost of shipping is a negligible part of the sales

---

※ ※ ※
zone pricing A pricing tactic in which customers in different geographic zones pay different transportation rates.

※ ※ ※
uniform delivered pricing A pricing tactic in which a firm adds a standard shipping charge to the price for all customers regardless of location.

※ ※ ※
freight absorption pricing A pricing tactic in which the seller absorbs the total cost of transportation.

price and the profit margin. Marketers are most likely to use freight absorption pricing in highly competitive markets or when such pricing allows them to enter new markets.

Discounting for Members of the Channel

As well as tactics used to sell to ultimate customers, marketers use discounting tactics to implement pricing strategies with members of the channel of distribution.

TRADE OR FUNCTIONAL DISCOUNTS

Whether a firm sells to businesses or directly to consumers, most pricing structures are built around list prices. A **list price** is set by the manufacturer for the end customer to pay. In pricing for members of the channel, marketers recognize that pricing must ensure that retailers and wholesalers can cover their costs of doing business and make a profit.

When manufacturers develop pricing tactics for channel intermediaries, they often use **trade** or **functional discounts**, because the channel members perform selling, credit, storage, and transportation services that the manufacturer would otherwise have to provide. Often, setting functional discounts is simplified when a firm uses set percentage discounts off list price for each channel level.

Let's look at an example of a channel of distribution that includes a manufacturer that sells to wholesalers that in turn sell to smaller retailers. The manufacturer may state trade discounts as list price less 40/20. The first number means that 40% of the list price is to cover the overhead and profit requirements for the retailer—the manufacturer is suggesting that the wholesalers sell to their retail customers at list less 40%. If the list price of a product is $200, the price to the retailers would be:

$$\$200 - (40\% \times 200) = \$200 - \$80 = \$120$$

The second number, the 20, is the discount percentage allowed for wholesalers to cover their costs of doing business and profit. Thus, the manufacturer's selling price to the wholesaler is discounted from the retailer's price and would be:

$$\$120 - (20\% \times 120) = \$120 - \$24 = \$96$$

Note that although we talk about trade discounts being determined by manufacturers, in reality the manufacturer has little if any control over the percentage discounts. In most industries, these are standard percentages based on the margins retailers and wholesalers require to cover their overhead and profits.

QUANTITY DISCOUNTS

Firms that sell to distribution channel members or end-user business customers often offer **quantity discounts**, or reduced prices, for purchases of larger quantities. Marketers commonly use quantity discounts as a way to encourage larger purchases from distribution channel partners.

Sometimes marketers offer buyers **cumulative quantity discounts**, which are based on a total quantity bought within a specified time period, such as a year. Cumulative quantity discounts encourage a buyer to stick with a single seller instead of moving from one supplier to another.

Cumulative quantity discounts may be rebates, in which case the firm sends the buyer a rebate cheque at the end of the discount period. In other cases, the discount is a credit against future orders. In either case, the buyer must wait until the end of the discount period to receive the discount. This delay makes cumulative quantity discounts less attractive, because the buyer must pay the non-discounted price for the goods all year long and not realize the discount until the end of the period. For businesses that operate with low gross margins, this can create some financial hardships.

Non-cumulative quantity discounts are based only on the quantity purchased with each individual order. Non-cumulative discounts encourage larger single orders, but do little to tie the buyer and the seller together. When a competitor makes a better discount offer, the buyer may switch.

In most cases, non-cumulative quantity discounts mean that the buyer pays a reduced price for the goods purchased—there is a simple cash discount. In other cases the discount

---

✳ ✳ ✳
list price The price the end customer is expected to pay as determined by the manufacturer.

✳ ✳ ✳
trade or functional discounts Discounts off list price of products to members of the channel of distribution that perform various marketing functions.

✳ ✳ ✳
quantity discounts A pricing tactic of charging reduced prices for larger quantities of a product.

✳ ✳ ✳
cumulative quantity discounts Discounts based on the total quantity bought within a specified time period.

✳ ✳ ✳
non-cumulative quantity discounts Discounts based only on the quantity purchased in individual orders.

offer is made in terms of free goods. For example, a grocer who buys 10 cases of peanut butter may get one case free.

Sometimes, offering quantity discounts can create problems for the manufacturer. For example, one Canadian publisher developed a four-volume set of encyclopedias, for which it developed a pricing structure with steep quantity discounts and a list price of $175 per set. Small, independent bookstores bought the encyclopedias priced at $125 per set, whereas large chain stores purchased in larger quantities at $75 or $80 a set. When the chain stores decided to give up some of their margin to increase sales and sold the sets at $99, below what the small independents paid the publisher, the manufacturer faced some very unhappy "former" customers.

CASH DISCOUNTS

Using money costs money, as anyone who's ever taken out a mortgage or a college loan understands. When a firm borrows money, it must pay interest for every day it has the use of the money. Conversely, if a firm has excess cash, it is able to invest that cash and make money from its money. Thus, having cash is an advantage. For this reason many firms try to entice their customers to pay their bills quickly by offering *cash discounts*. For example, a firm selling to a retailer may state that the terms of the sale are "2 percent 10 days, net 30 days." This means that if the retailer pays the producer for the goods within 10 days, the amount due is cut by two percent. The total amount is due within 30 days, and after 30 days, the payment is late.

SEASONAL DISCOUNTS

Seasonal discounts are price reductions offered during certain times of the year. Products such as snow blowers, lawn mowers, and water skiing equipment are priced in this way. If such products are sold only during a few months of the year, then the manufacturer must either build a large plant that has to be shut down during the off-season or build a large warehouse to store inventory until the season comes around again. Both of these options are unattractive; so to entice retailers and wholesalers to buy off-season and store the product at their locations until the right time of the year, a firm may offer seasonal discounts.

Pricing with Electronic Commerce

Many experts suggest that technology is creating a pricing revolution that is changing pricing forever—and creating the most efficient market ever. Because sellers are directly connected to buyers around the globe through the Internet, corporate networks, and wireless set-ups, marketers can offer consumers deals tailored to a single person at a single moment.[19]

The Internet has created a wired economy, enabling buyers to compare products and prices and enabling sellers to collect data about customers' buying habits. For example, hundreds of Internet online auctions allow shoppers to bid on everything from Beanie Babies to health and fitness equipment to a Ted Harrison painting. The impact on overall commerce isn't known yet. In specialty product areas, electronic exchanges act as intermediaries connecting buyers and sellers. Web search engines using sophisticated software robots, called "bots," help consumers by searching the hundreds of sellers on the Web to locate products, thus allowing consumers to find the lowest price and forcing Internet sellers to use price as a competitive strategy. Companies have found that by using private networks that link them with their customers, they can track inventories, costs, and demands and adjust prices instantly. A more thorough discussion of electronic commerce is found in Chapter 15.

Psychological Issues in Pricing

Much of what we've said about pricing depends on economists' notions of a customer who evaluates price in a logical, rational manner. For example, the concept of demand is expressed by a smooth demand curve, which assumes that if a firm lowers a product's price from $10 to $9.50 and then from $9.50 to $9 and so on, customers will simply buy more and more. In the real world, though, it doesn't always work that way. Let's look at the psychological issues of pricing.

Buyers' Pricing Expectations

Often consumers base their perceptions of price on what they perceive to be the customary or fair price. For example, for many years a candy bar or a pack of gum was five cents. Consumers would have perceived any other price as too high or low. It was a nickel candy bar—period. When costs went up or inflation kicked in, the candy makers shrank the size of the bar instead of changing the price. Eventually, inflation prevailed and consumers' salaries rose, and the candy bar goes for 15 to 20 times one nickel today—a price that consumers would have found unacceptable even a decade ago.

When the price of a product is above or even sometimes when it's below what consumers expect, they are less willing to purchase the product. If the price is above their expectations, they will perceive it as a rip-off. If it is below expectations, consumers may think the product quality is unsatisfactory. By understanding the pricing expectations of their customers, marketers are better able to develop pricing strategies that meet those expectations.

INTERNAL REFERENCE PRICES

Sometimes consumers' perceptions of the customary price of a product depend on their **internal reference price**—based on past experience, consumers have a set price or a price range in their mind that they refer to in evaluating a product's cost. The reference price may be the last price paid, or it may be the average of all the prices they know of similar products. No matter what the brand, the normal price for a standard loaf of sandwich bread is about $1.49. In some stores, it may be $1.39 and in others $1.59, but the average is $1.49. If consumers find a loaf of bread priced much higher than this—perhaps $2.99—they will feel it is overpriced and grab a competing brand. If they find bread priced significantly lower—perhaps $0.59 or $0.69—they may shy away from the purchase, wondering "what is wrong" with the bread. Clarion Grand Pacific customers, too, have an internal reference price for what a hotel room should cost.

> ✳ ✳ ✳
> **internal reference price** A set price or a price range in consumers' minds that they refer to in evaluating a product's price.

Marketers may try to influence consumers' expectations of what a product should cost by using reference pricing strategies. For example, manufacturers may show their price compared to competitors' prices in advertising. Similarly, a retailer will display a product next to a higher-priced version of the same or a different brand. The consumer must choose between the two products with different prices. Two quite different results are likely.

On the one hand, if the prices (and other characteristics) of the two products are fairly close, it is likely that the consumer will feel the product quality is similar. This is called an *assimilation effect*. The customer might think, "The price is about the same; they must be alike. I'll be a smart shopper and select the one that saves me a few dollars." And so the customer chooses the item that is priced lower, because the low price made it look attractive next to the high-priced alternative. This is why store brands of deodorant, vitamins, pain relievers, and shampoo sit beside national brands (see Exhibit 13.5), often accompanied by a shelf sign pointing out how much shoppers can save by purchasing the store brands.

On the other hand, if the prices of the two products are far apart, a *contrast effect* may result. In this case the consumer feels that the large difference in price means that there is a large difference in quality. "Gee, this lower-priced one is probably not as good as the higher-priced one. I'll splurge on the more expensive one." Using this strategy, an appliance store may place an advertised $800 refrigerator next to a $1199 model to make the customer believe the "bottom of the line" model just won't do.

PRICE-QUALITY INFERENCES

Imagine that you are in a shoe store looking for a new pair of running shoes. You notice one pair priced at $89.99. On another table you see a second pair displayed. It looks almost identical to the first pair, but the price is only $24.95. Which pair do you want? Which pair do you think is the better quality? Many of us will pay the higher price, because we believe the bargain-basement shoes won't be worth the price—at any price.

Exhibit 13.5

**Reference pricing
strategies: Pharmacists
sometimes need to
explain why a brand-name
drug costs more than a
generic drug.**

Consumers make *price–quality inferences* about a product when they use price as a cue or an indicator for quality. If consumers are unable to judge the quality of a product through examination or prior experience—direct evidence—they will usually assume that the higher-priced product is the higher-quality product.

Does it make sense to believe that a product is better quality just because it has a higher price tag? The answer is: sometimes. In many cases, it is true that a higher-priced product is better. Many of us have bought a bargain-priced pair of sneakers, a private-label brand of cereal, or a less expensive brand of cellophane tape only to be disappointed. These experiences lead rational decision makers to associate price with quality, when quality cannot be otherwise perceived, especially when they have little prior experience in evaluating the item.

Psychological Pricing Strategies

Setting a price is part science, part art. Psychological aspects of price are important for marketers to understand in making pricing decisions.

ODD-EVEN PRICING

We usually see prices reported in dollars and cents—$1.99, $5.98, $23.67, or even $599.99. Exhibit 13.6 shows this common practice. We see prices in even dollar amounts—$2, $10, or $600—far less often. The reason? Marketers have assumed that there is a psychological response to odd prices that differs from the responses to even prices. Research on the difference in perceptions of odd versus even prices has been inconclusive and has produced no substantive evidence that the use of odd prices is superior to even prices. But that doesn't mean that marketers should change this practice.

At the same time, there are some instances in which even prices are the norm or perhaps even necessary. Theatre and concert tickets, admission to sporting events, and lottery tickets tend to be priced in even amounts, so that ticket sellers don't have to make change. Professional fees are normally expressed as even dollars. If a lawyer charged $99.99 per hour, the client might wonder why he or she has a "bargain-priced" fee and may think less of the quality of the legal advice. Many luxury items such as jewellery, golf course fees, and resort accommodations use even dollar prices to set them apart from less costly substitutes.

PRICE LINING

* * *

price lining The practice of setting a limited number of different specific prices, called price points, for items in a product line.

Marketers often apply their understanding of the psychological aspects of pricing in a practice called **price lining**. This means that similar items in a product line sell at different prices, called price points. If you want to buy a personal computer, you will find that most manufacturers have one "stripped-down" model for about $1200, with an exact price of $1199 or $1189 or even $1219. Other desk-top systems are offered at prices around $1500,

$2000, $2500, $3000, $3500, and $4500. While consumers can spend much more than $4500 on a desk-top computer system, computer manufacturers have found that most consumers are prepared to pay $2000 to $3000 for a system. Rather than competing on price, these manufacturers compete on the features offered at each price point

Why is price lining a good practice? From the marketer's standpoint, price lining is a way to maximize profits. In theory, a firm would charge each individual customer the highest price that customer was willing to pay. If the most one specific person would be willing to pay is $1499 for a personal computer, then that would be their price. If another person would be willing to pay $1999, that would be their price. But charging each consumer a different price is really not possible. Having a limited number of prices that generally fall at the top of the range customers find acceptable is a more workable alternative. Firms that use price lining assume that demand is inelastic within certain ranges, but that if prices go above that range, demand will become elastic and customers will balk. Figure 13.4 shows an assumed demand curve for a product for which price lining is a good strategy. This figure shows price points within price bands for different computers in a manufacturer's product line.

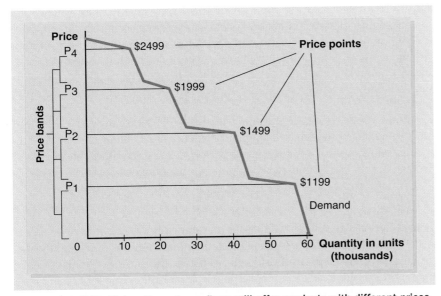

Figure 13.4 Price Lining: Sometimes firms will offer products with different prices to sell to more markets.

Legal and Ethical Considerations in Pricing

The free enterprise system is founded on the idea that the marketplace will regulate itself. Prices will rise or fall according to demand. Supplies of goods and services will be made available if there is an adequate profit incentive. Unfortunately, the business world includes the greedy and unscrupulous. The federal and provincial governments have found it necessary to enact legislation to protect consumers and to protect businesses from predatory rivals.

The Competition Bureau, a unit of Industry Canada, is responsible for ensuring that Canadian businesses (including businesses that operate in Canada) adhere to federal laws that are designed to maintain and encourage fair competition. Most of these laws are found within statutes of the *Competition Act*, but others are found in the *Consumer Packaging and Labelling Act*, the *Textile Labelling Act*, and the *Precious Metals Marking Act*. The *Competition Act* was recently amended to enable civil (as well as criminal) action to more quickly and effectively stop unfair, deceptive, or otherwise anti-competitive behaviour. In this next section, we will discuss these behaviours and some of the more important regulations to combat them. A more detailed discussion is available on the Competition Bureau Web site.

Competition Bureau
www.strategis.ic.gc.ca/SSG/
ct01250e.html

Deceptive Pricing Practices

Unscrupulous businesses may attempt to advertise or promote prices in a deceptive way. The *Competition Act* specifies that sellers cannot make a representation to the public that is false or misleading in a material respect. Thus, a retailer or other supplier must not claim that their prices are lower than a competitor's, unless it is true. Firms cannot promote a going-out-of-business sale, unless they are going out of business. Similarly, sellers cannot make false or misleading representation as to the ordinary selling price of a product. For example, a retailer cannot promote a 50%-off sale unless they have sold a substantial volume of the product at the "regular" or higher price within a reasonable period of time. An "introductory low price" cannot be promoted, unless the price goes up to its "regular" level within a reasonable period of time. What is "reasonable" and "substantial" is a matter for the civil courts to decide.

✳ ✳ ✳
bait and switch An illegal marketing practice in which an advertised price special is used as bait to get customers into the store with the intention of switching them to a higher-priced item.

Another deceptive pricing practice is the **bait and switch**, a tactic in which a retailer advertises an item at a very low price—the *bait*—to lure customers into the store, not have reasonable quantities available, and then try to get customers to buy a different, more expensive, item—the *switch*. They might tell the customer, "The advertised item is really poor quality. It doesn't have important features. There have been a lot of problems with that one. I can tell you're a really smart shopper—you know poor quality when you see it." Simply encouraging consumers to purchase a higher-priced item is an acceptable sales technique—called "trading up"—but it is a civil offence to advertise a lower-priced item when there are not reasonable quantities available. It is not considered "bait-and-switch" when a product is not available because of circumstances beyond the retailer's control or when customers are offered a "rain check," a promise to fulfill at a later date, when supplies are exhausted.

Other deceptive practices are selling a product at a price above the advertised price and double ticketing, or selling a product at the higher of two prices communicated to the consumer on, accompanying, or promoting the product. Selling at a price above the advertised price is a civil court issue, while double ticketing is a criminal offence.

Predatory Pricing

✳ ✳ ✳
predatory pricing The policy of selling products at unreasonably low prices to drive competitors out of business.

Predatory pricing is a policy of selling products at unreasonably low prices to drive a rival out of the market or substantially reduce competition, then raising prices to recoup the sacrificed returns and earn higher profits. Although predatory pricing is a criminal offence under section 50(1)(c) of the *Competition Act*, setting prices for the purpose of taking business away from competitors is normal competition. It is very difficult to prove that low prices are "unreasonable" or that an intentional "policy" is being followed, and few organizations have been charged under this section of the Act.

A low price is not necessarily a predatory price. **Loss-leader pricing**, for example, is a retailer's strategy of offering products below cost to draw consumers into their stores. Once in the store, the consumers are expected to buy other items with higher margins. Vancouver, for example, has a reputation for having the lowest CD prices in the world. Stores like A&B Sound, Sam the Record Man, and Future Shop, compete aggressively with international chains like HMV and Virgin Records. A $12.79 CD brings customers into the stores, where they tend to buy $30 to $40 worth of CDs, and may buy stereo equipment or other electronic products while they are there.[21]

Price Discrimination

The *Competition Act* also prohibits **price discrimination**. Price discrimination is a supplier practice of granting price concessions or other advantages to one purchaser, but not making them available to competing purchasers that are buying articles of like quality and quantity.[22] It applies only to the sale of goods, not leases, licences, or consignment of goods or the sale of services. It applies only to competing business purchasers, not end users or consumers, and it does not apply to concessions (such as discounts, rebates, guarantees, or shipping costs) negotiated on a particular transaction. As with the predatory pricing statute, price discrimination, a criminal offence, is difficult to prove. The Consumers Group for Fair Gas Prices, for example, took the case of Porter's Automotive Parts and Service in Foxtrap, Newfoundland, to the Competition Bureau, alleging that the major Canadian gasoline suppliers were selling gas to their own corporate-owned gas stations at a lower price than to the independents. The Competition Bureau found no evidence to support the allegation that gas suppliers had charged Porter's a higher price than another dealer in the area buying a similar volume.[23]

Price Maintenance

Price maintenance, or price fixing, occurs when two or more companies conspire to keep prices at a certain level. The Federal Court of Canada imposed a fine of $2.25 million on Chinook Group Limited of Toronto for its participation in an international conspiracy to fix prices and share markets for choline chloride, an important additive widely used in the animal feed industry.[24] A criminal offence under section 61 of the *Competition Act*, price maintenance can take two forms: horizontal and vertical.

HORIZONTAL PRICE FIXING

Horizontal price fixing occurs when competitors making the same product jointly determine what price they will charge. This kind of price fixing keeps prices high by eliminating competition. Canadian courts convicted and fined the head of a Swiss vitamin and fine chemicals company, who conducted conversations with other multinational vitamin producing companies to fix prices and allocate sales volumes for numerous bulk vitamins and related products.[25] In industries, such as the Canadian gasoline industry, in which there are few sellers, there may be no specific price-fixing agreement, but sellers will still charge the same price to "meet the competition." Such parallel pricing is not of itself considered price fixing. There must be an exchange of pricing information between sellers to indicate price-fixing actions.

VERTICAL PRICE FIXING

Sometimes manufacturers or wholesalers attempt to force retailers to charge a certain price for their product. This is called *vertical price fixing*, a criminal offence under the *Competition Act*. Retail stores are free to set whatever price they choose without interference or coercion by the manufacturer or wholesaler. Manufacturers and wholesalers can provide a "suggested retail price," but they cannot retaliate against retailers who chose not to follow the suggestion. Manufacturers or wholesalers are free to set prices when they own the retail outlet. The same is true for consignment selling, in which retailers do not actually ever own the product

The *Competition Act* prohibits a company from predatory pricing—selling below cost to drive a competitor out of business. The Competition Bureau has expressed concerns that Air Canada's purchase of Canadian Airlines and subsequent 80% share of the air travel market will result in anti-competition pricing. As WestJet moves to introduce flights in Central and Eastern Canada, there is potential for Air Canada to reduce fairs to a point that will drive the competition out.[20] In general, predatory pricing charges are hard to prove because reducing prices to stimulate business is the very essence of competition. Should a company have the right to charge whatever it would like for its products—even if it loses money in the short run—if this pricing decision is part of its overall business strategy?

✳ ✳ ✳
loss-leader pricing The pricing policy of setting prices below cost to attract customers into a store.

✳ ✳ ✳
price discrimination The illegal practice of offering the same product of like quality and quantity to different business customers at different prices, thus lessening competition.

✳ ✳ ✳
price maintenance The collaboration of two or more firms in setting prices, usually to keep prices high.

Real People, Real Decisions
How it worked out at Clarion Hotel Grand Pacific

Stephen Webb decided to pursue Option 2: tearing down the Quality Inn and building an addition to the Grand Pacific, with an estimated cost in excess of $20 million. He reworked existing phase two design plans left from the former owner. An architect and construction team helped him present the current owner with a proposal for the demolition of the Quality Inn and a large expansion of the Grand Pacific. The decision was approved, and construction began in the fall of 1999. Currently, the project is on target for the both the budget and completion date of May 2001. Advance group sales are going well, with the company expecting to maintain their number two ranking in market share in the city, while increasing yearly room rate averages. Local tourism continues to grow, with over a billion dollars being generated from the industry in Victoria alone. Benchmark targets for assessing the construction project's success will be based largely on revenues and profit contribution. Current estimates suggest the Grand Pacific will be seeing a payback on the construction investment within three and a half years, significantly less than the usual business expectations of five years for return on investment. This option also maximized the asset value of the property and realized the full potential of the premium location in Victoria's Inner Harbour.

but simply agree to offer it for sale and to accept a percentage of the selling price for their efforts.

BID RIGGING

***

bid rigging Collusion between suppliers responding to bid requests to lessen competition and secure higher margins.

Bid rigging is collusion between suppliers responding to a request for bids or tenders, where the suppliers reduce or eliminate competition in the bidding process and trade off opportunities to "win" the business with margins that are higher than would otherwise be attained. This might include: suppliers agreeing to submit token bids that are priced too high; suppliers abstaining from bidding or withdrawing bids; pre-selected suppliers submitting the lowest bid on a systematic or rotating basis; or suppliers not competing in designated geographic regions or for specific customers. These activities are all criminal offences.

Chapter Summary

1. Understand key pricing strategies.

The most commonly used pricing strategies are based on cost. Though easy to calculate and "safe," cost-based strategies do not consider demand, the competition, the stage in the product life cycle, plant capacity, or product image. Cost-based strategies include cost-plus pricing—markup on cost or markup on selling price—and price-floor pricing.

Pricing strategies based on demand require that marketers estimate demand at different prices to be certain they can sell what they produce. Such strategies include demand-backward pricing, which starts with a customer-pleasing price and works back to cost, and chain-markup pricing, which begins with an end-user price and works back through the channel. Variable pricing strategies establish negotiated prices based on what customers are willing to pay.

Strategies based on the competition may represent industry wisdom, but they can be tricky to apply. A price leader strategy is often used in an oligopoly, in which it is best for all to avoid competition. In parity pricing, a firm sets the same price as competitors.

Firms that focus on customer needs in developing pricing strategies may consider every day low price (EDLP) or value pricing strategies. If a new product has unique customer benefits and demand is inelastic, then a firm can charge a high skimming price to recover research, development, and promotional costs. If the firm needs to encourage more customers and discourage competitors from entering the market, then it may use a very low penetration price. Trial pricing means setting a low price for a limited time.

2. Explain pricing tactics for individual and multiple products.

To implement pricing strategies with individual products, marketers can use two-part pricing or payment pricing tactics. For multiple products, marketers can use price bundling, whereby two or more products are sold and priced as a single package. Captive pricing is often chosen when two items must be used together; one item is sold at a very low price and the other at a high, profitable price.

Geographic pricing tactics address differences in how far products must be shipped. With f.o.b. origin pricing, the seller pays only to have the product loaded for shipment. In zone pricing, a firm sets a limited number of different prices based on shipping distances. Uniform delivered pricing means that the same shipping cost is added to the product price no matter how far the product is actually shipped. In freight absorption pricing, the seller absorbs the costs of transportation.

Pricing for members of the channel can include trade or functional discounts, cumulative or non-cumulative quantity discounts to encourage larger purchases, cash discounts to encourage fast payment, and seasonal discounts to spread purchases throughout the year or to increase off-season or in-season sales.

Electronic commerce allows buyers to compare products and prices and enables sellers to adjust prices instantly when needed.

3. Describe the psychological aspects of pricing.

Consumers are not completely rational—they may express emotional or psychological responses to prices. Based on past experience, customers may use an idea of a customary or fair price as an internal reference price in evaluating products in the marketplace. Marketers sometimes use reference pricing strategies by displaying two products with different prices next to each other. A price–quality inference means that consumers use price as a cue for quality. Marketers also know that customers respond to odd prices differently than to even-dollar prices. Marketers can apply their understanding of the psychological aspects of pricing with price lining strategies, a practice of setting a limited number of different price ranges for a product line.

4. Understand some of the legal and ethical considerations in pricing.

Most marketers seek to avoid unethical or illegal pricing practices. Deceptive pricing practices include illegal bait-and-switch pricing and superficial discounting. The federal *Competition Act* prohibits predatory pricing, price discrimination, horizontal or vertical price maintenance, and bid rigging.

Chapter Review

Marketing Concepts: **Testing Your Knowledge**

1. Explain cost-plus pricing and price-floor pricing.

2. What are the advantages and disadvantages of pricing strategies based on demand? Explain demand-backward pricing and chain-markup pricing.

3. Explain how a price leadership strategy works and how it helps all of the firms in an oligopolistic industry. Explain parity pricing.

4. What is every day low pricing?

5. For new products, when is skimming pricing more appropriate and when is penetration pricing the best strategy? When would trial pricing be an effective pricing strategy?

6. Explain how marketers use two-part pricing, payment pricing, price bundling, and captive pricing tactics.

KEY TERMS

bait and switch (366)

bid rigging (368)

captive pricing (359)

chain-markup pricing (354)

cost-plus pricing (351)

cumulative quantity discounts (361)

demand-backward pricing (353)

demand-based pricing (353)

f.o.b. delivered pricing (359)

f.o.b. origin pricing (359)

freight absorption pricing (360)

internal reference price (363)

list price (361)

loss-leader pricing (367)

non-cumulative quantity discounts (361)

penetration pricing (357)

predatory pricing (366)

price bundling (359)

price discrimination (367)

price-floor pricing (352)

price leader (354)

price lining (364)

price maintenance (367)

quantity discounts (361)

skimming price (356)

trade or functional discounts (361)

trial pricing (357)

uniform delivered pricing (360)

value pricing or every day low pricing (EDLP) (355)

variable pricing (354)

zone pricing (360)

7. What are the advantages and disadvantages of f.o.b. origin pricing, f.o.b delivered pricing, zone pricing, uniform delivered pricing, and freight absorption pricing?

8. Why does it make sense for marketers to use trade or functional discounts, quantity discounts, cash discounts, and seasonal discounts in pricing to members of the channel?

9. Explain these psychological aspects of pricing: price–quality inferences; odd–even pricing; internal reference price; price lining.

10. Explain these unethical or illegal pricing practices: bait and switch; predatory pricing; price discrimination; price maintenance; bid rigging.

Marketing Concepts: Discussing Choices and Issues

1. Many very successful retailers use a loss-leader pricing strategy, in which they advertise an item at a price below their cost and sell the item at that price to get customers into their store. They feel that these customers will continue to shop with their company, and that they will make a profit in the long run. Do you consider this an unethical practice? Who benefits and who is hurt by such practices? Do you think the practice should be made illegal?

2. With a price leadership strategy, firms can avoid price competition and yet not be guilty of illegal collusion—getting together to set prices. Although it is legal, is a price leadership strategy ethical? How does a price leadership strategy hurt and how does it help the industry? What benefits does it provide and what problems does it pose for customers?

3. Every day low pricing strategies have met with limited success. What do you think are the advantages and disadvantages of EDLP? Are some products more suited to it than others? Why have customers not been more responsive to EDLP? What do you think its future will be?

4. Two-part pricing and payment pricing are pricing tactics that are designed to make price more palatable to customers and to better meet their needs. But do these policies always benefit consumers? What are the advantages and disadvantages of these pricing approaches for the average consumer? For business customers?

5. Technology is said to be creating a pricing revolution. How is electronic commerce changing pricing strategies? In what ways are such changes good for customers? In what ways are the changes good for sellers?

6. Retailers sometimes display two products that are similar but have different prices next to each other, hoping for an assimilation effect or for a contrast effect. Give some examples of products you have noticed displayed in this manner. What factors do you think make it more likely that one effect versus the other will occur? Do such practices help or hurt the consumer?

Marketing Practice: Applying What You've Learned

1. Assume that you have been hired as the assistant manager of a local store that sells fresh fruits and vegetables and some homemade baked goods. As you look over the store, you notice two things about the prices of the products. All of the products are priced using even numbers: $1 a pound for green beans, $2 each for cantaloupes, $3 for a loaf of cheese bread. You also notice that sometimes two different offerings of the same item are priced very close to each other. Small tomatoes are $1.25 a pound, and large tomatoes are $1.40 a pound. Large apples are $4 a bag, and small apples are $3.50 a bag. You feel that by understanding the psychological aspects of pricing you can develop pricing policies that will increase store sales. Outline your recommendations for price changes, and explain why each suggestion is important.

2. As the vice-president for marketing in a firm that markets computer software, you must regularly develop pricing strategies for new software products. Your latest product is a software package that automatically translates any foreign language e-mail messages into the user's preferred language. You are trying to decide on the pricing for this new product. Should you use a skimming price, a penetration price, or something in between? With a classmate taking the role of another marketing professional with your firm, argue in front of your class the pros and cons for each alternative.

3. Assume that you are working in the marketing department of a firm that manufactures furnaces and air conditioners. Previously, your firm has limited its operations to manufacturing units for other OEM companies. Now your firm is expanding. You will be manufacturing your product for sale with your own brand name and will be selling to heating and air-conditioning distributors across the country. Part of the plans for the new venture include how to cover the costs of shipping units to the customers from your plant in Mississauga, Ontario. You consider f.o.b. factory pricing, zone pricing, uniform delivered pricing, and

freight absorption pricing. Write a report presenting the advantages and disadvantages of each of these alternatives. What is your recommendation?

Marketing Mini-Project: **Learning by Doing**

The purpose of this mini-project is to help you become familiar with how consumers respond to different prices by conducting a series of pricing experiments.

For this project, select a product category that students such as yourself normally purchase. It should be a moderately expensive purchase, such as athletic shoes, a bookcase, or a piece of luggage. Then obtain two photographs of items in this product category or, better, two actual items. The two items should not appear to be substantially different in quality or in price.

Note that you will need to recruit separate research participants for each of the activities listed in the next section.

Experiment 1—reference pricing

a. Place the two products together. Place a sign on one with a low price. Place a sign on the other with a higher price (perhaps 50% higher). Ask your research participants to evaluate the quality of each of the items and tell you which one they would probably purchase.

b. Reverse the signs and ask other research participants to evaluate the quality of each of the items and tell you which one they would probably purchase.

c. Place the two products together again. This time place a sign on one with a moderate price. Place a sign on the other that is only a little higher (less than 10% higher). Again, ask research participants to evaluate the quality of each of the items and tell you which one they would probably purchase.

d. Reverse the signs and ask other research participants to evaluate the quality of each of the items and tell you which one they would probably purchase.

Experiment 2—odd-even pricing

For this experiment you will only need one of the items from experiment 1.

a. Place a sign on the item with the price ending in $.99 (for example, $59.99). Ask research participants to tell you if they think the price for the item is very low, slightly low, moderate, slightly high, or very high. Also ask them to evaluate the quality of the item and tell you how likely they would be to purchase the item.

b. This time place a sign on the item with the price ending in $.00 (for example, $59.00). Ask different research participants to tell you if they think the price for the item is very low, slightly low, moderate, slightly high, or very high. Also ask them to evaluate the quality of the item and tell you how likely they would be to purchase the item.

Develop a presentation for your class in which you discuss the results of your experiments and what they tell you about how consumers view prices.

Real People, Real Surfers: **Exploring the Web**

Choice Hotels International is the second largest hotel franchise company in the world, with nearly 5000 hotels, inns, all-suite hotels, and resorts in 37 countries. Clarion is just one of their many brands. Explore the Choice Hotels Web site at www.choicehotels.com and answer the following questions:

1. Make a list of the different hotels that Choice Hotels International operates. Based on what you see on the Internet, how does Choice Hotels International position each of these brands?

2. What market segments do you think Choice Hotels International is targeting with each of the hotel brands?

3. Describe how Choice Hotels International uses a price lining strategy with its hotels.

4. List and describe the different businesses (other than hotels) in which Choice Hotels International is involved.

5. Based on everything you have learned about the company, do you think Choice Hotels International describes itself as being in the "hotel business" or in some other way?

6. What is your evaluation of Choice Hotels International's Web site? Is it useful to consumers? To business customers? What recommendations for improvement would you make to Choice Hotels International?

WestJet Airlines

While the last decade brought sweeping changes to the Canadian airline industry with deregulation, increased access to international carriers, and the merger of Air Canada and Canadian, the last year has been particularly volatile. Bill Lamberton, vice-president of marketing and sales for WestJet Airlines, needs to decide whether to change key elements of WestJet's marketing strategy, including pricing, in light of: WestJet's expansion into central and eastern Canada; potential changes to Canada's competition act; the demise and then potential partial resurrection of Canada 3000; the entry of Air Canada's Tango Airlines into the discount airline market; and fallout of over-capacity and reduced demand following the September 11, 2001 terrorist attacks on the United States. In these uncertain times WestJet will need to be even more creative and careful with their strategy.

WestJet began in 1994 with the recognition that travellers, both for business and pleasure, were searching for a low-cost alternative for their short-haul flights. The company began with just three Boeing 737 aircraft, providing service to Vancouver, Kelowna, Calgary, Edmonton, and Winnipeg. Rather than challenging the competition, WestJet chose to adopt a "market stimulator" strategy—combining low fares with excellent personal service to attract customers who usually would choose alternatives to air travel—train, bus, or car.

Other carriers set different prices for tickets depending on the day of the week, the time of day, consumer demand (load), or whether a passenger stays over a Saturday night. But WestJet offers all of their fares as one-way tickets, with an everyday low price. This strategy allows passengers to travel when they want, without having to jump any of the "fences" other airlines put in place to get discount rates. WestJet has been able to keep costs down by being an industry leader in electronic ticketing and eliminating the expense and administration of issuing paper tickets; offering "short-haul" flights where meals and movies are not necessary for passenger comfort; standardizing on a limited number of airplane models to reduce maintenance and parts inventory costs; and flying in and out of airports that are less busy and thus don't charge as much for access. Low fares are only part of the strategy. As Lamberton points out, "WestJet understands that low fares may work for the first-time client, but customers also expect excellent service or they will not choose us again." The company encourages a professional yet fun attitude from their staff, which is appreciated by clients who might assume "no frills" means "no service."

The "market stimulator" strategy seems to be working. WestJet has recorded 20 consecutive quarters of profitability. In 2000 they were the second most profitable airline in North America (just after SouthWest Airlines) and in the fourth quarter of 2001 when the rest of the North American airline industry was reeling, WestJet recorded earnings of $9.4 million up 14% from 2000. WestJet now serves more than 20 Canadian cities including Ontario cities of Hamilton, London, Sudbury, Sault Ste. Marie, Thunder Bay, and Ottawa and well as Moncton, New Brunswick. While other airlines are cutting capacity, WestJet bought 4 new Boeing 737-700 aircraft in 2001 and another in the first quarter of 2002. These new planes provide increased reliability and 30% greater fuel efficiency, allowing longer flights.

With the demise of Canada 3000, Canada's second largest airline, in the fall of 2001, Bill Lamberton and the other WestJet executives are giving serious thought to taking over some of Canada 3000's slots at Toronto's Pearson International Airport. They are also considering adding Montreal and developing an eastern Canada hub out of Halifax that would also service St. John's, Newfoundland to become "Canada's low-fare, short-haul carrier." CanJet, a no-frills airline operating out of Halifax, had been bought by Canada 3000, before Canada 3000 went bankrupt, leaving room for Eastern expansion. With hubs in Calgary, Hamilton, and Halifax, and operations in Vancouver, Toronto, and Montreal, WestJet could become a national carrier and compete directly with Air Canada on long-haul flights across the country. This would require larger planes for direct flights between the west coast and central or eastern Canada, and

MARKETING IN ACTION

would put them in direct competition with Air Canada. Flying in and out of Toronto or Montreal would involve slower turnaround time for aircraft and access surcharges that would increase ticket prices.

It is not clear whether the "market stimulator" strategy, successful for short-haul flights, would be successful for longer-haul flights. Will consumers be willing to forgo some of the services like meals and movies to save money on the airfare? Will they be willing to travel to airports with less opportunity for connecting flights on other carriers?

Air Canada may also perceive expansion as a threat and attempt to change their marketing and pricing strategies to compete even more directly with WestJet. In 2001 Air Canada introduced "Tango," a no-frills short haul carrier focused mainly on central Canada. They have recently announced plans to expanded this service to 21 cities from coast to coast. With the demise of Canada 3000, Air Canada now has 80% market share in the Canadian airline industry and plans to increase this market share are being scrutinized by the federal government.

The Competition Bureau is currently investigating Air Canada for predatory pricing as a result of Air Canada dropping prices from more than $600 to less than $100 on the entry of CanJet and WestJet into eastern Canada routes. The Competition Bureau is arguing that Air Canada priced their product below their cost structure. Air Canada is arguing that they are simply matching prices. As there are currently no sanctions that the Competition Bureau can apply other than "cease and desist," they are planning to toughen the Competition Act to protect fair competition in the airline industry, act more quickly, and impose heavy fines of up to $15 million for violators. The federal government is also planning to impose a flat $12 flight tax to help offset increased costs of airport security. This tax would increase the price of most short-haul flights by 15% to 20% and would result in total taxes of more than 50% on short-haul tickets.

New competitors may also be in the offing—utilizing the assets and routes of Canada 3000 and maybe even the Canada 3000 brand name. These considerations were on the mind of Bill Lamberton as he decided whether intended expansion still makes sense and how such an expansion might best be accomplished.

THINGS TO THINK ABOUT

1. What expansion strategy would you recommend for WestJet?
2. Would you expect WestJet to encounter different consumer attitudes and behaviours in Central and/or Eastern Canada? Why or why not?
3. How integrated are price and other marketing mix considerations in WestJet's strategy?
4. Should WestJet consider going into the long-haul business? Would the same strategy work?
5. What implementation issues do you think might arise as WestJet expands their operations?

What Does That Have to Do with the Price of Bugs in China?

Computer Friendly Stuff learns to incorporate pricing decisions into the other elements of the marketing mix.

Why We Don't Let Chris Set Pricing...

Bill Martens speaking now. There was no way that I was about to let my partner, Chris Cole, write this case on pricing. Chris is a great guy, but when it comes to driving a hard bargain, he's more Mother Teresa than Bill Gates. I think he gets it from his mom. Last time she bought a car, she gave the salesman $200 over sticker price because "he was really nice."

Pricing questions arise almost daily at Computer Friendly Stuff. Chris now trusts me to make these decisions: This is good, because I enjoy the basic things in life, like eating. There are three general philosophies that apply to almost every pricing situation: "tight profits," "reasonable profits," and "very good profits." In the beginning, Chris favoured tight profits. I think he just liked the sound of it. He would walk around the office saying "Profits are tight!" and clench his fist.

But Chris also reasoned that since we were a fledgling company, we should use price as a way of attracting customers—small profits on some sales are better than large profits on non-existent sales. I favoured "reasonable profits," even though it didn't sound as dramatic. I didn't want to price too low and maybe find ourselves out of business. Also, we might be sending out a negative message about the quality of our product. Reasonable profits also give us some room to grow. The third philosophy, "very good profits," which neither of us favoured, dictates that we would price as high as we could in an attempt to earn as much as possible before sales drop or imitators hit the market. We eventually settled on a price objective somewhere between "tight" and "reasonable."

The next step was to accurately establish our cost of production. Normally, this is a fairly easy exercise. In our case, however, it was complicated, because we had to prorate the costs of our Computer Bug moulds over time. We also had to figure in costs for replacement moulds.

Once we had all of our costs of production straight, we used a rule of thumb to decide upon a profit margin for our "tight and reasonable" strategy. This left us with a suggested retail price of $17.99 in Canada. We then looked at the marketplace to compare prices. We looked at store shelves and saw that there were no comparable competing products, computer toys with screen savers, which was good news. We also noticed that most screen saver products were selling at about $20: These higher prices seemed reasonable because many of them featured well-known characters. We then tested our pricing strategy over the first year at various trade and Christmas shows. We found that a few dollars either way didn't seem to make a difference in demand. This strengthened my argument for starting at a higher price.

Drawbacks to Using a Rule of Thumb Pricing Strategy

During that period when we were selling directly to customers and to small retailers, our pricing strategy worked fine. However, as we grew and began to require the assistance of salespeople and distributors, we ran into a problem. The salespeople and distributors were crucial to get us into large retail chains. Unfortunately, our initial pricing strategy hadn't included enough of a margin to cover their costs. They required as much as 10% off the top of wholesale: That cut deeply into our profit.

Another problem with our rule of thumb pricing strategy was that it probably prevented us from adequately considering the other elements of the marketing mix, namely promotion. (Remember our misguided marketing plan from Part I: "Start at the top"?) When we were ready to open negotiations with large retail chains, we had no room to allow for such costs as cooperative advertising, where you split the cost of catalogue and Sunday newspaper advertising, special promotions, and special in-store placements with the

retail chain. This gets back to the lesson that we learned in Case 1: Products do not sell themselves. It is not enough to get into large retail chains. You have to promote the product.

A Solution to Our Problem

It was time to break the news to Chris. We assured him that he could still pound his fist and say "profits are tight," which seemed to please him, but the "tight and reasonable" strategy wasn't working. It was time to raise our wholesale price, which we could control, unlike our retail price, which was determined by the retail chains. As a result, the Canadian suggested retail price rose to $19.99.

Fortunately, the development of our second product, Monitor Morphs, benefited from this experience. From the beginning, we allowed enough money to account for all of our costs. Morphs cost slightly more to manufacture, so the prices are slightly higher than the Computer Bug ($24.99 suggested retail).

Everything Is Negotiable

After we spent so much effort in pricing these two products, you would think that our pricing work was done. Far from it. While we don't negotiate price with individual customers or small retail stores, we constantly negotiate special pricing with large retailers. There are many reasons for this. The main reason is that they make us do it. Large retailers wield a great deal of pricing leverage because they offer the most opportunity for high-volume sales. Deals at this level are also fairly complex and often include allocating money for promotional expenses. Another reason we negotiate price is that we often deal with international distributors and their fluctuating currency rates. In fact, sometimes the rates go too low. For example, our New Zealand distributors—our first big account—were hit hard by the Asian financial crisis of 1998. The exchange rate in New Zealand dropped so much that they couldn't make a profit as a middleman for imported toys. They went out of business, but were nice

enough to pass on their retail contacts to us, which led us to sell directly to the chains.

Summing it up, the best advice that we can give with regard to pricing is: It is an element that evolves constantly, and thus should be evaluated on a regular basis. Now that you see how we developed and priced our product, see the next case, in which we enter cyberspace.

Questions

1. In grid format, list the advantages and disadvantages of all three pricing strategies: tight profit margin, reasonable profit margin, and very good profitable margin. Which pricing strategy do you think is the best?

2. For the most part, CFS looked at a static pricing strategy. How easy will it be to change prices? Does CFS have to change its objectives to change prices? What future events could cause CFS to change its pricing strategy?

3. Compare CFS products with other consumer products, such as cars and fast food. How important is promotion for these products? How important is advertising? How important is a sales staff? Make a grid with your answers.

4. A South American distributor contacted CFS and wanted to buy Computer Bugs that were translated into Portuguese (the CD-ROM contents, the packaging, and the pamphlet). Given that they will have to spend time and money creating this version, how should CFS settle on a price for 5000 units? Go through the reasoning process.

Marketing Plan Questions

Refer to the Sample Marketing Plan in Appendix A as you answer these questions about developing and modifying a marketing plan for CFS.

1. For this year's marketing plan, explain how CFS is using price lining to develop a specific price point for each of the items in its product line.

2. Looking ahead to next year's marketing plan, what type of new product pricing is appropriate for CFS's forthcoming Chubby Stubbies product? Why?

CBC ☀ VIDEO CASE 1

Discount Travel

Excess capacity in the airline, resort, cruise, and other travel industries in the past decade has motivated operators to adopt a tiered pricing strategy, providing discounts for both early and last-minute bookings. This strategy was in response to the perishability of services—the logic being that any contribution margin is better than none at all; once a plane flies, a ship sails, or a night passes, seat or room revenue is lost forever. One consequence of this strategy is that consumers have learned to expect last-minute deals. Most travellers used to call up a travel agency and purchase a flight or a travel package several weeks or even months in advance. Now, many consumers are waiting for the last-minute sale or are demanding steep discounts to save hundreds of dollars.

Travel discounters, such as Sun Holidays, are servicing the needs and demands of the last-minute travellers—those who can act impulsively, are flexible in the timing of a trip, or are flexible in the destination, wanting simply to go, for example, "somewhere warm." And lots of consumers are able or willing to do this to save money. Sun Holidays, with seven offices across Canada, booked over $40 million of discount travel sales last year.

Discounters make money by negotiating commissions (typically up to 20%) with the operators and cutting their margins: By cutting the cost of product, they attract customers. It's a bit like a game of chicken. The operators would rather lower the prices and sell the space themselves or through a non-discount agency to retain higher margins. They may not be able to sell all of their capacity, however, and at some point—typically just before the Wednesday advertising copy deadline for the Saturday newspaper travel section—they offer the space and margins to the discounters, after hard negotiations where they hold their "cards" (key information relating to variable costs and capacity) close to maintain a strong bargaining position. The discounters with the largest customer base and best track record can negotiate the most space and best commissions and, thus, offer the lowest prices. That is what Binod Singh, founder of Sun Holidays, excels at—putting the squeeze on the operators. He doesn't care if the operators like him; he only cares that they need him because he offers the best deals and so delivers the most customers. His challenge is to keep pressure on the operators while not alienating them entirely.

It's a tough business. Agents use the margins negotiated with the operators in conjunction with further operator-based price discounts to attract last-minute customers. However, information technology, including discount travel faxes, e-mail, and Internet shopping "bots" (electronic price-comparing tools), enables customers to put the squeeze on the discounters to get the best travel deal possible. In the end, it's a profit game of who chickens first—the customer, discounter, or operator—before the sales or travel opportunity is lost forever.

It is not clear whether the discount strategy is good or bad for the industry. It puts continuous pressure on prices, but the operators have more yield management options and are able to generate some revenue from capacity that might not have generated revenue at all. The challenge is to protect the high-margin sales to those willing to pay more for certainty in their travel arrangements while accommodating the increasing demands of last-minute travellers.

Questions

1. How does Sun Holidays take advantage of the discount travel market?
2. How do suppliers interact with Sun Holidays to ensure that they maximize revenue?
3. How has technology changed the travel industry? How could technology benefit or hurt consumers and airlines in the future?
4. Given that the North American population is aging, will older travellers accept this new way of booking vacations? What about organized tours?
5. What effect might the airline mergers have on discount travel?

Source: This case was prepared by Hillary Samson and Brock Smith and is based on "Discount Travel," *Venture* #685 (14 April 1998).

CBC ⬤ VIDEO CASE 2

The Big Squeeze

Many small food manufacturers think that getting listed with one of the country's large grocery retailers is a ticket to prosperity. Think again. Canadian retail giants are putting "the squeeze" on food manufacturers across the country—using their size and bargaining position to reduce suppliers' profit margins. Competition to get listed with the retailers is intense and recent industry consolidation has left food manufacturers few channel choices to reach consumers. With the Loblaws purchase of Provigo in Quebec and Sobey's purchase of the Oshawa Group (IGA), two companies now control 58% of Canadian grocery retail. Further consolidation is expected in Western Canada.

Joelle Verdon of CIBC World Capital thinks that "the people who are most at risk are the small suppliers." Small suppliers, who don't have many other alternatives to reach consumers, don't have much choice but to acquiesce to the demands and whims of the retailers—and few are willing to air their complaints publicly, for fear of retaliation in the form of lost contracts or shelf space. Some of these suppliers view the retailers as bullies—flexing their muscles by forcing price cuts, accepting only parts of large orders, and otherwise breaking contracts.

Even large manufacturers like Kraft and Heinz are feeling the squeeze. Brands with third and fourth leading market share are being taken off the retail shelves and replaced with private label products, which are more profitable for the retailers. Private-label work, however, is considerably less profitable for manufacturers who lose their only real bargaining power—a brand name sought by consumers. This is a particular concern in Quebec where Loblaws is expected to introduce its President's Choice private label brand in Provigo stores, displacing brands from Quebec and other Canadian manufacturers.

The grocery chains argue that the squeeze is simply good business and a necessary measure to protect the industry against future competition from US retail giants such as Wal-Mart. Wal-Mart alone is twice the size of the entire Canadian grocery industry and commands considerable bargaining power with global manufacturers. Canadian retailers argue that they need efficient, low-cost suppliers to stay competitive.

While consolidation is also expected among food suppliers to increase their bargaining position, small suppliers are going to continue to be squeezed. They will need to find a new source of bargaining power or new channels to reach consumers.

Questions

1. What sources of bargaining power are available to small suppliers?
2. Do you agree with the retailers' perspective that they have to squeeze the suppliers in order to ward off potential US competition?
3. What would you expect the impact of this industry consolidation to be on Canadian consumers?

Source: This case was prepared by Brock Smith and is based on "Shelf Wars," *Venture* #742 (March 7, 2000).

Truly HARTMANN

Our approach and our every effort is dedicated to fostering human health and wellbeing. With our reliable products and services focusing on the areas of disease prevention, diagnostics, healing, patient care and hygiene, we help enhance the quality of life of those who trust in us.

The 9,600-plus HARTMANN employees in 27 different countries ensure that this promise is fullfilled.

PAUL HARTMANN AG
Paul-Hartmann-Straße 12
89522 Heidenheim
P.O. Box 1420
89504 Heidenheim
Germany
Phone   +49-73 21 / 3 60
Fax   +49-73 21 / 36 36 36
www.hartmann-online.com

14

Channel Management, Wholesaling, and Physical Distribution: Delivering the Product

When
you
have
completed
your
study
of this
chapter,
you
should
be able
to

CHAPTER OBJECTIVES

1. Explain what a distribution channel is and what functions distribution channels perform.

2. Describe some of the types of wholesaling intermediaries found in distribution channels.

3. Discuss the steps in planning distribution channel strategies.

4. Describe the important activities in the physical distribution of goods.

5. Discuss the distribution implications of the Internet.

Real People, Real Decisions ✓ ✗
Meet Ryan Hobenshield
A Decision Maker at HARTMANN Group

Ryan Hobenshield is an area sales manager for the HARTMANN Group, a leading European manufacturer of health care and hygiene products. With more than 8000 employees, and sales of more than a billion US dollars in 28 countries, the HARTMANN Group focuses on three product lines: 1) medical products such as bandages and tapes, adhesive plasters, and operating theatre products for hospitals, diagnostics devices such as thermometers and blood pressure monitors, wound care products such as dressings and bandages, for hospitals, doctors' offices, and clinics; 2) hygiene and health care products such as medical skin care products, incontinence products, and personal hygiene products for nursing homes, hospitals and home care; and 3) consumer products including cotton wool, diapers, feminine hygiene products, first aid kits, and bandages for household users. While approximately two thirds of HARTMANN sales come from the surgical and hygiene

lines, significant focus is being put on the newer consumer products.

Ryan Hobenshield first joined the HARTMANN Group in 1998 as a cooperative education work term student. After graduating with a B.Com in Entrepreneurship from the University of Victoria in 1999, he returned to HARTMANN as an assistant to the director of sales outside of Europe. After half a year of special projects and learning German, Hobenshield became the junior area sales manager for Australia and New Zealand. Six months later he was made area sales manager for Australia and New Zealand when the current sales manager went on a three-year maternity leave. In mid 2001 HARTMANN's daughter company in South Africa also came under his supervision. In his current position, Hobenshield is responsible for managing distributor relationships, developing new distributors and distribution channels, and building sales in his territory.

Chapters Online Inc.
www.chapters.ca

Indigo Online Inc.
www.indigo.ca

Place: The Final Frontier

Distribution may be the final "frontier" for competitive success. After years of hype, many consumers no longer believe that "new and improved" products really are new and improved. Aggressive pricing strategies are usually easily matched by competitors. Advertising and other forms of promotion are so commonplace that they have lost much of their impact. Marketers know that place may be the only one of the four Ps for which there is an opportunity for sustainable competitive advantage. That's why HARTMANN puts special emphasis on their distribution strategy.

David Hainline and his colleagues at Chapters Inc. are aware of the major criteria people use to choose a bookstore. Selection, pricing, and knowledgeable staff are certainly important, but the most important factor is the same answer realtors give when asked what three factors sell a house: location, location, location.

Because the convenience of buying a book is important to customers, book retailers such as Chapters and Indigo try to make *place* a competitive advantage. By place, we mean making goods and services available where and when customers need and want them. Banks and trust companies, for example, make it easy for people to access their services by locating instant tellers where people are likely to need money: malls, grocery stores, and airport lounges. Canadian Imperial Bank of Commerce, for example, teamed up with Loblaw Companies Limited to offer "President's Choice Financial," in-store no-fee banking, with low mortgage rates and no-minimum balance savings accounts paying interest above CIBC's own products.[1] The other major banks also have kiosks in supermarkets—this makes good sense since as many as 10 000 to 30 000 shoppers pass by each week.[2]

For those who don't even have time to run out to the grocery store, the Internet is fast becoming an important place for consumers to shop for everything from tulip bulbs to mortgages to exotic vacations. Chapters Online Inc. and Amazon.com Inc., among others, make books available to consumers any time and any place. As we discussed in Chapter 7, the Internet enables even small firms with limited resources to enjoy the same competitive advantages as their largest competitors in terms of making their products available to customers around the globe.

This chapter is about the science and art of distributing goods and services to customers. First, we'll discuss distribution channels and how marketers make smart decisions in developing distribution strategies. We'll also consider physical distribution, which is the process of moving finished goods from one point to another.

The Importance of Distribution: You Can't Sell What Isn't There!

You have identified and profiled your target market(s). You have created your product and priced it. You're not done. You need to get it to your customer. In today's marketplace, marketers such as HARTMANN must work hard to get their products to consumers, who no longer have the leisure time available to "shop 'til they drop" for goods and services.

What Is a Distribution Channel?

A **channel of distribution** is a series of firms or individuals that facilitates the movement of a product from the producer to the final customer. In many cases, channels include an organized network of manufacturers, wholesalers, and retailers that develop relationships and work together to make products conveniently available to eager buyers.

Distribution channels come in different shapes and sizes. The bakery around the corner where you buy your cinnamon rolls is a member of a channel, as is the baked goods section at the local supermarket, the espresso bar at the mall that sells biscotti to go with your double mocha cappuccino, and the bakery outlet store that sells day-old rolls at a discount.

A channel of distribution consists of, at a minimum, a producer—the individual or firm that manufactures or produces a good or service—and a customer. This is a *direct channel*. For example, when you buy a kilogram of strawberries at a farm where they're grown, that's a direct channel. Firms that sell their own products through catalogues, 800 numbers, or factory outlet stores use direct channels.

But channels often are *indirect*, because they include one or more **channel intermediaries**, firms or individuals such as wholesalers, agents, brokers, and retailers, that in some way help move the product to the consumer or business user. For example, strawberry farmers may choose to sell their berries to a produce wholesaler that, in turn, sell cases of the berries to supermarkets and restaurants that, in turn, sell to consumers.

Functions of Distribution Channels

Distribution channels perform a number of different functions that make the flow of goods from the producer to the customer possible. These functions must be handled by someone, be it the producer, a channel intermediary, or even the customer. They can be shifted from one member of the channel to another, such as when customers pick up new chairs from the warehouse instead of having them delivered to their home, but they cannot be eliminated. Channels that include one or more intermediaries can often accomplish certain distribution functions more effectively and efficiently than can a single organization.

Channels provide time, place, and ownership utility for customers. They make desired products available when, where, and in the sizes and quantities that customers want them. Take, for example, flowers such as those shown in Exhibit 14.1. The flowers are harvested and electronically sorted by growers, auctioned to buyers in Amsterdam, shipped by air to importers in Mississauga, where they are inspected for insects and disease, transported to wholesalers around the country, and finally distributed to local florists who make them available to their customers. The channel members—the growers, the auction house, the importers, the wholesalers, and the local florists—all work together to create just the right bouquet for flower lovers.

A second function of distribution channels is increasing the efficiency of the flow of goods from producer to customer. How would we buy groceries without our modern system of supermarkets? We'd have to get our milk from a dairy, our bread from a bakery, our tomatoes

✳ ✳ ✳
channel of distribution The series of firms or individuals that facilitates the movement of a product from the producer to the final customer.

✳ ✳ ✳
channel intermediaries Firms or individuals such as wholesalers, agents, brokers, or retailers that help move a product from the producer to the consumer or business user.

Exhibit 14.1	
An efficient distribution system facilitates getting flowers from greenhouses to lovers—all in the same day.	

and corn from a local farmer, and our flour from a flour mill. And forget about specialty items, like Twinkies or Coca-Cola. The companies that make these items would have to handle literally millions of transactions to sell to every individual who craved a junk-food fix.

Distribution channels create efficiencies by reducing the number of transactions necessary for goods to flow from many different manufacturers to large numbers of customers. This occurs in two ways. With **bulk breaking**, wholesalers and retailers purchase large quantities (usually cases) of goods from manufacturers but sell only one or a few at a time to many different customers. Channel intermediaries also reduce the number of transactions by **creating assortments**—providing a variety of products in one location—so that customers can conveniently buy many different items from one seller at one time.

Figure 14.1 provides a simple example of how distribution channels reduce hassles in our lives. This illustration includes five manufacturers and five customers. If each producer sold

* * *
bulk breaking Dividing larger quantities of goods into smaller lots to meet the needs of buyers.

* * *
creating assortments Providing a variety of products in one location to meet the needs of buyers.

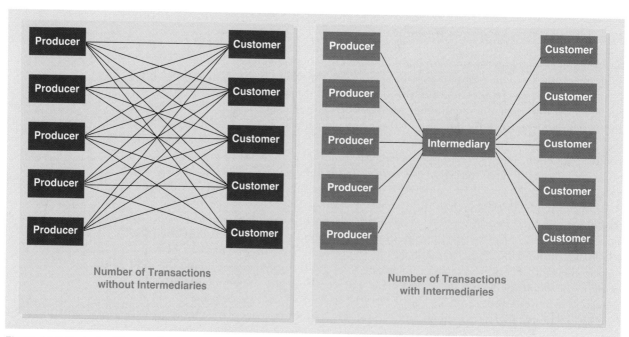

Figure 14.1 Reducing Transactions via Intermediaries

its product to each individual customer, 25 different transactions would have to occur, which is a very inefficient way to distribute products. But with a single intermediary who buys from all five manufacturers and sells to all five customers, the number of transactions is cut to 10. If there were 10 manufacturers and 10 customers, an intermediary would reduce the number of transactions from 100 to just 20. Do the math: Channels are efficient.

Channel intermediaries also perform a number of **facilitating functions**, which make the purchase process easier for customers and manufacturers. For example, intermediaries often provide important customer services, such as offering credit to buyers. Most of us like to shop at department stores because, if we are not happy with the product, we can take it back to the store, where customer service personnel are happy to give us a refund (at least in theory). These same customer services are even more important in business-to-business markets in which customers purchase larger quantities of higher-priced products than in consumer markets. Some wholesalers and retailers assist the manufacturer by providing repair and maintenance service for products they handle. An appliance, television, stereo, or computer dealer may serve as an authorized repair centre, provide maintenance contracts, and sell essential supplies to customers.

Finally, international distribution channels can make global marketing easier. Even small companies can be successful in global markets by relying on distributors that know local customs and laws.

We've discussed what a distribution channel is and some of the functions it performs. What are the different types of channel intermediaries and channel structures?

The Composition and Structure of Channels

How can you get your hands on a new Phish T-shirt? There are several ways. You could pick one up at your local music store or directly over the Internet. You might buy an "official Phish concert T-shirt" from vendors during a show. Alternatively, you might get a "deal" on a bootlegged, unauthorized version of the same shirt being sold from a suitcase by a shady guy standing *outside* the stadium. It might even be possible to buy it on the Home Shopping Network. Each of these distribution alternatives traces a different path from producer to consumer. Let's look at the different types of wholesaling intermediaries and at different channel structures. We'll focus on retailers, which are usually the last link in the chain, in the next chapter.

Types of Wholesaling Intermediaries

Wholesaling intermediaries are firms that handle the flow of products from the manufacturer to the retailer or business user. There are many different types of consumer and business-to-business wholesaling intermediaries. Some of these are independent, but manufacturers and retailers can own them, too. Table 14.1 summarizes the important characteristics of each.

INDEPENDENT INTERMEDIARIES

Independent intermediaries do business with many different manufacturers and many different customers. Because they are not owned or controlled by any manufacturer, they make it possible for many manufacturers like HARTMANN to serve customers throughout the world while keeping prices low.

Merchant wholesalers are independent intermediaries that buy goods from manufacturers and sell to retailers and other business-to-business customers. Because merchant wholesalers **take title** to the goods—they actually have legal ownership of the goods—they assume certain ownership risks and can suffer losses if products get damaged, become out-of-date or obsolete, are stolen, or just don't sell. At the same time, because they own the products, they are free to develop their own marketing strategies including setting the prices they charge their customers.

Full-service merchant wholesalers, as the name suggests, provide a wide range of services for their customers. These services may include delivery, credit, product-use assistance, repairs,

❋ ❋ ❋
facilitating functions Functions of channel intermediaries that make the purchase process easier for customers and manufacturers.

❋ ❋ ❋
wholesaling intermediaries Firms that handle the flow of products from the manufacturer to the retailer or business user.

❋ ❋ ❋
independent intermediaries Channel intermediaries that are not controlled by any manufacturer but rather do business with many different manufacturers and many different customers.

❋ ❋ ❋
merchant wholesalers Intermediaries that buy goods from manufacturers (take title to them) and sell to retailers and other business-to-business customers.

❋ ❋ ❋
take title To accept legal ownership of a product and the accompanying rights and responsibilities of ownership.

Table 14.1 Types of Intermediaries

Intermediary Type	Description	Advantages
Independent Intermediaries	Do business with many different manufacturers and many different customers	Used by most small to medium-size firms
Merchant Wholesalers	Buy (take title of) goods from producers and sell to organizational customers; either full or limited function	Allow small manufacturers to serve customers throughout the world while keeping costs low
Rack jobbers	Provide retailers with display units, check inventories, and replace merchandise for the retailers	Useful when retailers require merchandising services from manufacturers
Cash-and-carry wholesalers	Provide products for small business customers who purchase at wholesaler's location	To distribute low-cost merchandise for small retailers and other business customers
Truck jobbers	Deliver perishable food and tobacco items to retailers	For perishable items when delivery and some sales functions are required
Drop shippers	Take orders from and bill retailers for products drop-shipped from manufacturer	Facilitate transactions for bulky products
Mail-order wholesalers	Sell through catalogues, telephone, or mail order	For products sold to small organizational customers at a reasonable price
Merchandise Agents and Brokers	Provide services in exchange for commissions	Sellers do not give up legal ownership of product
Manufacturers' agents	Independent salespeople; carry several lines of noncompeting products	Supply sales function for small and new firms
Selling agents Export/import agents	Handle entire output of one or more products	Handle all marketing functions for small manufacturers
Commission merchants	Receive commission on sales price of product	Primarily in agricultural products markets
Merchandise brokers Export/import brokers	Identify likely buyers and bring buyers and sellers together	In markets where there are lots of small buyers and sellers
Manufacturer Owned	Operations limited to one manufacturer	Control
Sales branches	Like wholesalers, maintain some inventory in different geographic areas	When firms must provide service to customers in different geographic areas
Sales offices	Carry no inventory; in different geographic areas	Reduce selling costs and provide better customer service
Manufacturers' showrooms	Products attractively displayed for customers to visit	When desirable for customers to examine merchandise at a central location

Source: Adapted from J. Thomas Russell and W. Ronald Lane, *Kleppner's Advertising Procedure*, 11th ed. (Upper Saddle River, NJ: Prentice Hall, 1990); William Wells, John Burnett, and Sandra Moriarty, *Advertising: Principles and Practice*, 3d ed. (Upper Saddle River, NJ: Prentice Hall, 1995).

advertising and other promotion support, and market research. Full-service wholesalers often have their own sales force to call on businesses and organizational customers.

One type of full-service merchant wholesaler is a *rack jobber*. Rack jobbers supply retailers with such specialty items as health and beauty products, magazines, and books. Rack jobbers get their name because they own and maintain the product display racks in grocery, drug, and variety stores. These wholesalers visit their retail customers on a regular basis to maintain levels of stock and refill their racks with merchandise.

In contrast, *limited-service merchant wholesalers* provide fewer services for their customers. Like full-service wholesalers, they take title to merchandise, but they are less likely to provide such services as delivery, credit, or marketing assistance to retailers.

- *Cash-and-carry wholesalers* provide low-cost merchandise for retailers and industrial customers that are too small for other wholesalers' sales representatives to call on. Customers pay cash for products and provide their own delivery. Some popular cash-and-carry product categories include groceries, office supplies, building materials, and electrical supplies.

- *Truck jobbers* carry their products to small business customer locations for their inspection and selection. Truck jobbers often supply such perishable items as fruit, vegetables, and meats to small grocery stores. The bakery truck jobber shown in Exhibit 14.2 calls on supermarkets, checks the stock of bread on the shelf, removes any outdated items, and suggests how much bread the store needs to order.

- *Drop shippers* are limited-function wholesalers that take title to the merchandise but never actually take possession of it. Drop shippers take orders from and bill retailers

Exhibit 14.2

Bakery truck jobbers make sure supermarkets have enough bread to meet customer demands.

and industrial buyers, but the merchandise is shipped directly from the manufacturer. Because they take title to the merchandise, they assume the same risks as other merchant wholesalers. Drop shippers are important to both the producers and customers of bulky products such as coal, oil, or lumber.

- *Mail-order wholesalers* sell products to small retailers and other industrial customers, often located in remote areas, through catalogues rather than a sales force. They usually carry products in inventory and require payment in cash or by credit card before shipment. Mail-order wholesalers supply such products as cosmetics, hardware, sporting goods, and general merchandise.

Merchandise agents or brokers are another major type of independent intermediary. Agents and brokers provide services in exchange for commissions. They may or may not take possession of the product, but they never take title—they do not accept legal ownership of the product. Agents normally represent buyers or sellers on an ongoing basis, whereas brokers are employed by clients for a short period of time.

- *Manufacturers' agents*, also referred to as *manufacturers' reps*, are independent salespeople who carry several lines of noncompeting products. They have contractual arrangements with manufacturers, which outline territories, selling prices, and other specific aspects of the relationship. These agents have little, if any, supervision and are compensated with commissions based on a percentage of what they sell. Manufacturers' agents often develop strong customer relationships and provide an important sales function for small and new companies.

- *Selling agents*, including export–import agents, market a whole product line or one manufacturer's total output. They are often seen as independent marketing departments because they perform the same functions as full-service wholesalers but do not take title to products. Unlike manufacturers' agents, selling agents have unlimited territories and control the pricing, promotion, and distribution of their products. Selling agents are found in the furniture, clothing, and textiles industries.

- *Commission merchants* are sales agents who receive goods, primarily agricultural products, such as grain or livestock, on consignment—they take possession of products without taking title. Although sellers may state a minimum price they are willing to take for their products, commission merchants are free to sell the product for the highest price they can get. Commission merchants receive a commission on the sales price of the product.

- *Merchandise brokers* including export–import brokers are intermediaries that facilitate transactions in markets such as real estate, food, and used equipment in which there are many small buyers and sellers. Brokers identify likely buyers and sellers and bring the two together in return for a fee received when the transaction is completed.

✳✳✳
merchandise agents or brokers
Channel intermediaries that provide services in exchange for commissions but never take title to the product.

MANUFACTURER-OWNED INTERMEDIARIES

Sometimes manufacturers like HARTMANN set up their own channel intermediaries. In this way, they can have separate business units that perform all of the functions of independent intermediaries *and* maintain complete control over the channel.

- *Sales branches* are manufacturer-owned facilities that, like independent wholesalers, carry inventory and provide sales and service to customers in a specific geographic area. Sales branches are found in such industries as petroleum products, industrial machinery and equipment, and motor vehicles.
- *Sales offices* are manufacturer-owned facilities that, like agents, do not carry inventory but provide selling functions for the manufacturer in a specific geographic area. Because they allow members of the sales force to be located close to customers, they reduce selling costs and provide better customer service.
- *Manufacturers' showrooms* are manufacturer-owned or leased facilities in which products are permanently displayed for customers to visit. Manufacturers' showrooms are often located in or near large merchandise marts, such as the furniture market in High Point, North Carolina, where Palliser Furniture (see Chapter 12 Real People, Real Decisions) goes to showcase its products.

Types of Distribution Channels

Firms face many choices when structuring distribution channels. Should they sell directly to consumers and business users? Would they benefit by including wholesalers, retailers, or both in the channel? Would it make sense to sell directly to some customers but use retailers to sell to other customers? There is no single best channel for all products. The marketing manager must select a channel structure that creates a competitive advantage for the firm and its products based on the size and needs of the target market. Here are some factors marketers need to consider.

***
channel levels The number of distinct categories of intermediaries that populate a channel of distribution.

In developing place or distribution strategies, marketers first consider different **channel levels**, or the number of distinct categories of intermediaries that make up a channel of distribution. Many different factors have an impact on this decision. What channel members are available? How large is the market, how frequently do consumers purchase the product, and what services do they require?

Figure 14.2 summarizes the different structures a distribution channel can take. The producer and the customer are always members, so the shortest channel possible has two levels. Using a retailer adds a third level; a wholesaler adds a fourth level; and so on. Different channel structures exist for both consumer and business-to-business markets.

CONSUMER CHANNELS

The simplest channel is a direct channel. Why do some manufacturers sell directly to customers? One reason is that a direct channel may allow the manufacturer to serve its customers better and at a lower price than is possible using a retailer. By using direct channels, strawberry farmers make sure their customers have fresher strawberries than if they sell the berries through a local supermarket. Furthermore, if the farmers sell the berries through a supermarket, their price will be higher because of the supermarket's costs of doing business and required profit on the berries. In fact, sometimes the direct channel is the *only* way to sell the product, because using intermediaries may increase the price above what consumers are willing to pay.

One of the newest means of selling direct is through the Internet. Three years ago, Nick Clark and his family were trying to think of an idea for a family-owned business. The main difficulty was that the brothers, sisters, and spouses were scattered between Kelowna, Calgary, and Bowen Island, BC. The Internet provided an excellent opportunity for the whole family to work together. Tina Clark, Nick's sister-in-law, suggested that they market and distribute her father's smoked salmon, and BlackBear (www.blackbear.net) was created (see Exhibit 14.3). Although in business for only two and a half years, BlackBear has sent products from Moscow to Singapore. Their line has expanded from salmon to a wide range of products, which includes clothing and jewellery. Interestingly, retail stores found out

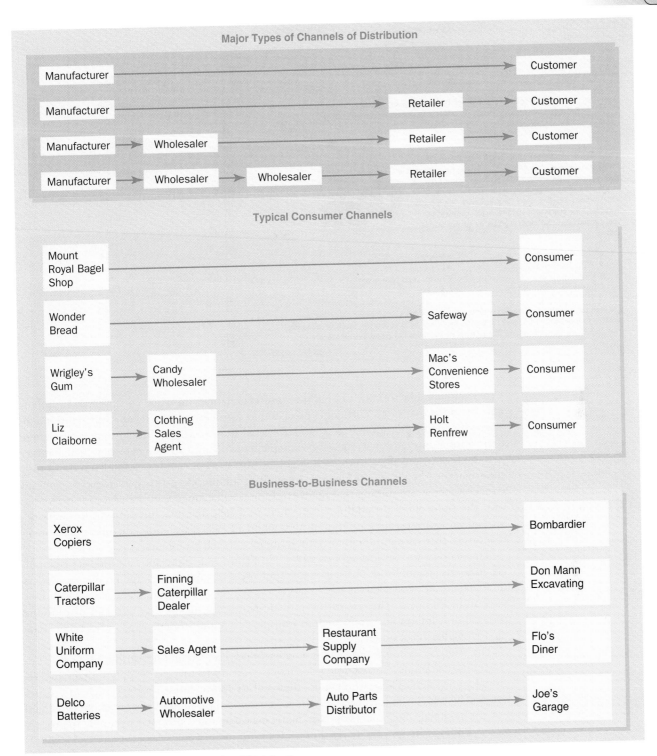

Figure 14.2 Different Types of Channels of Distribution

about BlackBear through the Internet and requested to carry the products through regular affiliated retail distribution channels.

Another reason to use a direct channel is control. When the manufacturer handles distribution, it maintains control of pricing, service, delivery—all elements of the transaction. Because distributors and dealers carry many products, it can be difficult to get their sales forces to focus on selling one product. In a direct channel, a producer works directly with customers, gaining insights into trends, customer needs and complaints, and the effectiveness of its marketing strategies.

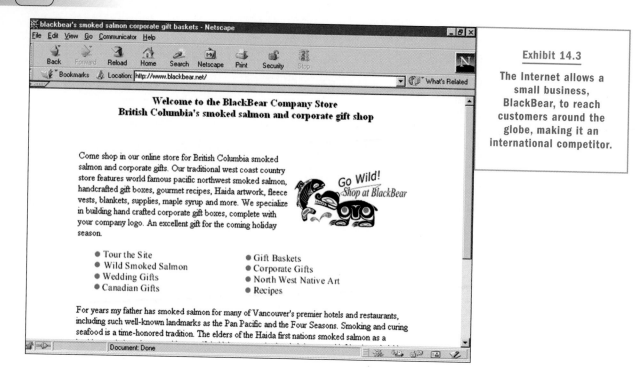

Exhibit 14.3

The Internet allows a small business, BlackBear, to reach customers around the globe, making it an international competitor.

Why do manufacturers choose to use indirect channels to reach consumers? An important reason is that often customers are familiar with certain retailers or other intermediaries—it's where they always go to look for what they need. Getting customers to change their normal buying behaviour—for example, convincing consumers to buy their laundry detergent or frozen pizza from a catalogue or over the Internet instead of from the corner supermarket—might be difficult, although e-commerce grocery businesses such as GroceryGateway are finding that many consumers will change their behaviour if presented with the right offer.[3] In addition, intermediaries help manufacturers in all the ways described earlier. By creating utility and transaction efficiencies, channel members make manufacturers' lives easier and enhance their ability to reach customers.

The *manufacturer-retailer-consumer channel* in Figure 14.2 is the shortest indirect channel. GE uses this channel when its sells small appliances through such large retailers as Zellers or Sears. Because the retailers buy in large volume, they can buy at a low price, which they pass on to shoppers. The size of these retail giants also means that they can provide the physical distribution functions, such as transportation and storage, which wholesalers handle for smaller retail outlets.

The *manufacturer-wholesaler-retailer-consumer channel* is a common distribution channel in consumer marketing. For example, a single ice-cream factory can supply four or five regional wholesalers. These wholesalers then sell to 400 or more retailers, such as grocery stores. The retailers in turn each sell the ice cream to thousands of customers. In this channel, the regional wholesalers combine many manufacturers' products to supply to grocery stores. Because the grocery stores do business with many wholesalers, this arrangement results in a broad selection of products.

BUSINESS-TO-BUSINESS CHANNELS

Business-to-business distribution channels, as the name suggests, facilitate the flow of goods from a producer such as HARTMANN to an organizational or business customer such as a hospital. Generally, business-to-business channels parallel consumer channels—they may be direct or indirect. The simplest indirect channel in industrial markets is the single intermediary—a merchant wholesaler referred to as an *industrial distributor* rather than a retailer—buying products from a manufacturer and selling them to business customers.

Direct channels are more common to business-to-business markets than to consumer markets, because business-to-business marketing often means selling high-dollar, high-profit items—a single piece of industrial equipment may cost hundreds of thousands of dollars—

Real People, Real Decisions
Decision Time at HARTMANN Group

Founded in 1818, HARTMANN began aggressive international expansion in the 1970s following a basic growth strategy: identify and partner with local merchant wholesalers, help those wholesalers grow the HARTMANN business, then buy the partner company when target sales penetration is achieved. HARTMANN is now in more than 20 countries with several wholly-owned subsidiaries as well as numerous partner wholesalers, including 5 in Australia and 1 in New Zealand. HARTMANN has been in Australia for 25 years with many different agents. The five current Australian partners have been successful in developing either the surgical or hygiene product lines, and in some cases both. These partners, however, were reluctant to develop the consumer product line, were not in a position to invest in its development, were only able to generate about $50 000 in sales each in a trial period, and were not capable of developing retailers. Hobenshield needed to find another option for developing HARTMANN consumer in Australia. He considered three alternatives:

Option 1 Go in on its own. HARTMANN could develop its own retail distribution company that would work on getting listings with key Australian retailers. HARTMANN would not have to share the expected profit, would retain direct control over sales forecasting, inventory management, and how the market was developed. They would also be able to train sales representatives in the HARTMANN model. An owned distributor would be able to develop its own in-house tools and tailor HARTMANN international marketing and communication strategy to the Australian context. The main downside would be the opportunity cost of taking two or three years to develop their own Australian company.

Option 2 Find another Australian distributor. Hobenshield could try to find a new business partner that had consumer health product expertise, established retail relationships, and the ability to take on 40% to 50% of the cost of developing the market. The partner would also need to be small enough that the opportunity would be viewed as a highly attractive expansion option and HARTMANN could in the future buy them out or without legal difficulty take over the cus-

tomers. Finding such a partner and developing a relationship of trust to the point where a partnership agreement might be struck would take six to eight months of effort and numerous trips to Australia. Then it might take six months to train the partners sales force, develop Australian communications materials, start getting listings, and stock inventory. This option would allow HARTMANN to get into the market a year or two earlier than going in on its own and an Australian partner would be able to provide expertise on local business practices and consumer behaviour.

Option 3 Expand with the existing New Zealand partner. When Hobenshield began exploring option 2, his New Zealand partner offered to develop both the New Zealand and Australian consumer markets. This partner was a strong performer with the HARTMANN medical and hygiene/health care product lines and had good relationships with hospitals and nursing homes in New Zealand and Australia. They also had a consumer goods division that was independent of their business-to-business division. This partner was known by Hobenshield to be aggressive—but Hobenshield was worried that they might be too aggressive and too independent. Recently, for example, they had not notified Hobenshield of a sales promotion relating to HARTMANN hygiene products, which had resulted in a temporary global inventory crisis. Hobenshield was worried that the consumer goods division might act like a rogue team in Australia with HARTMANN having little control over how the market was developed. HARTMANN's inventory management system was very efficient and Hobenshield didn't want an Australian partner that would make promises it could not keep and overload HARTMANN's distribution system before it was set up for volume in Australia and New Zealand. On the other hand, this partner had the resources and relationships to develop both the New Zealand and Australian markets quickly and could get started almost immediately. Quick entry into the market would help HARTMANN secure its position against other international competitors.

Now join Ryan Hobenshield and the HARTMANN decision team: Which option would you choose, and why?

---

to a market made up of only a few customers. In such markets, it pays for a company to develop its own sales force and sell directly to customers at a lower cost than if it used intermediaries.

DISTRIBUTION CHANNELS FOR SERVICES

Because services are intangible, there is no need to worry about storage, transportation, and the other functions of physical distribution. In most cases, the service travels directly from the producer to the customer. However, some services do need an intermediary, an *agent* who helps the parties complete the transaction. Examples include insurance agents, stockbrokers, and travel agents.

DUAL DISTRIBUTION SYSTEMS

Figure 14.2 shows simple distribution channels; but life is rarely that simple. Manufacturers, dealers, wholesalers, retailers, and customers alike may actually interact with more than one type of channel. These are *dual* or *multiple distribution systems.*

The pharmaceutical industry provides a good example of multiple channel usage. Pharmaceutical companies distribute their products in at least three channel types. First, they sell to hospitals, clinics, and other organizational customers directly. These customers buy in quantity, purchase a wide variety of products, and, because pills are dispensed one at a time rather than in bottles of 50, they require different product packaging than when the products are sold to other customers. Pharmaceuticals' second channel is an indirect consumer channel in which the manufacturer sells to large drug retailer chains that distribute the medicines to their stores across the country. Some of us would rather purchase our prescriptions in a more personal manner from a local independent drugstore. In this channel, the manufacturer sells to drug wholesalers that in turn supply these independents.

We have discussed what distribution channels and channel intermediaries are and the role of channel members in the distribution of goods and services. We know that not all channels are alike: Some are direct and simple, but indirect channels can be quite complex. The next section is about how marketers plan channel strategies to meet customer needs better than the competition—the all-important competitive advantage.

Planning a Channel Strategy

Do customers want products in large or small quantities? Do they insist on buying them locally, or will they purchase from a distant supplier? How long are they willing to wait to get the product? Intelligent marketers want to know. Distribution planning is best accomplished when marketers follow the steps in Figure 14.3. In this section, we'll look at how manufacturers decide on distribution objectives, examine what influences distribution decisions, and discuss how firms select distribution strategies and tactics.

Firms that operate within a channel of distribution—manufacturers, wholesalers, and retailers—may do some distribution planning. In this section, our perspective focuses on distribution planning of producers or manufacturers rather than intermediaries, because they, more often than intermediaries, take a leadership role in creating a successful distribution channel.

Channel Objectives

The first step in deciding on a distribution plan is to develop appropriate objectives that support the organization's overall marketing goals. How can distribution work with the other elements of the marketing mix to increase profits? To increase market share? To increase volume of sales?

In general, the overall objective of any distribution planning is to make a firm's product available when, where, and in the quantities customers want and need at a minimum cost. More specific distribution objectives, however, depend on characteristics of the product and the market. For example, if the product is bulky, a primary distribution objective may be to minimize shipping costs. If the product is fragile, a goal may be to develop a channel that minimizes handling. In introducing a new product to a mass market, a channel objective may be to provide maximum product exposure or to make the product available close to where customers live and work. Sometimes marketers make their product available where similar products are sold so that consumers can compare prices.

Evaluating the Environment

After setting the distribution objectives, marketers must consider their internal and external environments. The organization must examine such issues as its

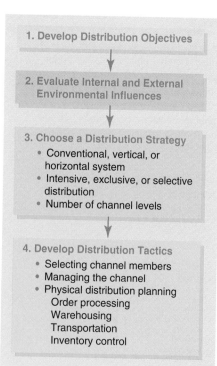

1. Develop Distribution Objectives

2. Evaluate Internal and External Environmental Influences

3. Choose a Distribution Strategy
- Conventional, vertical, or horizontal system
- Intensive, exclusive, or selective distribution
- Number of channel levels

4. Develop Distribution Tactics
- Selecting channel members
- Managing the channel
- Physical distribution planning
  Order processing
  Warehousing
  Transportation
  Inventory control

Figure 14.3 Steps in Distribution Planning

own ability to create distribution channels, what channel intermediaries are available, the ability of customers to access these intermediaries, and how the competition distributes its products. Should a firm use the same retailers as its competitors? Sometimes, to ensure customers' undivided attention, a firm sells its products in outlets that don't carry the competitors' products. In other cases, a firm uses the same intermediaries as its competitors because customers expect to find the product there. Finally, by studying competitors' distribution strategies, marketers can learn from their successes and failures. For example, if the biggest complaint of competitors' customers is delivery speed, developing a system that allows same-day delivery can make the competition pale in comparison.

Choosing a Distribution System

Planning distribution strategies means making at least three decisions. Distribution planning includes decisions about the number of levels in the distribution channel, but distribution strategies also involve decisions about channel relationships—whether a conventional system or a highly integrated system will work best. A final decision relates to the distribution intensity or the number of intermediaries at each level of the channel.

CONVENTIONAL, VERTICAL, AND HORIZONTAL MARKETING SYSTEMS

Participants in any distribution channel form an interrelated system. To develop a successful distribution strategy, marketers must consider the different types of systems and select the one that best meets their needs. In general, these systems take one of three forms: conventional, vertical, and horizontal marketing systems.

A **conventional marketing system** is a multiple-level distribution channel in which members work independently of one another. Their relationships are limited to simply buying and selling from one another. Each firm seeks to benefit with little concern for other channel members. Even though channel members work independently, most conventional channels are highly successful. For one thing, all members of the channel are working for the same goals—to build demand, reduce costs, and improve customer satisfaction. And the channel members know that it's in everyone's best interest to treat other channel members fairly.

A **vertical marketing system (VMS)** is a channel in which there is cooperation among channel members at two or more levels of the channel—the manufacturing, wholesaling, and retailing levels. Firms in a VMS work together and depend on each other, like links in a chain. Members share information and provide services to other members, recognizing that such coordination makes everyone more successful in reaching a desired target market.

There are three types of vertical marketing systems: administered, corporate, and contractual. In an administered VMS, channel members remain independent but voluntarily agree to work together. In a corporate VMS, firms have ownership control of some or all of a distribution channel such as when HARTMANN buys agent companies.

In a contractual VMS, cooperation is enforced by contracts, legal agreements that spell out each member's rights and responsibilities and how they will cooperate. In a wholesaler-sponsored VMS, wholesalers get retailers to work together under their leadership in a voluntary chain. Retail members of the chain use a common name, cooperate in advertising and other promotion, and even develop their own private-label products. Examples of wholesaler-sponsored chains are IGA (Independent Grocers' Alliance) food stores, Ace Hardware stores, and Island Farms Dairy (BC).

In other cases, retailers themselves organize a cooperative marketing channel system. A *retailer cooperative* is a group of retailers that has established a wholesaling operation to help them compete more effectively with the large chains. Each retailer owns shares in the wholesaler operation and is obligated to purchase a certain percentage of inventory from the cooperative operation. The Calgary Co-op and True Value Hardware Stores are examples of retailer cooperatives.

Franchise organizations are a third type of contractual VMS. In these organizations, channel cooperation is explicitly defined and strictly enforced through contractual arrangements in which a franchiser (a manufacturer or a service provider) allows an entrepreneur

✳✳✳
conventional marketing system
A multiple-level distribution channel in which channel members work independently of one another.

✳✳✳
vertical marketing system (VMS) A channel of distribution in which there is cooperation among members at the manufacturing, wholesaling, and retailing levels.

True Value Hardware Stores
www.truevalue.com

to use the franchise name and marketing plan for a fee. In most franchise agreements, the franchiser provides a variety of services for the franchisee, such as helping train employees, giving access to lower prices for needed materials, and helping pick a location with visibility. In return, the franchiser receives a percentage of revenue from the franchise owner. Usually the franchisees are also allowed to use the franchiser business format, but they are required to follow that format to the letter.[4] For example, a McDonald's franchisee is not allowed to change the menu or the physical decor of the restaurant. It's important that customers know that they can get the same Big Mac in Toronto that they will find in Corner Brook, Newfoundland.

Canada is the franchise capital of the world—with more than 1300 franchise operations and 64 000 outlets generating more than a million jobs and $100 billion a year in revenues.[5] Although relatively high-cost food-service franchises ($60 000 to $1 million) represent about 40% of all outlets, some of Canada's hottest franchises are in consumer and business services—Web site design, window cleaning, tutoring, maid services, and house painting—with franchise fees under $30 000. Some long-standing and some new franchise operations are listed in Table 14.2.

From the manufacturer's perspective, franchising a business is a way to develop widespread product distribution with minimal financial risk while, at the same time, maintaining control over product quality. From the entrepreneur's perspective, franchises, such as Great Canadian Bagel shown in Exhibit 14.4, are a popular way to get a start in business.

In a **horizontal marketing system,** two or more firms at the same channel level agree to work together to get their product to the customer. Air Canada and Lufthansa, for example, cooperate in providing passenger air service. To increase passenger volume for both airlines, they share a common flight code. This means that travel agents who book passengers on one of the airlines flights will be more likely to book a connecting flight on the other airline. To increase customer benefits, they also share frequent-flyer programs and airport clubs.[6]

INTENSIVE, EXCLUSIVE, AND SELECTIVE DISTRIBUTION

Distribution strategy decisions also mean determining how many wholesalers and retailers will carry the product within a given market. This may seem like an easy decision: Distribute the product through as many intermediaries as possible. However, if the product goes to too many outlets, there may be inefficiency and duplication of efforts. For example, if there are too many Honda dealerships in town, there will be many unsold Hondas sitting on dealer lots, and no single dealer will be successful. But, if there are not enough wholesalers or retailers carrying a product, total sales of the manufacturer's products (and profits) will not be maximized. If customers have to drive hundreds of miles to find a Honda dealer, they may settle for a Ford or a Chevy. Thus, a distribution objective may be to either increase or decrease the level of market penetration.

* * *

horizontal marketing system An arrangement within a channel of distribution in which two or more firms at the same channel level work together for a common purpose.

Table 14.2 Established and Emerging Franchises: A Sampler

Company Name	Description	Startup Costs
Tim Hortons	coffee shop and restaurant	$165 000
Chip King	windshield repair	$25 000
Harvey's	fast-food restaurants	$450 000
Chem-Dry Canada	carpet and upholstery cleaning	$20 000 and up
Chausseur's Panda Ltd.	children's shoes	$100 000
Mad Science Group, Inc.	after-school programs and birthday party entertainment that make science fun	$57 000
McDonald's	fast-food restaurants	$700 000
Subway	sandwich shops	$50 000
Baskin-Robbins	ice-cream shops	$150 000–180 000

Source: Adapted from Jeffrey A. Tannenbaum, "Franchisers Are Finding Some New Twists on Old Ideas," *Wall Street Journal*, 24 April 1995, B2; Veronica Byrd, "Hamburgers or Home Decorating? Businesses That Sell," *New York Times*, 4 October 1992, 10.

Exhibit 14.4

Great Canadian Bagel is a franchise bagel shop that is becoming a Canadian icon.

The three basic choices are intensive, exclusive, and selective distribution. Table 14.3 summarizes the five decision factors—company, customers, channels, constraints, and competition—and how they help marketers determine the best fit between distribution system and marketing goals.

Intensive distribution aims at maximizing market coverage by selling a product through all wholesalers or retailers that will stock and sell the product. Marketers use intensive distribution for such products as chewing gum, soft drinks, milk, and bread that are quickly consumed and must be frequently replaced. Intensive distribution is necessary for these products, because availability is more important than any other consideration in customers' purchase decisions.

In contrast to intensive distribution, **exclusive distribution** means limiting distribution to a single outlet in a particular region. Marketers sell pianos, cars, executive training programs, television programs, and many other products with high price tags through exclusive distribution arrangements. These strategies are typically used with products that are high priced and have considerable service requirements and when there are a limited number of buyers in any single geographic area. Exclusive distribution enables wholesalers and retailers to recoup the costs associated with long selling processes for each customer and, in some cases, extensive after-sale service.

Not every situation neatly fits a category in Table 14.3. For example, consider professional sports. Customers might not shop for games in the same way they shop for pianos. They might go to a game on impulse, and they don't require much individualized service. Nevertheless, professional sports employ exclusive distribution. The team's cost of serving customers is high, due to those million-dollar player salaries and multimillion-dollar stadiums.

The alert reader (especially one who is also a sports fan) may note that there are some exceptions to the exclusive distribution of sports teams: New York has two football teams and two baseball teams; Chicago fields two baseball teams. Market coverage that is less than intensive distribution, but more than exclusive distribution, is **selective distribution**. Selective distribution fits when demand is so large that exclusive distribution is inadequate, but selling costs, service requirements, or other factors make intensive distribution a poor fit. Although a White Sox baseball fan may not believe that the Cubs franchise is necessary (and vice versa), major league baseball and even some baseball fans think the Chicago market is large enough to support both teams (see Exhibit 14.5).

Selective distribution strategies are suitable for shopping products, such as household appliances, computers, and electronic equipment, for which consumers are willing to spend time visiting different retail outlets to compare product alternatives. For producers, selective distribution means freedom to choose only those wholesalers and retailers that have a

✳✳✳
intensive distribution Selling a product through all suitable wholesalers or retailers that are willing to stock and sell the product.

✳✳✳
exclusive distribution Selling a product only through a single outlet in a particular region.

✳✳✳
selective distribution
Distribution using fewer outlets than in intensive distribution but more than in exclusive distribution.

Table 14.3 Characteristics That Favour Intensive over Exclusive Distribution

Decision Factor	Intensive Distribution	Exclusive Distribution
Company	Oriented toward mass markets	Oriented toward specialized markets
Customers	High customer density	Low customer density
	Price and convenience are priorities	Service and cooperation
Channels	Overlapping market coverage	Nonoverlapping market coverage
Constraints	Cost of serving individual customers is low	Cost of serving individual customers is high
Competition	Based on a strong market presence, often through advertising and promotion	Based on individualized attention to customers, often through relationship marketing

good credit rating, provide good market coverage, serve customers well, and cooperate effectively. Wholesalers and retailers like selective distribution because it results in higher sales and profits than are possible with intensive distribution in which sellers often have to compete on price.

Developing Distribution Tactics

As with planning for the other marketing Ps, the final step in distribution planning is developing the distribution tactics necessary to implement the distribution strategy. These decisions are usually about the type of distribution system to use—a direct or indirect channel, a conventional or an integrated channel. Distribution tactics relate to the implementation of these strategies, such as selecting individual channel members and managing the channel.

SELECTING CHANNEL PARTNERS

When firms agree to work together in a channel relationship, they become partners in what is normally a long-term commitment. Like a marriage, it is important to both manufacturers and intermediaries to select channel partners wisely or they'll regret the match later. In evaluating intermediaries, manufacturers try to answer such questions as: Will the channel member contribute substantially to our profitability? Does the channel member have the ability to provide the services customers want? What impact will a potential intermediary

Exhibit 14.5

Selective distribution: Chicago baseball fans have a choice between the White Sox and the Cubs.

have on channel control? For example, what small to mid-size firm wouldn't jump at the chance to have its products distributed by retail giant Canadian Tire? With Canadian Tire as a channel partner, a small firm could double, triple, or quadruple its business. Actually, more than one firm, recognizing that size means power in the channel, have decided against Canadian Tire, because they are not willing to relinquish control of their marketing decision making.

Another important consideration in selecting channel members is competitors' channel partners. For example, because people spend time comparing different brands when purchasing a shopping product, firms need to make sure their products are displayed near similar competitors' products. If most competitors distribute their electric drills through mass merchandisers, a manufacturer has to make sure its brand is there as well.

A firm's dedication to social responsibility may also be an important determining factor in the selection of channel partners. Many firms have developed extensive programs to recruit minority-owned channel members.

MANAGING THE CHANNEL OF DISTRIBUTION

Once a manufacturer develops a channel strategy and aligns channel members, the day-to-day job of managing the channel begins. That's what Ryan Hobenshield does for HART-MANN. The **channel leader** is the dominant firm that controls the channel. A firm becomes the channel leader because it has power relative to other channel members. This power comes from different sources:

- A firm has *economic power* when it has the ability to control resources.
- A firm such as a franchiser has *legitimate power* if it has legal authority to call the shots.
- A firm has *reward* or *coercive power* if it engages in exclusive distribution and has the ability to give profitable products and to take them away from the channel intermediaries.

Although producers have traditionally held the role of channel leader, a firm at any level of distribution can emerge as a channel leader. When retailers were much smaller than they are now, manufacturers tended to assume leadership in consumer goods markets. Procter & Gamble, for instance, developed customer-oriented marketing programs, tracked market trends, and advised retailers on the mix of products most likely to build sales. As large retail chains evolved, such giant retailers as Canadian Tire and Home Depot began to assume a leadership role because of the sheer size of their operations.

Because manufacturers, wholesalers, and retailers depend on one another for success, channel cooperation helps everyone. Channel leaders like HARTMANN take actions that help make their partners more successful. High intermediary profit margins, training programs, cooperative advertising, and expert marketing advice are invisible to end customers but are important motivating factors in the eyes of wholesalers and retailers.[7] Victoria's Rogers' Chocolates, for example, has found ways to help its retail channel partners become more successful. By improving the speed and accuracy of reorders, retailers are able to maintain inventory levels necessary to satisfy customers while avoiding ordering errors.

Relations among members in a channel are not always wonderful. Because each firm has its own unique set of objectives, channel conflict may threaten a manufacturer's distribution strategy. Such conflict most often occurs between firms at different levels of the same distribution channel. Incompatible goals, poor communication, and disagreement over roles, responsibilities, and functions cause conflict. For example, a manufacturer is likely to feel the firm would enjoy greater success and profitability if intermediaries carry only its brands, but the intermediaries believe they will do better if they carry a number of brands.

Distribution Channels and the Marketing Mix

How are decisions about place interrelated with the other three Ps? For one thing, place decisions affect pricing. Marketers that distribute products through mass merchandisers such as Zellers and Canadian Tire will have different pricing objectives and strategies than those that sell to specialty stores.

Canadian Tire
www.canadiantire.com

✳ ✳ ✳
channel leader A firm at one level of distribution that takes a leadership role, establishing operating norms and processes that reduce channel conflicts, reduce costs, and enhance delivered customer value.

Rogers' Chocolates
www.rogerschocolates.com

SPOTLIGHT ON REAL PEOPLE *McAfee Associates*

Most software companies distribute their products in stores. William Larson, the 40-year-old CEO of McAfee Associates, does things differently. McAfee licenses its network security and management software programs that detect viruses and facilitate backup storage for two-year periods. Unlike other companies that sell major upgrades every 18 months or so, McAfee sends out mini-upgrades to licensees over the Internet—for free. Because distribution over the Internet is so inexpensive,

McAfee boasts a 95% gross margin, the highest in the software business. This form of distribution also builds loyalty—renewal rates among licensees run at 85%. Now McAfee has developed other management software products that it also sells over the Internet at prices as much as 50% lower than competitors. This distribution strategy ensures that this maker of anti-virus programs will stay healthy for some time to come.[8]

1. What distribution channel does McAfee use?
2. What other channels are available to the firm?
3. How does McAfee's distribution strategy differ from that of other software manufacturers?

good OR bad DECISION?

When a firm engages in illegal distribution practices, the marketer loses in a number of ways. The effort spent in building a distribution system is lost, competition gains ground, and courts may impose high fines on a guilty firm. To avoid costly setbacks, marketers must understand the basic legal constraints of channel arrangements. Here are some of the most common offenders:

- Exclusive dealing contracts: a written agreement allowing the retailer to carry a firm's products only if it does not carry other brands.

- Exclusive territories: an agreement stating that only one wholesaler or retailer will be allowed to sell the manufacturer's products in that geographic area.

- Tying contracts: an agreement in which a producer requires that a wholesaler or retailer purchase one or more of its other products along with the desired product.

Why do you think these practices spell bad business, and for whom?

✳ ✳ ✳

physical distribution The activities used to move finished goods from manufacturers to final customers, including order processing, warehousing, materials handling, transportation, and inventory control.

Distribution decisions can sometimes give a product a distinct position in its market. For example, Peter van Stolk, the creator of Jones Cola, realized that he couldn't compete with the US $200 million Coke and Pepsi spent on advertising, so he chose to try to increase sales through unusual distribution channels. Rather than remain unnoticed on supermarket shelves and convenience stores, van Stolk chose to distribute his product in tattoo and body-piercing parlours, hair salons, sex shops, and fashion stores—anywhere that Coke and Pepsi won't go or won't be taken. As well, the company recently signed an agreement to stock its soda in all 100 Future Shop stores, a very unusual distribution channel for a soft drink.[9]

So far we've been concerned with the distribution channels firms use to get their products to customers. Now, we'll look at the different day-to-day activities of these firms, as the product travels from producer to user—activities referred to as physical distribution.

Physical Distribution

Marketing textbooks tend to depict the practice of marketing as 90% planning and 10% implementation. In the real world, many managers would argue that this ratio should be reversed. Marketing success is very much the art of getting the timing right and delivering on promises. That's why marketers place so much emphasis on efficient physical distribution.

What Is Physical Distribution?

Physical distribution is the movement of finished goods from manufacturers to final customers. Physical distribution is how marketers physically get products where they need to be, when they need to be there, at the lowest possible cost. In most physical distribution decisions, firms must compromise between low costs and high customer service. For example, it would be nice to transport all goods quickly by air, but that is certainly not practical. Physical distribution includes order processing, warehousing, materials handling, transportation, and inventory control.

ORDER PROCESSING

Order processing includes the series of activities that occurs between the time an order comes into the organization and the time a product goes out the door. After an order is received, it is typically sent electronically to an office for record keeping and then to the warehouse to be filled. When the order reaches the warehouse, personnel there check to see if the item is in stock. If it is not, the order is placed on back-order status. That information is sent to the office and then to the customer. If the item is available, it is located in the warehouse, packaged for shipment, and scheduled for pickup by either in-house or external shippers.

Many firms have automated this process. Once an order is in the system, all of the other steps occur automatically. Inventories are continuously updated in computer databases so that a sales representative who calls on customers or telemarketers who take orders by phone know immediately whether the product is in stock.

WAREHOUSING

Whether we speak of fresh-cut flowers, canned goods, or computer chips, at some point goods (unlike services) must be stored. Storing goods allows marketers to match supply with demand. For example, toys and other gift items are big sellers at Christmas, but toy factories operate 12 months of the year. **Warehousing**—storing goods in anticipation of sale or transfer to another member of the channel of distribution—enables marketers to provide time utility to consumers by holding onto products until consumers need them (see Exhibit 14.6).

Part of developing effective physical distribution is deciding how many warehouses a firm needs, where, and what type they should be. A firm determines the location of its warehouse(s) by the location of customers and access to major highways, airports, or rail transportation. The number of warehouses often depends on the level of service customers require. If customers generally require fast delivery (today or tomorrow at the latest), then it may be necessary to store products in a number of different locations where they can be delivered to the customer within a few days.

Firms use private and public warehouses to store goods. With private warehouses, firms have a high initial investment but they also lose less inventory due to damage. Public warehouses are an alternative, allowing firms to pay for a portion of warehouse space. Most countries offer public warehouses in all large cities and many smaller cities to support domestic and international trade. A *distribution centre* is a warehouse that stores goods for short periods of time and that provides other functions, such as breaking bulk.

✳ ✳ ✳
warehousing Storing goods in anticipation of sale or transfer to another member of the channel of distribution.

MATERIALS HANDLING

Materials handling is the moving of products into, within, and out of warehouses. When goods come into the warehouse, they must be physically identified, checked for damage, sorted, and labelled. Next they are taken to a location for storage. Finally, they are recovered from the storage area for packaging and shipment. The goods may be handled over a dozen separate times. Procedures that limit the number of times a product must be handled decrease the likelihood of damage and reduce the cost of materials handling.

✳ ✳ ✳
materials handling The moving of products into, within, and out of warehouses.

Exhibit 14.6

By warehousing goods, marketers can match supply with demand.

TRANSPORTATION

Physical distribution decisions take into consideration the modes of transportation and the individual freight carriers a firm needs to use to move products among channel members. Making transportation decisions entails a compromise between minimizing cost and providing the service customers want. As shown in Table 14.4, modes of transportation, including railroads, pipelines, water transportation, motor carriers, and airways, differ in the following ways:

- *Dependability:* the ability of the carrier to deliver goods safely and on time.
- *Cost:* the total transportation costs for moving a product from one location to another, including any charges for loading, unloading, and in-transit storage.
- *Speed of delivery:* the total time for moving a product from one location to another, including loading and unloading.
- *Accessibility:* the number of different locations the carrier serves.
- *Capability:* the ability of the carrier to handle a variety of different products (e.g., large and small, fragile and bulky).
- *Traceability:* the ability of the carrier to locate goods in shipment.

Each mode of transportation has strengths and weaknesses that make it a good choice for different transportation needs. Table 14.4 summarizes these.

Railroads. Railroads are best for carrying heavy or bulky items, such as coal and other mining products, agricultural products, forest products, steel, automobiles, and large machines over long distances. Railroads are about average in their cost and provide moderate speed of delivery. Although rail transportation provides dependable, low-cost service to many locations, trains simply cannot carry goods to every community in the country, and they can't go over the oceans. These problems with rail transportation have been solved in recent years. *Piggyback services* allow low-cost rail transportation for shipping to a larger number of destinations. Truck trailers are loaded onto trains and carried as close to their destination as possible. Truck, train, and ship transportation has been similarly combined to provide *fishyback services.* Combining truck and air transportation is called *birdyback service.* Problems of excessive handling and damage have been reduced by *containerization,* in which large quantities of goods are sealed in large protective containers for transit.

Water. Ships and barges, like railroads, carry large, bulky, nonperishable goods and are very important in international trade. Water transportation is quite low in cost but is very slow.

Table 14.4 A Comparison of Transportation Modes

Transportation Mode	Dependability	Cost	Speed of Delivery	Accessibility	Capability	Traceability	Most Suitable Products
Railroads	average	average	moderate	high	high	low	heavy or bulky goods such as automobiles, grain, steel
Water	low	low	slow	low	moderate	low	bulky, nonperishable goods such as automobiles
Trucks	high	high for long distances; low for short distances	fast	high	high	high	a wide variety of products including those that need refrigeration
Air	high	high	very fast	low	moderate	high	high-value items such as electronic goods and fresh flowers
Pipeline	high	low	slow	low	low	moderate	petroleum products and other chemicals
Internet	high	low	very fast	potentially very high	low	high	services such as banking, information, and entertainment

Trucking. Arnold Bros. Transport Ltd. promises "on the road and on time!" Trucks or motor carriers, such as those operated by Arnold Bros. in Exhibit 14.7, are the most important carrier for consumer goods, especially for shorter hauls. Motor carrier transportation allows flexibility because trucks can travel to those locations missed by boats, trains, and planes. Trucks are also able to carry a wide variety of products, including perishable items.

Although costs are fairly high for longer-distance shipping, trucks are economical for shorter deliveries. Because trucks provide door-to-door service, product handling is minimal, reducing the chance of product damage.

Air. Air transportation is the fastest and most expensive transportation mode. It is ideal to move high-value items, such as some mail, electronic goods, fresh-cut flowers, and live lobsters. Passenger airlines, air-freight carriers, and express delivery firms such as Federal Express and Parcel Post provide air transportation. Air transportation, especially the overnight services provided by express delivery firms, is becoming more and more important in the development of international markets—particularly for e-commerce where customers expect fast delivery. Ships, however, remain the major mover of international cargo, with Vancouver, Halifax, and Montreal being Canada's busiest ports. Port Vancouver alone handles more than $89 million of trade per day.[10]

Pipeline. Pipelines are used to carry such petroleum products as oil and natural gas and a few other chemicals. Pipelines primarily flow from oil or gas fields to refineries. They are very low in cost, require little energy, and are not subject to disruption by weather.

The Internet. Although scientists haven't yet figured out how to transport goods electronically, marketers of services such as banking, news, and entertainment are taking advantage of distribution opportunities provided by the Internet. Even though the Internet has existed since the 1960s, we are only beginning to realize its potential to distribute goods and services. The Internet is revolutionizing many distribution channels. Small entrepreneurs as well as larger firms such as Roots, Molson Canada, and the Bank of Montreal, are rushing to set up Web sites to make their products readily available to a worldwide market.

INVENTORY CONTROL

A final activity of physical distribution is **inventory control**, developing and implementing a process to ensure that the firm always has goods available to meet customers' demands—no

✳ ✳ ✳
inventory control Activities to ensure that goods are always available to meet customers' demands.

Exhibit 14.7

Arnold Bros. Transport Ltd. is one of Canada's largest independent transportation companies and a leading player in the North American transportation scene.

more and no less. Firms store goods, or create an inventory, for many reasons. For manufacturers, the pace of production may not match seasonal demand, and it may be more economical to produce snow skis year round than to produce them only during the winter season. For channel members that purchase goods from manufacturers or other channel intermediaries, it may be economical to order a product in quantities that don't exactly parallel demand. For example, delivery costs make it prohibitive for a retail gas station to place daily orders for just the amount of gas people will use that day. Instead, stations usually order truckloads of gasoline, holding their inventory in underground tanks. Finally, the consequences of stock-outs may be very negative. Hospitals must keep adequate supplies of blood, IV fluids, drugs, and other supplies on hand to meet emergencies, even if some items go to waste.

Inventory control has a major impact on the costs of physical distribution. If supplies of products are too low to meet fluctuations in customer demand, a firm may have to make expensive emergency deliveries or lose customers to competitors. If inventories are above demand, unnecessary storage expenses and the possibility of damage or deterioration occur.

Increasingly manufacturers are turning to quick-response, continuous replenishment, and just-in-time inventory management systems to ensure that their products are available for customers when and where they are needed and to improve the bottom lines of all channel partners. VF Corporation, maker of Lee and Wrangler jeans, uses a computerized market-response system that keeps records on what consumers buy each day from the register scanners of each of their key retail partners, automatically enters an order based on what items have been sold, and ships new jeans to arrive within three days.[11]

These types of systems are only part of a general movement toward supply chain management (SCM). In the 1960s and 1970s, physical distribution management focused on outbound logistics—what happened after the product was produced. The focus was internal, on individual processes and systems used to get product from the warehouse to the retailer. In the 1980s, the focus was on logistics management—inbound and outbound efficiencies and effectiveness involving procurement, materials management, production and delivery—considered together. Now, organizations are focusing beyond their own domain and trying to manage the logistics of a supply chain—all the suppliers, suppliers' suppliers, manufacturing partners, and distributors involved in creating value for customers. The Internet is a key facilitating technology in this effort, as it enables channel partners to integrate their systems, exchange information, and track materials, parts, and products as they progress through the supply chain.

Channel members in the Canadian grocery industry, for example, have been cooperating since 1993 to implement an efficient consumer response (ECR) system that focuses on eliminating wasteful activities and inefficiencies in the food supply chain. Increasing international competition was the impetus behind this move to standardize key processes and infrastructure relating to product identification and bar-coding, electronic data interchange, continuous replenishment, value chain analysis, activity-based costing, unsaleables, and deductions (from standard margins). Phil Lanzarotta, co-chair of the ECR supply chain executive committee, explains "that to really be efficient and compete on a world-class scale, we need to all get together on the back end (of the business) … and compete on the execution of marketing."[12]

Chapter Summary

1. Explain what a distribution channel is and what functions distribution channels perform.

A distribution channel is a series of firms or individuals that facilitates the movement of a product from the producer to the final customer. Channels provide time, place, and ownership utility for customers and reduce the number of transactions necessary for goods to flow from many manufacturers to large numbers of customers by breaking bulk and creating assortments. Channel members make the purchasing process easier by providing important customer services.

Real People, Real Decisions
How it worked out at HARTMANN Group

Hobenshield and the HARTMANN decision team chose to implement Option 3: Expand with the existing New Zealand partner. Hobenshield thought that HARTMANN would miss out on three or four million dollars in sales if they waited two or three years to develop their own wholly-owned subsidiary. Identifying and developing a relationship with a new Australian distributor would also delay market entry. The New Zealand partner could realize the market potential very quickly. Hobenshield and his HARTMANN superiors thought that there would be less risk going with a partner they knew and had performed well with the other product lines, even though HARTMANN had not previously dealt with the consumer products division of the partner. As a hedge against the potential risk that the New Zealand partner would be too independent and aggressive, Hobenshield gave them the

HARTMANN consumer products distribution rights for New Zealand with an option for Australia based on their New Zealand performance after six months. This would allow Hobenshield to work with the consumer products representatives in starting to develop the New Zealand market before extending the partnership to Australia.

Three months after entering into the new agreement with the New Zealand partner, Hobenshield went to New Zealand to assess their progress. As a result of this visit HARTMANN and the partner have entered into an exclusivity agreement with a large New Zealand based retail/wholesale outlet (75 stores), which means efficient, full container orders starting soon. The Australia option will be reassessed at the end of 2002 when the New Zealand business has further developed.

2. Describe some of the types of wholesaling intermediaries found in distribution channels.

Wholesaling intermediaries are firms that handle the flow of products from the manufacturer to the retailer or business user. Merchant wholesalers are independent intermediaries that take title to a product and include both full-function wholesalers and limited-function wholesalers. Merchandise agents and brokers are independent intermediaries that do not take title to products. Manufacturer-owned channel members include sales branches, sales offices, and manufacturers' showrooms.

Distribution channels vary in length from the simplest two-level channel to longer channels with three or more channel levels. Consumer distribution channels include direct distribution, in which the producer sells directly to consumers, and indirect channels, which may include a wholesaler and/or a retailer. Business-to-business channels may also be either direct or indirect and often include industrial distributors. Distribution channels for services are usually direct but may include an agent intermediary. Many firms are part of more than one type of channel, participating in dual or multiple distribution systems.

3. Discuss the steps in planning distribution channel strategies.

Marketers begin channel planning by developing channel objectives and considering important environmental factors. Conventional marketing systems include multiple levels of intermediaries that work independently. Vertical marketing systems (VMS) are channels in which there is cooperation at the different levels and may be administered, corporate, or contractual. Horizontal marketing systems are composed of firms at one channel level that work together.

Distribution planning also includes decisions about the number of channel members at each level. Intensive distribution includes all possible intermediaries, exclusive distribution has only one intermediary per region, and selective distribution includes a few but not all outlets in a region. Distribution tactics include the selection of individual channel members and management of the channel.

4. Describe the important activities in the physical distribution of goods.

Physical distribution involves the movement of goods from the manufacturer to the customer in, hopefully, the most efficient and effective manner possible. Physical distribution includes order processing, warehousing, materials handling, transportation, and inventory control.

KEY TERMS

bulk breaking (382)

channel intermediaries (381)

channel leader (395)

channel levels (386)

channel of distribution (381)

conventional marketing system (391)

creating assortments (382)

exclusive distribution (393)

facilitating functions (383)

horizontal marketing system (392)

independent intermediaries (383)

intensive distribution (393)

inventory control (399)

materials handling (397)

merchandise agents or brokers (385)

merchant wholesalers (383)

physical distribution (402)

selective distribution (393)

take title (383)

vertical marketing system (VMS) (391)

warehousing (397)

wholesaling intermediaries (383)

5. Discuss the distribution implications of the Internet.

The Internet is revolutionizing many distribution channels. It provides a means of direct distribution for banking, news, information, entertainment, and other services, where both large and small organizations have equal access to consumers and business-to-business customers around the world. By partnering with physical distribution companies like Federal Express, consumer and industrial goods companies can provide same- or next-day delivery for online purchases. The Internet is also facilitating supply chain management initiatives, as it enables channel partners to integrate their systems, exchange information, and track shipments.

Chapter Review

Marketing Concepts: Testing Your Knowledge

1. What is a channel of distribution? What are channel intermediaries?

2. Explain the functions of distribution channels.

3. List and explain the types of independent and manufacturer-owned wholesaling intermediaries.

4. What is a direct channel? An indirect channel?

5. Explain the steps in distribution planning.

6. What are conventional, vertical, and horizontal marketing systems?

7. Explain intensive, exclusive, and selective forms of distribution.

8. What is a channel leader?

9. What activities are involved in physical distribution?

10. What are the advantages and disadvantages of shipping by rail? By air? By ship? By truck?

11. What is supply chain management?

Marketing Concepts: Discussing Choices and Issues

1. You have probably heard someone say, "The reason products cost so much is because of all the intermediaries." Do intermediaries increase the cost of products? Would consumers be better off or worse without intermediaries?

2. Many entrepreneurs choose to start a franchise business rather than "go it alone." Do you think franchises offer the typical businessperson good opportunities? What are some positive and negative aspects of purchasing a franchise?

3. As colleges and universities are looking for better ways to satisfy their customers, an area of increasing interest is the distribution of their product—education. Describe the characteristics of your school's channel(s) of distribution. What types of innovative distribution might make sense for your school to try?

Marketing Practice: Applying What You've Learned

1. Assume that you have recently been hired as the director of marketing for a medium-sized furniture manufacturer. Your firm specializes in producing small tables and chests, each of which is made unique with a hand-painted design. As your firm is beginning to expand into new regions of the country, you must consider whether an intensive, selective, or exclusive distribution system is best for your product.

   a. Develop an outline listing the pros and cons of each type of system for your product.

   b. Decide which you will recommend, and say why.

2. As the one-person marketing department for a candy manufacturer (your firm makes high-quality, hand-dipped chocolates of only natural ingredients), you are considering making changes in your distribution strategy. Your products have previously been sold through a network of food brokers who call on specialty food and gift stores. But you think that it would be good for your firm to develop a corporate VMS (vertical integration). In such a plan, a

number of company-owned retail outlets would be opened across the country. The president of your company has asked that you present your ideas to the company executives. In a role-playing situation with one of your classmates, present your ideas to your boss, including the advantages and disadvantages of the new plan compared to the current distribution method.

3. Assume that you have recently been given a new marketing assignment by your firm. You are to head up development of a distribution plan for a new product line—a series of do-it-yourself instruction videos for home gardeners. These videos would show consumers how to plant trees and shrubbery and bulbs, how to care for their plants, how to prune, and so on. You know that in developing a distribution plan, it is essential that you understand and consider a number of internal and external environmental factors. Make a list of the information you will need before you can begin developing the distribution plan. How will you adapt your plan based on each of these factors?

Marketing Mini-Project: **Learning by Doing**

In Canada, the distribution of most products is fairly easy. There are many independent intermediaries (wholesalers, dealers, distributors, and retailers) that are willing to cooperate to get the product to the final customer. Our highway system combines with rail, air, and water transportation to provide excellent means for moving goods from one part of the country to another. In many other countries, the means for distribution of products are far less efficient and effective.

For this mini-project, you and one or more of your classmates should first select a consumer product, probably one that you normally purchase. Then use either or both library sources and other people (e.g., retailers, manufacturers, dealers, classmates) to gather information to do the following:

1. Describe the path the product takes to get from the producer to you. Draw a model to show each of the steps the product takes. Include as much as you can about transportation, warehousing, materials handling, order processing, and inventory control.

2. Select another country in which the same or a similar product is sold. Describe the path the product takes to get from the producer to the customer in that country.

3. Determine if the differences between the two countries cause differences in price, availability, or quality of the product.

4. Make a presentation to your class on your findings.

Real People, Real Surfers: **Exploring the Web**

Chapters Online Inc. (www.chapters.indigo.ca) is one of many book retailers that are seeking to develop a competitive advantage through distribution, by offering customers online shopping services. Some other leaders in Internet shopping are Amazon.com (www.amazon.com) and Barnes & Noble (www.bn.com).

Explore these or other book and music selling sites. Based on your experience, answer these questions:

1. Describe the online shopping services offered by Chapters.

2. Describe the online shopping services offered by the other retailers you have researched.

3. What differences do you see in the online shopping services offered to consumers by the different book sellers?

4. Distribution planning seeks to make products available to customers when and where they want them. Do all customers want book shopping services available on the Internet? What book-related services do you think consumers and business customers want on the Internet? What services do you think they would prefer through a different distribution channel? Which segments of customers do you think prefer online book shopping to the in-store experience?

5. Of the book sellers that you have studied, which do you think provides a competitive advantage for customers like yourself, and why?

6. What is your overall opinion of the book seller Web sites you visited? What is it about the sites that makes them appealing to potential customers? Is adequate information about the service provided? Is one site easier to navigate than the other? Based on the design of the Web site, which customers do you think each book seller is most interested in attracting?

Moosehead Brewery

Steven Poirier, vice-president of sales and marketing for Moosehead Brewery, considered his options for increasing sales of the popular Moosehead brands of beer. Having operated as a craft brewery for 127 years in Saint John, New Brunswick, Moosehead Brewery now distributes its beer to every province in Canada, except Saskatchewan and Quebec, and sells it internationally in over 60 countries. Although Moosehead is a profitable company, Poirier and the other executives realized that there was still unused capacity in their production facilities. To increase efficiency, Moosehead investigated the viability of additional distribution markets. Quebec seemed like the next logical step for distribution. The province is densely populated, with 7.3 million residents, and is the second largest beer consumption market in Canada, consuming 5.3 million hectolitres a year. As Quebec and New Brunswick are neighbouring provinces, distribution costs would be significantly less than shipping to other markets.

Poirier considered the company's usual marketing strategy. Moosehead's basic strategy focuses on selling their product as a premium Canadian lager. Their approach in each market differs, based on volume, market conditions, as well as distributor and government regulations. Within Canada, Moosehead starts out with a strong licensee push to generate trial and awareness, as this is the most cost-effective way to promote the product. They then begin to overlay advertising through print, radio, and outdoor billboards and signs. They could use a similar strategy in Quebec, taking into account language and cultural differences.

Poirier, very familiar with the Canadian food and beverage industry—having worked for Bacardi Rum and McCain Foods—realized that there would be challenges to distributing Moosehead products in Quebec. New Brunswick and Quebec have historically struggled with high inter-provincial trade barriers, and there were strong labour and corporate lobby groups that wanted to keep Moosehead out of the province.

The push against Moosehead was being led by a smaller Quebec brewery, whose product is not selling well in the New Brunswick market. The Quebec company believes that the New Brunswick regulations are causing the poor sales. Their product, however, is sold at a very high premium price and is a Belgian-styled beer, quite different in taste from English-styled ales and lagers. It is also difficult to compare the regulations of out-of-province product, as the New Brunswick and Quebec practices are structured differently.

New Brunswick marks up out-of-province beer by an additional $59 per hectolitre, but also guarantees 100% retail distribution. Quebec, however, is not involved in the liquor industry, so it does not offer any distribution services. Subcontracting the distribution costs a company a minimum of $48 per hectolitre, but this does not provide any guarantee of listings. To list the product, most breweries need to account for another $24 per hectolitre. Moosehead believes that these factor will contribute to higher costs when selling in Quebec. However, this is not recognized by the provincial regulators.

Other challenges involve physical distribution and channel management. In British Columbia and Ontario, all alcoholic beverages are sold through government-owned liquor distribution branches (LDB). Trucks carrying Moosehead beer have relatively few stops to deliver product to the LDBs. In-store promotions are typically coordinated centrally and are similar for each of the government retail outlets, making promotion management fairly straightforward. In Alberta and Quebec, however, alcohol is sold to independent retailers or retail chains. Each retailer is responsible for negotiating contracts as well as for obtaining and promoting product. The breweries also have to assume the cost of warehousing the inventory. Selling beer in these provinces is similar to selling other retail products, such as cola or toothpaste, and requires a stronger channel management program. Moosehead would also have to ensure that the labels follow Quebec language regulations.

To balance these challenges, Moosehead already has a very high brand awareness in Quebec. Their initial studies indicate that retailers are very interested in stocking Moosehead beer, and

MARKETING IN ACTION

the company is confident that it will attain high-volume sales. Sales are excellent in areas surrounding Quebec. Although the two major Canadian breweries enjoy a 90% market share, Moosehead has the largest market share of the "smaller breweries." Poirier feels he could maintain Moosehead's premium image and pricing in the Quebec market because of this brand awareness.

After much thought and analysis, Poirier thought that entering the Quebec market made sense for Moosehead. It was not clear, however, how best to do this. Poirier knew that he needed to devise a market entry strategy for Quebec, make marketing mix decisions consistent with this strategy and the Quebec market, and focus particularly on distribution and relationship management issues. There would be implementation issues, but he didn't know if any of these would be insurmountable.

THINGS TO THINK ABOUT

1. What marketing mix and market entry strategy would you recommend for Moosehead?
2. How would you manage Moosehead's relationships with Quebec retailers and other key stakeholders?
3. What issues, barriers, or limitations would need to be overcome to implement your strategy? Do any of these seem insurmountable?
4. What additional research or analysis would you want to conduct before implementing your launch strategy?

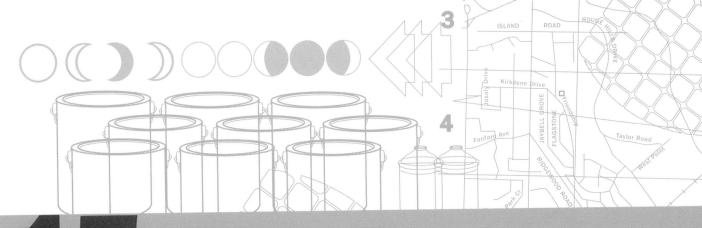

15

Retailing and E-tailing

When you have completed your study of this chapter, you should be able to

CHAPTER OBJECTIVES

1. Define retailing and describe how retailers evolve over time.

2. Classify retailers by their selection of merchandise.

3. Understand the importance of store image to a retail position-ing strategy, and explain some

of the actions a retailer can take to create a desired image in the marketplace.

4. Describe the opportunities and barriers to e-tailing.

5. Describe the major forms of non-store retailing.

Real People, Real Decisions
Meet Göran Carstedt
A Decision Maker at IKEA

IKEA is the world's largest-volume furniture chain, with 166 stores in 30 countries and sales of over 10 billion Euro. There are currently 9 stores in Canada and plans to open a second store in Montreal in 2003. IKEA's mission is to "...offer a wide range of home furnishing items of good design and function, at prices so low, that the majority of people can afford to buy them." The company was founded by Ingvar Kamprad, who arrived at the name IKEA by combining his initials with the first letters of the Swedish farm, Elmtaryd, and parish, Agunnaryd, where he grew up.

Göran Carstedt joined the organization in 1990, when he was named president of IKEA North America, headquartered outside of Philadelphia. Before working in retailing, he had spent most of his career in the Swedish auto industry. After

receiving a PhD in marketing from the University of Umes in 1974, Carstedt joined Volvo as manager of market planning in the Car Division. He was president of Volvo France for several years, and from 1985 until he joined IKEA, he was president of Volvo Svenska Bil AB. Since September 1995, when Jan Kjellman was named president of IKEA North America, Carstedt has been president of IKEA Europe and he is also overseeing the company's newly established corporate marketing staff.

Sources: Solomon, M. and Stuart E., *Marketing: Real People, Real Choices*, Second Edition, Prentice Hall: 2000; www.IKEA.ca; "Furniture giant IKEA spending $60 million to build second Montreal store," Canadian Press Newswire, January 16, 2002.

Retailing: Special Delivery

Shop 'til you drop! For many people, obtaining the product is half the fun. Others would rather walk over hot coals than spend time in a store. Marketers need to find ways to deliver products and services that please both types of consumers. **Retailing** is the final stop on the distribution path—the process by which goods and services are sold to consumers for their personal use.

A retail outlet is often more than simply a place where you buy something. The retailer adds or subtracts value from the offering with its image, inventory, service quality, location, and pricing policy. In many cases, the shopping experience is what is being bought as well as the products we take home. That's what visitors to the Discovery Channel store in Washington, DC, get when they meet up with a life-size model of a *Tyrannosaurus rex* on the main floor of the four-level store. The place feels like a museum with such attractions as a cockpit from a vintage World War II plane.[1] Similarly, part of IKEA's strategy is to make the store a shopping destination with experiences that encourage shoppers to spend more time there.

Retailers are a special breed of marketers. They assemble and present products, often from many different manufacturers, in ways that make them appealing and accessible, and often develop unique and exciting store images that are similar to the product branding strategies we've already discussed. In this chapter, we explore the different types of retailers, comparing and contrasting them along some key dimensions, keeping in mind that today's shoppers have so many retail choices—boutiques, department stores, ordering by phone, and clicking on a Web site. How does a retailer—whether a traditional one operating a store or a non-store retailer selling via television, phone, or computer—lure the consumer? These important marketing questions get more difficult to answer as the competition for customers intensifies. We start with an overview of where retailing has been and where it's going.

Retailing: A Mixed (Shopping) Bag

Retailing is big business. About one in eight Canadian workers is employed in retailing, and the sales from more than 180 000 retail stores represents about 6.2% of Canada's gross do-

✳ ✳ ✳
retailing The final stop in the distribution channel by which goods and services are sold to consumers for their personal use.

IKEA
www.ikea.com

mestic product.[2] Although we tend to associate huge chains like IKEA, Canadian Tire, and The Bay with retailing activity, most retailers (about 75%) are independent small businesses.[3] Some retailers, such as Home Depot and Costco, are also wholesalers, which provide goods and services to businesses as well as end consumers. We saw how the wholesaling process works in the previous chapter. Now, we'll focus on the process that delivers goods and services to individuals for their personal use.

Retailers provide many benefits to consumers. Some save people time or money by providing an assortment of merchandise under one roof. Others search the world for the most exotic delicacies, allowing shoppers access to goods they would otherwise never see. Still others, such as Chapters and Indigo bookstores, provide us with interesting environments in which to spend our leisure time and, they hope, our money.

The Evolution of Retailing

Retailers have taken many forms over time, including the simple peddler who hawked his wares from a horse-drawn cart, a majestic urban department store, an intimate boutique, and a huge hypermarket which sells everything from potato chips to snow tires. Old types of retailers routinely give way to new variations, as economic, social, and cultural developments change the face of society. That horse-drawn cart has been replaced by the cart that sits in the middle of your local mall, selling new-age jewellery or monogrammed golf balls to passers-by en route to grab a plate of sushi in the food court or catch a movie at a state-of-the-art theatre. As times change, different types of retailers emerge, often replacing older, outmoded types. How can we understand and predict what the dominant types of retailing will be tomorrow or 10 years from now to be sure that we keep in step?

THE WHEEL OF RETAILING

One of the oldest and simplest explanations for these changes is the **wheel-of-retailing hypothesis**. This states that new types of retailers find it easiest to enter the market by offering goods at lower prices than competitors.[4] After they gain a foothold, they gradually trade up, improving their facilities, increasing the quality of merchandise, and offering amenities like parking and gift wrapping. This upscaling results in greater investment and operating costs, so the store must raise its prices to remain profitable, which then makes it vulnerable to still newer entrants that can afford to charge lower prices. And so the wheel turns. The wheel of retailing helps to explain the development of some, but not all, forms of retailing. For example, some retailers never trade up; they simply continue to occupy a niche as discounters. Others, such as upscale specialty stores, start out at the high end. Let's take a look at a more satisfying explanation.

✳ ✳ ✳
wheel-of-retailing hypothesis A theory that explains how retail firms change, becoming more upscale as they go through their life cycle.

THE RETAIL LIFE CYCLE

Retailers sell products; but in a way, retailers also *are* products, because they provide benefits such as convenience or status to consumers and they must offer a competitive advantage over other retailers to survive. A better way to understand how retailers evolve is the **retail life cycle**. Like the product life cycle, this perspective recognizes that retailers are born, they live, and eventually they die. The life cycle approach allows us to categorize retail stores in terms of the conditions they face at different points in the cycle.[5]

✳ ✳ ✳
retail life cycle A process that focuses on the various retail life cycle stages from introduction to decline.

In the *introduction* stage, the new retailer is often an aggressive entrepreneur who takes a unique approach to doing business. This may mean competing on the basis of low cost, as the wheel of retailing suggests. However, the new guy on the block may enter the market by offering a distinctive assortment or a different way to distribute items, such as through the Internet. In this initial stage, profits are low due to high development costs.

As the business enters the *growth* stage, the retailer catches on with shoppers, and sales and profits rise. But a new idea doesn't stay new for long. Others start to copy it, and competition increases, so the retailer needs to expand what it offers. Often the retailer responds by opening more outlets and developing systems to distribute goods to these new stores, which may cut profits, as the firm invests in new buildings and fixtures.

In the *maturity* stage, the industry has overexpanded, and intense competition makes it difficult to maintain customer loyalty. Profits decline, as retailers resort to price cutting to

Exhibit 15.1

Full-service gas stations fight off decline by adding products to their retail mix.

Office Depot
www.officedepot.com

keep their customers. This pattern applies to department stores like The Bay and fast-food chains like McDonald's. Office supply superstores are entering the mature phase of the retail life cycle, which means they need to find ways of differentiating themselves other than price. For example, in 1998, Office Depot enlisted the help of cartoon character Dilbert, the stereotypical cubicle dweller, to forge a distinctive identity claiming: "Business is crazy. Office Depot makes sense."[6]

In the *decline* stage, retail businesses, like the general store or the peddler, become obsolete, as newer ways of doing business emerge. The outmoded retailer does not have to fold its tent at this stage: Marketers that anticipate these shifts can avert decline by changing to meet the times. For example, full-service gas stations had difficulty competing with self-service discount outlets. Many responded by adding variety stores to their retail mix for drivers wanting to buy a tank of gas and groceries at the same location, as seen in Exhibit 15.1. Canada Safeway is doing the opposite—adding gasoline to their retail mix.[7]

The Evolution Continues: What's "in Store" for the Future?

As our world continues to rapidly change, retailers are scrambling to keep up. Three important factors motivate innovative merchants to reinvent the way they do business.

DEMOGRAPHICS

As noted in Chapter 8, keeping up with changes in population characteristics is at the heart of many marketing developments. Retailers can no longer afford to stand by and assume that their customer base is the same as it has always been. They are coming up with new ways to sell their products to diverse groups. Major demographic factors altering the face of retailing include:

- *Convenience for working women:* Some retailers are expanding their hours of operation, because many harried women have time to shop only at night. Others, including dry cleaners and pharmacies, are adding drive-up windows to meet demands for convenience and security. In some areas, from financial services to interior decorating and clothing, enterprising individuals have turned time shortage into a business opportunity by offering their services as shopping consultants for those unwilling or unable to shop on their own. Many major department stores also fill this need by offering the services of their own in-house consultants at no charge.

- *Catering to specific age segments:* Retailers are recognizing that there are many opportunities to specialize in providing for the needs of different age groups. For example, IKEA is responding to its me-too rivals by developing Children's IKEA, which sells furniture and related products for kids. The company recruited psychologists to assist in

Exhibit 15.2

Food for future thought: New database technology puts supermarkets in the high-tech fast lane.

creating 600 new products for this market, from egg-shaped cribs to fabric dolls.[8]

- *Recognizing ethnic diversity:* Although members of every ethnic group can usually find local retailers that understand and cater to their specific needs, larger companies must tailor their strategies to the cultural makeup of specific areas. George Michel, president of the Toronto-based Burger King Restaurants of Canada, for example, recognized that catering to multiculturalism would benefit the company. With 25% of the Toronto population of Chinese descent, Michel began the "Now we're speaking the same language" ad campaign in Cantonese, focusing on strategic locations. Burger King also rolled out its veggie burger to ethnic markets to appeal to non–beef-eating East Indian and East Asian markets.[9] Canada's native peoples represent an underserved market niche. In the three Prairie provinces they make up at least 10% of the population, half of them are under 30, their education levels are soaring, and land-claim settlements (across Canada) are forecasted to be $15 billion over the next decade.[10]

TECHNOLOGY

Technology is revolutionizing retailing. In-store video channels entertain customers by giving messages about local events or showing ads.[11] Some stores feature talking posters that contain a human body sensor that speaks up when a shopper approaches.[12] Other stores (see Exhibit 15.2) are experimenting with wireless networks that allow shoppers to scan in their own items as they shop, eliminating the need for checkout lines.[13] When shoppers enter a store, whatever chip-enabled device they are carrying—a cellphone, palm computer, or smart card—interacts with a store's computer system to update the shopper's buying profile and provide the shopper with individualized communications, coupons, and other incentives.[14] And widespread use of the personal computer has turned many homes into virtual malls, as consumers surf the Web from the comfort of their own chairs.

Some of the most profound changes are not even visible to shoppers, such as advanced electronic **point-of-sale (POS) systems**, which collect sales data, are hooked directly into the store's inventory control system, and place timely orders to ensure that the store does not stock out of an item. Birks Jewellers, for example, uses their new POS system for this purpose; but in the future, the chain expects to use it for such marketing applications as analyzing trends and planning local sales.[15]

Other technological innovations will radically change the way we shop in the future. One leading retailer predicts that in the year 2010: "Each consumer will have a personal preference card, so a store will know your tastes, clothing sizes, and even your current household decor. When shopping for furniture, a design consultant will call up a 3-D image of your living room, and show you how your new purchases will actually look in the room. Or, forget about endlessly trying on clothes—holographic imaging will let you 'see' yourself in a new suit or dress."[16] As Exhibit 15.3 shows, sophisticated body scanners already exist that can read a person's exact dimensions and send this information to machines that produce clothing precisely tailored to individual proportions.

GLOBALIZATION

As we saw in Chapter 4, the world is becoming a smaller place. Retailers are busy expanding to other countries and bringing with them innovations and management philosophies

✳ ✳ ✳
point-of-sale (POS) systems
Retail computer systems that collect sales data and are hooked directly into the store's inventory control system.

Exhibit 15.3

Body scanners can read a person's exact dimensions and send this information to machines that produce precisely tailored clothing.

that change the way local firms do business. Many international retailers, such as IKEA, Blockbuster Entertainment, Home Depot, and Toys 'R' Us (see Exhibit 15.4), are prominent in Canadian retailing, while some Canadian retailers such as Roots, La Senza, and Mark's Work Wearhouse have made significant inroads in the United States and other parts of the world.[17] Cinnaroll Bakeries Ltd., a Western Canadian cinnamon bun retailer, has 10 Cinnzeos franchises in the Philippines, is expected to open 30 more there by 2002, and has signed an agreement for 50 more Cinnzeos throughout Southeast Asia.[18]

Types of Retailers

We've seen that exciting things are happening in the world of retailing. But the field of retailing covers a lot of ground—from mammoth department stores to sidewalk vendors to Web sites. This section provides an overview of the different types of retailers. Retail managers need to understand the competitive environment in which they operate to make decisions about the ways to offer their merchandise to the public and to compare the productivity of their business to similar retailers.

Classifying Retailers by What They Sell

✽ ✽ ✽
merchandise mix The total set of all products offered for sale by a firm, including all product lines sold to all consumer groups.

One of the most important strategic decisions a retailer makes is *what* to sell—its **merchandise mix**. This choice is similar to settling on a market segment as discussed in Chapter 8:

Exhibit 15.4

International retailers, such as Toys 'R' Us, are prominent in Canadian retailing.

If a store's merchandise mix is too limited, it may not have enough potential customers; if it is too broad, the retailer runs the risk of being a "jack of all trades, master at none." A retailer's **merchandise assortment**, or merchandise mix, is the variety and selection of products it sells. It has both breadth and depth.

Merchandise breadth, or variety, is the number of different product lines available. A *narrow assortment*, such as that found in convenience stores, means that its customers can buy only a limited selection of product lines, such as candy, cigarettes, and soft drinks. A *broad assortment*, such as that in a warehouse store, means there is a wide range of items from eyeglasses to barbecue grills.

Merchandise depth is the variety of choices available for each specific product. A *shallow assortment* means that the selection within a product category is limited, so a factory outlet store may sell only white and blue men's dress shirts all made by the same manufacturer and only in standard sizes. In contrast, a men's specialty store may feature a *deep assortment* of dress shirts, but not much else, in exotic shades and in hard-to-find sizes. Figure 15.1 illustrates these assortment differences for one product, science fiction books.

The strategy of carrying a mixture of merchandise items that are not directly related to each other is called **scrambled merchandising**. This strategy is exemplified by Blockbuster Entertainment Group, which defines its merchandise mix in terms of products a customer might want when spending an evening at home, including food items and other goods. In addition to stocking your favourite James Bond video, the stores sell candy, soda, and even private-label popcorn to complete the couch potato experience.

In deciding what merchandise assortment to offer, retailers need to strike a balance between the profitability of the mix and ensuring that they have the depth and breadth required to satisfy their customers. On the profitability side, they consider the markup on particular items, projected sales volume, and gross margin (revenues minus cost of goods sold, calculated as a percentage of sales). Gross margin, however, does not consider the costs of operating the store. Knowing a store's gross margin is useful, because it is a performance measure that allows the retailer to compare how it is doing relative to similar stores. The retailer also can compare how much different product lines within the store are contributing to profits. Usually, stores that mark up items substantially will have higher gross margins than those that sell products closer to what they actually cost the store to buy.

Inventory turnover, or *stock turn*, is the average number of times a year a retailer expects to sell its inventory. For example, a candy store owner can expect to sell the "same" pack of gum hundreds or thousands of times a year. A jewellery store owner may need to sell only one diamond ring per year to make the same profit as the gum retailer selling a thousand packs a year. So the candy store owner hopes to sell a greater volume of merchandise to compensate for razor-thin margins. All retailers, regardless of gross margin, try to encourage more rapid turnover, because this helps guarantee that their merchandise will be "fresh" and that expenses associated with storing the products will be minimized. Overly rapid turnover, however, results in greater costs, because products must be bought in smaller quantities. Then the retailer can't take advantage of volume discounts offered by the manufacturer or wholesaler, and delivery charges are higher for small shipments. Successful retailers try to balance gross margin and inventory turnover. The Gap, for example, started by selling items with thin profit margins, such as inexpensive jeans and T-shirts. When competitors began imitating this strategy, the company boosted profits by modifying its merchandise mix to include more higher-margin items, such as hats and handbags.[19]

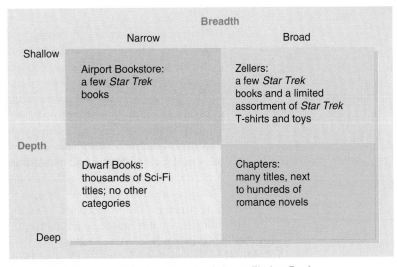

Figure 15.1 **Merchandise Selection for Science Fiction Books**

✳ ✳ ✳
merchandise assortment The range of products sold.

✳ ✳ ✳
merchandise breadth The number of different product lines available.

✳ ✳ ✳
merchandise depth The variety of choices available for each specific product.

✳ ✳ ✳
scrambled merchandising A merchandising strategy that offers consumers a mixture of merchandise items that are not directly related to each other.

✳ ✳ ✳
inventory turnover The average number of times a year a retailer expects to sell its inventory.

STORE TYPES

We have seen that retailers differ in the breadth and depth of their assortments. Let's review some of the major forms these retailers take.

Convenience stores, such as Mac's or 7-Eleven, are neighbourhood retailers that carry a limited number of frequently purchased items, including basic food products, newspapers, and sundries. They cater to consumers willing to pay a premium for the ease of buying staple items close to home. In other words, they meet the needs of those who are pressed for time, who buy items in smaller quantities, or who shop at irregular hours.

Supermarkets, such as Loblaws or Safeway, are food stores that carry a wide selection of edibles and non-edible products. Although the large supermarket is a fixture in North America, it has not caught on to the same extent in other parts of the world. Europeans, for example, are used to walking or bicycling to small stores near their homes. They tend to have smaller food orders per trip and to shop more frequently. Wide variety is less important than quality and local ambience, though those habits are changing as huge hypermarkets have grown in popularity.

Specialty stores, such as La Senza, Mark's Work Warehouse, and Lee Valley Tools (Exhibit 15.5), have narrow and deep inventories. They do not sell a lot of product lines, but they offer good selection of brands within the lines they do sell. Some retailers are even establishing specialty store-within-stores, such as The Bay's in-store vitamin boutique.

General merchandise discount stores, such as Zellers and Wal-Mart, offer a broad assortment of items at low prices and with minimal service. Some discount stores, such as Army & Navy and Toronto's Honest Ed's, are **off-price retailers**. These stores obtain surplus merchandise from manufacturers and offer these brand-name, fashion-oriented goods at low prices.

Warehouse clubs, such as Costco and the Loblaws warehouse stores, are a new version of the discount store. These establishments do not even pretend to offer any of the amenities of a store; a bargain mentality is reinforced by merchandise that is displayed, often in its original box, in a cavernous, bare-bones facility. These clubs often charge a modest membership fee to consumers and small businesses, which buy a broad assortment of food and non-food items in bulk sizes. The typical warehouse shopper is likely to have a large family and a relatively high income and can afford to pay several hundred dollars to "stock up" on staples during one shopping trip.[20]

Factory outlet stores, such as Danier Leather Factory Outlet, are another type of discount retailer. These stores are owned by a manufacturer and sell off its defective merchandise or excess inventory.[21] Although the assortment is not wide, because a store carries only products made by one manufacturer, a recent trend is for different factory outlet stores to cluster together in the same location to form an *outlet mall*.

Department stores, such as The Bay and Sears, sell a broad range of items and offer a deep selection organized into different sections of the store. Department stores have encountered serious problems in recent years, exemplified by the bankruptcy of Eaton's and its subsequent sale to Sears.

✳ ✳ ✳

off-price retailers Retailers that buy excess merchandise from well-known manufacturers and pass the savings on to customers.

Exhibit 15.5

Lee Valley Tools is a specialty store targeting woodworking, gardening, and other hobby enthusiasts.

Specialty stores have lured department store shoppers away with deeper, more cutting-edge fashion selections and better service. They have also been squeezed by mass merchandisers, catalogues, and e-commerce retailers, which can offer many of the same items at lower prices, because they don't have to shoulder expenses involved in elaborate fixtures or high salaries for knowledgeable salespeople.

Hypermarkets combine the characteristics of warehouse stores and supermarkets. Popular in Europe and Latin America, these huge establishments are several times larger than other stores. A supermarket might be 40 000 to 50 000 square feet, whereas a hypermarket takes up 200 000 to 300 000 square feet, the equivalent of four football fields. They offer one-stop shopping, often for over 50 000 items, and feature restaurants, beauty salons, and children's play areas. They haven't caught on as well in North America, where so many discount stores, malls, and supermarkets are available, and consumers find the hypermarkets to be so large that finding items and checking out is too time-consuming.[22]

✳ ✳ ✳
hypermarkets Retailers with the characteristics of both warehouse stores and supermarkets; hypermarkets are several times larger than other stores and offer virtually everything from grocery items to electronics.

Real People, Real Decisions
Decision Time at IKEA

IKEA came to North America in the early 1980s, first to Canada and then to the US. As Göran Carstedt puts it, IKEA North America's strategy is to appeal to the American customer "by speaking English with a Swedish accent." IKEA's unique recipe for success caught on quickly, and the company now sells about $1.5 billion worth of products a year in North America. IKEA stores are usually found outside city limits but close to main roads to keep costs down by minimizing the distance from suppliers.

Such phenomenal success is bound to be copied, and that's just what happened. An American-owned clone of IKEA, called STØR, opened three stores in the Los Angeles area (STØR was a made-up name that was intended to imply it was Swedish). Although IKEA entered the US market on the east coast, management felt that it needed to go head-to-head with STØR in the LA marketplace. If STØR was too successful, IKEA feared it would expand to other locations and create problems later.

IKEA opened its first LA store in Burbank and two years later a second store in Fontana. IKEA then acquired STØR. IKEA closed one of its former rival's smaller stores, which was located in a very successful shopping centre called the Del Amo Fashion Center in Torrance, and reopened two others under the IKEA brand name.

Still, Carstedt had a problem. Although IKEA now had four stores operating in the LA area, there was not one close enough to attract the customers who had shopped at STØR in Torrance. IKEA began to shop around for sites near Torrance, keeping in mind the company's strategy of locating in a highly visible area, preferably right off a major highway—in this case, the San Diego Freeway. The overall objective was to have five stores in place by year end. A number of potential sites were identified, but each had drawbacks.

Option 1. Choose the STØR site in Torrance. This was, however, only 110 000 square feet, much smaller than IKEA needed to stock the more than 10 000 items an average store carries as part of its strategy of offering a wide assortment to shoppers.

Option 2. Three properties in the same area as the STØR site were possibilities. However, one was on a dump site, and the other two were contaminated. There might be delays in getting construction started if one of these were chosen. This delay would mean lost business, and the undesirable sites might negatively affect IKEA's store image.

Option 3. A site was available at Carson Mall, a strip mall with three department stores. On the positive side, the shopping centre was located at an exit of the San Diego Freeway, the most heavily travelled highway in the world. About 250 000 cars pass by this intersection every day. On the negative side, Carson Mall suffered from a poor image. It had a bad reputation in the community as an unsafe place to shop. The company hired a local research firm to conduct a telephone survey, which found that only 60% of the area residents said they would shop at IKEA if it were located at the Carson Mall. To make matters worse, only 14% said that they had shopped at the Carson Mall in the last three months.

Now, join Göran Carstedt and the IKEA decision team: Which option would you choose, and why?

Developing a Store Positioning Strategy:
Retailing as Theatre

Although stores can be distinguished by the breadth and depth of their assortments, we are less likely to say "I'll go to that store because their assortment is broad," and are more likely to say "That place is neat, I like going there." Stores can entertain us, they can bore us, they can make us angry or make us sad. In today's competitive marketplace, retailers have to do more than offer good inventory at reasonable prices. They need to position their stores so that they offer a competitive advantage over other stores also vying for the shopper's attention. Let's see how they do that.

Walk into REI, a Seattle-based store that sells gear for climbing, cycling, skiing, and camping. REI is more than that, though. As Exhibit 15.6 shows, the store features a 65-foot-high, artificial climbing rock, a vented area for testing camp stoves, and an outdoor trail to check out mountain bikes. Buying a water pump? Test it in an indoor river. Eyeing that new Gore-Tex jacket? See how it holds up in a simulated rainstorm.[23]

In Chapter 11, we saw that staging a service is much like putting on a play. Similarly, many retailers recognize that much of what they do is really theatre. At a time when it is possible to pick up a phone or log onto a computer to buy many items, a customer must have a reason to make a trip to a store instead. True, you can probably buy that jacket over the Internet, but try getting your computer to rain on it.

Shoppers are an audience to entertain. The "play" can cleverly employ stage sets (store design) and actors (salespeople) that together create a "scene." For example, think about buying a pair of sneakers. Athletic shoe stores are a far cry from the old days, when a tired shoe salesman (much like Al Bundy in the TV show *Married with Children*) waded through box after box of shoes as kids ran amok across dingy floors. Now salespeople may be dressed in black-striped referee outfits, and stores like Foot Locker are ablaze with neon, with the shoes displayed in clear acrylic walls appearing to float.[24] All these special effects make the buying experience less about buying and more about having an experience. As one marketing strategist commented, "The line between retail and entertainment is blurring."[25]

Ontario's Liquor Control Board (LCBO) recognized the importance of entertainment to attract customers and motivate purchases. They created a 20 000-square-foot mega liquor store in Toronto's Bayview Village shopping centre (Exhibit 15.7), which has 1600 different wines, 250 foreign and domestic beers, music listening stations, a gift-wrapping centre, and a demonstration kitchen for cooking presentations and wine tasting seminars—turning what was once a mundane trip to the liquor store into a great shopping experience.[26] What tools are available to the retailing playwright?

Exhibit 15.6

The REI store in Seattle provides a unique shopping experience.

Store Image

When people think of a store, they often have no trouble describing it in the same terms they might a person. They use words like *exciting, depressed, old-fashioned, tacky,* or *elegant*. **Store image** is how the target market perceives the store—its market position relative to the competition. For example, Holt Renfrew's department store is seen by many as chic and fashionable, especially compared to a more traditional competitor such as The Bay. These images don't just happen. Just as brand managers do for products, store managers work hard to create a "personality."

In developing a desirable store image, the resourceful retailer has a number of choices. Ideally, all of these elements should work together to create a clear, coherent picture that meets consumers' expectations of what that particular shopping experience should be.

Atmospherics is the use of colour, lighting, scents, furnishings, sounds, and other design elements to create a desired setting. Marketers manipulate these to create a certain "feeling" about the retail environment. US retailer Kinney's Colorado Stores, which sell high-end outdoor clothing, has taken this to an extreme. Their stores are designed to make the shoppers feel they're out in nature: The stores pipe in new-age background music, interrupted occasionally by the sound of a thunderstorm or a babbling brook. Motion sensors in the ceiling activate displays as a shopper approaches—a person who walks near an arrangement of beach shoes, for example, may hear the sound of waves crashing.[27] The owners of these stores believe that getting people "into the mood" makes them more likely to buy what they see.

STORE DESIGN: SETTING THE STAGE

The elements of store design should correspond to management's desired image. A bank lobby needs to convey respectability and security, because people need to be reassured about the safety of their money. In contrast, a used bookstore might create a disorderly look, so shoppers will think treasures lie buried beneath piles of tattered novels. One of the most innovative restaurant store designs in Canada is the Movenpick Marché in Toronto's BCE Place. This 400-seat restaurant has several rooms, each decorated in different styles, such as French bistro. The cafeteria-style restaurant offers stations throughout the store where customers can watch their dinner of sushi, spit-roasted Cornish hen, or fresh pasta being prepared. An in-store bakery, ice-cream parlour, and fruit and vegetable stand allow customers to complete their grocery shopping after dinner, a feature especially attractive to busy businesspeople.

Some specific design decisions management must make are:

- *Store layout.* This is the arrangement of merchandise in the store. The placement of fixtures such as shelves, racks, and cash registers is important, because store layout determines **traffic flow**—how shoppers move through the store and what areas they pass or avoid. A *grid layout,* usually found in supermarkets and discount stores, consists of rows of neatly spaced shelves that are at right angles or parallel to one another. This configuration is useful when management wants to systematically move shoppers down each aisle, ensuring that they pass through such high-margin sections as deli and meat. Figure 15.2 illustrates how a grid layout in a supermarket helps to regulate traffic flow.

✳ ✳ ✳
store image The way a retailer is perceived in the marketplace relative to the competition.

✳ ✳ ✳
atmospherics The use of colour, lighting, scents, furnishings, and other design elements to create a desired store image.

✳ ✳ ✳
traffic flow The direction in which shoppers move through the store and what areas they pass or avoid.

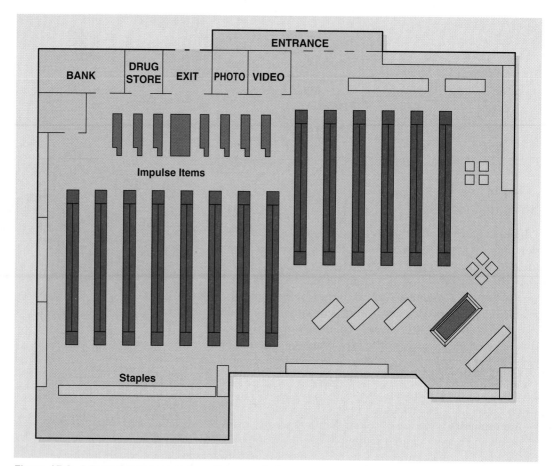

Figure 15.2 A Typical Grid Layout for a Supermarket

A typical strategy is to place staple goods in more remote areas. The designers know that traffic will move to these areas, because staples are purchased frequently. They try to place impulse goods in spots shoppers will pass on their way elsewhere; then they place eye-catching displays to catch people's attention. In contrast, a *free-flow layout* is more often used in department and specialty stores, because it is conducive to browsing. A retailer might arrange merchandise in circles or arches or perhaps in separate areas, each with its own distinct image and merchandise mix.

- *Fixture type and merchandise density.* Just as we form impressions of people from the way they decorate their homes, our feelings about stores are affected by furnishings, fixtures (shelves and racks that display merchandise), and even how much "stuff" is packed into the sales area. Generally, clutter conveys a lower-class store. Upscale stores allocate space for sitting areas, dressing rooms, and elaborate displays of merchandise. A southern California shopping centre called the Lab attracts its target audience of mall rats aged 18 to 30 by using unusual furnishings—concrete walls, a fountain made of oil drums, and an open-air living room filled with thrift-shop furniture to craft a laid-back image its patrons call "the anti-mall."

- *The sound of music.* An elegant restaurant softly playing Mozart in the background is worlds apart from a raucous place such as the Hard Rock Café, where loud rock 'n' roll is essential to the atmosphere. One owner of a 7-Eleven convenience store discovered the power of music when he figured out how to deter groups of teenagers who were loitering in his store. He piped in "classics" from the 1940s and 1950s, and soon they were gone.[28]

- *Colour and lighting.* Marketers use colour and lighting to set a mood. Red, yellow, and orange are warm colours (fast-food chains use a lot of orange to stimulate hunger), whereas blue, green, and violet signify elegance and cleanliness. Light colours make one feel more serene, whereas bright colours convey excitement. Nova Scotia's Bolands

food stores, for example, moved all their fruits and vegetables onto one 12-foot wall of produce, painted the wall black, and highlighted the whole section with spotlights. This treatment, added to the addition of a few new and exotic varieties of produce, drew customers to the produce and increased sales.[29]

THE ACTORS: STORE PERSONNEL

Store personnel should complement a store's image. Each employee has a part to play, complete with props and costumes. Movie theatres sometimes dress ushers in tuxedos, and many store employees are provided with scripts to use when they present products to customers. At the Loblaws store at Queen's Quay (see Exhibit 15.8), for example, counter staff help to create a fun and entertaining atmosphere by engaging customers with banter and hucksterisms—the seafood counter clerk, for example, yelling "fresh fish, get your fresh fish here."[30]

Although the presence of knowledgeable sales personnel is important to shoppers, they generally rate the quality of service they receive from retail personnel as low, often because stores don't hire enough people to wait on their customers.[31] In one survey, 62% of shoppers said they had decided to not buy a product in a store in the past six months because sales clerks were unavailable to help them.[32] Retailers are working hard to upgrade service quality, though they often find that the rapid turnover of salespeople makes this a difficult goal to achieve. Perhaps they can learn from Japanese retailers: A visitor to a Japanese store is greeted by an enthusiastic, polite employee who bows profusely.[33]

PRICING POLICY: HOW MUCH FOR A TICKET TO THE SHOW?

When consumers form an image of a store in their minds, the *price points*, or price ranges, of its merchandise often play a role. Ed Mirvish uses humour and poetry to communicate his concept of Honest Ed's, for example: "Honest Ed's for the birds—his prices are cheap, cheap, cheap." Similarly, Daffy's, a US off-price retailer, advertises: "Friends Don't Let Friends Pay Retail." In recent years, department stores have been hurt by consumers' desires for bargains. The response of many department stores was to run frequent sales, a strategy that often backfired because many consumers would buy *only* when the store held a sale. As we saw in Chapter 13, many stores, such as Zellers and Home Depot, have reduced the number of sales they run in favour of an everyday low-pricing (EDLP) strategy. Loblaws supports their premium shopping experience with prices that are often slightly higher than the competitors'. They have recognized, however, that premium merchandise and pricing need to be supported by premium store designs, and that the building itself contributes a lot to the customer experience.[34]

Building the Theatre: Store Location

Realtors list the three most important factors in buying a home as "location, location, and location." The same is true in retailing. Wal-Mart's success is not due to what it is but *where* it is. Wal-Mart was the first mass merchandiser to locate in small and rural market areas. When choosing a site, its planners consider such factors as proximity to highways and major traffic routes. By carefully selecting "undiscovered" areas, the company has been able to negotiate inexpensive leases in towns with expanding populations, an important strategy for Wal-Mart because it means access to markets hungry for a store that offers such a wide assortment of household goods.[35] This section reviews some important aspects of retail locations.

TYPES OF STORE LOCATIONS

As Figure 15.3 shows, there are four basic types of retail locations—a business district, a shopping centre, a free-standing entity, or a non-traditional location.

- *Business districts.* A *central business district (CBD)* is the traditional downtown business area in a town or city. Many people are drawn to the area to shop or work, and public transportation is usually available. CBDs have suffered in recent years due to concerns about security, lack of parking, and the lack of customer traffic on evenings and weekends. To combat these problems, many cities provide such incentives as tax breaks to encourage the opening of stores and entertainment areas like Toronto's St. Lawrence Market as shown in Figure 15.3. These vibrant developments are called *festival marketplaces,* and they have done much to reverse the fortunes of aging downtown areas.

West Edmonton Mall
www.westedmall.com

- *Shopping centres.* A shopping centre is a group of commercial establishments owned and managed as a single property. They range in size and scope from *strip centres* to massive *super-regional centres,* such as the West Edmonton Mall, shown in Figure 15.3, the world's largest retail centre—a 492 370-square-metre complex complete with a theme-room hotel, amusement park, water park, full-sized indoor skating rink, deep sea adventure area that houses dolphins and submarines, casino, and shooting gallery.[36] Strip malls offer quick and easy access to basic conveniences such as dry cleaners and video rentals, though shoppers seeking more exotic goods need to look elsewhere. Shopping malls offer variety and the ability to combine shopping with entertainment. On the other hand, rents tend to be higher, so it's difficult for stores such as home-improvement centres to be profitable. In addition, small specialty stores may find it hard to compete with a mall's *anchor stores,* the major department stores that typically draw many shoppers.

- *Free-standing retailers.* Some stores, usually larger ones such as IKEA (Figure 15.3), are free-standing, located by themselves in a separate building. These retailers benefit from lower rents and fewer parking problems. However, the store must be attractive enough on its own to be a destination point for shoppers, because it can't rely on spillover from consumers visiting other stores at the same place.

- *Non-traditional store locations.* Innovative retailers find new ways to reach consumers. Many entrepreneurs use *carts,* small, movable stores that can be set up in many locations including inside malls, airports, or other public facilities, or *kiosks* that are slightly larger and offer store-like facilities, including telephone hookups and electricity. As Exhibit 15.9 shows, Sunglass Hut sells nothing but sunglasses in its kiosk. Its assortment is narrow and deep. Carts and kiosks are relatively inexpensive and a good way for new businesses to get started. Mall operators need to be careful about regulating carts, because they may block a store or sell merchandise that is incompatible with a desired image.

SITE SELECTION: CHOOSING WHERE TO BUILD

Retailers used to simply choose to build a store on a site where an adequate number of people saw it. Sam Walton, the founder of Wal-Mart, used to fly over an area in a small plane until he found a spot that appealed to him. No more. Now such factors as long-term population patterns, the location of competitors, and the demographic makeup of an area factor into retailers' decisions. The choice of where to open a new store should reflect the company's overall growth strategy. It should be consistent with long-term goals and be in a place that allows the company to best support the outlet. For example, a chain with stores and an extensive warehouse system in Ontario may not be wise to open a new store on Vancouver Island, because the store would be an "orphan" cut off from the company's supply lines.

Location planners look at many factors when selecting a site. A store's targeted consumer segment is a key determinant of where it locates. For example, a new, growing community would be appealing for hardware stores that can supply hammers and drywall to home-

A central business district is often found in downtown areas. Although North American retailers have been deserting city centres for the past 20 years, these downtown areas are now staging a comeback. Such sophisticated developments as Toronto's St. Lawrence Market (shown here) and Queen's Quay, Winnipeg's The Forks, and Vancouver's Granville Market are bringing shoppers back to the city cores.

A shopping centre features one or more anchor stores, usually major department stores that initially attract shoppers, who then discover the other small, specialty stores in the centre. Shopping centres have the advantages of (1) providing heavy traffic flow (especially for small stores that would not attract so many people if they were on their own), (2) the sharing of costs (such as advertising and promotion) among tenants, and (3) a clean (and usually safe) environment. It seems likely that large malls will continue to evolve as entertainment centres and for recreational shopping, featuring a greater mix of movie theatres, restaurants, and hobby and bookstores.[a] The West Edmonton Mall is the world's largest retail centre, featuring a wide variety of shopping and entertainment experiences.

A freestanding store is not located near other stores. This locational strategy, used by some big chains like Kids 'R' Us, has the advantage of offering a lack of direct competition, lower rents, and adaptability. The store has the freedom to alter its selling space to accomodate its own needs. On the other hand, the store had better be popular because it cannot rely on the drawing power of neighbour stores to provide it with customer traffic.

A nontraditional location offers products to shoppers in convenient places. Canadian banks and financial institutions are opening branches and kiosks in large grocery stores. McDonald's has located inside Wal-Mart stores to entice customers to take a McBreak from shopping.

[a] Chip Walker "Strip Malls: Plain But Powerful," *American Demographics*, October 1991, 48(4).

Figure 15.3 Types of Store Locations

owners, whereas upscale dress stores and travel agencies might find better locations in more established areas where people have the income to spend on fashion items and vacations. Planners also want to find a place that is convenient to customers in the store's **trade area**, the geographic zone that accounts for the majority of its sales and customers.[37] A *site evaluation* considers such specific factors as traffic flow, number of parking spaces available, ease of delivery access, visibility from the street, local zoning laws that determine the types of buildings, parking, and signage allowed, as well as such cost factors as the length of the lease and the amount of local taxes.

Planners also consider such population characteristics as age profile (Is the area witnessing an influx of new families?), community life cycle (Is the community relatively new, stable, or in decline?), and mobility (How often are people moving in and out of the area?). Planners also have to consider the degree of competition they will encounter by locating in one place rather than another.

✳ ✳ ✳
trade area A geographic zone that accounts for the majority of a store's sales and customers.

E-tailing and Other Non-Store Retailing

Many products are readily available in places other than traditional "bricks and mortar" stores. For example, the familiar Avon ladies, who sell cosmetics and other beauty products to millions of women around the world, show that a retailer need not be a store. Avon is continuing to explore new ways to give customers access to its products. Customers can place orders by phone, fax, catalogue, via the Internet, or through a sales representative. Avon is currently testing a 30-minute infomercial to sell its products on television.[38]

Avon's success at giving customers alternatives to traditional store outlets illustrates the increasing importance of **non-store retailing**, which is any method a firm uses to complete an exchange that does not require a customer visit to a store. North Americans spend almost $70 billion through catalogues, TV shopping channels, the Internet, and other non-store formats.[39] Many retail stores even offer non-store alternatives to buying their merchandise, such as using catalogues and Web sites. As the founder of the Neiman-Marcus department store acknowledged: "If customers don't want to get off their butts and go to your stores, you've got to go to them."[40]

Two major types of non-store retailing are **e-tailing** and **direct marketing**: Customers are exposed to merchandise through print, broadcast, or electronic media and then purchase the products over the Internet, by phone, or by mail. In this section, we'll review the major forms of non-store retailing, starting with the newest—buying on the Internet.

E-tailing

Throughout this book, we have talked about electronic commerce—conducting business transactions and communication over networks and through computers. In Chapter 7, we discussed electronic commerce's place in business-to-business (B2B) markets. In this chapter, our focus is on e-tailing, electronic commerce in business-to-consumer (B2C) markets. There are other forms of electronic commerce that are beyond the scope of this book, including: consumer-to-consumer (C2C) activities, such as those facilitated by E-bay and other auction sites; consumer-to-business (C2B) activities, such as those facilitated by priceline.com and other reverse auction sites; business-to-government (B2G) activities, such as lobbying efforts of the Canadian Hemp Growers Association (www.hempro.com/chga); and government-to-business (G2B) activities, such as the industry and market information provided by IndustryCanada.com or government bid (tender) sites such as MERX (merx.cebra.com).

LOTS OF SIZZLE, BUT IS THERE STEAK?

Despite considerable hype about the "new economy," even in light of the dot-com share valuation meltdown, online sales accounted for just 0.2% of total sales in the Canadian

✳ ✳ ✳

non-store retailing Any method used to complete an exchange with a product end user that does not require a customer visit to a store.

✳ ✳ ✳

e-tailing Offering products for sale directly to consumers via the Internet.

✳ ✳ ✳

direct marketing Exposing a consumer to information about a good or service through a non-personal medium and convincing the customer to respond with an order.

economy in 1999.[41] Canadian e-tailers generated $890 million in sales in 2000, up 46% from 1999. That figure represented about 12% of all online revenue (B2B is 80%), but less than 0.5% of all retail sales.[42] In the US e-tailers fared better with sales of about US$26 billion in 2000 and US$33 bilion in 2001, representing 1% of all US retail sales.[43] Although e-tail sales increases have slowed since the late 1990s when they were doubling or tripling each year, Industry Canada and market research firms still forecast annual growth of 50% to 70% through 2005 and expect worldwide e-commerce sales of US$1.9 to $3 trillion.[44] So even in the aftermath of some "dot.bombs," there is still a lot of excitement about e-tail opportunities.

CANADA SLOW OFF THE MARK

Canadian retailers and **pure play e-tailers**—those that only have electronic sales—have been slow to develop online solutions for Canadian consumers, however, and Canadian consumers have been slow to warm up to online buying, despite having greater Internet access than US consumers.[45] A joint study by the Boston Consulting Group and the Retail Council of Canada found that almost 60% of Canadian and American consumers have shopped online, but fewer Canadians than Americans (43% versus 51%) have ever purchased online. Where the average Canadian spent $220 over five transactions in 1999, the average American spent $705 over 11 transactions.[46] Part of the reason for this difference may be the lower availability of Canadian e-tail sites; however, Canadians also have greater concerns about Internet security and privacy than do American consumers, and Canadians experience a higher rate of failed purchase attempts (12% of orders are never filled, compared to 6% in the US).[47] Overall, only 1.9% of Canadian visits to e-tail sites result in a sale, or conversion. Figure 15.4 illustrates some key factors that influence conversion rates.

Although Canada ranks second in the world in many Internet use categories,[48] Canadians run the risk of being late entrants into e-commerce and e-tail business. There are high fixed costs in the technology and people required to support the businesses, which could make late entry a problem. And the global market is quickly consolidating—as much as 75% of all B2C commerce is generated through five major players: eBay, Yahoo!, America OnLine, Amazon.com, and Buy.com.[49] E-commerce is still in its infancy, however, and the gold rush is still on. Opportunities abound for creative e-commerce solutions that provide value to consumers.

✳ ✳ ✳

pure play e-tailer A retailer that offers product for sale only via the Internet.

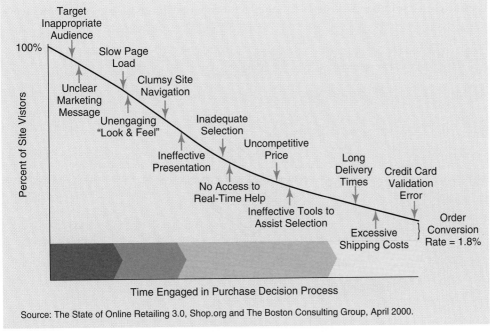

Source: The State of Online Retailing 3.0, Shop.org and The Boston Consulting Group, April 2000.

Figure 15.4   Conversion Rates Are Influenced by Many Factors

WHO SHOPS ONLINE?

Almost 60% of Canadian have tried to buy something online.[50] Traditionally (a couple of years ago), Internet shoppers tended to be better educated, younger men who were better off financially. Increased access to the Internet at work, school, libraries, and home, however, have reduced demographic differences in online shopping. The profile of online consumers now mirrors those of other shoppers: Online shoppers are now, on average, older, increasingly female, less affluent, and less highly educated than they once were.[51]

Canadian teenagers, however, are a special subset of the general population. Eighty-five percent of the 2.4 million teens in Canada use the Internet regularly (an average of 9.3 hours a week), but only 10% of them have purchased something online.[52] EcomCard Inc. of Markham, Ontario, hopes to change that. They have introduced a pre-paid card, similar to a phone card, that can be established with a desired sum, used to purchase products online, and then disposed of when all the money is spent, removing concerns of parents and other consumers about using traditional credit card numbers online.[53]

WHY DO THEY SHOP ONLINE?

✳ ✳ ✳

bots Electronic robots or shopping agents that help consumers find products and prices on the Internet

Consumers shop online to achieve a variety of benefits, known as the six Cs: cost, choice, convenience, customization, communication, and control (see Figure 15.5). Many consumers shop online to get lower prices and to reduce the psychological cost of comparison shopping: Product information is just a click away, and there are **bots**, electronic shopping agents that help consumers find the lowest prices. Cost is one of the reasons Canadians have been slower to buy online. Many products are available only through US e-tailers, and transportation costs, import duties, and unfavourable exchange rates make online purchases less attractive from a cost savings perspective.

Other consumers shop online because of choice and convenience—accessibility to products from around the corner to around the world, the ability to buy them from the comfort of their home or office, and the ability to have them delivered right to their homes or, in the case of gifts, directly to others, gift wrapped with a personalized card. Lingerie sellers, like Montreal-based Linda Lingerie (www.lindalingerie.com), La Senza (www.lasenza.com) (see Exhibit 15.10), and La Vie en Rose (www.lavieenrose.com), provide a convenient, more private online shopping experience that is particularly attractive to men buying lingerie for women.[54] They make it convenient by using standard sizing, offering easy-to-follow sizing charts, making product out of Lycra which accommodates different sizes and shapes, and having flexible return policies.

For others, the main motivation is customization—being able to buy something made specifically for your needs. Procter & Gamble, for example, hired Calgary-based interactive

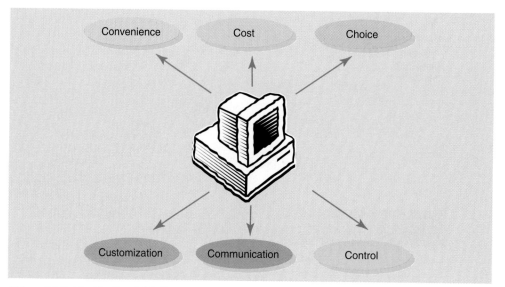

Figure 15.5 The Six Cs of E-tailing

Exhibit 15.10

Lingerie retailer La Senza stresses convenience as a main benefit to shopping online.

marketing agency Critical Mass to create Reflect.com (www.reflect.com), a site that allows consumers to buy cosmetic products that have been customized and packaged just for them.[55]

Still others are attracted to buying online because of their ability to have interactive communication with e-tailers. **Push technology** allows marketers to automatically send customers relevant information, specified by consumer preferences; while e-mail, chat rooms, and call centres allow consumers to talk back. Women-oriented Internet **portals** (gateways to the Internet), such as Canadian Shenetworks.com and Women.ca (see the Spotlight feature in this chapter) are attracting the attention of marketers seeking to connect with women consumers.

Finally, online shopping gives customers greater control over the shopping experience, and allows them to engage e-tailers on their own terms and make more informed purchase decisions. Internet portals, such as Canoe.ca and Sympatico.ca assist consumers to navigate the Internet, find products, and make informed choices.

WHAT DO THEY BUY?

Although still in its infancy, electronic commerce is transforming the way we shop. Buyers now have access to millions of stores around the world without leaving their computers, and often they can easily get crucial information before making a purchase. For example, Intel is working on a site for Ticketmaster that allows the customer to move around a virtual replica of a concert hall or a sports arena to test the view from different seats before buying tickets: Try doing that over the phone.[56] Clearwater Fine Foods of Nova Scotia (www.cffi.com) sells fresh lobster, shipped to your door anywhere in North America within 24 hours. Ordering might be done by fax, but it's easier to track your dinner over the Internet using software supplied by courier companies like UPS and Federal Express.

Travel services, computer hardware and software, financial services, and collectibles represented 70% of North American e-tail sales in 1999.[57] However, high-growth categories included auto sales (up 2300%), health and beauty (up 780%), and toys (up 440%), and computer, books, music, and video sales are expected to meet or beat 10% market penetration by the end of 2000.[58] What do these products have in common? Products that can actually be delivered electronically over the Internet, such as computer software, news, music, videos, electronic games, financial services, airline and other tickets, and maybe even books are naturals for e-tailing—the convenience of buying these products online may soon make other forms of distribution obsolete.

Traditional players in the music industry, for example, are threatened by MP3 technology and the ability of audiophiles to source high-quality recordings from each other using free software such as Gnutella, and through sites such as MP3.com and Napster.com.[59] There are over 5000 Internet radio stations to tune into (such as www.theiceberg.com). And companies like Penguin Radio and Kerbango Inc. are creating Internet radios: It won't be long before pocket-sized and smaller wireless devices will let "streamies" (consumers who use streaming media) play and record CD-quality music and receive increasingly higher-

✱ ✱ ✱

push technology Internet tools that allow marketers to send information they think is relevant to consumers directly to their computers.

✱ ✱ ✱

portals Gateways to the Internet that assist consumers to navigate the Internet and customize their experience.

Online Radio Stations
www.theiceberg.com

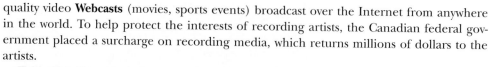

✳ ✳ ✳

Webcast Real-time transmission of encoded video under the control of a server to multiple recipients, who all receive the same content at the same time.[60]

quality video **Webcasts** (movies, sports events) broadcast over the Internet from anywhere in the world. To help protect the interests of recording artists, the Canadian federal government placed a surcharge on recording media, which returns millions of dollars to the artists.

Table 15.1 illustrates other consumer products that have the potential to do well online. This is not an exhaustive list: Every day innovative entrepreneurs are demonstrating business models for selling new product categories online. MagiCorp Inc., of Toronto, for example, aims to market "international connectedness" with an ambitious plan to create 30 cyber-connected entertainment complexes called TribeNation (www.tribenation.com) starting in Hong Kong, Montreal, Toronto, and Seattle in the Spring of 2001.[61] Aimed at 16- to 25-year-olds around the world, TribeNation will be physical entertainment multiplexes, offering a wide range of activities related to extreme sports, fashion, design, music, new media, games, and travel among many other themes—these will be Webcast, along with other events such as concerts, festivals, and interviews, to other TribeNation venues. Thus the physical complexes provide Web-based content for each other and allow young people from all over the world to connect, interact, play, and party at a venue or online.

Critical Success Factors

We are just beginning to see the enormous potential of electronic commerce in retailing. The success of this non-store format will depend on the ability of retailers to offer sites that are entertaining and informative, and that are worth revisiting again and again even after the novelty wears off. Gap, for example, offers a Web site with a page (shown in Exhibit 15.11) that allows the shopper to mix and match colours and styles on the computer, a service that can't be matched by a conventional catalogue. Blast Radius, a three-year-old Vancouver-based Web design company with production offices in Toronto, New York, and Los Angles, won gold and silver Clio awards for the interactive sites they designed for Casio

Gap
www.gap.com

Table 15.1 Consumer Products That Have the Potential to Do Well Online

Characteristic	Description	Example
Straight rebuys	Consumers have product and brand experience and just want another one as conveniently and cost effectively as possible	packaged goods, household items, health, flowers, personal care products
Commodities	No or few perceived differences between brands and price is a key buying criteria	produce, electricity, recycling services, telephone services
"Low-touch" items	Items that don't need to be tried on or fitted, felt, or smelled (Although once body shapes and sizes are determined as depicted in Exhibit 15.3, even custom clothes can be bought online.)	
Have high retail margins	Direct to consumer distribution may provide significant cost savings	toys, cosmetics, clothes
Can be customized	Can be targeted to very narrow audiences around the world	computers, cars, clothing, music
Expensive to inventory	Difficult and expensive to offer wide selections in traditional retail settings	cars, computers, household appliances
Invite comparison shopping	Products that are highly differentiated or where they are many options and where consumers can save time and effort by comparing product features and prices	consumer electronics, household furniture and fixtures
Difficult to find	Where supply is limited or geographically inaccessible	collectibles, specialty goods, antiques, art

SPOTLIGHT ON REAL PEOPLE *Shenetworks.com*

Women are now almost equal to men in their use of the Internet. Internet entrepreneurs Natasha Kong and Nicole Blades saw an opportunity to give women in their 20s an alternative to the drivel and irrelevant content about babies and menopause of magazines and online 'zines such as Moxie.ca, iVillage.com, woman.com, and chickclick.com.[62] The Shenetworks.com Web site is a funky mix with links grouped under names such as SheCooks, SheMoney, SheErotic, SheGrooves, and SheBytes. It is positioned to capture the young wired woman by addressing "real deal" issues and interests. The site promises "clean, consistent, clutter-free aesthetic, minus the tired man-nailing strategies and recycled weight loss tips...delivering targeted, accessible, relevant content, all in one space."

Blades graduated with honours from York University in 1994 with a BA in mass communications and a BA in psychology, and then moved to New York City to join NBC talk show *Sally Jessy Raphael* as a public relations representative. Kong's career in new media began in 1994 when she co-founded Random Media Core, a creative house based in downtown Toronto. As creative director, she developed Web sites and corporate identity for clients including TV Guide Telemedia (tvguidelive.com), Sega City, RCA, and Absolut Vodka.

In the aftermath of the "dot.bomb" fallout in 2001, Kong and Blade's revenue model of selling space to advertisers targeting young women dried up. The site has been taken down temporarily while they try to find a model that will support their growing technology needs. This may be a challenge. Springboard.ca, a woman's portal launched in early 2001 by Rogers Media, did not last the year. Moxie.ca was still running in the spring of 2002 but faces the same challenge—making a profit by providing value to a target market.

1. What do you consider the critical success factors for Shenetworks.com and other gender focused portals?
2. Compare and contrast some women focused Web sites. Are they direct competitors or are they positioned differently?
3. Is segmenting by gender appropriate for an internet portal or does this result in too broad a target market?

(www.gshock.com) and Lego (www.lego-media.com), respectively.[63] These sites keep consumers involved, bring them back, and help build brand loyalty.

Branding (discussed in Chapter 10) is particularly important in e-tailing, as customers need to know what to look for online and need some way to assess the trustworthiness of online suppliers. That's why many e-tailers are spending, on average, 32% of revenues on marketing communications, where traditional retailers typically spend about five percent.[64]

Exhibit 15.11

Advanced technology allows the Gap to let surfers mix and match its apparel items on the company's Web site.

Generating awareness, establishing credibility, and building trust can be expensive if attempted on a global scale. Forrester Research estimates that e-commerce companies spent as much as $2.5 billion on conventional advertising in 1999, with America OnLine spending half of it.[65] We'll see in Chapters 16 and 18, however, that there are other, often more cost-effective alternatives to advertising for building consumer awareness and trust.

A second critical success factor is building loyalty. This is where Canadian e-tailers excel, with 47% of their revenues coming from repeat customers compared to 31% for US e-tailers.[66] As Figure 15.6 shows, speed of delivery, cost of delivery, responsiveness of customer service, and return policy are key factors in driving customer satisfaction, a key determinant of customer loyalty.

Branding and customer loyalty are also key issues for traditional retailers. Where e-tail organizations really stand out is in their **scalability**, their ability to get bigger without a big rise in expenses. Once a Web site is set up, it is accessible anywhere in the world. It also allows marketers such as Amazon.com to almost infinitely expand the depth and breadth of their product assortment, as long as they can deliver the product to the customer.

✱ ✱ ✱
scalability The ability of organizations to get bigger without a big rise in expenses.

BARRIERS TO SUCCESS

Despite all the hoopla, e-tailing is not without disadvantages, and it won't replace stores anytime soon. One drawback is that customers must wait a few days to receive the products, which are often sent via private delivery services, so shoppers can't achieve instant gratification by walking out of a store clutching their latest "finds." Customer fulfillment continues to be a major stumbling block for e-tailers, as only 71% of orders are completely filled (delivered to the customer) in Canada and 83% in the US.[67]

This is why Chapters, as discussed in Chapter 14, decided to create their own fulfillment company. One might think that traditional retailers such as Future Shop would have a distribution advantage over pure play e-tailers, but the distribution systems that are effective for shipping large orders to centralized locations (stores) are not effective for shipping small orders to distributed locations (homes). This is a problem that Toronto-based Oxford Properties Group Ltd. plans to address with a series of depots called The Depot (www.Empori.com) in major office towers across Canada.[68] These depots will allow e-tailers to ship product to centralized locations convenient for pickup by customers.

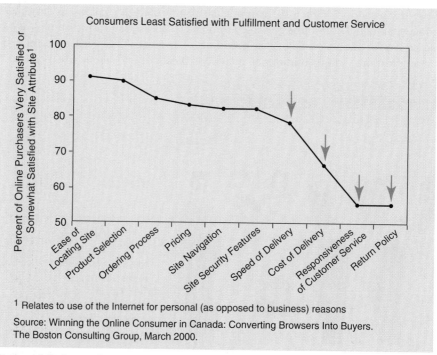

[1] Relates to use of the Internet for personal (as opposed to business) reasons
Source: Winning the Online Consumer in Canada: Converting Browsers Into Buyers. The Boston Consulting Group, March 2000.

Figure 15.6 Determinants of E-Customer Satisfaction

Another problem is that people need "touch-and-feel" information before buying many products. For this reason, companies such as Tupperware, Amway, and Mary Kay discourage Internet sales. Executives at Tupperware want shoppers to be able to "burp" their plastic containers to appreciate their airtight qualities.[69] This is one reason that Just White Shirts and Black Socks (www.executive-lifestyle.com) of Mississauga decided to open a bricks-and-mortar warehouse outlet in Toronto to support their Internet and mail-order sales (see Exhibit 15.12)—some buyers just have to touch the fabric and feel the weight of the cotton.[70] Product returns are a big problem with e-tailing, as one in every 10 products ordered on the Internet comes back to the company that sent it out.[71]

Many consumers are still reluctant to buy over the Internet due to their concerns about security. They are understandably reluctant to provide such sensitive information as credit card numbers. Technological advances, such as digital signatures, may help to ensure that valuable personal information is secure, and pre-paid e-cards, such as the one offered by EcomCard Inc., may reduce the risk of others using your credit card number.[72] The governments of Ontario and Saskatchewan have passed e-commerce bills to ensure that electronic contracts, documents, and signatures have the same legal effect as non-electronic versions to protect both consumers and businesses.[73]

As major marketers beef up their presence on the Web, some are concerned that inventory sold online will cannibalize store sales. That is not a concern of Future Shop: This electronics retailer has one of Canada's busiest Web sites, with over 100 000 visits each month. The site is fully integrated with their stores in a "clicks and mortar" concept, so that consumers can decide to buy online or just browse online and go to a traditional Future Shop store to purchase. The retail stores provide their customers with a tangible point of reference, places where they can go and see the products.[74]

Manufacturers also face a problem. If they sell their products directly on the Web, they will anger stores that carry their merchandise. Companies such as Mattel are experimenting with online marketing (www.barbie.com) and are finding that consumers appreciate access to hard-to-find items, such as Share a Smile Becky, a wheelchair-bound friend of Barbie that many small toy stores don't stock. Still, these companies must be sure they don't antagonize the many stores on which they still rely to sell their products.[75] Levi

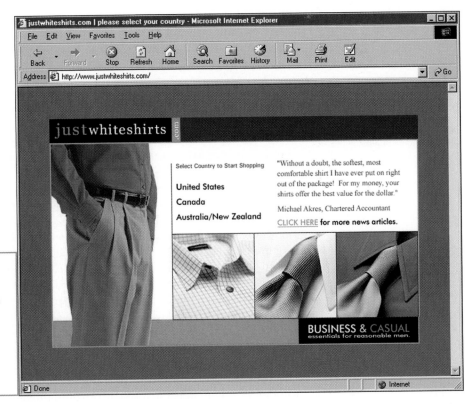

Exhibit 15.12

Some non-store retailers are opening traditional storefronts to support their brands.

Strauss, for example, decided to pull out of online sales in response to very strong objections by their channel partners.[76]

In addition, electronic retailing has the potential to increase price competition, because the Web surfer can look for the same branded item offered on numerous Web sites and just buy it wherever it's cheapest, regardless of whether the business is located next door or in another continent. Indeed, shopping bots already scan cyberspace for bargains; these electronic agents (such as the ones found at www.compare.net and www.webmarket.com) automatically access many sites and compare prices.

However, there's a fly in the ointment. Many retailers—those competing on dimensions other than price, such as image or sales support—don't want to cooperate and are finding ways to block the "bots." For example, CDNow, one of the Web's hottest music retailers, wants to discourage people from buying CDs at one site simply because they're a few cents cheaper. CDNow offers hundreds of thousands of albums, but it also provides "value added" in the form of music reviews and commentaries from fans and critics, and recommendations based on the surfer's past purchases at the site. Some online retailers program their pages to refuse entry to "bots," whereas others try to confuse them by changing the site's format so that the shopping robot doesn't know where to look for pricing information. Another tactic is to lower a product's base price but then tack on additional hidden costs for shipping and handling.[77]

CDNow
www.cdnow.com

Direct Marketing

Although e-tailing has gained significant attention in the marketplace, there are more established forms of non-store retailing, by which customers are exposed to merchandise through print or electronic media and then purchase the products by phone or mail. It's big business. Direct marketing, or direct response marketing, generated $45 billion in sales in Canada in 1999.[78] Let's look at the most popular types of direct marketing, starting with the oldest—buying through the mail. The communications functions of direct marketing will be discussed in Chapter 16.

MAIL ORDER

In 1872, Aaron Montgomery Ward and two partners put up $1600 to mail a one-page flyer that listed their merchandise with prices, hoping to spur a few more sales for their retail store.[79] The mail-order industry was born. Today, consumers can buy just about anything through the mail. Mail order comes in two forms: catalogues and direct mail.

CATALOGUES

✳ ✳ ✳
catalogue A collection of products offered for sale in book form, usually consisting of product descriptions accompanied by photos or illustrations of the items.

A **catalogue** is a collection of products offered for sale in book form, usually consisting of product descriptions accompanied by photos or illustrations of the items. Catalogues came on the scene within a few decades of the invention of moveable type in the fifteenth century, but they've come a long way since then.[80] The early Canadian catalogues pioneered by innovators such as Sears and Eaton's were designed for people in remote areas who lacked access to stores.

Today, the catalogue customer is likely to be an affluent career woman with access to more than enough stores but who does not have the time or desire to go to them. Canadians spend about $2 billion through domestic and foreign catalogues.[81] Catalogue mania extends well beyond clothing and cosmetics purchases. Dell and Gateway 2000, direct-selling computer companies, each have annual sales of over $1 billion. Bridgehead, an Ottawa-based Oxfam affiliate, has a catalogue that features housewares, gifts, foods, and other items imported through "fair trade" deals from the Third World. Although the Internet is starting to replace the function of catalogues, large retailers such as Sears, Canadian Tire, and IKEA continue to make extensive use of catalogues to make shopping more convenient for consumers. The trend, however, is to replace much of the catalogues with Internet sales.[82] Zellers, however, uses catalogues and the Internet to reach key target audiences. They recently created a new Zellers Special Delivery Baby Catalogue and online baby-gift registry. Baby-related tips are offered throughout the catalogue courtesy of *Today's Parent* magazine, and there is as an integrated loyalty program for Club Z members and their babies.[83]

DIRECT MAIL

Unlike a catalogue retailer that offers a variety of merchandise through the mail, **direct mail** is a brochure or pamphlet offering a specific product or service at one point in time. Although e-mail is increasingly used for the same purpose, Canada Post expects to continue to deliver about 4.7 billion pieces of direct mail each year.[84] The Toronto Blue Jays use direct mail to sell season tickets and group tickets. In 1999, they sent about 20 000 packages to their season base, 150 000 to early bird customers, and 40 000 to group sales clients. The club surpassed its goal of 14 000 season ticket sales, and had reached 80% of its goal for group sales only a few months into the campaign.[85] A direct mail offer has an advantage over a catalogue because it can be personalized. Direct mail also is widely used by charities, political groups, and other not-for-profit organizations.

Direct Selling

Direct selling occurs when a salesperson presents a product to one individual or a small group, takes orders, and delivers the merchandise. This form of non-store retailing works well for such products as vacuum cleaners, nutritional products, and educational materials—products that require a great deal of information to sell. Most people involved in direct selling are independent agents who buy the merchandise from the company and then resell it to consumers.

DOOR-TO-DOOR SALES

Although door-to-door selling is popular in some countries such as China, it is declining in North America, because few women are home during the day and those who are home are reluctant to open their doors to strangers. Companies that used to rely on door-to-door sales have had to adapt their retailing strategies. Finding that many of its female customers work during the day, Avon now sells to them at the office during lunch and coffee breaks. Similarly, Tupperware features rush-hour parties at the end of the workday and finds that about 20% of its sales come from outside the home. An employee of Mary Kay cosmetics, which has also adopted this strategy, offered another explanation for its success: "Working women buy more in the office because they are not looking at the wallpaper that needs replacing. They feel richer away from home."[86]

PARTIES AND NETWORKS

About three-quarters of direct sales are made in the consumer's home, sometimes at a home shopping party, at which a company representative makes a sales presentation to a group of people who have gathered at a friend's.[87] People who attend may get caught up in the "group spirit," buying things they would not normally buy if alone.[88] This technique is called a **party plan system**.

Another form of non-store retailing, epitomized by the Amway Company, is **multilevel marketing**, or network marketing. In this system, a master distributor recruits other people to become distributors as well. Master distributors sell the company's products to the people they entice to join and receive commissions on all the merchandise sold by the people they recruit. Despite the growing popularity of this technique, some network systems are illegal. They are really **pyramid schemes** in which the initial distributors profit by selling merchandise to other distributors, and very little product ever gets bought by consumers.[89]

TELEMARKETING

Telemarketing is direct selling conducted over the telephone. It is definitely easier and less expensive than door-to-door selling. Recent surveys indicate that one out of six North Americans felt it difficult to resist a telemarketing pitch; on the other hand, about one in three complained of feeling cheated at one time by a telemarketer.[90]

Automatic Vending

Coin-operated vending machines are a tried-and-true way to sell convenience goods, especially cigarettes and drinks. These machines are appealing, because they require minimal space and personnel to maintain and operate.

✳✳✳
direct mail A brochure or pamphlet offering a specific product or service at one point in time.

✳✳✳
direct selling An interactive sales process, in which a salesperson presents a product to one individual or a small group, takes orders, and delivers the merchandise.

✳✳✳
party plan system A sales technique that relies heavily on people getting caught up in the "group spirit," buying things they would not normally buy if alone.

✳✳✳
multilevel marketing A system in which a master distributor recruits other people to become distributors, sells the company's product to the recruits, and receives a commission on all the merchandise they sell.

✳✳✳
pyramid schemes An illegal sales technique, in which the initial distributors profit by selling merchandise to other distributors, with the result that consumers buy very little product.

✳✳✳
telemarketing A sales technique, in which direct selling is conducted over the telephone.

good OR bad DECISION?

When it is abused, telemarketing embodies the most negative aspects of marketing. Even though some consumers are open to telephone sales pitches, many resent being interrupted at home. Sometimes, it's hard to tell the difference between a legitimate sales call and a scam. Many telemarketing scams hawk fishy credit card deals, scholarships, and vacation packages. Nearly 20% of scams involve the sale of vitamins.[91] Many governments are now considering enacting tougher regulations on the telemarketing industry. Should marketers be allowed to "break and enter" into consumers' homes via the telephone to push their products, even if what they are selling is legitimate? What rules would you impose on telemarketing?

✱ ✱ ✱

direct-response TV Television programming, such as informercials or shopping channels, that elicits direct orders for products from the viewing public.

Some of the most interesting innovations are state-of-the-art vending machines, which dispense everything from Ore-Ida french fries to software. French consumers can even purchase Levi's jeans from a machine called Libre Service, shown in Exhibit 15.13, which offers the pants in 10 different sizes. Due to their frenetic lifestyles, the Japanese are avid users of vending machines. These machines, a cluster of which can be found on many street corners, dispense virtually all of life's necessities, plus many luxuries people in other countries would not consider obtaining from a machine. The list includes jewellery, fresh flowers, frozen beef, pornography, business cards, underwear, and even the names of possible dates.[92]

In general, vending machines are best suited to the sales of inexpensive merchandise and food and beverages. Most consumers are reluctant to buy pricey items from a machine. New vending machines may spur more interest, however, as technological developments such as video kiosk machines that let people see the product in use, the ability to accept credit cards as payment, and inventory systems that signal the operator when malfunctions or stockouts occur loom on the horizon.

Direct-Response Television

Almost as long as there has been television there has been **direct-response TV** (DRTV)—television programming that is intended to elicit direct orders, typically by phone, from viewers. Where the original DRTV pioneers were entrepreneurs who couldn't get their products into traditional channels, their approach of selling products on TV was so successful that it soon became mainstream for more established companies and brands.[93] DRTV is still an important marketing tool for two reasons: It works and it is measurable, so you can tell how well it is working.

INFOMERCIALS

Infomercials are half-hour or hour-long commercials that resemble a talk show but are actually intended to sell something. Although infomercials still carry a low-class, sleazy stereotype, more than 40 major North American companies have used this format, including heavyweights from American Airlines and Apple Computer to Visa and Volkswagen. A survey by *TV Guide* found that 72% of respondents have watched at least one infomercial, and

Exhibit 15.13

Levi Strauss sells jeans in vending machines to French consumers.

Real People, Real Decisions
How it worked out at IKEA

Göran Carstedt and his colleagues chose Option 3. They decided to enter the Carson Mall but only on the condition that the mall owner do a major renovation. Mall management agreed to spend $12 to $17 million to do a complete renovation of the centre, which was renamed Southwest Plaza. This meant installing roof windows to bring in natural light, redoing the exterior facade, and adding a fourth department store, an additional 50 000 square feet of retail space, and a multiscreen movie theatre.

This IKEA store is now the second largest in LA. Building on its LA success IKEA opened stores in Seattle and San Diego and plans to enter San Francisco soon. Göran Carstedt has now left IKEA to lead the formation of the Society for Organizational Learning.

about one-third made a purchase as a result.[94] Top-selling categories include cosmetics, self-improvement products, fitness products, kitchen appliances, music, and videos. And this is hardly just a North American phenomenon—DRTV sales in Japan of $1.5 billion per year equal those in the United States.[95]

HOME SHOPPING NETWORKS

Television channels that exist solely to sell products let shopping junkies indulge themselves without leaving their living rooms.[96] In Canada, shoppers can frequent the Home Shopping Channel; the US equivalent is QVC, which sells products at the rate of $39 per second around the clock. To date, the typical North American home shopping customer is in a low-income bracket, and the most frequently purchased product is inexpensive jewellery.

Chapter Summary

1. Define retailing and describe how retailers evolve over time.

   Retailing is the process by which goods and services are sold to consumers for their personal use. The wheel-of-retailing hypothesis suggests that new retailers compete on price and, over time, become more upscale, leaving room for other new, low-price entrants. The retail life cycle theory suggests retailing institutions are introduced, grow, reach maturity, and then decline. Three factors that motivate retailers to change are changing demographics, technology, and globalization.

2. Classify retailers by their selection of merchandise.

   Retailers can be classified according to the type of products sold, whether they carry items having high or low gross margins and high or low turnover rates. Merchandise assortment is described in terms of breadth and depth, which refer to the number of product lines sold and the amount of variety available for each.

3. Understand the importance of store image to a retail positioning strategy, and explain some of the actions a retailer can take to create a desired image in the marketplace.

   Store image is the result of many elements working together to create a desirable shopping experience and to ensure that shoppers view a store favourably compared to the competition. Colour, lighting, scents, furnishings, and other design elements, or atmospherics, are used to create a "feel" for a store environment. Atmospheric decisions include: store layout, which determines traffic flow and influences the desired customer behaviour in the store; the use of store fixtures and open space; the use of sound to attract (or repel) certain types of customers; and the use of colour and lighting that can influence customers' moods. The number and type of store personnel are selected to complement the store image. Pricing of products sold in the store contributes to shoppers' perceptions. A store's location also contributes to its image: Major types of retail locations include central business districts, shopping centres, free-standing retailers, and non-traditional locations such as kiosks.

4. Describe the opportunities and barriers to e-tailing.

Online shopping allows the Web surfer to efficiently collect information about a range of product alternatives and buy a product from retailers, regardless of their geographic location. Some issues that need to be resolved include the security of online transactions, the desire of many shoppers to handle a product before buying, the resistance of some online retailers to opening up their inventories to automated price comparisons, and the hesitation of some retailers that operate actual stores to cannibalize sales by offering items over the Internet.

5. Describe the major forms of non-store retailing.

Non-store retailing includes e-tailing and direct marketing, such as traditional mail-order shopping, direct-selling, vending machines, direct-response television shopping, and on-line shopping. Mail-order retailing includes catalogues and direct-mail advertisements sent to consumers. Popular direct selling techniques include the home shopping party, door-to-door sales, and telemarketing. The growing electronic marketplace uses both the power of more traditional television infomercials and home shopping networks and the growing popularity of computer online services and the World Wide Web.

Chapter Review

Marketing Concepts: Test Your Knowledge

1. How does the wheel-of-retailing hypothesis explain changes in retail outlets? How does the retail life cycle concept explain these changes?

2. What are some environmental trends that will have a major impact on the future of retailing?

3. How are gross margins and turnover rates used to classify retailers? Describe the differences in merchandise assortments for convenience stores, supermarkets, specialty stores, discount stores, department stores, and hypermarkets.

4. What is meant by store atmospherics? How can the elements of atmospherics be used to increase the store's success? How are store personnel a part of store image?

5. What are the different types of store locations? What are the advantages and disadvantages of each?

6. How do retail store location planners evaluate potential store sites?

7. Describe the major types of non-store retailing.

8. Describe some of the changes that are expected in the growing electronic marketplace.

9. Explain the different types of direct marketing.

Marketing in Action: Applying What You've Learned

1. All your life you've wanted to be an entrepreneur and own your own business. Now you're ready to graduate and you've decided to open a combination coffee shop and bookstore in a location near your college or university. You know that to attract both the student market and other customers from the local community, you will have to carefully design the store image. Develop a detailed plan that specifies how you will use atmospherics to create the image you desire.

2. In your job with a marketing consulting firm, you often are asked to make recommendations for store location. Your current client is a local caterer that is planning to open a new retail outlet for selling take-out gourmet dinners. You are examining the possible types of locations: the central business district, a shopping centre, free-standing entity, or some non-traditional location. Outline the advantages and disadvantages of each type of location. Present your recommendations to your client.

3. Assume you are the vice-president of marketing for Elegant Evenings, a chain of women's lingerie stores. Your firm sells exclusive designer lingerie in boutiques located in shopping

malls across the country. With a changing marketplace, your firm is considering whether there is a need to develop some type of non-store retailing operation. You consider the opportunities for marketing your products via

a. catalogues

b. direct mail

c. television infomercials

d. television home shopping network

e. World Wide Web

Outline the pros and cons of each for your firm.

4. Assume you are the director of marketing for a national chain of convenience stores. Your firm has about 80 stores located in central and eastern Canada. The stores are fairly traditional both in design and in the merchandise they carry. Because you want to be proactive in your marketing planning, you are concerned that your firm may need to consider significant changes due to the current demographic, technological, and global changes in the marketplace. You think it is important to discuss these things with the other executives at your firm. Develop a presentation that includes:

a. a discussion of the demographic changes that will affect your stores.

b. a discussion of the technological changes that will affect your stores.

c. a discussion of how global changes may pose problems and opportunities for your organization.

d. your recommendations for how your firm might meet the challenges faced in each of these areas.

Learning More by Experience: A Mini-Project

This project is designed to help you understand how store atmospherics play an important role in consumers' perceptions of a retail store.

1. Select two retail outlets where students in your college or university are likely to shop. Try to select two stores that have different images but that sell the same types of products.

2. Visit each store and write down a detailed description of its atmosphere—colours, materials used, types of displays, lighting fixtures, product displays, store personnel, and so on.

3. Survey some of the students in your college or university. Develop a brief questionnaire asking about the perceptions of the two stores you are studying. Include questions about the quality of merchandise, prices, competence and friendliness of the store personnel, the attitude of management toward customer service, and so on. What is the "personality" of each store?

4. Develop a report of your findings. Compare the description of the stores with the results of the survey. Explain how the different elements of the store atmosphere create each store's image.

Real People, Real Surfers: Exploring the Web

Many retailers now have Internet sites. The Hudson's Bay Company (www.hbc.com/bay), Sears (www.sears.ca), and Future Shop (www.futureshop.com) are three examples. Explore these or other retailer sites and answer the following questions.

1. Describe each retailer's Web site. What information is available on each site? How easy was each to navigate? What information did you find interesting and useful on each site? What did you find that you didn't expect to find at a retailer site? What was lacking at each site?

2. How do the retailers' Web sites communicate the image or personality of their stores? How are they alike? How are they different? If you had no information except that available on the Web, would you know what types of products are sold, whether the products sold are expensive, prestige products or low-priced products, and what types of consumers each retailer is attempting to attract to their stores? How does each site use graphics or other design elements to represent the "setting" as retailers do in their stores? How do they communicate the type of consumer they consider to be their primary market?

3. Why do you think customers visit a retailer's Web site? To find a local store? To learn about career opportunities? To find out whether a certain product is available in the store? To shop online? Or for some other reason? How well does each site you explored satisfy these customer needs?

4. What recommendations would you make to each retailer to improve its Web site?

Gap

Gap is unlike any other North American retailer. Under the leadership of chief executive Mickey Drexler, Gap has gone from just another retail chain to become one of the most recognized North American and global brands, and is as well known as Gillette, Coca-Cola, and Disney. Drexler's challenge is to keep the momentum going. Once the underdog icon of "invisible cool," the Gap is now perceived by many as simply being another mega-retailer. Earnings have recently fallen short of market expectations, putting downward pressure on the Gap's share value. While annual sales are around US $9 billion and a new store opens almost every day, there is pressure to recapture the Gap's "mojo," or source of magic.

In 1969, Donald and Doris Fisher opened the first Gap store (as in "generation gap") in San Francisco, where they sold Levi's jeans and discounted record albums and tapes to lure customers. After Drexler came on board in 1976, Gap grew from a meagre 200 outlets to over 4100 stores worldwide and 224 in Canada under such brand names as The Gap, Baby Gap, Old Navy, and Banana Republic. They recently bought a 738 000-square-foot warehouse in Brampton, Ontario, to support the launch of up to 30 Old Navy stores in Canada.

Experts in retailing suggest that Drexler has more influence on North American style than any other individual, including such designers as Ralph Lauren and Liz Claiborne. Drexler believes clothing should be simple, not complicated. Although most clothing companies want their clothing to symbolize something important such as money, power, class, virility, sex, privilege, competitiveness, or worldliness, Gap tries to be ordinary, unpretentious, and understated.

But Gap's success is due to more than just clothing design. Gap does a better job of marketing itself than the competition. Great advertising, for example, did much to establish Gap's image. The "Individual of Style" ad campaign included black and white photos of Kim Basinger in an oversized white Gap men's shirt and pearls and Dizzy Gillespie in a black Gap mock turtleneck. The "Who Wore Khakis?" campaign centred on extraordinary people and reminded consumers that "Ernest Hemingway Wore Khakis" and "Pablo Picasso Wore Khakis." In 1997, Gap introduced a television ad campaign for its Easy Fit jeans, starring Lena Horne and LL Cool J. Such advertising successfully convinced millions of consumers from modern art aficionados to rap fans that they should wear the same clothes that these cultural icons wear. The recent "Khakis Swing" and "Khakis A Go-Go" ads had energy, movement, and excitement that made people want to wear Gap clothes. Recently, however, the Gap has gone away from its traditional positioning. The campaigns "Everybody in Khakis," "Everybody in Vests," and "Everybody in Cords" struck a discord with viewers: They seemingly reminded them that "everybody" wears Gap clothing—and that's not particularly cool.

Much of Gap's past success can be attributed to continuously innovating to meet changing customer needs. Gap Kids, begun in 1986 when Drexler couldn't find good-looking clothes for his son, was an instant success. In 1994, when discount shopping in stores such as Zellers and Target (US) was the hot growth area in retailing, Drexler launched Old Navy stores in the US, another great Gap success story. In 1998, Old Navy cosmetics were introduced and Gap-to-go delivered khakis and 21 other basic Gap items to customers in New York offices, just like pizza. Gap Online started in 1997. Banana Republic now mails out catalogues. In fall 1998, GapBody stores that sell underwear, pyjamas, fragrances, soaps, and candles were opened. Some of Drexler's ideas have been less successful. For example, GapShoes opened in 1992 but closed two years later. Gap bought the Banana Republic chain in 1983, but the chain nearly went under in the late 1980s when safari clothing went out of style. Overall, Drexler managed to grow the company from $1.93 billion in sales in fiscal 1990 to $11.64 billion in fiscal 1999.

Today Gap is facing a financial and positioning crisis brought on by a slew of imitators like Levi's Dockers brand and American Eagle Outfitters, another top teen retail chain that has recently entered the Canadian market. In response to increased competition Gap tried to appeal to a younger, even fringe, audience with the introduction of far-out fashion elements like oddly

MARKETING IN ACTION

printed tees and bright hues. This confused shoppers who could already get cheerful and cheap designer imitations from Old Navy, Le Chateau, and other youth oriented chains. Net income across Gap companies fell 96% in the first nine months of fiscal 2001 (ended November 3) and by the end of December the Gap chain had recorded 19 straight months of declining sales. The question facing Drexler and Gap executives is what to do now.

Maureen Atkinson, a retail analyst with J.C. Williams Group of Toronto, suggests that the Gap needs to clearly differentiate the Gap and Old Navy brands. "Essentially, they've over-expanded with a product that's not well-differentiated. They have all these different units, [Gap, Old Navy and Banana Republic], which are very similar, except for their price structure...The question is, why would I buy a turtleneck at the Gap and pay $25 for it, when I could buy something that looks the same to the average consumer at Old Navy for $15?...What they have to do is not just sort out the customer target, but also their merchandise, which has to be more distinctive...When you have problems, there's a tendency to take fewer risks, and to go back to the things that were successful before. They go back to the same old, but that doesn't work."[97]

Andy Macaulay, a partner and planner with the marketing communications firm Zig of Toronto suggests that "basics with a bit more fashionability is where they should be. Part of their magic, before they caught this cold, was that they provided basics with an edge. The product had enough fashionability just to be distinctive...They've got a strong property and, of course, it needs to evolve with fashion changes, but I don't think it's fundamentally broken. My advice would be to continue to capitalize on its distinctiveness."

Pascale LeBlanc, a partner with youth-focused creative and communication consultant Big Orbit of Toronto, also recommends changes in Gap's marketing and merchandising strategy, suggesting that "the Gap has suffered from marketing too broadly. They seem to believe that they can be everything to all people. Most of their financial problems are self-inflicted mainly due to cannibalizing the Gap with Old Navy...They should stick with selling basics like jeans and cool T-shirts instead of trying to offer everything for [every] demographic. Their [marketing] messages do not seem to reach out to the audience but always ask them to look inward at their definition of the Gap brand. In doing this, they may have lost their grip on their customers."

He further adds, "We believe that Canadian retailers targeting 11- to 22-year-olds should adopt a 'youth boutique, in-store' approach. Today's kids like to shop in a 'youth-approved' environment. Marketing strategies need to consider creating an exciting, modern, urban, customer-friendly environment staffed with people who strongly relate to the target audience. Position the design and implementation of a retail mix to create a positive image of your retail store in the customer's mind. For example, the store design, layout of merchandising, display and visuals must be consistent because they are all a part of communicating the brand image...The in-store ambiance must evolve and react quickly to the changing needs of the target audience. Include a mix of elements, such as visuals that depict young people enjoying an active lifestyle with friends, event/concert billboards, high-tech sound systems, video screens showing the 'live your life' attitude, lounge areas where kids can relax and interact."[98]

Sources: "Gap shares drop 21% on profit warning," *Financial Post*, 4 August 2000: C3; "Old Navy assault will jolt retailers," Canadian Press, 12 December 1999; Nina Munk, "Gap gets it right," *Fortune*, 2 August 1998: 68–82.

THINGS TO THINK ABOUT

1. What is/are the problem(s) facing Mickey Drexler?
2. What factors are important in understanding this problem?
3. What are the alternatives?
4. What are your recommendations for solving the problem?
5. How could Gap implement your recommendations?

Caught Up in the Web

After discovering who its primary customer is, CFS enters the business-to-business market and learns about market segmentation.

Computer Friendly Stuff finds the Web not so friendly, then finds it friendly again.

From the beginning, we were excited about the Internet potential for Computer Friendly Stuff. The demographics were perfect for us: Our customers were computer users, and the Web is made up of computer users. It was almost too good to be true. We had visions of an automated Web site taking worldwide orders 24 hours a day, while we sat around all day watching TV in our PJs.

Fuelling our confidence were some of the built-in advantages of the Internet. One was the purity of the sales demographic. A person who is online is, by definition, a computer user, and thus a potential customer. It was a great fit for us. Another advantage to selling online is that our customers would be able to download a sample of one of our CD-ROMs before deciding to buy. We knew from our earlier market experiences that our products are well received once they are in customers' hands, and here was a way to get to customers quickly and simply. Our margins would be much better online, because overhead is lower. Lastly, the demographic that buys online is the demographic that is most likely to pass along good word of mouth via the Web. A lot of these people are Web junkies just looking for things to talk about online. We had just the product for them.

The funny thing is that the Internet was more of a hindrance than a help to us in the early days. Even though it has vast potential, we underestimated the Internet's complexity and were not prepared for it. In fact, our Internet experience has thus far been most helpful in forcing us to come to terms with an uncomfortable reality about our company: We are much better at creating innovative products than we are at selling them.

We've Found 56 239 Matches for "Computer Bug"

We began our Internet adventure by securing the name www.computerbug.com for our site. We were thrilled that we got it. In retrospect, it was a dumb name for a site. Just try to do a search on "computer bug" and the problem becomes clear—there are already hundreds of thousands of computer bug sites. These are actually sites where people are talking about the computer bugs that screw up their computers, not our fantastic toy that will add meaning to their lives. The result was that people couldn't find our site using search engines. They had to know exactly what they were looking for. We will eventually change the site to something better, like www.computerfriendly.com, but for now, we will just make do.

The next step was to build a really cool site. Incredibly fun, but also incredibly time consuming. Six months later, we did a complete overhaul to make it even cooler. And what happened? We got some orders. In fact, we got just enough orders to be annoying. We found ourselves spending too much time each day taking orders, running credit cards, packaging our product, and shipping. The irony was that we had enough orders to take a big chunk of our day, but not enough to make any money off them or to warrant hiring others to handle them. That was when we realized that we were approaching things incorrectly. We had developed a Web site, but not a Web strategy. By trying to create a presence as Web retailers, we were taking time away from what we were good at, which was creating new products.

We Need an Internet Sales Strategy

A couple of factors explained the initial failure of our Internet venture. One was that in 1996, people were still very uncomfortable giving their credit card information online. That is less of a problem today. A bigger problem was that we didn't market the site. We had not developed any kind of Internet sales strategy.

We knew that we needed outside help, and we got it. Our first step was to research how other small companies achieved success online. We understood that, at

least initially, we would not be able to imitate the model of superstar companies like Amazon.com, because we lacked the capital. Our research pointed us to three distinct selling strategies. We had tried the first, which was to operate our own site, taking full responsibility for selling, marketing, and shipping our products.

The second strategy was to use a site that sells our product but requires us to ship our products to customers. This arrangement has been successful for us. One of the companies that we have partnered with is Gift Tree (www.gifttree.com). Gift Tree has been successful in helping small companies that, like us, lack the marketing muscle to get people to their sites. In exchange for a set percentage, they list products on their site. We provide all product shots and product descriptions. This has been a financial success for us, but it has left very little time for lounging around in our PJs. First, most of the orders from Gift Tree are single units. Second, we have to ship the units ourselves, which is time consuming and costly. As a result, we give Gift Tree a smaller percentage than a normal retailer.

We also learned a few things about Internet customer behaviour from our Gift Tree experience. We can always tell when our product is listed on the front page of Gift Tree's site, because our number of orders increases dramatically. This tells us that people don't like to go very far into the site to find something. The closer you are to the front, the better your chances, just like in the old *Yellow Pages*. It goes to show that the more things change the more they stay the same.

The third type of Internet sales strategy is similar to retailing in a store. There are sites that purchase items from us, take orders on their site, and ship it themselves. This costs them more, because they have to warehouse the stock, but they have complete control over the level of customer service they provide. For example, if we screw up a Gift Tree order (and we have), we have to resolve the problem. At 911 Gifts, one of our partners in this third approach, the Web reseller is responsible for customer service. We prefer this type of site as it is the easiest for us to supply. We ship out bulk orders, and the site is responsible for selling its stock.

After all of our time and energy, we realized that our site is best used as an online catalogue, not a retail site. We decided to leave that to the experts. Despite our growing sophistication regarding Internet sales, we are still doing less than 10% of our sales on the Internet. But we are steadily improving our performance.

So back to stating the obvious: The Internet is here to stay. Have to do well on the Internet. It's the future. But nothing is easy, especially if you haven't figured out your initial strategy first. As we'll see in the final case, though, we still needed live bodies—a sales force—to help sell our products.

Questions

1. The Internet can be an advertising medium as well as (or rather than) a sales medium. Why do some companies see it this way?

2. Go to the CFS Web site. Has CFS done a good job advertising its product? Why or why not? What would you suggest it does?

3. The Internet can be seen as a product information medium. Go to the CFS Web site and comment on its effectiveness in conveying product information. What are some of the benefits of Computer Bugs and Monitor Morphs, as described in the Web site?

4. Comment on the usefulness of the product name "computer bug" considering the problems that came up with Internet search engines. What product names does the Internet force one to avoid? What are the characteristics of a good product name for the Internet?

5. Should CFS consider advertising for its products on other company Web sites? If so, what sites?

Marketing Plan Questions

Refer to the Sample Marketing Plan in Appendix A as you answer these questions about developing and modifying a marketing plan for CFS.

1. For this year's marketing plan, indicate whether CFS's Internet strategy should emphasize direct or indirect distribution to take advantage of the explosive growth of electronic commerce. Explain how this emphasis affects the company's plans for physical distribution.

2. Looking ahead to next year's marketing plan, what kind of channel conflict could CFS encounter if it signs up a much larger number of Internet retailers to sell its products? Does CFS have sufficient power to become a channel leader on the Internet? Explain your answer.

CBC 🍁 VIDEO CASE 1

DentureBrite

Neophyte business owners Shauna Sailer and Theresa Sulek were discovering the difficulty in securing distribution channels for their product DentureBrite, a battery-powered water bath for dentures. With a warehouse full of product and few orders, the driven pair frantically travelled between California and Toronto trying to build sales.

As many entrepreneurs have learned, even the best ideas don't sell themselves. Small business owners often spend months or years trying to convince retail partners to carry and sell their products. Their expectations are raised as distributors show an interest; only to be disappointed when final purchase orders are not negotiated. Sulek and Sailer stocked a warehouse with $160 000 worth of DentureBrites, based on an anticipated sale to a US drugstore chain, only to see the order cancelled at the last minute. The product was not returnable to the manufacturer in China. In May 1998, the partners found themselves paying inventory costs while trying to convince retailers to stock DentureBrite on their shelves.

With a $19 million denture cleansing market in Canada and a $200 million market in the US, it seemed to Sailer and Sulek that there must be a room for a new innovative product. Although they believed that DentureBrite was a superior denture cleaning system, they needed to convince retailers to give it some shelf space and the opportunity to be sold to consumers. They had to decide whether to focus on Canadian retailers or the larger American chains, such as Target and Walgreens. The latter could potentially garner volume sales, but they were constantly being pressured for shelf space. And DentureBrite was competing against internationally recognized brands, such as Efferdent and Polident, that had established relationships with retailers.

Communication was also an issue. By relying too heavily on retail brokers, the pair had no information on why their product wasn't breaking into the desired markets. They scheduled a meeting with the American brokers who were presenting DentureBrite to retailers, hoping that they would place on order. Because shelves are fully stocked, the brokers must convince store buyers that sales of DentureBrite will exceed others products that could occupy the same space. However, because campaigns in the US and Canada were not coordinated, the product's image was weakened. With their Canadian broker, Sailer and Sulek discovered that they needed to better define expectations and sales targets. The pair were finding themselves doing much of what a distributor should do, such as checking product on shelves, instead of focusing on running the business. After only one year, they decided to release their Canadian broker and move to a Toronto-based national firm.

Unlike the old broker, the new firm had its own sales representatives and did not rely on contracting out the regional sales. The new distribution company was working much better, with aggressive sales pitches to such Canadian companies as Zellers and Sears. Sulek and Sailer also managed to get some mail-order catalogue orders to use up some of the warehoused products. By the end of the year, the company was starting to look like it would overcome its challenges and become a success story.

Questions

1. What challenges did the DentureBrite entrepreneurs face with their retail brokers?
2. What tactics could the competition use to make it difficult for DentureBrite to succeed?
3. What distribution channels were working for DentureBrite? Identify other possible distribution channels and discuss how they might affect sales.
4. Do you think DentureBrite should have different campaigns in Canada and the US?
5. What could the company do to increase the likelihood of capturing shelf space in the large American chains?

Source: This case was prepared by Hillary Samson and is based on "Denture Queens," *Venture* #701 (27 October 1998).

CBC VIDEO CASE 2

Risk-E-Business

Retailers such as Chapters Inc., Future Shop, and The Bay are spending millions of dollars to offer online shopping experiences to Web-savvy consumers. But, other than unsupported claims by some of the larger US chains, no one knows whether money can be made in e-tail businesses, and setting one up can cost a fortune. Making money may not be the only objective: Interactive Internet sites can help build brand equity and develop closer, more intimate ties with consumers. Danier Leather, for example, uses a digital video camera to record behind-the-scenes looks at their traditional advertising photo shoots. This material—outtakes, the actual shoot, and interviews with the models and photographers—is displayed on its Web site, so that interested consumers can feel they are part of the action.

With projections of phenomenal Internet growth, retailers—both large and small—face competitive pressure to develop an online presence and e-tail sales. They all want in, but not at any cost. David Pecaut of the Boston Consulting Group cautions that "there is enormous range in what it costs to go on line. You'll see small retailers, some of them start to put up websites for under a hundred thousand dollars and begin to sell products on line, shipping one and two at a time via United Parcel Service or something like that. But for the bigger retailers it can be very expensive."

Chapters has spent over $22 million on developing Chapters Online. "It really is an amazing misconception, I think, by most people who are not in e-commerce, that it's two guys in a garage," says Larry Stevenson, CEO of Chapters. "I think that what we are trying to do is to make sure that we are the Canadian leader in e-tailing. And the way to do that is to spend enough to be there." Start-up costs for technology, credit card capabilities, security features, the Web site itself, and staffing were over $8 million, and, as we saw in Chapter 14, Chapters had to create a completely new distribution channel. To tell people where to find the Web site, they spent $3.7 million on start-up advertising. All these expenses, and Chapters isn't predicting that they will make any money on the Internet any time soon.

Not everyone has deep pockets and patient investors. Danier Leather is considering one of three IBM e-business solutions, at a cost of $250 000 to $450 000. But they are worried that IBM sales projections are optimistic and ongoing operating costs may be underestimated. Jim Carroll, Internet and e-commerce author, thinks that Danier may be deeply disappointed by its Internet sales: "They will discover that still the majority of people are gonna want to buy leather products in a real store because they want to try it on and see that it fits." But Jeffery Wortsman, CEO of Danier Leather, doesn't think they have much choice: Consumers are demanding service in three retail channels—stores, catalogues, and the Internet. The challenge will be to limit the risk.

Questions

1. If e-commerce is so risky, why are many large and small retailers getting into it?
2. Why might e-commerce be more suited to a lingerie company like La Senza?
3. Why do large companies need to invest so much more in e-commerce technology and systems than small companies?
4. Based on your understanding of e-commerce, what types of firms are likely to show a profit in their e-tail activities?

Source: This case was prepared by Brock Smith and is based on "E-commerce: Retail's Risky Venture?" *Venture* #723 (5 October 1999).

16

Integrated Marketing Communications and Relationship Management

When you have completed your study of this chapter, you should be able to

CHAPTER OBJECTIVES

1. Explain integrated marketing communications and its implementation, and why some marketers resist it.

2. List, describe, and contrast the elements of the communications mix.

3. Explain the steps involved in developing a communications plan.

4. Explain the philosophy and practices of relationship marketing.

5. Explain the role of databases in facilitating marketing communications and relationship management.

Real People, Real Decisions ✔ ✘

Meet David Edward
A Decision Maker at Cormark Communications

As president of Cormark Communications, David Edward leads a team of marketing professionals who practise integrated marketing communications. Cormark Communications is a full-service agency, with offices in London, Toronto, and Calgary. It is a member of Maxxcom, a communications holding company, which has created the fourth largest advertising network in Canada. Cormark provides communications counsel, strategic planning, advertising, promotion, and direct marketing to a diverse client base in the financial services, life sciences, agriculture, business-to-business, packaged goods, and retail sectors. Cormark's success is built on its people, attitude, and philosophy—exemplified by their mission of "doing great work, making a fair and reasonable profit and having fun." One of Cormark's major clients is Pfizer Animal Health, headquartered in London, Ontario.

After earning a BBA from Wilfrid Laurier University, Edward gained 16 years of agency management experience

with Ogilvy & Mather, Saatchi & Saatchi, and Grey Canada, managing such clients as Toyota, British Airways, SmithKline Beecham, American Express, and Effem Foods. In addition to his presidential duties, Edward takes an active role in the strategic management of Pfizer and other key clients. The Cormark Pfizer Animal Health Team also includes Kingsley Snelgrove and Sandy Watt: Snelgrove is a vice-president account director with 11 years of client service experience, 20 years of senior agricultural marketing management experience, and a BSc (Agriculture) from the University of Guelph; Watt, the account director on the Pfizer Companion Animal Division business at Cormark, has 12 years of agency management experience working at MacLaren McCann, Leo Burnett, and Young & Rubicam for major clients like Unilever, Kraft Canada, Pillsbury, Kodak, and Hostess Frito-Lay.

Tailoring Marketing Communications to Customers

UPS Canada
www.ups.com/canada

❋ ❋ ❋
promotion The coordination of a marketer's communications efforts to influence attitudes or behaviour toward a product or service.

❋ ❋ ❋
marketing communications Informing consumers and customers about the relative value of products, and developing trust and other relational bonds that facilitate ongoing exchange relationships.

David Edward knows that to reach customers, it is essential to get to know them and to talk their language—to communicate well. Sometimes, it's as simple as creating an image for your product or company that matches customer preferences. For example, when research showed that the image of courier service UPS Canada was that of a boring, traditional, and old-fashioned company, they knew that change was needed. A new communications campaign was developed to liven up UPS's image. It focused on their trusted and approachable drivers overcoming all obstacles to deliver their packages, with a tagline of "Moving at the speed of your business." It worked. Customers now use words like "dynamic" and "contemporary" to describe the company.[1]

The coordination of a marketer's efforts to influence attitudes or behaviour used to be commonly called **promotion**. While this term fit well as one of the four Ps of the marketing mix, it implies a one-way (asymmetrical) conversation from marketer to customer. Promotion-oriented companies focus on disseminating favourable information about products and services to mass audiences, or on using research to develop messages to persuade specific, targeted audiences to engage in desired behaviour.[2] Today, technologies ranging from the Internet to digital wireless communication to "smart" products allow marketers to become much more interactive with customers. Many consumers expect to enter into a dialogue with an organization—to be informed, not manipulated, and to be assisted in making decisions, not sold.

Marketing communications is the term now used most frequently to describe the vital roles of informing consumers and customers about the relative value of products, and developing trust and other relational bonds that facilitate ongoing exchange relationships. Marketing communications plays these roles for every type of business, whether its goal is to sell suits to executives or to encourage government to decrease taxes on gasoline. New two-way (symmetrical) approaches to communications strategies help build better relationships—there is greater mutual understanding with two-way ongoing dialogue, more balance in relationships, and consequently greater commitment to brands and companies on the part of consumers and customers that usually results in greater long-term profitability.[3]

Marketing communications can take many forms—quirky television commercials, sophisticated magazine ads, Internet banner ads using the latest interactive technology, glaring billboards, funky T-shirts, or blimps drifting lazily over football stadiums. Some of these communications activities are intended to communicate key messages to target audience. Others provide incentives to buy specific products. In each case, the communication is intended to accomplish specific goals:

- Communications *inform* consumers about new goods and services, and where they can be obtained.[4]
- Communications *remind* consumers to continue using products.
- Communications *persuade* consumers to choose one product over others.
- Communications *build* relationships with customers.

Communications Strategy

Virtually everything an organization says and does is a form of communication. The ads it creates, the packages it designs, even the uniforms its employees wear contribute to the picture people have of the company and its products. In a broad sense, every element of the marketing mix is actually a form of communication. After all, the price of a product, where it is sold, and even the nature of the product itself contribute to the impression of the item in people's minds.

Integrated Communications Strategy

In the past, companies made little effort to coordinate the messages consumers received. An advertising campaign would run independently of a sweepstakes, which in turn had no relation to a series of company-sponsored community events. The consumer, however, does not see these items in isolation but instead as one stream of communication. It was often confusing and ineffective. But let's see how the rules are changing in the marketing communication business.

COORDINATING COMMUNICATIONS MESSAGES

A broader view of the communications process, as shown in Figure 16.1, has spurred the development of an exciting new perspective on communication strategy. As defined by a leading

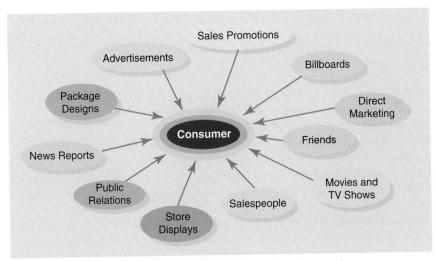

Figure 16.1 The Integrated Marketing Communications Perspective

* * *
integrated marketing communications (IMC) A strategic business process that marketers use to plan, develop, execute, and evaluate coordinated, measurable, persuasive brand communication programs over time with targeted audiences.

researcher in this area, **integrated marketing communications (IMC)** is "a strategic business process used to plan, develop, execute and evaluate coordinated, measurable, persuasive brand communication programs over time with consumers, customers, prospects and other targeted, relevant external and internal audiences."[5] In a survey of marketing executives, IMC was rated the most important factor in marketing strategy—more important than consumer lifestyle changes, economic trends, new retail formats, or globalization.[6]

The IMC philosophy recognizes that customers absorb information about a product or an organization from many sources, not all of which are formal communication messages or even under the marketer's control. It takes the recipients' perspective—anticipating every opportunity in which they see information about the good, service, or organization—and then ensures that each of these exposures communicates the desired message and elicits the intended response.[7] This approach still relies on a variety of communication tools and approaches, but it emphasizes that they must all be used in harmony to reach targeted consumers.

Tourism B.C. follows an IMC strategy in their "Destination Management System"—a low-cost integrated system aimed at impacting consumer buying decisions.[8] They start with identifying consumer needs and interests, then develop programs to motivate consumers involving distribution outlets (including sales offices), a Web site, a call centre, print ads, direct television (DRTV), direct mail, and a Getaway Guide distributed as a 28-page newspaper free-standing insert. The current "BC Escapes" campaign was launched in 1998 using this IMC strategy, targeting high-income, time-compressed consumers in San Francisco, Los Angeles and Chicago with all-inclusive four- or five-day spring getaway offers. In 2000, BC Escapes was expanded to target other US and Canadian cities and attracted nearly 60 000 visitors, generating $43 million in revenue from a $5 million campaign investment. Tourism B.C. attributes their success to the IMC strategy with a direct call to action and a 100% accountable, measurable tracking system.

THE EMERGING IMC PERSPECTIVE

The IMC perspective is still new and evolving. At many companies, it is more of an idea than a reality. However, many advertising agencies, communication companies, and marketing organizations are beginning to develop their own ideas of what an IMC strategy should look like. These approaches tend to share a number of characteristics:

- They focus on customers' need for communications rather than on the message.
- They rely on the use of a customer database or detailed primary research to precisely focus their audiences and messages.
- They strive to send consistent messages using diverse communications vehicles.
- They plan for carefully timed message deliveries to provide a continuous stream of consistent information to recipients.
- They use several communication tools plus product design and packaging to communicate.

Roadblocks to IMC

The idea of coordinating all elements of communication seems so sensible that you may wonder why all communications strategies are not done this way. Unfortunately, many marketers resist the IMC approach or have trouble implementing it.[9]

The approach requires changes in the way marketers plan and implement communication strategies. Many companies are financially driven rather than customer driven, and there is a general resistance to change in organizations. Finally, many executives specialize in one aspect of communication, such as advertising or sales promotion, and are reluctant to branch out into other areas.

The IMC approach can assign relatively more importance to aspects of communication other than advertising. Some executives are reluctant to divert part of their communications budget from glamorous ads to coupons or contests, and some advertising agencies don't want to relinquish this piece of their business to other companies specializing in running sweepstakes or hosting town hall meetings.

Brand managers and associate brand managers develop communication strategies at lower levels after senior planners have already developed the larger marketing strategy. But the IMC approach requires upper-level management to view other aspects of the marketing mix, such as packaging or pricing decisions, as part of the communication strategy. A successful IMC approach requires a company-wide commitment, from the CEO down, to putting the customer first and communicating interactively with customers in many different channels. Some firms find it hard to change their habits.

Some advertising agencies have not bought into the concept of IMC. Since they often do not have the full services required to deliver comprehensive programs, the solutions they offer their clients focus on their area of specialization, such as advertising or public relations.

The Communications Mix

We've discussed integration as key to effective communication strategy. Now let's look at the elements that marketers must coordinate in their IMC efforts. Within the marketing mix, the communication elements that the marketer controls or influences are the **communications mix**. These include advertising, sales promotions, public relations, direct marketing, personal selling, and word-of-mouth. The term *mix* implies that a company's communication strategy is focused on more than one element, so part of the challenge is to combine these different communications tools effectively. Another challenge is to ensure that the communications mix works in harmony with the overall marketing mix, which combines elements of communication with distribution, price, and product decisions to position the firm's offering in people's minds. These other marketing mix elements, after all, also communicate. A product design, for example, can send a powerful message: Honda Motor Company introduced to the Japanese market a model called the City, which it deliberately designed to attract young drivers. The car featured a very high roof that made the City look like a toy. This playful quality appealed to Japan's young consumers, and the design theme was reinforced by fun and carefree communication messages.[10]

***
communications mix The major elements of marketer-controlled communications, including advertising, sales promotions, marketing public relations, direct marketing, and personal selling.

Honda Motor Company
www.honda.com

Communications Mix Elements

Marketing communications can be categorized along two basic dimensions: the type of communication and the source (see Table 16.1). From the customer's perspective, there are two types of communication: marketers are trying to deliver a message about their product or organization or they are providing an incentive to purchase or otherwise change consumer behaviour.[11] The customer identifies the source of these messages or incentives as either the organization or a presumed independent source, such as friends, magazine editorials, or expert opinion. There are also two main methods of transmitting messages and incentives—those that communicate to a mass audience and those that communicate person to person. This latter distinction is becoming blurred, however, as technological advances such as the Internet, smart checkout scanners, and interactive television enable what has traditionally been considered tools of mass media—advertising, sales promotion, and

Table 16.1 Types of Marketing Communications

		Identified as Marketer	Not Identified as Marketer
METHOD OF TRANSMISSION	**Mass Media**	Advertising, Sales promotion	Public relations
	Personal	Personal selling	Word of mouth

public relations—to be used to reach individual consumers with personal appeals. In this section, we'll briefly describe the elements of the communications mix, which are covered in more detail in other chapters. Some of the pros and cons of each element are also presented in Table 16.2.

ADVERTISING

✳ ✳ ✳

advertising Non-personal, paid communication from an identified sponsor, primarily using mass media.

For many, **advertising** is the most familiar and visible element of the communications mix. Advertising is non-personal communication from an identified sponsor using paid space, primarily in mass media. Because it can convey rich and dynamic images, such as the ones in the Dunlop Tire ad in Exhibit 16.1, advertising creates and reinforces a distinctive brand identity. This helps marketers both persuade customers to select their product and build bonds with buyers by presenting them with familiar brand images and logos time after time. Advertising is also useful in communicating factual information about the product or reminding consumers to buy their favourite brand. However, advertising sometimes suffers from a credibility problem, because cynical consumers tune out messages they think are biased or are intended to sell them something they don't need. It can also be very expensive for firms, so they must take great care to ensure their messages are effective.

PERSONAL SELLING

The most personal way to communicate with consumers is by direct interaction, which can occur in person, by phone, or even over an interactive computer link. Personal selling occurs when a company representative comes in direct contact with a customer or group of customers to inform them about a product or service and to encourage them to make a purchase. This type of communication activity is most often seen in the business-to-business

Table 16.2 A Comparison of Elements of the Communications Mix

Communications Element	Pros	Cons
Advertising	The marketer has control over what the message will say, when it will appear, and who is likely to see it.	Often expensive to produce and distribute. May have low credibility and/or be ignored by audience.
Sales promotion	Provides incentives to retailers to support one's products. Builds excitement for retailers and consumers. Encourages immediate purchase and trial of new products. Price-oriented promotions cater to price-sensitive consumers.	Short-term emphasis on immediate sales rather than a focus on building brand loyalty. The number of competing promotions may make it hard to break through the promotional clutter.
Public relations	Relatively low cost. High credibility.	Lack of control over the message that is eventually transmitted, and no gurarantee that the message will ever reach the target. Hard to track the results of publicity efforts.
Personal selling	Direct contact with the customer gives the salesperson the opportunity to be flexible and modify the sales message to coincide with the customer's needs. The salesperson can get immediate feedback from the customer.	High cost per contact with customer. Difficult to ensure consistency of message when it is delivered by many different company representatives. The credibility of salespeople often depends on the quality of their company's image, which has been created by other promotion strategies.

TESTED FOR THE UNEXPECTED. DUNLOP

Exhibit 16.1

This German ad uses bizarre imagery to attract customers to its advertising.

market, but everyone has experienced a door-to-door representative selling Girl Guide cookies or sales clerks in clothing stores asking if they can be of assistance. Salespeople are a valuable communications medium, because customers can ask questions and the salesperson can immediately address objections and relay product benefits.

Personal selling can be tremendously effective, especially for big-ticket consumer items and for industrial products for which the "human touch" and developing tailored solutions is essential. It can be so effective that some marketers, if given a choice, might well abandon other forms of communication and simply dispatch a salesperson to every customer's house or office. Unfortunately, this form of communication is also the most expensive, and it can be difficult to ensure that all salespeople are delivering the same message with the same impact.

DIRECT MARKETING

Direct marketing was introduced in Chapter 15 as a form of non-store retailing. The tools of direct marketing—catalogues, direct mail, the Internet, and direct response television—also play a significant communications role and are part of the communications mix. Some of these tools, such as the Internet and direct mail, are interactive: They can be customized to elicit measurable direct responses from individual customers and allow marketers to provide further customized information based on that response. Use of these interactive tools is called **interactive marketing**. The desired response is typically an order—a first-order response. But other intermediate responses might be desired, such as a request for more information, agreeing to a sales demonstration, or providing feedback on a provided sample—second-order responses. Coupon Radio, a car radio system that is now being tested, lets drivers request more information (e.g., about a band they hear on the radio, or to get names and addresses of retailers that sell an advertised product), all while cruising

✳ ✳ ✳
interactive marketing Two-way communications, in which customized marketing communications elicit a measurable response from individual customers.

along in their cars.[12] It may sound strange, but another kind of second-order response is a request to *not* receive any more information from the company. We assume that a priority of any communication campaign is to get more customers. Interactive marketers sometimes operate with the opposite goal in mind: to *reduce* their customer base. They know that their efforts will be most effective when they are communicating only with customers who are interested in what they have to offer.

Direct marketing typically focuses on short-term, single transaction responses or a set of responses leading to a purchase decision. Database marketing, a related concept that will be discussed later in the chapter, focuses on building ongoing relationships and brand loyalty over time. The secret to effective direct marketing is developing an effective customer database, which contains enough detail in its target market profiles about customer needs, wants, interests, preferences, purchase behaviour, consumption behaviour, and media habits to enable the marketer to tailor messages to very specific categories of consumers. In the case of direct mail, messages are often personalized, not only by using the consumers' name and address, but also by using personal information from the database in the content of the message.

PUBLIC RELATIONS

* * *
public relations Communications strategies to build good relationships with an organization's publics.

Public relations is a set of communication tools that organizations use to establish and maintain contact with the various publics (stakeholders) on whom their success depends. Public relations components of the communications mix seek to nurture a long-term positive relationship between the organization and its customers, suppliers, distributors, employees, shareholders, legislators, and other parties who affect or are affected by the achievement of the organization's objectives, and a positive image for the organization and its products in the long term. Public relations activities include writing press releases, staging events, commissioning surveys of people's feelings about issues related to a product, signing and working with a celebrity spokesperson, and responding to product recalls or other crises. These are all activities that consumers identify with the organization. Public relations efforts can also focus on getting journalists to develop stories about their products: **publicity**. The communication results of publicity efforts are typically identified by consumers as being from an independent source.

* * *
publicity Unpaid communication about an organization appearing in the mass media.

SALES PROMOTION

Sales promotions are programs, such as contests or store demonstrations, that marketers design to build interest in or encourage purchase of a product or service during a specified time period. Unlike other forms of communication that are message oriented, sales promotions are incentives, which are primarily intended to stimulate immediate action, such as coupons, rebates, or bonuses that might stimulate a purchase. Increasingly, however, organizations such as airlines (e.g., Air Canada), grocery stores (e.g., Canada Safeway), and gas stations (e.g., Petro-Canada) are using continuity or loyalty programs, which give discounts, bonuses, or redeemable "points" to members or frequent customers with the intention of building long-term loyalty to the organization. Sales promotions are a form of mass appeal, because they target groups of consumers or retailers to receive special offers or merchandise, invite these people to participate in some activity, or call attention to some event or product feature.

OTHER ELEMENTS

The IMC concept, illustrated in Figure 16.1, suggests that marketers can use many other communications elements to communicate messages and incentives to customers—word-of-mouth communication, brand placement (such as in movies or on TV shows), third-party endorsements (such as Greenpeace recommending an environmentally friendly product), and third-party incentives (such as government subsidies for buying emergency preparedness kits). Marketers don't control third-party endorsements or incentives, but they can influence the third parties through public relations and political lobbying.

Word-of-mouth communication occurs when consumers tell their friends, relatives, or other people about their product experiences. A recommendation from a friend or relative

SPOTLIGHT ON REAL PEOPLE *Will the Real Consumers Please Stand Up!*

Rob Assimakopoulos, Procter & Gamble brand manager for liquid Cheer laundry detergent, spearheaded a new communication tactic in Canada after working on a similar concept in Argentina, called performance advertising. Initially posing as regular shoppers in a retail store, actors suddenly burst into action to perform two-minute, fashion-show–themed skits that promote the idea that "Liquid Cheer loves your clothes as much as you do." "There's a spontaneity and human quality to the concept that just isn't possible with other forms of advertising," says Assimakopoulos.[13]

1. Do you think that this type of communication will be effective, in the short term and in the long term?
2. Who is the target audience for this communication?
3. What are the drawbacks to this kind of communication, and how might they be overcome?

Exhibit 16.2

The Women's Group: Marketing Solutions of Toronto created a national Olay Tell-a-Friend sampling program to encourage word-of-mouth referrals.

can be a powerful influence on the buying behaviour of others. Marketers try to influence positive word-of-mouth by creating positive product experiences for customers, but also through communications. Procter & Gamble, for example, encourages consumers to talk to others about Olay skin products by advertising sales promotions that provide incentives for referrals (see Exhibit 16.2).

Developing a Communications Plan

The marketing manager has to identify the specific combination of communication tools that will meet the company's objectives in the most effective and cost-efficient way. Think of the manager as an artist who must choose just the right blend of "paints" to create a picture of the organization and its products that is pleasing to the public. When crafting such a picture, the manager must make numerous decisions about the best way to blend these elements. To ensure that companies develop an IMC strategy, the smart manager first develops a **communications plan**, a framework for developing, implementing, and controlling the firm's communication activities.[14]

Before we can even start planning, however, we need to review our target market profiles (Chapter 8) and further refine or develop them, as necessary, into **target audiences** for our communications messages. There may be more than one target audience within a target market. For example, if the audiences have different media watching and reading habits,

* * *
communications plan A framework that outlines the strategies for developing, implementing, and controlling the firm's communication activities.

* * *
target audience A highly segmented group of people who receive and respond similarly to marketing messages.

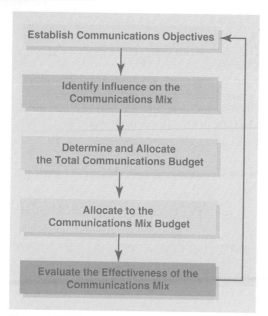

Figure 16.2 Stages in Developing the Communications Plan

live in different geographic areas reached by different TV or radio stations, or are persuaded by different types of information or appeals. To make our communications more effective we need to know their values, attitudes, interests, opinions, and anything else that might affect how they receive, process, store, and use information. This additional information helps marketers to hone their integrated communications strategies to successfully reach consumers with the right message, in the right place, at the right time, and with the right offer.

Toronto-based ICOM Information and Communications Inc. is helping Canadian and American marketers do just that. ICOM collects intelligence through bi-annual mail surveys on 2.2 million households in Canada and 18 million in the US. Each year, they add about one million new names in the Canadian market alone. If a marketer wants a list of Canadian women aged 35 to 50, who garden, use hand cream, and buy books by mail, ICOM can process the request in seconds.[15]

Effectively segmenting the market into target audiences is the first step in the strategic IMC planning process. Just as with any other strategic decision-making process, developing the communications plan includes several additional stages. While a detailed communications plan could be the focus of a whole other textbook, the major stages are shown in Figure 16.2. Let's review each.

Establish Communications Objectives

The point of developing a communications strategy is to connect the marketing plan to consumers, to let them know that the organization has a product to meet their needs in a timely and affordable way. It's bad enough when a product comes along that people don't want or need; perhaps a bigger marketing sin is to have a product that they do want, but fail to let them know about it. That's what communications firms like Cormark Communications work hard to avoid.

As creative as some advertisers or salespeople are, it is rare that any one communication element could cause a consumer who has never heard of a product to become aware of it, prefer it over competing products, and buy it on the spot. An exception is novelty or impulse items, which are bought on a whim. Think of this communications road as an uphill climb (see Figure 16.3)—as the hill gets steeper, the later steps, which are forming a preference for the product and actually buying it, get tougher. During this climb, many people drop out, so only a small proportion of the target market actually reaches the top of the hill to becomes loyal customers. Each part of this path can entail different communications objectives to "push" people to the next level in their decision processes (see Chapters 6 and 7 for a review of decision models).

To understand how this process works, consider how a company would have to adjust its communications objectives as it tries to establish a presence in the market for a new men's cologne called Hunk. Let's say that the primary target market for the cologne is single men, aged 18 to 24, who care about their appearance and who are into health, fitness, and working out. The company would want to focus on some communications methods (such as advertising) and less on others (such as personal selling). These are some steps the company might take to promote Hunk:

- *Create awareness.* The first step is to make members of the target market aware that there's a new brand of cologne on the market. This would be accomplished by simple, repetitive advertising in magazines, on television, and on the radio that feature the brand name. The selection of the specific magazines, television shows and radio stations would be based on knowing what men 18 to 24 years are reading, watching, and listening to. The company might even undertake a *teaser campaign*, in which interest is heightened by not revealing the exact nature of the product (e.g., newspaper ads that simply proclaim, "Hunk is coming!"). The communication objective might be to create an 80% awareness of Hunk cologne among 18- to 24-year-old men in the first two months in the three Prairie provinces.

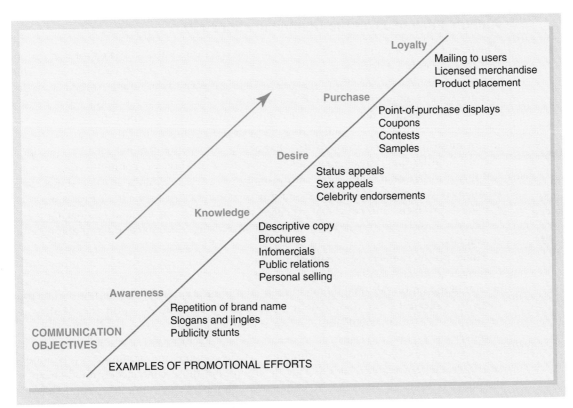

Figure 16.3 Up the Communications Road

- *Inform the market.* The next step would be to provide prospective users with knowledge about the benefits the new product has to offer, that is, how it is positioned relative to other fragrances (see Chapter 8). Perhaps the cologne has a light, slightly mentholated scent that smells vaguely like liniments men use after a workout. Communication efforts would focus on messages and images that emphasize this position. The objective at this point might be to communicate the connection between Hunk and muscle building, so that 75% of the target market becomes interested in the product.

- *Create desire.* The next task is to create favourable feelings toward the product and to convince at least some portion of this group that it is preferable to other colognes they now wear. Communications at this stage might emphasize splashy advertising spreads in magazines, perhaps including an endorsement by a well-known celebrity "hunk," such as Arnold Schwarzenegger. The specific objective might be to create positive attitudes toward Hunk cologne among 50% of the target market and brand preference among 30% of the target market.

- *Encourage trial.* The company now needs to get some of the men who have formed a preference for the product to splash it on. A communications plan might encourage trial by mailing samples of Hunk to members of the target market, inserting scratch-and-sniff samples in bodybuilding magazines, placing elaborate displays in stores that dispense money-saving coupons, or even sponsoring a contest in which the winner gets to have Arnold Schwarzenegger as his personal trainer for a day. The specific objective now might be to encourage trial of Hunk among 25% of 18- to 24-year-old men in the first two months in the three Prairie provinces.

- *Build loyalty.* Now, the company must focus on building loyalty: convincing customers to keep buying the cologne after they've gone through the first bottle. Communications efforts must maintain ongoing communications with current users to reinforce the bond they feel with the product. This will be accomplished with some mix of strategies, including periodic advertising, special events for users, and maybe even the development of a workout clothing line bearing the fragrance's logo. The objective might be to develop and maintain regular usage of Hunk cologne over 18 months among 10% of men from 18 to 24 years old in the three Prairie provinces.

Identify Influences on the Communications Mix

The one perfect communications mix that the manager can pull off the shelf for every good or service does not exist; the mix must be carefully tailored to match each situation. The manager must take into account how various characteristics of the situation are likely to determine which communications tools will work best.

One crucial issue in determining the communications mix is whether the company is relying on a **push strategy** or a **pull strategy**. A push strategy means that the company is seeking to move its products through the channel by convincing channel members to offer them and entice their customers to select these items. In this case, communication efforts will focus on personal selling and sales promotions, such as exhibits at trade shows. The company relying on a pull strategy is counting on consumers to learn about and express desire for its products, thus convincing retailers to respond to this demand by stocking these items. In this case, efforts will focus on media advertising to stimulate interest among end consumers.

Some products need personal selling, whereas others are best sold in other ways. Industrial goods and services, as well as big-ticket consumer items, are more likely to have a greater emphasis on personal selling in their communication mix; whereas it would be too costly for Colgate to hire door-to-door salespeople to promote its toothpaste. Many consumer products, such as cologne, tend to rely more on advertising, especially when the buyer selects the brand because of an image the manufacturer has carefully created for it. Using consumer sales promotion techniques such as coupons and premiums is very important to Procter & Gamble's sales of Tide detergent, but those same tactics would cheapen the image of Rolex or Mercedes. To compete for shoppers' attention, many companies allocate part of their communication efforts to in-store displays and even live product demonstrations to add the personal touch.

The communications mix must vary over time, because some elements are better for accomplishing the marketer's objectives at different points in time than are others. As we saw in the Hunk cologne example, the stage of the product life cycle (see Chapter 10) influences the communications mix.

In the introduction phase, the objective is to build awareness of the product among consumers and to rely on a push strategy. Advertising is the primary communication tool for creating awareness, and a publicity campaign to generate news reports about the new product may help. At this stage, sales promotion can be used to incent consumers to try a new product or service. Distributors are also often given incentives to stock the new item.

In the growth phase, communication efforts must start to focus on communicating specific product benefits. Advertising increases, whereas sales promotions that encourage trial often decline, because people are more willing to try the product without being offered an incentive.

The opposite pattern often occurs during the maturity phase in which many people have tried or used the product. As sales stabilize, the goal is to persuade people to switch from a competitor's product, often when they see few important differences between competitors in a category. Sales promotions, particularly coupons and special price deals, increase.

All bets are off during the decline phase. As sales plummet, the company dramatically reduces spending on all elements of the communications mix. Sales will be driven by the continued loyalty of a small group of users who keep the brand alive until it is sold to another company or discontinued as part of a harvesting strategy (see Chapter 2). The decline in sales further discourages the company from investing any more money in promoting the product, which may be left to wither on the vine. Alternatively, the company may decide to try to revive the brand and dedicate a modest budget to restoring sales.

This was the case with Clorox Canada. Market research found that by the late 1990s, the Glad garbage bags brand was time-worn. Clorox needed to revive its whole line of garbage bags and food protection products: They decided to go "retro" and revived a famous Canadian ad icon, the Man from Glad (see Exhibit 16.3). They took him out of the old suburban setting and placed him in the technical surroundings of a high-performance testing lab, where he watched technicians demonstrate the strength and dependability of Glad products to the slogan "Glad. Depend on it." Canadians watched new Man from Glad tele-

* * *
push strategy Moving products through the channel by convincing channel members to offer them.

* * *
pull strategy Moving products through the channel by building desire for the products among consumers, who convince retailers to stock the items.

Exhibit 16.3

Clorox Canada restored sales of Glad garbage bags by reviving the "Man from Glad" icon.

vision ads, read magazine ads, saw promotions in their local grocery store, and responded very positively. The re-emphasis on the Man from Glad has put Glad close to surpassing its main competitor to take over the top position in the disposable container category.[16]

Determine and Allocate the Total Communications Budget

In an ideal world, setting the budget for communications would be simple: Spend whatever it takes to accomplish the stated objectives. In reality, firms often view communications costs as an expense rather than as an investment that will lead to greater profits. When sales are declining or the company is operating in a difficult economic environment, it is often tempting to cut costs by reducing spending on advertising, sales promotions, and other "soft" activities whose contributions to the bottom line are hard to quantify. When this is the case, marketers must try to justify these expenses to others in the firm.

Economic approaches to budgeting rely on marginal analysis (discussed in Chapter 12), in which the organization spends money on communications as long as the revenues realized by these efforts continue to exceed the costs of the communications themselves. This perspective assumes that promotions are always intended solely to increase sales when, in fact, these activities may have other objectives, such as enhancing a firm's image. Also, the effects of communications often lag. For example, a firm may have to spend a lot on communications when it first launches a product without seeing any return on this investment for quite awhile. Because of these limitations, most firms rely on two budgeting techniques: top down and bottom up.

Top-down budgeting techniques require top management to establish the overall amount that the organization wishes to devote to communication activities, and this amount is then divided among advertising, public relations, and other communication departments.

The most common top-down technique is the **percentage-of-sales method**, in which the communication budget is based on last year's sales or on estimates for this year's sales. The percentage is an industry average provided by trade associations that collect objective information on behalf of member companies. The advantage of this method is that it reminds the organization that spending on communication does result in profits.

Unfortunately, this method implies that sales cause communication outlays, rather than viewing sales as the outcome of communication efforts. As sales drop, firms might be re-

* * *

top-down budgeting techniques Allocation of the promotion budget that is based on the total amount to be devoted to marketing communications.

* * *

percentage-of-sales method A method for promotion budgeting, in which the promotion budget is based on a percentage of either last year's sales or on estimates for this year's sales.

luctant to spend more on communication, when the drop might be due to environmental changes, such as a change in economic conditions or a rival's recent introduction of a new product. If so, cutting communication spending might not help the firm in the long run.

The *competitive-parity method* is simply matching whatever competitors are spending. Some marketers think this approach is justified, saying the decision simply mirrors the best thinking of others in the business. However, this method often results in each player maintaining the same market share year after year. This method also assumes that the same dollars spent on communication by two different firms will yield the same results, but spending a lot of money doesn't guarantee a successful communication. Firms certainly need to monitor their competitors' communication activities, but they must combine this information with their own objectives and abilities.

The problem with top-down techniques is that budget decisions are based more on established practices than on communication objectives. Another approach is to begin at the beginning: Identify communication goals and allocate enough money to accomplish them. That is what **bottom-up budgeting techniques** attempt. For example, some marketers construct a *payout plan* that attempts to predict the revenues and costs associated with a product over several years and matches communication expenditures to this pattern—spending more on communication in the first year to build market share, for example, and then less after the product catches on.

This bottom-up logic is at the heart of the **objective-task method**, which is gaining in popularity. Using this approach, the firm first defines the specific communication goals it hopes to achieve, such as increasing by 20% the number of consumers who are aware of the brand. It then tries to determine what kind of communication efforts it will take to meet that goal. Although this is the most rational approach, it is hard to implement, because it obliges managers to specify their objectives and attach dollar amounts to them. This method requires careful analysis and a bit of "guesstimating."

Allocate the Budget to a Specific Communications Mix

Once the organization has decided how much to spend on communications, it must divide its budget among the elements in the communications mix. Although advertising used to get the lion's share of the communications budget, sales promotions are now playing a bigger role in marketing strategies. As MasterCard's vice-president of promotions observed, marketers who once relied on sales promotions solely to create a short-term response now see them as "a permanent, integral part of the brand."[17] For example, although the typical NASCAR racing car, such as the one in Exhibit 16.4, is covered with the logos of tobacco

✳ ✳ ✳
bottom-up budgeting techniques Allocation of the promotion budget that is based on identifying promotional goals and allocating enough money to accomplish them.

✳ ✳ ✳
objective-task method A promotion budgeting method in which an organization first defines the specific communications goals it hopes to achieve and then tries to calculate what kind of promotional efforts it must take to meet these goals.

Exhibit 16.4

Many companies have shifted their promotional dollars to sponsor sporting events, such as NASCAR racing.

and motor oil companies, other marketers such as Hewlett-Packard, Universal Studios, and even banking giant HSBC (Hong Kong and Shanghai Banking Corp.) are changing their communications mix by sponsoring racing teams. They are joining the race to capture the attention of the 460 million people who watch these events as they are broadcast to 201 countries.[18] Several factors influence how companies divide up the communications pie:

Nestlé
www.nestle.com

- *Organizational factors:* Characteristics of the specific firm influence how it allocates its money. These characteristics are the complexity and formality of the company's decision-making process, preferences within the company for advertising versus sales promotions or other elements in the communications mix, past experiences with specific communications vehicles, as well as the "comfort level" of the firm's advertising and communications agencies with developing different kinds of marketing communications. Nestlé, the giant Swiss company, for example, shifted about 20% of its advertising budget into sales promotion and direct-response efforts over a two-year period after the company determined that its communications dollars would be more effective there.[19]

- *Market potential:* Consumers in some markets will be more likely to buy the product. For example, the marketers of Hunk might find that men in blue-collar occupations would be more interested in the product than men in professional occupations. It makes sense for marketers to allocate more resources to television shows, radio stations, magazines, and other media or communication vehicles that also target people in blue-collar occupations.

- *Market size:* As a rule, larger markets are more expensive places in which to communicate. The costs of buying media (such as spots on local television) are higher in major metropolitan areas. But the sheer density of highly populated areas makes it easier to reach large numbers of consumers at the same time. Advertising is good for mass-market products, whereas personal selling is good for specialized or highly technical products.

Evaluate the Effectiveness of the Communications Mix

The final stage in managing the communications mix is to decide whether the plan is working. The marketer needs to determine whether the communications objectives are adequately translated into marketing communications that are reaching the right target market.

It would be nice if a marketing manager could simply report, "Our new $3 million communications campaign for our revolutionary glow-in-the-dark surfboards resulted in $15 million in new sales!" Unfortunately, it is not so easy. Because there are many factors at work in the marketing environment, other events such as a manufacturing problem encountered by a rival board manufacturer, a coincidental photograph of a movie star riding one of the boards, or even renewed interest in surfing may have caused those new sales instead.

Still, there are ways to monitor and evaluate the company's communications efforts. The catch is that the effectiveness of some forms of communication are easier to determine than others. As a rule, sales promotions are the easiest to evaluate because they occur during a fixed period of time and can be directly tied to sales. Advertising researchers measure brand awareness, recall of product benefits communicated through advertising, and even the image of the brand before and after an advertising campaign. The firm can analyze and compare the performance of salespeople in different territories, though again it is often difficult to rule out other factors that make some sales forces more effective than others. Public relations activities are perhaps the hardest to assess, because they often are intended to result in building favourable relationships over a longer period of time.

EVALUATING INTEGRATED MARKETING COMMUNICATIONS

The IMC perspective takes a broad view of the world: Learning about a good or service comes from many sources, and beliefs develop over time. For these reasons, traditional measurement techniques that focus on the impact of one message at one point in time are not adequate to assess the impact of an entire communications program. Instead, marketers track consumer responses to communications efforts and interactions with the brand and/or company over time.[20] They also conduct research to assess consumer attitudes

Real People, Real Decisions
Decision Time **at Cormark Communications**

The Cormark Pfizer Animal Health Team was given the task of launching a new pharmaceutical product for the treatment of arthritis in dogs. Rimadyl had been successfully launched in the US market the previous year, and Pfizer was looking for similar success in Canada.

The US campaign was a high-budget, multilayered communication campaign that targeted both consumers and veterinarians. Media included television, magazines, direct mail, video production, in-clinic collateral, and veterinary detail pieces. The benchmark had been established, and a successful strategy and campaign had been developed. Cormark's task was to ensure similar success for Pfizer's first major direct-to-consumer launch of a product in Canada. A typical new product launch could take six months to plan and execute—Cormark and Pfizer Canada had 90 days. The agency had three options:

Option 1. Cormark could use existing US materials. The US agency responsible for the launch of Rimadyl was also a member of the Maxxcom network. Cormark had access to all materials, the strategy, and the teams responsible for the US launch. There were no issues in sourcing material. In fact, Cormark's professional relationship with the US agency meant materials could be sourced and used at a savings for the Pfizer Canada client. Cormark used this relationship to understand the strategy and how the materials were used in the marketplace. Given the success in the US and the market similarities, using the US materials would offer several benefits. It would be cost efficient—costs sunk into production of material could be allocated to media spending or other marketing activities to promote the launch—and time efficient—time otherwise spent on the production of communications materials could be spent on other marketing activities, particularly important given the launch timetable. In addition, using the materials would seem to provide some guarantee of success in the Canadian market.

Option 2. Cormark could build on a good thing by taking the best of the available US launch materials and adapting them for use in Canada. Given the variety of materials and the multitude of messages, they could tailor a campaign for Canada that would be based on the "best of the best." This option would ensure a role for the agency in the launch.

Materials could be adapted to address perceived market differences or any differences in consumer behaviour that might exist between Canadians and Americans. Costs would be minimized, as adaptation would be limited to copy platforms and claims. Strategic direction and major sunk production costs would be preserved. In the interests of synergy, North-South relationships, and cost, this option would be a pragmatic way to preserve Canadian identity in the communications.

Option 3. Cormark could create new communications materials for the Canadian launch, thus taking advantage of the learning in the US and building on its success. With the US results in hand and access to the strategy, Cormark could create materials designed to beat the US benchmark and provide Pfizer Canada the opportunity to better the US results with a Canadian success story. A case could be made that market conditions and consumer behaviour were not identical to those in the US launch. In the US, Rimadyl was a first in class product belonging to a new generation of non-steroid anti-inflammatory drugs (NSAIDs) while in Canada Rimadyl was second to market. In addition, there was the important French market to consider in Canada, which often requires separate strategy and communications materials. A "made in Canada" solution would ensure that Cormark and Pfizer Canada controlled the launch and managed the launch process to Canadian standards and Canadian expectations. An investment in new Canadian materials takes a longer-term view of the market in terms of payback and assumes that original work meets the financial hurdles and budget requirements for the launch.

Cormark and Pfizer Canada concluded that all of the options could be achieved in the 90-day launch timetable. They conducted qualitative research with consumers and veterinarians to probe usage and attitudes: The Cormark team concluded that the US strategy and its key messages were effective with Canadian consumers, who were generally similar to their US counterparts; but Canadian veterinarians held different perspectives.

Now, join David Edward and the Cormark-Pfizer decision team. Which option would you choose, and why?

toward the brand and/or organization. Although they don't always accurately predict purchases, customers' attitudes toward an item still are important pieces of information, especially when changes in attitudes are tracked over time. Ideally these pieces of information are collected on an ongoing basis and fed back into a database, where they will be used to update and refine the integrated strategy.[21]

Communications Theory

We've identified the stages to constructing a communications strategy; now we'll explore the specific ways that communications build the paths between producers and consumers.

The Communications Model

With either one-way or two-way communications, the consumer is the focal point: A message is transmitted on some medium from a sender to a receiver who (it is hoped) is paying attention and understands the sender. Regardless of how messages are sent, whether as a hat with a Roots logo on it or a sales pitch from an Aveda representative, messages are designed to capture receivers' attention and relate to their needs. With two-way communications, the receiver sends a message back to the original sender, opening a dialogue between the parties.

Any ways that marketers reach out to consumers, from simple highway billboards to customized messages sent via e-mail to busy executives, are part of the basic communications process. The **communications model** specifies that a number of elements are necessary for communication to occur—a source, a message, a medium, and a receiver. Figure 16.4 shows the communications model.

✳ ✳ ✳
communications model The elements necessary for meaning to be transferred from a sender to a receiver.

ENCODING BY THE MARKETER

It is one thing for marketers to create an idea about a product in their minds and quite another to express that idea so that other people get the same picture. **Encoding** is the process of translating an idea into a form of communication that will convey the desired meaning. Consider how different companies have used a dog to symbolize their brands. Microcell's Fido, a personal communication (PCS) product, has successfully used dogs in its communications to help us draw linkages to their services being as faithful and companionable as "man's best friend" (see Exhibit 16.5). RCA has introduced a second dog (a puppy) into its logo to communicate that they are always innovating—the best of old and new. And Greyhound Bus Lines has successfully used a greyhound dog to convey fast and sleek service. Many other animals have been used by many other companies to convey brand meaning: Can you think of some?

✳ ✳ ✳
encoding The process of translating an idea into a form of communication that will convey meaning.

THE SOURCE

The **source** is the organization or individual sending the message. Marketers must choose a real person (e.g., company president Dave Thomas for Wendy's fast-food restaurants), hire an actor or model (e.g., Canadian country singer Shania Twain for Revlon), or create a character (e.g., Mr. Peanut for Planters Peanuts) who will represent the source.

✳ ✳ ✳
source An organization or individual that sends a message.

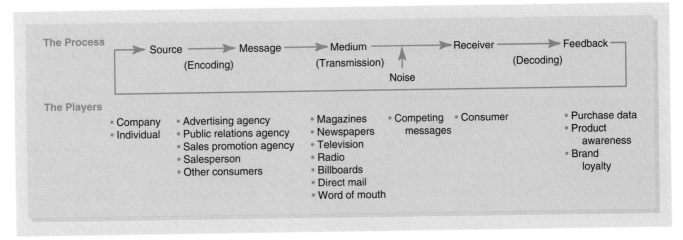

Figure 16.4 The Communications Model

Exhibit 16.5

The name "Fido" and the image of a dog convey the idea that this PCS is faithful and companionable.

THE MESSAGE

The **message** is the actual communication sent from a sender to a receiver. The message should ideally accomplish four objectives (though a single message can rarely do all of these): It should get *attention*, hold *interest*, create *desire*, and produce *action*. These communications goals are known as the **AIDA model**. Here we'll review some different forms the message can take, as well as how the information in the message can best be structured.

Type of appeal: Because there are many ways to say the same thing, marketers must choose what type of appeal, or message strategy, they will use when encoding the message. To illustrate how the choice of an appeal can result in a different communication, compare two strategies selected by rival car companies to promote similar automobiles. A few years ago, Toyota and Nissan both introduced a large luxury car that sold for over $50 000. Toyota's advertising for its Lexus model used a *rational appeal*, which focused on the technical advancements in the car's design. This approach is often effective for promoting products that are technically complex and that are a substantial investment.

In contrast, Nissan's campaign for its Infiniti model used an *emotional appeal*, an attempt to arouse good feelings in the consumer. The new car was introduced with a series of print and television ads, which focused on the Zen-like experience of driving and featured long shots of serene landscapes. As one executive with the campaign explained, "We're not selling the skin of the car; we're selling the spirit."[22]

Structure of the appeal: Many marketing messages are similar to debates or trials, in which someone presents arguments and tries to convince the receivers to shift their opinions accordingly. The way the argument is presented can be important. Most messages merely present one or more positive attributes about the product or reasons to buy it: These are *supportive arguments* or *one-sided messages*. An alternative is to use a *two-sided message*, with both positive and negative information. Two-sided ads can be quite effective, but marketers do not use them very often.[23] A related issue is whether the argument should draw conclusions: Should the ad say only "our brand is superior," or should it add the message that the consumer should buy the brand? The answer depends on the consumer's motivation to think about the ad and the complexity of the arguments. If the message is personally relevant, people will pay attention to it and spontaneously draw their own conclusions. However, if the arguments are hard to follow or the person's motivation to follow them is lacking, it is safer for the ad to make these conclusions explicit.[24]

THE MEDIUM

No matter how the message is encoded, it must then be transmitted via a **medium**, a communications vehicle used to reach members of a target audience. This vehicle can be television, radio, a magazine, personal contact, a billboard, or even a product logo printed on a coffee mug. Ideally the attributes of the product should match those of the medium. For example, magazines with high prestige are more effective at communicating messages about overall product image and quality, whereas specialized magazines do a better job of conveying factual information.[25]

✳✳✳

message The communication in physical form that goes from a sender to a receiver.

✳✳✳

AIDA model The communication goals of attention, interest, desire, and action.

✳✳✳

medium A communications vehicle through which a message is transmitted to a target audience.

DECODING BY THE RECEIVER

Communication cannot occur unless there is a **receiver** to intercept the message. Assuming that the customer is even paying attention—a big assumption in our overloaded, media-saturated society—the meaning of the message is interpreted in light of that individual's unique experiences. **Decoding** is the process whereby a receiver assigns meaning to a message. We hope that the target consumer will decode the message the way we had intended. Effective communication occurs only when the source and the receiver have a mutual *frame of reference*. They must share the same understanding about the world. Grabbing the receiver's attention is more likely if the message source is someone the receiver likes, the message is creatively executed, and the medium is one the receiver typically notices. Furthermore, it helps if the subject of the message is something that is personally relevant. The most enticing shampoo ad in the world probably won't be noticed by a bald man.

To improve the abilities of organizations to focus their communications efforts on receptive receivers, companies are slicing the mass market into smaller and smaller target audiences. In a truly interactive environment, communications efforts will look more like door-to-door selling than like television advertising. Even the Coca-Cola Company, which has long been known for extravagant network productions, is looking for alternatives to big-budget, mass-market commercials. One recent campaign, produced by Creative Artists Agency, has 24 ads in many moods and styles developed for 20 different television networks. These range from one done in a "quick-cut" style for MTV to a *Star Trek*–style spot called "Spaceship," intended to appeal to teenage boys.[26] These changes make sense, because the more recipients can identify with the message, the greater the probability they will reach for a Coke.

NOISE

The communications model also acknowledges that messages often are blocked by **noise**, which is anything that interferes with effective communication. Competing marketing communications cause noise, as do other things happening in the environment that divert the receiver's attention. Marketers try to minimize noise by placing their messages where there is less likely to be distractions or competition for consumers' attention. For example, companies such as Calvin Klein often buy a block of advertising pages in a magazine to be sure the reader sees only pictures of their clothing. Some advertisers such as MasterCard (see Exhibit 16.6) are now using black and white ads in colour magazines or on television to break through the noise.

FEEDBACK

To complete the communications loop, the source receives **feedback**, or reactions, from receivers. These reactions to the message help the marketer gauge the appeal's effectiveness and fine-tune it. Obtaining feedback reminds us of the importance of conducting marketing research to verify that a firm's strategies are working. The area of feedback is where newer symmetrical communications techniques based on IMC outperform the traditional asymmetrical approaches. By listening to the feedback provided by consumers and

***
receiver The organization or individual that intercepts and interprets the message.

***
decoding The process by which a receiver assigns meaning to the message.

***
noise Anything that interferes with effective communication.

***
feedback Receivers' reactions to the message.

tickets:
$45

programs:
$11

binoculars:
$160

a real live elvis sighting:
priceless

there are some things money can't buy.   **MasterCard**   for everything else there's MasterCard.

www.mastercard.ca

Exhibit 16.6

MasterCard's "Priceless" campaign uses black and white print and television ads to break through the noise of colour images.

customers, organizations can be more responsive to the information needs of consumers and develop closer and stronger relationships with them. Developing these relationships, seen as increasingly important, is the focus of the remainder of the chapter.

Relationship Marketing

✳✳✳

relationship marketing The philosophy and practice of developing long-term relationships with key stakeholders.

Marketers are increasingly recognizing that, in addition to other marketing mix decisions, they need to manage relationships with customers, suppliers, distributors, employees, and other key stakeholders, not just communicate with them. In fact, many would argue that forging and sustaining long-term relationships is the only source of sustainable competitive advantage, as strong ties or bonds between an organization and its customers and other key stakeholders are difficult for competitors to break.[27] **Relationship marketing** is the philosophy and practice of developing long-term relationships with key stakeholders. It recognizes that not all stakeholders and customers are of equal strategic importance to the organization and that the commitment and loyalty of key stakeholders needs to be cultivated, nurtured, developed, and protected. This is accomplished by managing all the interactions a customer has with an organization. Relationship marketing is consistent with the underlying philosophy of IMC. However, it goes beyond integrating and coordinating communications to key stakeholders, and focuses on integrating and coordinating all of the experiences stakeholders have with an organization to develop relational bonds or ties.

Relational bonds of trust and commitment translate into profit. In business-to-business marketing contexts, 20% of customers often present 80% of sales and sometimes more than 100% of a company's profits (they lose money on other customers). In both business-to-business and consumer marketing contexts, it is significantly less expensive to keep a customer (or a supplier or distributor) than it is to earn the business of a new one, or to win back the business of a customer or other stakeholder who has left. In addition, customers and other stakeholders in strong relationships may be less price sensitive, recognizing the time, effort, and expense required to have their needs understood and met elsewhere. For these reasons and the difficulty competitors face in convincing loyal customers, suppliers, and distributors to switch from strong established relationships, relationships are a strategic asset of an organization.

✳✳✳

customer relationship marketing (CRM) Relationship marketing focused on delivering customer satisfaction and improved customer retention.

Relationship marketing to customers is called **customer relationship marketing (CRM)**. CRM views customers as key assets of an organization, who represent a stream of future income and profitability. CRM focuses on delivering customer satisfaction and improved customer retention by prioritizing customers based on their economic and other value to the organization and managing all of the interactions that the organization, its people and its products have with the customer. This requires learning about customers, opening two-way communication, providing customized solutions, tracking the interactions, providing a common, consistent, and seamless face to the customer, and developing systems for disseminating customer information throughout an organization. Such systems are particularly important so that employees, whether in marketing, customer service, accounting, or another point of customer contact, understand the history that the company has with that customer and can further build the relationship from that foundation. CRM is becoming such an increasingly popular business philosophy that the software systems used as the backbone for managing customer relationships represent an industry that is expected to grow at a 43% compounded rate over the next five years and reach US$11 billion worldwide by 2003 and $378 million in Canada.[28]

Even colleges and universities are adopting CSM systems. The University of Western Ontario's division of information technology (IT) services, for example, purchased PeopleSoft's Vantive CRM solution to handle the support needs of 35 000 students, faculty, and staff.[29] The system allows IT staff to quickly access diagnostic information, record customer details and track customer problems in a central repository, coordinate customer services, and better customize services and payment options.

Three key trends are driving this increased focus on customer satisfaction and retention. First, customer expectations are continuously increasing: Today's consumers are smart,

Exhibit 16.7

Harry Rosen uses postcards and other means to keep in touch with customers.

Ermenegildo Zegna

highly informed, and critical consumers, who demand more than satisfactory experiences every time they interact with an organization. This is illustrated by the public outcry over the problems Air Canada faced in merging with Canadian Airlines: Delayed and cancelled flights, lost baggage, and threatened strikes are no longer tolerated by consumers.[30] Customers expect organizations to know who they are and to know the history of the relationship. Second, global competition means consumers can easily find other companies and solutions if their expectations are not met. Finally, information technology—scanners, powerful affordable computers, database software, and the Internet—combine to enable organizations to track and share customer information and implement enterprise-wide CSM solutions in ways not previously possible.

Databases: A Key Relationship Marketing Tool

The goal of the relationship marketer is to track interactions with customers, develop a dialogue with them, provide relevant, responsive communications which further a sense of relationship, and develop bonds of trust, commitment, and loyalty. That's what men's clothier Harry Rosen Inc. of Toronto is doing when it collects information from each customer at the time of purchase. Any time a customer shops at any store across Canada, the purchase information is saved in the system. Rosen uses the information to call customers who have not been in recently about a special offer on the brand they usually buy, call major purchasers to ensure they remain satisfied, mail out its catalogue to the best customers, or customize invitations to designer shows. Exhibit 16.7 illustrates a Harry Rosen postcard used to communicate special offers. Bob Humphrey, chairman and CEO of Harry Rosen, says that generally their direct marketing efforts generate about 70% of their sales.

Harry Rosen Inc.
www.harryrosen.com

As this example illustrates, underlying effective relationship marketing is the development of a customer database that allows the organization to learn about the preferences and behaviours of its customers and track the interactions the customer has with the employees and products of the organization. This is the foundation on which relationships can be built. Maintaining a customer database is not a new idea.

What *is* new is to use the database as the core of the company's marketing activities rather than as a simple repository of information. That's what cosmetics chain Faces is doing through its stand-alone boutiques in malls across Canada (see Exhibit 16.8). Their focus is on building customer relationships and customizing interactions with customers by getting to know them better. To do this, they implemented a detailed database that tracks purchase behaviour and other details about each customer. This information is then used to send customers direct mail information that they should be interested in, such as a new fall lipstick shade for fair-skinned women. The system also allows them to offer specially targeted gifts, premiums, or discounts to customers to say "thank you" and hopefully motivate consumers to buy more product.[31]

DATABASE MARKETING

Databases are used extensively to support relationship marketing efforts; they also provide a foundation for direct marketing. Direct marketing involves generating a measurable response or a series of responses from customers over a short period of time, intended to

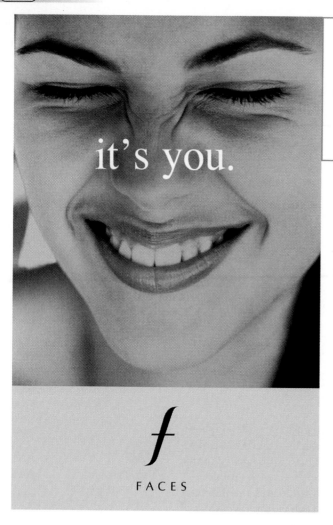

it's you.

f

FACES

Exhibit 16.8

Cosmetics chain Faces uses a customer database to support its relationship marketing efforts.

result in a purchase. When the intent of the marketing activity is to develop an ongoing relationship with a customer, this is **database marketing**. Database marketing is the use of direct marketing tools and techniques to establish and develop on-going customer relationships. Database marketing helps marketers achieve a number of objectives:[32]

- *Enables interactive communication.* Recall that interactive marketing requires a response from the consumers. They must take some action, such as filling out an order form or calling an 800 number for product information. For example, H.J. Heinz sent a mail piece to female cat owners that asked the provocative question, "Does he sleep with you?" If the woman completed a brief survey that told the company more about her pet food preferences, she received a personalized thank-you note that mentioned her pet by name.[33] She was also entered into the company's database, so that she would receive future communications about her feline friend. This type of interactivity gives marketers more than one opportunity to develop a dialogue with the customer, and possibly to create add-on sales by engaging the customer in a discussion about the product and related items or services in which she might be interested.

***

database marketing The use of direct marketing tools and techniques to establish and develop ongoing customer relationships.

- *Can locate new customers.* In some cases, a marketer can create new customers by directing its communications to likely prospects who have characteristics similar to current users. For example, the brand manger for Palmolive soap, in an effort to convert users to the new lemon Palmolive dish soap, could find out why people use Ivory and create specific messages or offers for them. The same could then be done for Excel dish soap users. As discussed in Chapter 5, a number of market research companies in Canada can provide this level of information to marketers.

- *Can stimulate cross-selling.* Database marketers can more easily offer related products to their customers. If consumers have expressed interest in a particular product category, odds are that they will also be good candidates for similar items. This explains why consumers are bombarded with mail offers for computer software, magazines, or clothing after purchasing a similar product over the phone or through a catalogue.[34]

- *Provides measurable results.* A common complaint marketers voice is that they can't pinpoint what impact a communication campaign had on their target market. Who can say for sure that a $100 000 commercial motivated people to switch colas? Because database marketers know exactly who received a specific message, they can measure the effectiveness of each communication. Responses are *trackable*. The marketer can assess the proportion of message recipients that responded, compare the effectiveness of different messages, and compile a history of which consumers are most likely to respond over time. Farm equipment manufacturer John Deere targeted 20 000 farmers who were loyal to other brands. Using a list of farmers who owned competing equipment, the company sent prospects a series of four mailings spaced over eight weeks, each with an inexpensive gift, such as a stopwatch, that was related to the theme of saving time and money by replacing existing equipment. The campaign brought 5800 farmers into the showroom, yielding a 29% response rate. Nearly 700 of these consumers bought new equipment, resulting in more than $40 million in new business.[35]

Database marketing has been used particularly effectively by the New Brunswick Department of Economic Development, Tourism and Culture to attract American visitors to the Bay of Fundy.[36] Using primary and secondary data, they developed a database of visitor buying patterns, activities, interests, opinions, media habits, and travel motivations, which gave a clear picture of who was visiting the Bay of Fundy region and why (see Exhibit 16.9). Using this profile, the tourism department sent 200 000 pieces of direct mail to potential American visitors. They received 39 999 inquiries for further information, and 19% of the people making those inquiries showed up at the Bay of Fundy that year. Armed with this success, the tourism department conducted focus groups to further understand American visitors and test new communication materials. They learned that most visitors came for a short visit, were motivated by convenient access, and lived within the northeastern US. A second direct mail campaign that focused on major northeastern US cities resulted in 66 435 enquiries and 32 000 visits to the Bay of Fundy. The total budget for the Bay of Fundy initiative was $800 000. The investment returned over $8 million to the New Brunswick economy and over $2 million in extra tax revenue for the government. Not a bad investment! The example illustrates the power of database marketing and developing rich target market profiles.

Other Relationship Marketing Tools

Marketers use a variety of tools and tactics to establish, develop, and maintain relationships with customers and other key stakeholders. To establish a relationship, marketers attempt to create a sense of one, using such vehicles as e-mail, newsletters, and recognition or loyalty programs. They recognize and thank customers, using postcards, thank-you cards, and electronic greeting cards. They provide opportunities for customer involvement by soliciting feedback, involving customers in focus groups, and inviting customers to planning sessions. There are many other tools and tactics for keeping in contact with customers. You have probably experienced some of these as a consumer yourself. The key is to make the communication desired by customers—make it relevant to them, be sincere in your request for a relationship, and be respectful of their time and privacy. Relationship marketing can be overdone—annoying customers and resulting in negative associations and personal boycotts of brands—opposite to what was intended.[40] Furthermore, some customers simply

To reach likely customers, many companies buy response lists from professionals called list managers. These contain addresses of people who have an interest in the product or who have bought a related item in the past. For example, a response list sold to casinos was called the "Compulsive Gamblers Special," because it promised to provide the names of people with "unquenchable appetites for all forms of gambling."[37]

The growing use of sophisticated databases is not sitting well with some consumer groups, which are concerned about invasion of privacy. In late 1998, the European Union passed a law to limit the ability of companies to sell consumer data. The new directive allows citizens to decline to be included in private databases, so that data collected for one purpose, such as a credit card purchase, cannot be sold elsewhere. The Canadian federal government passed a similar law, Bill C-6, in April 2000, instructing that: "Beginning January 1, 2001, you will need the consent of an individual to collect information, to use information, to transfer information and for use of the information for other than the original purpose for which you collected it."[38] US trade negotiators are fighting these laws, claiming that they restrict free trade.[39] Should marketers have the right to buy private information about the purchasing habits of consumers to sell other products and services to them?

Exhibit 16.9

New Brunswick's tourism department uses database marketing to attract visitors to the Bay of Fundy region.

Real People, Real Decisions
How it worked **out at Cormark Communications**

The Cormark team chose Option 2, maintaining the US strategic platform but rebuilding key sections of the strategy to meet the needs of the Canadian marketplace. They concluded that the communications materials were directionally right but needed some modification to fit the Canadian marketplace and regulatory context, particularly for the veterinary market. They based this decision primarily on their market research. The hybrid option of customizing the US strategy allowed Cormark and Pfizer Canada to control the Canadian product launch and move directionally correct and successful US material to strategically accurate and insightful material that was right for the Canadian market.

There were two significant differences in the Canadian launch program. One was the significantly smaller budget requiring tighter targeting of messaging for efficiency. The second was a higher degree of emotion in the message. Cormark learned through research that consumers were moved by the restoration of the dog–owner relationship that could be achieved by the use of the product.

In implementing the strategy, Cormark developed a launch blueprint for Canada. The agency determined the key audiences within the broader consumer and veterinarian target markets and determined how best to reach them. Within three months of launch, Rimadyl exceeded the annual volume objective. Post-campaign research indicated that awareness by the target markets was higher than expected. Rimadyl is well on its way to becoming a major product in the category. Since the launch, other international markets have requested the Canadian launch materials for their own local use.

don't want to have a close relationship with their grocery store, bank, or other service or good provider. They want to be left alone. Determining a customer's relationship orientation helps marketers to develop appropriate relationship strategies.

Chapter Summary

1. Explain integrated marketing communications and its implementation, and why some marketers resist it.

   Integrated marketing communications (IMC) programs allow marketers to communicate with consumers on a continual basis by coordinating the communications messages and media. IMC often uses customer databases to stay in touch with the market. In an IMC strategy, contact management means that communications occur when customers will be receptive to them. The type of message is influenced by the communications objectives, the characteristics of the customer group, and the exposure situation. The effectiveness of the IMC strategy may be assessed through transactional data, by customers' second-order responses, or by customer attitudes. Some marketers resist IMC, because it requires changing accepted ways of doing things, decreases emphasis on advertising, puts an increased focus on communications, and requires major changes in advertising agencies.

2. List, describe, and contrast the elements of the communications mix.

   The five major elements of marketing communications are known as the communications mix. Personal selling provides direct contact between a company representative and a customer. Direct marketing is direct impersonal communication focused on short-term, single transaction responses or a set of responses leading to a purchase decision. Advertising is non-personal, paid-for communication from an identified sponsor using mass media. Sales promotions stimulate immediate sales by providing incentives to the trade or to consumers. Publicity and public relations activities seek to influence the attitudes of various publics.

3. Explain the steps involved in developing a communications plan.

The communications plan begins with communications objectives, usually stated in terms of communications tasks, such as creating awareness, knowledge, desire, product trial, and brand loyalty. Which communications mix elements will be used depends on the overall strategy—a push versus a pull strategy, the type of product, and the stage of the product life cycle. Communications budgets are often developed, using the percentage-of-sales, competitive-parity, or objective-task methods. Money from the total budget is then allocated to various elements of the communications mix, based on characteristics of the organization, the market potential, and the size of the market. Finally, marketers monitor and evaluate the communications efforts to determine if objectives are being reached.

4. Explain the philosophy and practices of relationship marketing.

Relationship marketing is the philosophy and practice of developing long-term relationships with key stakeholders. It recognizes that not all stakeholders and customers are of equal strategic importance to the organization and that the commitment and loyalty of key stakeholders needs to be cultivated, nurtured, developed, and protected. This is accomplished by managing all the interactions a customer has with an organization. Databases and information technology enable marketers to establish, develop, and maintain relationships with customers and other key stakeholders.

5. Explain the role of databases in facilitating marketing communications and relationship management.

Database marketing, interactive marketing that uses a customer database, allows marketers to develop dialogues and build relationships with customers. Marketers use database marketing to create programs that are more flexible, reward loyal users, locate new customers, offer related products to existing customers (i.e., cross-selling), and track customer responses.

Chapter Review

Marketing Concepts: Testing Your Knowledge

1. What is integrated marketing communications (IMC)? What is contact management and how is it a part of IMC?

2. What is communication? What are the goals of communication?

3. List and describe the elements of the communications mix.

4. List and explain the steps in the development of a communications plan.

5. Why should communication objectives be phrased in terms of communications tasks? What are some examples of communications task objectives?

6. How does the communications mix vary with push versus pull strategies? How does it vary in different stages of the product life cycle (PLC)?

7. Explain each of the following budgeting methods:

   a. percentage-of-sales method

   b. competitive-parity method

   c. objective-task method.

8. Describe the traditional communications model.

9. What is relationship marketing?

10. What is database marketing? What are some reasons that database marketing is growing in popularity?

Marketing Concepts: Discussing Choices and Issues

1. Increasingly, marketers are seeking new ways to communicate with consumers. Advertising is being placed on washroom walls, in high-school cafeterias, and even in the halls of uni-

---

KEY TERMS

advertising (448)

AIDA model (460)

bottom-up budgeting techniques (456)

communications mix (447)

communications model (459)

communications plan (451)

customer relationship marketing (CRM) (462)

database marketing (464)

decoding (461)

encoding (459)

feedback (461)

integrated marketing communications (IMC) (446)

interactive marketing (449)

marketing communications (444)

medium (460)

message (460)

noise (461)

objective-task method (456)

percentage-of-sales method (455)

promotion (444)

public relations (450)

publicity (450)

pull strategy (454)

push strategy (454)

receiver (461)

relationship marketing (462)

source (459)

target audience (451)

top-down budgeting techniques (455)

versity and college classroom buildings. Develop debate arguments for and against this proliferation of commercial messages.

2. One reason to build a database is to advance a political or social agenda by identifying and mobilizing a core of supporters. For example, Philip Morris has built a database with 26 million names, which the tobacco company uses to rally customers to the cause of smokers' rights. What are the ethical issues related to this usage of databases?

3. Consumers are becoming concerned that the proliferation of databases is an invasion of the individual's privacy. Do you feel this is a valid concern? How can marketers use databases effectively and, at the same time, protect the rights of individuals?

4. Some argue that IMC is just a passing fad in marketing communications. What do you think?

Marketing Practice: **Applying What You've Learned**

1. As a marketing consultant, you are frequently asked by clients to develop recommendations for communications strategies. Outline your recommendations for the use of different communications mix elements for one of the following products:

   a. a new brand of laundry detergent

   b. a familiar brand of cereal

   c. a political candidate

   d. equipment for a new manufacturing facility.

2. As the director of marketing for a small firm that markets specialty salad dressings, you are in the process of developing a communications plan. With one or more of your classmates, develop suggestions for each of the following. Then, in a role-playing situation, present your recommendations to the client.

   a. communications objectives

   b. a method for determining the communications budget

   c. the use of a push strategy or a pull strategy

3. Assume you are an account executive with an advertising agency. Your assignment is to develop recommendations for advertising for a new client, a health and fitness centre. Give your recommendations for:

   a. how to use interactive marketing

   b. how to develop a database for interactive marketing.

4. As a member of the marketing department for a manufacturer of sports equipment, you have been directed to select a new agency to do the communications for your firm. You have asked two agencies to submit proposals. One agency recommends an integrated marketing communications plan, and the second agency has developed recommendations for a traditional advertising plan. Write a memo to explain each of the following to your boss.

   a. what is different about an integrated marketing communications plan?

   b. why is the IMC plan superior to merely advertising?

   c. why do some agencies resist changing from traditional communications planning?

Marketing Mini-Project: **Learning by Doing**

This mini-project is designed to help you understand how organizations use database marketing.

1. With a group of fellow students, contact a local small business (e.g., a restaurant, dry cleaner, hardware store, bookstore). Ask the manager whether they make use of any database marketing activities such as the ones discussed in this chapter.

2. Obtain the cooperation of the business owner or a manager in working with you to develop recommendations for a new database marketing plan or for improving the existing plan. Your recommendations might include the following:

   a. how to obtain names for an initial or expanded database.

   b. what information should be included in the initial database.

   c. what information should be regularly added to the database.

d. how the business might use the database for communicating with existing customers, obtaining new customers, increasing the sales volume for existing customers, planning for future expansion, monitoring and improving customer satisfaction, and making changes in the business strategy.

Real People, Real Surfers: **Exploring the Web**

More and more firms are finding that database marketing is a good way to provide interactive communications that build relationships with customers. The Internet provides an excellent way to both build a database and communicate one-on-one with customers. Although individual sites change frequently, some sites that have in the past provided multiple opportunities for interactive communications with customers and for building a database are:

iVillage (www.ivillage.com)

Indigo (www.indigo.ca)

Disney (www.disney.com)

Lane Bryant (www.lanebryant.com)

Hallmark (www.hallmark.com)

Explore these or other sites that provide opportunities for consumers to register, answer questionnaires, or in some other way use Internet connections to build a database. After completing your exploration of each site, answer these questions:

1. Based on the design of the Web site, what customers is each firm targeting? How do you know that?

2. In what ways does each Web site facilitate interactive communications between the firm and customers?

3. How does each firm use the Internet to gather information on customers? What information is gathered? Which site does a superior job of gathering information and why?

4. How do you think the firm might use the information it gathers through the Internet in database marketing activities? How can the information be used to build relationships with customers and prospective customers?

5. How does each firm use the site to practise integrated marketing communications?

6. What recommendations do you have for each site to improve the interactive opportunities on its Web site?

Orchard Park Shopping Centre

Alison Love, marketing manager at Orchard Park Shopping Centre, reviewed the first year results of the mall's "Stores… and Lots of Them" communication strategy. Although the results could not necessarily be directly tied to the $170 000 campaign, shopper visits to the mall had increased by 5.2% in the past year, and sales had increased by 14.3%, or $9.35 million. Love wanted to leverage this success and develop the second stage of a three-year plan to reposition and reconfirm the Orchard Park as a retail leader in the marketplace.

Orchard Park is a 673 000-square-foot regional mall in Kelowna, a thriving city of 130 000 people in BC's Okanagan Valley. Anchored by four major department stores and offering 150 specialty stores, it caters to residents of Kelowna, as well as those of Vernon and Penticton (populations of 50 000 each) which are an hour away, and of outlying areas who are willing to drive as long as 2.5 hours to access Orchard Park's store selection.

Kelowna had recently seen significant big box development, new "power strip" centres, and the addition of over one million square feet of retail space. This growth created greater draw to Kelowna but also greater competition for Orchard Park Shopping Centre, whose sales and market share had been in decline for five years. Love recognized, however, that Orchard Park offered the broadest selection of stores in the marketplace by far, and that it had the most popular names in retailing, which were not offered elsewhere in the region. She also realized that Orchard Park had never capitalized on its greatest asset—the depth and breadth of its retail mix—but had assumed that customers already knew. Orchard Park management decided that for the first year of a three-year plan, they would develop an advertising campaign to communicate this strength to the marketplace. They hired Virginia Boggie and Victoria-based Suburbia Studios to help them do it.

Suburbia Studios is a full-service communications agency with an international reputation; it had grown quickly in the past five years from a home-based business. Suburbia was charged with developing an advertising campaign that would:

- Affirm Orchard Park's position as a premiere shopping destination, offering the best selection of the most popular retailers in its primary and secondary trade areas.

- Increase awareness in its primary and secondary trade areas of the diverse selection of stores and services available.

- Provide a means to promote numerous ongoing store openings.

- Increase total shopper visits and sales by 5% in the first year.

To achieve these objectives, Suburbia developed an aggressive advertising campaign that consistently communicated a single unified theme—Orchard Park has stores… and lots of them!—targeted at women aged 25 to 54. As the centre's primary and secondary market areas extend over an hour's drive in any direction, Suburbia determined that a multi-media advertising campaign was necessary to deliver the key message effectively. They chose television as the primary advertising medium, since its reach extends to all corners of the centre's vast trading area, to be supported by newspaper advertising and busboards to provide regional coverage at a reasonable cost. They purchased three seasonal television flights to coincide with major merchandizing periods in the year and overlapping the television schedule; and virtually every busboard available in the region, thereby dominating the medium and enabling Orchard Park to drive their message home to customers on the go. They placed newspaper advertisements during each flight in the only daily newspaper providing regional coverage to further support and reinforce the message.

To create a meaningful impression of "stores… and lots of them," the names of key Orchard Park retailers were featured in the campaign in five store categories. Suburbia wanted the stores to speak for themselves in the TV campaign, so they produced six unique, distinctive, and lighthearted 15-second commercials. Each spot was set to a customized soundtrack without voice-

MARKETING IN ACTION

overs and opened with a witty, animated headline designed to pique the viewer's curiosity and to set the stage for a humorous vignette. At the end of the commercials, the designated merchandise category was revealed along with the names of eight featured stores, which were set in motion to encourage viewers to read each name. By using the 15-second format, Orchard Park was able to run the ads as "book ends" or back to back, further reinforcing the "lots of them" claim. By using a "snapshot" from each commercial, the bus board and newspaper ads mirrored the TV campaign. Six different retailers were featured on each busboard, further reinforcing the "lots of them" message. To ensure that the newspaper ads would stand out, they ran teasers in the form of banner ads as a lead-in to the centre's ads, which followed on the next page.

Total production costs for the campaign were about $100 000, and media placement costs were about $70 000. The TV ads reached 98% of the target audience, an average of 10.5 times per flight, generating 1029 gross rating points (GRP) per flight and 3087 GRPs for the campaign. The campaign also had a long "shelf life" in that the spots could easily be updated by changing store names.

As Love reflected on the success of this campaign, she wondered what they could do next to keep the momentum going. They had successfully used advertising in the first year of the repositioning strategy, but Love recognized that other elements of the communications mix might be added to develop an integrated communications strategy.

Public relations and publicity, in particular, would be important this year, as Orchard Park was going to undergo a major renovation and expansion. Plans were also underway to develop an "e-tail" initiative to allow consumers to patronize Orchard Park stores online. Thinking that Boggie might be able to help organize her thoughts, she picked up the phone and called Suburbia Studios.

Sources: Briefing documents and award submissions provided by Suburbia Studios and Orchard Park Shopping Centre.

THINGS TO THINK ABOUT

1. What were key elements of the first-phase strategy that contributed to its success?
2. Is it time for Orchard Park to consider key secondary messages? If so, what might these be?
3. What communications strategy would you recommend for the second and third phases of the strategy?
4. Taking an integrated marketing communications perspective, what other elements or aspect of Orchard Park Shopping Centre should Love consider focusing on?

en tidning från stiftelsen Non-Violence och Sveriges Bryggerier

alkohål i huvet

Linda Norrman
Skugges
alkoharnär

Vilken alkohol är du?

**Sex
– bättre med
eller utan?**

vinn en resa
till miami

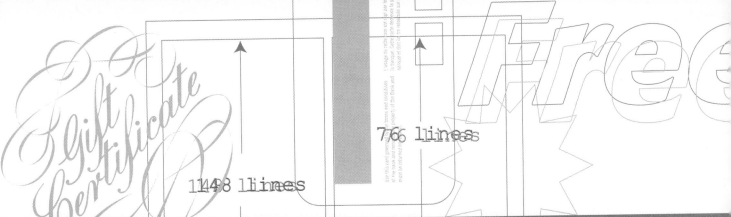

17

Advertising

CHAPTER OBJECTIVES

1. Tell what advertising is and describe the major types of advertising.

2. Describe the major players in the advertising process.

3. Tell how advertisers develop an advertising campaign.

4. Describe the major advertising media and the important considerations in media planning.

5. Explain how advertisers evaluate the effectiveness of the campaign.

6. Discuss the challenges facing advertising.

Real People, Real Decisions ✔ ✘

Meet Anna Olofsson
A Decision Maker at A&O Analys

Anna Olofsson is account manager at A&O Analys (www.analys.nu), a Swedish advertising agency that focuses on strategic marketing consultation. A&O Analys works with food industry and high-tech companies, with a special interest in the adolescent market. Olofsson has been a lecturer in marketing at Umes Business School in

northern Sweden, where she did research on how popular culture influences the behaviours and product preferences of adolescents. She is also a columnist for the Swedish Advertising Association's trade magazine *Resumé* and for the digital magazine *Roaming* (www.roaming.net). She has written a book on the consumption patterns of Generation X.

Promotional Messages: And Now, for a Word from Our Sponsor . . .

❋ ❋ ❋
advertising Non-personal communication paid for by an identified sponsor using mass media to persuade or inform.

Wherever we turn, we are bombarded by ads in the form of television commercials, radio spots, banner ads on the Internet urging us to "click here," or huge billboards screaming "Buy Me!" **Advertising** is non-personal communication paid for by an identified sponsor using mass media to persuade or inform an audience.[1] Advertising can be fun, glamorous, annoying, informative, or ineffective. Advertising can be straightforward, providing valuable facts. It can also be magical, making products come alive.

Advertising has been with us a long time. In ancient Greece and Rome, advertisements of sorts appeared on walls and on tablets. Today, we get messages about products almost wherever we are, whether cruising down the road or around the Web, and we even hear them on mobile phones. Furthermore, advertising is often unparalleled in its ability to create desire for these goods or services by transporting us to imaginary worlds in which users of these items are happy, beautiful, or rich. In this way, advertising allows the organization to communicate its message in a favourable way and to repeat the message as often as it deems necessary for it to have an impact on receivers.

Types of Advertising

The amount of money spent on advertising every year in Canada is close to $6 billion.[2] Although almost every business advertises, some businesses are bigger spenders than others. Retail companies spend the most money on advertising activities in Canada, accounting for 16.6% of total national advertising expenditures. The next largest categories of spenders, in order, are automotive companies, food companies, financial services, and telecommunications companies. Because so much is spent on advertising, marketers must decide which type of ad will work best, given the organizational and marketing goals. The advertisements an organization runs can take many forms.

PRODUCT ADVERTISING

❋ ❋ ❋
product advertising An advertising message that focuses on a specific good or service.

When people give examples of advertising, they are likely to recall the provocative poses in Calvin Klein ads, a ranting Molson Joe, or dancers in Gap ads. These are examples of **product advertising**, in which the message focuses on a specific good or service. Product advertising usually has one of three purposes. If a product is in the introductory stage of the product life cycle, advertising will educate people about the new product and what it does. Other product ads emphasize a brand's features and try to convince the target market to choose it over other options. Finally, many of the ads we see are designed to ensure that peo-

Exhibit 17.1

Institutional advertising can be used to build a corporate reputation.

ple won't forget about the product and the things they already know about it. These messages are often used for products that are already well established in the market.

INSTITUTIONAL ADVERTISING

Rather than focusing on a specific brand, **institutional advertising** promotes the activities, personality, or point of view of an organization or company, as in the ad for Pfizer shown in Exhibit 17.1. Another use of institutional advertising is to build demand for a product category, such as the Canadian egg producers ads that encourage consumers to "Get Cracking."

Some institutional messages state a firm's position on an issue to sway public opinion, a strategy called **advocacy advertising**.[3] For example, the R.J. Reynolds company ran an ad titled "Of Cigarettes and Science," which attempted to refute arguments about the relationship between smoking and health. **Public service advertisements** (PSAs) are advertisements the media runs free of charge for not-for-profit organizations that serve society in some way, or to champion an issue such as increasing literacy or discouraging drunk driving. The ad for Camp Chrysalis in Exhibit 17.2 won a Canadian Marketing Award in 2000 in the Public Service Campaign category. Often advertising agencies will take on one or more public service campaigns on a pro bono basis (for free).

Who Does Advertising?

An **advertising campaign** is a coordinated, comprehensive plan that carries out promotion objectives and results in a series of advertisements placed in media over a period of time. For example, the long-running advertising campaign for Buckley's Mixture—"It tastes awful. And it works."—has included both print advertising and a series of humorous television commercials that all work together to build brand loyalty for the cough medicine. In fact, the Buckley's campaign is considered one of the most effective in Canadian advertising history. The brand is the number-one selling cough syrup in Canada, even though they spend far less on advertising every year ($458 600) than their closest competitor, Robitussin Dm ($1.7 million).[4]

Creating and executing an advertising campaign often requires many companies working together and a broad range of skilled people to do the job right. Some firms may do their own advertising by creating an *in-house agency*. In many cases, though, the firm retains one or more outside advertising agencies to develop advertising messages on its behalf. A *limited-service agency* provides one or more specialized services, such as media buying or creative development (we'll see what these tasks are later). A *full-service agency* provides most or all of the services needed to mount a campaign, including research, creation of ad copy and art, media selection, and production of the final messages. In keeping with the move to integrated communications strategies discussed in Chapter 16, most Canadian advertising agencies have transformed themselves into full-service *communications services companies*, which provide clients with advice and service in all areas of communications decision making, including advertising. The five largest Canadian marketing communications services

---

✳✳✳
institutional advertising An advertising message that promotes the activities, personality, or point of view of an organization or company.

✳✳✳
advocacy advertising A type of public service advertising provided by an organization that is seeking to influence public opinion on an issue because it has some stake in the outcome.

✳✳✳
public service advertisements Advertising run by the media without charge for not-for-profit organizations or to champion a particular cause.

✳✳✳
advertising campaign A coordinated, comprehensive plan that carries out promotion objectives and results in a series of advertisements placed in media over a period of time.

PRAY THAT DONATIONS ARE ALL YOU EVER SEND TO OUR CAMP.

CAMP CHRYSALIS AIDS RETREAT

Exhibit 17.2

A public service advertisement.

companies, by revenue, are Cossette Communication Group Inc., MacLaren McCann Canada Inc., The Young & Rubicam Group of Companies Ltd., Maxxcom Inc., and BBDO Canada Inc.[5] Many different tasks are required to produce an advertising campaign. The ad in Exhibit 17.3 humorously illustrates the "birth" of an advertising concept, highlighting some of the major players who participate in the delivery. Big or small, an advertising agency or communications services company joins the talents of specialists who together craft a message and make the communications concept a reality.

- *Account Management:* The *account executive*, or *account manager* or *suit*, is the "soul" of the operation. This person develops the campaign's strategy for the client. The account executive supervises the day-to-day activities on the account, and is the primary liaison between the agency and the client. The account executive has to ensure that the client is happy while verifying that people within the agency are executing the desired strategy.

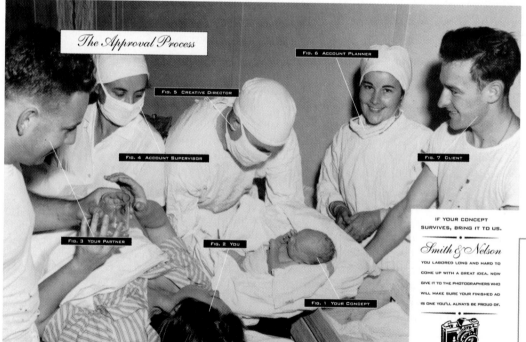

The Approval Process

Fig. 6 Account Planner

Fig. 5 Creative Director

Fig. 4 Account Supervisor

Fig. 7 Client

Fig. 3 Your Partner

Fig. 2 You

Fig. 1 Your Concept

IF YOUR CONCEPT SURVIVES, BRING IT TO US.

Smith & Nelson

YOU LABORED LONG AND HARD TO COME UP WITH A GREAT IDEA. NOW GIVE IT TO THE PHOTOGRAPHERS WHO WILL MAKE SURE YOUR FINISHED AD IS ONE YOU'LL ALWAYS BE PROUD OF.

Exhibit 17.3

This trade ad illustrates the "birth" of an advertising concept.

Real People, Real Decisions
Decision Time at A&O Analys

Anna Olofsson was asked to tackle an important issue for a client, the Swedish Brewers' Association. The objective was not to sell more alcohol, but to keep young people from drinking it. The Swedish social minister was concerned about an increase in youth drinking, and he asked the beer producers to inform teens about the consequences of adolescent drinking. The trade association wanted Olofsson to create public service advertising messages that would address this social problem in Sweden while letting the public know that the beer industry was concerned.

Although drinking habits in Sweden slowly are changing to a more southern European style of drinking wine with dinner, many young people start to drink alcohol on weekends when they are as young as 13. Although temperance organizations routinely visit schools to talk about the dangers of drinking, alcohol consumption among adolescents is rising.

First, Olofsson conducted focus groups and surveys to learn about the reasons kids drink. The answer was not surprising: Kids drink to get drunk. They enjoy the feeling of intoxication. When they are drunk they say they feel more sociable and attractive. To them, the only negative aspect of drinking alcohol is the fear of getting so drunk that they cannot run from a violent situation, often a fight for the boys and rape for the girls. Many girls also feared that long-term alcohol use would ruin their looks.

The research showed that the kids tuned out messages saying that they should avoid alcohol altogether. They also believed that they already had heard everything there is to know about alcohol. The feedback from the kids was clear: The source of alcohol messages could not be government authorities or temperance organizations, because these groups had no credibility with young people.

Who *would* be a credible source? Olofsson thought of a Swedish organization called the Non-Violence Project (NVP), which sends young speakers to schools to promote peaceful solutions to problems. She arranged to have the NVP collaborate with the Swedish Brewers' Association to get out the message to kids concerning the relationship between alcohol and violence.

But how could they create an advertising message to appeal to a group that claimed to know everything about drinking? What should they say? How, when, and where should they say it? Olofsson considered these options.

Option 1. Focus on the belief that drinking makes you popular. This campaign would emphasize the risk of looking stupid in front of one's friends after getting too drunk. But there was a risk that this would make the brewers a target for the temperance movement. And would the kids buy yet another advertisement about the evils of drinking?

Option 2. Focus on the fear of violence, which Swedish teens say is their chief concern about getting drunk. This campaign would emphasize that when you get drunk, it's much easier to get hurt and harder to defend yourself if someone else becomes violent. But a fear appeal can be ineffective if it hits too close to home and leads the audience to ignore the message or deny its relevance. Also, Olofsson would need to develop separate campaigns to address boys' fear of being beaten and girls' fear of being raped.

Option 3. Admit that adults don't know what to do about the problem, and ask the kids themselves to pitch in to find a solution. This campaign would not be preachy so wouldn't alienate kids. Rather, it would seek to obtain solutions that had not occurred to the older generation. Still, the big effect in changing attitudes toward drinking would be delayed until hearing from kids and creating ads from their feedback. Olofsson then had to determine how to use the adolescents in the campaign, if they even wanted to participate.

Now, join Anna Olofsson and the A&O Analys decision team: Which option would you choose, and why?

- *Creative Services:* *Creatives* are the "heart" of the communications effort. These are the people who actually dream up and produce the ads. They include the agency's creative director, copywriter, and art director. Creatives are the artists who breathe life into marketing objectives and craft messages that (hopefully) will excite, arouse, or interest consumers.

- *Research and Marketing Services:* Researchers are the "brains" of the campaign. They collect and analyze information that will help account executives develop a sensible strategy. They assist creatives in getting consumer reactions to different versions of ads, or by providing copywriters with details on the target group.

- *Media Planning:* The media planner is the "legs" of the campaign. The media planner helps to determine which communications vehicles are the most effective and recommends the most efficient means for delivering the ad by deciding where, when, and how often it will appear.

Developing the Advertising Campaign

The advertising campaign is much more than creating a cool ad and hoping that people notice it. It should be intimately related to the organization's overall promotional goals. That means the firm (and its outside communications services company if it uses one) must have a good idea of whom it wants to reach, what it will take to appeal to this market, and where and when the messages should be placed to have the best chance of making an impact. Let's review the steps required to do this.

Identify the Target Market

The best way to communicate with an audience is to understand as much as possible about them, and what turns them on and off. An ad that uses the latest slang may relate to teenagers but not to their parents. This explains why Anna Olofsson took pains to talk with numerous young drinkers about alcohol and discover why anti-drinking messages didn't have much impact.

The target market is identified from research and segmentation decisions, which we discussed in Chapter 8. Researchers try to get into the customers' heads to understand just how to create a message that they will understand and respond to. For example, an account executive working on a campaign for Pioneer Stereo was assigned to hang out with guys who were likely prospects to buy car stereos. His observations resulted in an advertising campaign that incorporated the phrases they used to describe their cars: "My car is my holy temple, my love shack, my drag racer of doom...."[6]

Establish Message and Budget Objectives

Advertising objectives should be consistent with the marketing plan. That means that both the underlying message and its costs need to be related to what the marketer is trying to say about the product and what the marketer is willing or able to spend.

SETTING MESSAGE GOALS

Message goals can be increasing brand awareness, boosting sales by a certain percentage, or even changing the image of a product. In the 1990s, Canadian Tire embarked on advertising designed to improve its image and refocus on its core businesses: leisure and living, automotive and sporting goods. In an award-winning ad entitled "Bike Story," a depression-era boy is shown receiving a new red bicycle from Canadian Tire. The story touched the hearts of Canadian consumers and re-established Canadian Tire as an important national retailer.[7] Sometimes the objective is simply to get people to recognize that they need the product at all. That was the task facing an Indian advertising agency R K Swamy/BBDO, as it began work on a campaign for its client Apple Computer. In 1995, about 12 500 personal computers, only five percent of the total in India, were used in homes. Apple wanted to motivate its target market, middle-class Indian consumers, to buy a computer for household management, children's education, and entertainment.

Apple and R K Swamy/BBDO found that the key consumer expectations for a home computer centred around low price, ease of use, and reliability. The agency developed a campaign for Apple's Macintosh Performa to communicate with potential customers on these terms.[8] The agency positioned the Performa as the ideal computer for the family by highlighting its ease of use, value for the money, and multimedia capability.

SETTING THE BUDGET

A firm allocates a percentage of its overall marketing budget to advertising. This budget level depends on how much and what type of advertising the company can afford. Major corporations such as General Motors of Canada advertise heavily through expensive media

Apple Computers
www.apple.com/ca

(e.g., television) for multiple products throughout the year. Other firms need to be more selective: Smaller firms are more likely to put their advertising dollars into less expensive media, such as direct mail or trade publications. The major approaches and techniques to setting overall promotional budgets such as the percentage-of-sales and objective-task methods discussed in Chapter 16 are also used to set advertising budgets.

Design the Ad

Creative strategy is the process that turns a concept into an advertisement. It's one thing to know what a company wants to say about itself and its product, and quite another to figure out exactly how to say it. The creative process has been described as the "spark between objective and execution." The Novell ad in Exhibit 17.4 demonstrates how even business-to-business products, such as computer software and services, can come to life with the right creative strategy. As we saw in Chapter 16, for an advertising message to be effective, it should satisfy four requirements that marketers call AIDA: attention, interest, desire, and action.

It is unlikely that one ad can do all that, but the goal of an advertising campaign is to present a series of messages and repeat it to a sufficient degree so that the customer will progress through the AIDA stages. To do this, advertising creatives (art directors, copywriters, photographers, and others) must develop a "big idea," a concept that expresses aspects of the product, service, or organization in a tangible, attention-getting, memorable manner, like the Brazilian ad in Exhibit 17.5 that proclaims "Your feet are ready for summer."

When designing the ad, advertisers come up with many ingenious ways to express a concept. An **advertising appeal** is the central idea of the ad. Some

good OR bad DECISION?

The Canadian government has traditionally been one of the largest advertisers in Canada. In 1999, the Canadian government spent $59.9 million on advertising to inform Canadians about government services and to build good feelings for "brand Canada," especially in Quebec. Then in June 2000, the federal government announced that it was going to spend an additional $90 million, money taken from surplus tax revenue, over three years. This additional money would go toward advertising programs and other communications initiatives, such as a mobile Canadian pavilion to travel across the country promoting the services offered by the federal government. Some critics claim that such large expenditures are a poor use of taxpayers' money in light of the need for funds to address major social problems such as poverty and hunger. Other critics argue that the advertising is simply being used as a way to promote the ruling political party. Do you think advertising by the Canadian federal government is a good use of tax dollars? What should be the goals of government advertising?[9]

✽ ✽ ✽
creative strategy The process that turns a concept into an advertisement.

✽ ✽ ✽
advertising appeal The central idea or theme of an advertising message.

eProvisioning solutions:
the way to get everyone in your company
working in uNison.

As part of the Novell₈ one Net vision, the employee eProvisioning Solution Framework gives you a simple way to provide, change or update the information, communication resources and applications employees need to be 100 percent productive on their first day and every day thereafter. (Plus, you'll have the security to revoke their access just as simply if an employee's status changes.) This increased productivity optimizes revenue and accelerates profit growth, going straight to your company's bottom line. That's the power of the Novell eProvisioning Solution Framework. **To find out how Novell and its partners can make eProvisioning solutions work for you, visit** www.novell.com/eprovisioning

Novell.
the power to chaNge

© Copyright 2001 Novell, Inc. All rights reserved. Novell is a registered trademark and the power to change is a trademark of Novell, Inc., in the United States and other countries.

Exhibit 17.4

Business products like software can be given a distinctive identity through advertising.

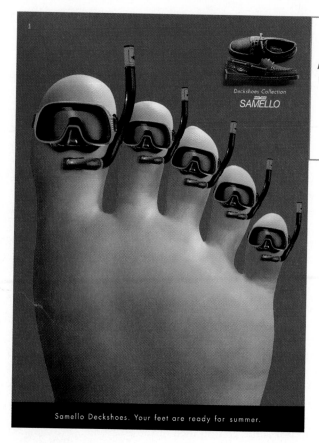

Samello Deckshoes. Your feet are ready for summer.

Exhibit 17.5

Advertising creatives find unique ways to express a concept.

advertisers use an emotional appeal complete with dramatic colour or powerful images, whereas others bombard the audience with facts. Some feature sexy people or stern-looking experts (even professors from time to time). Different appeals can work for the same product, from a bland "talking head" to a montage of animated special effects. An attention-getting way to say something profound about cat food or laundry detergent is more art than science, but we can describe some common appeals.

* *Reasons Why:* A **unique selling proposition (USP)** gives consumers a single, clear reason why one product is better at solving a problem. The format focuses on a need and points out how the product can satisfy it. For example, "m&m's melt in your mouth, not in your hands."

* *Comparative Advertising.* A *comparative advertisement* explicitly names two or more competitors. The Pepsi challenge is an example of a comparative advertising campaign that has been used successfully over a long period of time. Comparative ads like the Pepsi Challenge can be very effective, but there is a risk of turning off consumers who don't like the negative tone. This is especially a problem in cultures that don't take kindly to impolite messages. For instance, Tokyo's five major television networks pulled a Pepsi comparative ad, because Japanese viewers found it offensive to be too blunt.[10]

* *Demonstration:* The ad shows a product "in action" to prove that it performs as claimed. "It slices, it dices!" This appeal helps sell products that people "use."

* *Testimonial:* A celebrity, an expert, or a "typical person" states the product's effectiveness. The use of *celebrity endorsers* is a common but expensive strategy. It is particularly effective for mature products, which need to differentiate themselves from competitors. 3M Canada, for example, used comedian Steve Smith (otherwise known as Red Green) as the spokesperson for one of its mature products—the Scotch brand duct tape.[11]

* *Slice-of-Life:* A slice-of-life format presents a (dramatized) scene from everyday life. Today, advertisers are trying to expand their definition of "everyday life." An ad for Spray 'n' Wash Stain Stick from Dow Chemical, for example, shows a mother and her Down syndrome child. The mother comments, "The last place we need another chal-

✳ ✳ ✳

unique selling proposition (USP) An advertising appeal that focuses on one clear reason why a particular product is superior to any others.

3M Canada
www.3M.com/intl/CA/english

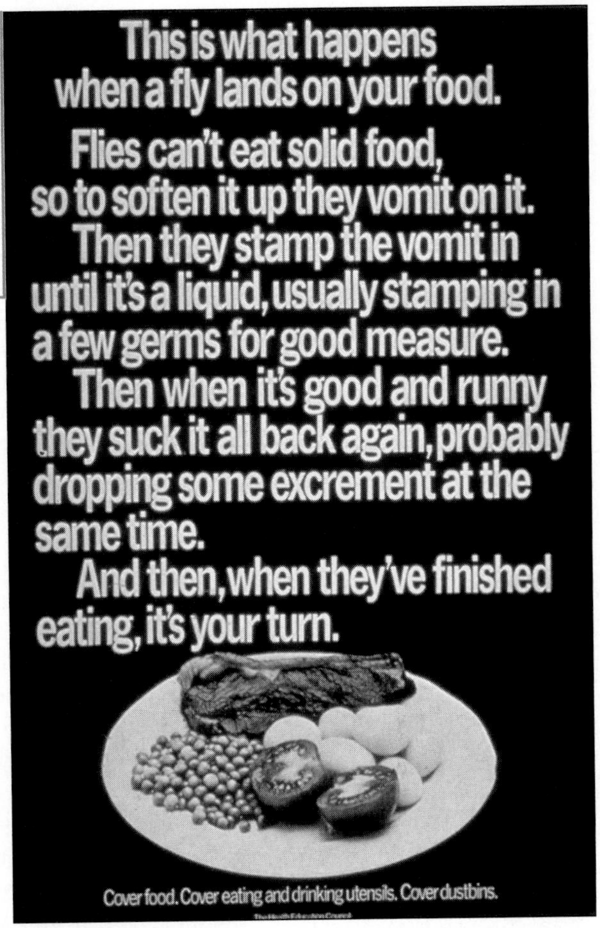

Exhibit 17.6

A graphic fear appeal.

This is what happens when a fly lands on your food.

Flies can't eat solid food, so to soften it up they vomit on it. Then they stamp the vomit in until it's a liquid, usually stamping in a few germs for good measure. Then when it's good and runny they suck it all back again, probably dropping some excrement at the same time. And then, when they've finished eating, it's your turn.

Cover food. Cover eating and drinking utensils. Cover dustbins.

lenge is the laundry room." One advertising critic described the spot as "the most crassly contrived slice-of-life in advertising history." But the American National Down Syndrome Congress applauded the ad and awarded Dow its annual media award.[12]

- *Lifestyle:* A lifestyle format shows a person or persons attractive to the target market in an appealing setting. The advertised product is "part of the scene," implying that the person who buys it will attain the lifestyle. For example, a commercial shown on MuchMusic might depict a group of snowboarders having fun and then taking time to drink a McCain fruit drink. A fantasy format is a variation of the lifestyle approach in which the viewer is encouraged to imagine being transported to a novel or exotic situation. Ads for some Canadian lotteries show fantasy lifestyles that ticket purchasers can achieve if they win the lottery. R K Swamy/BBDO used a lifestyle appeal to sell the Performa by focusing on how the machine empowers children to pursue their potential. They created print ads and television commercials that plugged the Performa by showing parents and children using it to expand their horizons. The goal was to create ad messages that are warm and friendly, "feel-good" ads that would humanize the technology behind Apple's products and show potential buyers how the home computer could improve their lives.

- *Fear Appeals:* This format highlights the negative consequences of using or not using a product. A classic 1970 British ad (see Exhibit 17.6) promoted the use of clean eating utensils. One of Anna Olofsson's options is to use a fear appeal to capitalize on young drinkers' anxiety about getting beaten or raped because they're too drunk to defend themselves.

- *Sex Appeals:* Some ads appear to be selling sex rather than products. This was the case in a recent ad for Carlsberg beer, run by Labatt Breweries of Canada, in which three women are shown discussing a boyfriend's willingness to perform a particular sexual act. These ads and many others rely on sexuality to get consumers' attention.

- *Humorous Appeals:* Humorous ads can be an effective way to break through advertising clutter. But humour can be tricky: What is funny to one person may be offensive to another. Different cultures also have different senses of humour.

Pretest What Will Be Said

Once the creatives have developed a way to communicate, how does the agency know if the ideas will work? Advertisers try to minimize mistakes by getting reactions to ad messages before they are actually placed. Much of this **pretesting**, the research that goes on in the early stages of a campaign, centres on gathering basic information that will help planners make sure they've accurately defined the product's market, consumers, and competitors. This information comes from quantitative sources, such as syndicated surveys, and qualitative sources, such as focus groups, which we discussed in Chapter 5.

As the campaign takes shape, the players need to determine how well the specific advertising concepts under development will perform. **Copy testing** measures the effectiveness of

✱ ✱ ✱
pretesting A research method that seeks to minimize mistakes by getting consumer reactions to ad messages before they appear in the media.

✱ ✱ ✱
copy testing A marketing research method that seeks to measure the effectiveness of ads by determining whether consumers are receiving, comprehending, and responding to the ad according to plan.

ads. It seeks to determine whether consumers are receiving, comprehending, and responding to the ad according to plan. There are several copy-testing techniques.

- *Concept testing* helps determine if initial ideas will work. Respondents, who are often drawn from the target market for which the ad is intended, evaluate different creative ideas or rough copies of ad layouts.

- *Test commercials* let consumers respond to a rough version of what a television message will look like. This preliminary treatment may take the form of an *animatic* or *storyboard*, such as the one shown in Exhibit 17.7, which is a series of sketches showing frame by frame what will happen in the finished commercial.

- *Finished testing* is testing audience reactions to a fully produced commercial to see if it has motivated them to buy the product. This occurs before the commercial actually airs on television. Because production of a "real" commercial is expensive, most testing is conducted before this point.

Choose the Media

✳✳✳

media planning The process of developing media objectives, strategies, and tactics for use in an advertising campaign.

Media planning is a problem-solving process for getting a message to a target audience in the most effective fashion. The decisions include audience selection and where, when, and how frequent the exposure should be. There is no such thing as one perfect medium for advertising. The choice depends on the specific target audience, the objective of the message, and the budget. For the advertisement to be effective, the media planner must match up the profile of the target market with that of specific media vehicles. For example, 80% of Chinese Canadian consumers in Vancouver read Chinese Canadian newspapers.[13] Thus, a marketer trying to reach this segment might allocate a significant share of the advertising budget to buying space in these newspapers.

✳✳✳

aperture The best place and time to reach a person in the target market group.

The media planner's first task in deciding where to place the advertising message is to find out when and where people in the target market are most likely to be exposed to the communication. This is the **aperture**, the best "window" to reach that type of person. For example, many people who drive to work in the morning listen to the radio, so their aperture would include this medium at this time.

TYPES OF MEDIA: WHERE TO SAY IT

What does a 52-inch television with Dolby Surround-Sound have in common with a matchbook? Each is a media vehicle that permits an advertiser to communicate with a potential customer. Depending on the intended message, each medium has its advantages and dis-

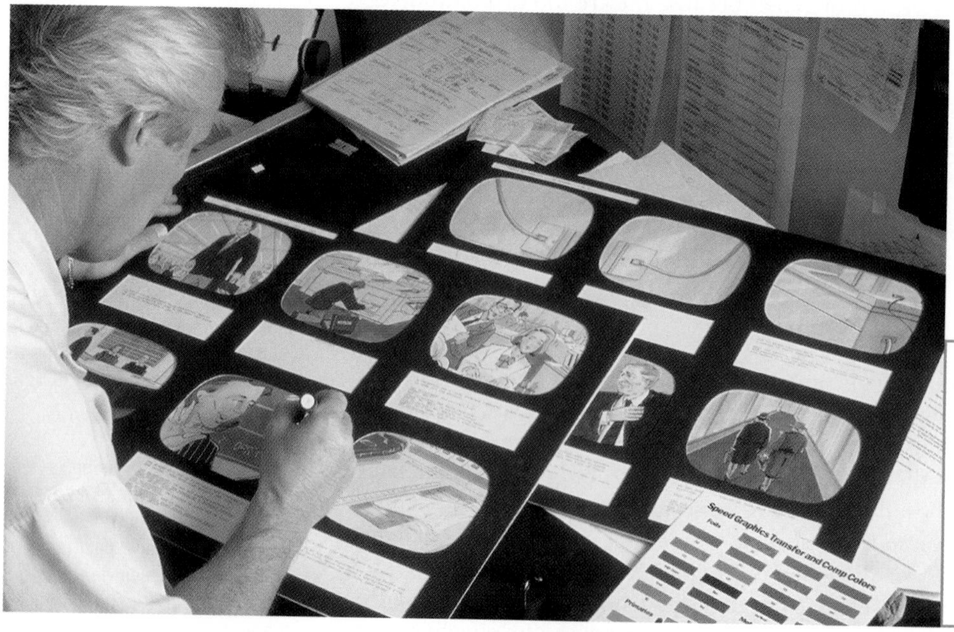

Exhibit 17.7

A storyboard presents preliminary ideas for an advertisement.

advantages. Let's look at the major categories of media. The pros and cons of each type are summarized in Table 17.1.

Television. Because of television's ability to reach so many people at once, this medium is a favourite choice for regional or national companies. Ninety-nine percent of Canadians live in households that have a TV; and on an average day, 77% of Canadians watch TV at least once.[14] There are two English (CBC and CTV) and two French (Radio-Canada and TVA) national television networks in Canada, which can offer both regional and national advertising exposure. There are 18 regional networks, three of which are in French. Yet another option for TV advertising is specialty channels, which provide a specific programming format (The Comedy Network) or audience (Women's Television Network) and can, therefore, provide easy access to a particular market segment.

Table 17.1 Pros and Cons of Selected Media Vehicles

Vehicle	Pros	Cons
Television	Extremely creative and flexible. Network TV is a cost-effective way to reach a mass audience. Specialty TV allows the advertiser to reach a selected group at relatively low cost. Messages have high impact because of the use of sight and sound.	The message is quickly forgotten unless it is repeated often. The audience is increasingly fragmented. Although the relative cost of reaching the audience is low, prices are still high on an absolute basis—often too high for smaller companies. A 30-second spot on a primetime TV sitcom costs over $45 000. Rising costs have led to more and shorter ads, which cause greater clutter.
Radio	Good for selectively targeting an audience. Relatively low cost, both for producing a spot and for running it repeatedly. Radio ads can be modified quickly to reflect changes in the marketplace. Use of sound effects and music allows listeners to use their imagination to create a vivid scene.	Listeners often don't pay full attention to what they hear. The small audience of most stations means ads must be repeated frequently. Not appropriate for products that must be seen or demonstrated to be appreciated.
Newspapers	Wide exposure provides extensive market coverage. Flexible format permits the use of colour, different sizes, and targeted editions. Useful for comparison shopping. Allows local retailers to tie in with national advertisers.	Most people don't spend much time reading the newspaper. Readership is especially low among teens and young adults. Short life span—people rarely look at a newspaper more than once. Very cluttered ad environment. The reproduction quality of images can be poor.
Magazines	Audiences can be narrowly targeted by specialized magazines. High credibility and interest level provide a good environment for ads. Advertising has a long life and is often passed along to other readers. Visual quality is excellent.	Can be expensive. The cost of a full-page, four-colour ad in a general-audience magazine typically exceeds $30 000. Long deadlines can reduce flexibility. The advertiser must generally use several magazines to reach the majority of a target market.
Internet Banner Advertising	Narrow targeting possible. Can be cost effective. Measurable.	Easily ignored. Very cluttered environment. Security/privacy issues may prevent consumers from clicking on banner ads.
Outdoor	Most of the population can be reached at low cost. Good for supplementing other media.	Hard to communicate complex messages. Hard to demonstrate a product's effectiveness. Controversial and disliked in many communities.

Source: Adapted from J. Thomas Russell and W. Ronald Lane, *Kleppner's Advertising Procedure*, 11th ed. (Upper Saddle River, NJ: Prentice Hall, 1990); William Wells, John Burnett, and Sandra Moriarty, *Advertising: Principles and Practice*, 3d ed. (Upper Saddle River, NJ: Prentice Hall, 1995).

One disadvantage of advertising on television is cost. In addition to the cost of placing ads in media, production costs range from $80 000 to $250 000 for a 30-second television ad.[15] This high cost of production has led some companies to consider advertising on TV without using commercials. *Product placement* is a method of advertising on television (and in movies), where the product is seen as part of the TV show (or movie) rather than in a separate ad. Recent product placements in Canadian TV shows include Nortel phones used on *The Newsroom*, Polaroid cameras used on *The X-Files* and *PSI Factor*, and BMWs used by characters on *Traders*. MMI Product Placement, the largest product placement company in Canada, claims that the advantages of product placement include image reinforcement when a "star" uses the product, brand awareness, extensive reach (during reruns as well as during first runs), and the protection of the product from zapping (since consumers often use zapping to avoid ads, not TV shows).[16]

Radio. One advantage of radio advertising is flexibility. Marketers can change commercials quickly, often on the spot by an announcer and a recording engineer.[17] Radio is attractive to advertisers seeking low cost and the ability to reach specific consumer segments. There are hundreds of radio stations in Canada, with formats ranging from contemporary hit radio to classical.[18] The growth of online radio also presents future opportunities for reaching large numbers of consumers in a cost-effective manner.

Newspapers. The newspaper is one of the oldest media vehicles. Retailers in particular have relied on newspaper ads since before the turn of the century to inform readers about sales and deliveries of new merchandise. Newspapers are an excellent medium for local advertising and for events (such as sales) that require a quick response. Many newspapers, such as *The Globe and Mail* and the *National Post*, offer online versions of their papers to expand their exposure.

Magazines. Magazine ads provide high-quality images and can reach specific segments of consumers. New technologies such as *selective binding* allow publishers to personalize their editions so that advertisements for local businesses can be included in issues mailed to specific locations. *Desktop publishing* software allows magazines to close their pages just before going to press—no more long lead times that used to plague advertisers that wanted to hit their market with timely information.

Directories. Directory advertising is the most "down-to-earth," information-focused advertising medium. Today, the *Yellow Pages* has revenues of over $9.5 billion, and more than 6000 directories are published in North America alone. These listings are usually references used just before the consumer makes the decision to buy, so the advertiser has the opportunity to influence the buyer immediately before the decision.

Computer media that transmit advertisements via e-mail and the Internet are growing in popularity, as increasing numbers of consumers get online. Worldwide Internet advertising revenues are projected to reach $16.5 billion by the year 2005.[19] As the ad for DoubleClick in Exhibit 17.8 shows, one potential advantage of

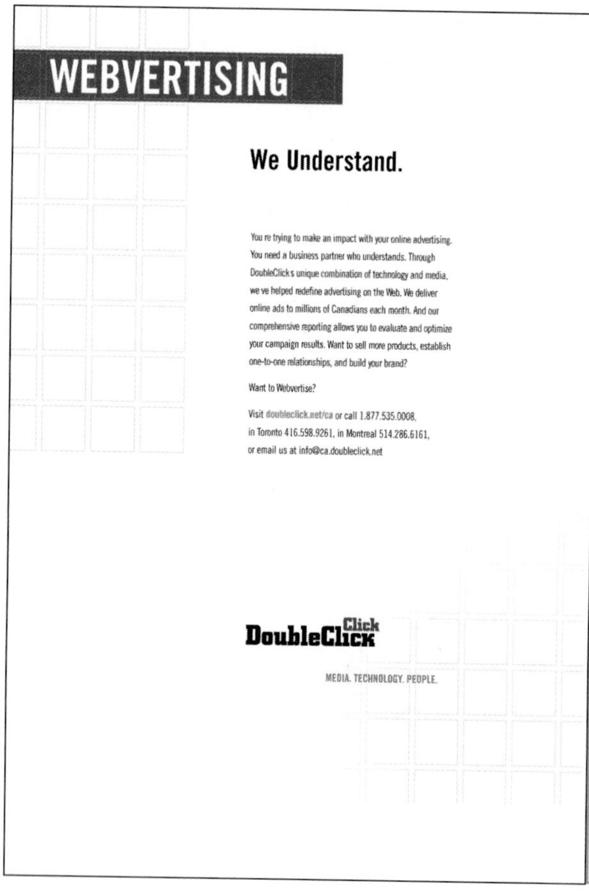

The Globe and Mail
www.globeandmail.ca

✳ ✳ ✳
computer media
Communications media that transmit information through the Internet or via e-mail messages.

WEBVERTISING

We Understand.

You're trying to make an impact with your online advertising. You need a business partner who understands. Through DoubleClick's unique combination of technology and media, we've helped redefine advertising on the Web. We deliver online ads to millions of Canadians each month. And our comprehensive reporting allows you to evaluate and optimize your campaign results. Want to sell more products, establish one-to-one relationships, and build your brand?

Want to Webvertise?

Visit doubleclick.net/ca or call 1.877.535.0008, in Toronto 416.598.9261, in Montreal 514.286.6161, or email us at info@ca.doubleclick.net

DoubleClick
MEDIA. TECHNOLOGY. PEOPLE.

Exhibit 17.8

Reaching their target market with advertising is important to media planners.

banner advertising online is that advertisers can reach a large and diverse number of consumers. However, some critics believe that most banner advertising goes unnoticed by Internet users, making it an ineffective advertising strategy.

Currently the majority of banner advertising on the Internet is done on portal sites, such as canoe.ca, www.canada.ca, or sympatico.ca, gateways through which Web surfers frequently pass on their way to other sites. Canadian banner advertising is also done through network vendors like DoubleClick (www.doubleclick.net/ca) that allow advertisers to target consumer groups using filters, including where the consumer lives, day or time of day when they access the site, or the Internet Service Provider (ISP) they use.

A company's Web site, although not a paid form of advertising, is becoming an increasingly important way to communicate interactively with consumers and support other forms of advertising. Kellogg Canada has set up several Web sites to support its advertising and communication goals for individual products. For example the site for Kellogg's Special K cereal (www.specialK.kelloggs.ca) uses the slogan from their television and magazine ads, "Look good on your own terms," and is designed for women, the cereal's primary target market. As users enter the site, they are shown an ad for Special K before the Web page loads. Once on the site, visitors can see recipes using the product, participate in chat rooms, or ask questions of fitness and nutrition experts. Through its Web site, Kellogg Canada is able to reinforce advertising activities in more traditional media and potentially reach new consumers with their ads and other promotional messages.

Kellogg Canada
www.kelloggs.ca

The Internet is also increasingly being used by companies to encourage word-of-mouth communications. Knowing that consumers often use chat rooms and Web sites to discuss products, companies have devised strategies to encourage positive word-of-mouth advertising through these informal advertising channels. This approach, called *viral marketing*, was used by Virgin Music Canada when promoting a new alternative band A Perfect Circle. The company wanted to target fans of the rock band Tool (one of the members of A Perfect Circle is also the lead singer for Tool), who tend to be Internet-savvy 15- to 25-year-old males. The company obtained the names of fans of Tool from *Watch* magazine, a Canadian publication that targets teens. Virgin Canada then selected five fans from Toronto and provided them with downloadable song samples from A Perfect Circle and information about the band. Virgin was hoping that these fans would then discuss the new band in online chat rooms and on other Web sites; this did happen. The five chosen teens were pleased that they were the first five kids to find out about the band and were happy to share their "find" with others online.[20]

Out-of-home media, such as blimps, transit ads, and billboards, reach people in public places. This medium works best when it tells a simple, straightforward story.[21]

✳ ✳ ✳
out-of-home media
Communications media that reach people in public places.

Marketers are constantly searching for new ways to get their messages out to busy people. Ads in movie theatres are popular with certain advertisers. For example, since TV viewers are also frequent movie goers, several TV networks, such as Global and the Discovery Channel (Canada), use ads in movie theatres to promote new shows.[23]

In addition, *place-based media*, which transmit messages in public places, can be an effective way to reach a captive audience. Kitchener, Ontario–based Timeline Technologies operates video screens that transmit ads while consumers are pumping gas at gas stations. IGRABBER is a Canadian company that sells ad space on more than 1000 mini-billboards in laundromats across the country.[24]

MEDIA SCHEDULING: WHEN TO SAY IT

After choosing the advertising media, the planner then creates a **media schedule** that specifies the exact media to use, when, and how often the message should appear. Figure 17.1 shows a hypothetical media schedule for the promotion of a new video game. Note that much of the advertising reaches its target audience in the months just before Christmas, and that much of the expensive television budget is focused on advertising during specials just before the holiday season. The company's Web site is used in the media schedule as a constant reinforcement of the paid advertising placed in other media.

✳ ✳ ✳
media schedule The plan that specifies the exact media to use and when.

The media schedule outlines the planner's best estimate of which media will be most effective in attaining the advertising objective(s), and which specific media vehicles will do

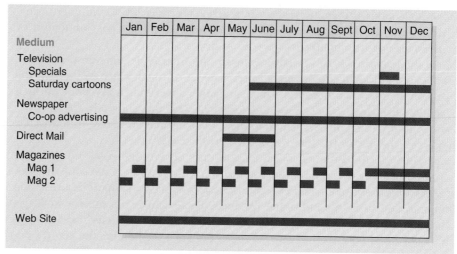

Figure 17.1 A Media Schedule for a Video Game

the most effective job. The media planner considers such factors as the match between the demographic and psychographic profile of a target audience and the people reached by a media vehicle, the advertising patterns of competitors, and the capability of a medium to convey the desired information adequately. The planner must also consider the compatibility of the product with editorial content: After all, viewers might not respond well to a light-hearted ad for a new snack food during a sombre documentary on world hunger.

When analyzing media, the planner is interested in assessing **advertising exposure**, the degree to which the target market will see an advertising message in a specific medium. Media planners talk in terms of **impressions**, which measure the number of people who will be exposed to a message placed in one or more media vehicles. For example, if one million people watch a miniseries on CTV, each time an advertiser runs an ad during that program, it receives one million impressions. If the advertiser's spot runs four times during the program, the impression count would be four million, even though some of these impressions would represent repeated exposure to the same viewers.

To calculate the exposure a message will have if placed in a certain medium, planners consider two factors: reach and frequency. **Reach** is the percentage of the target market that will be exposed to the media vehicle. This measure is particularly important for widely used products when it's important to get the message to as many consumers as possible. **Frequency** is the number of times a person in the target group would be exposed to the message. This is important with products that are complex or are targeted to relatively small markets for which multiple exposures to the message are necessary to make an impact.

For example, say a media planner wants to get Club Med advertising to university and college students. The advertiser learns that 25% of that target market reads at least a few issues of *Rolling Stone* each year (reach). The advertiser may also determine that these students are likely to see three of the twelve monthly ads that Club Med will run in *Rolling Stone* during the year (frequency). Now, the planner calculates the magazine's **gross rating points (GRPs)** by multiplying reach times frequency, which in this case compares the effectiveness of *Rolling Stone* to alternative media. By using this same formula, the planner can then compare the GRP number of another magazine or the GRP of placing an ad on television or on a bus or any other advertising medium.

Although some media vehicles deliver superior exposure, they may not be cost efficient. More people will see a commercial aired during the Stanley Cup playoffs than during a 3:00 a.m. rerun of a horror movie. But the advertiser could run late-night commercials every night for a year for the cost of one 30-second Stanley Cup spot. For example, a 30-second ad on CBC that would be shown across the country could cost as little as $100 or as much as $46 000, depending on when it was run. Similarly, a 30-second ad on TSN could be as little as $100 or as much as $20 000.[25]

SPOTLIGHT ON REAL PEOPLE *Amoeba Corporation*

Amoeba Corporation is an advertising agency formed in 1997 by three young Canadian entrepreneurs: Mikey Richardson, Michael Kelar, and Syam Smolkin. Two of the three partners studied at the Ontario College of Art and Design, and all three have a particular interest in the graphic design and creative side of advertising. Their philosophy in designing advertising has always been to question the traditional approach, a philosophy that is clearly working. After just a few years of operation, the company has become an important player in the Canadian advertising world.

Although they wanted to stay "unconventional," the company has ended up with some very conventional clients. Within three years of starting the agency, the entrepreneurs had designed ads for such high-profile accounts as Molson Canadian, Nike, the Bank of Montreal, and the Toronto Maple Leafs. Molson has been one of the most important clients for Amoeba, which provided input into the content of the Molson "I Am" advertising campaign, designed the Web site (www.iam.ca), and redesigned the "I Am" logo. Because the campaign received so much publicity, the work with Molson positioned Amoeba as a creative company that understands "cool." Their youthful perspective was also valuable in their work for the "Keep It Weird" concept for YTV, a contract that was worth about $400 000 to the company.

The success of Amoeba has meant that the company is growing rapidly, something that is both exciting and worrisome to its founders. As Kelar says, "We never want to become a traditional advertising agency, with all those account execs running around, not letting anyone else in the office work on their accounts. We want to be a creative house, and there is nothing that says a creative house can't produce good ads."[22]

1. Can Amoeba remain primarily a "creative house" as it starts to add employees and clients?
2. What are some ways that a creative atmosphere can be promoted in an advertising agency like Amoeba?
3. One of the benefits Amoeba brings to its clients is a youthful perspective. The founders of Amoeba are part of the target market for many of the companies they are working for, which means they understand the consumer well. Is it possible to create good advertising for a target group if you are not a member of that group? Do you think Amoeba could create effective ads for people 55 and older?

Amoeba Corporation
www.amoebacorp.com

✳ ✳ ✳
cost per thousand (CPM) A measure used to compare the relative cost effectiveness of different media vehicles that have different exposure rates: the cost to deliver a message to 1000 people or homes.

To compare the relative cost-effectiveness of different media and of spots run on different vehicles in the same medium, media planners use a measure called **cost per thousand (CPM)**. This figure compares the relative cost effectiveness of different media vehicles that have different exposure rates and reflects the cost to deliver a message to 1000 people. For example, the cost for a Canadian company to do banner advertising on DoubleClick averages $30 to $40 CPM.[26] A medium's popularity with consumers determines how much advertisers must pay to put their message on it. Television networks are concerned with getting good ratings, because their advertising rates are determined by how many viewers their programming attracts. Similarly, magazines and newspapers try to boost circulation and Web sites to justify raising ad rates.

MEDIA SCHEDULING: HOW OFTEN TO SAY IT

After deciding where to advertise, the planner must decide when and how often. What time of day? Frequently for a few weeks, or occasionally for a long time? After selecting the media schedule, the planner turns to the overall pattern the advertising will follow.

A *continuous schedule* maintains a steady stream of advertising throughout the year. This is most appropriate for products that sell on a regular basis, such as shampoo or bread. Some advertising professionals maintain that continuous advertising sustains market leadership even if total industry sales fall.[27] On the downside, some messages can suffer from *advertising wearout*, because people tune out the same old ad messages.

A *pulsing schedule* varies the amount of advertising throughout the year, based on when the product is likely to be in demand. A sunscreen manufacturer might advertise year round but more heavily during the summer months. *Flighting* is an extreme form of pulsing in which advertising appears in short, intense bursts alternating with periods of little to no activity. It can produce as much brand awareness as a steady dose of advertising at a much lower cost, if the messages from the previous flight were noticed and made an impact.

Evaluating Advertising

A retail advertiser once complained: "I am certain that half the money I spend on advertising is completely wasted. The trouble is, I don't know which half."[28] Now that we've seen how advertising is created and executed, we need to consider how we decide if it's working.

Research findings generally support the wisdom of spending money on advertising. Studies by media companies and trade groups show that increased advertising boosts sales, and that increased product usage is linked to advertising exposure.[29] Still, there's no doubt that a lot of advertising is ineffective, so it's important for firms to evaluate their efforts to increase the impact of their messages. Direct measures of advertising effectiveness are difficult to design. It is hard to determine just how many sales were the result of a specific ad campaign. Measuring the effectiveness of banner advertising is easier, since the number of visitors coming to a Web site through a banner ad is directly measurable. Ads placed in more traditional media, such as magazines, can be evaluated on their ability to persuade people to do something specific. For example, in the Adobe ad in Exhibit 17.9, the company wants people to visit the "defytherules" site; if Adobe wanted to measure the effectiveness of the ad, it might use number of visits to the Web site advertised as one measure of this. Most often, however, advertisers research consumer response to advertising through posttesting.

Posttesting

posttesting Research conducted on consumers' responses to actual advertising messages they have seen or heard.

Posttesting is conducting research on consumers' responses to advertising messages they have seen or heard (as opposed to pretesting, which collects reactions to messages before they're actually placed in "the real world"). Ironically, many creative ads that are quirky or even bizarre make an advertising agency look good within the industry but are ultimately unsuccessful, because they don't communicate what needs to be said about the product it-

www.defytherules.com

Adobe® software lets you do the impossible on the Web. Go. See for yourself. Inspiration becomes reality.™

Adobe

Exhibit 17.9

The number of people visiting the "defytherules" Web site would be one way of measuring the effectiveness of this ad.

self. As one consultant observed, "There is so much emphasis on the creative aspect of the ads, sort of 'Aren't we clever?' that the message is lost."[30]

In some cases, the ads are popular but they send the wrong message to consumers. For example, a lot of people remember Joe Isuzu, the lying car salesman whose television commercials were popular for two years but were no help to Isuzu's car sales during that time.[31] As one advertising executive explained, "The humor got in the way. All you remembered was that car salesmen are dishonest, and the car salesman you remembered most was from Isuzu."[32] Three measures of the impact of an advertisement are *unaided recall, aided recall,* and *attitudinal measures.* **Unaided recall** tests, by telephone survey or personal interview, how much of an ad a person remembers during a specified period of time, sometimes by asking the person to write down what the ad said. An **aided recall** test uses clues to prompt answers. For example, a researcher might show a group of consumers a list of brands and ask them to choose which items they have seen advertised within the past week. **Attitudinal measures** probe a bit more deeply by testing consumer beliefs or feelings about a product before and after being exposed to messages about it. If, for example, Dove antiperspirant's ads about the product being good for the skin make enough consumers believe that this is an important attribute for antiperspirants, marketers can consider the advertising campaign successful.

Challenges Facing the Advertising Industry

In addition to evaluating the quality of specific advertising messages, marketers must also think hard about the overall effectiveness of advertising as a promotional strategy, especially as other forms of promotion threaten to overshadow it. There was a time in the 1970s and 1980s when it seemed that advertising agencies could do no wrong. Spurred by the popularity of new product categories, such as personal computers and compact disc players, that needed heavy promoting, ad revenues soared. Things slowed down in the 1990s, and although the industry is healthier now, it still faces several threats, as many marketers are choosing to allocate less of their promotional budget to advertising and shifting money into other areas, such as sales promotions. Challenges include:

- *Erosion of brand loyalty.* Consumers are becoming cynical due to the constant barrage of advertisements, and buyers are more likely to choose brands based on price rather than image. When consumers buy on the basis of price only, image-oriented advertising, which stresses such intangible qualities as sex appeal or style, is not very effective.

- *Technology gives power back to the people.* Modern technology has given consumers the Internet, interactive TV, television remotes, and VCRs. No longer passive "couch potatoes," consumers have the power to have their voice heard online and to avoid ads by "zipping," or fast-forwarding, through commercials or by "zapping" them when channel-surfing.

- *Greater emphasis on point-of-purchase factors.* Consumers make many purchase decisions when they are actually shopping. This realization has forced many marketers to shift away from advertising toward other elements of the promotion mix, such as in-store sales promotions and publicity events.

- *The rules are changing.* Although advertising has always been a competitive business, executives in communications services companies are now finding that they must also compete with other industries for business. Formerly loyal clients such as Coca-Cola are turning to computer wizards and even to Hollywood talent agencies to produce mind-bending commercials, using the latest special effects technology, or to recruit movie directors and other specialists who are able to create gripping stories about everyday products.

- *The advertising environment is cluttered.* Many messages compete for customers' attention. About 1600 magazines are published in Canada every year, and there are more than 900 radio stations and 108 daily newspapers, all of which depend on advertising revenue to survive. The average household can view several television channels; during prime time, commercials account for 10.5 minutes of each programming hour.[33] Many people feel overwhelmed by the barrage of ads, and a lot of messages simply get lost.

- *Some consumers are turned off by advertising.* Some advertising messages are so persistent or obnoxious that people tune them out. One survey said 60% of consumers polled

✻ ✻ ✻
unaided recall A research technique conducted by telephone survey or personal interview that asks how much of an ad a person remembers during a specified period of time.

✻ ✻ ✻
aided recall A research technique that uses clues to prompt answers from people about advertisements they might have seen.

✻ ✻ ✻
attitudinal measures A research technique that probes a consumer's beliefs or feelings about a product before and after being exposed to messages about it.

Adbusters
www.adbusters.org

agreed with the statement "advertising insults my intelligence."[34] Other people feel that ads have little or no credibility, because product claims are untrue or exaggerated. Canadian-based Adbusters presents strong criticisms of the credibility and usefulness of advertising messages and the advertising industry itself through a quarterly magazine and through its Web site. Spoof ads on the Web site make fun of such familiar advertising campaigns as those for Calvin Klein Obsession and Absolut Vodka.

How the Advertising Industry Is Meeting the Challenges

These discouraging factors have forced advertising professionals to demonstrate that advertising can deliver powerful, persuasive messages to vast numbers of consumers in a cost-efficient manner. One solution is to continue to create images that are fun, artistic, or powerful to remind us that "a picture is worth a thousand words." In addition, advertisers are looking to the future to anticipate changes and be sure that their messages will always have a place in society. These are some ways they're doing this:

- *Global Reach.* Advertisers are trying to establish brand images globally, so that customers around the world will respond to their messages and allow firms to expand their markets by appealing to many people with the same messages (see Chapter 4). Dentsu's advertising for Lexus cars in Japan targets higher-income Japanese, but the creative execution depicts a young North American law professor as the ideal driver of the car. Even though the person in the ad is a foreigner, the agency is counting on this "upscale" image to travel across national boundaries.

- *Diversity.* Consumers are becoming quite vocal about advertising they feel singles out a group in a negative way. Nike ads starring cartoon character Porky Pig drew fire from the National Stuttering Project, which argued that advertisers that make fun of speech disabilities make it difficult for stutterers to get respect.[35] As Chapter 6 discussed, many

Real People, Real Decisions
How it worked out at A&O Analys

The campaign used a combination of Options 2 and 3. To get maximum attention from the adolescents, the message used a fear appeal by creating a slogan that was a play on words: "Alco-hole in your head?" The objective of the campaign was to encourage adolescents to come up with ideas to help their younger friends develop more moderate drinking behaviours by entering an advertising contest. The prize was a trip to Miami to meet with the American equivalent of the Non-Violence Project. The information campaign used a mixture of personal appearances and media. Representatives from the Non-Violence Project visited 10% of Sweden's colleges and talked to students about their drinking behaviour in a humorous way.

In addition, three 60-second commercials aired, showing how even moderate use of alcohol can snowball into a dangerous situation. The commercials used a number of rising young actors and actresses to increase interest. They depicted social drinkers who suddenly found themselves in potentially dangerous situations. The only written copy in the commercial was the address for the "Alco-hole in your head" home page so the viewer could surf the net for more information and enter the ad competition. A magazine called *Alco-hole in Your Head* (one issue cover is shown as the opening image for this chapter) also arrived at the home of every 18-year-old in Sweden. The magazine contained articles about sex, violence, and alcohol, as well as entry forms for the advertising competition.

Posttest research showed that 89% of those who received the magazine read at least parts of it. Ninety-two percent thought the campaign was trustworthy, 76% said it made them think about how their friends used alcohol, and half of the group said they reflected about their own drinking habits. Olofsson was particularly encouraged that almost half of the target market had saved the magazine. In addition, many adolescents sent their entries to the ad competition. The winner submitted a script with lines for a teen saying, "I drink in order to feel good!" while in the background listeners hear the sound of someone vomiting.

Canadian companies now practise multicultural marketing and are working hard to better reflect the cultural diversity of their target markets by including people of different ethnic groups in their advertising.

- *Technology.* Many agencies use new technology to deliver advertising messages—such as e-mail—often with a touch of personalization. Chrysler Corporation recently introduced Command, a system that coordinates the company's databases to learn about customers. This system allows Chrysler to customize its advertising to customer preferences. Command does this by ensuring that drivers receive ads for only those models in which they're most likely to be interested, so the information they receive is timely and welcome rather than intrusive.[36] Other marketers are hard at work developing Web sites and *e-zines*, which include advertisements you can click on only if you want to see and hear them—and making these messages so interesting that you *will* want to see and hear them.

Chapter Summary

1. Tell what advertising is and describe the major types of advertising.

   Advertising is non-personal communication from an identified sponsor using mass media to persuade or influence an audience. Advertising informs, reminds, and creates consumer desire. Product advertising is used to persuade consumers to choose a specific product or brand. Institutional advertising is used to develop an image for an organization or company, or to express opinions (advocacy advertising), or support a cause (public service advertising).

2. Describe the major players in the advertising process.

   Advertising begins with the client or advertiser, which may be a manufacturer, distributor, retailer, or institution. Some companies have in-house advertising departments, but most rely on the services of advertising agencies. Advertising agencies or communications services companies create ads (or other promotions) and arrange for their delivery to the target market. Typical agency personnel and departments include account management who supervises the account, creative services who dream up and produce ads, research and marketing services who collect and analyze target market information, and media planners who recommend and buy the appropriate media.

3. Tell how advertisers develop an advertising campaign.

   Development of an advertising campaign begins with developing message and budget objectives—what the advertising campaign seeks to accomplish and what it is expected to cost. Next, advertisers develop a creative strategy that should create attention, interest, desire, and action. Some of the frequently used types of advertising appeals are unique selling propositions (USP), comparative advertising, demonstrations, testimonials, slice-of-life ads, lifestyle ads, fear appeal ads, sex appeal ads, and humorous ads. To avoid mistakes, pretesting or copy testing of advertising before placing in the media may include concept testing, testing of television advertising animatics or storyboards, and finished ad testing.

4. Describe the major advertising media and the important considerations in media planning.

   A media plan determines where and when advertising will appear. Broadcast media choices include television and radio. Print media are newspapers, magazines, and directories. Computer-based media provide opportunities for Internet banner advertising and the use of Web sites as an advertising vehicle. Out-of-home media include outdoor advertising (primarily billboards) and place-based media. In developing media schedules, planners consider the size and characteristics of each media vehicle's audience, the objectives of the media plan—reach and frequency, the advertising of competitors, and the capabilities of the media. Planners examine the comparative cost efficiency of each media vehicle, using cost per thousand (CPM). Media planners must also decide whether to use a continuous, pulsing, or flighting schedule.

KEY TERMS

advertising (474)

advertising appeal (479)

advertising campaign (475)

advertising exposure (486)

advocacy advertising (475)

aided recall (489)

aperture (482)

attitudinal measures (489)

computer media (484)

copy testing (481)

cost per thousand (CPM) (487)

creative strategy (479)

frequency (486)

gross rating points (GRPs) (486)

impressions (486)

institutional advertising (475)

media planning (482)

media schedule (485)

out-of-home media (485)

posttesting (488)

pretesting (481)

product advertising (474)

public service advertisements (475)

reach (486)

unaided recall (489)

unique selling proposition (USP) (480)

5. Explain how advertisers evaluate the effectiveness of the campaign.

Advertisers need to conduct research to determine if specific advertisements are effective. Posttesting research may include recall tests or attitudinal measures, which examine whether the message had an influence on the target market.

6. Discuss the challenges facing advertising.

As other types of promotion threaten to overtake advertising, advertisers face a number of challenges. These include erosion of brand loyalty, threats from technology, greater emphasis on point-of-purchase communications, new communications industries, a cluttered advertising environment, and increased consumer disapproval of advertising. Advertisers respond by seeking to establish global brand images, reflecting cultural diversity in ads, and personalizing messages by using technology.

Chapter Review

Marketing Concepts: Testing Your Knowledge

1. What is advertising and what is its role in marketing?

2. What are the types of advertising that are most often used?

3. List and describe the various departments in an advertising agency.

4. What is an advertising campaign?

5. What is a creative strategy? Describe some of the different advertising appeals.

6. What are the strengths and weaknesses of television, radio, newspapers, magazines, out-of-home media, and the Internet for advertising?

7. What information does a media planner use in developing an effective media schedule?

8. What are continuous, pulsing, and flighting media schedules?

9. How can advertisers make sure their advertising is effective before it is placed in the media and after the audience has been exposed to the advertising in the media?

10. What are the challenges facing advertising today? How have advertisers responded to these challenges?

Marketing Concepts: Discussing Choices and Issues

1. Some people are turned off by advertising because they say it is obnoxious, that it insults their intelligence, and that advertising claims are untrue. Others argue that advertising is beneficial and actually provides value for consumers. What are some arguments on each side? How do you feel?

2. In recent years, for various reasons, many advertisers have been decreasing the amount spent on advertising. What are the reasons for this change? What do you think will happen to advertising spending during the next five to ten years?

3. Advertisers who spend millions of dollars for ads during special events such as the Olympics may be more interested in achieving aesthetic goals—having the most highly rated ad—than in selling products. Does it make sense for advertisers to focus on aesthetic goals rather than on marketing goals? Explain.

4. Technology through the Internet, television remotes, VCRs, and digital television is giving today's consumers more and more control over the advertising images they see. How has this affected the advertising industry so far? Do you think this will affect it in the future? What are some ways that advertising can respond to this?

Marketing Practice: Applying What You've Learned

1. As an account executive for a communications services firm, you have been assigned to a new client, a manufacturer of a popular brand of toothpaste. As you begin development of the creative strategy, you are considering different types of appeals:

a. USP

b. comparative advertising

c. a fear appeal

d. a celebrity endorsement

e. a slice-of-life ad

f. sex appeal

g. humour

Outline the strengths and weaknesses of using each of these appeals for advertising the toothpaste.

2. Assume that you are working in the media department of an advertising agency. You have been asked your opinion on which media to use for advertising for a local retail clothing store.

a. Write a memo that compares newspapers, magazines, television, radio, and outdoor advertising as vehicles for this media plan.

b. Write a memo assessing the appropriateness of each of these media for advertising a national brand of dog food.

3. Spend some time looking through magazines. Find an ad that fits each of the following categories:

a. USP strategy

b. testimonial

c. lifestyle format

d. humour appeal

Critique each ad. Tell who the target market appears to be. Describe how the appeal is executed. Discuss what is good and bad about the ad. Do you think the ad will be effective? Why or why not?

Marketing Mini-Project: **Learning by Doing**

The purpose of this mini-project is to give you an opportunity to experience the advertising creative process.

1. With one or more classmates, create (imagine) a new brand of an existing product, such as a laundry detergent, toothpaste, perfume, or soft drink.

2. Decide on an advertising appeal for your new product.

3. Create a series of at least three different magazine ads for your product, using the appeal you selected. Your ads should have a headline, a visual, and copy to explain your product and to persuade customers to purchase your brand.

4. Present your ads to your class. Discuss the advertising appeal you selected, and explain your ad executions.

Real People, Real Surfers: **Exploring the Web**

Much of the advertising you see every day on television and in magazines is created by communications services companies and advertising agencies. Some of these companies are large, some very small. Some offer clients specialized services, such as "new media" advertising, while others offer a wide variety of services. To make their company stand out from the others, the different agencies develop unique personalities or corporate philosophies. Visit the Web sites of several large and small Canadian communications companies.

Cossette Communications Group (www.cossette.com)

BBDO Canada (www.bbdo.ca)

Amoeba Corporation (www.amoebacorp.com)

Palmer Jarvis DDB (www.palmerjarvisddb.com)

Sonic Boom (www.sonicboom.com)

Critical Mass (www.criticalmass.ca)

Explore the Web sites to see how they differ. Then answer these questions.

1. What is the mission of each company? How does each company attempt to position itself?

2. Who are some of the major clients of the firm?

3. How does the site demonstrate the creative ability of the company? Does the site do a good job of communicating the mission of the company? Explain.

4. If it is available, tell a little about the history of the company.

5. Of the companies you visited, which would you most like to work for and why?

6. As a client, based on your exploration of the Web sites, which company would you choose for your business and why?

MARKETING IN ACTION

Brand Canada

Developing an appealing brand identity has become an important part of attracting international investment to Canada. While the US, which is much larger in terms of population, has a strong brand image that doesn't require much active promotion internationally, Canada's image is more prone to misconceptions or simply lack of knowledge and therefore needs the help of a branding strategy. To compete effectively for investment dollars in the future, Canada needs a proactive branding strategy, incorporating an international advertising campaign, which will convince international investors that Canada is a good investment opportunity.

The image of Canada internationally is not as favourable as it should be. A study of international executives found that Canada was ranked 12th as an investment choice, despite the fact that a 2002 study conducted by management consulting firm KPMG found that the cost of doing business in Canada over a 10 year period is lower than doing business elsewhere in North America, Europe or Japan. Canadian cabinet minister Pierre Pettigrew made the following observation about brand Canada: "I am struck by how other nations view Canada. We are still seen as a nice country, with Mounties, maple syrup and hockey. We are not yet recognized as an economy fired by information technology, fuelled by telecommunications and fortified by the fifth-largest aerospace industry in the world. This outdated view of Canada has to change...."

In the past, the only significant advertising Canada has done internationally was for tourism, much of it highlighting Canada's natural beauty and wildlife. While this advertising is appropriate for appealing to certain tourist segments, it also reinforces images of Canada that are not consistent with those of a competitive nation that offers exciting business opportunities for investors. Even Canadians themselves don't have a good idea of the Canadian business identity. One study found that 46% of Canadians still think Canada's number one export is wood pulp, when it actually accounts for only about 5% of total exports.

One of the problems Canada faces in establishing its brand identity is proximity to the United States. Canada is often viewed by international business people as an extension of the US, and large Canadian companies, such as Nortel Networks, are often perceived as being American. One of Canada's challenges is to establish a brand image that communicates that Canada is the largest trading partner of the US, a key competitive advantage for international business people who may be looking at Canada as a gateway to entering the US market.

Recognizing that brand Canada has a weak image in Japan, the Canadian ambassador to Japan has already launched a rebranding of Canada. A recent survey in Japan revealed that Canada was perceived as a dull and "stodgy" country, with only 3% of respondents indicating that Canada was a source of high technology. Visits to Japan by Margaret Atwood, performances by Cirque du Soleil, and other events highlighting Canadian high tech executives are some activities that the ambassador is using to help reformulate the Japanese perception of brand Canada.

Branding consultants considering how to improve brand Canada on a broader scale internationally have suggested a multimillion-dollar, international advertising campaign aimed at building a strong technology-focused brand, while still retaining some of the traditional images (such as the Maple Leaf) that people around the world strongly associate with Canada. One consultant even suggested hiring Mike Myers to promote the fact that although most people think that he (like many Canadian products) is American, he's Canadian. Another consultant sums up the situation this way: "Canada has for too long branded itself as the land of vacations, of beavers and nice folks....Let people know the beaver has fangs. Cover your Maple Leaf in computer chips."

Sources: Miro Cernetig, "Canada isn't working," *Report on Business Magazine*, May 2001; "Canada still number one," press release, 29 January 2002, http://napoleon.ic.gc.ca/scdt/bizinvst/interface2.nsf/engdoc/0.html.

THINGS TO THINK ABOUT

1. What key messages about brand Canada do the international business community need to hear?
2. Develop an advertising campaign that can be used to convince international investors to invest in Canada. What countries should be targeted with the campaign? What media should be used?

HARRY POTTER

and the Prisoner of Azkaban

J.K. ROWLING

DOUBLE SMARTIES AWARD-WINNING AUTHOR

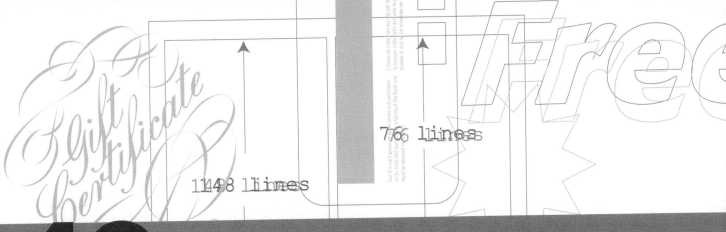

18

Sales Promotion, Public Relations, and Personal Selling

When you have completed your study of this chapter, you should be able to

CHAPTER OBJECTIVES

1. Explain the role of public relations.

2. Describe the steps in developing a public relations campaign.

3. Explain what sales promotion is and describe some of the different types of trade and consumer sales promotion activities.

4. Explain the important role of personal selling in the marketing effort.

5. List the steps in the personal selling process.

6. Explain the job of the sales manager.

Real People, Real Decisions ✔ ✘

Meet Desiree Walsh and Tessa Vanderkop
Decision Makers at Raincoast Books

Marketing decisions are often a team effort, and that is certainly the case at Raincoast Books. Raincoast is the Vancouver-based publishing company that holds the Canadian rights to J.K. Rowling's popular series of books featuring the adventures and exploits of Harry Potter—the bespectacled orphaned wizard, attendee of Hogwarts School of Witchcraft and Wizardry, and bane of the evil Lord Voldemort. Raincoast Books, with over 100 employees, is a book publisher, distributor, and wholesaler—a unique combination in the Canadian book industry. Two key decision makers at Raincoast Books are Desiree Walsh and Tessa Vanderkop, who lead a team of marketing professionals responsible for the Canadian marketing and promotion of J.K. Rowling's books, with particular focus on the fourth book in the series, *Harry Potter and the Goblet of Fire*.

Desiree Walsh is director of marketing at Raincoast Books, a position she has held for three years. She has been working in publishing for eight years (six at Raincoast) in various capacities, including telemarketing representative and trade catalogue coordinator. Marketing was the furthest thing from her mind while she was at Wellesley College where she received a BA in Chinese studies in 1986. Tessa Vanderkop, publicity manager for the past six months, has been with Raincoast for five years, starting as an in-house sales rep and working her way through the marketing and publicity department. Vanderkop has a BA in history and English from Simon Fraser University.

Raincoast Books
www.raincoast.com

Fido
www.fido.ca

Advertising's Not the Only Game in Town!

Organizations that follow an integrated marketing communications (IMC) strategy recognize that advertising is only one element of the communications mix. Microcell Solutions, for example, supports their Fido (PCS phone) brand's communications strategy with a strong public relations program, sales promotion, and personal selling. In the greater Toronto area, their Microcell's objective was to increase awareness and trial of Fido and leverage the emotional relevancy of the brand to reach customers one-to-one.[1] They linked a variety of experiences—key messages, images, sounds, and activities to the brand under the theme "Fun & Freedom." They launched the campaign with a "Fido mobile," a vintage 1942 bus pulled by a dozen dogs, which attracted significant media attention. Fun & Freedom events were held throughout greater Toronto—augmented by free photographing of prospective customers and their pets, having dogs perform tricks to demonstrate Fido's feature and benefits, and allowing prospective customers to make free calls anywhere in Fido's coverage area. Fido also chose to involve Canine Vision Canada in the campaign, because both Fido and guide dogs represent freedom to their masters. Advertising supported the public relations efforts by visually linking Fido to fun and freedom imagery, such as sunglasses, beach balls, and fireworks. Sales promotions, including a grand prize sweepstakes and at-event contests for T-shirts, baseball caps, Fido phones, and airtime packages, further enhanced the overall strategy. The campaign was successful in making the Fido brand personally relevant to thousands of pet owners.

This novel way to create interest in a PCS brand combined three different communication techniques, in addition to advertising, to make an impact: public relations (including free publicity covering the Fido Mobile), sales promotion (contests and free airtime to get people to try the phone), and personal selling (delivering messages to pet owners in person). In this chapter, we'll look at these three forms of promotion communication, common additions to advertising in a firm's communications mix. We start with public relations, which is what Raincoast Books excels at.

Public Relations

Chapter 16 noted that **public relations (PR)** helps build mutually beneficial long-term relationships and improve the image of an organization with key stakeholders—consumers, the media, shareholders, legislators, and interest groups. Public relations is crucial to an organization's ability to create and sustain a favourable relationships, corporate goodwill, and overall image. There are many types of public relations that focus on different activities and stakeholders:

* Publicity and media relations: unpaid communications about an organization and/or its products appearing in the mass media.
* Corporate public relations: managing the overall reputation and image of the organization.
* Crisis management: plans for the management of corporate crises, including boycotts, recalls, natural disasters, strikes.
* Employee relations: internal programs designed to foster positive relationships among and between organization employees.
* Financial relations: effective communications directed toward investors, regulators, and other financial stakeholders.
* Public affairs: lobbying efforts aimed at influencing policy decisions at the federal, provincial, and municipal levels of government.
* Community relations: grassroots management of relationships with local community stakeholders, including business owners, major employers, schools, kids' groups, and community organizations.

Although public relations is a powerful element of the communications mix, it is often overlooked by marketers, primarily because it doesn't have the creative and visual appeal of creating an "ad." Public relations is powerful because it is interactive, helping to foster relationships (recall from Chapter 16 the value of relationship marketing). It allows corporations

***

public relations (PR) Communications strategies to build good relationships and corporate image with an organization's stakeholders, including consumers, stockholders, and legislators.

to build social goodwill, which can often protect them against future public issues and concerns. It also provides a higher level of credibility and believability when the communication is presented through third parties like reporters, experts, celebrities, or independent organizations such as the Consumers' Association of Canada. Finally, public relations provides an inexpensive way to reach not only consumers but also other stakeholders important to the interests of an organization.

Objectives of Public Relations

Public relations specialists need to operate at many levels to ensure that various stakeholders receive coordinated, and accurate messages about the firm. As we saw with the Fido example, public relations strategies are often used in concert with advertising, sales promotions, and personal selling to accomplish communication objectives related to:

- *Introducing new products:* When Al Galbraith earned the chance to sell 246 homes in the village at Cornwallis Park, a former military base in Nova Scotia, he enlisted a PR agency to help him develop an innovative public relations and advertising campaign. It was expected to take two years to sell the well-maintained, three- and four-bedroom homes, some of which had ocean views; Galbraith sold them all in seven weeks. One key was price—the homes were $29 900 to $49 900. A second key was getting media attention. Galbraith and his PR agency created news releases to catch the public interest angles—the developer was targeting former service men and other retirees who didn't have a lot of money, and was revitalizing a down-trodden region of Nova Scotia; these were picked up across the country.[2]

Ocean Spray Cranberries Ltd.
www.oceanspray.com

- *Supporting current products:* Ocean Spray Cranberries Ltd. sponsored research at Harvard Medical School that confirmed the "folk wisdom" that cranberry juice is an effective way to treat urinary tract infections. With the help of PR agency Cohn & Wolfe in Toronto, Ocean Spray sent press kits to food editors and other writers with a focus on health and seniors' lifestyles to promote the study published in the *New England Journal of Medicine* and to offer interviews with the leader of the research team, Dr. Jerry Avorn.[3] The strategy was to promote the product category, not the brand, but sales of Ocean Spray Cranberry juice increased significantly after the PR program.

- *Influencing government legislation:* Concerned about public outcry over the price of gasoline, Petro-Canada and other distributors developed a PR campaign to explain that more than half the price consumers pay for gasoline is tax.[4] This was intended, in part, to deflect public influence onto the federal and provincial governments.

- *Enhancing the image of an organization or entity:* Faced with international criticism about possible human rights abuses and restriction of trade, the Chinese government established an office in charge of "overseas propaganda" to present a more favourable image of China to the rest of the world.[5]

- *Calling attention to a firm's involvement with the community:* To help improve their corporate images, Canadian insurance companies, such as Royal Insurance, are providing financial aid and employees' time to support community initiatives, such as injury awareness campaigns, sailing regattas, block parent associations, and neighbourhood watch. These companies have realized what others organizations that support little league teams, youth associations, and community events have known all along—being involved in community interests helps win friends and influence people.[6] Many companies find value in sponsorship of large-scale events, such as the Benson & Hedges Symphony of Fire, the DuMaurier Montreal International Jazz Festival (see Exhibit 18.2), or the Molson Indy. Public relations specialists work behind the scenes to ensure that a sponsored event receives ample press coverage and exposure for the organization.

- *Demonstrating social responsibility:* With help from Toronto-based social marketing firm Manifest Communications, Swedish telecom giant Ericsson launched a program called Ericsson Response, a worldwide initiative to aid the cause of disaster relief by providing mobile and satellite telephones systems to humanitarian relief workers.[7] Crabtree & Evelyn of London, Ontario, donates $2 for every bath gel sold in the month of October to the Canadian Breast Cancer Foundation, which helps raise the company's visibility.[8]

Exhibit 18.2

A sponsored event is a form of public relations.

- *Developing positive employee or investor relations:* Petro-Canada uses PR to influence, albeit indirectly, government legislation. They have also undertaken an internal communications program in an effort to enlist their 4500 employees in the cause to redirect public concern about gas prices—recognizing that their employees are their best ambassadors.[9] Husky Injection Molding Systems introduced a program that allows its 3000 workers to earn company shares for acting green and helping others. While this has social responsibility and community involvement messages, it also makes employees more committed to the organization and helps shape organization culture.[10] Electronic bulletin boards, newsletters, golf tournaments, and staff picnics are among many vehicles used to develop positive employee relations. Company tours, open houses, annual reports, quarterly reports, annual general meetings, technical briefings, and one-on-one interviews are some of the methods used to develop relationships with investors and potential investors.

- *Handling communication issues and crises:* A few years ago, PepsiCo was rocked by claims that hypodermic needles had been found in Diet Pepsi cans. The company assembled a crisis team to map out a response and supplied video footage of its bottling process to reassure people that foreign objects could not be inserted at the factory. The claims turned out to be false, and PepsiCo ran ads designed to let people know there was nothing to worry about. Pepsi's calm, coordinated response averted a public relations disaster. Similarly, Bridgestone/Firestone Canada Inc. decided to act proactively and voluntarily recalled a million sport-utility vehicle (SUV) tires when it was learned that some Firestone tires had failed in the United States under the conditions of high temperatures, high speed, and low tire pressure. This PR initiative will cost Bridgestone/Firestone over $212 million in Canada but is expected to foster stronger long-term relationships with SUV owners.[11] McDonald's, on the other hand, decided to sue a London, England–based environmental group in the 1980s to prevent it from publishing a pamphlet that accused McDonald's of numerous wrongdoings. McDonald's won the suit, but it took ten years and cost $23 million in legal fees, and the proceedings were covered by the global media for a decade. Supporters of the defendants established a Web site (www.mcspotlight.org) that is still frequently updated to bring public scrutiny to McDonald's business practices.[12]

Planning a Public Relations Campaign

A public relations campaign is a coordinated effort to communicate with one or more of the firm's stakeholders. It requires a three-step process of developing objectives, executing, and evaluating.

The organization must first develop clear objectives for the PR program that define the message it wants people to hear. Raincoast Books, for example, wanted to ensure that they got the "most bang for the time" in terms of favourable publicity surrounding J.K. Rowling's visit to Canada. After determining the objective, the PR specialists create a campaign strategy, which includes these elements:

- a statement of the problem
- a situation analysis
- specification of target audiences (publics)
- messages to be communicated
- specific program elements to be used
- a timetable and budget
- discussion of how the program will be evaluated

The International Apple Institute, a trade group devoted to increasing the consumption of apples, had to decide if a campaign should get consumers to cook more with apples, drink more apple juice, or buy more fresh fruit. Because fresh apples brought a substantially higher price per pound to growers than apples used for applesauce or apple juice, the group decided to push the fresh fruit angle. It used the familiar theme "An apple a day..." and mounted a focused campaign to encourage people to eat more apples by placing articles extolling the fruit's health benefits in consumer media.

Execution of the campaign means deciding precisely how the message should be communicated to the stakeholder(s) of interest. An organization can get out its positive messages in many ways (see Table 18.1), ranging from news conferences and sponsorship of charity events to creating such attention-getting promotions as the Oscar Mayer "Wienermobile" shown in Exhibit 18.3.

Sometimes, these efforts involve lobbying government officials to persuade them to vote a certain way on pending legislation, or writing speeches for company executives to deliver. PR specialists may provide input on corporate identity materials, such as logos, brochures, building design, and even stationery, which communicate a positive image for the firm. Or the organization can simply try to get media exposure for the achievements of an employee who has done some notable charity work or for a product it developed that saved someone's life. For example, the Canadian pharmaceutical firm Boehringer Ingelheim (Canada) Ltd. sent large My Buddy dolls, as shown in Exhibit 18.4, wearing respirator masks to Canadian pediatricians. The dolls helped doctors ease their young patients' fears about putting a mask over their mouths and noses. In return, Boehringer Ingelheim received a lot of favourable publicity when newspapers across the country featured the campaign.

As the My Buddy doll example illustrates, **publicity** is a powerful PR tool. The most common way for public relations specialists to communicate to the media is through a **press release**, a description of some event that an organization produces itself and sends to the

✳ ✳ ✳
publicity Unpaid communication about an organization appearing in the mass media.

✳ ✳ ✳
press release Information that an organization distributes to the media about its activities, intended to appear as publicity.

Table 18.1 Tools of Public Relations

Interactive	Proactive	Responsive	Indirect & Associative
E-mail	Newsletters	Letters to Customers	Social/Cause Advertising
Web Sites	News Releases	Annual Reports	Public Service Announcements
Open Houses	Video News Releases	Bulletin Boards	Celebrity Endorsement
Ceremonies	Disaster Planning	Suggestion Boxes	Product Placement
Meetings	Issues Management	Surveys	Fundraising
Events	Lobbying	Environmental Scanning	Sponsorship
Speeches/Addresses	Brochures		Advertorials
Trade Shows & Exhibits	Pamphlets		
News Conference			
Annual General Meeting			
Corporate Social Events			
Employee Volunteering			

Note: Categories are illustrative; public relations tools can be used in different ways to reach different objectives.

Exhibit 18.3

Oscar Mayer created an eye-catching "Wienermobile" to draw the attention of hot dog consumers.

media in the hope that a reporter will write an article about it. A newer version of this idea is a video news release (VNR), aimed at the broadcast media, that tells the story in a film format. Some of the most common types of press releases are:

- *Timely topics* deal with hot topics in the news. Levi Strauss promoted casual Fridays (and presumably sales of its casual dress pants such as Dockers and Slates) by highlighting how different corporations around the country are adopting a relaxed dress code.

- *Research stories* summarize research projects, such as articles that universities send out that highlight recent breakthroughs from faculty members or public opinion polls that are released by political parties. Ralston Purina released the results of a survey that asked people how they show love to their pets: It was picked up by media across the country, earning 22 million impressions based on readership, viewership, and circulation of the media.[13]

- *Consumer information releases* provide information to help consumers make better product decisions. The British Columbia Ministry of Health's Food Safe Program distributes helpful tips about properly preparing foods for Thanksgiving, barbecuing, and other seasonal activities.

Ralston Purina Canada Inc.
www.purina.ca

One barrier to greater reliance on public relations campaigns by many organizations is the PR focus on long-term relationships across a wide variety of stakeholders, making it difficult to assess the effectiveness of specific program elements. For example, no one knows precisely what impact a series of appearances by company executives on talk shows or sponsorship of a charity event has on sales: Any one effect cannot be isolated. Marketers do, however, use such research tools as focus groups, interviews, and

Exhibit 18.4

Boehringer Ingelheim did a good deed by distributing these dolls and received positive publicity for its actions.

Real People, Real Decisions

Decision Time **at Raincoast Books**

The July 8, 2000, launch of *Harry Potter and the Goblet of Fire* was wildly successful, with bookseller demand for the novel exceeding the publisher's supply of 300 000 copies. It was a very unusual launch for a book in that no previews of the novel were released to critics or dealers for review. This strategy to use secrecy in the launch proved that you don't need to have a huge paid advertising budget to have a successful campaign. The launch relied heavily on public relations to meet its communications objectives. As the book retailers were required (a request backed by worldwide release date in major English-speaking countries) to keep the boxes sealed until midnight of July 7 local time, many decided to stay open past midnight while others planned grand openings the morning of July 8.

To encourage this activity, Raincoast decided to spend some of their promotional budget on posters, bookmarks, stickers, and party kits with wands, lightning bolt tattoos, and other "wizard" theme items, which they distributed to bookstores that had placed advanced orders with Raincoast for the new book. The kits helped individual stores hold sleepovers, dress-up contests, essay contests, and other special parties and activities—250 celebrations in total across the country. Public relations activities are often directed toward getting free publicity, and the response to the *Goblet of Fire* was phenomenal. Raincoast believes that there was free coverage of the launch of the book in all major cities in Canada. Television, radio, magazine, and newspaper journalists all wrote about the release of the new book; and in many cases, the story was front page and top story coverage. Many media outlets covered the story more than once, with cameras and reporters showing up at the midnight parties to capture the excitement. Raincoast could never have purchased the same amount of coverage with paid advertising.

Awareness levels for the launch of the new book were the highest of any book (or entertainment product, for that matter) ever released. This public relations strategy did even more, however. It strengthened pre-existing relationships between Raincoast and key book retailers and between the book retailers and children and their parents in local markets. Coordination of delivery was key, as Raincoast had to ensure delivery to book retailers and wholesalers within a very specific and short time frame to meet the international release date of July 8. Raincoast began a system of Harry Potter faxed newsletters and e-mails to keep all of their customers informed about events and distribution procedures. The launch of the Goblet of Fire helped raise the profile of stores with the local media through the combination of the stores' relationships with local media and the great interest in the story. Raincoast, in effect, helped local book retailers to increase their profile in the community. In addition, many book retailers used the opportunity to tell readers and par-

ents about other "Harry Potter–like" books that their readers might enjoy, turning kids onto reading, while increasing sales. These results could give Raincoast a distinct advantage when negotiating with these resellers on other titles or when presenting future lists to their customers.

Raincoast decided to only use a small portion of their $200 000 promotional budget on the launch, as an author's tour was anticipated in the fall (and indeed J.K Rowling agreed to come to Canada in October 2000). Walsh and Vanderkop now needed to decide how to best use Rowling's time and where to focus the remainder of the promotional budget to keep the Harry Potter momentum (and sales) going.

Option 1. Raincoast could maximize the exposure of the author by organizing a multi-city tour throughout Canada. This would enable several booksellers to feature Rowling in their stores, and would build sales into Christmas. However, the organizational logistics were somewhat difficult, as security, travel, and accommodations would need to be arranged in each city. By including several cities, though, more young fans would be able to meet their idol.

Option 2. Raincoast recognized that Rowling's recent tour of the United States had been hectic and exhausting. A second option was put forth to cover only two cities, Toronto and Vancouver, to allow for interviews and promotions. Raincoast would have to choose only two bookstores for the events, however, potentially alienating some of their long-term customers. A strong advertising campaign would promote the author's readings as well as the release date of the second novel in paperback, *Harry Potter and the Chamber of Secrets*.

Option 3. Walsh and Vanderkop also examined the possibility of having Rowling visit Toronto and Vancouver, under the auspices of authors' festivals in those cities. By timing Rowling's visit to coincide with established festivals, Raincoast could help make them even bigger literary happenings. Rather than appearing on stage alone, Rowling would be part of panels and reading groups and would have a chance to meet with and talk to other writers. This would give her a chance to connect with the Canadian literary community, share experiences, and perhaps learn from others as much as they learned from her. While this option would exclude all bookstore appearances and eliminate the need to choose one over the other, it was not clear how the bookstores would react to a lack of participation with Rowling. Young fans would also miss out on meeting her.

Now, join Desiree Walsh and Tessa Vanderkop and the Raincoast Books decision team: Which option would you choose, and why?

SPOTLIGHT ON REAL PEOPLE *Canadian Tire*

Eymbert Vaandering, vice-president of marketing at Canadian Tire, heads a team that developed an integrated marketing communications campaign, the "Big Spender Giveaway" contest, aimed at increasing customer loyalty and both in-store and online traffic. In 2000 Canadian Tire ran a "Big Spender" ad campaign that profiled customer uses of Canadian Tire money— the long-standing loyalty program where customers receive "money" coupons when they buy merchandise with cash, debit card, or a Canadian Tire credit card. The fall 2001 campaign, featuring three grand prizes of $50 000 in Canadian Tire money and $200 000 in other Canadian Tire prizes, integrated the loyalty benefits of Canadian Tire money with the creative equity of the "Big Spender" ad campaign. The campaign deployed multi-channel media that included TV and radio, an in-store contest supported by flyers, Canadian Tire credit card statement inserts, point-of-purchase displays in stores and at Canadian Tire gas bars, and an online scavenger hunt contest, implemented in partnership with Sympatico Lycos.

The campaign was a big hit with customers and became one of the most successful integrated retail and online promotions run in Canada. It allowed Canadian Tire to reach more than seven million unique Sympatico users, reminded customers about Canadian Tire, got them more excited about and involved with the brand, served as a reminder about a previous campaign, and built both traffic and sales in-store and online, providing a strong competitive advantage.[14]

1. How did Canadian Tire utilize the concept of integrated marketing communications?
2. How might Canadian Tire make better use of public relations in its "Big Spender Giveaway" campaign?

quantitative surveys (described in Chapter 5) to measure PR effectiveness by tracking changes in attitudes, opinions, and behaviours over time. Measuring media exposure from publicity efforts is relatively more straightforward, although it is more difficult to gauge what impact that coverage has had. Table 18.2 describes some of the most common publicity measurement techniques.

Canadian Tire
www.canadiantire.ca

Table 18.2 Measuring Effectiveness of Publicity Efforts

Method	Description	Pros	Cons
In-house assessment conducted by a public relations manager	Analyze media coverage in publications, looking for number of mentions and prominence of mentions.	Relatively inexpensive because the major cost is the manager's time.	Cannot guarantee objectivity in the analysis; crucial to specify up front what the relevant indicators are.
Awareness and preference studies	Assess company's standing in the minds of customers relative to competition.	Good for broad-based strategy setting or to demonstrate the progress of a large program.	Difficult to connect results to specific PR events and to identify which actions had what level of impact on awareness; very expensive.
Counting of press clippings	The basic measurement tool in PR.	Provides a quantifiable measure of press coverage; relatively inexpensive.	Quantitative only; does not consider the *content* of the press coverage.
Impression counts	Measure the size of the potential audience for a given article.	Because a similar measure is used to assess advertising effectiveness, provides a common measure for comparison.	Usually limited to the circulation of selected publications, so this method does not include pass-along readership; can be expensive.

Source: Adapted from Deborah Holloway, "How to Select a Measurement System That's Right for You," *Public Relations Quarterly*, Fall 1992, 15–17.

Sales Promotion

Walking into your student union, you have to be prepared to be ambushed by people eager for you to enter a contest, taste a new candy bar, or take home a free T-shirt with a local bank's name on it. These are examples of **sales promotions**, programs marketers design to build interest in or encourage you to purchase a product or service during a specified time period.[15] Sales promotions can sometimes be elaborate and far-reaching. For example, a successful promotional effort by Diet Coke capitalized on the enormous popularity of the television sitcom *Friends* when the company distributed bottle caps with the names of the show's main characters on them. Each week, a different character was shown drinking a bottle of Diet Coke in a commercial immediately after the show, and holders of caps with that person's name won a prize.

How does a sales promotion differ from advertising? They are similar in that they are both paid messages from identifiable sponsors intended to bring about a change in behaviour or attitudes. In some cases, the sales promotion itself is publicized using a traditional advertising medium, such as the Diet Coke commercials that ran after *Friends*. But although many advertising campaigns are carefully crafted to create long-term positive feelings about a brand, company, or store, sales promotions tend to focus on more short-term objectives, such as an immediate boost in sales of Diet Coke. There are exceptions, however. Perpetual promotions like McDonald's Monopoly game, Canadian Tire's "Canadian Tire money," and Tim Hortons' "Roll-up-the-rim-to-win" contest are all examples of sales promotions targeted to support or reward an existing customer base, rather than boost short-term sales.[16] Marketers also recognize that a series of short-term sales promotions can help to create long-term brand associations, image, and equity.

Coca-Cola
www.coca-cola.com

Sales promotions are very useful if the firm has an immediate objective, such as quickly bolstering sales for a brand or encouraging consumers to try a new product. The objective may be to create enthusiasm among dealers who carry the product by convincing them to take a chance on a new product or provide more shelf space for an item they carry. Thus, like advertising, sales promotions can be targeted to channel partners and to the firm's own employees in the form of trade promotions as well as to end consumers. Table 18.3 summarizes these techniques.

Trade Promotions

Trade promotions take one of two forms. Some sales promotions give the retailer a discount on the product's cost or on the expense of advertising it to encourage the store to stock the item and be sure it's given a lot of attention. Other sales promotions generate awareness and increase sales by creating enthusiasm among salespeople.

DISCOUNTS AND DEALS

One form of trade promotion is a price break. A manufacturer can reduce a channel partner's costs through sales promotions that give a discount on its own products. For example, a manufacturer can offer a **merchandise allowance**, which reimburses the retailer for in-store support such as shelving. A **case allowance** provides a discount to the retailer or wholesaler based on the volume of product ordered.

INDUSTRY BOOSTING AND BOASTING

Other types of trade sales promotions increase the visibility of a manufacturer's products to channel partners. Whether an elaborate exhibit at a convention or a coffee mug with the firm's logo mailed to clients, these efforts seek to keep the company's name topmost when distributors and retailers make decisions about which products to stock and push. These forms of sales promotions include:

- *Trade shows.* Hundreds of industry **trade shows** are held in Canada each year, and over 9000 shows are held in the US. These are major vehicles for manufacturers to show off their product lines to wholesalers and retailers.[17] Large trade shows are often held in big hotels or convention centres where many companies set up elaborate exhibits to show their products, give away samples, distribute product literature, and troll for new

Table 18.3 Sales Promotion Techniques: A Sampler

Technique	Primary Target	Description	Example
Trade show	Industry	Many manufacturers showcase their products to convention attendees.	The National Kitchen and Bath Association organizes several shows a year. Manufacturers display their latest wares to owners of kitchen and bath remodelling stores.
Incentive program	Sales force	A prize is offered to employees who meet a prespecified sales goal or who are top performers in a given time period.	Mary Kay cosmetics awards distinctive pink cars to its top-selling representatives.
Point-of-purchase displays	Trade and consumers	In-store exhibits make retail environment more interesting and attract consumers' attention.	The Farnam Company: As somber music plays in the background, a huge plastic rat draped in a black shroud lies next to a tombstone to promote the company's Just One Bite rat poison.
Push money	Trade	Salespeople are given a bonus for selling a specific manufacturer's product.	A retail salesperson at a formal wear store gets $1 every time he or she rents a particular tuxedo for a prom or wedding.
Promotional products	Trade	A company builds awareness and reinforces its image by giving out items with its name on them.	Beer companies send liquor store owners posters of attractive women wearing company T-shirts.
Cooperative promotions	Trade	Companies team up to promote their products jointly.	CompuServe and Universal Pictures ran a promotion for the mystery/thriller film *Sneakers*. CompuServe users were invited to break a series of codes contained in a special "Sneakers" file and win a trip to Hollywood.
Coupons	Consumers	Certificates for money off on selected products, often with an expiration date, used to encourage product trial.	Colgate-Palmolive offers 79 cents off a bottle of Teen Spirit deodorant.
Samples	Trade and consumers	Retailers might get a demonstration product to help in sales presentations; consumers get a free trial size of the product.	A small bottle of Pert shampoo arrives in the mail.
Contests/ sweepstakes	Trade and consumers	A sales contest rewards wholesalers or retailers for performance; consumers participate in games or drawings to win prizes; builds awareness and reinforces image.	The Publishers' Clearing House announces its zillionth sweepstakes.
Bonus packs	Consumers	Additional product is given away with purchase; rewards users.	Maxell provides two extra cassettes with purchase of a pack of ten.
Gifts with purchase	Consumers	A consumer gets a free gift when a product is bought; reinforces product image and rewards users.	A free umbrella comes with the purchase of Lagerfeld's Photo cologne.

Source: Some material adapted from Ajay Bhasin, Roger Dickinson, William A. Robinson, and Christine G. Hauri, "Promotion Investments That Keep Paying Off," *Journal of Consumer Marketing*, Winter 1989, 31–36; "One Sneaky Campaign," *Incentive*, November 1992, 93.

business contacts. Some large Canadian companies, such as Home Hardware Stores Ltd. and Shoppers Drug Mart, focus their marketing strategies on private trade shows where key suppliers can interact more closely with buyers and store managers and do more deal making than is possible in a standard show where suppliers interact with many competing customers.[18]

- *Promotional products.* We have all seen them—coffee mugs, visors, T-shirts, key chains, and countless other doodads emblazoned with a company logo. These are *promotional products.* Unlike licensed merchandise sold in stores, these goodies are given away free to build awareness of the sponsor. Although some of these freebies are distributed directly to consumers, many are intended for channel partners, such as retailers and vendors, to build name recognition and loyalty.

• *Incentive programs.* In addition to motivating distributors and customers, some promotions are designed to light a fire under the firm's own sales force. These incentives, known as **push money**, may come in the form of cash bonuses, trips, or prizes. Mary Kay cosmetics is famous for giving its more productive distributors pink cars as a reward for their efforts. Involving employees in a promotion is a great way to get them excited about what they sell. When Frito-Lay sponsored a promotion giving away six million bags of their new Nacho Cheese Doritos around the United States in one day, one objective was to psych up its own employees. Frito-Lay had its salespeople distribute the free goodies to people on the street, and a full-page ad in *USA Today* featured employees who worked on the brand.[19]

Consumer Promotions

Since 1970, Gillette has run the Gillette Cavalcade of Sports promotion, using large prizes, huge display, and major sports stars to draws consumers across Canada into retail outlets to buy popular and less well-known Gillette products. Each year, they fine tune the $2 million promotion to keep it fresh, but the basic strategy is impact—go big or go home. Year after year, it works, and the company experiences a 30% dollar sales increase during the event.[20]

Gillette's efforts and the Fido example, discussed earlier in the chapter, illustrate how major companies are creating unusual and attention-getting forms of promotion. As with trade promotions, sales-boosting efforts try to stimulate purchases by attracting consumers with price breaks or attracting their attention with novel incentive.

PRICE-BASED CONSUMER PROMOTIONS

Many sales promotions aim for consumers' wallets. They emphasize short-term price reductions or refunds, thus encouraging people to choose a brand—at least while the deal is on.

• *Coupons.* Try to pick up any Wednesday newspaper without spilling a pile of coupons. Coupons are certificates redeemable for money off a purchase and are the most common price promotion. Indeed, they are the most popular form of sales promotion overall. Over 3.1 billion coupons are distributed annually in Canada, with redemptions valued at $100 million.[21] Consumers can also now find coupons online at sites like www.savingyoumoney.com.

• *Price deals, refunds, and rebates.* Manufacturers often offer temporary price reductions to stimulate sales. This price deal may be printed on the package itself, or it may be a price-off flag or banner on the store shelf. Sometimes companies offer **rebates**, which allow the customer to recover part of the product's cost directly from the manufacturer. Chapters Inc. offered a new twist on the common "scratch & save" promotion by offering Web surfers a chance to scratch a real-sounding card on their Web site.

• *Special packs.* Another form of price promotion is giving the shopper more of the product instead of lowering its price.[22] A *special pack* can be a separate product given away along with another product. Zellers, for example, gave away free 3-D glasses with the purchase of a Cadbury TimeOut chocolate bar in a three-way promotion with CanWest Global Television to increase viewership of the season finale of the TV series *3rd Rock from the Sun.*[23]

ATTENTION-GETTING CONSUMER PROMOTIONS

Attention-getting consumer promotions stimulate interest in and publicity for a company's products. Labatt Breweries, for example, recently made a 14-stop tour of Ontario parks and beaches to promote its Kokanee brand of beer. The tour included a 25-foot-high inflatable glacier, bikini and muscleman contests, ultimate Frisbee games, and kayak races.[24] Some typical types of attention-getting promotions are:

Contests and sweepstakes. A contest is a test of skill, while a sweepstakes is based on chance. Guinness Import Company's "Win Your Own Pub in Ireland" contest gave away an actual pub to winners of an essay contest "Why Guinness Is My Perfect Pint."[25] Tim Hortons' "Roll-up-the-rim-to-win" contest has become so ingrained in Canadian culture that Tim Hortons ran an advertising campaign in which a traveller "proved" Canadian citizenship by spouting the "Roll-up-the-rim-to-win" slogan.[26]

Premiums. **Premiums** are items offered for free to people who have bought a product. A premium is often a novelty item, such as the free, removable tattoos called Barqtoos that Barq's root beer gives away to its customers. A Pokemon card in a box of cereal, a replica Stanley Cup in cases of Labatt's Blue, or a movie pass in Humpty-Dumpty potato chips are all examples of premiums. The latest craze in premiums is prepaid phone cards that enhance brand identification. Many companies are jumping on the phone card bandwagon, offering cards emblazoned with pictures of sports heroes, products, and even rock bands. Phone cards make ideal premiums, because they are compact in size, brand logos or graphics provide opportunities for repeat exposure, and the issuer can track card usage and build databases by determining where calls originate.[27]

Sampling. How many people at one time or another have managed to scrape together an entire meal by scooping up free food samples at their local grocery store? **Sampling** gets people to try a product by distributing trial-size versions in stores, on street corners, or through the mail. PowerBar Foods used extensive sampling to launch its PowerBar Harvest bar in Ontario and Quebec (see Exhibit 18.5). They distributed 240 000 mini-samples and coupons in subway stations, bars, and fitness clubs to reach their target market of active 18- to 34-year-olds.

Point-of-purchase promotion. A **point-of-purchase (POP) promotion** attempts to influence consumers in the store by catching their attention with displays or signs.[28] Marketers are challenged to come up with new and innovative POP displays that will grab people's attention. For example, Bausch & Lomb conducted a promotion in Spain to encourage consumers with good vision to buy contact lenses to change their eye colour. The in-store display allowed shoppers to see what they would look like with five different colours of eyes before they actually inserted the contacts.[29] POP activities also include the use of *in-store media*, including placards on shopping carts or even closed-circuit television, which promote specific products. As the CEO of one company that produces these in-store messages put it, "Does it make any sense to spend millions of dollars talking to people in their living rooms and cars and then let them wander around a supermarket with 30 000 product choices without something to remind them to buy your product?"[30]

✳ ✳ ✳
premium An item included without charge with a purchased product.

✳ ✳ ✳
sampling Distributing trial-size versions of a product for free to encourage people to try it.

✳ ✳ ✳
point-of-purchase (POP) promotion The use of signs or displays to influence purchases at the store.

Exhibit 18.5

PowerBar Foods uses sampling to generate awareness and trial for new products.

Introducing New Vanilla Crisp Flavour.

Number 1 never tasted so good.

Don't Bonk.

good OR bad DECISION?

Alberta poet Edward Brennan earned infamy in Canadian sales promotion history when he was taken to court and found guilty under Section 206(1)(f) of the federal Criminal Code of running an illegal lottery.[33] This section of the Criminal Code is a 100-year-old law that prohibits the "disposing of goods...by any game of chance...or mixed chance and skill, in which the [contestant or] competitor pays money." Brennan had been giving out tickets to people who bought his latest book of poetry, holding a draw each week for a prize of $50 and holding a draw at the end of the year for a Ford Mustang—a sales promotion contest similar to thousands of others run across the country. Brennan had followed standard industry practice of obliging winners to answer a skill-testing question and allowing contestants to enter the contest without buying a book by submitting facsimiles of the book cover by mail. These provisions were thought to satisfy the Criminal Code, as the intent of Section 206 (1)(f) was to curb illegal gambling, not restrict sales promotions. A year after the conviction, an Alberta Court of Appeal acquitted Brennan of running an illegal lottery. This acquittal, however, may not provide a protective precedent for others running sales promotions, and it is still not clear what is allowed under the law. Industry advocates are reluctant to seek amendments to the Criminal Code lest clarity result in unwanted restrictions being placed on common industry practices. Should there be any restrictions on sales promotions? Should contestants have to purchase a product to be eligible?

LOYALTY GENERATING PROMOTIONS

Continuity programs, membership programs, and *loyalty programs* are all terms used to describe the practice of awarding discounts, bonuses, or such other incentives as redeemable "points" to frequent and other high-value customers. These programs are increasingly recognized as the best retention marketing tactic. They are used to recognize the importance of the customer, reward their ongoing patronage, establish long-term ties or bonds to the organization, and encourage loyalty. An added benefit is enabling the organization to observe and track their purchase behaviour. More than 71% of Canadian consumers participate in at least one loyalty program, and over 67% take part in four or five different programs.[31] While some companies such as Air Canada (Aeroplan) and Petro-Canada (Petro-Points) have independent loyalty programs, smaller companies are able to participate in joint programs such as Air Miles, where points earned from purchases from a variety of participating organizations can be redeemed for travel on a number of sponsor airlines or for merchandise (such as theatre tickets) from member organizations.

PROMOTION STRATEGY

Ideally, the objective of every sales promotion should be to cement the product's position in the marketplace. This may mean building awareness for a new product, enticing retailers to stock it, or kick-starting sales for an item during Christmas season. Once marketers have determined the objectives of a sales promotion, they must decide what the program will look like. If the objective is to encourage users of a competing product to try the item, a sampling program might work best. If the objective is to encourage loyal users to increase their interest in the brand, the firm might sponsor a contest or sweepstakes. If the company wants to increase its shelf space allocation, it might try a price break to retailers. Many marketers also are discovering the virtues of **cross-promotion**, in which two or more companies combine forces to create interest in their different products or services using a single promotional tool. That was the plan behind the cross-promotion between Heinz and the producers of *Pokemon, the First Movie* (see Exhibit 18.6).

A key issue for marketers is over-redemption: having too many customers redeem coupons, satisfy contest requirements, or buy cross-promoted product.[32] The classic example of this was Maytag Corporation's 1993 offer of free round-trip airline tickets to British customers who bought Hoover-brand appliances. They placed severe restrictions on the dates of travel to limit redemption but hadn't counted on unemployed people buying the appliances just to go on the trip. It cost Maytag US$36 million to honour the promotion, and then they faced a flood of "nearly new" second-hand Hoover appliances being sold by customers who never really wanted the appliance. Marketers can now buy over-redemption insurance.

cross-promotion Two or more companies combining forces and using a single promotional tool to create interest in their products or services.

※ ※ ※

Exhibit 18.6

A cross-promotion lets companies join forces to communicate about their products.

Personal Selling

The final piece of the promotion pie is personal selling, which is a far more intimate way to talk to the market. **Personal selling** is a company representative coming in direct contact with customers to inform them about a good or service to get a sale. Many organizations rely heavily on this immediate form of communication. The "personal touch" can be a lot more influential than information we get from mass media. And, for business-to-business marketers such as Xerox, personal selling accounts for a big chunk of sales. Many industrial products and services are too complex or expensive to be adequately explained or demonstrated in an impersonal trade advertisement.

Another advantage of relying on a good sales force is that salespeople are the firm's eyes and ears in the field. They pay attention to which competitors' salespeople are calling on customers, what new competing products have been delivered to their customers, and what new literature is on the customers' desks. Personal selling has special importance for students, because many graduates with a marketing background will enter sales jobs. Let's take a close look at how personal selling works and how sophisticated salespeople work hard to develop long-term relationships with customers.

✳ ✳ ✳
personal selling The part of the promotion mix that involves direct contact between a company representative and a customer.

The Role of Personal Selling

When a man calls an 800 number to order a new desktop PC configured with a snappy DVD drive so his kids can play the latest Hollywood blockbuster, he is dealing with a company salesperson. When he sits in on a presentation at work by a computer technician who demonstrates a new spreadsheet software package, he is dealing with a company salesperson. And when that same man agrees over dinner at a swanky restaurant to buy a new computer network for his company, he also is dealing with a company salesperson.

For many firms, some form of personal selling is essential for a transaction (the sale) to occur, so this type of communication is an important part of an organization's overall marketing plan. Generally, a personal sales effort is more important when a firm engages in a *push strategy*, in which the goal is to push the product through the channel of distribution. As a vice-president at Hallmark Cards observed, "We're not selling *to* the retailer, we're selling through the retailer. We look at the retailer as a pipeline to the hands of consumers."[34] Personal selling also is likely to be crucial in business-to-business contexts when direct interaction with upper-level management is required to clinch a big deal—and often when intense price negotiations will occur before the deal is signed. In addition, inexperienced buyers may need the hands-on assistance that a salesperson can provide. Organizations selling products that consumers buy infrequently, such as computers, lawn mowers, and college educations, often place greater emphasis on personal selling, as do firms selling complex or very expensive products that need a salesperson to explain, justify, and sell them.

Hallmark
www.hallmark.com

If personal selling is so effective, why don't firms just scrap their advertising and sales promotion budgets and hire more salespeople? There are some drawbacks that limit the role played by personal selling in the communications mix.

First, when the dollar amount of individual purchases is low, it doesn't make sense to use personal selling. The cost per contact with a customer is much higher than with other forms of communication. After all, the median cost for a typical sales call is over $3200, due to salary, travel, a company car, and other expenses.[35] In comparison, the cost per contact of a national television commercial is low, even though the total cost to run the ad is high. A 30-second, prime-time commercial may be $30 000 to $40 000 (plus production costs) but with millions of viewers, the cost may be only $10 or $15 per 1000 viewers—little more than a penny per viewer.

Because salespeople—even if they are *really* energetic—can call on only a limited number of customers in a day, reliance on personal selling is effective only when a reasonable number of the customers the salespeople do see make a purchase. Because the cost of field salespeople is so great, **telemarketing**, in which person-to-person communication takes place via the telephone or fax machine, is growing in popularity. Pharmaceutical companies Novartis, Janssen-Ortho, and Becton Dickinson, for example, make extensive use of tele-

✳ ✳ ✳
telemarketing The use of the telephone or fax to sell directly to consumers and business customers.

marketing to launch new products. Armed with a good database and software that can handle 8000 to 10 000 outbound faxes per hour, they can communicate product information to all the 6500 pharmacies and dispensaries in Canada within one hour. They then follow up the same or next day with phone calls from a team of professional, knowledgeable telemarketers who can each place about 80 calls per day. This enables the pharmaceutical companies to effectively reach their target audience with timely information far more quickly than a regiment of in-store reps.[36]

The type of salespeople and the roles they perform vary in different firms. The person who processes a computer purchase over the phone is an **order taker**, a salesperson whose primary function is to facilitate transactions that the customer initiates. Most retail salespeople are order takers; but often wholesalers, dealers, and distributors also employ salespeople to wait on customers. The computer technician is a **technical specialist**, who contributes expertise in the form of product demonstrations, recommendations for complex equipment, and set-up of machinery. The technical specialist's job is to provide *sales support* rather than actually closing the sale, meaning that the technical specialist promotes the firm and tries to stimulate demand for a product to make it easier for others to actually make the deal.

Sometimes a person whose job is to lay this groundwork is known as a **missionary salesperson**.[37] Missionary salespeople promote the firm and try to stimulate demand for a product but don't actually complete a sale. And this support person may even be part of a sales team. Xerox, for example, competes for big accounts by sending out teams of specialists: Each Team Xerox includes customer service personnel, financial experts, and even top management in the case of important customers.[38] Finally, the person who actually convinces the customer to shell out for the computer network, probably after several weeks or months of discussions, is an **order getter**. Order getters work creatively to develop relationships with customers or to generate new sales. These salespeople find new customers, persuade customers to buy, and close the sale.

Approaches to Personal Selling

Personal selling is one of the oldest forms of communication, but the image of this profession has been tarnished by smooth-talking hucksters who would say anything to make a sale. In the latter part of the twentieth century, personal selling has largely redeemed itself as a profession. In most industries, it has moved from a transactional, hard-sell marketing approach to a relationship marketing approach.

TRANSACTIONAL MARKETING: PUTTING ON THE HARD SELL

The *hard sell* is a high-pressure process. We've all been exposed to the pushy electronics salesperson who puts down the competition by telling shoppers that if they buy elsewhere they will be stuck with an inferior sound system that will fall apart in six months. These hard-sell tactics are a form of **transactional selling**, a sales technique that focuses on making an immediate sale with little or no attempt to develop a relationship with the customer. As customers, we feel manipulated by the hard sell and resent it. This technique and its depiction in movies like *GlenGarry GlenRoss* and plays like *Death of a Salesman* also contribute to the negative image many of us have of obnoxious salespeople. But not all transactional marketers are obnoxious. Jacques Gatien, president of Atlantic Promotions of Longueuil, Quebec (see Exhibit 18.7) has earned a reputation as the "jovial huckster." He is the brains behind a $115 million company that sells products like the Oskar snowbrush, Pant Saver car mat, Starfrit Rotato, T-Rex rake, and other useful products, using a combination of advertising and in-store demonstrations. His motto is: "The more you can use a demonstration to sell a product, the easier it is to sell."[39]

RELATIONSHIP SELLING: COUNTERING THE TARNISHED IMAGE

Rather than transactional selling, today's professional salesperson is more likely to practise **relationship selling**—seeking to develop a mutually satisfying relationship with the customer.[40] Relationship selling involves winning, keeping, and developing customers. *Winning* customers means converting interested prospects into people who are convinced

---

***

order taker A salesperson whose primary function is to facilitate transactions that the customer initiates.

***

technical specialist Sales support personnel with a high level of technical expertise who assist in product demonstrations.

***

missionary salesperson A salesperson who promotes the firm and tries to stimulate demand for a product but does not actually complete a sale.

***

order getter A salesperson who works creatively to develop relationships with customers or to generate new sales.

***

transactional selling A form of personal selling that focuses on making an immediate sale with little or no attempt to develop a relationship with the customer.

***

relationship selling A form of personal selling in which the salesperson seeks to develop a mutually satisfying relationship with the consumer so they can work together to satisfy each other's needs.

Exhibit 18.7

Jacques Gatien uses in-store product demonstrations to show customers how useful his products are.

that the product or service holds value for them. *Keeping* customers means ensuring that the product or service delivers what was promised. *Developing* customers means satisfying them so that they can be counted on to provide future business.[41]

The Role of Personal Selling in the Communications Mix

The salesperson's job can be made easier with support from public relations and advertising. The business customer, having already seen the supplier's advertisements or product releases, is likely to welcome that vendor's representative. Responses to toll-free numbers included in advertising and sales promotions can provide hot sales leads to follow up with prospective customers who have already expressed interest in learning more about the product. And many salespeople obtain valuable leads at industry trade shows attended by thousands of prospective customers.

The Selling Process

Selling is seldom boring. Every customer, every sales call, and every salesperson are unique. Some salespeople are successful primarily because they know so much about what they sell. Others are successful because they've built strong relationships with their customers over time, and these people look forward to their visits to "chew the fat." And most salespersons understand and engage in a series of activities necessary to bring about a transaction.

Sales of complex or expensive products require careful planning. To be successful in these, the salesperson must follow the **creative selling process**—seeking out customers, analyzing their needs, determining how product attributes provide benefits, and then deciding how best to communicate that information to the targeted customers. As Figure 18.1 shows, there are seven steps in the process.

PROSPECT CUSTOMERS

Prospecting is the process of identifying and developing a list of potential customers, called *prospects* or *sales leads*. Leads can come from existing customer lists, telephone directories, and commercially available databases. The local library usually contains directories of businesses (including those published by provincial and federal agencies) and directories of association memberships. Some companies generate sales leads through their advertising or sales promotions by letting customers request more information (in Chapter 16, we called this a *second-order response*). One way to generate leads is through *cold calling*, when the salesperson contacts prospects "cold," without prior introduction or permission. Because it always helps to know someone rather than starting off cold, salespeople might instead seek *referrals* from other customers. Current clients who are satisfied with their purchase often give referrals, which is yet another reason to maintain good customer relationships.

QUALIFY PROSPECTS

Just because people are willing to talk to a salesperson doesn't mean they will turn out to be good sales leads. Along with identifying potential customers, salespersons need to

* * *

creative selling process The process of seeking out customers, analyzing their needs, determining how product attributes might provide benefits for them, and then communicating that information.

* * *

prospecting A part of the selling process that includes identifying and developing a list of potential or prospective customers.

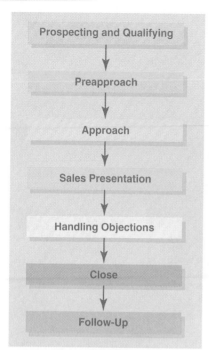

Figure 18.1 Steps in the Creative Selling Process

✳ ✳ ✳
qualify prospects A part of the selling process that determines how likely prospects are to become customers.

✳ ✳ ✳
preapproach A part of the selling process that includes developing information about prospective customers and planning the sales interview.

✳ ✳ ✳
approach The first step of the actual sales presentation in which the salesperson tries to learn more about the customer's needs, create a good impression, and build rapport.

✳ ✳ ✳
sales presentation The part of the selling process in which the salesperson seeks to persuasively communicate the product's features and the benefits it will provide after the sale.

qualify prospects to determine how likely they are to become customers. Salespeople qualify prospects by asking themselves such questions as: Are the prospects likely to be interested in what I'm selling? Are they likely to switch their allegiance from what they are currently using? Is the potential sales volume large enough to make a relationship with them profitable? Can they afford the purchase? If they must borrow money to buy my product, is their credit history acceptable?

DO A PREAPPROACH

The **preapproach** consists of compiling background information about prospective customers and planning the sales interview. Important purchases are not made lightly, so it is foolish for a salesperson to blindly call on a qualified prospect and risk losing the sale due to a lack of preparation. Salespeople try to learn as much as possible about qualified prospects before initiating a sale, such as their past history of purchases, their current needs, and, in some cases, personal information about their likes and dislikes.

Salespeople can find information about a prospect from a variety of sources. In the case of larger companies, financial data, names of top executives, and other information about business can be found in such publications as *Standard & Poor's 500 Directory* or the *Million Dollar Directory*. The inside scoop on a prospect, however, frequently comes from informal sources, such as noncompeting salespeople who have dealt with the person before. This background information helps salespeople to plan their strategy and the goals they will try to achieve when the prospect is contacted.

MAKE THE APPROACH

After the groundwork has been laid with the preapproach, it is time to **approach**, or contact, the prospect. During the important first minutes when the salesperson initiates contact with the prospective customer, several key events occur. The salesperson tries to learn even more about the prospect's needs, create a good impression, and build rapport. If the salesperson made contact with the prospect through a referral, the salesperson will probably acknowledge this connection: "Barbara Price with Amida Industries suggested I call on you."

During the approach, the customer is deciding whether the salesperson has something beneficial to offer. The old saying, "You never get a second chance to make a good first impression," certainly rings true in this situation. A professional appearance is a signal to the prospect that the salesperson means business and is competent to handle the sale. Successful salespeople are always well groomed and wear appropriate business dress; they don't chew gum, use poor grammar or inappropriate language, mispronounce the customer's name, or seem uninterested in the job.

MAKE THE SALES PRESENTATION

Many sales calls involve a formal **sales presentation**, in which the salesperson lays out the benefits of the product and why it is better than what competitors are offering. *Proof statements*, such as data on past sales, testimonials, guarantees, or research results, help to make the salesperson's pitch credible. And in the most effective sales presentations, the salesperson gets the would-be customer to participate by asking questions or, as we saw with Jacques Gatien, allowing the customer to try the product.

Some sales presentations are canned, which means a script has been written in advance and the same message is delivered to every prospect. This technique often provides a series of verbal prompts to which the customer is expected to respond in the desired manner. For example, office supplies salespeople might start all of their pitches with, "Would you like to see a new line of products that will revolutionize the way you run your office?" That standardized approach works fine in some cases, but the most effective sales presentations are those that are tailored to the specific needs of the customer. For example, a salesperson instead might say, "Would you be interested in getting better-quality report binders at a lower price?" after discovering during the preapproach that the office manager was under pressure from the boss to cut costs on office supplies.

Such technologies as laptop and palm computers, presentation software, digital projectors, and the Internet are enhancing the ability of sales people to make effective presentations. "Web-push" technology, for example, transmits information via any combination of telephone and Internet-enabled communication formats to a desktop computer, allowing presenters to simultaneously talk to, visually interact with, and otherwise communicate with remote audiences using in-sync multiple media formats.[42]

OVERCOME CUSTOMER OBJECTIONS

It is rare that a prospect accepts whatever the salesperson has to say and immediately makes an order. The effective salesperson anticipates *objections*, or reasons why the prospect is unwilling to commit to a purchase, and is prepared to overcome them by providing additional information or persuasive arguments. In fact, the salesperson should *welcome* objections, because they show that the prospect is at least interested enough to have considered the offer and seriously weigh its pros and cons. Handling the objection successfully may move a prospect to the decision stage. For example, the salesperson might say, "Ms Robbins, you've said before that you don't have room to carry our new line of sleeping bags, although you admit that you may be losing some sales by carrying only one brand with very few different models. If we could determine how much business you're losing, I'd be willing to bet you'd make room for our line, wouldn't you?"

CLOSE THE SALE

A common mistake made by salespeople is that they work very hard to open the door for the prospect but don't get the prospect to walk through that door. **Sales closing** occurs when the salesperson asks the customer straight out to buy the product and complete the transaction.

There is a variety of techniques good salespeople use to close the sale. A *last objection close* asks customers if they are ready to purchase, providing any concerns they have about the product can be addressed: "Are you ready to order if we can show you a 20% cost savings associated with using this software?" In a *trial close*, on the other hand, the salesperson acts as if the purchase is inevitable; all that's left is to wrap up the details: "What quantity would you like to order?" In some cases, the salesperson applies a bit more pressure by using a *standing-room-only close*, in which the salesperson indicates that if the customer does not buy now, there may not be the opportunity in the future. No matter what technique is used, it's important to close the sale rather than just assuming the transaction will happen "magically" on its own.

✳ ✳ ✳
sales closing The stage of the selling process in which the salesperson asks the customer to buy the product.

FOLLOW-UP AFTER THE SALE

Sales follow-up includes arranging for delivery, payment, and purchase terms. It also means the salesperson making sure the customer received the order and is satisfied. Follow-up also allows the salesperson to *bridge* to the next purchase. Once a relationship develops with a customer, the selling process is only beginning. Even as one cycle of purchasing draws to a close, a good salesperson is already laying the foundation for the next one.

✳ ✳ ✳
sales follow-up After-sales activities that provide important services to customers.

Sales Management

No firm can succeed with just one star salesperson. Personal selling is a team effort, and this form of communication usually requires careful planning to ensure that a firm's salespeople are in the field when and where customers need them. **Sales management** is the process of planning, implementing, and controlling the personal selling function of an organization. These are some major decisions sales professionals who oversee this function must make.

✳ ✳ ✳
sales management The process of planning, implementing, and controlling the personal selling function of an organization.

SETTING SALES FORCE OBJECTIVES

Sales force objectives state what the sales force is expected to accomplish and when. Sales managers develop specific sales force performance objectives, such as "acquire 100 new customers," "generate $100 million in sales," or even "reduce travel expenses by two percent." Some firms also state goals for customer satisfaction, new customer development, new product suggestions, training, or community involvement.

Sales managers also work with their salespeople to develop individual goals. *Performance goals* are measurable outcomes, such as total sales and total profits per salesperson.

Behavioural goals specify the actions salespeople must accomplish, such as the number of prospects to identify, the number of sales calls they need to make, and the number of sales presentations they must deliver.

CREATING A SALES FORCE STRATEGY

* * *

sales territory A set of customers often defined by geographic boundaries, for whom a particular salesperson is responsible.

IBM
www.ibm.com

A sales force strategy specifies how the firm will structure, size, and compensate its sales force. Each salesperson has the responsibility for a **sales territory**, a set group of customers. The territory structure allows salespeople to have an in-depth understanding of customers and their needs because they call on the same people repeatedly and get to know them on a personal level. The most common way to structure territories is by geographic boundaries to minimize travel and other field expenses. Thus, a sales territory might be Regina, Saskatchewan, the Prairie provinces, Western Canada, or even all of Canada, depending on the size of the sales force and how many customers are found in an area.

If the product line is technically complex or quite diverse, however, it may be better to structure sales territories based on different classes of products rather than location. This enables the salesperson to provide greater expertise to a set of customers with similar needs. Still another structure is industry specialization in which salespeople focus on a single industry or a small number of industries. For example, IBM went from a geographic sales force structure to one in which its salespeople were assigned to one of 14 different industries. In making the change, IBM executives cited a need to have salespeople who "speak the language of its customers and understand their industries."[43]

Putting a salesperson out into the field is an expensive proposition; so the number of people pounding the pavement for the company affects its profitability. For this reason, determining the optimal number of salespeople is an important decision. A larger sales force may increase sales, but it will also increase costs. A smaller sales force will keep costs down, but this strategy can backfire—competitors with larger sales forces may be able to develop strong customer relationships, because each of their salespeople doesn't have to call on as many customers.

RECRUITING, TRAINING, AND REWARDING SALESPEOPLE

Because the quality of a sales force can make or break a firm, recruiting and hiring the right set of people to do the job is a top priority for sales managers. Many firms recruit people who are strategic thinkers, who have technical knowledge pertaining to the industry, and who have excellent interpersonal skills.[44] Companies use various methods to screen potential salespeople. Interviews reveal communication skills, interpersonal skills, and information about interests and capabilities. Paper-and-pencil tests can determine quantitative skills and competence in areas not easily assessed through interviews.

Although some people feel that a successful salesperson is born, not made, even the most skilled communicator has much to learn. *Sales training* allows salespeople to learn about the organization and its products and to develop the skills, knowledge, and attitudes necessary for high levels of performance. For example, training programs at Xerox focus on ways to identify customer problems. The Xerox Document University, a training facility with 250 classrooms and a curriculum of 180 courses, provides an 11-week training program for new salespeople and continuing training throughout the salesperson's career.[45] The publisher Southwestern Company runs a different sort of sales training program: Every summer, almost 4000 college students attend the company's sales school where they attend pep rallies (see Exhibit 18.8), meet with sales managers, and learn how to sell books door-to-door.

An important way to motivate salespeople is by paying them well, and often this means tying compensation to performance. There are several payment systems commonly used to motivate salespeople. A *straight commission plan* is payment based solely on a percentage of sales the person closes. Under a *commission-with-draw plan*, earnings still are based on commission but the salesperson also receives a regular payment, or "draw," which may be charged against future commissions if current sales are inadequate to cover the draw. With a *straight salary compensation plan*, the salesperson is paid a set amount regardless of sales performance. Sometimes straight salary plans are augmented by use of a *quota-bonus plan*, in

Exhibit 18.8

Sales schools train college students to sell by finding novel ways to motivate them.

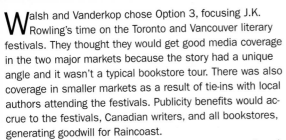

which salespeople are paid a salary plus a bonus for sales they make above their assigned quota.

Although most salespeople like to work independently, supervision is essential for an effective sales force. Sales managers often require salespeople to develop monthly, weekly, and daily *call reports*, plans of action detailing which customers were called upon and what happened during the call. These reports allow the sales manager to track what the salespeople are doing in the field, and they provide marketing managers with timely information about customers' responses, competitive activity, and changes in the firm's customer base.

Real People, Real Decisions

How it worked out at Raincoast Books

Walsh and Vanderkop chose Option 3, focusing J.K. Rowling's time on the Toronto and Vancouver literary festivals. They thought they would get good media coverage in the two major markets because the story had a unique angle and it wasn't a typical bookstore tour. There was also coverage in smaller markets as a result of tie-ins with local authors attending the festivals. Publicity benefits would accrue to the festivals, Canadian writers, and all bookstores, generating goodwill for Raincoast.

To satisfy young readers, Rowling gave public readings in both Toronto and Vancouver and the Toronto SkyDome reading was the largest reading ever held. The organizers of both festivals worked with sponsors on promotions, including contests, to raise the profile of the events and Rowling's participation.

By 2001 Harry Potter mania had swept Canada and the world, propelled by an aggressive international marketing strategy by Warner Bros. The first of a projected seven Harry Potter movies, *Harry Potter and the Philosopher's Stone*, set a box office record with earnings of almost US$240 million in just 24 days. Extensive merchandising efforts with

Hasbro, Mattel, and Lego have put Harry Potter imagery on cards, board games, video games, notebooks, train sets, clothes, lunch boxes, bedding, and anything else kids might want. Warner Bros. believes the franchise could be worth more than the US$1 billion it has earned in merchandising its Batman films.

With 130 million books sold, a $50 million signing bonus and 5% royalty on all Harry Potter merchandise, a multimillion dollar movie rights payment and 1% of all box office and video receipts, Rowlings is on her way to becoming the first billionaire author.

The Harry Potter mania has been a unique experience for Walsh and Vanderkop; rather than trying to "create the buzz" for an author and her work, they have been trying to "manage the buzz" and make sure as many stakeholders as possible benefit from the phenomenon.

Sources: Keith McArthur, "Fan frenzy greets new Harry Potter," *The Globe and Mail*, 8 July 2000; Maurice Chittenden and Robert Winnett, "Rowling set to become first billionaire author: Literature's 'biggest brand name since Shakespeare' reaps the rewards of huge toy and movie royalties," *The Ottawa Citizen*, 25 November 2001, p. A1.

Chapter Summary

1. Explain the role of public relations.

   The purpose of public relations is to build mutually beneficial long-term relationships and improve the image of an organization with key stakeholders, including consumers, the media, shareholders, legislators, and interest groups. An important part of this is managing publicity. Public relations is important in introducing new products, influencing legislation, enhancing the image of a city, region, or country, and calling attention to a firm's community involvement.

2. Describe the steps in developing a public relations campaign.

   A public relations campaign begins with setting objectives, creating and executing a campaign strategy, and planning how the PR program will be evaluated. PR specialists often use print or video news releases to communicate timely topics, research stories, and consumer information.

3. Explain what sales promotion is and describe some of the different types of trade and consumer sales promotion activities.

   Sales promotions are short-term programs designed to build interest in or encourage purchase of a product. Trade promotions include merchandise allowances, trade shows, promotional products, and incentive programs including push money. Consumer sales promotions include coupons, price deals, rebates, special packs, contests and sweepstakes, premiums, sampling programs, point-of-purchase promotions, and continuity (loyalty) programs.

4. Explain the important role of personal selling in the marketing effort.

   Personal selling occurs when a company representative directly informs a client about a good or service to get a sale. Personal selling is more important for push strategies. Because of the high cost per customer contact for field sales, telemarketing is growing in popularity. Different types of salespeople include order takers, technical specialists, missionary salespeople, and order getters. Today's salesperson is less likely to practise transactional selling, that is, hard-sell tactics. Instead, salespeople today often engage in relationship selling, seeking to develop mutually satisfying relationships with customers.

5. List the steps in the personal selling process.

   The steps in the personal selling process include prospecting, qualifying the prospects, the preapproach, the approach, making the sales presentation, overcoming customer objections, closing the sale, and follow-up after the sale.

6. Explain the job of the sales manager.

   Sales management means planning, implementing, and controlling the selling function. The responsibilities of a sales manager are setting sales force objectives and creating a sales force strategy, including specifying sales territories, recruiting, training, and rewarding salespeople.

Chapter Review

Marketing Concepts: Testing Your Knowledge

1. What is public relations? What is publicity?

2. What are some frequently used objectives of public relations?

3. What are the steps in planning a public relations campaign?

4. What is sales promotion? When is sales promotion more likely to be an important part of the promotion mix?

5. Explain some of the different types of trade sales promotions marketers frequently use.

6. Explain some of the different types of consumer sales promotions marketers frequently use.

7. What is the role played by personal selling within the total marketing function?

8. What is the difference between transactional selling and relationship selling?

9. What are order getters, order takers, missionary salespeople, and technical specialists?

10. List the steps in the creative selling process.

11. Describe the major decisions made by sales managers.

Marketing Concepts: **Discussing Choices and Issues**

1. Some critics denounce public relations specialists, calling them "flacks" or "spin doctors," whose job is to cover up the truth about a company's problems. What is the proper role of public relations within an organization? Should PR specialists try to put a good face on bad news?

2. Companies sometimes teach consumers a "bad lesson" with the overuse of sales promotion. As a result, consumers expect the product always to be "on deal." What are some examples of products for which this has occurred? How do you think companies can prevent this?

3. In general, professional selling has evolved from hard sell to transactional selling. Does the hard-sell style of selling still exist? If so, in what types of organizations? What do you think the future holds for these organizations? Will the hard sell continue to succeed?

4. One reason cited by experts for the increase in consumer catalogue shopping is the poor quality of service available at retail stores. What do you think about the quality of most retail salespeople you come in contact with? What are some ways retailers can improve the quality of their sales associates?

Marketing Practice: **Applying What You've Learned**

1. As a public relations professional employed by your college or university, you have been asked to develop recommendations for improving your school's public relations program. Write a memo to your college or university president with your recommendations.

2. Assume that you are a public relations professional working for a firm whose business is the incineration of hazardous waste. Outline your recommendations for a public relations campaign for the coming year.

3. Assume that you are a member of the marketing department for a firm that produces several brands of household cleaning products. Your assignment is to develop recommendations for trade and consumer sales promotion activities for a new brand of laundry detergent. Develop an outline of your recommendations for sales promotions for the new detergent.

4. Timing is an important part of a sales promotion plan. When is the best time to mail out samples, to offer trade discounts, to sponsor a sweepstakes? Assume the introduction of the new laundry detergent in question 3 is planned for April 1. Place the activities you recommended in question 3 on a 12-month calendar. In a role-playing situation, present your plan to your supervisor. Be sure to explain why you have included certain types of promotions and the reasons for your timing of each promotion activity.

5. You have been newly hired as a field salesperson by a firm that markets college and university textbooks. As part of your training, your sales manager has asked that you develop an outline of what you will say in a typical sales presentation. Write that outline.

6. As a sales manager for a firm that sells heavy construction equipment, you are evaluating the current sales force compensation plan. Currently, salespeople are paid straight commission, but you are thinking that moving to straight salary or a combination salary and commission plan might be better.

   a. With one of your classmates taking the other side, present your arguments for each option in a role-playing situation.

   b. In a similar role-playing situation, present arguments for different compensation plans that might be used in a retail clothing store.

   c. In a similar role-playing situation, present arguments for different compensation plans that might be used by a new car sales force.

Marketing Mini-Project: **Learning by Doing**

Many college and university students say that they are "absolutely, completely lost" when it comes to knowing what type of job they want, much less how to look for the ideal job. This project gives you experience in the beginning steps in the creative selling process; but in this case, your potential customers are potential employers and the "product" you will be selling is yourself. You might find the information included on the Pearson Education Canada Companion Web Site (www.pearsoned.ca/solomon) helpful for this project.

1. Your first task is to identify a list of characteristics of jobs you might find attractive—your target market. You may consider such characteristics as:

   a. geographic location

   b. size of company (local, regional, national, international)

   c. type of business

   d. job responsibilities

   e. skills required

2. One method used by salespeople for identifying potential job prospects is through networking. Therefore, with one or more members of your class, seek to talk with other people for their suggestions and to find out if they know of any jobs that have the characteristics you have outlined for your target market.

3. Using the resources of your school or your college or university library, generate a list of potential employers that seem to match your target market.

4. Using library resources or personal contacts if available, find out as much as you can about each potential employer.

5. Based on the information you have gathered, classify these employers as A, B, or C leads. "A" leads warrant more of your time and effort. "C" leads warrant the least level of time and effort, because you have determined that their fit with your target market is not very good.

6. With your group, present your findings to your class.

Real People, Real Surfers: **Exploring the Web**

A problem that has confronted marketers for several years is how to efficiently distribute coupons. Some companies find the Internet to be a useful medium for this. In fact, a number of Web sites have been developed solely for the purpose of distributing coupons, including:

www.valpak.com

www.couponscanada.com

www2.hotcoupons.com/coupon/canada/

www.valupage.com

www.suzicoupon.com

Visit several of these Web sites, or use an Internet search engine to identify other coupon sites. Then evaluate the different sites you've visited by answering the following questions.

1. Generally describe each coupon Web site you visited. What kinds of coupons were there? How do consumers take advantage of the offers?

2. What about the design of each Web site is most useful to you as a consumer?

3. Do you think the coupons offered by the Web sites are useful to many consumers? Do you think consumers visit the Web site on a regular basis? What do you think would be some of the characteristics of the type of consumer most likely to be a regular visitor to these sites?

4. As a marketer, would you be likely to try to distribute coupons for your products over the Web sites? Why or why not?

5. How would you improve each of the Web sites you visited?

MARKETING IN ACTION

Molson Canadian

"Hey, I am not a lumber jack or a fur trader, and I don't live in an igloo or eat blubber or own a dog sled, and I don't know Jimmy, Sally or Suzie from Canada although I am certain they're really, really nice. I have a Prime Minister not a president. I speak English and French, not American, and I pronounce it about, not a boot. I can proudly sew my country's flag on my back pack. I believe in peace keeping not policing, diversity not assimilation, and that the beaver is a truly proud and noble animal. A toque is a hat, a chesterfield is a couch. And it is pronounced zed, not zee, zed. Canada is the second largest landmass, the first nation of hockey, and the best part of North America, my name is Joe, and I am Canadian. Thank you."

These are the immortal words of "Joe," a typical patriotic Canadian who is fed up with not being recognized as different from an American. "The Rant," inspired by Toronto agency Bensimon Byrne D'Arcy, was a wildly successful advertising and public relations coup for Molson Canadian, which recently resuscitated its "I Am Canadian" brand positioning. "The Rant" ad received front-page headlines, media coverage in the US, and talk show invitations for Brett Marchand, Molson's vice-president of marketing. On July 1, Molson ended "The Rant" campaign on a high note, by sending "Joe" across the country to make live rants at Canada Day celebrations from Halifax to Victoria.

"The Rant" ad was one of the most successful beer ads ever and became a true cultural phenomenon. Participants in *National Post Online*'s Armchair Critic, a weekly online opinion poll, gave the ad an 81% approval rating—the second highest score ever given to an ad.

Producing an ad that appealed to Canadian nationalism was certainly risky. Canadians are known to be proud of their country and culture but have traditionally been reserved about displaying it, considering blatant nationalism to be inappropriate and too American. Molson's market research suggested otherwise: Patriotic messages, if done tastefully and with a touch of Canadian self-deprecating humour, would be received well by Canadians, particularly by those in their 20s.

The problem facing Marchand and the rest of the Molson marketing team was "what next?" How do you build on, replicate, or otherwise maintain the success of a smash hit? Alanis Morissette couldn't do it after her hit album "Jagged Little Pill"; Michael Jackson didn't do it after "Thriller"; and Mike Myers didn't really do it with his Austin Powers sequel. It's not easy to live up to expectations. The problem with hit albums, movies, or advertising is that the sequels almost always pale by comparison; and even if you can keep the momentum going for awhile (*Rocky I, II, III, IV*), creative ideas eventually run dry or miss the mark.

This is what critics have been saying about "Stereotypes," Molson's sequel to "The Rant." Also based on the "I Am Canadian" positioning, "Stereotypes" features several twentysomethings repeating clichés about Canadians—such as being overly polite, reserved, and humble—while images flash in the background revealing the truth to be quite the opposite. These images include hockey player Phil Esposito elbowing international opponents and sports fans being quite unreserved. Jack Bensimon, president of Bensimon Byrne D'Arcy, explains the strategy as wanting to "build on the success of 'The Rant' with a spot that shows what it really means to be Canadian. On the one hand, we're proud of who we are, but on the other, we know how to have fun and throw great parties." Armchair Critic voters disagreed: Only 41% thought the ad effective, tying "Stereotypes" with a Gap ad for the second-least liked commercial. A number of respondents noted, for example, that the theme song of this ad, which touted Canadian nationalism, was performed by an American band.

Molson did better with the third spot of the "I Am Canadian" revival, "No Doot About It." In this spot, a nameless Canadian working in the US is taunted by office mate Greg about Canadian

MARKETING IN ACTION

stereotypes—such as "Do you want a donut?"—until the Canadian loses it. Hockey fight–style, he "jerseys" Greg (pulls Greg's suit jacket over Greg's head), a classic move to temporarily disable an opponent. The ad, which recaptures the self-deprecating humour of "The Rant," had scored well with young men in test screenings and went on to be nominated for a Bessie award.

The latest Molson Canadian campaign, referred to as "The Toast" ("Here's to you Canada"), tries to show consumers that Molson Canadian is the one true beer for the proudly Canadian guy. It features a new immigrant with a Scottish-Irish accent who tells viewers what he likes about Canada. To further connect multicultural drinkers to the campaign, Molson (with the help of Citizenship and Immigration Canada) sponsored the swearing in of new Canadians during several games in the NHL playoffs. While the viewing audience seemed to like the ad, critics claimed it recaptured the magic of "the Rant" only superficially.

In the end, building brand equity and sales among targeted 19- to 35-year-old men is what counts. "The Rant," though very popular, gained its notoriety mainly outside the beer's target market and did not have a big impact on sales. Whether Armchair Critics like an ad is also irrelevant. What matters is that the target market likes and is motivated by the ad. Similarly, the ads can't be judged in isolation; as a campaign, they work together to meet multiple objectives. These are some of the thoughts of the Molson Canadian marketing team, who continue to struggle with the issue of "what next?" The team is now led by Andrew Barrett, a 34-year-old executive with packaged goods experience with Pillsbury and Procter & Gamble, who has replaced Brett Marchand as vice-president of Molson Canadian. Barrett and his team must decide whether they should continue to generate creative under the "I Am Canadian" positioning or whether is it time to move on and create a new campaign. There might also be opportunities to extend these campaigns with public relations elements and develop an integrated marketing communications strategy.

Sources: "I am drunk: Real Canadian raucous, Molson declares [The Rant]," *Canadian Press Newswire*, 16 June 2000; "Sequel to 'I Am Canadian' ads to feature obnoxious American," *Canadian Press Newswire*, 29 July 2000; Patrick Allossery, "The sequel just isn't as good, or is it? [Stereotypes vs. Rant ads]," *Financial Post*, 26 June 2000: C7; Paul Brant, "Armchair critic: Molson follow-up to Rant ad doesn't measure up: just 43% like stereotypes," *Financial Post*, 17 July 2000: C4; Astrid Van Den Broek, "Molson pours on more stereotypes," *Marketing Magazine Online*, 26 June 2000; Chris Daniels, "Canucks vs. Yanks," *Marketing Magazine Online*, 22 May 2000; Astrid Van Den Broek, "A toast to more colour in beer ads: recent campaigns reflect the diverse backgrounds of today's beer drinkers," *Marketing Magazine Online*, 4 June 2000; Lisa Francilia, "The Creative Eye," *Marketing Magazine Online*, 14 May 2001.

THINGS TO THINK ABOUT

1. What criteria should be used to judge the effectiveness of the most recent set of "I Am Canadian" spots?
2. If new "I Am Canadian" spots were created, what should be their focus, theme, and style?
3. If a new campaign were created, what should be the objective, key messages, themes and tactics?
4. How might public relations be used in conjunction with these campaigns?
5. How could integrated marketing communications concepts be applied?

PART VI CASE

May the Sales Force Be with You

Computer Friendly Stuff realizes the power of (sales) people.

Guys, I Think We Need Some Salespeople

Welcome to the last CFS case. If you have read all of the other CFS cases, you may have suspected two things. First, we really started to grow as a company after we hired a sales force. Second, the CFS introduction is, indeed, not on the test.

We had our share of success before summer 1998, but it was that summer's addition of a sales force that really kicked things into high gear for us. For example, we had approached a well-known computer chain with more than 500 locations with no success. One of our sales reps Bill Benetton signed on with us after we met at a trade show. Two weeks after joining us, Bill brought in a $21 000 initial order from that same computer chain. Clearly, his addition made the difference. We would have spent years trying to achieve that type of success. Not all sales happened that quickly or easily, but things have generally moved along much more quickly than when we were trying to do it ourselves.

Originally, we never thought we'd need a sales force. We thought we had such a great product, we'd just sell it to stores ourselves, thereby eliminating the cost of salespeople. Naive. It's all about access to retail chains, and salespeople give you access. Once we realized that in early 1998, we began to canvas for sales reps. We had no idea where to look. We read ads in the back of trade show magazines and sent samples to rep groups, but this was a fairly haphazard way to go about things. We needed someone who knew the ropes. We needed an industry insider. We needed Joel Wildman.

Joel Wildman is a toy man the same way other men are car men. He thinks, eats, and breathes toys. He wants his son to be a toy man, too, so he brings his young son to the Toy Fair in New York City each year. But it isn't just father-and-son bonding. Joel wants to know if his son thinks a toy is cool. As Joel says, "He's not just my son, he's my own teenage focus group." It's enough to bring a tear to your eye. But it worked for us.

Joel's son walked by our booth last year, liked what he saw, and the rest is history.

Joel is now our national sales manager. He's been terrific, having brought an ideal mix of experience and expertise to our sales effort. He works out of his office in Florida. We see him face-to-face only three or four times a year, at trade shows or meetings, but we speak on the phone several times a day. He fills two roles for us: He hires and manages our sales force and he oversees licensing.

Joel brought us our initial sales reps, but we have continued to acquire additional reps through trade shows. Now when they approach us, we simply hand them over to Joel, who evaluates them in terms of our needs in a particular territory. As of this writing, we have 32 reps selling across North America, and some of them work all three markets: computers, toys, and gifts.

A Sales Force Costs Money!

Should a company use salaried salespeople or freelance sales reps who work on commission? Money provided the answer. We didn't have enough money for salaries, so we had to get freelance reps to work on commission. Fortunately, as it turns out, that is exactly what a young company should be doing. Startup companies are mainly concerned with access. They need someone to get them in the door with a Toys 'R' Us. They pay a lot of money to reps for that access, somewhere between five and ten percent of the wholesale price. Established companies don't need that type of access. If we were Hasbro or Mattel, we wouldn't have trouble getting Toys 'R' Us to meet with us. Thus, established companies are more concerned with servicing accounts. They use salaried reps and pay much lower commissions (one to two percent). When established companies launch new products, they rely on their marketing departments to promote the product, and their salespeople take on more of a facilitating role.

CFS sales reps are on commission, and we pay them five to ten percent. On top of this, we have other significant costs, including the many industry trade shows that we do each year. Trade shows are our bread and butter in terms of finding new leads and maintaining our industry presence, but our reps rely on them as well. They use the shows as a forum to meet with their buyers. Together with Joel, we map out our annual plans for trade show attendance and we update our plan constantly throughout the year. For example, we spent more than $20 000 attending trade shows in the first two months of 2000 alone.

Freelance reps carry multiple product lines from different companies, and ours are no exception. That is bad, because you compete with their other lines. It is good, because it means that they are responsible for their own expenses, including airfare, meals, hotels, and rental cars. The toy industry is particularly brutal, because it requires the reps to travel extensively. Over the course of a year, some of our reps will hopscotch the globe, meeting with the same toy buyers at the same type of trade shows. Why? Because that is the way it is done. They will see the buyers at the pre–Toy Fair in New York in August, Hong Kong in October, Hong Kong again in January at the Hong Kong Toy Show, in Dallas in January at the Dallas Toy Show, and in New York in February at the Toy Fair. You can imagine how expensive it would be if we had to cover all of those costs, in addition to our own. Luckily, our other two markets (computers and gifts) don't require the same amount of repetition.

A Simple Way to Ensure Your Sales force Is Motivated...

We have never worried about Joel Wildman's motivation. He is excited about our products and is a natural go-getter. We pay Joel a monthly advance on his commissions and cover all travel expenses. A bigger issue is how to motivate the sales force that works under Joel. He plays a key role here. He provides his reps with all the tools they need to sell our products, including press kits and samples. He also provides a constant flow of information to all the reps: sales success stories, special offers, and general updates. Some people might ask, after all that, what do you do to get your reps' attention if they aren't selling your products? Easy. You fire them. If a freelance rep is working on commission and you aren't seeing results, there is little more that you can do about it. They obviously have other priorities. Part ways and move on to someone who is going to make things happen for you.

Complexity in the Business-to-Business World

The thing that we find most interesting about sales reps is their ability to negotiate the complex business-to-business deals that major retail chains require. In a perfect world, deals would go like this: We sell 1000 Computer Bugs to a major US retail chain at our wholesale price of $8.99. The chain pays us upon receipt and then sells the Bugs at their retail price of $17.99. Everyone goes home happy.

Here is what happens in the real world: The chain begins by telling us they want a better wholesale price than $8.99. The chain also tells us that they plan to advertise our product in their catalogue, which is mailed out to two million customers, but they want $3000 to split the advertising cost. Further, they give us the option of being placed in an ideal store location for two weeks during the Christmas season (end of aisle or by the cash registers), but that will cost us an additional $2000. Then the chain wants 60-day terms. This means that we front the cost of manufacturing, but we don't get paid for two months after we ship. Finally, the chain wants the order on consignment: If it doesn't sell, they reserve the right to ship back unsold product. Oh, and they don't want to pay for any of the shipping either way.

Confusing? Unfair? Yes. That is why you need good reps. They have the experience to walk in and negotiate down many of these costs. You'd be amazed at what they can finagle. It seems to boil down to the relationships that they have with the buyers. A lot of "scratching of each other's backs" goes on in an effort to make the deal work.

What Does the Future Hold?

CFS has grown tremendously during its first four years. We still have a long way to go, but we feel that we are off to a great start. One thing is certain: We will continue to experience the same type of brain-wracking tough marketing decisions that we have faced in years past. For example, we hope to reach the point where we'll need salaried sales reps. This will bring an entirely new set of questions regarding the way we promote products and motivate reps. We're ready for the challenge. Don't forget to check in with us from time to time at www.computerbug.com.

Questions

1. At what point do you think it is reasonable for CFS to take on a salaried sales force? Is it a question of size of a company or the characteristics of a particular industry?

2. What are the similarities and differences between commissioned multiline reps and a salaried sales force?

3. Does it matter that Joel Wildman doesn't work at the CFS home office? What are the advantages and disadvantages of this type of arrangement?

4. What type of special promotions would you offer to the CFS sales force? Draw up a flyer announcing a special promotion.

Marketing Plan Questions

Refer to the Sample Marketing Plan in Appendix A as you answer these questions about developing and modifying a marketing plan for CFS.

1. For this year's marketing plan, design a trade promotion to attract potential buyers to CFS's exhibit at the upcoming Toy Fair. Indicate how the sales reps, the buyers, and CFS will benefit from this promotion.

2. Looking ahead to next year's marketing plan, what sales force objectives should CFS set for its sales reps? How will these objectives help CFS reach its overall goals?

CBC ⊕ VIDEO CASE 1

Up Close and Personal

The effectiveness of conventional, mass advertising is being questioned by those marketing decision makers who want to develop closer relationships with individual consumers. Mass advertising in magazines, television, and other media can be an efficient way to reach large numbers of consumers. However, how many of the estimated 1500 ads per day that each consumer is exposed to actually get noticed?

Customizing advertising messages to match customer needs can increase the likelihood that consumers pay attention, because the messages are meaningful to them. One company that has experienced success with a customization approach is the furniture retailer IKEA. IKEA is trying to establish a closer relationship with its three million Canadian customers, so it has developed a database containing the names and addresses of people who have either made an IKEA purchase or who have requested information about the retailer. IKEA uses this database to communicate in a meaningful way with customers, such as targeting direct mail pieces like flyers or catalogues to those consumers who would be most interested. For example, all of the people in the database who purchased an IKEA bed in the previous six months might be sent a flyer for an upcoming IKEA bed linen sale.

The Royal Bank has also established a database marketing program, which they use in customizing advertising and direct marketing appeals. To better understand individual needs of potential home buyers, for instance, the bank sends out questionnaires to all of the people in its 8.6 million–name database who have an apartment number in their address. The questionnaire asks these people whether they are considering a home purchase, when they will be buying, what type of home they will be considering. The bank uses the responses to tailor their marketing response: To consumers planning to purchase within one year, they send a direct mail flyer about how to buy a home; to consumers indicating an earlier purchase intent, they send a package by courier containing information about specific mortgage rates as well as other Royal Bank financial services they may be interested in. Royal Bank telemarketers also phone all of the questionnaire respondents to try to better understand their needs and interest them in appropriate Royal Bank products.

Customized communication is evolving into interactive communication, using such tools as toll-free phone numbers and Web sites. Companies use Web sites to simply provide information to consumers, to better understand them, and to provide them with an opportunity to interactively communicate with the company. Real-time communications like live help and on-site retail assistance are becoming common on the Web, and consumers are demanding even more interactivity as their experience with online communications increases.

Men's clothing retailer Harry Rosen takes a more low-tech, but still interactive, approach to relationship marketing, by hosting in-store parties for his customers. He is convinced that getting to know consumers better and communicating with them in a more individualized way will lead to long-term, perhaps even lifetime, relationships, a goal that most marketing decision makers share.

Questions

1. Identify several methods companies can use to establish more personal relationships with their consumers.
2. Some proponents of relationship marketing argue that one reason it is effective is because it makes consumers feel special and valued by the company. Do you agree? Do you think the methods used by IKEA, Royal Bank, and Harry Rosen would make consumers feel valued?
3. How does the integrated communications perspective discussed in Chapter 16 relate to a focus on relationship marketing?

Source: This case was prepared by Auleen Carson and is based on "Relationship Marketing," *Venture* #684 (7 April 1998).

CBC ⬤ VIDEO CASE 2

Attracting the Wrong Customer

Through advertising, publicity, sales promotions, and other elements of the communications mix, marketers invest considerable time, effort, and money attracting customers. Large and small organizations alike have found that some customers are simply not worth having. Grumpy, demanding, or cheapskate customers can actually cost you money: It takes more resources to service and satisfy them than the profit you generate on their purchases. And sometimes, they don't even purchase. "No shows" are a bane of such service organizations as massage parlours, dentist offices, and doctor offices, which have to strike a balance between the cost of no shows in terms of idle staff and the cost, in terms of customer satisfaction, of extra booking and having everyone show up and wait.

Ian Gordon of TCI Convergence Ltd. suggests that organizations should "fire" the customers they lose money on. These are the customers who set up accounts with shipping companies and never ship anything. These are the customers who buy only when products are on sale. These are the customers who complain about everything, looking for concessions and other "make-goods." These are the customers who buy on the Internet three sizes of a clothing product and send two (or all) of them back. It is particularly hard for new businesses to turn away business, but not all business is worth it.

It is not hard to find out who these 25 to 30% of customers are. Many companies have a mountain of customer information gathered from scanners and smart cash registers, credit card summaries, call centres, and customer feedback programs that can be mined with simple software tools to identify the most profitable and least profitable customers. Clearnet, for example, tries to assess the value of every customer. They steeply discount the sales of cell phones to attract a long-term stream of monthly phone usage. If a customer is not generating sufficient revenue to warrant Clearnet's investment in the phone, Clearnet first tries to get them to use it more and then tries to reduce the cost of servicing the customer by reducing service levels. As a last resort, they will cut off the phone service, buy back the phone for what the customer paid for it, and politely suggest that another service provider would better meet that customer's needs.

Firing a customer needs to be done with some tact, particularly in Canada where there are only 10 to 12 million households, and companies can't risk alienating too many of them. A common strategy is to reduce service levels or otherwise make the product offer less attractive to those unattractive customers, so that they choose to go to another service or product provider and don't realize that you did not want their business. The challenge is to not attract them in the first place. This takes a strong understanding of target market profiles and messages that would attract desired customers and not others.

Questions

1. What elements would you include in an information system to identify unprofitable or otherwise unattractive customers?
2. Should airlines such as Air Canada be able to drop routes that cost more to service than is generated through customer ticket sales?
3. What public relations issues do you see in "firing" a customer?

Source: This case was prepared by Brock Smith and is based on "Firing Your Customer," *Venture #710* (26 January 1999).

Appendix A A Sample Marketing Plan: Computer Friendly Stuff

Situation Analysis

COMPANY BACKGROUND

Computer Friendly Stuff (CFS) was founded in May 1996 with the goal of creating and marketing toys and accessories to make computers more fun to use. CFS is pioneering the integrated computer toy/accessory category, which is expected to grow as computer use expands both domestically and internationally. Currently, little competition exists in this new category, although more competition is anticipated in the coming years.

The initial product, introduced in mid-1997, was the Original Computer Bug computer toy, a plastic character designed to adhere to the side or top of a computer monitor. An integrated add-on product was a series of humorous screen savers and animations featuring the Bug, available on CD-ROM in Windows 95 format. The second product, introduced in 1998, was Monitor Morphs. This product consists of bendable arms that adhere to a computer monitor, plus an integrated series of goofy-face screen savers and animations on CD-ROM in Windows 95 format.

As an entrepreneurial company, CFS has a flat, functional organization structure. Key personnel are:

- *Chris Cole, co-founder and co-president.* Cole is responsible for the creation, design, packaging, and production management of all CFS products.

- *Bill Martens, co-founder and co-president.* Martens is responsible for international and domestic distribution and marketing. He also serves as a financier.

- *Joel Wildman, national sales manager.* Wildman is responsible for maintaining the sales force of independent sales reps. He also handles licensing negotiation and advises on overseas production.

- *Brett Moreland, communications director.* Moreland manages publicity and market research for all CFS products.

- *Dan Mack, creative development manager.* Mack works with Cole on all product concepts and copy for marketing literature and packaging.

- *Jeff Harvey, senior designer.* Harvey is responsible for software interface, animation, music composition, and package design.

- *Abel Ramirez, designer.* Ramirez is responsible for animation, package design, sales literature design, and Web site development.

MARKETS

In the broadest sense, the overall consumer market for CFS products is anyone who uses a personal computer. This market is exploding, with worldwide personal computer sales increasing at a rate of over 20% per year. In 1999, there were 105 million personal computers sold in the US alone. Despite this strong sales growth, fewer than half of all US and Canadian households own a PC, compared with greater than 90% penetration of televisions. As a result, the North American market for PCs is expected to continue expanding for some time, as is the market in Asia and other areas around the world.

Within the overall North American consumer market, CFS is targeting two specific segments. Based on feedback about the strong appeal of the Bug character, one important segment is youngsters, aged 7 to 14. This represents a sizable segment. According to Statistics Canada and US Bureau of the Census data, the North American population of boys and girls aged 5 to 14 is almost 45 million; the segment of 7 to 14 year olds is estimated at 40 million.

The second consumer segment being targeted is women aged 30 to 65 who use computers. According to Statistics Canada and US Bureau of the Census data the population of women in North America aged 35 to 64 totals 61 million. Assuming that 20% of those women are employed in a professional work setting, this segment is estimated at 12.2 million.

To reach the consumer market, CFS is targeting three broad reseller markets: computers, toys, and gifts. CFS sells through wholesalers to selected retailers and through independent sales reps directly to major national retail chains. CFS products are also available on Web retail sites such as Gift Tree and on the company Web site (www.computer-bug.com). CFS products are available in the North American market as well as in New Zealand, the UK, Latin America, Asia, and the Middle East.

COMPETITION

No direct competition exists in the integrated computer toy and accessory category. Many screen saver products are available at the retail level, and many are offered without charge on the Web, but none of these products incorporate adhesive toy attachments for the monitor. Thus, the ability to create humorous and imaginative computer toy and accessory combinations is a distinctive competency for CFS.

The closest competing product is a Warner Brothers Taz Mousepad and Screen Saver, which sells for $16.99 with a single screen saver on 3.5-inch disk. The Warner Brothers product enjoys high brand awareness, due to the popularity of the Taz licensed character. It also benefits from national distribution through Warner Brothers Studio Stores and other outlets. Other screen savers featuring brand-name licensed characters (but no computer toy) sell for about $20.

In recent years, interactive toys based on licensed characters such as Barney have been introduced, at relatively high price points (approximately $100). Because these are geared primarily toward younger children and are unrelated to PC use, they are not considered competition for CFS products.

From a competitive standpoint, CFS products are positioned as fun, unique, and value added. They retail at a slightly higher price than the Warner Brothers product, but they also provide significantly more in terms of software and innovation. Whereas buyers receive only one Taz screen saver when they buy the Warner Brothers product, they receive 10 screen savers with the CFS product. The CFS characters are humorous, new, and distinctive, and feedback demonstrates their widespread appeal among the market segment of youngsters aged 7 to 14.

PRODUCTS

CFS is expanding its line of products that make computers more fun. At present, the product line consists of:

The Original Computer Bug computer toy (introduced in 1997). This is a plastic character designed to adhere to the side or top of a computer monitor, without marring the monitor's finish. It is integrated with a CD-ROM containing a series of screen savers, wallpapers, and animations of the Bug, for Windows 95 format. This add-on product can be sold separately or bundled with the Bug toy. A Macintosh version of the CD-ROM was introduced in September 1999.

The Original Computer Bug computer toy has been repackaged into a brightly-coloured blister pack with legs. This package enhances the consumer appeal of the package. It also allows the product to stand on a shelf or hang from a peg, depending on the retailer's merchandising preference. More packaging changes, however, are needed to emphasize the integrated CD-ROM and explain the product.

Monitor Morphs (introduced in 1998). This product comes with two adhesive, bendable arms that attach to the sides of a computer monitor to hold pens, paper, or other office supplies. The product also includes a CD-ROM in Windows 95 format with an integrated series of screen savers with giant animated faces. When installed, the product appears to transform the user's monitor into a giant head with arms sticking out. A Macintosh version of the CD-ROM was introduced in September 1999.

CHANNELS

CFS's primary emphasis is on the retail channel, specifically toy stores, gift stores, and computer and software stores. To reach the retail channel, CFS uses wholesalers for select accounts and independent sales representatives for other accounts. The appointment of a national sales manager has boosted CFS's ability to sell into the retail channel. To build awareness and generate leads, CFS also participates in such industry conventions as the Toy Fair. CFS's largest retail accounts have been the Electronics Boutique, a 500-store US chain, and Radio Shack Canada, another 500-store chain.

The Internet is a secondary channel for CFS. Online retail outlets currently account for 10% of CFS's annual sales. This proportion is expected to increase as electronic commerce grows, and CFS arranges for distribution through major online outlets. The CFS site also allows consumer orders, although this is not a major channel for the company at present.

ENVIRONMENT

Economic considerations. CFS products sell well in periods of prosperity, when the economy is strong, consumer confidence is on the upswing, and computer sales are also growing. Although CFS has no experience marketing during a recession, sales are likely to plateau or, in the worst case, possibly decline as the business cycle swings away from growth.

Demographic considerations. The North American population of children aged 7 to 14 is projected to remain stable through 2005, which means this targeted segment will remain at about 40 million. The North American population of women aged 35 to 64 is projected to grow to 68 million by 2005. If 20% are assumed to be in professional work settings, this targeted segment will represent 13.6 million women by 2005.

Social and cultural considerations. The ongoing shift to a service economy in North America means more knowledgeable workers sitting in front of PCs. At the same time, computers are becoming commonplace in businesses and, to a lesser extent, homes around the world. Over time, these two trends will support higher demand for integrated computer toys and accessories.

Political and legal considerations. No import/export restrictions currently affect CFS products. Special legal and regulatory guidelines would apply if the products were geared for children under three years old, but these are currently not an issue since the target market is children aged seven and older. Any future television campaigns developed by CFS will have to conform to regulatory guidelines governing advertising that targets children.

Technological considerations. The consumer market is split into two PC platforms: Windows/IBM-compatible PCs and Apple/Macintosh PCs. The original CFS products were designed for Windows 95, with Macintosh versions added later. The huge popularity of Apple's iMac makes that platform even more attractive for future CFS products. Microsoft continues to release newer versions of Windows, but CFS products are designed to be compatible with these newer versions, which means consumers will still be able to run their screen savers after any Windows upgrade. An area of possible future concern is an increase in pirating, which could cut into revenues and profits.

PREVIOUS RESULTS

Sales of CFS products have steadily increased since 1997, the first full year of operation.

Company sales performance:

1997 gross sales	$ 47 000
1998 gross sales	105 000 (123% increase over 1997)
1999 gross sales	380 000 (262% increase over 1998)
2000 gross sales (projected)	750 000 (98% increase over 1999)

Product sales performance:

1997	
Computer Bug toy	$10 000
Bug and screen saver	37 000

1998	
Computer Bug toy	$15 000 (50% increase over 1997)
Bug and screen saver	72 000 (95% increase over 1997)
Monitor Morphs	18 000 (introduced in October)

1999	
Bug and screen saver	$ 80 000 (12% increase over 1998)
Monitor Morphs	160 000 (790% increase over 1998)
Corporate Friendly Stuff services	140 000 (new division in 1999)

2000 (projected)	
Bug and screen saver	$100 000 (25% increase over 1999)
Monitor Morphs	250 000 (56% increase over 1999)
Corporate Friendly Stuff services	400 000 (185% increase over 1999)

Seasonality of sales:

Eighty percent of product sales have occurred during the year-end holiday season. This seasonality is the direct result of the high proportion of gift and toy stores currently carrying CFS products. Broadening the distribution to include more computer and electronics stores will significantly reduce this seasonality and spread sales more evenly throughout the year. In turn, this will improve cash flow.

SWOT and Issue Analysis

Strengths. One internal strength of CFS is the creative, skilled employee team. All employees apply their creative talents to every project. Employees have appropriate technical skills and have proven their ability to adapt to the ever-changing demands of an entrepreneurial startup. A second strength is the high-performance organizational culture, which focuses on quality and customer satisfaction—with a sense of humour. A third strength is the flexibility and cost savings gained by outsourcing production functions.

Weaknesses. One internal weakness of CFS is limited financial resources to fund heavy promotional campaigns or large-scale expansion activities to meet unexpectedly high demand. Also, if CFS had an established reputation and a proven product track record, it would be better able to compete for distribution opportunities in major chains.

Opportunities. One external opportunity for CFS is the increase in computer use—both domestically and internationally—which is creating a huge potential market for CFS products. Another opportunity is the increase in electronic commerce, which is likely to increase the proportion of CFS products purchased through online retailers. In addition, both Marvel Comics and Warner Brothers have expressed interest in licensing their characters for CFS products, an arrangement that could greatly expand CFS's public awareness and open new promotion and distribution opportunities. The possible licensing of the Original Computer Bug for a Saturday morning cartoon series is another opportunity. Given the co-founders' experience and connections in the entertainment industry, this opportunity could lead to extremely wide public awareness and much higher sales of tie-in products.

Threats. One external threat is the relative lack of awareness of CFS brands among the target audiences. The Warner Brothers licensed characters enjoy widespread brand awareness, whereas the Original Computer Bug and Monitor Morphs are much less widely known at present. Another threat is vulnerability to imitations produced by companies with more financial resources and larger distribution networks. In addition, CFS products have a limited lifespan because they are designed for desktop PC monitors; as laptops and flat screen monitors become more popular, CFS will need new products designed specifically for these uses. Finally, the current seasonality of CFS products is problematic for cash flow.

Critical Issues. One critical short-term issue for CFS is its ability to negotiate favourable licensing arrangements for established characters from Warner Brothers or other sources. Another critical issue is ensuring compatibility of CFS products with future Windows operating systems, as well as designing products for the growing market of laptops and flat-screen monitor users. The third critical issue for CFS is its continuing to develop new products to stay ahead of any deep-pocketed competitors that may imitate CFS's existing products. A fourth critical issue is obtaining suitable distribution in North America and in world markets to boost sales while spreading sales more evenly throughout the year.

Mission and Objectives

The mission of CFS is to design and market integrated computer toys and accessories that offer the benefit of making computers fun to use at home or in the workplace. CFS is targeting two consumer segments, youth aged 7 to 14 and professional women aged 35 to 65. CFS's distinctive competency is the ability to create humorous and imaginative computer toy and accessory combinations.

MARKETING OBJECTIVES

- To increase the number of retail outlets carrying CFS products by 300% within one year.

- To improve market penetration by boosting the number of additional products purchased by existing customers by 25% within two years.

- To introduce two new products by year-end.
- To research brand awareness of CFS among targeted segments as a baseline and then set objectives for boosting brand awareness by year-end.
- To improve market development by expanding distribution of current products to at least two new international markets within six months.

SALES OBJECTIVES

- To increase gross sales by 300% within one year and by 250% within two years.
- To increase sales of Monitor Morphs by 200% within one year.
- To maintain sales growth of at least 150% for Computer Bug Toys for the next year.
- To achieve first-year gross sales of at least $70 000 for each new product introduced in the next year.

Target Markets and Positioning

CFS is using a target market strategy to focus on selected consumer and organizational segments. CFS has segmented the consumer market on the basis of demographics (age and gender) and behaviour (computer usage at home or office and propensity to give gifts). CFS has segmented the organizational market on the basis of NAICS/SIC codes.

Consumer segments. The segment of youngsters, aged 7 to 14, is estimated at 40 million. The segment of professional women, aged 35 to 65, is estimated at 12.2 million. Informal research—feedback from trade shows, Christmas shows, fan mail, and in-store appearances—indicates that the youth segment reacts very positively to the Bug character and the humorous screen savers. Secondary market research shows that professional women buy more gifts than men, so they are a good target for buying CFS products for gift-giving occasions.

Organizational segments. To reach the two targeted consumer segments, CFS is targeting three reseller markets: computers, toys, and gifts. These can be identified by their NAICS/SIC codes. Toy stores are NAICS code 45112 (SIC 5945); gift stores are NAICS code 45322 (SIC 5947); and computer and software stores are NAICS code 44312 (SIC 5734). CFS sells through wholesalers to selected retailers in these segments and, through independent sales reps, sells directly to major national retail chains in these segments. CFS products are also available on retail Web sites that sell toys and gifts.

CFS products are positioned as fun, unique, and value added, with the major benefit of making computer use more fun. The products have a distinctive and humorous brand personality, which supports this major benefit. The Computer Bug carries the slogan, "I'm the Bug you *want* to have in your computer!" and Monitor Morphs carry the slogan, "Morph your monitor!"

Product Strategies

The two existing products, Computer Bug and Monitor Morphs, are moving from the growth to the maturity stage of the product life cycle. Although both continue to sell well, CFS needs additional new products to achieve its ambitious sales objectives. New product sales will also balance a drop in sales that might occur if one or more of the original products becomes a fad and then quickly loses its appeal.

CFS plans to develop both the product line and product mix. The product line will be lengthened by adding new licensed characters and different Computer Bugs and Monitor Morphs. The product mix will be broadened by adding new products such as Chubby Stubby stuffed animals, cute creatures with stubby legs.

CFS will build on the product franchise and extend the product life cycle of the Computer Bug by investigating opportunities to license the character for a television cartoon show or for other types of products. In contrast, Monitor Morphs are expected to have a more compressed product life cycle, unless CFS is able to arrange licensing of established characters, a move that would extend the appeal and sales possibilities for this product.

As new product development progresses on Chubby Stubby products, CFS has forged alliances with Asian suppliers that will make prototypes for free in exchange for the right to manufacture the products. This new product, like all CFS products, will be legally protected by trademarks and patents. Chubby Stubby products will be test marketed through key retail accounts before being introduced to all North American and global retail outlets. The new product launch will be accompanied by targeted consumer and trade promotions to boost retail acceptance and spark consumer interest.

To support point-of-sale merchandising, CFS is changing its packaging in two key ways. First, increasing the size of the clear window through which the Computer Bug is viewed will make the CD-ROM more visible inside the blister pack. Second, new, brighter graphics will explain the product more clearly and call attention to the integration of the computer toy and the screen saver CD-ROM.

Pricing Strategies

Pricing is a key ingredient for boosting profits that can be reinvested to support CFS's plans for rapid sales growth. It also affects consumers' perceptions of product quality and value. In addition, product pricing must cover sufficient gross margin for retailers as well as commissions for the independent sales representatives and wholesalers who sell CFS products; otherwise, CFS will be unable to expand its distribution base.

In managing wholesale and retail prices, CFS considers production costs, competitive prices, retail and wholesale margins, and consumer reaction. By testing, CFS has confirmed that a slight increase in retail price will not adversely affect consumer demand. CFS uses price lining, assigning different prices to different products in the product line. Therefore, CFS has set retail prices for its existing product line as:

Computer Bug w/CD-ROM	$19.99
Monitor Morphs w/CD-ROM	$24.99

The national sales manager has authority to negotiate with large retail chains that request discounts for volume, advertising allowances, and other pricing adjustments. CFS also plans to use seasonal discounts, coinciding with major holidays and trade shows, to encourage purchasing during specific periods. In addition, pricing in international markets is adjusted sale by sale to account for ever-changing foreign currency rates. As competition develops, CFS plans to consider revising wholesale and retail prices as necessary to support sales growth, protect market share, and support distribution objectives.

Channel (Place) Strategies

Distribution is an important component for increasing sales of CFS products in all markets. CFS targets three categories of resellers: toy stores, computer stores, and gift stores. The primary CFS channel strategy involves indirect distribution, selling through wholesalers and manufacturers' agents (independent reps supervised by a CFS national sales manager) to the targeted retailers, who then sell to the consumer market. These independent reps have developed relationships with buyers for the top North American retail chains, so they can demonstrate CFS products and negotiate orders and pricing.

CFS plans to increase its selective distribution among toy, computer, and gift stores that can display the product appropriately and reach the targeted consumer segments. This will achieve the goals of increasing the number of retail outlets carrying CFS products by 300% and placing CFS products in 10 major North American chains during this year. To obtain distribution in these large national chains, CFS plans to support its products with pricing allowances, trade promotions, and consumer promotions. For example, CFS will produce and distribute 50 000 consumer promotion flyers for in-store display this year. In the coming year, CFS will test response to placing products in mail-order catalogues geared toward the targeted consumer segments.

CFS also sells directly to consumers through its Web site, although this is currently a secondary strategy. Selling through online retailers, however, will be an increasingly important part of channel strategy, given the explosive growth of electronic commerce. Therefore, CFS's priority in online distribution is to sell through Internet retailers that take title to the goods and handle all order processing and shipment. Online retailers that sell CFS products but require fulfillment by CFS will be a much lower priority because of the complications and costs of physical distribution.

Promotion Strategies

CFS will use promotion to educate the target audience about the features and benefits of its products, build brand awareness and preference, support the distribution strategy, and build long-term customer relationships. As CFS works toward its distribution goals, it is putting more emphasis on personal selling. Other promotional techniques will include consumer and trade sales promotion, limited advertising, and public relations.

Personal selling. CFS has a network of 32 manufacturers' agents who sell CFS to resellers. These independent salespeople receive a commission of 5 to 10% of the wholesale price of all the CFS products they sell. Joel Wildman serves as CFS national sales manager, hiring and managing the agents, approving pricing adjustments, negotiating licensing deals, and working with CFS management to set sales goals. This year, CFS will begin evaluating agents on a bimonthly basis to ensure efficient, appropriate coverage of the reseller market. These frequent reviews will also allow CFS to monitor sales to key accounts more closely and replace agents quickly if they do not achieve sales goals. To support personal selling tactics, CFS will provide additional promotional materials and product demonstration models earlier in the selling season. By mid-year, CFS will introduce a new incentive program of bonuses and promotions for the independent salespeople.

Consumer sales promotion. To better educate consumers about CFS products and build brand awareness, CFS will distribute 50 000 in-store point-of-sale flyers to participating resellers this year. CFS also will continue to send someone in a seven-foot Computer Bug mascot costume to promote products through monthly in-store appearances. In addition, CFS is using sampling—putting demonstration versions of all products on every CD-ROM—to support the market penetration goal of boosting the number of additional products purchased by existing customers by 25% within two years. Within three months, CFS plans to design new point-of-purchase displays to improve product placement and encourage more impulse buying in stores.

Trade sales promotion. In addition to providing resellers with new point-of-purchase displays to support sales, CFS is allocating $15 000 as push money to encourage sales of Monitor Morphs at computer chains. CFS has also budgeted $90 000 to cover the cost of exhibiting at trade shows in the coming year and will spend up to $20 000 on cooperative promotions through major retailers.

Advertising. Tests of magazine advertising have shown low sales response, because CFS products cannot be demonstrated in print media. Television advertising would be ideal for demonstrating the Computer Bug and Monitor Morphs, but the high costs of production and media put this medium out of reach for a young, entrepreneurial company. CFS will therefore concentrate on co-op advertising, partnering with resellers that stock the product to share the costs of local advertising, including television, newspapers, magazines, and direct mail. These advertising messages will emphasize the "fun" benefits and the unique brand personality.

Public relations. CFS has successfully used public relations to showcase products to the consumer audience, especially in the US market. CFS products have been featured in the *Chicago Tribune, BUZZ* magazine, and *CBS This Morning*. In the coming year, CFS will expand the public relations effort to include the top children's magazines; the top working women's magazines; the 50 largest US newspapers; the top children's cable networks; all national television morning shows; and local morning television shows in the top 20 US markets. Each television show will receive a special package including a customized demonstration CD-ROM (mentioning the program and the anchors by name). When attending trade shows, the Computer Bug mascot will visit targeted media outlets in the local area. All these public relations tactics will be timed to coincide with specific selling periods, such as back-to-school and Christmas.

Marketing Research, R&D

As CFS products gain wider distribution, more research is needed about brand awareness and perceptions among professional women, one of the two targeted consumer segments. Therefore, CFS will commission exploratory research early this year, using personal interviews and focus groups to uncover women's attitudes, feelings, and buying behaviours toward CFS products.

Informal marketing research is helpful in assessing children's reactions to existing products and testing ideas for new products. Throughout this year, CFS will insert youth-oriented notices into products sold in toy stores, inviting children to submit their comments through e-mail (after asking their parents' permission). The Web site will also invite children to answer a brief online questionnaire about new products (reassuring parents that no identifying personal data will be collected). Before Chubby Stubby stuffed animals are test marketed, CFS will conduct focus group research to gauge consumer reaction to the product and to various marketing mix strategies.

Controls

CFS will use several tools to evaluate and control activities implemented under this marketing plan. First, CFS will use monthly trend analyses to examine sales by channel, type of reseller, chain, agent, and geographic area. These analyses will enable CFS to take corrective action when necessary.

Second, CFS will monitor customer and reseller feedback weekly to quickly identify problems, such as in product quality, and to stay abreast of competitive moves. This will allow CFS to respond more quickly.

Third, CFS will conduct a marketing audit in mid-year and again at year-end to evaluate the effectiveness and efficiency of the marketing programs. In this way, CFS will be able to pinpoint areas for improvement and prepare contingency plans for emerging problems.

Note: Some details of this plan have been changed to protect proprietary information.

Appendix B Marketing Math

To develop marketing strategies to meet the goals of an organization effectively and efficiently, it is essential that marketers understand and use a variety of financial analyses. This appendix provides some of these basic financial analyses, including a review of the income statement and balance sheet as well as some basic performance ratios. In addition, this appendix includes an explanation of some of the specific calculations that marketers use routinely in determining price.

Income Statement and Balance Sheet

The two most important documents used to explain the financial situation of a company are the income statement and the balance sheet. The **income statement** (which is sometimes referred to as the profit and loss statement) provides a summary of the revenues and expenses of a firm—that is, the amount of income a company received from sales or other sources, the amount of money it spent, and the resulting income or loss that the company experienced.

The major elements of the income statement are

Gross sales: the total of all income the firm receives from the sales of goods and services.

Net sales revenue: the gross sales minus the amount for returns and promotional or other allowances given to customers.

Cost of goods sold (sometimes called the *cost of sales*): the cost of inventory or goods that the firm has sold.

Gross margin (also called *gross profit*): the amount of sales revenue that is in excess of the cost of goods sold.

Operating expenses: expenses other than the cost of goods sold that are necessary for conducting business. These may include salaries, rent, depreciation on buildings and equipment, insurance, utilities, supplies, and property taxes.

Operating income (sometimes called *income from operations*): the gross margin minus the operating expenses. Sometimes accountants prepare an *operating statement*, which is similar to the income statement except that the final calculation is the operating income—that is, other revenues or expenses and taxes are not included.

Other revenue and expenses: income and/or expenses other than those required for conducting the business. These may include such items as interest income/expenses and any gain or loss experienced on the sale of property or plant assets.

Taxes: the amount of income tax the firm owes calculated as a percentage of income.

Net income (sometimes called *net earnings* or *net profit*): the excess of total revenue over total expenses.

Table B1 shows the income statement for an imaginary company, DLL Incorporated. DLL is a typical merchandising firm. Note that the income statement is for a specific year and includes income and expenses from January 1 through December 31 inclusive. The following comments explain the meaning of some of the important entries included in this statement.

- DLL Inc. has total or gross sales during the year of $253 950. This figure was adjusted, however, by deducting the $3000 worth of goods returned and special allowances given to customers and by $2100 in special discounts. Thus the actual or net sales generated by sales is $248 850.

- The cost of goods sold is calculated by adding the inventory of goods on January 1 to the amount purchased during the year and then subtracting the inventory of goods on December 31. In this case, DLL had $60 750 worth of inventory on hand on January 1. During the year the firm made purchases in the amount of $135 550. This amount, however, was reduced by purchase returns and allowances of $1500 and by purchase discounts of $750, so the net purchase is only $133 300.

There is also an amount on the statement labelled "Freight-In." This is the amount spent by the firm in shipping charges to get goods to its facility from suppliers. Any expenses for freight from DLL to its customers (Freight-Out) would be an operating expense. In this case, the Freight-In expense of $2450 is added to net purchase costs. Then these costs of current purchases are added to the beginning inventory to show that during the year the firm had a total of $196 500 in goods available for sale. Finally, the inventory of goods held on December 31 is subtracted from the goods available, for the total cost of goods sold of $136 200.

For a manufacturer, calculation of the cost of goods sold would be a bit more complicated and would probably include separate figures for such items as inventory of finished goods, the "work-in-process" inventory, the raw materials inventory, and the cost of goods delivered to customers during the year.

- The cost of goods sold is subtracted from the net sales revenue to get a gross margin of $112 650.

Table B.1   DLL Inc. Income Statement for the Year Ended December 31, 20XX

Gross Sales			$253 950
Less: Sales Returns and Allowances		$ 3 000	
Sales Discounts		2 100	5 100
Net Sales Revenue			$248 850
Cost of Goods Sold			
Inventory, January 1, 20XX			$ 60 750
Purchases		$135 550	
Less: Purchase Returns and Allowances		1 500	
Purchase Discounts		750	
Net Purchases		$133 300	
Plus: Freight-In		2 450	135 750
Goods Available for Sale			196 500
Less: Inventory, December 31, 20XX			60 300
Cost of Goods Sold			$136 200
Gross Margin			112 650
Operating Expenses			
Salaries and Commissions		15 300	
Rent		12 600	
Insurance		1 500	
Depreciation		900	
Supplies		825	
Total Operating Expenses			31 125
Operating Income			81 525
Other Revenue and (Expenses)			
Interest Revenue		1 500	
Interest Expense		(2 250)	(750)
Income before Tax			80 775
Taxes (40%)			32 310
Net Income			$ 48 465

- Operating expenses for DLL include the salaries and commissions paid to its employees, rent on facilities and/or equipment, insurance, depreciation of capital items, and the cost of operating supplies. DLL has a total of $31 125 in operating expenses, which is deducted from the gross margin. Thus DLL has an operating income of $81 525.

- DLL had both other income and expenses in the form of interest revenues of $1500 and interest expenses of $2250, making a total other expense of $750, which was subtracted from the operating income, leaving an income before tax of $80 775.

- Finally, the income before tax is reduced by 40 percent ($32 310) for taxes, leaving a net income of $48 465. The 40 percent is an average amount for federal and provincial corporate income taxes incurred by most firms.

The **balance sheet** lists the assets, liabilities, and stockholders' equity of the firm. Whereas the income statement represents what happened during an entire year, the balance sheet is like a snapshot; it shows the firm's financial situation at one point in time. For this reason, the balance sheet is sometimes called the *statement of financial position.*

Table B2 (page 536) shows DLL Inc.'s balance sheet for December 31. Assets are any economic resource that is expected to benefit the firm in the short or long term. Current assets are items that are normally expected to be turned into cash or used up during the next twelve months or during the firm's normal operating cycle. Current assets for DLL include cash, securities, accounts receivable (money owed to the firm and not yet paid) inventory on hand, prepaid insurance, and supplies: a total of $84 525. *Long-term assets* include all assets that are not current assets. For DLL, these are property, plant, equipment, furniture, and fixtures less an amount for depreciation, or $45 300. The total assets for DLL are $129 825.

A firm's *liabilities* are its *economic obligations,* or debts that are payable to individuals or organizations outside the firm. *Current liabilities* are debts due in the coming year or in the firm's normal operating cycle. For DLL, the current liabilities—the accounts payable, unearned sales revenue, wages payable, and interest payable—total $72 450. *Long-term liabilities* (in the case of DLL, a note in the amount of $18 900) are all liabilities that are not due during the coming cycle. *Stockholders' equity* is the value of the stock and the corporation's capital or retained earnings. DLL has

$15 000 in common stock and $23 475 in retained earnings for a total stockholders' equity of $38 475. Total liabilities always equal total assets—in this case, $129 825.

Important Financial Performance Ratios

How do managers and financial analysts compare the performance of a firm from one year to the next? How do investors compare the performance of one firm with that of another? Often, a number of different financial ratios provide important information for such comparisons. Such ratios are percentage figures comparing various income statement items to net sales. Ratios provide a better way to compare performance than simple dollar sales or cost figures for two reasons. They enable analysts to compare the performance of large and small firms, and they provide a fair way to compare performance over time, without having to take inflation and other changes into account. In this section we will explain the basic operating ratios. Other measures of performance that marketers frequently use and that are also explained here are the inventory turnover rate and return on investment (ROI).

OPERATING RATIOS

Measures of performance calculated directly from the information in a firm's income statement (sometimes called an operating statement) are called the *operating ratios*. Each ratio compares some income statement item to net sales. The most useful of these are the *gross margin ratio, the net income ratio, the operating expense ratio, and the returns and allowances ratio*. These ratios vary widely by industry but tend to be important indicators of how a firm is doing within its industry. The ratios for DLL Inc. are shown in Table B3.

- The **gross margin ratio** shows what percentage of sales revenues are available for operating and other expenses and for profit. With DLL, this means that 45 percent, or nearly half, of every sales dollar is available for operating costs and for profits.

- The **net income ratio** (sometimes called the *net profit ratio*) shows what percentage of sales revenues are income or profit. For DLL, the net income ratio is 19.5 percent. This means that the firm's profit before taxes is about 20 cents of every dollar.

Table B.2 DLL Inc. Balance Sheet: December 31, 20XX

Assets			
Current Assets			
Cash		$ 4 275	
Marketable Securities		12 000	
Accounts Receivable		6 900	
Inventory		60 300	
Prepaid Insurance		300	
Supplies		150	
Total Current Assets			84 525
Long-Term Assets—Property, Plant and Equipment			
Furniture and Fixtures	$42 300		
Less: Accumulated Depreciation	4 500	37 800	
Land		7 500	
Total Long-Term Assets			45 300
Total Assets			$129 825
Liabilities			
Current Liabilities			
Accounts Payable	$70 500		
Unearned Sales Revenue	1 050		
Wages Payable	600		
Interest Payable	300		
Total Current Liabilities		72 450	
Long-Term Liabilities			
Note Payable		18 900	
Total Liabilities			91 350
Stockholders' Equity			
Common Stock		15 000	
Retained Earnings		23 475	
Total Stockholders' Equity			38 475
Total Liabilities and Stockholders' Equity			$129 825

Table B.3 (Hypothetical) Operating Ratios for DLL Inc.

Gross margin ratio	=	$\dfrac{\text{gross margin}}{\text{net sales}}$	=	$\dfrac{\$112\ 650}{248\ 850}$	= 45.3%
Net income ratio	=	$\dfrac{\text{net income}}{\text{net sales}}$	=	$\dfrac{\$\ 48\ 465}{248\ 850}$	= 19.5%
Operating expense ratio	=	$\dfrac{\text{total operating expenses}}{\text{net sales}}$	=	$\dfrac{\$\ 31\ 125}{248\ 850}$	= 12.5%
Returns and allowances ratio	=	$\dfrac{\text{returns and allowances}}{\text{net sales}}$	=	$\dfrac{\$\ 3000}{248\ 850}$	= 1.2%

- The **operating expense ratio** is the percentage of sales needed for operating expenses. DLL has an operating expense ratio of 12.5 percent. Tracking operating expense ratios from one year to the next or comparing them with an industry average gives a firm important information about how efficient its operations are.
- The **returns and allowances ratio** shows what percentage of all sales are being returned, probably by unhappy customers. DLL's returns and allowances ratio shows that only a little over 1 percent of sales are being returned.

INVENTORY TURNOVER RATE

The *inventory turnover rate*, also referred to as the stockturn rate, is the number of times inventory or stock is turned over (sold and replaced) during a specified time period, usually a year. Inventory turnover rates are usually calculated on the basis of inventory costs, sometimes on the basis of inventory selling prices, and sometimes by number of units.

For our example, DLL Inc., we know that for the year, the cost of goods sold was $136 200. Information on the balance sheet enables us to find the average inventory. By adding the value of the beginning inventory to the ending inventory and dividing by 2, we can compute an average inventory. In the case of DLL, this would be

$$\frac{\$60\ 750 + \$60.300}{2} = \$60\ 525$$

Thus

$$\text{Inventory turnover rate (in cost of goods sold)} = \frac{\text{costs of goods sold}}{\text{average inventory at cost}} = \frac{\$136\ 200}{\$60\ 525} = 2.25 \text{ times}$$

RETURN ON INVESTMENT (ROI)

Firms often develop business objectives in terms of return on investment, and ROI is often used to determine how effective (and efficient) the firm's management has been. First, however, we need to define exactly what a firm means by investment. In most cases, firms define investment as the total assets of the firm. In order to calculate the ROI, we need the net income found in the income statement and the total assets (or investment), which is found on the firm's balance sheet.

Return on investment is calculated as follows:

$$\text{ROI} = \frac{\text{net income}}{\text{total investment}}$$

For DLL Inc., if the total assets are $129 825, then the ROI is

$$\frac{\$48\ 465}{\$129\ 825} = 37.3\%$$

Sometimes return on investment is calculated by using an expanded formula.

$$\text{ROI} = \frac{\text{net profit}}{\text{sales}} \times \frac{\text{sales}}{\text{investment}}$$

$$= \frac{\$48\ 465}{\$248\ 850} \times \frac{\$248\ 850}{\$129\ 825} = 37.3\%$$

This formula makes it easy to show how ROI can be increased and what might reduce ROI. For example, there are different ways to increase ROI. First, if the management focuses on cutting costs and increasing efficiency, profits may be increased while sales remain the same.

$$\text{ROI} = \frac{\text{net profit}}{\text{sales}} \times \frac{\text{sales}}{\text{investment}}$$

$$= \frac{\$53\ 277}{\$248\ 850} \times \frac{\$248\ 850}{\$129\ 825} = 41.0\%$$

But ROI can be increased just as much without improving performance simply by reducing the investment—by maintaining less inventory, for instance.

$$\text{ROI} = \frac{\text{net profit}}{\text{sales}} \times \frac{\text{sales}}{\text{investment}}$$

$$= \frac{\$48\ 465}{\$248\ 850} \times \frac{\$248\ 850}{\$114\ 825} = 42.2\%$$

Sometimes, however, differences among the total assets of firms may be related to the age of the firm or the type of industry, which makes ROI a poor indicator of performance. For this reason, some firms have replaced the traditional ROI measures with *return on assets managed* (ROAM), *return on net assets* (RONA), or *return on stockholders' equity* (ROE).

Price Elasticity

Price elasticity, discussed in Chapter 12, is a measure of the sensitivity of customers to changes in price. Price elasticity is calculated by comparing the percentage change in quantity to the percentage change in price.

$$\text{Price elasticity of demand} = \frac{\text{percentage change in quantity}}{\text{percentage change in price}}$$

$$E = \frac{(Q_2 - Q_1)/Q_1}{(P_2 - P_1)/P_1}$$

where Q = quantity and P = price.

For example, suppose the manufacturer of jeans in Chapter 13 increased its price from $30 a pair to $35. But instead of 40 000 pairs being sold, sales declined to only 38 000 pairs. The price elasticity would be calculated as follows:

$$E = \frac{(38\ 000 - 40\ 000)/40\ 000}{(\$35 - 30)/\$30} = \frac{-0.05}{0.167} = 0.30$$

Note that elasticity is usually expressed as a positive number even though the calculations create a negative value.

In this case, a relative small change in demand (5 percent) resulted from a fairly large change in price (16.7 percent), indicating that demand is inelastic. At 0.30, the elasticity is less than 1.

On the other hand, what if the same change in price resulted in a reduction in demand to 30 000 pairs of jeans? Then the elasticity would be

$$E = \frac{(30\ 000 - 40\ 000)/40\ 000}{(\$35 - 30)/\$30} = \frac{-0.25}{0.167} = 1.50$$

In this case, because the 16.7 percent change in price resulted in an even larger change in demand (25 percent), demand is elastic. The elasticity of 1.50 is greater than 1.

Note: Elasticity may also be calculated by dividing the change in quantity by the average of Q1 and Q2 and dividing the change in price by the average of the two prices. We, however, have chosen to include the formula that uses the initial quantity and price rather than the average.

Economic Order Quantity

The amount a firm should order at one time is called the *economic order quantity* (EOQ). Every time a firm places an order, there are additional costs. By ordering larger quantities less frequently, the firm saves on these costs. But it also costs money to maintain large inventories of needed materials. The EOQ is the order volume that provides both the lowest processing costs and the lowest inventory costs. The EOQ can be calculated as follows:

1. Determine the **order processing cost**. This is the total amount it costs a firm to place an order from beginning to end. Typically, this might include the operating expenses for the purchasing department, costs for follow-up, costs of record keeping of orders (data processing), costs for the receiving department, and costs for the processing and paying of invoices from suppliers. The simplest way to calculate this is to add up all these yearly costs and then divide by the number of orders placed during the year.

2. Next, calculate the **inventory carrying cost**. This is the total of all costs involved in carrying inventory. These costs include the costs of capital tied up in inventory, the cost of waste (merchandise that becomes obsolete or unuseable), depreciation costs, storage costs, insurance premiums, property taxes, and opportunity costs.

The formula for calculating EOQ is

$$\text{EOQ} = \sqrt{\frac{2 \times \text{units sold (or annual usage)} \times \text{ordering cost}}{\text{unit cost} \times \text{inventory carrying cost (\%)}}}$$

For example, suppose an office supply store sells 6000 cases of pens a year at a cost of $12 a case. The cost to the store for each order placed is $60. The cost of carrying the pens in the warehouse is 24 percent per year (this is a typical inventory carrying cost in many businesses.) Thus, the calculation is

$$\text{EOQ} = \sqrt{\frac{2 \times 6000 \times \$60}{\$12 \times 0.24}} = \sqrt{\frac{\$720\ 000}{\$2.88}} = 500$$

The firm should order pens about once a month (it sells 6000 cases a year or 500 cases a month).

Endnotes

CHAPTER 1

1. Andrew Wahl, "Tickets to rise," *Canadian Business*, 30 April 1999: 26–32.
2. "AMA board approves new definition," *Marketing News*, 1 March 1985: 1.
3. Michael R. Solomon, "Deep-seated materialism: The case of Levi's 501 jeans," in Richard Lutz (ed.) *Advances in Consumer Research* 13, Las Vegas: Association for Consumer Research, 1986: 619–22.
4. Peter F. Drucker, *Management: Tasks, Responsibilities, Practices*, New York: Harper & Row, 1972: 64–5.
5. Kevin Helliker, "Can wristwatch whiz switch Swatch cachet to an automobile?" *The Wall Street Journal*, 4 March 1994: A1-2; Ferdinand Protzman, "Off the wrist, onto the road: A Swatch on wheels," *New York Times*, 5 March 1994: 39.
6. "McCain drops genetically altered spuds," *Calgary Herald*, 29 November 1999: D5.
7. Peter Drucker, *Management*, New York: Harper & Row, 1973.
8. Statistics Canada, "The daily for September 29, 1999."
9. Randall Lane, "Prepackaged celebrity," *Forbes*, 20 December 1993: 86.
10. John W. Schouten, "Selves in transition: Symbolic consumption in personal rites of passage and identity reconstruction," *Journal of Consumer Research*, 17 March 1991: 412–25; Michael R. Solomon, "The wardrobe consultant: Exploring the role of a new retailing partner," *Journal of Retailing* 63, 1987: 110–28; Michael R. Solomon and Susan P. Douglas, "Diversity in product symbolism: The case of female executive clothing," *Psychology & Marketing* 4, 1987: 189–212; Joseph Z. Wisenblit, "Person positioning: Empirical evidence and a new paradigm," *Journal of Professional Services Marketing* 4(2), 1989: 51–82.
11. Linda Grant, "Mattel gets all dolled up," *U.S. News & World Report*, 13 December 1993: 72(4).
12. Eve Lazarus, "Lemon-aid," *Marketing Magazine*, 11 October 1999.
13. Bill Saporito, "Behind the tumult at P&G," *Fortune*, 7 March 1994: 74(6).
14. Theodore Levitt, "Marketing myopia," *Harvard Business Review*, July–August 1960: 45–56.
15. *Canadian Business*, 26 December 1997: 66–7.
16. "IKEA insists suppliers protect environment," *The Globe and Mail*, 25 November 1999.
17. Rockwell International, *Annual Report*, 1992.
18. Ani Hadjian, "Communicate, innovate," *Fortune*, Autumn/Winter 1993: 25.
19. Leslie Cauley, "Wrestling's TV audience grows and advertisers jump into ring," *The Wall Street Journal Interactive Edition*, 28 April 1998.
20. "Wrestling cage match," *Marketing Magazine*, August 1999: 16-17.
21. Conrad Phillip Kottak, "Anthropological analysis of mass enculturation," in Conrad P. Kottak (ed.) *Researching American Culture*, Ann Arbor, MI: University of Michigan Press, 1982: 40–74; Joseph Campbell, *Myths, Dreams, and Religion*, New York: Dutton, 1970.
22. Sal Randazzo, "Advertising as myth-maker; brands as gods and heroes," *Advertising Age*, 8 November 1993: 32.
23. Vernon Silver, "How he got there he hasn't a clue," *New York Times*, 16 May 1993: K3.
24. "Dear Chrysler: Outsiders' advice on handling the odometer charge," *The Wall Street Journal*, 26 June 1987: 19.
25. Larry Edwards, "The decision was easy," *Advertising Age* 2, 26 August 1987: 106. For research and discussion related to public policy issues, see Paul N. Bloom and Stephen A. Greyser, "The maturing of consumerism," *Harvard Business Review*, November/December 1981: 130–9; George S. Day, "Assessing the effect of information disclosure requirements," *Journal of Marketing*, April 1976: 42–52; Dennis E. Garrett, "The effectiveness of marketing policy boycotts: Environmental opposition to marketing," *Journal of Marketing* 51, January 1987: 44–53; Michael Houston and Michael Rothschild, "Policy-related experiments on information provision: A normative model and explication," *Journal of Marketing Research* 17, November 1980: 432–49; Jacob Jacoby, Wayne D. Hoyer, and David A. Sheluga, *Misperception of Televised Communications*, New York: American Association of Advertising Agencies, 1980; Gene R. Laczniak and Patrick E. Murphy, *Marketing Ethics: Guidelines for Managers*, Lexington, MA: Lexington Books, 1985: 117–23; Lynn Phillips and Bobby Calder, "Evaluating consumer protection laws: Promising methods," *Journal of Consumer Affairs* 14, Summer 1980: 9–36; Donald P. Robin and Eric Reidenbach, "Social responsibility, ethics, and marketing strategy: Closing the gap between concept and application," *Journal of Marketing* 51, January 1987: 44–58; Howard Schutz and Marianne Casey, "Consumer perceptions of advertising as misleading," *Journal of Consumer Affairs* 15, Winter 1981: 340–57; Darlene Brannigan Smith and Paul N. Bloom, "Is consumerism dead or alive? Some new evidence," in Thomas C. Kinnear (ed.) *Advances in Consumer Research* 11, Provo, UT: Association for Consumer Research, 1984: 569–73.
26. Quoted in Alice Z. Cuneo, "SegaSoft Online games tap into cultlike mind-set," *Advertising Age*, 7 April 1997: 3.
27. William Leiss, Stephen Kline, and Sut Jhally, *Social Communication in Advertising: Persons, Products, and Images of Well-Being*, Toronto: Methuen, 1986; Jerry Mander, *Four Arguments for the Elimination of Television*, New York: Morrow, 1977.
28. George Stigler, "The economics of information," *Journal of Political Economy*, 1961: 69.
29. William Leiss, Stephen Kline, and Sut Jhally, *Social Communication in Advertising: Persons, Products, and Images of Well-Being*, Toronto: Methuen, 1986.

CHAPTER 2

1. David Greising, "I'd like the world to buy a Coke," *Business Week*, 13 April 1998: 70–6.
2. Theodore Levitt, "Marketing myopia," *Harvard Business Review*, September-October 1975: 1ff.
3. Seth Lubove, "Aim, focus and shoot," *Forbes*, 26 November 1990: 67, 68, 70.
4. Joshua Levine, "Badass sells," *Forbes*, 21 April 1997: 142–8.
5. Jeffrey Zygmont, "In command at Campbell," *Sky*, March 1993: 52–62.
6. http://www.viacom.com/thefacts.tin
7. Linda Grant, "Outmarketing P&G," *Fortune*, 12 January 1998: 150–2.
8. Ricahrd W. Melcher, "Why Zima faded so fast," *Business Week*, 10 March 1997: 11–4.

9. Greg Burn, "What price the Snapple debacle," *Business Week*, 14 April 1997: 42.

10. Julia Flynn, "Ikea's new game plan," *Business Week*, 6 October 1997: 99, 102.

11. Thomas Petzinger Jr., "The front lines: Aly Abulleil finds facts by tracking feelings," *The Wall Street Journal Interactive Edition*, 4 September 1998.

12. Dyan Machan, "Is the Hog going soft?" *Forbes*, 10 March 1997: 114–9.

13. Justin Martin, "Are you as good as you think you are," *Fortune*, 30 September 1996: 142–52.

14. Mike McKesson,"Blazer aims for high sales," *Times Union*, 8 September 1994: C-12.

15. Tom Seery, "RV makers targeting new niche," *Post and Courier (Charleston, SC)*, 25 May 1997: 1–2D.

16. Mercedes M. Cardona, "Crayola breaks ad effort to target parents' nostalgia," *Advertising Age*, 21 July 1997: 35.

17. Kathleen Kerwin, "Not your father's Corvette," *Business Week*, 23 December 1996: 44.

18. Ian P. Murphy, "Southwest emphasizes brand as others follow the low-fare leader," *Marketing News*, 4 November 1996: 1–2.

19. Gail DeGeorge, "Dilbert to the rescue," *Business Week*, 4 May 1998: 166.

20. Ronald Henkoff, "Growing your company: Five ways to do it right," *Fortune*, 25 November 1996: 78–88.

21. Charles P. Wallace, "Adidas: Back in the game," *Fortune*, 18 August 1997: 176–82.

22. Jeff Jensen, "Nike to slice marketing by $100 mil," *Advertising Age*, 23 March 1998: 1, 46.

23. www.pg.com

24. Terence P. Paré, "How to find out what they want," *Fortune*, Autumn/Winter Supplement 1993: 39–41.

CHAPTER 3

1. *1992 Annual Report*, Rockwell International.

2. www.thebodyshop.ca

3. Quote by John Shad, former chairman of the US Securities and Exchange Commission, in N. Craig Smith and John A. Quelch, *Ethics in Marketing*, Homewood, IL: Richard D. Irwin, 1993.

4. KPMG Canada, *1999 KPMG Business Ethics Survey*, www.kpmg.ca/ethics/v1/99ethcse.html.

5. "Shareholders and General Public Say Corporations Should Balance Profits with Social Responsibilities, Poll Reveals," press release, Canadian Democracy and Corporate Accountability Commission, http://www.corporate-accountability.ca, 9 January 2002.

6. Joseph Pereira, "Toys 'R' Us says it decided to pull Sega's Night Trap from store shelves," *Wall Street Journal*, 17 December 1993: B5F.

7. www.transparency.org/documents/cpi/2001/cpi2001.html

8. Jan Phersson-Broberg, CEO, Daydream Software, personal communication, 14 August 1998, www.daydream.se/.

9. www.nortelnetworks.com/corporate/community/ethics/living.html

10. Rajendra S. Sisodia, "We need zero tolerance toward ethics violations," *Marketing News*, March 1990: 4,14.

11. "When gift giving goes too far," *Sales and Marketing Management*, June 1995: 15.

12. Peter Cheney, "Heavy lifting with light fingers," *The Globe and Mail*, 27 February 1999: A12.

13. www.mbnet.mb.ca/crm/law/cac01.html

14. www.geocites.com/WallStreet/Floor/3105/RIGHTS.html

15. Information on product recalls in Canada is available on the CBC Web site at: www.cbc.ca/consumer/market/recalls/index.html.

16. Marge Goodnuff, interview, 26 May 1998.

17. Joan C. Szabo, "Business pitches in after Andrew," *Nation's Business*, October 1992:37–9.

18. Mark Abley, *The Ice Storm: January, 1998*, Montreal: McClelland and Stewart.

19. Advertising Standards Canada, "1998 Ad Complaints Report," www.canad.com.

20. Alfred G. Haggerty, "Bang! Bang! Selling life insurance: when bullets fly," *National Underwriter*, October 1990: 14.

21. Advertising Standards Canada, "Gender Portrayal Guidelines," www.canad.com.

22. Advertising Standards Canada, "1998 Ad Complaints Report," www.canad.com.

23. www.thebodyshop.ca

24. Angela Kryhul, "Do the right thing," *Marketing Magazine*, 5 June 2000, www.marketingmag.ca.

25. www.environmentalchoice.com

26. Catherine Arnst, Stanley Reed, Gay McWilliams, and De'Ann Weimer, "When green begets green," *Business Week* 10 November 1997: 98–106.

27. Catherine Arnst, Stanley Reed, Gay McWilliams, and De'Ann Weimer, "When green begets green," *Business Week* 10 November 1997: 98–106.

28. www.nortelnetworks.com/corporate/community/awards.html.

29. Emily Thornton, Keith Maughton, and David Woodruff, "Toyota's green machine," *Business Week*, 15 December 1997: 108–9.

30. Nancy Arnott "Marketing with a passion," *Sales & Marketing Management*, January 1994: 64–71.

31. www.avon.com/about/women/global/current_programs.html.

32. Nancy Arnott, "Marketing with a passion," *Sales & Marketing Management*, January 1994: 64–71.

33. Jeffrey Gandz, "A business case for diversity," www.equalopportunity.on.ca/enggraf/gandz/castu.html.

34. www.equalopportunity.on.ca/enggraf/business/labert.html.

35. Patricia Digh, "America's largest untapped market: Who they are, the potential they represent," *Fortune*, 2 March 1998: S1–S12.

36. "National survey reveals that canadian consumers' concerns about quality are not being heard," press release, National Quality Institute, www.nqi.ca/new_web/english/html/prod_csq.html.

37. John Holusha, "Global yardsticks are set to measure 'quality'," *The New York Times* 23 December 1992: D6.

38. www.nqi.ca.

39. www.nqi.ca.

40. Stanley Brown, "Now it can be told," *Sales & Marketing Management*, November 1994: 34, 38.

41. Patrick Bultema, "From cost center to profit center: The changing bent of support operations," *Fortune*, 10 July 1995: S2–S3.

42. Don E. Schultz, "Maybe we should start all over with an IMC organization," *Marketing News*, 25 October 1993: 8.

43. Kevin Kelly and Peter Burrows, "Motorola: Training for the millennium," *Business Week*, 28 March 1994: 158–63.

44. www.cdma.org/new/nr_newmedia2.html.

45. Conference Board of Canada, "Spring 1999 provincial outlook: Smooth surface disguises turbulent economic

waters," press release, 8 June 1999, www2.confboard.ca/press/1999/posp99.html.

46. Melissa Levy, "Manufacturing showed growth during October," *Wall Street Journal*, 2 November 1993: A2.

47. Michael McCullough, "The truth is out there," *Marketing*, 28 September 1998:10.

48. Patrick Bultema, "From cost center to profit center: The changing bent of support operations," *Fortune*, 10 July 1995: S2–S3.

49. "Canada's Competition Act and the Competition Bureau," The World Wide Legal Information Association, wwlia.org/~wwlia/ca-comp1.html.

50. Stephanie Whittaker, "The push to drop Quebec's ad ban," *Marketing*, 22 March 1999: 24.

51. "Competition Bureau obtains record fine in deceptive tele-marketing case and launches public education campaign to fight phone fraud," news release, Competition Bureau, 5 May 1999, www.strategis.ic.gc.ca/SSG/ct01521e.html.

52. P. Rajan Varadarajan, Terry Clark, and William M. Pride, "Controlling the uncontrollable: Managing your market environment," *Sloan Management Review*, Winter 1992: 39–47.

53. "Packaging draws protest," *Marketing News*, 4 July 1994: 1.

CHAPTER 4

1. Bernadette Johnson, "Honeydew finds a place in U.S.," *Strategy Magazine*, 5 July 1999, www.strategymag.com/articles/st26038.asp.

2. David Todd, "Special report: Multicultural marketing; Nike takes it to the streets: Concentrates World Cup outdoor campaign in Toronto's Portuguese and Italian neighborhoods," *Strategy Magazine* 17, August 1998: 26.

3. Linda Himelstein, "The swoosh heard 'round the world," *Business Week*, 12 May 1997: 76.

4. "So you know your exports, eh?" *Canadian Business*, 10 January 2000: 42.

5. Patricia Smith, "10 steps for taking on the world with exports," *Business Sense* 3(1), November/December 1999: 19-20.

6. Statistics Canada, CANSIM Matrices 3651 and 3652.

7. Lara Mills, "Buckley's sets its sights on the U.S." *Marketing Magazine*, 16 November 1998: 3.

8. Sara Hope Franks, "Overseas, it's what's inside that sells," *Washington Post National Weekly Edition*, 5–11 December 1994: 21.

9. Louis Uchitelle, "Gillette's world view: One blade fits all," *New York Times*, 4 January 1994: C3.

10. Andrew Higgins, "Lacking money, Russian firms do business in twilight of barter," *Wall Street Journal Interactive Edition*, 27 August 1998.

11. Sak Onkvisit and John J. Shaw, *International Marketing: Analysis and Strategy* 2nd ed., New York: Macmillan, 1993.

12. World Trade Organization, "Growth, jobs, development and better international relations: How trade and the multilateral trading system help," www.wto.org/wto/ministl/stak_e_3.html; http://www.wto.org/english/news_e/pres01_e/pr249_e.htm#table1.5.

13. World Trade Organization, press release, 19 March 1998, accessed via www.wto.org/wto/intltrad/internat.htm, 27 August 1998.

14. Peter Verburg, "We think, therefore we prosper," *Candian Business*, 10 January 2000: 44.

15. Peter Verburg, "We think, therefore we prosper," *Canadian Business*, 10 January 2000: 44.

16. Michael E. Porter, *The Competitive Advantage of Nations*, New York: The Free Press, 1990.

17. Michael R. Czinkota and Masaaki Kotabe, "America's new world trade order," *Marketing Management* 1(3), 1992: 47–54.

18. Sak Onkvisit and John J. Shaw, *International Marketing: Analysis and Strategy* 2nd ed., New York: Macmillan, 1993.

19. Ernest Beck, "Russians resist foreign vodka, frustrating western distillers," *Wall Street Journal Interactive Edition*, 15 January 1998.

20. Sak Onkvisit and John J. Shaw, *International Marketing: Analysis and Strategy* 2nd ed., New York: Macmillan, 1993.

21. www.dfait-maeci.gc.ca/english.

22. Sak Onkvisit and John J. Shaw, *International Marketing: Analysis and Strategy* 2nd ed., New York: Macmillan, 1993.

23. David Stipp, "Farewell, my logo," *Fortune*, 27 May 1996: 130.

24. David Stipp, "Farewell, my logo," *Fortune*, 27 May 1996: 130.

25. Masaaki Kotabe and Maria Cecilia Coutinho de Arruda, "South America's free trade gambit," *Marketing Management* 38(10), Spring 1998, accessed via proquest.umi.com, 22 May 1998.

26. Harvey S. James, Jr. and Murray Weidenbaum, *When Businesses Cross International Borders: Strategic Alliances and Their Alternative*, Westport, CT: Praeger, 1993.

27. William C. Symonds, "Border crossings," *Business Week*, 22 November 1993: 40(3).

28. Department of Foreign Affairs and International Trade, www.dfait-maeci.gc.ca/nafta-alena/score-e.asp.

29. "AFS clears the air in Mexico," Department of Foreign Affairs and International Trade, www.dfait-maeci.gc.ca/nafta-alena/success2-e.asp.

30. Harvey S. James, Jr. and Murray Weidenbaum, *When Businesses Cross International Borders: Strategic Alliances and Their Alternative*, Westport, CT: Praeger, 1993.

31. Michael Solomon, Gary Bamossy, and Søren Askegaard, *Consumer Behavior: A European Perspective*, London: Prentice Hall International, 1999.

32. Thane Peterson, "The Euro," *Business Week*, 27 April 1998: 90–4.

33. Steven Prokesch, "Selling in Europe: Borders fade," *New York Times*, 31 May 1990: D1.

34. David Todd, "Great Canadian Bagel makes slow but sure gains in Moscow," *Strategy Magazine*, 14 February 2000: 27.

35. Peter Fuhrman and Michael Schuman, "Where are the Indians? The Russians?" *Forbes*, 17 July 1995: 126(2).

36. Statistics Canada Internet site, www.statcan.ca/english/Pgbd/People/Population/demo23b.

37. Charles D. Schewe and Anne L. Balazs, "Role transitions in older adults: A marketing opportunity," *Psychology and Marketing* 9, March/April 1992: 85–99; Ricardo Sookdeo, "The new global consumer," *Fortune*, Autumn/Winter 1993: 68(8).

38. Dilip Subramanian, "Economic slowdown fails to dampen ad spends by India's top marketers," *Marketing Magazine*, 6 September 1999: 7.

39. Karen Yates, "Advertising's heart of darkness," *Advertising Age*, 15 May 1995: I-10, I-15; Cyndee Miller, "Exploring Africa: Untapped market scares most companies," *Marketing News*, 21 July 1997: 1(2); Matt Murray, "Weight Watchers hopes to fatten its ledgers with Zimbabwe focus," *Wall Street Journal Interactive Edition*, 25 August 1997.

40. Bill Saporito, "Where the global action is," *Fortune*, Autumn/Winter 1993: 62(4).

41. Bill Saporito, "Where the global action is," *Fortune*, Autumn/Winter 1993: 62(3).

42. Bill Saporito, "Where the global action is," *Fortune*, Autumn/Winter 1993: 63(2).

43. Kevin Cete, "East Germans scout for good buys in West," *Advertising Age*, 11 December 1990: 40.

44. "Peru: Privatization is principal policy for attracting foreign investment," *Wall Street Journal*, 27 October 1993: B7.

45. World Trade Organization, press release, 19 March 1998, accessed via www.wto.org/wto/intltrad/internat.htm, 27 August 1998.

46. "The European connection," *Latin Trade* 5(11), November 1997: 391, accessed via www3.xls.com, 27 August 1998.

47. Nathaniel C. Nash, "A new rush into Latin America," *New York Times*, 11 April 1993: Sec. 3, 1(2); Calvin Sims, "KFCTries for a turnaround in Chile," *New York Times*, 27 December 1994: D8.

48. Warren S. Hersch, "Study reveals Asian crisis benefit U.S. PC industry," *Computer Reseller News*, 16 May 1998, accessed via proquest.umi.com, 28 May 1998; Joseph Chang, "Investment in Asia," *Chemical Market Reporter*, 23 March 1998, accessed via http: //proquest.umi.com, 28 May 1998.

49. Brian Dunn, "Quebec juice maker Lassonde is out to become a major North American player," *Marketing Magazine* 2 November 1998, www.marketing mag.ca.

50. Lara Mills, "Inniskillin warms to U.S. icewine sales," *Marketing Magazine*, 30 November 1998: 3.

51. Statistics Canada, CANSIM, Matrices 3651 and 3685.

52. Chris Daniels, "Canada shows Japan its colors," *Marketing Magazine*, 26 October 1998: 6.

53. "Risky business," CBC *Venture*, 8 February 2000, www.cbc.ca/business/programs/venture/on_venture.html.

54. "Risky business," CBC *Venture*, 8 February 2000, www.cbc.ca/business/programs/venture/on_venture.html.

55. Sara Hope Franks, "Overseas, it's what's inside that sells," *Washington Post National Weekly Edition*, 5–11 December 1994: 21.

56. Bernadette Johnson, "Honeydew pegs future on U.S. sales," *Strategy Magazine*, 14 February 2000: 26.

57. William C. Symonds, "Border crossings," *Business Week*, 22 November 1993: 40(3).

58. Michael O'Neal, "Does New Balance have an American soul?" *Business Week*, 12 December 1994: 86, 90.

59. World Trade Organization, press release, 19 March 1998, accessed via http: //www.wto.org/wto/intltrad/internat. htm, 27 August 1998.

60. James A. Morrissey, "Industry mulls issue of apparel sweatshops," *Textile World*, August 1997: 94.

61. Michael Janofsky, "Levi Strauss: American symbol with a cause," *New York Times*, 4 January 1994: C4; Russell Mitchell, "Managing by values," *Business Week*, 1 August 1994: 46(7); Mitchell Zuckoff, "Taking a profit, and inflicting a cost," *Boston Globe*, 10 July 1994: 1(2).

62. Joanna Ramey, "Levi's will resume production in China after 5-year absence," *Women's Wear Daily*, 9 April 1998: 1(2).

63. Carla Cook, "Stephanie Konkin, 23, Whitehorse" in "13 stories," *Realm*, 2 May 2000, www.realm.net.

64. Alecia Swasy, "Don't sell thick diapers in Tokyo," *The New York Times*, 13 October 1993: F9.

65. Richard W. Pollay, "Measuring the cultural values manifest in advertising," *Current Issues and Research in Advertising* 6(1), 1983: 71–92.

66. Daniel Goleman, "The group and the self: New focus on a culturual rift," *New York Times*, 25 December 1990: 37; Harry C. Triandis, "The self and social behavior in differing cultural contexts," *Psychological Review* 96, July 1989: 506; Harry C. Triandis, Robert Bontempo, Marcelo J. Villareal, Masaaki Asai, and Nydia Lucca, "Individualism and collectivism: Cross-culturual perspectives on self-ingroup relationships," *Journal of Personality and Social Psychology* 54, February 1988: 323.

67. Paul M. Sherer, "North American and Asian executives have contrasting values, study finds," *Wall Street Journal*, 8 March 1996: B1, 2B.

68. "New Japanese fads blazing trails in cleanliness," *Montgomery Advertiser*, 28 September 1996: 10A; Andrew Pollack, "Can the pen really be mightier than the germ?" *New York Times*, 27 July 1995: A4.

69. George J. McCall and J. L. Simmons, *Social Psychology: A Sociological Approach*, New York: The Free Press, 1982.

70. Alison Leigh Cowan, "Caterpillar: Worldwide watch for opportunities," *New York Times*, 4 January 1994: C4.

71. Norihiko Shirouzu, "P&G's Joy makes a splash in Japan's dish soap market," *Wall Street Journal Interactive Edition*, 10 December 1997.

72. www.getcustoms.com.

73. Philip R. Cateora, *Strategic International Marketing*, Homewood, IL: Dow Jones-Irwin, Inc., 1985.

74. "Canada signs OECD Convention on combatting bribery," Department of Foreign Affairs and International Trade, www.dfait-macci.gc.ca/english/news/press_releases/97_press/97_214E.html.

75. William Echikson, "The trick to selling in Europe," *Fortune*, 20 September 1993: 82.

76. Wendy Cuthbert, "Faces adapts to local market," *Strategy Magazine*, 14 February 2000: 25.

77. David Mick, "Consumer research and semiotics: Exploring the morphology of signs, symbols, and significance," *Journal of Consumer Research* 13, September 1986: 196–213.

78. Marian Katz, "No women, no alcohol, learn Saudi taboos before placing ads," *International Advertiser*, February 1986: 11–2.

79. Steve Rivkin, "The name game heats up," *Marketing News*, 22 April 1996: 8.

80. Aaron Lam, "Bruce Poon Tip," *Business Sense* 1(1), Spring 1999: 23–5; "G.A.P. Adventures Inc.," *Profit Magazine, 100 Fastest Growing Companies*, www.profit100.com; G.A.P. Adventures Inc. corporate Web site: www.gap.ca.

81. Michael Solomon, Gary Bamossy, and Søren Askegaard, *Consumer Behavior: A European Perspective*, London: Prentice Hall International, 1999.

82. Alexander Hiam and Charles D. Schewe, *The Portable MBA in Marketing*, New York: John Wiley & Sons, 1992.

83. Harvey S. James, Jr. and Murray Weidenbaum, *When Businesses Cross International Borders: Strategic Alliances and Their Alternative*, Westport, CT: Praeger, 1993.

84. Sak Onkvisit and John J. Shaw, *International Marketing: Analysis and Strategy* 2nd ed., New York: Macmillan, 1993.

85. Ikechi Ekeledo and K. Sivakumar, "Foreign market entry mode choice of service firms: A contingency perspective," *Journal of the Academy of Marketing Science* 26(4), 1998: 274–92.

86. "Yogen Fruz World-Wide Inc.," *Profit Magazine*, www.prift100.com, 2 May 2000.

87. Peter Morton, "Telesat gets chance at U.S. markets," *National Post*, 3 February 2000.

88. Rod McQueen, "Made in Canada global strategies," *Financial Post* 91(40), 5 March 1998: MGB3–4.

89. Andrew Tanzer, "Sweet Chinese siren," *Forbes*, 20 December 1993: 78(2).

90. An influential argument for this perspective can be found in Theodore Levitt, "The globalization of markets," *Harvard Business Review*, May–June 1983: 92–102.

91. Juliana Koranteng, "Reebok finds its second wind as it pursues global presence," *Advertising Age International*, January 1998: 18.

92. Terry Clark, "International marketing and national character: A review and proposal for an integrative theory," *Journal of Marketing* 54, October 1990: 66–79.

93. Norihiko Shirouzu, "Snapple in Japan: How a splash dried up," *Wall Street Journal*, 15 April 1996: B1(2).

94. Sara Hope Franks, "Overseas, its what's inside that sells," *Washington Post National Weekly Edition*, 5–11 December 1994: 21.

95. William Echikson, "The trick to selling in Europe," *Fortune*, 20 September 1993: 82.

96. Nikhil Deogun and Jonathan Karp, "For Coke in India, Thumbs Up is the real thing," *Wall Street Journal*, 29 April 1998: B1(2).

97. Bernadette Johnson, "Clearly Canadian launches in U.S. first," *Strategy Magazine*, 14 February 2000: 28.

98. Bradley Johnson, "Unisys touts service in global ads," *Advertising Age* 3(2), 15 February 1993: 59.

99. Ashish Banerjee, "Global campaigns don't work; multinationals do," *Advertising Age*, 18 April 1994: 23.

100. Sinclair Stewart, "Tim Hortons brews new U.S. campaign," *Strategy Magazine*, 27 September 1999: 3.

101. Eve Lazarus, "Kokanee brews up fans in the U.S.," *Marketing Magazine*, 29 March 1999, www.marketingmag.ca.

102. Sak Onkvisit and John J. Shaw, *International Marketing: Analysis and Strategy* 2nd ed., New York: Macmillan, 1993.

103. "Kodak alleges Fuji photo is dumping color photographic paper in the U.S.," *Wall Street Journal*, 22 February 1993: B6.

104. Andrea Mandel-Campbell, "McCain tries to thaw South American biz," *Marketing Magazine*, 7 October 1996: 5.

105. Louise Kramer, "Virgin brings cola to U.S. markets," *Advertising Age*, 1 May 1998: 3(2).

CHAPTER 5

1. Ken Deal, "The eyes and ears of business," *Marketing Magazine*, 17 May 1999: 18.

2. Chris Flanagan, "Proof positive," *Marketing Magazine*, 17 May 1999: 15.

3. SurveySite Web site, www.surveysite.com.

4. Michael R. Solomon and Elnora W. Stuart, *Marketing: Real People, Real Choices*, Upper Saddle River, NJ: Prentice Hall, 1997.

5. Robert Baxter, Mercedes-Benz North America, personal communication, June 1996.

6. Statistics Canada Web site, www.statcan.ca/english/IPS/Data/63-224-XPB.html.

7. Christel Beard and Betsy Wiesendanger, "The marketer's guide to on-line databases," *Sales &Marketing Management*, January 1993: 36(6).

8. Cyndee Miller, "Sometimes a researcher has no choice but to hang out in a bar," *Marketing News*, 3 January 1994: 16(2).

9. Annetta Miller, "You are what you buy," *Newsweek*, 4 June 1990: 59(2).

10. "Special report: Research: What role should research play?" *Strategy Magazine*, 1 September 1997: 23.

11. David Kiley, "At long last, Detroit gives consumers the right of way," *Adweek*, 6 June 1988: 25–7.

12. Jack Weber, "Absorbing some changes," *Quirk's Article # 101*, November 1994, accessed via www.quirks.com, 26 January 1998.

13. "Special report: Research: What role should research play?" *Strategy Magazine*, 1 September 1997: 23.

14. Leslie Kaufman, "Enough talk," *Newsweek*, 18 August 1997: 48–9.

15. "Special report: Research: What role should research play?" *Strategy Magazine*, 1 September 1997: 23.

16. Nancy Vonk, "Fun with dull numbers," *Marketing Magazine*, 10 April 2000: 26.

17. Kelly Shermach, "Art of communication," *Marketing News*, 8 May 1995: 2.

18. David Bosworth, "Bayer posts DM survey to health care professionals," *Strategy Magazine*, 16 August 1999: D5.

19. Erica Zlomislic, "Special report: Legitimate researchers combat 'sugging'," *Strategy Magazine*, 14 April 1997: 40.

20. Fawzia Sheikh, "Kiosks ASK shoppers for their views," *Marketing Magazine*, 15 February 1999: 3.

21. Rebecca Piirto Heath, "The digital interviewer," *Marketing Tools*, August 1997: 28(3).

22. Peter Krasilovsky, "Surveys in cyberspace," *Marketing Tools*, November/December 1996: 18(4).

23. Michael J. McCarthy, "James Bond hits the supermarket: Stores snoop on shoppers' habits to boost sales," *Wall Street Journal*, 25 August 1993: B1(2).

24. Chris Daniels, "Real life research," *Marketing Magazine*, 17 May 1999: 15–6.

25. Chris Daniels, "Real life research," *Marketing Magazine*, 17 May 1999: 15–6.

26. Mike Galetto, "Turning trash to research treasure," *Advertising Age*, 17 April 1995: I-16.

27. Michael J. McCarthy, "James Bond hits the supermarket: Stores snoop on shoppers' habits to boost sales," *Wall Street Journal*, 25 August 1993: B1(2).

28. Barnaby J. Feder, "Test marketers use virtual shopping to gauge potential of real products," *New York Times*, 22 December 1997: D3.

29. Alan Radding, "Consumer worry halts databases," *Advertising Age*, 11 February 1991: 28.

30. Jan Larson, "It's a small world, after all," *Marketing Tools*, September 1997: 47–51.

31. Tara Parker-Pope, "Nonalcoholic beer hits the spot in Mideast," *Wall Street Journal*, 6 December 1995: B1(2).

32. SurveySite Web site (www.surveysite.com).

33. Rebecca Piirto Heath, "Wake of the flood," *Marketing Tools*, November/December 1996: 58–63.

34. Mario A. Abate, "Applications and analyses in single-source data: Experiences of the American Chicle Group Warner Lambert," *Journal of Advertising Research* 29, December/January 1989/90: 53–6.

35. Peter R. Peacock, "Data mining in marketing: Part I," *Marketing Management*, Winter 1998: 9–18.

36. Peter R. Peacock, "Data mining in marketing: Part I," *Marketing Management*, Winter 1998: 9–18.

37. Bruce L. Stern and Ray Ashmun, "Methodological disclosure: The foundation for effective use of survey research," *Journal of Applied Business Research* 7, 1991: 77–82.

38. Alan E. Wolf, "Most colas branded alike by testy magazine," *Beverage World*, 31 August 1991: 8.

39. Janet Simons, "Youth marketing: Children's clothes follow the latest fashion," *Advertising Age*, 14 February 1985: 16.

40. Gary Levin, "New adventures in children's research," *Advertising Age*, 9 August 1993: 17.

41. Terence P. Pare, "How to find out what they want," *Fortune*, Autumn/Winter 1993: 39(3).

42. Alan J. Greco and Jack T. Hogue, "Developing marketing decision support systems in consumer goods firms," *Journal of Consumer Marketing* 7, 1990: 55–64.

43. Ann Walmsley, "Be prepared," *Report on Business Magazine*, July1998, www.robmagazine.com/archive/98ROBjuly/html.future.html.

44. Edward Cornish, *The Study of the Future: An Introduction to the Art and Science of Understanding and Shaping Tomorrow's World*, Washington, DC: World Future Society, 1977; examples provided by Professor Fredric Kropp, Bond University, Australia, personal communication, 12 August 1998.

45. S.J. Diamond, "Trend tracking," *Los Angeles Times*, 29 March 1993: E1, www.speakers.com/popcorn.htm/, accessed 2 August 1998.

CHAPTER 6

1. James R. Bettman, "The decision maker who came in from the cold," in Leigh McAllister and Michael Rothschild (eds.) *Advances in Consumer Research* 20, Provo, UT: Association for Consumer Research, 1990; John W. Payne, James R. Bettman, and Eric J. Johnson, "Behavioral decision research: A constructive processing perspective," *Annual Review of Psychology* 4, 1992: 87–131; Robert J. Meyer and Barbara E. Kahn, "Probabilistic models of consumer choice behavior," in Thomas S. Robertson and Harold H. Kassarjian (eds.) *Handbook of Consumer Behavior*, Englewood Cliffs, NJ: Prentice Hall, 1991: 85–123.

2. "Condoms cause concern among student consumers," *Chronicle, The Univeristy of B.C. Alumni Magazine* 53 (2), Summer 1999.

3. Ronald Alsop, "Agencies scrutinize their ads for psychological symbolism," *The Wall Street Journal*, 11 June 1987: 27.

4. Abraham H. Maslow, *Motivation and Personality*, 2nd ed., New York: Harper & Row, 1970.

5. Robert A. Baron and Donn Byrne, *Social Psychology: Understanding Human Interaction*, 5th ed., Boston: Allyn & Bacon, 1987.

6. Rebecca Piirto Heath, "You can buy a thrill: Chasing the ultimate rush," *American Demographics I*, June 1997: 47–51.

7. Linda L. Price and Nancy Ridgway, "Development of a scale to measure innovativeness," in Richard P. Bagozzi and Alice M. Tybout (eds.) *Advances in Consumer Research* 10, Ann Arbor, MI: Association for Consumer Research, 1983: 679–84; Russell W. Belk, "Three scales to measure constructs related to materialism: Reliability, validity, and relationships to measures of happiness," in Thomas C. Kinnear (ed.) *Advances in Consumer Research* 11, Ann Arbor, MI: Association for Consumer Research, 1984: 291; Gordon R. Foxall and Ronald E. Goldsmith, "Personality and consumer research: Another look," *Journal of the Market Research Society* 30(2) 1988: 111–25; Ronald E. Goldsmith and Charles F. Hofacker, "Measuring consumer innovativeness," *Journal of the Academy of Marketing Science* 19(3) 1991: 209–21; Terence A. Shimp and Subhash Sharma, "Consumer ethnocentrism: Construction and validation of the CETSCALE," *Journal of Marketing Research* 24, August 1987: 282.

8. Emily Yoffe, "You are what you buy," *Newsweek*, 4 June 1990: 59.

9. Jeffrey F. Durgee, "Self-esteem advertising," *Journal of Advertising*, 14(4) 1986: 21.

10. Mark Etting, "How to make perfect patties," *Marketing Magazine*, 26 October 1998: 47.

11. Benjamin D. Zablocki and Rosabeth Moss Kanter, "The differentiation of life-styles," *Annual Review of SociologyI*, 1976: 269–97.

12. Alfred S. Boote, "Psychographics: Mind over matter," *American Demographics*, April 1980: 26–9; William D. Wells, "Psychographics: A critical review," *Journal of Marketing Research* 12, May 1975: 196–213.

13. Alan R. Hirsch, "Effects of ambient odors on slot-machine usage in a Las Vegas casino," *Psychology & Marketing* 12(7), October 1995: 585–94.

14. Marianne Meyer, "Attention shoppers!" *Marketing and Media Decisions* 23, May 1988: 67.

15. Eben Shapiro, "Need a little fantasy? A bevy of new companies can help," *The New York Times*, 10 March 1991: F4.

16. Brad Edmondson, "Pass the meat loaf," *American Demographics*, January 1989: 19.

17. Robert La Franco, "Wallpaper sonatas," *Forbes*, 25 March 1996: 114; Louise Lee, "Background music becomes hoity-toity," *The Wall Street Journal*, 22 December 1995: B1(2).

18. Bernice Kanner, "Trolling in the aisles," *New York*, 16 January 1989: 12; Michael Janofsky, "Using crowing roosters and ringing business cards to tap a boom in point-of-purchase displays," *The New York Times*, 21 March 1994: D9.

19. Stephanie Whittaker, "Stopping them cold," *Marketing Magazine*, 5 April 1999.

20. Wendy Cuthbert, "Gadgets and gizmos," *Strategy Magazine*, 27 September 1999: 21.

21. John P. Robinson, "Time squeeze," *Advertising Age*, February 1990: 30–3.

22. Leonard L. Berry, "Market to the perception," *American Demographics*, February 1990: 32.

23. Richard W. Pollay, "Measuring the cultural values manifest in advertising," *Current Issues and Research in Advertising*, 1983: 71–92.

24. Michael Adams, "Clouds over Canada: The new social climate," www.erg.enviornics.net/news/default.asp?aID=400.

25. "Cashing in on the new nationalism," *Marketing Magazine*, 22 May 2000: 26.

26. Shawna Steinberg, "Oh, Canada in the spotlight," *Marketing Magazine*, 2 November 1998: 10–1.

27. Chris Daniels, "Canucks vs. Yanks," *Marketing Magazine*, 22 May 2000: 26–7.

28. Tony Spencer, "Going Canadian," *Marketing Magazine*, 7 September 1998: 23.

29. Helena Katz, "Distinctly Quebecois," *Marketing Magazine*, 26 April 1999: 13.

30. Jack Kohane, "Wampole Canada taps into sappy idea," *Marketing Magazine*, 5 October 1998: 2.

31. Brandon Watson, "The new frontiers," *Marketing Magazine*, 21 June 1999: 14.

32. Astrid Van Den Broek, "Speaking the same language," *Marketing Magazine*, 21 June 1999: 13.

33. "Canada's hole-y grail," *Marketing Magazine*, 6 September 1999: 30.

34. Richard P. Coleman, "The continuing significance of social class to marketing," *Journal of Consumer Research* 10, December 1983: 265–80.

35. J. Michael Munson and W. Austin Spivey, "Product and brand-user stereotypes among social classes: Implications for advertising strategy," *Journal of Advertising Research* 21, August 1981: 37–45.

36. Stuart U. Rich and Subhash C. Jain, "Social class and life cycle as predictors of shopping behavior," *Journal of Marketing Research* 5, February 1968: 41–9.

37. Brian Dunn, "So hip it sells," *Marketing Magazine*, 14 June 1999: 16.

38. Michael Shnayerson, "The champagne city," *Vanity Fair*, December 1997: 182–202.

39. Robert D. Hof, "Special report: Internet communities," *Business Week*, 5 May 1997: 63(8).

40. Nathan Kogan and Michael A. Wallach, "Risky shift phenomenon in small decision-making groups: A test of the information exchange hypothesis," *Journal of Experimental Social Psychology* 3, January 1967: 75–84; Nathan Kogan and Michael A. Wallach, *Risk Taking*, New York: Holt, Rinehart and Winston, 1964; Arch G. Woodside and M. Wayne DeLozier, "Effects of word-of-mouth advertising on consumer risk taking," *Journal of Advertising*, Fall 1976: 12–9.

41. Donald H. Granbois, "Improving the study of customer in-store behavior," *Journal of Marketing* 32, October 1968: 28–32.

42. Len Strazewski, "Tupperware locks in new strategy," *Advertising Age*, 8 February 1988: 30.

43. Kara K. Choquette, "Not all approve of Barbie's MasterCard," *USA Today*, 30 March 1998: 6B.

44. Kathleen Debevec and Easwar Iyer, "Sex roles and consumer perceptions of promotions, products, and self: What do we know and where should we be headed," in Richard J. Lutz (ed.) *Advances in Consumer Research* 13, Provo, UT: Association for Consumer Research, 1986: 210–4; Lynn J. Jaffe and Paul D. Berger, "Impact on purchase intent of sex-role identity and product positioning," *Psychology & Marketing*, Fall 1988: 259–71.

45. Kathleen Debevec and Easwar Iyer, "Sex roles and consumer perceptions of promotions, products and self"; Deborah E. S. Frable, "Sex typing and gender ideology: Two facets of the individual's gender psychology that go together," *Journal of Personality and Social Psychology* 56(1), 1989: 95–108; Lynn J. Jaffe and Paul D. Berger, "Impact on purchase intent of sex-role identity and product positioning," Keren A. Johnson, Mary R. Zimmer, and Linda L. Golden, "Object relations theory: Male and female differences in visual information processing," in Melanie Wallendorf and Paul Anderson (eds.) *Advances in Consumer Research* 14, Provo, UT: Association for Consumer Research, 1986: 83–7; Leila T. Worth, Jeanne Smith, and Diane M. Mackie, "Gender schematicity and preference for gender-typed products," *Psychology & Marketing* 9, January 1992: 17–30.

46. James Pollock, "Home Hardware drops handyman slogan," *Marketing Magazine*, 24 Feburary 1997: 2.

47. Everett M. Rogers, *Diffusion of Innovations*, 3rd ed., New York: Free Press, 1983.

48. Steven A. Baumgarten, "The innovative communicator in the diffusion process," *Journal of Marketing Research* 12, February 1975: 12–8.

CHAPTER 7

1. *US Statistical Abstract*, 1997: 330.

2. B. Charles Ames and James D. Hlaracek, *Managerial Marketing for Industrial Firms*, New York: Random House Business Division, 1984; Edward F. Fern and James R. Brown, "The industrial/consumer marketing dichotomy: A case of insufficient justification," *Journal of Marketing*, Spring 1984: 68–77.

3. Andrew A. Duffy, "WorldBid gears down for new era," *Victoria Times Colonist*, May 17, 2001, p. D10; press releases from WorldBid.com; James Careless, "Cornering the B2B Markets," *Marketing Magazine Online*, June 18, 2001.

4. www.census.gov/pub/epcd/www/naics/html.

5. Terry Lefton, "Sprint positions as biz solution," *Brandweek*, 11 July 1994: 6.

6. Statistics Canada, Consolidated federal, provincial, territorial, and local government revenue and expenditures, www.statcan.ca/english/pgdb/State/Government.

7. Government of Canada Web site, canada.gc.ca/depts.

8. MERX home page, www.merx.ca/english2/about.html.

9. Daniel H. McQuiston, "Novelty, complexity, and importance as causal determinants of industrial buyer behavior," *Journal of Marketing*, April 1989: 66–79.

10. J. Joseph Cronin Jr. and Michael H. Morris, "Satisfying customer expectations: The effect on conflict and repurchase intentions in industrial marketing channels," *Journal of the Academy of Marketing Science*, Winter 1989: 41–9; Thomas W. Leigh and Patrick F. McGraw, "Mapping the procedural knowledge of industrial sales personnel: A script-theoretic investigation," *Journal of Marketing*, January 1989: 16–34; William J. Qualls and Christopher P. Puto, "Organizational climate and decision framing: An integrated approach to analyzing industrial buying," *Journal of Marketing Research*, May 1989: 179–92.

11. Ruby Roy Dholakia, "Decision-making time in organizational buying behavior: An investigation of its antecedents," *Journal of the Academy of Marketing Science*, Fall 1993: 281–92.

12. Neville Nankivell, "Total change: Canadian companies reach out online," *Financial Post*, 26 April 2000: E3.

13. Ruby Roy Dholakia, "Decision-making time in organizational buying behavior: An investigation of its antecedents," *Journal of the Academy of Marketing Science*, Fall 1993: 281–92.

14. Simon Tuck "Point2.com mines success in heavy equipment," *The Globe and Mail*, 22 June 2000: T1.

15. Simon Tuck, "The B2B boom," *The Globe and Mail*, 16 March 2000: T1.

16. Neville Nankivell, "Total change: Canadian companies reach out online," *Financial Post*, 26 April 2000: E3.

17. Debbie Barrett, "Taking a page from efficiency's book: Tiny technology tools save city workers lots of frustration and create new ways to bond," *Technology in Government* 6(9), Spring 1999: 29.

18. Tom Venetis, "Extranets take over for EDI," *Computer Dealer News*, 15(39), 15 October 1999: 15.

19. Kimberly Chapman, "A matter of life and death," *Network World Canada* 9(15), 13 August 1999: 20.

20. Kevin Ferguson, "Purchasing in packs," *Business Week*, 1 November 1999.

21. Marie Clarke, "Strategies: Pulling together," *Canadian Business* , November 1988.

22. Wendy Stueck, "Onvia lets small firms buy like big business," *The Globe and Mail*, 22 June 2000: T9.

23. Faye W. Gilbert, Joyce A. Young, and Charles R. O'Neal, "Buyer–Seller relationships in just-in-time purchasing environments," *Journal of Organizational Research*, February 1994: 29, 111–20.

CHAPTER 8

1. Industry Canada, *Small Business Quarterly*, Spring 2000, www.strategis.ic.gc.ca.

2. Sinclair Stewart, "Grand & Toy launches The Stockroom," *Strategy Magazine*, 7 June 1999: D10.

3. Joseph Pereira, "Going to extremes: Board-riding youths take sneaker maker on fast ride uphill," *Wall Street Journal Interactive Edition*, 16 April 1998.

4. Jamie Beckett, *San Francisco Chronicle*, April 1998, accessed via ssnewslink.

5. David K. Foot and Daniel Stoffman, *Boom, bust and echo 2000: Profiting from the demographic shift in the new millennium*, Macfarlane Walter & Ross, Toronto, 1998.

6. David K. Foot and Daniel Stoffman, *Boom, bust and echo 2000: Profiting from the demographic shift in the new millennium*, Macfarlane Walter & Ross, Toronto, 1998.

7. David K. Foot and Daniel Stoffman, *Boom, bust and echo 2000: Profiting from the demographic shift in the new millennium*, Macfarlane Walter & Ross, Toronto, 1998: 124.

8. "Kids with cash," *Marketing Magazine*, 29 November 1999: 76.

9. Liza Finlay, "A lot more than just a piggy bank," *Marketing Magazine*, 4/11 January 1999: 14.

10. Statistics Canada, Cansim Matrix #6367, www.statcan.ca/english/pgdb/people/populat/demo10a.htm.

11. Jennifer Lawrence, "Gender-specific works for diapers—almost too well," *Advertising Age*, 8 February 1993: S-10.

12. Astrid Van Den Broek, "Not so tough a sell," *Marketing Magazine*, 19/26 July 1999.

13. Charles M. Schaninger and William D. Danko, "A conceptual and empirical comparison of alternate household life cycle markets," *Journal of Consumer Research* 19, March 1993: 580–94.

14. James Careless, "Condos find their niche," *Marketing Magazine*, 25 January 1999: 12.

15. *Statistics Canada Daily*, 12 June 2000, www.statcan.ca; Statistics Canada, *The Population Census of Canada, 1996*.

16. Bill Keenan, "Snob appeal," *Marketing Magazine*, 8 May 2000: 15.

17. Michael R. Solomon, Judith L. Zaichkowsky, and Rosemary Polegato, *Consumer Behaviour: Buying, Having and Being*, Canadian Edition, Toronto: Prentice Hall Canada Inc., 1999: 476.

18. Danny Kucharsky, "Quebec's distinct specialty TV," *Marketing Magazine*, 20 March 2000: 22.

19. "1996 Census: Ethnic origin, visible minorities," *Statistics Canada Daily*, 17 February 1998.

20. Judy Waytiuk, "The new Native niche," *Marketing Magazine*, 22 May 2000: 13.

21. Julie McCann, "Native niches," *Marketing Magazine*, 14 September 1998: 15–7.

22. Ken Waldie, "Out of the gate, financing aboriginal enterprises," *Summit*, November 1998: 56.

23. "1996 Census: Ethnic origin, visible minorities", *Statistics Canada Daily*, 17 February 1998.

24. Eun-Mi (Liz) Adams, "The big piece of the mosaic," *Marketing Magazine*, 21 June 1999: 16–7.

25. "1996 Census: Ethnic origin, visible minorities," *Statistics Canada Daily*, 17 February 1998.

26. Eun-Mi (Liz) Adams, "The big piece of the mosaic," *Marketing Magazine*, 21 June 1999: 16–7.

27. Astrid Van Den Broek, "Cozying up to kosher," *Marketing Magazine*, 5 June 2000:18–9.

28. Carey Toane, "Veering off from the mainstream," *Marketing Magazine*, 5 June 2000: 24.

29. Eun-Mi (Liz) Adams, "The big piece of the mosaic," *Marketing Magazine*, 21 June 1999: 16–7.

30. "The rich list: How the rich spend their money," *The National Post*, 22 April 2000, www.nationalpost.com/content/features/richlist/spend.html.

31. Jo Marney, "When the urge hits," *Marketing Magazine*, 29 March 1999.

32. Canada Post Web site, www.canadapost.ca/cpc2/dirmlfiles/geopost.pdf.

33. Margaret Carlson, "Where Calvin crossed the line," *Time*, 11 September 1995: 64.

34. Lewis Alpert and Ronald Gatty, "Product positioning by behavioral life styles," *Journal of Marketing* 33, April 1969: 65–9; Emanuel H. Demby, "Psychographics revisited: The birth of a technique," *Marketing News*, 2 January 1989: 21; William D. Wells, "Backward segmentation," in Johan Arndt (ed.) *Insights into Consumer Behavior*, Boston: Allyn & Bacon, 1968: 85–100.

35. Bill Guns, president, SRI Consulting, personal communication, 1998.

36. Environics Research Group Web site, www.erg.environics.net/tribe/default.asp.

37. Craig Saunders, "Peachtree invests in brand-building," *Strategy Magazine*, 27 March 2000: 1.

38. Robert L. Burr, "Market segments and other revelations," *Journal of Services Marketing* 1, Fall 1987: 59–67.

39. Judann Pollack, "Kraft's Miracle Whip targets core consumers with '97 ads," *Advertising Age*, 3 February 1997: 12.

40. "Vital signs," *Financial Post*, 1 April 1999: C8.

41. "How Ocean Spray gave cranberries some sparkle," *The New York Times*, 26 November 1992: D1.

42. Thomas V. Bonoma and Benson P. Shapiro, *Segmenting the Organizational Market*, Lexington, MA: Lexington Books, 1983.

43. Catherine Arnst, "PC makers head for SOHO," *Business Week*, 28 September 1992: 125.

44. Debbie Shork, "A matter of taste," *Marketing Magazine*, 22 May 2000: 14.

45. Eve Lazarus, "Sizing up the sizzle," *Marketing Magazine*, 5 June 2000: 17.

46. Heather Paris and Henry Wong, "Toyota sells functional fun," *Marketing Magazine*, 20 March 2000: 27.

47. William Echikson, "Aiming at high and low markets," *Fortune*, 22 March 1993: 89.

48. Kathleen Martin-James, "Peak pita performance," *Marketing Magazine*, 10 April 2000: 18.

49. Chip Bayers, "The promise of one to one (A love story)," *Wired*, May 1998: 130.

50. "Nike global adds critical mass," *Marketing Magazine*, 5 June 2000: 3.

51. Linda Himelstein, "Levi's is hiking up its pants," *Business Week*, 1 December 1997: 70; Bob Morris, "Extreme sport, extreme chic, extreme hype," *New York Times Online*, 8 February 1998.

52. Ian P. Murphy, "Beverages don't mean a thing if they ain't got that zing," *Marketing News*, 14 April 1997: 1.

53. Chris Daniels, "Little porn shop going mainstream," *Marketing Magazine*, 29 May 2000.

54. Eve Lazarus, "Lemon-aid," *Marketing Magazine*, 11 October 1999: 15.

55. Martin R. Lautman, "End-benefit segmentation and prototypical bonding," *Journal of Advertising Research*, June/July 1991: 9–18.

56. Astrid van den Broek, "Brand makeovers," *Marketing Magazine*, 26 April 1999.

57. Shawna Cohen, "Energizing elixirs," *Marketing Magazine*, 3 April 2000: 12–3.

CHAPTER 9

1. Information obtained from the Woodstream Corporation.
2. Gabriella Stern, "If you don't feel like fetching the rental car, it fetches you," *The Wall Street Journal*, 9 June 1995, B1(2).
3. Wendy Cuthbert, "Virtual impulse buying a reality," *Strategy Magazine*, 3 January 2000: D12.
4. George Anders, "Vital statistic: Disputed cost of creating a drug," *The Wall Street Journal*, 9 November 1993: B1.
5. Edmund L. Andrews, "When imitation isn't the sincerest form of flattery," *The New York Times*, 9 August 1990: 20.
6. Caryne Brown, "Making money making toys," *Black Enterprise*, November 1993: 68–77.
7. Roman G. Hiebing and Scott W. Copper, *Instructor's Manual: The Successful Marketing Plan*, Lincolnwood, IL: NTC Business Books, 1992.
8. Lindsay Elliott, "What were they thinking?" *Realm*, Winter 1998: 29.
9. James Dao, "From a collector of turkeys, a tour of a supermarket zoo," *The New York Times*, 24 September 1995: F12.
10. NRG Group Web site, www.thenrggroup.com.
11. John Gray, "U.S. optical company eyes Vancouver market," *Strategy Magazine*, 15 February 1999: 7.
12. Craig Saunders, "Canada test ground for Korean appliance manufacturer," *Strategy Magazine*, 5 June 2000: 5
13. "Test marketing a new product: When it's a good idea and how to do it," *Profit Building Strategies for Business Owners*, March 1993: 14.
14. William M. Bulkeley, "PictureTel to introduce $6,000 system to make PCs work as video telephones," *The Wall Street Journal*, 16 July 1993: B8.
15. Mark De Wolf, "Barq's bites into Canadian root beer market," *Strategy Magazine*, 7 July 1997: 8.
16. Michael J. Himowitz, "At last, digital cameras worth the price," *Fortune*, 22 June 1998: 148.
17. Everett Rogers, *Diffusion of Innovations*, New York: Free Press, 1983: 247–51.
18. "Please excuse Johnny, he needs new shoes," *Montgomery Advertiser*, 29 March 1997: C1.
19. Beth Hitchcock, "Pore wars," *Marketing Magazine*, 12 April 1999: 16–7.
20. Christopher Power, Kathleen Kerwin, Ronald Grover, Keith Alexander, and Robert D. Hof, "Flops," *Business Week* 3332, 16 August 1993: 77.
21. Everett Rogers, *Diffusion of Innovations*, New York: Free Press, 1983: Chapter 6.
22. Statistics Canada, *Market Research Handbook*, www.statscan.ca; and Statistics Canada, "Selected dwelling characteristics and household equipment," 1995, 1993, 1991, 1990, 1987, 1984, 1981, www.statscan.ca.
23. Thomas S. Robertson and Yoram Wind, "Organizational psychographics and innovativeness," *Journal of Consumer Research* 7, June 1980: 24–31.

CHAPTER 10

1. Julie McCann, "Marketers caught up by Beetle mania," *Marketing Magazine*, 29 June 1998: 3.
2. David Todd, "Dentyne Ice locks lips with youth target," *Strategy Magazine*, 8 May 2000: B14.
3. Wendy Cuthbert, "Big Rock brews up marketing push: Alberta brewer wants stronger foothold in Ontario and B.C.," *Marketing Magazine*, 20 July 1998: 1.
4. Astrid Van Den Broek, "Souped-up design," *Marketing Magazine*, 26 October 1998: 14–6.

5. Brian Dunn, "Taking on Tropicana," *Marketing Magazine*, 2 November 1998: 16.
6. Astrid Van Den Broek, "Germ warfare," *Marketing Magazine*, 29 November 1999: 15.
7. Richard W. Stevenson, "The brands with billion-dollar names," *The New York Times*, 28 October 1988: A1.
8. Jo Marney, "Too much of a good thing," *Marketing Magazine*, 24 January 2000: 21.
9. www.ford.com/archive/edselhistory.html; www.lvrj.com/lvrj home/1998/Mar-29-Sun=1998/news/; www.theautochannel. com/content/news/date/ 19960426/news00601.html.
10. "Warner-Lambert strips Listerine," *Marketing Magazine*, 3 July 2000: 2.
11. Ed Brown, "Thwacking away for 66 years," *Fortune*, 4 August 1997: 40.
12. Andrea Coutu, "Covering their assets," *Realm*, Spring 1999: 33; Body Blockers Web site at www.bodyblockers.com.
13. Gail Tom, Teresa Barnett, William Lew, and Jodean Selmonts, "Cueing the consumer: The role of salient cues in consumer perception," *Journal of Consumer Marketing*, 1987: 23–27.
14. Suzanne Steel, "Hudson's Bay Company set to join KFC, CIBC, IBM, O&Y and TD," *Financial Post*, 11 February 1999.
15. Zena Olijnyk, "Hudson's Bay drops idea of shortening name," *Financial Post*, 12 February 1999: 1.
16. Andrea Haman, "Top client, financial services: Clarica clarifies things," *Strategy Magazine*, 31 July 2000: B4.
17. Hugh Graham, "Launch annals of marketing," *Report on Business Magazine*, October 1998: 16–7.
18. David Aaker and Erich Joachimsthaler, "Brand leadership," *Brandweek*, 21 February 2000.
19. Stan Sutter, "Lessons in ingenuity," *Marketing Magazine*, 15 May 2000: 30; and Shawna Cohen, "The Pill is controversial once again," *Marketing Magazine*, 15 May 2000: 3.
20. Lesley Daw, "Pillsbury turnover," *Marketing Magazine*, 14 July 1997: 11–2.
21. Susan Caminiti, "How to win back customers," *Fortune*, 14 June 1993: 118; Craig Saunders, "Holt's launches private label promo blitz," *Strategy Magazine*, 31 July 2000: 3.
22. Norma Ramage "Private-label H2O," *Marketing Magazine*, 11 October 1999: 3.
23. Betsy Spethmann and Karen Benezra, "Co-Branding or be damned," *Brandweek*, 21 November 1994: 21–4.
24. Keith McArthur, "Co-branding roulette," *The Globe and Mail*, 14, June, 2000: www.theglobeandmail.com.
25. David Todd, "Out with the old, in with the new," *Strategy Magazine*, 13 March 2000: 33.
26. Angela Kryhul, "MAC make-up isn't just for drag queens," *Marketing Magazine*, 20/27 December 1999: 15.
27. "Put your snapshot here," *Digital Marketing in Marketing Magazine*, 13 March 2000: 4.
28. "New tobacco regulations become law," press release, Health Canada, 28 June 2000, www.hc-sc.gc.ca/english/ archives/releases/2000/2000_67e.htm.
29. Jack Neff, "P&G redefines the brand manager," *Advertising Age*, 13 October 1997: 1,18,20.
30. Pam Weisz, "Lever plans P&G-like moves," *Brandweek*, 10 January 1994: 1,6.
31. Gary Hoover, Alta Campbell, and Patrick J. Spain, *Hoover's Handbook of American Business* 1994, Austin: The Reference Press, 1994.

32. James B. Treece, "The great refrigerator race," *Business Week*, 15 July 1993: 78–81; "Whirlpool wins prize of $30 million to build efficient refrigerator," *The Wall Street Journal*, 30 June 1993: B8.

33. Zachary Schiller, "Frigidaire's run for the cold cash," *Business Week*, 15 July 1993: 81.

CHAPTER 11

1. Astrid Van Den Broek, "Hydro rebranding for deregulation," *Marketing Magazine*, 8 May 2000: 3.

2. Statistics Canada, *Non-Profit Sector Knowledge Base Project-Brief Report Series*, June 2000, Catalogue #75F0033MIE.

3. Laura Koss Feder, "Branding culture," *Marketing News*, 5 January 1998: 1 (2).

4. Helena Katz, "Law firm ads break mold," *Marketing Magazine*, 6 July 1998: 14.

5. Gene R. Laczniak, "Product management and the performing arts," in Michael P. Mokwa, William M. Dawson, and E. Arthur Prieve, eds., *Marketing the Arts*, New York: Praeger Publishers, 1980: 124–38.

6. Michael R. Solomon, "The wardrobe consultant: Exploring the role of a new retailing partner," *Journal of Retailing* 63, Summer 1987, 110–28.

7. Philip Kotler, "Overview of political candidate marketing," *Advances in Consumer Research* 2, 1975: 761–9.

8. Michael R. Solomon, "Celebritization and commodification in the interpersonal marketplace," unpublished manuscript, Rutgers University, 1991.

9. Irving J. Rein, Philip Kotler, and Martin R. Stoller, *High Visibility*, New York: Dodd, Mead & Company, 1987.

10. Charla Krupp, "Can Cyndi Lauper bring back the headdress?" *Glamour*, January 1987: 138 (2).

11. Astrid Van Den Broek, "Nunavut tentative on tourism push," *Marketing Magazine*, 8 March 1999: 2.

12. Eve Lazarus, "Tourism gets dirty in B.C.," *Marketing Magazine*, 11 October 1999: 4.

13. Chris Daniels, "A tourism departure," *Marketing Magazine*, 2 July 2000: 8.

14. Jacqueline Foley, "Picking a philanthropic partner," *Marketing Magazine*, 7 Septmeber 1998 (www.marketingmag.ca).

15. Astrid Van Den Broek, "Benevolent dictators," *Marketing Magazine*, 7 September 1998 (www.marketingmag.ca).

16. Gustav Niebuhr, "Where religion gets a big dose of shopping-mall culture," *New York Times*, 16 April 1995: 1 (2).

17. "New Church uses marketing to appeal to baby boomers," *Marketing News*, 12 April 1993: 11.

18. "Employment by industry, population 15 years of age and over," Statistics Canada, CANSIM, Matrix 3472, www.statcan.ca/english/pgdb/Economy/Economic/econ40.htm.

19. John A. Czepiel, Michael R. Solomon, and Carol F. Surprenant, eds., *The Service Encounter: Managing Employee/Customer Interaction in Service Businesses*, Lexington, MA: D.C. Heath and Company, 1985.

20. Lee D. Dahringer, "Marketing services internationally: Barriers and management strategies," *Journal of Services Marketing* 5, Summer 1991: 5–17, Table 2.

21. Jim Carlton, "Support lines' busy signals hurt PC makers," *Wall Street Journal*, 6 July 1995: B1 (2).

22. Lou W. Turkey and Douglas L. Fugate, "The multidimensional nature of service facilities: Viewpoints and recommendations," *Journal of Services Marketing* 6, Summer 1992: 37–45.

23. David H. Maister, "The psychology of waiting lines," in J. A. Czepiel, M. R. Solomon, and C. F. Surprenant, eds., *The Service Encounter: Managing Employee/Customer Interaction in Service Businesses*, Lexington, MA: Lexington Books, 1985: 113–24.

24. Richard Gibson, *Wall Street Journal Interactive Edition*, 3 September 1998.

25. Norma Ramage, "Flames score with marketing plan," *Marketing Magazine*, 6 December 1999: 4.

26. Astrid Van Den Broek, "ING expansion includes cafés and Web," *Marketing Magazine*, 5 April 1999: 4.

27. Michael T. Kaufman, "About New York: The nail salon of the 90s: Massages for the clothed," *The New York Times*, 1 December 1993: B3.

28. Rachel Lipton, "You don't have to be a celebrity…to live like one," *National Post*, 24 April 1999: 25.

29. Jenifer Chao, "Airports open their gates to profits," *Montgomery Advertiser*, 26 January 1997: 16A.

30. Adam Bryant, "An airborne battle of services," *The New York Times*, 19 October 1994: D1 (2).

31. Isabel Wilkerson, "New funeral options for those in a rush," *The New York Times*, 25 February 1989: A16.

32. Mary Nemeth, "Smarts for cheap," *Canadian Business*, 31 December 1999: 100–4.

33. Astrid Van Den Brock, "Trying to become a genuinely different kind of bank," *Marketing Magazine*, 20/27 December 1999: 13.

34. Gilbert A. Churchill Jr. and Carol F. Surprenant, "An investigation into the determinants of customer satisfaction," *Journal of Marketing Research* 19, November 1983: 491–504; John E. Swan and I. Frederick Trawick, "Disconfirmation of expectations and satisfaction with a retail service," *Journal of Retailing* 57, Fall 1981: 49–67; Peter C. Wilton and David K. Tse, "Models of consumer satisfaction formation: An extension," *Journal of Marketing Research* 25, May 1988: 204–12; Ann L. McGill and Dawn Iacobucci, "The role of post-experience comparison standards in the evaluation of unfamiliar services," in John F. Sherry Jr. and Brian Sternthal, eds., *Advances in Consumer Research* 19, Provo, UT: Association for Consumer Research, 1992: 570–8.

35. Cynthia Webster, "Influences upon consumer expectations of services," *Journal of Services Marketing* 5, Winter 1991: 5–17.

36. Mary Jo Bitner, "Evaluating service encounters: The effects of physical surroundings and employee responses," *Journal of Marketing* 54, April 1990: 69–82.

37. Edwin McDowell, "Ritz-Carlton's keys to good service," *New York Times*, 31 March 1993: D1 (2).

38. Michael Selz, "Chain aims to hammer dents out of auto-collision repair," *Wall Street Journal Interactive Edition*, 31 July 1998.

39. Lewis P. Carbone and Stephan H. Haeckel, "Engineering customer experiences," *Marketing Management* 3, Winter 1994, reprint.

40. Lewis P. Carbone and Stephan H. Haeckel, "Engineering customer experiences," *Marketing Management* 3, Winter 1994: reprint, Exhibit 4.

41. Valarie A. Zeithaml, "How consumer evaluation processes differ between goods and services," in Christopher H. Lovelock, *Services Marketing*, 2nd ed., Englewood Cliffs, NJ: Prentice Hall, 1991: 39–47.

42. Kenneth Wylie, "Customer satisfaction blooms; rivalry at top grows," *Advertising Age*, 18 October 1993: S-1 (2).

43. Valarie A. Zeithaml, Leonard L. Berry, and A. Parasuraman, "Communication and control processes in

the delivery of service quality," *Journal of Marketing* 52, April 1988: 35–48.

44. Jody D. Nyquist, Mary F. Bitner, and Bernard H. Booms, "Identifying communication difficulties in the service encounter: A critical incident approach," in John A. Czepiel, Michael R. Solomon, and Carol F. Surprenant, eds., *The Service Encounter: Managing Employee/Customer Interaction in Service Businesses*, Lexington, MA: D. C. Heath, 1985: 195–212.

45. Michael P. Mokwa, William M. Dawson, and E. Arthur Prieve, eds., *Marketing the Arts*, New York: Praeger Publishers, 1980.

46. "Opera company employs racy ads," *Montgomery Advertiser*, 28 September 1996: 10A.

47. A. Parasuraman, Valarie A. Zeithaml, and Leonard L. Berry, "SERVQUAL: A multiple-item scale for measuring consumer perceptions of service quality," *Journal of Retailing* 64, Spring 1988: 12–40; Valarie A. Zeithaml, A. Parasuraman, and Leonard L. Berry, "Strategic positioning on the dimensions of service quality," in Teresa A. Swartz, David E. Bowen, and Stephen W. Brown, eds., *Advances in Services Marketing and Management: Research and Practice*, vol. 1, Greenwich, CT: JAIPress: 207–28.

48. Michael Janofsky, "Domino's ends fast-pizza pledge after big award to crash victim," *The New York Times*, 22 December 1993: A1 (2).

49. Anita Lahey, "The Last market," *Marketing Magazine*, 10 August 1998: 10–1.

CHAPTER 12

1. Laura Pratt, "Trading places," *Financial Post Magazine*, March 1998: 97–100.

2. Michael L. Rothschild, "Marketing communications in nonbusiness situations or why it's so hard to sell brotherhood like soap," *Journal of Marketing*, Spring 1979: 11–20.

3. Kenneth Labich, "What will save the U.S. airlines," *Fortune*, 14 June 1993: 98–101.

4. Leslie Vreeland, "How to be a smart shopper," *Black Enterprise*, August 1993: 88.

5. Melissa Campanelli, "The price to pay," *Sales and Marketing Management*, September 1994: 96.

6. Anita Lahey, "Wholesale war," *Marketing Magazine*, 27 April 1998.

7. Jim Carlton, "Microsoft takes aim at Novell by cutting software price $35,000," *The Wall Street Journal* 222, 22 September 1993: B6.

8. Peter Verburg, "His party, your hangover," *Canadian Business*, 27 August 1999: 36–9.

9. Andrew E. Serwer, "What price brand loyalty?" *Fortune*, 10 January 1994: 103–4; Richard Gibson, "General Mills to cut prices of 3 cereals and curb discounts," *The Wall Street Journal* 222(116), 14 December 1993: A10; Richard Gibson, "Kellogg boosts prices on many cereals; average 2.6% rise may meet resistance," *The Wall Street Journal*, 8 February 1994: A3, A8.

10. Judann Pollack, "Post's price play rocked category, but did it work," *Advertising Age*, 1 December 1997: 24.

11. Betsy McKay, "Coca-Cola sets prices at premium," *The Globe and Mail*, 16 November 1999: B18.

12. Joseph Pereira, "Early coupon campaign by Toys "R" Us may spark price war among discounters," *The Wall Street Journal*, 29 October 1993: B1.

13. Norma Ramage, "Nevada Bob's tries new brand stance," *Marketing Magazine*, 13 September 1999.

14. Gabriella Stern, "P&G gains little from diaper price cuts," *The Wall Street Journal*, 28 October 1993: B12.

15. Alex Taylor III, "Soaring sales—but at a price," *Fortune*, 12 November 2001; Steve Erwin, "GM truck sales jump; Ford, Chrysler sales sink," *Ottawa Citizen*, 2 November 2001, p. E3.

16. Rahul Jacob, "The economy: Girding for worse," *Fortune*, 18 October 1993: 10.

17. Yumiki Ono, "As discounting rises in Japan, people learn to hunt for bargains," *The Wall Street Journal*, 31 December 1993: 1, 8.

18. George Burns, "McDonald's: Now it's just another burger joint," *Business Week*, 17 March 1997: 38; Bill McDowell and Laura Petrecca, "Burger King ads take slap at McD's," *Advertising Age*, 10 February 1997: 12.

19. "Canada ordered to cut dairy export subsidies," *The Guardian (Charlottown)*, 14 October 1999: B7.

20. Jacob Rahul, "Beyond quality and value," *Fortune*, Autumn/Winter 1993: 8(3).

21. Alisa Priddle, "Japanese car makers gaining ground," *The Edmonton Journal*, 8 December 1998: 18.

22. Lloyd Robertson, "Prairie farmers say the need as much as one billion dollars in aid to deal with a looming crisis in farm income," broadcast transcript, CTV National News, 4 November 1998.

23. Steve Mertl, "Forest industry battles switch to boardroom," *Times Colonist (Victoria)*, 12 October 1999: E1.

24. William G. Flanagan, "Thanks for the subsidies," *Forbes*, 7 July 1997: 120–7.

25. Eve Lazarus, "Selling sparkle: When it comes to marketing, Canada's first diamonds are no longer in the rough," *Marketing Magazine Online*, July 23, 2001.

CHAPTER 13

1. Steward Washburn, "Pricing basics: Establishing strategy and determining costs in the pricing decision," *Business Marketing*, July 1985, reprinted in Valerie Kijewski, Bob Donath, and David T. Wilson, eds., *The Best Readings from Business Marketing Magazine*, Boston: PWS-Kent Publishing Co., 1993: 257–69.

2. Steven Theobald, "Bay boss reverses upmarket tide," *The Telegram (St. John's)*, 3 July 1999: 26

3. Shawn Tully, "Can Boeing reinvent itself?" *Fortune* 127, 8 March 1993: 66–73.

4. Tony Wong, "Some like it hot at Coca-Cola: Soft-drink maker exploring vending machines that raise the price of a can of pop when the weather warms up," *The Toronto Star*, 29 October 1999: Section Head, NEWS.

5. Susanne Craig, "Wal-Mart has radically changed the retail scene," *The Financial Post*, 21 December 1996: 41.

6. "Challenging the high price at the pumps: Consumers force an inquiry on the gas industry," *Maclean's* 109(23), 3 June 1996: 17,19.

7. Michael MacDonald, "Charge against Irving Oil just a distraction: Liberal MP," *Canadian Press Newswire*, 1 October 1999.

8. Betsy McKay, "Coca-Cola sets prices at premium," *The Globe and Mail*, 16 November 1999: B18.

9. Zachary Schiller, "'Value pricing' pays off," *Business Week*, 1 November 1993: 32–3.

10. Jack Neff, "Diaper battle puts EDLP on injured list," *Advertising Age*, 14 August 1995: 3, 33.

11. Jan Wong, "Coffins at your disposal," *The Globe and Mail*, 1997, accessed via ssnewslink.

12. Jennifer Merritt, "The belle of the golf balls," *Business Week*, 29 July 1996: 6.

13. Sebastian Rupley, "The PowerPC revolution," *PC/Computing*, February 1994: 129–31; Marc Dodge, "New power chips," *PC/Computing*, February 1994: 116–7.

14. Jim Carlton, "Apple to launch Macintosh PowerPCs priced at level to gain market share," *Wall Street Journal*, 14 March 1994: B4.

15. Michael D. Mondello, "Naming your price," *Inc.*, July 1992: 159.

16. Paul Marck, "Telus pilot program serves up everything but the popcorn," *Edmonton Journal*, 22 February 2000: A-1.

17. Douglas Lavin, "Goodbye to haggling: Savvy consumers are buying their cars like refrigerators," *Wall Street Journal*, 20 August 1993: B1, B3.

18. William C. Symonds, "Would you spend $1.50 for a razor blade?" *Business Week*, 27 April 1998: 46.

19. Amy E. Cortese and Marcia Stpeanek, "Good-bye to fixed pricing?" *Business Week*, 4 May 1998: 71–84.

20. "Federal watchdog has concerns over airline merger, says Globe," *Canadian Press Newswire*, 7 October 1999.

21. Mike Roberts, "World beats a path to Vancouver's cheap CDs," *The Province (Vancouver)*, 1 August 1999: B1.

22. "Price discrimination enforcement guidelines," news release, Competition Bureau, Industry Canada, 1992-08-17.

23. Chris Flanagan, "Gas price group takes on the giants," *The Telgram (St. John's)*, 20 May 1999: 1.

24. Ryan Cleary, "Price-fixing charge dismissed," *The Telegram (St. John's)*, 21 March 2000: 1.

25. "Canadian participant in an international price-fixing conspiracy for a feed additive fined $2.25 million," news release, Competition Bureau, Industry Canada, 1999-09-24; "Former Roche executive convicted and fined for international conspiracies under the *Competition Act*," news release, Competition Bureau, Industry Canada, 1999-09-27.

CHAPTER 14

1. Thu Hien Dao, "Banks jump on kiosk bandwagon," *Financial Post* 2(58), 1 January 2000: C6.

2. G. Bruce Knecht, "Banks bag profits with supermarket branches," *The Wall Street Journal*, 20 May 1994: B1, B8.

3. Zena Olijnyk, "GroceryGateway struggles to meet heavy demand: phenomenal growth. Hoping for help from warehouse and new software," *Financial Post*, 18 May 2000: C9.

4. Jeffrey A. Tannenbaum, "Chain reactions," *Wall Street Journal*, 15 October 1993: R6.

5. Charise Clark, "The new face of franchising: From cool concepts to creative financing methods, franchising offers hot new growth opportunities," *Profit: The Magazine for Canadian Entrepreneurs* 18 (8), December 1999/January 2000: 36–40.

6. Robert L. Rose and Bridget O'Brian, "United, Lufthansa form marketing tie, dealing a setback to American Airlines," *The Wall Street Journal*, 4 October 1993: A4.

7. Allan J. Magrath, "The gatekeepers," *Across the Board*, April 1992: 43–6.

8. Scott Woolley, "The new distribution," *Forbes*, 4 November 1996: 164–5.

9. Eve Lazarus, "The longshot," *Marketing Magazine*, 27 October 1997.

10. Lori Kittelberg, "Labour trouble halts $89m in daily trade at Vancouver Port," *Hill Times*, 15 November 1999: 20.

11. Scott Woolley, "Replacing inventory with information," *Forbes*, 24 March 1997: 54–8.

12. Paul Briggs, "Food for thought: There are lessons to be learned for all logistics professionals from the Canadian grocery industry's collective approach to supply chain management," *Canadian Transportation Logistics* 103 (1), January 2000: 30, 32.

13. Ross Laver, "Fairly tales and monsters," *Maclean's*, 20 March 2000: 40.

CHAPTER 15

1. Jennifer Steinhauer, "Interactive stores make shopping an experience," *New York Times News Service* online, 28 February 1998.

2. Jacobson Consulting Inc., *The Retail Sector in Canada*, report prepared for the Retail Council of Canada, www.retail-council.org.

3. Michael Levy and Barton A. Weitz, *Retailing Management*, 3rd ed., Boston: Irwin/McGraw-Hill, 1998.

4. Stanley C. Hollander, "The wheel of retailing," *Journal of Retailing*, July 1960: 41.

5. William R. Davidson, Albert D. Bates, and Stephen J. Bass, "The retail life cycle," *Harvard Business Review*, November–December 1976: 89.

6. Gail DeGeorge, "Dilbert to the rescue," *Business Week*, 4 May 1998: 166.

7. "Safeway gas stations pose challenge to big oil," *The Globe and Mail*, 15 August 2000: B10.

8. Julia Flynn, "IKEA's new game plan," *Business Week*, 6 October 1997: 99 (2).

9. Astrid van den Broek, "Speaking the same language: Burger King cooks up a multicultural marketing menu," *Marketing Magazine*, 21 June 1999.

10. Judy Waytiuk, "The new native niche," *Marketing Magazine*, 22 May 2000: 13.

11. Robert E. Calem, "Coming to a cash register near you: Multimedia," *New York Times*, 31 July 1994: F7.

12. Marianne Meyer, "Attention shoppers!" *Marketing and Media Decisions*, May 1988: 67–70.

13. Gary Robins, "Wireless POS systems," *STORES*, February 1994: 47 (2).

14. Raju Mudhar, "Food for future thought: New database technology puts supermarkets in the high-tech fast lane," *Marketing Magazine*, 18 October 1999.

15. Diane Forget, chief systems, POS, Henry Birks & Sons, personal communication.

16. Alfred F. Lynch, "Training for a new ball game: Retailing in the 21st century," *The Futurist*, July/August 1992: 36–40.

17. Arthur Good and Stephen Granovsky, "Retail goes global," *Canadian Business Review* 22(2), Summer 1995: 31–3.

18. Norma Ramage, "Canadian cinnamon buns savoured in Asia," *Marketing Magazine*, 19 June 2000: 6.

19. Mitchell Russell, "The Gap dolls itself up," *Business Week*, 21 March 1994: 46.

20. Julie Liesse, "Welcome to the club," *Advertising Age* 2, 1 February 1993: 3 (2).

21. Debra Hazel, "The factory outlets' best of times: Belz's and other centers beat the recession," *Chain Store Age Executive*, November 1992: 39–42.

22. Michael Levy and Barton A. Weitz, *Retailing Management*, 3rd ed., Boston: Irwin/McGraw-Hill, 1998.

23. Jennifer Steinhauer, "Interactive stores make shopping an experience," *New York Times News Service* online, 28 February 1998.

24. "A wide world of sports shoes: Fixtures enhance appeal of world foot locker," *Chain Store Age Executive*, January 1993: 176–81.

25. Wendy Marx, "Shopping 2000," *Brandweek* 20 (2), 9 January 1995: 20.

26. Chris Eby, "A toast to opening of booze behemoth," *National Post*, 24 February 1999: B1.

27. "The sound of retail," *Chain Store Age*, January 1996: 3C–6C.

28. "Lobbyists against noise pollution pick up some unexpected allies," *Wall Street Journal*, 1 June 1990: B1.

29. "Design therapy: New trends in supermarket design can create moods that can enhance sales," *Canadian Grocer* 107(2), February 1993: 102–10.

30. George Condon, "Retailing as entertainment!: Is it fun to shop in your store?" *Canadian Grocer* 112(6), July/August 1998: 14–9.

31. "Service: Retail's no. 1 problem," *Chain Store Age*, 19 January 1987.

32. Elaine Underwood, "Mall busters, like crime, a boon for home shopping," *Brandweek*, 17 January 1994: 18 (2).

33. Stephanie Strom, "Bold stroke in Japan's art of retailing," *New York Times*, 23 April 1993: D1 (2).

34. Zena Olijnyk, "Supermarket chic. He's been raising food retailing to new heights: Architect Leslie Rebanks has transformed what used to be big boxes that sold groceries into cultural phenomena," *Financial Post*, 24 April 2000: C1,C4.

35. Kate Fitzgerald, "All roads lead to ... ," *Advertising Age*, 1 February 1993: S-1.

36. "Service memorial for Jacob Ghermazian," Canadian Press Newswire, 4 January 2000.

37. Michael Levy and Barton A. Weitz, *Retailing Management*, 3rd ed., Boston: Irwin/McGraw-Hill, 1998.

38. Pat Sloan, "Avon looks beyond direct sales," *Advertising Age*, 22 February 1993: 32; Seema Nayyar, "Avon calling, by fax, phone, and infomercial," *Brandweek*, 22 February 1993: 22–3.

39. John Browning and Spencer Reiss, "Encyclopedia of the new economy, Part I," *Wired*, March 1998: 105 (8).

40. Stratford Sherman, "Will the information superhighway be the death of retailing?" *Fortune*, 18 April 1994: 99(5), 110.

41. Thomas Watson, "Much-hyped e-commerce a bust so far," *National Post*, 11 August 2000: A1.

42. http://retailinteractive.ca/SSG/ri00910e.html?he=1

43. http://www.census.gov/Press-Release/www/2000/cb00-40.html

44. Boston Consulting Group and Retail Council of Canada, *The Canadian Online Retailing Report*, joint research project, June 19, 2000, www.bcg.com/media_center; "E-commerce: Shopping around the Web," *The Economist*, 26 February 2000: 65-93; A.C. Neilsen, *The Canadian Internet Survey*, Industry Canada, 12 April 2000.

45. Boston Consulting Group and Retail Council of Canada, *The Canadian Online Retailing Report*, joint research project, June 19, 2000, www.bcg.com/media_center.

46. Boston Consulting Group, "Canadian retailers and consumers missing out on online opportunity," press releases, www.bcg.com/media_centre.

47. Boston Consulting Group and Retail Council of Canada, *The Canadian Online Retailing Report*, joint research project, June 19, 2000, www.bcg.com/media_center.

48. Angus Reid Media Center, "Face of the Web study pegs global Internet population at more than 300 million," www.angusreid.com/media/content.

49. "E-commerce: Shopping around the Web," *The Economist*, 26 February 2000: 65–93.

50. Boston Consulting Group and Retail Council of Canada, *The Canadian Online Retailing Report*, joint research project, June 19, 2000, www.bcg.com/media_center.

51. http://www.shop.org/research/summary.htm

52. Daniel McHardie, "Web-surfing teens turn off the TV," *The Globe and Mail*, 24 May 2000: A1.

53. Daniel McHardie, "EcomCard after teens with new e-card," *The Globe and Mail*, 7 August 2000: B1.

54. Danny Kucharsky, "Log-ons & lace," *Marketing Magazine*, 24 January 2000.

55. John Grey, "Internet rewriting marketing rules: P&G," *Strategy: The Canadian Marketing Report*, 13 March 2000: 5.

56. Richard Covington, "Companies find the net helps trap surprising source of revenue," *International Herald Tribune*, accessed via ssnewslink, 23 February 1998.

57. Boston Consulting Group and Retail Council of Canada, *The Canadian Online Retailing Report*, joint research project, June 19, 2000, www.bcg.com/media_center.

58. "E-commerce: Shopping around the Web," *The Economist*, 26 February 2000: 65–93.

59. David Akin, "Don't shoot the MP3 player: The record industry should admit that MP3 is its best prospect for selling music and start using it," *Financial Post*, 13 May 2000: D11.

60. Ted Haynes, *The Electronic Commerce Dictionary*, The Robleda Company, August 1995.

61. Lian Morfitt, "Toronto firm set to create global magic," *The Globe and Mail*, 15 August 2000: B1.

62. Fawzia Sheikh, "New portal players are jockeying to be the top Canadian women's destination online," *Marketing Magazine*, 17 July 2000.

63. Eve Lazarus, "Blast off," *Marketing Magazine*, July 2000: 12.

64. Patricia Sellers, "Inside the first e-Christmas," *Fortune*, 1 February 1999: 71; Boston Consulting Group and Retail Council of Canada, *The Canadian Online Retailing Report*, joint research project, June 19, 2000, www.bcg.com/media_center.

65. Alan Middleton, "Branding in an e-com world," *Marketing Magazine*, 13 March 2000.

66. Boston Consulting Group and Retail Council of Canada, *The Canadian Online Retailing Report*, joint research project, June 19, 2000, www.bcg.com/media_center.

67. Boston Consulting Group and Retail Council of Canada, *The Canadian Online Retailing Report*, joint research project, June 19, 2000, www.bcg.com/media_center.

68. Marina Strauss, "Depots aim to solve delivery dilemma," *The Globe and Mail*, 28 July 2000.

69. Lisa Napoli, *New York Times News Service Online*, 26 February 1998, accessed via ssnewslink.

70. Andrew Tausz, "The Internet rewards Dell's directness," *Financial Post*, 17 April 2000: E1.

71. Robert Thompson, "Product returns: E-com's dirty little secret," *eBusiness Journal*, April 2000: 22, 24.

72. John Browning and Spencer Reiss, "Encyclopedia of the new economy, Part I," *Wired*, March 1998: 105 (8).

73. Richard Mackie, "Ontario unveils e-biz act," *The Globe and Mail*, 14 June 2000: B5.

74. "Future Shop is a veteran of the e-commerce world," *The Globe and Mail*, 30 November 1999: E21.

75. Dana Canedy, "Buying Barbie, Legos and Beanie Babies online," *New York Times News Service*, 27 July 1998.

76. "E-commerce: Shopping around the Web," *The Economist*, 26 February 2000: 65–93.

77. Rebecca Quick, "Internet's robot shoppers are unable to roam free," *Wall Street Journal Interactive Edition*, 3 September 1998.

78. "DM spending hits $8 billion," *Marketing Magazine*, 8 May 2000.

79. Frances Huffman, "Special delivery," *Entrepreneur*, February 1993: 81 (3).

80. Paul Hughes, "Profits due," *Entrepreneur*, February 1994: 74 (4).

81. Margaret Nearing, "A comfy place to shop: Canadians' increasing fondness for catalogue ordering is spurring red-hot sales growth," *Marketing Magazine*, 7 December 1998.

82. Zena Olinjnyk, "Sears shuts call centre: Internet more profitable," *Financial Post*, 12 May 2000: C6.

83. "Zellers delivers baby catalogue," *Marketing Magazine*, 21 June 1999: 3.

84. David Carr, "The limits of e-mail," *Marketing Magazine*, 24 April 2000.

85. "Baseball club aims to score a direct mail triple," *Marketing Magazine*, 3 May 1999 .

86. Kate Ballen, "Get ready for shopping at work," *Fortune*, 15 February 1988: 95.

87. Michael Levy and Barton A. Weitz, *Retailing Management*, 3rd ed., Boston: Irwin/McGraw-Hill, 1998; Len Strazewski, "Tupperware locks in new strategy," *Advertising Age*, 8 February 1988: 30.

88. Peter Wilkinson, "For your eyes only," *Savvy Woman*, January 1989: 68.

89. Mario Brossi and Joseph Marino, *Multilevel Marketing: A Legal Primer*, Washington, DC: Direct Selling Association, 1990.

90. Linda Lipp, "Telephones ringing off the hook," *Journal and Courier*, 19 May 1994.

91. Denise Gillene, "FBI launches 12-state telemarketing sweep," *Los Angeles Times*, 5 March 1993: D1.

92. James Sterngold, "Why Japanese adore vending machines," *New York Times*, 5 January 1992: A1 (2).

93. Ian French, "Brand-based DRTV that sells: Rules to live by in the brave new world of direct response," *Marketing Magazine*, 24 April 2000.

94. Tim Triplett, "Big names crowd the infomercial airwaves," *Marketing News*, 28 March 1994: 1 (2).

95. Gary Arlen, "DRTV: Beyond the fringe!" *Marketing Tools*, October 1997: 37–42.

96. "How Videotex offers special potential in France," *Business Marketing Digest* 17, 1992: 81–4.

97. Lisa D'Innocenzo, "How would you reposition the Gap?" *Strategy*, 28 January 2002, page 3.

98. Lisa D'Innocenzo, "How would you reposition the Gap?" *Strategy*, 28 January 2002, page 3.

CHAPTER 16

1. Rob Pashko, "No more yawns," *Marketing Magazine*, 31 January 2000.

2. J. Grunig, *Excellence in Public Relations and Communications Management*, New Jersey: Lawrence Erlbaum Associates, Inc., 1992.

3. J. Grunig, *Excellence in Public Relations and Communications Management*, New Jersey: Lawrence Erlbaum Associates, Inc., 1992.

4. Leiss et al., *Social Communication*; George Stigler, "The economics of information," *Journal of Political Economy*, 1961: 69.

5. Don E. Schultz and Heidi F. Schultz, "Transitioning marketing communications into the twenty-first century," *Journal of Marketing Communications* 4(1), March 1998: 9–26.

6. Scott Hume, "Integrated marketing: Who's in charge here?" *Advertising Age*, 22 March 1993: 3(2).

7. Don E. Schultz, Stanley I. Tannenbaum, and Robert F. Lauterborn, *Integrated Marketing Communications: Pulling It Together and Making It Work*, Chicago: NTCBusiness Books, 1993; Melanie Wells, "Purposeful grazing in ad land," *Advertising Age*, 11 April 1994: S-12.

8. Lesley Young, "Great escapes," *Marketing Magazine Online*, 20 August 2001.

9. Don E. Schultz, Stanley I. Tannenbaum, and Robert F. Lauterborn, *Integrated Marketing Communications: Pulling It Together and Making It Work*, Chicago: NTC Business Books, 1993.

10. Katsumi Hoshino, "Semiotic marketing and product conceptualization," in Jean Umiker-Sebeok (ed.), *Marketing and Semiotics: New Directions in the Study of Signs for Sale*, Berlin: Mouton de Bruyter, 1987: 41–56.

11. D. Schultz and B. Barnes, *Strategic Brand Communication Campaigns*, 5th ed., Lincolnwood IL: NTC Publishing, 1999.

12. Michael Wilke, "A radio entrepreneur reaches for the interactive age," *New York Times*, 4 September 1994: F7.

13. "P&G stages live advertising," *Marketing Magazine*, 1 May 2000.

14. George E. Belch and Michael A. Belch, *Introduction to Advertising & Promotion: An Integrated Marketing Communications Perspective* 2nd ed., Homewood, IL: Irwin, 1993.

15. "The marketing factory," *Marketing Magazine*, 14 February 2000.

16. "The Man from Glad—He's back," *Marketing Magazine*, 20 March 2000.

17. Jonathan Berry, "Wilma! What happened to the plain old ad?" *Business Week*, 6 June 1994: 54–5.

18. Tom Buerkle, "Advertisers find a formula they like in auto racing," *International Herald Tribune* [on-line] 10 March 1998, accessed via ssnewslink.

19. Patricia Sellers, "Winning over the new consumer," *Fortune*, 27 July 1991: 113.

20. Don E. Schultz, Stanley I. Tannenbaum, and Robert F. Lauterborn, *Integrated Marketing Communications: Pulling It Together and Making It Work*, Chicago: NTC Business Books, 1993.

21. John F. Yarbrough, "Putting the pieces together," *Sales and Marketing Management*, September 1996: 70.

22. Michael Lev, "For car buyers, technology or Zen," *New York Times*, 22 May 1989: D1.

23. Linda L. Golden and Mark I. Alpert, "Comparative analysis of the relative effectiveness of one- and two-sided communication for contrasting products," *Journal of Advertising* 16, 1987: 18–25; Kamins, "Celebrity and noncelebrity advertising in a two-sided context,"; Robert B. Settle and Linda L. Golden, "Attribution theory and advertiser credibility," *Journal of Marketing Research* 11, May 1974: 181–5.

24. Frank R. Kardes, "Spontaneous inference processes in advertising: The effects of conclusion omission and involvement on persuasion," *Journal of Consumer Research* 15, September 1988: 225–33.

25. Gert Assmus, "An empirical investigation into the perception of vehicle source effects," *Journal of Advertising* 7, Winter 1978: 4–10; Stephen Baker, *Systematic Approach to Advertising Creativity*, New York: McGraw-Hill, 1979.

26. Patricia Sellers, "The best way to reach your buyers," *Fortune*, Autumn/Winter 1993: 15 (4).

27. James P Masciarelli, "Are you managing your relationships?" *Management Review New York* 87(4): 41–5.

28. "CRM sales outperform all enterprise applications," *National Post*, 17 May 2000: E2.

29. "CRM teaches university's IT department about customers," *National Post*, 17 May 2000: E9.

30. Mark MacKinnon, "Flying Air Canada's unfriendly skies," *The Globe and Mail*, 5 August 2000.

31. "Database marketing: A view of customer loyalty," *Marketing Magazine*, 16 August 1999.

32. Curt Barry, "Building a database," *Catalog Age*, August 1992: 65–8.

33. Martin Everett, "This one's just for you," *Sales and Marketing Management*, June 1992: 119–26.

34. G. Bruce Knecht, "American Express embraces co-brands," *Wall Street Journal*, 17 February 1994: B1.

35. Martin Everett, "This one's just for you," *Sales and Marketing Management*, June 1992: 119–26.

36. Donalee Moulton, "Selling the Bay of Fundy's sizzle," *Marketing Magazine*, 24/31 August 1998.

37. S.C. Gwynne, "How casinos hook you," *Time*, 17 November 1997: 69.

38. Lara Mills, "Playing hard to get: Consumers reluctant to give out personal information will be tough to cozy up to, especially under the rules of the new federal privacy law," *Marketing Magazine*, 24 April 2000.

39. Robert Kuttner, "The U.S. could use a dose of Europe's privacy medicine," *Business Week*, 16 November 1998: 22.

40. Virginia Matthews, "Relationship marketing flawed," *Marketing Magazine*, 21 February 2000.

CHAPTER 17

1. William Wells, John Burnett, and Sandra Moriarty, *Advertising: Principles and Practice*, 2nd ed., Englewood Cliffs, NJ: Prentice Hall, 1992.

2. A.C. Nielsen Canada, "1999 advertising trends in Canada," www.acnielsen.ca/sect_adtrends/adtrends-en.htm.

3. Bob D. Cutler and Darrel D. Muehling, "Another look at advocacy advertising and the boundaries of commercial speech," *Journal of Advertising* 20, December 1991: 49–52.

4. Lara Mills, "Campaigns with legs," *Marketing Magazine*, 15 May 2000: 12–4.

5. "The rankings," *Marketing Magazine*, 25 June 2001.

6. Leslie Kaufman, "Enough talk," *Newsweek*, 18 August 1997: 48–9.

7. "How Canadian Tire refocused and solved its identity crisis," *Marketing Magazine*, 20/27 December 1999: 13.

8. R K Swamy/BBDO, *R&D: Relevance and Difference at Work*, June 1996, Bombay, India; Priya Raj, Director Client Services, R K Swamy/BBDO, personal communication, January 1998.

9. Stan Sutter, "Your tax dollars at work," *Marketing Magazine*, 3 July 2000: 22.

10. Juliette Walker, "Pepsi-Coke spat raises questions about ad policies," *Japan Times Weekly International Edition*, 24–30 June 1991: 7.

11. "Green promotes 'handyman's helper,'" *Marketing Magazine*, 3 July 2000: 3.

12. Kevin Goldman, "Ad with disabled child stirs controversy," *Wall Street Journal*, 3 September 1993: B8.

13. Eun-Mi (Liz) Adams, "The big piece of the mosaic," *Marketing Magazine*, 21 June 1999: 16–7.

14. Canadian Media Directors' Council, *1999/2000 Canadian Media Directors' Council Media Digest*: 16.

15. James Careless, "Where's the price tag," *Marketing Magazine*, 31 January 2000.

16. Philip Hart, "Product placement comes of age in Canada," *Marketing Magazine*, 18 November 1996: 20.

17. Phil Hall, "Make listeners your customers," *Nation's Business*, June 1994: 53R.

18. Canadian Media Directors' Council, *1999/2000 Canadian Media Directors' Council Media Digest*: 27.

19. www.cyberatlas.internet.com/markets/advertising/article/0,,5941_440981,,00.html.

20. Andrea Zoe Aster, "Virgin Music tries viral marketing," *Marketing Magazine*, 1 May 2000: 2.

21. Lisa Marie Petersen, "Outside chance," *Mediaweek*, 15 June 1992: 20–3.

22. John Gray, "Hosers with attitude," *Canadian Business*, 15 May 2000: 70–2.

23. Astrid Van Den Broek, "TV networks' ads go to the movies," *Marketing Magazine*, 3 April 2000: 3.

24. Altaf M. Khan, "New ways to get in faces," *Marketing Magazine*, 10 April 2000: 33.

25. Canadian Media Directors' Council, *2000/2001 Canadian Media Directors' Council Media Digest*: 17.

26. www.Doubleclick.net/ca.

27. Bristol Voss, "Measuring the effectiveness of advertising and PR," *Sales and Marketing Management*, October 1992: 123–4.

28. Charles Goodrum and Helen Dalrymple, *Advertising in America: The First 200 Years*, New York: Harry N. Abrams, 1990.

29. Bristol Voss, "Measuring the effectiveness of advertising and PR," *Sales and Marketing Management*, October 1992: 123–4.

30. Kevin Goldman, "The message, clever as it may be, is lost in a number of high-profile campaigns," *Wall Street Journal*, 27 July 1993: B1(2).

31. Charles Goodrum and Helen Dalrymple, *Advertising in America: The First 200 Years*, New York: Harry N. Abrams, 1990.

32. Kevin Goldman, "Knock, Knock. Who's there? The same old funny ad again," *Wall Street Journal*, 2 November 1993: B10.

33. William Wells, John Burnett, and Sandra Moriarty, *Advertising: Principles and Practice*, 3rd ed., Englewood Cliffs, NJ: Prentice Hall, 1995.

34. William Wells, John Burnett, and Sandra Moriarty, *Advertising: Principles and Practice*, 3rd ed., Englewood Cliffs, NJ: Prentice Hall, 1995.

35. Kevin Goldman, "From witches to anorexics, critical eyes scrutinize ads for political correctness," *Wall Street Journal*, 19 May 1994: B1(2).

36. Gary Levin, "Keeping in touch easy with database," *Advertising Age*, 28 March 1994: S-8.

CHAPTER 18

1. Danielle D'Agostino, "Teaching brands new tricks: Fido's PR campaign worked by leveraging off the visual icon of the dog," *Marketing Magazine*, 28 February 1999: 28.

2. Michael Bernard, "The great house sale," *Marketing Magazine*, 23 February 1998.

3. Anita Lahey, Michael McCullough, and Gail Chiasson, "Placing products," *Marketing Magazine*, 12 August 1996.

4. Patrick Allossery, "Petro-Canada to list its costs per litre in public relation bid: Posted on the pumps," *Financial Post*, 14 March 2000: C6.

5. Ni Chen and Hugh M. Culbertson, "Two contrasting approaches of government public relations in mainland China," *Public Relations Quarterly*, Fall 1992: 36–41.

6. John Swinimer, "Untarnished: Rolling up their sleeves to polish up what is widely seen as a mudied image, insurance companies and industry associations are cleaning it off by getting involved in worthy causes and community projects," *Canadian Underwriter*, February 1993: 12–3.

7. "Ericsson, Manifest team on aid," *Marketing Magazine*, 8 May 2000.

8. Anita Lahey, Michael McCullough, and Gail Chiasson, "Placing products," *Marketing Magazine*, 12 August 1996.

9. Patrick Allossery, "Petro-Canada to list its costs per litre in public relation bid: Posted on the pumps," *Financial Post*, 14 March 2000: C6.

10. Tony Van Alphen, "Husky Injection Molding adds altruism to the mix," *Canadian Press Newswire*, 21 January 2000.

11. Roma Luciw, "Bridgestone recalls Canadian tires: About a million of affected brands are on selected SUVs and trucks," *The Globe and Mail*, 11 August 2000: A1.

12. Rick Hall, "Lessons of the McLibel case," *Marketing Magazine*, 25 January 1999.

13. Anita Lahey, Michael McCullough, and Gail Chiasson, "Placing products," *Marketing Magazine*, 12 August 1996.

14. Eymbert Vaandering, "Hey, Big Spender," *Marketing Magazine Online*, 14 January 2002.

15. Howard Stumpf and John M. Kawula, "Point of purchase advertising," in S. Ulanoff (ed.), *Handbook of Sales Promotion*, New York: McGraw Hill, 1985; Karen A. Berger, *The Rising Importance of Point-of-Purchase Advertising in the Marketing Mix*, Englewood, NJ: Point-of-Purchase Advertising Institute.

16. Liza Finlay, "Perpetual promotions," *Marketing Magazine*, 31 May 1999: 11–2.

17. Melinda Grenier Guiles, "Wooing press and public at auto shows," *Wall Street Journal*, 8 January 1990: B1.

18. Fawzia Sheikh, "Do your own thing," *Marketing Magazine*, 14 July 1997: 14.

19. Jennifer Lawrence, "Tracy-Locke Division works for the big event," *Advertising Age*, 17 May 1993: S-2, S-7.

20. Louise Gagnon, "The big one," *Marketing Magazine*, 14 April 1997: 12.

21. Dagmara Lewkowicz, "Couponing shifts away from food: The real growth is in categories like hair care," *Marketing Magazine*, 13 April 1998.

22. Don E. Schultz, William A. Robinson, and Lisa A. Petrison, *Sales Promotion Essentials*, 2nd ed., Lincolnwood, IL: NTC Business Books, 1993.

23. "Show and sell," *Marketing Magazine*, 16 June 1997.

24. "Sampling debuts PowerBar in East," *Marketing Magazine: Newsline*, 7 June 1999.

25. Kate Fitzgerald, "Guinness looks to its past to fresh 5th pub giveaway," *Advertising Age*, 30 March 1998: 46.

26. Liza Finlay, "Perpetual promotions," *Marketing Magazine*, 31 May 1999: 11–2.

27. Kerry J. Smith, "It's for you," *PROMO: The International Magazine for Promotion Marketing*, August 1994: 41(4); Sharon Moshavi, "Please deposit no cents," *Forbes*, 16 August 1993: 102.28. *The Point-of-Purchase Advertising Industry Fact Book*, Englewood, NJ: The Point-of-Purchase Advertising Institute, 1992.

29. "Bausch & Lomb makes eyes with consumers in Spain," *PROMO: The International Magazine for Promotion Marketing*, October 1994: 93.

30. Patricia Sellers, "Winning over the new consumer," *Fortune*, 29 July 1991: 113.

31. Lara Mills, "Marketers face up to new challenges," *Marketing Magazine*, 24 May 1999: 4.

32. Lara Mills, "Too much of a good thing," *Marketing Magazine*, 19/26 August 1996.

33. Anita Lahey, "Letting sleeping dogs lie," *Marketing Magazine*, 14 April 1997: 14.

34. Jaclyn Fierman, "The death and rebirth of the salesman," *Fortune*, 25 July 1994: 38(7), 88.

35. "A user's guide to the sales manager's budget planner," *Sales and Marketing Management*, 28 June 1993: 6–10.

36. Greg Weatherdon, "The telemarketing edge: Combining it with broadcast faxing creates a powerful tool for drug companies," *Marketing Magazine*, 19 October 1998: 25.

37. Dan C. Weilbaker, "The identification of selling abilities needed for missionary type sales," *Journal of Personal Selling & Sales Management* 10, Summer 1990: 45–58.

38. W. David Gibson, "Fielding a force of experts," *Sales and Marketing Management*, April 1993: 88–92; Henry Canaday, "Team selling works!" *Personal Selling Power*, September 1994: 53–8.

39. Jack Branswell, "The gadget king," *Marketing Magazine*, 12 June 2000.

40. Martin Everett, "This is the ultimate in selling," *Sales and Marketing Management*, August 1989: 28.

41. Maurice G. Clabaugh Jr. and Jessie L. Forbes, *Professional Selling: A Relationship Approach*, New York: West, 1992.

42. André Mazerolle and Eva A. Lau, "A teleconference on steroids: Web-push technology offers the next best thing to being there at a press conference," *Marketing Magazine*, 15 March 1999.

43. Melissa Campanelli, "Reshuffling the deck," *Sales and Marketing Management*, June 1994: 83–90.

44. W. David Gibson, "Fielding a force of experts," *Sales and Marketing Management*, April 1993: 88–92.

45. W. David Gibson, "Fielding a force of experts," *Sales and Marketing Management*, April 1993: 88–92.

Credits

CHAPTER 1

2 Lanyon Phillips Communications Inc., Bill Downie, Art Director and Peter Lanyon, Chairman/Chief Creative Officer; 4 Vancouver Sun Photo/Dick Didlick; 6 Willie L. Hill/The Image Works; 7 Durex Canada a division of SSL Canada Inc.; 8 (top) Courtesy of the Calgary Zoo & Pattison Outdoor; 8 (bottom) Reebok; 12 Kaepa Shoes/Complete Sportswear; 13 Churchill & Klehr Photography; 16 Ford Motor Company, Detroit; 19 Peter Jones/Reuters/Corbis; 20 Churchill & Klehr Photography; 21 Courtesy of the American Association of Advertising Agencies; page 22 Lanyon Phillips Communications Inc., Bill Downie, Art Director and Peter Lanyon, Chairman/Chief Creative Officer.

CHAPTER 2

28 Palmer Jarvis DDB; 30 Dick Hemingway; 38 Linda Farwell Photography; 39 Courtesy of Loblaws Co. Ltd.; 40 Andersen Windows, Inc.; 42 Dave G. Houser/Corbis; 44 Chevrolet-Central Office; 45 Office Depot; 46 Michael Newman/PhotoEdit

CHAPTER 3

54 Ethical Funds Inc.; 56 Ethical Funds Inc.; 58 Courtesy of Daydream Software AB (publ), Sweden; 64 AP/Canapress/Richard Drew; 65 (top) ©2000 Avon Canada Inc.; 65 (bottom) Dick Hemingway; 67 Alene M. McNeill; 68 Courtesy of DaimlerChrysler Canada Inc.; 70 Courtesy of Primus Canada; 74 Courtesy of Neilson Dairy; 76 Concerned Children's Advertisers; 77 Ethical Funds Inc.

CHAPTER 4

84 Alain Benainous/Liaison Agency, Inc.; 86 Peter Einstein; 88 Nike Advertising; 89 W.K. Buckley Limited 95 Photo courtesy of Canadian Tourism Commission; 97 J. Nordell/The Image Works; 98 The Procter & Gamble. Used by permission; 100 Clearly Canadian Beverage Corp.; 105 (top) MTV, Music Television; 105 (bottom) Hosaka Naoto/Liaison Agency, Inc.; 106 Ogilvy & Mather; 107 Paradiset DDB

CHAPTER 5

120, 122 Courtesy of SurveySite; 123 Ad courtesy of Ford Motor Company; 126 Released with permission by Dun and Bradstreet Canada; 127 (top) Michael Newman/PhotoEdit; 127 (bottom) Columbia Information Systems; 132 Louie Psihoyos/Matrix International, Inc.; 133 General Mills; 134 Paul Shambroom/Photo Researchers, Inc.; 136 Reprinted from *Marketing Tools* magazine, with permission." 1998, PRIME-DIA/Intertec, PO Box 4284, Stamford, CT 06907-4284; 137 Courtesy of SurveySite

CHAPTER 6

144 Courtesy of d-Code; 146 Courtesy Robert Barnard d-Code; 148 Courtesy of Sympatico and Fuel Advertising; 149 Permission of Yellow.ca; 151 Leo Burnett Company, Ltd.; 152 Courtesy of Benetton; 154 Printed with permission of Imperial Oil; 155 Benjamin Moore Co., Limited; 156 Kellogg Canada Inc.; 158 XTRA! Canada's Gay & Lesbian Media Group; 160 James Leynse/SABA Press Photos, Inc.; 161 Courtesy of www.canoe.ca; 163 Courtesy of Parasuco Jeans Inc.; 165 Courtesy of Royal Mutual Funds Inc.

CHAPTER 7

172 Courtesy of Michel Bendayan; 174 Courtesy of Ritvik Holdings Inc.; 175 Courtesy of Bombardier Inc.; 177 (top) Courtesy of Nortel Networks; 177 (bottom) Neil Rabinowitz/Corbis; 179 BMW of North America, Inc.; 182 Metro Transit -Halifax Regional Municipality; 183 Mita Copystar America, Inc.; 185 Bob Daemmrich/The Image Works; 187 Ralf-Finn Hestoft/SABA Press Photos, Inc.

CHAPTER 8

200 Ford Motor Company of Canada, Ltd.; 202 Roman Pylypczak Photography; 204 Joe McBride/Tony Stone Images; 207 Courtesy of Royal Bank/Aboriginal Banking, artwork by Linda Rostad; 208 Courtesy of CFMT-TV; 213 Soya World Inc.; 214 Beef Information Centre; 216 Hard Candy, Inc.; 220 CORBIS/S.I.N.

CHAPTER 9

232, 234 Courtesy of Roots Canada Limited; 235 Churchill & Klehr Photography; 240 Research In Motion Ltd.; 242 UPI/Corbis; 243 Kraft Canada Inc.; 245 Ann States/SABA Press Photos, Inc.; 246 Procter & Gamble Inc.; 250 Warner-Lambert Canada Inc.; 251 "Barq's" trademarks are used with permission; 252 Jergens Canada Inc.; 254 David Madison/Tony Stone Images; 255 (top) Changepoint PSA; 255 (bottom) Roots Canada Inc.

CHAPTER 10

260 Canada Cutlery Inc.; 262 Dick Hemingway; 263 (top) Volkswagen of America, Inc.; 263 (bottom) Volkswagen of America/FPG International LLC; 265 Photo used with permission of Bombardier Inc. Traxter ™ XT, are trademarks of Bombardier Inc. and/or its subsidiaries; 266 Courtesy of Procter & Gamble Inc.; 268 Samsung Canada Inc; 269 Warner-Lambert Canada Inc.; 270 Jessica Wecker Photography; 272 (top) Kraft Canada Inc.; 272 (bottom) ©2000. Clarica Life Insurance Company. All rights reserved.; 273 The A&W Rootbeer Company; 276 Courtesy T. Marzetti & Co., Columbus, OH.; 279 AP/Wide World Photos

CHAPTER 11

286, 307 Charity.ca; 288 Dick Hemingway; 289 (top) Canapress/Kevin Fryer; 289 (bottom) McMichael Canadian Art Collection; 290 Courtesy of the Confederation Centre of the Arts; 292 Courtesy of Ontario Tourism and Fuel Advertising; 293 (top) Indiana University; 293 (bottom) Health Canada; 294 © 2000 Gowling Lafleur Henderson LLP; 301 Courtesy of the Bank of Montreal; 302 (top) TELUS Corporate Communications; 302 (bottom) Lewis P. Carbone and Stephan H. Haeckel, "Engineering Customer Experiences," Marketing Management 1994, U.3, 3, Exhibit 4. Courtesy of the American Marketing Association

CHAPTER 12

318, 320 Palliser Furniture Ltd.; 321 MADD; 323 Gucci America Inc.; 324 Tursack Incorporated; 326 Saturn; 329 SuperStock, Inc.; 331 Cliff Otto/Los Angeles Times; 332 Ballard Power Systems; 340 Teri Stratford; 342 Lee Valley Tools Ltd.; 346 BHP Billiton Diamonds Inc.

CHAPTER 13

348 Clarion Hotel Grand Pacific; 350 Courtesy of Clarion Hotel Grand Pacific and Mr. Stephen Webb; 353 Michael Newman/PhotoEdit; 355 Courtesy of Sanyo; 357 Texas Instruments Incorporated; 360 Malaysia Airlines/Albert Pointdexter; 364 Blair Seitz/Photo

Researchers, Inc.; **365** Majorie Farrell/
The Image Works

CHAPTER 14

378 Courtesy of Ryan Hobenshield; **380**
Courtesy of HARTMANN Group; **382**
John Elk III; **385** L. Migdale/Stock
Boston; **388** BlackBear Company Store;
393 Alene M. McNeill; **394** Jim Whitmer;
397 SuperStock, Inc.; **399** Arnold Bros.
Transport Ltd.

CHAPTER 15

406 IKEA; **408** IKEA International; **410**
Courtesy of Petro-Canada; **411** Domnion
Stores/Alene M. McNeill; **412 (top)** R.A.
Flynn, Inc./TC2; **413 (bottom)**
Fujifotos/The Image Works; **414** Lee
Valley Tools Ltd; **416** Courtesy REI; **417**
Alene M. McNeill; **419** Dick Hemingway;
421 (top right) Canapress/Dave Buston;
421(bottom right) PhotoEdit, Jim Mone;
421 (bottom left) AP/Wide World
Photos; **421 (top left)** Toronto Corporate

Services; **422** Samcor Communications
Company; **425** Courtesy of La Senza; **427**
The Gap; **429** Just White Shirts & Black
Socks; **432** M. Antman/The Image Works

CHAPTER 16

442 Courtesy Cormark Communications;
444 Dave Chidley; **449** BBDO
Duesseldorf; **451** Oil of Olay-Division of
Procter & Gamble; **455** GLAD is a regis-
tered trademark of the GLAD Products
Company and is used with permission.
Copyright 1999, The GLAD Products
Company. Reprinted with permission;
456 Canapress/David Duprey; **460**
Microcell Solutions Inc.; **461** Courtesy of
Master Card; **463 (top)** Ermenegildo
Zegna Canada; **463 (bottom)** Faces Inc.;
465 Courtesy of the Province of New
Brunswick Resources

CHAPTER 17

472, 474 A Och O Analys; **475** Pfizer
Canada Inc.; **476 (top)** Courtesy of Camp

Chrysalis; **476 (bottom)** Courtesy of
Smith & Nelson; **479** Courtesy of Novell;
480 DM9 Advertising; **481** Saatchi &
Saatchi; **482** Tom Lyle/Medichrome/
The Stock Shop, Inc.; **484** Digital Pulp,
2000; **488** Adobe and the Adobe logo
are trademarks of Adobe Systems
Incorporated.

CHAPTER 18

496 Courtesy of Raincoast Books; **498** Al
Harvey/The Slide Farm; **499** Microcell
Solutions Inc.; **501** Canapress/Paul
Chaisson; **503 (top)** Oscar Mayer Foods;
503 (bottom) Boehringer Ingelheim
(Canada) Ltd.; **509** Courtesy of PowerBar
Foods Canada; **510** H. J. Heinz Company
of Canada Ltd.; **513** Phil Norton/Gazette
Photos Montreal; **517** The Southwestern
Company

Company/Name Index

Subject Index

follows the introduction of a new product in the marketplace, 267–269

inventory control: Activities to ensure that goods are always available to meet customers' demands, 399

inventory turnover: The average number of times a year a retailer expects to sell its inventory, 413

involvement: The relative importance of perceived consequences of the purchase to a consumer, 147

ISO 9000: Criteria developed by the International Standards Organization to regulate product quality internationally, 66

Italian Canadian community, 207

J

joint demand: The demand for two or more goods that are used together to create a product, 179

joint venture: A strategic alliance in which two or more firms form a new entity, allowing the partners to pool their resources for common goals, 103

just in time (JIT): Inventory management and purchasing processes that manufacturers and resellers use to reduce inventory to very low levels and ensure that deliveries from suppliers arrive only when needed, 191–192

K

keiretsu, 90

knock-off: A new product that copies with slight modification the design of an original product, 243

L

labelling regulations, 277

laggards: The last consumers to adopt an innovation, 253

language barriers
cultural environment, 99
data collection, 134

late majority: The adopters who are willing to try new products when there is little or no risk associated with the purchase, when the purchase becomes an economic necessity, or when there is social pressure to purchase, 252

learning: A relatively permanent change in behaviour caused by acquired information or experience, 153

behavioural learning theories, 153–154
classical conditioning, 153
cognitive learning theory, 154
observational learning, 154
operant conditioning, 153
stimulus generalization, 153–154

legal environment, 74–75
adapting to, 75
federal laws, 74
global marketing environment, 95–96
human rights issues, 96
labelling regulations, 277
local content rules, 95
provincial laws, 74
regulatory agencies, 75

less developed country (LDC): A country at the earliest stage of economic development, 93

licensing: An agreement in which one firm gives another firm the right to produce and market its product in a specified location in return for royalties; an agreement in which one firm sells another firm the right to use a brand name for a specific purpose and for a specific period of time, 103, 275

lifestyle: The pattern of living that determines how people choose to spend their time, money, and energy and that reflects their values, tastes, and preferences, 158
format, 481
marketing, 158

lighting, 418–419

limited problem solving, 147

limited-service agency, 475

limited-service merchant wholesalers, 384

list price: The price the end customer is expected to pay as determined by the manufacturer, 361

local content rules: A form of protectionism stipulating that a certain proportion of a product must consist of components supplied by industries in the host country, 95

location
vs. standardization, 104–105
store. *See* store location

longitudinal design: Technique that tracks the responses of the same sample of respondents over time, 129

loss-leader pricing: The pricing policy of setting prices below cost to attract customers into a store, 367

low-involvement purchases, 147

M

macroenvironment, 72–73

magazines, 484

mail order, 430

mail order wholesalers, 385

maintenance, repair, and operating (MRO) products: Goods that a business customer consumes in a relatively short time, 241

manufacturer brands: Brands that the manufacturer of the product owns, 274

manufacturer-owned intermediaries, 386
manufacturers' showrooms, 386
sales branches, 386
sales offices, 386

manufacturer-retailer-consumer channel, 388

manufacturer-wholesaler-retailer-consumer channel, 388

manufacturers' agents, 385

manufacturers' showrooms, 386

Margaritaville myth, 19

margin: The difference between the cost of the product and the selling price of the product, 322

marginal analysis: A method that uses cost and demand to identify the price that will maximize profits, 337–338

marginal cost: The increase in total cost that results from producing one additional unit of a product, 337

marginal revenue: The increase in total revenue (income) that results from producing and selling one additional unit of a product, 337

market: All of the customers and potential customers who share a common need that can be satisfied by a specific product, who have the resources to exchange for it, who are willing to make the exchange, and who have the authority to make the exchange, 6
objectives, 42–43
scope of, 88–89

market development: Growth strategies that introduce existing products to new markets, 38

market fragmentation: Creation of many consumer groups due to a diversity of distinct needs and wants in modern society, 202

market fulfillment approach, 291

market manager: A manager who is responsible for developing and implementing the marketing plans for products sold to a specific customer group, 278

"AS IS" LICENSE AGREEMENT AND LIMITED WARRANTY